THE FORMATION OF THE CLASSICAL ISLAMIC WORLD

General Editor: Lawrence I. Conrad

Volume 24

The Qur'an

Style and Contents

THE FORMATION OF THE CLASSICAL ISLAMIC WORLD

General Editor: Lawrence I. Conrad

1	**Byzantium on the Eve of Islam**	*Averil Cameron*
2	**The Sasanian East on the Eve of Islam**	*Shaul Saked*
3	**The Arabs and Arabia on the Eve of Islam**	*Frank E. Peters*
4	**The Life of Muḥammad**	*Uri Rubin*
5	**The Arab Conquests**	*Fred M. Donner*
6	**The Articulation of State Structures**	*Fred M. Donner*
7	**Problems of Political Cohesion**	*R. Stephen Humphreys*
8	**Arab-Byzantine Relations**	*Michael Bonner*
9	**The Turks in the Early Islamic World**	*C.E. Bosworth*
10	**Patterns of Everyday Life**	*David Waines*
11	**Agricultural Production and Pastoralism**	*Michael G. Morony*
12	**Manufacturing, Mining and Labour**	*Michael G. Morony*
13	**Trade, Exchange and the Market Place**	*A.L. Udovitch*
14	**Property and Consumption**	*Baber Johansen*
15	**Cities in the Islamic World**	*Hugh Kennedy*
16	**Nomads and the Desert**	*Hugh Kennedy*
17	**Society and the Individual**	to be announced
18	**Muslims and Others**	*Albrecht Noth*
19	**Christian Communal Life**	*Sidney H. Griffith*
20	**The Jewish Communities**	*David Wasserstein*
21	**Archaeology and Early Islam**	*Donald Whitcomb*
22	**Numismatics and Monetary History**	*Michael Bates*
23	**Art and Architecture**	*Jonathan Bloom*
24	**The Qur'ān: Style and Contents**	*Andrew Rippin*
25	**The Qur'ān: Formative Interpretation**	*Andrew Rippin*
26	**The Development of Ritual**	*G.R. Hawting*
27	**The Formation of Islamic Law**	to be announced
28	**The Development of *Ḥadīth***	*Harold Motzki*
29	**Historiographical Traditions**	*Lawrence I. Conrad*
30	**Early Islamic Theology**	*Josef van Ess*
31	**Eschatology and Apocalyptic**	*Wilferd Madelung*
32	**Visions of Community**	*Wadād al-Qāḍī*
33	**Shī'ism**	*Etan Kohlberg*
34	**The Khawārij**	*Ridwan al-Saiid*
35	**The Emergence of Mysticism**	*Bernd Radtke*
36	**The Philological Tradition**	*Ramzi Baalbaki*
37	**Poetry and Poetics**	*Suzanne Stetkevych*
38	**Arabic Prose Literature**	*Fedwa Malti-Douglas*
39	**The Rise of Islamic Philosophy**	*Everett Rowson*
40	**The Rise of Arab-Islamic Medicine**	*Lawrence I. Conrad*
41	**The Exact Sciences**	*Jamil Ragep*
42	**Magic and Divination**	*Emilie Savage-Smith*
43	**Education and the Transmission of Knowledge**	*Claude Gilliot*
44	**The Islamic Manuscript Tradition**	*Jan Just Witkam*
45	**Islamic North Africa**	*Elizabeth Savage*
46	**The Formation of al-Andalus I**	*Manuela Marín*
47	**The Formation of al-Andalus II**	*Maribel Fierro / Julio Samsó*

THE FORMATION OF THE CLASSICAL ISLAMIC WORLD

General Editor: Lawrence I. Conrad

Volume 24

The Qur'an:

Style and Contents

edited by
Andrew Rippin

Ashgate

VARIORUM

Aldershot • Brookfield USA • Singapore • Sydney

Published in the series **The Formation of the Classical Islamic World** by

Ashgate Publishing Limited
Gower House, Croft Road
Aldershot, Hampshire
Great Britain

Ashgate Publishing Company
131 Main Street
Burlington, Vermont 05401–5600
USA

ISBN 0–86078–700–1

British Library CIP Data
The Qur'an: Style and Contents. – (The Formation of the Classical Islamic World 24)
1. Koran – Criticism, interpretation etc. – History. 2. Koran – Language, style. I. Rippin, Andrew
297.1'226'01

US Library of Congress CIP Data
The Qur'an: Style and Contents / edited by Andrew Rippin.
p. cm. – (The Formation of the Classical Islamic World 24)
Includes bibliographical references.
1. Koran – Language, style. 2. Koran – Koran – Evidence, authority, etc.
I. Rippin, Andrew, 1950– . II. Series.
PJ6696.Q73 2000
297.1'226–dc21 99–058416

This volume is printed on acid-free paper.

Printed and bound in Great Britain

THE FORMATION OF THE CLASSICAL ISLAMIC WORLD-24

CONTENTS

ACKNOWLEDGMENTS

CHAPTER 1: Chaim Rabin, "Islam and the Qumran Sect", Chaim Rabin, *Qumran Studies* (New York, 1957), pp. 112–130. Copyright © 1957 by Oxford University Press. Reprinted by permission.

CHAPTER 2: Neal Robinson, "Jesus and Mary in the Qur'ān: Some Neglected Affinites", *Religion* 20 (London, 1990), pp. 161–75. Copyright © 1990 by Harcourt Brace & Company.

CHAPTER 3: Translation of: M. Causse, " Théologie de rupture et théologie de la communaute; études sur la vocation prophetic de Moise d'après le Coran", *Revue d'Histoire et de Philosophie Religieuses* 44 (Paris, 1964), pp. 60–82. Copyright © 1964 by Presses Universitaires de France. Translation by Gwendolin Goldbloom; Copyright © 2001 by Ashgate Publishing Ltd.

CHAPTER 4: Ilse Lichtenstadter, "And Become Ye Accursed Apes", *Jerusalem Studies in Arabic and Islam* 14 (Jerusalem, 1991), pp. 153–75. Copyright © 1990 by the Max Schloessinger Memorial Foundation, Institute of Asian and African Studies, the Hebrew University of Jerusalem.

CHAPTER 5: D.Z.H. Baneth ,"What Did Muḥammad Mean When he Called his Religion Islam? The Original Meaning of *aslama* and its Derivatives", *Israel Oriental Studies* 1 (Tel Aviv, 1971), pp. 183–90. Copyright © 1971 by the Faculty of Humanities at the University of Tel Aviv.

CHAPTER 6: Jacques Waaredenburg, "Towards a Periodization of Earliest Islam According to Its Relations with other Religions", R. Peters, ed., *Proceedings of the 9th Congress of the Union Européenne des Arabisants et Islamisants* (Leiden, 1981), pp. 304–26. Copyright © 1981 by E.J. Brill.

CHAPTER 7: Fred Leemhuis, "Qur'ānic Siğğil and Aramaic *sgyl*", *Journal of Semitic Studies* 27 (Oxford, 1982), pp. 47–56. Copyright © 1982 by Oxford University Press. Reprinted by permission.

CHAPTER 8: Michael B. Schub, "Two Notes", *Zeitschrift für arabische Linguistik* 18 (Wiesbaden, 1988), pp. 95–97. Copyright © 1988 by Harrassowitz Verlag Wiesbaden.

CHAPTER 9: W.A. Bijlefeld, "A Prophet and More than a Prophet? Some Observations on the Qur'ānic Use of the Terms 'Prophet' and 'Apostle'", *The Muslim World* 59 (Hartford, Connecticut 1969), pp. 1–28. Copyright © 1990 by the Hartford Seminary.

CHAPTER 10: William A. Graham "The Earliest Meaning of Qur'ān", *Die Welt des Islams* 23–24 (Leiden, 1984), pp. 101–39. Copyright © 1984 by E.J. Brill.

CHAPTER 11: Thomas J. O'Shaughnessy, "The Qur'ānic View of Youth and Old Age", *Zeitschrift der morgenländischen Gesellschaft* 141 (Stuttgart, 1991), pp. 33–5. First published by Franz Steiner Verlag Wiesbaden GmbH, Stuttgart. Copyright © 1991 by Thomas J. O'Shaughnessy.

CHAPTER 12: Translation of: Jacques Jomier, "Le nom divin 'al-Raḥmān' dans le Coran", *Mélanges Louis Massignon* (Damascus, 1957), pp. 361–81. Copyright © 1957 by Institut Français d'études Arabes de Damas. Translation by Andrew Rippin; Copyright © 2001 by Ashgate Publishing Ltd.

CHAPTER 13: Devin J. Stewart "Saj' in the Qur'ān: Prosody and Structure", *Journal of Arabic Literature* 21 (Leiden, 1990), pp. 101–39. Copyright © 1990 by E.J. Brill.

CHAPTER 14: Translation of: Angelika Neuwirth, "Einige Bemerkungen zum besonderen sprachlichen und literartischen Charakter des Koran", *Deutscher Orientalistentag 1975* (Stuttgart, 1977), pp. 736–39. Copyright © 1977 by Angelika Neuwirth. Translation by Gwendolin Goldbloom; Copyright © 2001 by Ashgate Publishing Ltd.

CHAPTER 15: Richard Bell, "The Beginnings of Muḥammad's Religious Activity", *Transactions of the Glasgow University Oriental Society* 7 (Glasgow, 1934–35), pp. 16–24. Copyright © 1934–35 by *Transactions of the Glasgow University Oriental Society.*

CHAPTER 16: Uri Rubin, "Abū Lahab and Sūra CXI", *Bulletin of the School of Oriental and African Studies* 42 (Oxford, 1979), pp. 13–28. Copyright © 1990 by Oxford University Press. Reprinted by permission.

CHAPTER 17: Translation of: Robert Brunschvig, "Simples remarques negatives sur le vocabulaire du Coran", *Studia Islamica* 5 (Paris, 1956), pp. 19–32. Copyright © 1956 by Maisonneuve et Larose. Translation by Gwendolin Goldbloom; copyright © 2001 by Ashgate Publishing Ltd.

CHAPTER 18: Translation of: Mohammed Arkoun, "Introduction: Bilan et perspectives des études Coraniques", Mohammed Arkoun, ed., *Lectures du Coran* (Paris, 1982), pp. v–xxxiii. Copyright © 1982 by Mohammed Arkoun. Translation by Scott Lucas: Copyright © 2001 by Ashgate Publishing Ltd.

CHAPTER 19: Michael Sells, "Sound, Spirit, and Gender in *Sūrat al-qdar*", *Journal of the American Oriental Society* 111 (Ann Arbor, 1991), pp. 239–59. Copyright © 1990 by American Oriental Society.

CHAPTER 20: Norman O. Brown, "The Apocalypse of Islam", Norman O. Brown, *Apocalypse and/or Metamorphosis* (Berkeley, 1991), pp. 155–70. Copyright © 1990 by the University of California Press.

CHAPTER 21: S. Parvez Manzoor, "Method Against Truth: Orientalism and Qur'ānic Studies", *Muslim World Book Review* 7 (Leicester, 1987), pp. 33–49. Copyright © 1987 by the Hartford Seminary.

Every effort has been made to trace all the copyright holders, but if any have been inadvertently overlooked, the publishers will be please to make the necessary arrangement at the first opportunity.

GENERAL EDITOR'S PREFACE

Since the days of Ignaz Goldziher (1850–1921), generally regarded as the founder of Islamic studies as a field of modern scholarship, the formative period in Islamic history has remained a prominent theme for research. In Goldziher's time it was possible for scholars to work with the whole of the field and practically all of its available sources, but more recently the increasing sophistication of scholarly methodologies, a broad diversification in research interests, and a phenomenal burgeoning of the catalogued and published source material available for study have combined to generate an increasing "compartmentalisation" of research into very specific areas, each with its own interests, priorities, agendas, methodologies, and controversies. While this has undoubtedly led to a deepening and broadening of our understanding in all of these areas, and hence is to be welcomed, it has also tended to isolate scholarship in one subject from research in other areas, and even more so from colleagues outside of Arab-Islamic studies, not to mention students and others seeking to familiarise themselves with a particular topic for the first time.

The Formation of the Classical Islamic World is a reference series that seeks to address this problem by making available a critical selection of the published research that has served to stimulate and define the way modern scholarship has come to understand the formative period of Islamic history, for these purposes taken to mean approximately AD 600–950. Each of the volumes in the series is edited by an expert on its subject, who has chosen a number of studies that taken together serve as a cogent introduction to the state of current knowledge on the topic, the issues and problems particular to it, and the range of scholarly opinion informing it. Articles originally published in languages other than English have been translated, and editors have provided critical introductions and select bibliographies for further reading.

A variety of criteria, varying by topic and in accordance with the judgements of the editors, have determined the contents of these volumes. In some cases an article has been included because it represents the best of current scholarship, the "cutting edge" work from which future research seems most likely to profit. Other articles—certainly no less valuable contributions—have been taken up for the skillful way in which they synthesise the state of scholarly knowledge. Yet others are older studies that—if in some ways now superseded—nevertheless merit attention for their illustration of thinking or conclusions that have long been important, or for the decisive stimulus they have provided to scholarly discussion. Some volumes cover themes that have emerged fairly recently, and here it has been necessary to include articles from outside the period covered by the series, as illustrations of paradigms and methodologies that may prove useful as research develops.

In the present state of the field of early Arab-Islamic studies, in which it is routine for heated controversy to rage over what scholars a generation ago would have regarded as matters of simple fact, it is clearly essential for a series such as this to convey some sense of the richness and variety the approaches and perspectives represented in the available literature. An effort has thus been made to gain broad international participation in editorial capacities, and to secure the collaboration of colleagues representing differing points of view. Throughout the series, however, the range of possible options for inclusion has been very large, and it is of course impossible to accommodate all of the outstanding research that has served to advance a particular subject. A representative selection of such work does, however, appear in the bibliography compiled by the editor of each volume at the end of the introduction.

The interests and priorities of the editors, and indeed, of the General Editor, will doubtless be evident throughout. Hopefully, however, the various volumes will be found to achieve well-rounded and representative syntheses useful not as the definitive word on their subjects—if, in fact, one can speak of such a thing in the present state of research—but as introductions comprising well-considered points of departure for more detailed inquiry.

A series pursued on this scale is only feasible with the good will and cooperation of colleagues in many areas of expertise. The General Editor would like to express his gratitude to the volume editors for the investment of their time and talents in an age when work of this kind is grossly undervalued, to the translators who have taken such care with the articles entrusted to them, and to Dr John Smedley and his staff at Ashgate for their support, assistance and guidance throughout.

Lawrence I. Conrad

INTRODUCTION
The Qur'ān: Style and Contents

Andrew Rippin

THE EUROPEAN WORLD has been fascinated with the Qur'ān since at least the twelfth century AD, when the first translation of the scripture into Latin was written by Robert of Ketton.[1] That translation was motivated by a plain polemical spirit: it was to allow arguments to be constructed which would counter Muslim accusations of the deficiencies of the Bible and to facilitate missionary activity. It is in relation to this heritage that much subsequent scholarship on the Qur'ān—and the Muslim reaction to it—must be understood. As well, it needs to be recognized that the European study of the Qur'ān, at least in some senses, was an outgrowth of studies internal to the Muslim world. European scholars worked within the assumptions of historical context, textual formation and progressive revelation with which Muslims had explored the Qur'ān, even if they did so without the theological perspective of the Islamic faith itself. It may therefore be suggested that the early history of the discipline of Qur'ānic studies is the result of the interplay of those two dimensions—the Muslim presuppositions and the Christian polemical approach. Only in the latter part of the twentieth century have these aspects been fully brought into question.

The Sources of the Qur'ān

Approaching the Qur'ān with modern scholarly aspirations[2] for the first time is a task generally credited[3] to Abraham Geiger (d. 1874), most famous as the founder and leader of the German Jewish Reform movement. Writing in Latin, Geiger submitted a contest entry to the University of Bonn in 1832 which was published in German under the title *Was hat Mohammed aus dem Judenthume aufgenommen?* in 1833.[4] Geiger's approach marks

[1] See Hartmut Bobzin, "Latin Translations of the Koran: a Short Overview", *Der Islam* 70 (1993), 193–206.

[2] By this I mean the critical dispassionate (i.e. non-polemical) search for knowledge, unconstrained by ecclesiastical institutional priorities. Obviously, this is not uncontentious. For example, see Hava Lazarus-Yafeh, *Intertwined Worlds: Medieval Islam and Bible Criticism* (Princeton, 1992), who argues that medieval Jewish (especially Ibn Ezra) Biblical studies—a field much indebted to Islamic scriptural studies—are the intellectual precursor of Spinoza and all subsequent scholarship. See my review in *BSOAS* 56 (1993), 363–64.

[3] See, e.g., T. Nöldeke/F. Schwally, *Geschichte des Qorāns*, II (Leipzig, 1919), 208.

[4] English translation by F.M. Young, *Judaism and Islam* (Madras, 1898).

the beginning of the European (and subsequently Euro-American) scholarly quest for traceable sources of the Qur'ān within Judaism and, to a lesser extent, Christianity. His study is distinct from virtually all that preceded it in that, perhaps most significantly, he was willing to accept Muḥammad as sincere in his religious mission rather than as an "impostor", as the polemical works of earlier times had generally portrayed him. But Geiger's study was also motivated by what could be considered the underlying thrust of post-Enlightenment work in general: curiosity, to which no particular value was added over and above the desire to know the previously unknown. It would be a mistake, on the other hand, to feel that Geiger's work simply "appears", as it were, without any sense of precedent, for a history of scholarship leads up to this point;[5] the work of Lodovico Marracci in 1698[6] and George Sale in 1734[7] can hardly be overlooked. However, the subsequent scholarly community has always treated Geiger's work as seminal in the history of the discipline (as the continued reprinting of its English translation confirms).

Geiger's 1833 study, then, wished to contextualize Muḥammad, but, from the perspective of the way in which Qur'ānic studies have developed in the intervening century and a half, it is notable that he did not emphasize the movement of history in the development of Qur'ānic themes. As an example, note should be taken of his appendix, "Statements in the Qur'ān hostile to Judaism", which, while positing a historical transition and a new strategy on the part of Muḥammad after the change of the *qibla* from Jerusalem to Mecca, still speaks of this in terms of simple comparisons and does not tie any of the cited examples to a specific historical context (e.g. the "break" with the Jews as later historians have put it). The fact of Jewish parallels was sufficient as an explanatory device for Geiger to contextualize his interpretation within a generally ahistorical framework.

It is important to remember that the point of such studies of "influence" on Muḥammad has always been to clarify the meaning of the Qur'ān, not to construct a reductive catalogue of influences, although it has sometimes

[5]See, e.g., H. Bobzin, *Der Koran im Zeitalter der Reformation* (Beirut, 1995). For a valuable overview of Geiger and his significance within the context of the Haskala, see the observations in Lawrence I. Conrad, "The Pilgrim from Pest: Goldziher's Study Trip to the Near East (1873–74)", in Ian Netton, ed., *Golden Roads: Migration, Pilgrimage and Travel in Mediaeval and Modern Islam* (London, 1993), 110–59, esp. 122–25.

[6]See Johann Fück, *Die arabischen Studien in Europa bis in den Anfang des 20. Jahrhunderts* (Leipzig, 1955), 94–95. This is a useful source for much information on the history of the discipline.

[7]See, for example, the appreciation of Sale's work in W.M. Watt, "On Interpreting the Qur'ān", *Oriens* 25–26 (1976), 41–42.

appeared that the latter was the case. The argument has always been (and must be if there is to be any legitimacy in these studies) that interpretation of a text must take place in a context and that the context of Judaism is one which provides a coherent and self-confirming interpretation. Of course, others have argued for different contexts and this is what has made the entire approach so problematic: pagan Arab,[8] ancient Near Eastern,[9] Christian,[10] Samaritan,[11] and sectarian Jewish[12] contexts, among many others, have all been suggested.[13] The material on Judaism as a background to the Qur'ān, however, is undoubtedly the most impressive in terms of its quantity, and, to the extent that a scholarly consensus has arisen, an emphasis on the Jewish context seems to predominate.[14] The debate over the nature of that Jewish environment, however, may be seen within the work of Chaim Rabin (Chapter 1), in which he isolates the symbolism, mythology and terminology of the Jewish Qumrān community and sees its continued presence in the Qur'ān.[15] A recent book by Steven Wasserstrom[16] provides an excellent

[8]E.g. M.M. Bravmann, *The Spiritual Background of Early Islam: Studies in Ancient Arab Concepts* (Leiden, 1973).

[9]E.g. Geo Widengren, *Muhammad, the Apostle of God, and his Ascension* (Uppsala, 1955).

[10]E.g. Richard Bell, *The Origins of Islam in its Christian Environment* (London, 1926); K. Ahrens, "Christiches im Qoran: eine Nachlese", *ZDMG* 84 (1930), 15–68, 148–90; John Bowman, "The Debt of Islam to Monophysite Syrian Christianity", in E.C.B. MacLaurin, ed., *Essays in Honour of Griffithes Wheeler Thatcher 1863–1950* (Sydney, 1967), 191–216; more extreme is Giulio Basetti-Sani, *The Koran in the Light of Christ* (Chicago, 1977).

[11]Joshua Finkel, "Jewish, Christian and Samaritan Influences on Arabia" in R.W. Barstow, ed., *The Macdonald Presentation Volume* (Princeton, 1933), 147–66; Patricia Crone and Michael Cook, *Hagarism: the Making of the Islamic World* (Cambridge, 1977).

[12]Marc Philonenko, "Une expression qoumranienne dans le Coran", in *Atti del terzo congresso di studi arabi e islamici* (Naples, 1967), 553–56; Yoram Erder, "The Origin of the Name Idrīs in the Qur'ān: a Study of the Influence of Qumrān Literature on Early Islam", *JNES* 49 (1990), 339–50.

[13]A good overview of the subject of "influence" is found in Tryggve Kronholm, "Dependence and Prophetic Originality", *Orientalia Succana* 31–32 (1982–83), 47–70.

[14]See, among many possibilities, the studies of Joseph Horowitz, "Jewish Proper Names and their Derivatives in the Koran", *HUCA* 2 (1925), 147–227; *idem*, *Koranische Untersuchungen* (Berlin and Leipzig, 1926); Heinrich Speyer, *Die biblischen Erzählungen im Quran* (Gräfenheinlichen, *ca.* 1933); Charles C. Torrey, *The Jewish Foundation of Islam* (New York, 1933); Abraham I. Katsh, *Judaism in Islam: Biblical and Talmudic Backgrounds of the Koran and its Commentaries* (New York, 1954).

[15]Note may also be taken of the idea of a psychological profile as an interpretative strategy. This always takes place, however, within a historical framework for contextualization purposes. See, e.g., D.B. Macdonald, review of R. Bell, *Origins of Islam*, in *MW* 16 (1926), 309–10.

[16]*Between Muslim and Jew: the Problem of Symbiosis under Early Islam* (Princeton, 1995).

overview of this problem of the identity of Jewish groups in the initial and formative periods of Islam, indicating the extent to which this remains an matter for scholarly debate.

Studies on Biblical personalities as portrayed within the Qur'ān are limited versions of the same tendency towards contextualization within an overall framework of other religions, although frequently the point is rendered quite subtle within the mass of detail. The idea of looking at the figure of Jesus in the Qur'ān—one of the most overworked subjects in the field, for certain—ends up being an implicit or even explicit comparison with a definition of Christianity, in that these studies address the question, "How does the Qur'ān differ from or remain the same as this or that view of Christianity on the figure of Jesus?"[17] Neal Robinson's treatment of Jesus and Mary (Chapter 2) provides one such example by examining the way in which these two figures are incorporated into the structure of Qur'ānic narratives and how the stories have been "affected" by the life story of Muḥammad. Likewise, Maurice Causse's study of Moses (Chapter 3) examines the nature of theological (re-)telling of the stories of the prophets by focusing on the ways in which Moses is a "model" of the prophetic mission.

While the overriding motif of all such investigations may be the fitting of the stories of the prophets (and of the Qur'ān as a whole) into the life of Muḥammad, underlying all of them is the implicit comparison between the Qur'ānic rendition of the story and the Biblical version (which it is generally assumed that the reader knows). The tools of comparison are essential to the task of eliciting meaning, but that comparison is still situated within a framework of historico-religious contextualization, as suggested by the very items selected for comparison. Some scholars have provided studies which tackle just a single item of Qur'ānic discourse without necessarily putting forth an entire theory on the background and interpretational framework for reading the Qur'ān. An article by Ilse Lichtenstadter (Chapter 4) provides an example of a word study in which the mythological background of the "dog-headed ape", traced here to ancient Egypt and transmitted through Christian legend, is examined for its assistance in understanding the Qur'ānic story of the Jews being turned into apes as referred to in Sūra

[17]See, e.g., Geoffrey Parrinder, *Jesus in the Qur'ān* (London, 1965); Neal Robinson, *Christ in Islam and Christianity: the Representation of Jesus in the Qur'ān and the Classical Muslim Commentaries* (Basingstoke, 1991); Jane Dammen McAuliffe, *Qur'ānic Christians: an Analysis of Classical and Modern Exegesis* (Cambridge, 1991); and, generally, Don Wismer, *The Islamic Jesus: an Annotated Bibliography of Sources in English and French* (New York, 1977).

2:65 and other passages.[18]

Debates over context remain a vital part of Qur'ānic studies, if only because the apparent Arabian milieu of some of the Qur'ān makes it so difficult to provide an entirely convincing picture of the Qur'ān wholly within a Jewish–Christian context. Discussions of the term *islām* itself—a topic extensively discussed by scholars[19]—provides one such example, and is dealt with in the study of D.H. Baneth (Chapter 5). The argument over the extent to which *islām* as a term conveys an ethos derived from ancient Arabia (as Baneth suggests) or is to be intimately linked to the Biblical Abraham, in his role as a *ḥanīf* or pious follower of the one God and the model for every righteous Muslim, illustrates the centrality of the discussion but also its inconclusiveness. Jacques Waardenburg's contribution (Chapter 6) on the "periodization" of early Islam only emphasizes this fact by analyzing the changes which he sees the early community passing through, as reflected in the very concept of "religion" (*dīn*) as used in the Qur'ān itself, but based around the attitudes reflected in the text towards its religious "surroundings".

The Philological and Semantic Approaches to the Qur'ān

Underlying the most successful of these "influence" studies is solid philological scholarship, in much of which one can still see the traces of the work of one of the greatest philologists of the Semitic traditions, Theodor Nöldeke (d. 1930). His lasting monument to Qur'ānic scholarship, *Geschichte des Qorāns*, has a history similar to that of Geiger's work. Written originally in Latin, submitted in 1856 as a dissertation and awarded the winning prize in a Parisian competition for a study of the "critical history of the text of the Qur'ān", the work was first published in an expanded German edition in 1860. A second edition of the work appeared in three volumes, with Volumes I and II edited and rewritten by Friedrich Schwally (1909, 1919), and Volume III written by Gotthelf Bergsträsser and Otto Pretzl (1938). Overall, Nöldeke's work has set the agenda for the subsequent generations of Qur'ānic scholarship in reflecting the concerns of chronology and Biblical background, but it is in its philological insights that its most lasting value is to be seen. Its treatment of language, stress upon etymology, and insights into grammar all provide the model for philological study of the Qur'ān, and the material provided by Nöldeke continues to be a valued source of reference for later

[18]On this motif, also see William M. Brinner, "The Image of the Jew as *Other* in Medieval Arabic Texts", *IOS* 14 (1994), 227–40, esp. 235–40.

[19]See H. Ringgren, *Islām, 'Aslama and Muslim* (Uppsala, 1949), and sources quoted therein.

scholarship. The most significant subsequent work continuing in this line is Rudi Paret's *Der Koran. Kommentar und Konkordanz* (Stuttgart, 1971, 1977), a by-product of Paret's Qur'ān translation and a tool to which all later Qur'ān scholars have been greatly indebted because of its extensive cross-referencing of linguistic details within the text of the Qur'ān and its attention to scholarship surrounding the derivation and meaning of lexical items.

While Nöldeke and Paret have accomplished the immense task of examining the whole of the Qur'ān, individual studies abound which demonstrate the continued value of the philological approach. One such summary of this field is by Arthur Jeffery, *The Foreign Vocabulary of the Qur'an* (Baroda, 1938), whose work remains the major source of basic information and opinion in the area. Valuable additional contributions continue to be made, however. Fred Leemhuis (Chapter 7) demonstrates the usefulness of understanding other languages, ranging from Sumerian to Akkadian, Hebrew, and Aramaic, in coming to grips with the single Qur'ānic word, *sijjīl*. Likewise, M.B. Schub brings philology and grammar into conjunction with traditional Muslim exegesis of the Qur'ān in his study of the Hebrew background to *akhlada* meaning "to incline (towards the earth)" in sūra 7, verse 176, and in his special attention to the translation of Arabic verbal tenses in sūra 109 (Chapter 8).

A major development in the study of the Qur'ān arrived with the publications of Toshihiko Izutsu, whose works have been praised by Muslim and non-Muslim scholars alike. While a parallel movement was taking place in Biblical studies,[20] Izutsu's works, *The Structure of Ethical Terms in the Koran* (Tokyo, 1959) and *God and Man in the Koran* (Tokyo, 1964), as well as the rewritten version of the former work, *Ethico-Religious Concepts in the Qur'ān* (Montreal, 1966) appear uninfluenced by research in the Biblical field (in either a theoretical manner or in matters of detail). The chronological development of the two fields at roughly the same time is perhaps best understood in light of developments in the field of linguistics.[21] The semantic method is set out by Izutsu in systematic fashion at the beginning of his *Ethico-Religious Concepts*, but its thrust is based on one idea: that the meaning of words inheres in the context, not in the individual words themselves. Thus, on one level, this approach could well be characterized as being in direct opposition to the philological method with its stress on etymology as determining meaning. However, in terms of the level at which

[20] Represented most significantly in James Barr, *Semantics of Biblical Language* (Oxford, 1961).

[21] Specifically Stephen Ullmann, *The Principles of Semantics*, 2nd ed. (Oxford, 1957).

the investigations take place (i.e. at the word level in the Arabic text) and their textual (rather than linguistic) presuppositions, the two methods may well be considered related. The influence of the "semantic method", which may be thought of as an attempt to impose some sense of organization upon the more intuitive ideas of philology,[22] is plain to see in many studies of individual words and word patterning in the Qur'ān, although it is frequently linked to other scholarly preoccupations (such as "chronology" or "influences"). Willem A. Bijlefeld's work (Chapter 9) on *nabī* and *rasūl* in the Qur'ān, published in 1969, is a good example of the use of the idea of context *within* the text of the Qur'ān to determine meaning. Coping with the mass of raw data in a study such as this is also facilitated by the imposition of a chronology upon the text, an element which Izutsu resisted in his own work (cf. the idea of "synchronic semantics" versus "diachronic semantics", a much rehearsed debate within Biblical studies). William Graham's article (Chapter 10) on the meaning of the word *qur'ān* itself raises issues of the derivation of the word from the Syriac and the historical use of the word both before Islam and after the revelation of the scripture. The stress of the article, through its systematic examination of the use of the word in context within the Qur'ān, is upon the meaning of the word as "reciting aloud" with the sense of "scripture" only being imposed through a "reading back" of later ideas onto the text.[23] Governed by thematic as well as chronological concerns, the work of Thomas J. O'Shaughnessy (Chapter 11) likewise employs a detailed examination of words, for example in looking at the term *yatīm* meaning "fatherless child", in order to extract specific Qur'ānic attitudes regarding youth which, according to O'Shaughnessy's study, vary chronologically throughout the text. Jacques Jomier's article (Chapter 12) examines the name of God, *al-Raḥmān*, in the Qur'ān within a chronological framework, with the conclusion that the name was used within a specific timeframe in the career of Muḥammad and that it was tied to the development of specific themes within his preaching. The intertwining of chronology with theme is thus emphasized and provided with an explanation, in this case that this was a way for a new teaching to be introduced within the Meccan context.

---

[22] Cf. James Barr, *Comparative Philology and the Text of the Old Testament* (Oxford, 1968; 2nd ed. Winona Lake, 1987).

[23] William A. Graham, *Divine Word and Prophetic Word in Early Islam* (The Hague and Paris, 1977); and *idem*, *Beyond the Written Word: Oral Aspects of Scripture in the History of Religions* (Cambridge, 1987), are both elements in Graham's ongoing study of this problem.

The Style of the Qur'ān

In 1910 Theodor Nöldeke published his "Zur Sprache des Korans", a study of the language of the Qur'ān which is the earliest and remains the most extensive systematic discussion of the linguistic and stylistic differences between the Qur'ān and what has come to be known as Classical Arabic.[24] The question of what these differences might mean underlies the tangled problem of the language of the Qur'ān itself. Theories abound concerning the relationship between the style of the Qur'ān and the status of the language within the text. Was this the language of the poets at the time of Muḥammad, or was it the spoken language? Has the Arabic of the text been "adjusted" to fit the later emerging ideas of Classical Arabic? What does one make of the remaining orthographic and grammatical peculiarities of the text when compared to later standards? Are those variations the result of dialectical differences, inadequacies in script, errors, or language development? Karl Vollers,[25] Paul Kahle,[26] John Wansbrough,[27] Michael Zwettler[28] and Kees Versteegh,[29] to select only the most prominent names, have all attempted some sort of understanding of this problem. Aspects of these discussions underlie many later studies of Qur'ānic style. It is the work of Nöldeke, however, which continues to provide the essential collation of the facts and overview of the subject.[30] Some of the problematic nature of the language of the Qur'ān and how to define it is well illustrated by the article of D.J. Stewart (Chapter 13), which works through the question of the poetical nature of the text, how that may be defined and how it stands in the context of other early Arabic literary productions.

[24]Theodor Nöldeke, "Zur Sprache des Korans. II: Stilistische und syntaktische Eigentümlichkeiten der Sprache des Korans", in his *Neue Beiträge zur semitischen Sprachwissenschaft* (Strassburg, 1910), 5–23.

[25]See Karl Vollers, *Volkssprache und Schriftsprache im alten Arabien* (Strassburg, 1906).

[26]E.g. Paul Kahle, "The Qur'ān and the 'Arabīya", in S. Löwinger and J. Somogyi, eds., *Ignaze Goldziher Memorial Volume*, I (Budapest, 1948), 163–82.

[27]John Wansbrough, *Quranic Studies: Sources and Methods of Scriptural Interpretation* (Oxford, 1977), 85–117.

[28]Michael Zwettler, *The Oral Tradition of Classical Arabic Poetry: Its Character and Implications* (Columbus, 1978), 97–188. Zwettler has an excellent summary of the debate and the various positions taken by previous scholars.

[29]Kees Versteegh, *Pidginization and Creolization: the Case of Arabic* (Amsterdam, 1984).

[30]It may be observed that this work has not always received its due attention within scholarship despite a translation into French by G.H. Bousquet, *Remarques sur les particularités stylistiques et syntaxiques de la langue du Coran* (Paris, 1953); see also John Burton, "Linguistic Errors in the Qur'ān," *JSS* 33 (1988), 181–96, for Muslim exegetical treatments of some of the more problematic passages.

Recent works dealing with these problems have provided increasingly systematic attempts—that is, they have attempted to come up with a single theory that will explain the situation as it is perceived to exist—to devise a solution.[31] Undoubtedly the most successful of recent years has been that of Angelika Neuwirth,[32] but other attempts, such as those of de Crapona[33] and Lüling[34] have drawn some attention also. Neuwirth sees strict formulaic construction techniques structuring the Qur'ān which reflect a liturgical oral background of "cola" as building blocks for the text.[35] That observation suggests that a careful literary structure is to be found in each *sūra* of the Qur'ān, as Neuwirth's article (Chapter 14) argues.

Underlying many of these discussions, and as a clear preoccupation of much scholarship on the style (and the interaction of style and theme) of the Qur'ān in general, has been the interplay between style and chronology, starting from observations on the marked difference between certain *sūras* written in the ancient soothsayer format of *saj'*,[36] and the long, prose *sūras* containing legal material, presumed within both the Muslim and the European scholarly traditions to stem in general from Muḥammad's time in Mecca and Medina respectively. Here it is possible to see a relationship to Biblical studies,[37] at least in the methodological insights of the latter, especially as exemplified by the works of Julius Wellhausen and the idea of the "Documentary Hypothesis".[38]

It is worth remembering what the accomplishment of Wellhausen was:

> Wellhausen did not invent literary critical methods; he merely applied them very skillfully. His own particular contribution was

---

[31]Earlier attempts may be noted: D.H. Müller, *Die Propheten in ihrer ursprünglichen Poesie* (Vienna, 1896); R. Geyer, "Zur Strophik des Qurân," *WZKM* 22 (1908), 265–86.

[32]Angelika Neuwirth, *Studien zur Komposition der mekkanischen Suren* (Berlin, 1981).

[33]Pierre Crapon de Crapona, *Le Coran: aux sources de la parole oraculaire. Structures rythmiques des sourates mecquoises* (Paris, 1981).

[34]G. Lüling, *Über der Ur-Qur'ān. Ansätze zur Rekonstruktion vorislamischer christlicher Strophenlieder im Qur'ān* (Erlangen, 1974).

[35]"Cola" are also discussed in A.H. Mathias Zahniser, "The Word of God and the Apostleship of 'Īsā: a Narrative Analysis of Āl 'Imrān (3): 33–62", *JSS* 36 (1991), 77–112. "Cola" are defined as "breath units of speech, the number of syllables which can be encompassed in a single breath" (88).

[36]See Régis Blachère, *Histoire de la littérature arabe des origines à la fin du XVe siècle de J.-C* (Paris, 1964), II, 187–241; and D.J. Stewart, "*Saj'* in the Qur'ān", Chapter 13 in this volume.

[37]Some of the following material comes from my article "Reading the Qur'ān with Richard Bell", *JAOS* 112 (1992), 641–43.

[38]See Brevard S. Childs, "Wellhausen in English", *Semeia* 25 (1983), 85. Wellhausen's most significant work, *Prolegomena zur Geschichte Israels*, was published in 1878.

> to link together the results of literary criticism with an entirely fresh conception of the history of Israel (and of early Christianity), completely rejecting the church's traditional view of biblical history. His method was to turn directly from the chronological or geographical placing of a written source or a redactor to the outward events of that particular period, for the biblical writers were much influenced by the national or religious political life of their day, and did not consider the old traditions merely as such. They intended their work to have some effect upon contemporary conditions. *This direct connection between determining sources and historical events* is the main characteristic of Wellhausen's treatment to different historical fields.[39]

Viewing scripture in relation to historical development (and as having been reformulated in light of that history) is the fundamental argument here, and only a few words need to be changed in the preceding quotation in order to make it applicable to the core motives and assumptions of Qur'ānic scholarship at the beginning of the twentieth century. The scholarly position has always been that, with a clear understanding of the development of Muḥammad's life, the Qur'ān may be rearranged so that it "makes sense" in terms of history (or, paraphrasing Wellhausen, this is to be done by "constructing history well"). In the case of the Qur'ān furthermore, as has been suggested earlier in this essay, the traditional Muslim sources themselves support, if not in fact encourage, the basic principles lying behind the work of post-Enlightenment scholarship. That is, the ideas of form criticism (in the most general understanding of that method) may be put in conjunction with the material of Muslim tradition such that the latter is pushed to the (logical) extreme of its implications. Muslims speak of the Qur'ān as being written, prior to its collection, on "stones, palm leaves and the hearts of men"; a literary hypothesis for the origins of the text, one which would account for the text's apparent disjointedness, virtually jumps out at the scholar familiar with form criticism when faced with such Muslim testimony. If the distinction between the "J" and the "E" strands of Genesis suggested, to some people, two literary texts being woven together, then, on the evidence of the Muslim tradition itself, the same could be envisioned for the Qur'ān: a weaving together of a text, involving duplications and abrupt breaks, just as in the Bible.

[39]Klaus Koch, *The Growth of the Biblical Tradition: the Form-Critical Method* (New York, 1969), 70, emphasis in the original.

Gustav Weil, in his 1844 publication *Historisch-kritische Einleitung in den Koran*, provided the first attempt[40] (refined in the 2nd edition of the book published in 1872) at a systematic chronological ordering of the *sūra*s of the Qur'ān by tying an understanding of the history of Muḥammad to the text and arriving at what is now the scholarly standard of three Meccan periods and one Medinan. Most of his insights were based on stylistic considerations and, as Welch has pointed out,[41] a general acceptance of the Muslim lists of *sūra* ordering, if not the principles under which those were established. In doing this, some scholars would claim, chronological re-orderings of the Qur'ān have worked in the opposite direction from traditional Muslim scholarship while dealing with something which, on the surface, appears to be concerned with the same topic. Muslim chronology revolved around a life account of Muḥammad (*sīra*) which was both created by and exegetical of the Qur'ān. European scholarship in its early period tended to take the *sīra* and place it back onto the Qur'ān, disregarding the possibility that the *sīra* accounts had, in fact, been produced by exegesis of the scripture. Regardless, the approach became important in the study of the Qur'ān. Significant refinements were added to the approach of Weil by Nöldeke in 1860 in his *Geschichte des Qorāns* and Hartwig Hirschfeld in 1886 and 1902.[42] Jacob Barth's posthumous article "Studien zur Kritik und Exegese des Qorāns"[43] was the first to suggest (from a scholarly perspective) that the Qur'ān had suffered extensively from disruptive editing. In his article he speaks of the need to rearrange sections of the text such that they "make sense". This he put in opposition to Nöldeke's assumption of the fundamental structural coherence of major units of the text as it is now organized, such that, with a limited number of exceptions, entire *sūra*s may

[40] *Historisch-kritische Einleitung in der Koran* (Bielefeld, 1844; 2nd ed. 1872). To suggest that this be recognized as the first attempt at chronology is to argue a significant point. As I have asserted elsewhere, Muslim attempts at ordering the *sūra*s of the Qur'ān are in fact based upon principles quite different from European historical concerns and are done with quite different aims in mind: they do not entail "chronology" as that word is used by modern historians. See my "The Function of *asbāb al-nuzūl* in Qur'ānic Exegesis", *BSOAS* 51 (1988), 1–20.

[41] A.T. Welch, "Ḳur'ān", *EI*², V, 417a.

[42] *Beiträge zur Erklärung des Koran* (Leipzig, 1886); *New Researches into the Composition and Exegesis of the Qoran* (London, 1902). An excellent presentation of German scholarship on Islam of this period in light of Romanticism and Historicism is to be found in Baber Johansen, "Politics and Scholarship: the Development of Islamic Studies in the Federal Republic of Germany", in Tareq Y. Ismael, ed., *Middle East Studies: International Perspectives on the State of the Art* (New York, 1990), esp. 75–90.

[43] *Der Islam* 6 (1916), 113–48. Barth (1851–1914) was a student of H.L. Fleischer and T. Nöldeke; see the obituary by C.H. Becker in *Der Islam* 6 (1916), 200–202.

be taken as blocks and dated as such. Nöldeke does occasionally see displacement in the text, but clearly prefers not to privilege such a reconstructive method.[44] Barth did not develop a theory as to how or why these reformulations took place, except to speak of the vagaries of the collection process; it was Richard Bell's contribution to provide a more extensive explanation and to apply the principles throughout the Qur'ānic text. Bell developed the chronological impulse to a certain logical conclusion, but it was not followed by many scholars to such an extreme. Bell's article on "The Beginnings of Muhammad's Religious Activity" (Chapter 15) is just one example[45] of his attempt to re-organize the Qur'ān piece by piece. Bell's Qur'ān translation[46] and commentary[47] provide a more detailed analysis, working out these same principles.

Despite the lack of acceptance of Bell's specific ideas by scholarship in general, both the impulse and the procedure is clear to see, especially in some semantic studies of the Qur'ān, as already mentioned, in which ordering the *sūra*s at least by the three Meccan periods and the one Medinan (Weil's basic insight) frequently becomes a principle by which the vast quantity of semantic material may be organized. This is true of the work of Causse (Chapter 3), for example, who puts a good measure of trust in the re-ordering of the *sūra*s of the Qur'ān as determined by Régis Blachère in his French Qur'ān translation and introduction,[48] while the works of O'Shaughnessy (Chapter 11) and Bijlefeld (Chapter 9) both rely heavily on Nöldeke in combination with other scholars. The results of such studies tend to be self-confirming: using the chronological framework produces a systematic picture of the development of semantic information which may then be used to re-date elements which do not fit into the basic scheme. Certainly such a method has its circularity, most would admit, but it is often held out that such a study might prove persuasive if it combined a number of such thematic and semantic elements to produce a single cohesive and coherent pattern; a study of this type, however, has not yet been undertaken.[49]

[44]See, for example, his treatment of Qur'ān 29:18–22 in Nöldeke/Schwally, *Geschichte des Qorāns*, I, 157.

[45]See A. Rippin, "Reading the Qur'ān with Richard Bell", 639 n. 4, for a full bibliography of Bell's work.

[46]R. Bell, *The Qur'ān, Translated, with a Critical Re-arrangement of the Surahs* (Edinburgh, 1937–39).

[47]R. Bell, *A Commentary on the Qur'ān* (Manchester, 1991).

[48]R. Blachère, *Le Coran* (Paris, 1949–50; 2nd ed. 1966); idem, *Introduction au Coran* (Paris, 1947; 2nd ed. 1977).

[49]See Welch, "Ḳur'ān", V, 418.

Other Issues

To those knowledgeable in the field, it may appear that certain issues which have been the source of much attention in scholarship are not included directly in this volume. Certainly the subtitle of this volume clearly reflects the focus of attention of articles within the volume itself. However, matters related to the text of the Qur'ān, such as its variants, its historical construction, its chronology and its collection have been omitted, even though there exists a large volume of scholarship devoted specifically to those fields. One reason for this is that studies on the style and content of the Qur'ān raise issues of interest to the larger historical picture of the rise of Islam (which is the focus of this series of books), whereas textual studies do so to a much more limited extent. Furthermore, and perhaps more saliently, the issues which underlie all textual studies make their presence felt in each and every case of the scholarly treatment of the style and the content of the Qur'ān as covered in this volume. Consider the significance of the Flügel edition of the text of the Qur'ān, first published in 1834, and followed by a concordance in 1842.[50] In publishing a text that was eclectic by reading and non-Muslim by design, Flügel made the text fit better within the rules of Classical Arabic orthography by omitting the "additional" vowel signs and reading hints which are found within the developed Muslim *muṣḥaf* (but which are likewise ignored within the Muslim exegetical tradition except when crucial to establishing a tradition of interpretation). Most Western Qur'ānic scholarship in the past used the Flügel edition both for ease of reading and consistency in textual citation. As a result, a legacy of difficulty in communication between traditional Muslim scholars and those working within the tradition of the printed book has lingered on. Furthermore, the starting point of that scholarship is a questionable text-critical foundation, one which allowed textual emendation (even if only to a very limited extent) without any historical justification.[51] While studies of Qur'ān manuscripts flourish, they have not, as yet,[52] affected the actual canon of scripture which is subjected to scholarly study.

[50]See R. Smitskamp, "Flügel's Koran edition", *'Ālam al-kutub* 15 (1994), 533–35.

[51]Useful collections of articles on this aspect of Qur'ānic studies (as well as others) are to be found in Rudi Paret, ed., *Der Koran* (Darmstadt, 1975) and Ibn Warraq, *The History of the Koran: Classic Essays on Islam's Holy Book* (Amherst, 1998).

[52]The studies of a collection of early Yemenite manuscripts may yet have an effect. See Gerd-R. Puin, "Observations on Early Qur'ān Manuscripts in Ṣan'ā'", in S. Wild, ed., *The Qur'ān as Text* (Leiden, 1996), 107–11; also see the popular journalism article by Toby Lester, "What is the Koran?", *The Atlantic Monthly*, January 1999, 43–56.

Other matters are more specific: the so-called mysterious letters at the beginning of some *sūras* have proven to be an intractable problem despite the best efforts of some brilliant minds both within and outside the Muslim community.[53] Such studies, when analyzed as a whole, display the same methodological perspectives and approaches as the field as a whole: the desire to reconstruct a historical situation in which the letters will "make sense"; whether this be internal to the text or external to it, the impetus is the same as that of looking for interpretational context or examining the style of the Qur'ān.

A Glimpse of the Future

The future of the discipline of Qur'ānic studies may be more of the same—the desire for coherence created through solid philological and semantic study put forth in increasingly systematic form—but it may also lie in new directions.

One area, only touched upon slightly above, sees a role to be played in the study of Muslim classical interpretational literature (*tafsīr*) in order to clarify the meaning of the Qur'ān. While strictly speaking this is a matter of more concern for a subsequent volume in this series, the work of Uri Rubin (Chapter 16) does display an example of an approach which strives after the (or "the original") meaning by scouring the classical exegetical sources for items that are deemed likely to be historically true because they would not have been preserved otherwise (frequently because they are contrary to later Muslim dogmatic ideas about the personality of Muḥammad or the nature of revelation).

Fascinating, too, as a vision of future directions, are attempts to understand the Qur'ān in terms of its significance, its difference, and, perhaps most notably, its contribution to culture in general, within a broader cultural framework. While Robert Brunschvig's article (Chapter 17) is, on one level, a simple semantic study, the idea of a study of what the Qur'ān is *not*, as related to linguistic features of the society within which it exists, raises all sorts of possibilities for the future. Indeed, this is one of the directions of liberating thought that is conveyed within the work of Mohammed Arkoun, an example of which is included as Chapter 18 in this volume. He employs the categories of "thought", "unthought" and "unthinkable" in the context of the ways in which the Qur'ān has created, enriched and limited society. This idea also suggests a significance to the study of Brunschvig that

[53]See the fairly complete bibliography and treatement of the topic in Welch "Ḳur'ān", V, 412–14; a new addition is Keith Massey, "A New Investigation into the 'Mystery Letters' of the Quran", *Arabica* 43 (1996), 497–501.

goes beyond the "simple observations" which the latter makes on Qur'ānic and non-Qur'ānic vocabulary. Arkoun's article (and the entire corpus of his scholarly writing) is a call for a broadly based, multi-disciplinary approach to the Qur'ān, one in which scholars themselves are involved in re-defining the meaning of the Qur'ān in a manner appropriate to today's society. This remains a powerful vision of change in the direction of scholarship on the Qur'ān, although it is one which, at the end of the twentieth century, has hardly been acted upon.

Other lines of investigation truly do display new approaches to the Qur'ān, combining different perspectives, different assumptions and different goals. Michael Sells's article (Chapter 19) looks at the interplay of sound and gender in creating meaning within a specific unit of the text. While based to a limited extent upon psychological and physiological aspects of the auditor's reaction to the text and thus highly speculative, the significance of Sells's work lies in its willingness to leave the domain of the philological in order to concentrate on a different dimension, one which essentially argues that the meaning of a text does not inhere in the text itself but in the reader's creation of the meaning.[54] Likewise, Norman O. Brown's article (Chapter 20) brings the outsider's vision to the reading of the Qur'ān. Neither a scholar of Arabic nor of Islam, Brown's is a reading which tries to understand the experience of the text for what it conveys.

The "monological" reading of the Qur'ān, an impulse which lies behind the philological tradition of scholarship and held in common (somewhat ironically perhaps) with contemporary Islamist readings of the Qur'ān, is the main target of the "post-modern" ethos. It would be an unfortunate misreading of the Muslim exegetical tradition to suggest that "through many centuries the Qur'ān has seemed univocal and coherent to a substantial community of people; that its meaning, far from being considered 'nomadic', has appeared clearly settled."[55] One only need to contemplate the *Tafsīr* of al-Qurṭubī for a few moments to realize the joy in which Muslims beheld both the potentialities and the ambiguities of the Qur'ān. But an extensive discussion of that aspect of the topic will take us further into a discussion of the formative period of *tafsīr* than is appropriate for this volume. Whether the "post-modern" emphases will "solve the problem" of the very apparent conflict over the values of scholarship as mapped out by Parvez Manzoor in his article (Chapter 21) is open to question. Manzoor, whose frequent writings

[54]Likewise, Michael Fischer and Mehdi Abedi, *Debating Muslims: Cultural Dialogues in Postmodernity and Tradition* (Madison, 1990), 95–149.

[55]Daniel Madigan, "Reflections on some Current Directions in Qur'ānic Studies", *MW* 85 (1995), 350.

display a lucid command and biting critique of the jargon of contemporary intellectual trends in European thought,[56] is one in a long line of critics of Euro-American scholarship on the Qur'ān, but his article is, in many respects, one of the most perceptive ever written.[57] The epistemological issues with which modern scholarship grapples are precisely those which Manzoor isolates as *the* issue, and rightly so. It is here that post-modern thinking, too, has posed the greatest challenge to the legacy of post-Enlightenment thought.

[56] See his regular contributions to *Muslim World Book Review*.

[57] A comparison between Manzoor and Fazlur Rahman is interesting in this regard; see the latter's "Islamic Studies and the Future of Islam" in M.H. Kerr, ed., *Islamic Studies: a Tradition and its Problems* (Malibu, 1980), 125–33 (esp. 130–32).

BIBLIOGRAPHY

Tools for the Study of the Qur'ān

Allard, Michel. *Analyse conceptuelle du Coran sur cartes perforées*. Paris, 1963.

Jeffery, Arthur, ed. *Materials for the History of the Text of the Qur'ān*. Leiden, 1937.

________. *The Foreign Vocabulary of the Qur'an*. Baroda, 1938.

Kassis, Hanna E. *A Concordance of the Qur'ān*. Berkeley, 1983.

Mir, Mustansir. *Verbal Idioms of the Qur'ān*. Ann Arbor, 1989.

________. *Dictionary of Qur'ānic Terms and Concepts*. New York, 1987.

Paret, Rudi. *Der Koran: Kommentar und Konkordanz*. Stuttgart, 1971; 2nd ed. 1977.

Penrice, John. *A Dictionary and Glossary of the Kor-ān with Copious Grammatical References and Explanations of the Text*. London, 1873.

Bibliographies of Studies of the Qur'ān

Bijlefeld, Willem A. "Some Recent Contributions to Qur'anic Studies: Selected Publications in English, French, and German, 1964–1973", *Muslim World* 64 (1974), 79–102, 172–79, 259–74.

Jeffery, A. "The Present Status of Qur'ānic Studies", *Middle East Institute: Report on Current Research*, Spring 1957, 1–16.

Neuwirth, Angelika. "Koran", in *Grundriss der arabischen Philologie*, II, ed. H. Gätje (Wiesbaden, 1987), 96–135.

Tadros, F.M. *The Holy Koran in the Library of Congress: a Bibliography*. Washington, D.C., 1993.

Introductions to the Study of the Qur'ān

Blachère, Régis. *Le Coran*. Series *Que sais-je?* Paris, 1966; 2nd ed. 1969.

________. *Introduction au Coran*. Paris, 1959.

Nöldeke, Theodor. *Geschichte des Qorāns*: I: *Über den Ursprung des Qorāns*, II: *Die Sammlung des Qorāns*, III: *Die Geschichte des Korantexts*. Leipzig, 1909–38.

Watt, W. Montgomery. *Bell's Introduction to the Qur'ān*. Edinburgh, 1977.

History of the Study of the Qur'ān

Bobzin, Hartmut. *Der Koran im Zeitalter der Reformation. Studien zur Frühgeschichte der Arabistik und Islamkunde in Europa*. Stuttgart, 1995.

Studies on Specific Qur'ānic Topics

Ahrens, K. *Mohammed als Religionsstifler*. Leipzig, 1935.

Ambros, Arne A. "Eine Lexikostatistik des Verbs im Koran", *Weiner Zeitschrift für die Kunde des Morgenlandes* 77 (1987), 9–36.

———. "Gestaltung und Funktionen der Biosphäre im Koran", *Zeitschrift der Deutschen Morgenländischen Gesellschaft* 140 (1990), 290–325.

Arkoun, Mohammed. *Lectures du Coran*. Paris, 1982.

Bakker, Dirk. *Man in the Qur'ān*. Amsterdam, 1965.

Baljon, J.M.S. "The Amr of God in the Koran", *Acta Orientalia* 23 (1958), 7–18.

———. "'To Seek the Face of God' in Koran and Hadith", *Acta Orientalia* 21 (1953), 254–66.

Barth, J. "Studien zur Kritik und Exegese des Qoran", *Der Islam* 6 (1916), 113–248.

Bauer, H. "Über die Anordnung der Suren und über die geheimnisvollen Buchstaben im Qoran", *Zeitschrift der Deutschen Morgenländischen Gesellschaft* 75 (1921), 1–20.

Beck, E. "Die Gestalt des Abraham am Wendepunkt der Entwicklung Muhammeds, Analyse von Sure 2,118 (124)–135 (141)", *Le Muséon* 65 (1952), 73–94.

———. "Iblis und Mensch, Satan und Adam. Der Werdegang einer koranischen Erzählung", *Le Muséon* 89 (1976), 195–244.

———. "Die Sure ar-Rum", *Orientalia* N.S. 13 (1944), 334–55; 14 (1945), 118–42.

Bell, Richard. *A Commentary on the Qur'ān*. 2 vols. Ed. C. Edmund Bosworth and M.E.J. Richardson. Manchester, 1991.

Bellamy, J.A. "Al-Raqīm or Al-Ruqūd? a Note on Sūrah 18: 9", *Journal of the American Oriental Society* 111 (1991), 115–17.

———. "Fa-Ummuhu Hāwiyah: a Note on Sūrah 101: 9", *Journal of the American Oriental Society* 112 (1992), 485–87.

Bergsträsser, Gotthelf. *Verneinungs- und Fragepartikeln und Verwandtes im Ḳur'ān. Ein Beitrag zur historischen Grammatik des Arabischen*. Leipzig, 1914.

Bouman, J. *Gott und Mensch im Koran. Eine Strukturform religiöser Anthropologie anhand des Beispiels Allah und Muhammad.* Darmstadt, 1977.

Chouémi, M. *Le verbe dans le Coran: racines et formes.* Paris, 1966.

Corbon, J. "Notes sur le vocabulaire de prédication des premières sourates mekkoises", *Mélanges de l'Université Saint-Joseph* 36 (1959), 149–95.

Cragg, Kenneth A. *The Event of the Qur'ān: Islam in Its Scripture.* London, 1971; 2nd ed. Oxford, 1994.

________. *The Mind of the Qur'ān.* London, 1973.

Denny, Frederick Mathewson. "The Meaning of 'Ummah' in the Qur'ān", *History of Religions* 15 (August 1975), 34–70.

________. "Some Religio-Communal Terms and Concepts in the Qur'ān", *Numen* 24 (1977), 26–59.

Esack, Farid. *Qur'ān, Liberation and Pluralism: an Islamic Perspective on Interreligious Solidarity against Oppression.* Oxford, 1997.

Haddad, Y.Y. "The Conception of the Term Dīn in the Qur'ān", *Muslim World* 64 (1974), 114–23.

Hirschfeld, Hartwig. *New Researches Into the Composition and Exegesis of the Qoran.* London, 1902.

________. *Beiträge zur Erklärung des Koran.* Leipzig, 1886.

Horovitz, J. "Jewish Proper Names and Derivatives in the Koran", *Hebrew Union College Annual* 2 (1925), 145–227 (repr. separately Hildesheim, 1964).

________. *Koranische Untersuchungen.* Berlin and Leipzig, 1926.

Humphreys, R. Stephen. "Qur'ānic Myth and Narrative Structure in Early Islamic Historiography", in F.M. Clover and R.S. Humphreys, eds., *Tradition and Innovation in Late Antiquity* (Madison, 1989), 271–90.

Ibn Warraq. *The History of the Koran: Classic Essays on Islam's Holy Book.* Amherst, New York, 1998.

Izutsu, Toshihiko. *Ethico-Religious Concepts in the Qur'ān.* Montreal, 1966.

________. *The Structure of the Ethical Terms in the Koran: a Study in Semantics.* Tokyo, 1959.

________. *God and Man in the Koran.* Tokyo, 1964.

Jeffery, Arthur. *The Qur'ān as Scripture.* New York, 1952.

Jomier, Jacques. *Les grands thèmes du Coran.* Paris, 1978; English trans. *The Great Themes of the Qur'an.* London, 1997.

Katsh, Abraham I. *Judaism in Islam: Biblical and Talmudic Backgrounds of the Koran and Its Commentaries.* New York, 1954.

Kronholm, Tryggve. "Dependence and Prophetic Originality in the Koran", *Orientalia Succana* 31–32 (1982–83), 47–70.

Leemhuis, F. *The D and H Stems in Koranic Arabic: a Comparative Study of the Function and Meaning of the fa"ala and 'af'ala Forms in Koranic Usage*. Leiden, 1977.

________. "A Koranic Contest Poem in Sūrat Aṣ-Ṣāffāt?", in G.J. Reinink and H.L.J. Vanstiphout, eds., *Dispute Poems and Dialogues in the Ancient and Medieval Near East* (Leuven, 1991), 165–77.

Lichtenstadter, Ilse. "Origin and Interpretation of Some Koranic Symbols", in G. Makdisi, ed., *Arabic and Islamic Studies in Honor of Hamilton A.R. Gibb* (Cambridge, Mass., 1966), 426–36.

________. "A Note on the *Gharāniq* and Related Qur'ānic Problems", *Israel Oriental Studies* 5 (1975), 54–61.

Lohmann, T. "Die Gleichnisreden Muhammeds im Koran", *Mitteilungen des Instituts für Orientforschung* 12 (1966), 75–118, 241–87.

Marshall, David. *God, Muhammad and the Unbelievers: a Qur'anic Study*. Richmond, 1999.

Martin, Richard C. "Understanding the Qur'ān in Text and Context", *History of Religions* 21 (1982), 361–84.

________. "Text and Contextuality in Reference to Islam", *Semeia* 40 (1987), 125–45.

Masson, D. *Le Coran et la révélation judéo-chrétienne*. Paris, 1958); 2nd ed., *Monothéisme coranique et monothéisme biblique*. Paris, 1976.

Michaud, Henri. *Jésus selon le Coran*. Neuchâtel, 1960.

Mooren, T. "Monothéisme coranique et anthropologie", *Anthropos* 76 (1981), 529–61.

Moubarac, Youakim. *Abraham dans le Coran*. Paris, 1958.

________. *Le Coran et la critique occidentale. Pentalogie islamo-chrétienne*. Beirut, 1972–73.

________. "Moise dans le Coran", in *Moise, l'Homme de l'Alliance* (Paris, 1955), 373-91.

Nagel, Tilman. "Vom 'Qur'ān' zur 'Schrift'—Bells Hypothese aus religionsgeschichtlicher Sicht", *Der Islam* 60 (1983), 143–65.

Nelson, K. *The Art of Reciting the Qur'an*. Austin, 1985.

Neuwirth, Angelika. "Der Horizont der Offenbarung. Zur Relevanz der einleitenden Schwurserien für die Suren der frühmekkanischen Zeit", in Udo Tworuschka, ed., *Gottes ist der Orient—Gottes ist der Okzident: Festschrift für Abdoldjavad Falaturi zum 65. Geburtstag* (Köln and Vienna, 1991), 3–39.

________. *Studien zur Komposition der mekkanischen Suren*. Berlin, 1981.

Nöldeke, Theodor. "Zur Sprache des Korans II: Stilistische und syntaktische Eigentumlichkeiten der Sprache des Korans", in his *Neue Beiträge zur semitischen Sprachwissenschaft* (Strassburg, 1910), 5–23.

O'Shaughnessy, Thomas J. *Creation and the Teaching of the Qur'ān*. Rome, 1985.

________. *The Development of the Meaning of Spirit in the Koran*. Rome, 1953.

________. *The Koranic Concept of the Word of God*. Rome, 1948.

________. *Muhammad's Thoughts on Death: a Thematic Study of the Qur'ānic Data*. Leiden, 1969.

Paret, Rudi. *Mohammed und der Koran. Geschichte und Verkundigüng des arabischen Propheten*. Stuttgart, 1957; 5th ed. 1980.

Parrinder, Geoffrey. *Jesus in the Qur'an*. London, 1965.

Pautz, Otto. *Muhammeds Lehre von der Offenbarung quellenmäszig untersucht*. Leipzig, 1898.

Rahbar, Muhammad Daud. *God of Justice: a Study on the Ethical Doctrine of the Qur'ān*. Leiden, 1960.

Reuschel, Wolfgang. *Aspekt und Tempus in der Sprache des Korans*. Frankfurt, 1996.

Ringgren, Helmer. *Islam, 'Aslama and Muslim*. Uppsala, 1949.

________. "Sin and Forgiveness in the Koran", *Temenos* 2 (1966), 98–111.

Rippin, Andrew. "The Commerce of Eschatology", in S. Wild, ed., *The Qur'ān as Text* (Leiden, 1996), 125–35.

________. "The Poetics of Qur'ānic Punning", *Bulletin of the School of Oriental and African Studies* 57 (1994), 193–207.

Roberts, Robert. *The Social Laws of the Qur'ān: Considered, and Compared with Those of the Hebrew and Other Ancient Codes*. London, 1925.

Robinson, Neal. *Discovering the Qur'an: a Contemporary Approach to a Veiled Text*. London, 1996.

Roest Crollius, A.A. *The Word in the Experience of Revelation in Qur'ān and Hindu Scriptures*. Rome, 1974.

Rudolph, W. *Die Abhängigkeit des Qorans von Judentum und Christentum*. Stuttgart, 1922.

Sabbagh, I. *La métaphore dans le Coran*. Paris, 1943.

Seale, M.S. *Qur'an and Bible*. London, 1978.

Shahid, Irfan. "A Contribution to Koranic Exegesis", in G. Makdisi, ed., *Arabic and Islamic Studies in Honour of Hamilton A.R. Gibb* (Leiden, 1965), 563–80.

———. "Two Qur'ānic Sūras: Al-Fīl and Qurayš", in Wadād al-Qāḍī, ed., *Studia Arabica et Islamica: Festschrift For Iḥsān 'Abbās on His Sixtieth Birthday* (Beirut, 1981), 429–36.

Sidersky, C. *Les origines des légendes musulmanes dans le Coran et dans les vies des prophètes*. Paris, 1933.

Sister, Moses. "Metaphern und Vergleiche im Koran", *Mitteilungen des Seminars für Orientalische Sprachen* 34 (1931), 104–54.

Speyer, H. *Die biblischen Erzählungen im Qoran*. Hildesheim, 1961; 1st ed. 1931.

Stanton, H.U. Weitbrecht. *The Teaching of the Qur'ān, with an Account of its Growth and a Subject Index*. London, 1919.

Torrey, Charles C. *Commercial–Theological Terms in the Qur'ān*. Leiden, 1892.

———. *The Jewish Foundation of Islam*. New York, 1933.

Waardenburg, Jacques. "Koranisches Religionsgespräch. Eine Skizze", in G. Widengren, *et al.*, eds., *Liber Amicorum: Studies in Honour of C.J. Bleeker* (Leiden, 1969), 208–53.

———. "Un débat coranique contre les polythéistes", in K. Bolle *et al.*, eds., *Ex Orbe Religionum: Studia Geo Widengren* (Leiden, 1972), II, 143–54.

———. "Faith and Reason in the Argumentation of the Qur'ān", in *Perennitas: studi in onore di A. Brelich* (Rome, 1980), 619–33.

Wagtendonk, K. *Fasting in the Koran*. Leiden, 1968.

Waldman, M.R. "The Development of the Concept of *Kufr* in the Qur'ān", *Journal of the American Oriental Society* 88 (1968), 442–55.

———. "New Approaches to 'Biblical' Materials in the Qur'ān", *Muslim World* 75 (1985), 1–16.

Walker, John. *Bible Characters in the Koran*. Paisley, 1931.

Wansbrough, John. *Quranic Studies: Sources and Methods of Scriptural Interpretation*. Oxford, 1977.

Watt, William Montgomery. "The Qur'ān and Belief in a 'High God'", in Rudolph Peters, ed., *Proceedings of the Ninth Congress of the Union Européenne des Arabisants et Islamisants* (Leiden, 1981), 327–33.

———. *Muhammad's Mecca: History in the Qur'ān*. Edinburgh, 1988.

———. "His Name is Aḥmad (cxi,6)", *Muslim World* 43 (1953), 110–17.

Weil, Gustav. *Historisch-kritische Einleitung in den Koran*. Bielefeld, 1844.

Welch, Alford T. "Allah and Other Supernatural Beings: the Emergence of the Qur'ānic Doctrine of Tawḥīd", *Journal of the American Academy of Religion Thematic Studies* 47 (1979), 733–58.

——— "Muhammad's Understanding of Himself: the Koranic Data", in R.G. Hovannisian and S. Vryonis, eds., *Islam's Understanding of Itself* (Malibu, 1983), 15–52.

Zahniser, A.H. Mathias. "The Word of God and the Apostleship of 'Īsā: a Narrative Analysis of Āl-'Imrān (3), 33–62", *Journal of Semitic Studies* 36 (1991), 77–112.

Zwettler, Michael. "A Mantic Manifesto: the Sūra of 'The Poets' and the Qur'ānic Foundations of Prophetic Authority", in James L. Kugel, ed., *Poetry and Prophecy: the Beginnings of a Literary Tradition* (Ithaca, 1990), 75–119.

1

ISLAM AND THE QUMRAN SECT

Chaim Rabin

LEST the theory that some late remnants of the Qumran sect survived in Arabia until the seventh century A.D. appear too fanciful from the outset, it is necessary to state that there are certain questions we must ask ourselves and to which the Scrolls themselves cannot provide the answer. These are:

1. What became of the sect after it left Qumran in what—judging by the abandonment of its library—seems to have been precipitate flight?[1]

2. On any dating of the sect, how can we explain that some of its teachings and terminology reappear in the last quarter of the first millennium? The theory of an earlier discovery of Cave No. I suffers from the fact that no such event is mentioned in the literature of the circles supposedly most deeply influenced.[2]

The probability that the suggestions made in the following pages are at least in part correct is enhanced by the circumstance that they deal not with major ideas—where independent origin in different places and 'mental climate' are complicating factors—but with small and secondary details, mainly of a philological nature. Since the latter are in many cases firmly anchored in a definite literary background, they can have been borrowed only by direct contact. They concern such matters as are admitted to be borrowed, even in the view of those scholars who believe Muhammad's religious ideas to have been largely original.[3]

The problem of the outside influences which went into the make-up of early Islam has attracted the attention of scholars ever since 1833, when Geiger published his youthful effort *Was hat Mohammed aus dem Judenthume aufgenommen?*[4] In 1867 Sprenger[5]

[1] It is hardly likely to have fled into Roman-occupied Judaea.

[2] No Jewish record exists of the discovery reported in the famous letter of Timotheus.

[3] e.g. Fück, *ZDMG* xc (1936), 509–25.

[4] Up-to-date bibliography in Katsh, *Judaism in Islam*, 1954.

[5] *Das Leben und die Lehre des Mohammed* (2nd edn., 1869).

demonstrated that much in Muhammad's religious outlook—including his theory of revelation and of his own prophetic office—cannot be explained on the basis of (Rabbinic) Jewish influence alone. Wellhausen[1] in 1887 coined the dictum: 'Von den Juden stammt nicht der Sauerteig, aber allerdings zum grossen Teile das Mehl, das später zugesetzt wurde.' In the present century T. Andrae[2] and K. Ahrens[3] made an attempt to show that much of the 'flour' was also Christian, while Torrey[4] brought to light much new material in support of Jewish origin, drawn especially from more intensive comparative study of the Koranic stories about O.T. prophets and Talmud and midrash.[5] In this connexion we may mention the effort of J. Finkel[6] to find the missing link in non-Rabbinic or pre-Rabbinic Jewish sects, and Gaster's[7] theory of Samaritan influence upon Muhammad. Amongst the partisans of Christian influence, too, there has been a tendency to seek the proximate source in Nestorianism or in Judaeo-Christian sects, such as the Ebionites,[8] Docetists, or Elkesaites.[9] The prominence of Gnostic traits in Islam moved C. Clemens[10] in 1921 to ascribe to Manichaeism a decisive influence upon it.

[1] *Reste arabischen Heidentums*, 2nd edn. (1927), p. 242.

[2] *Der Ursprung des Islams und das Christentum*, 1926.

[3] 'Christliches im Quran', *ZDMG* lxxxiv (1930), 15–68, 148–90.

[4] *Jewish Foundations of Islam*, 1933.

[5] The possibilities of this are by no means exhausted; see, e.g., Yahuda, *Goldziher Memorial Volume*, i (1948), 280–308, who brings further elucidation from recently-published Yemenite midrashim. We may add that Haman's presence at Pharaoh's court (by identification with his ancestor Amalek, who is in the midrash one of Pharaoh's advisers) may be alluded to in Alkabeẓ's *Mĕnoth ha-Levi* (Venice, 1585, f. 153b), which says Haman found one of the treasures buried by Joseph. Joseph's vision of the *burhān* (Ethiopic = 'light') of his Lord (12. 24) may connect with the late midrash where God threatens Joseph that He will cast away the *Even Shĕthiyyah* and reduce the world to Chaos (Ginzberg, *Legends*, ii. 54)—the *Even Shĕthiyyah* being the source of the first light at the Creation (ibid. i. 12).

[6] 'Old-Israelitish Tradition in the Koran', *PAAJR* ii (1931), 7–21; 'Jewish, Christian and Samaritan Influences on Arabia', *D. B. Macdonald Presentation Volume* (1933), pp. 147–66.

[7] 'Samaritans', in *Enc. Isl.* iv. 124–9.

[8] Whose identity with the Qumran sect has been advocated by J. L. Teicher.

[9] On this group, who have some points of contact with the Qumran sect, see Waitz, in *Harnack-Ehrung* (1921), pp. 87–104; Brandt in *Enc. Rel. and Ethics*, s.v.; Cullmann, *Le probl. littér. et hist. du roman pseudo-clémentin* (1930), pp. 170–83.

[10] In *Harnack-Ehrung* (1921), pp. 249–62.

In view of this inconclusive search it seems not unreasonable to test also possible connexions with the Qumran sect, especially as the latter lies at the intersection of almost all the previous lines of inquiry: it has close contact both with Rabbinic and non-Rabbinic Judaism, shows certain Gnostic traits,[1] and has numerous connections both with the early Church and the Judaeo-Christian sects. Thus features common to it, Islam, and one of the foregoing can provide further support for a connexion between it and Islam, provided such a connexion has been made probable by traits common to the Qumran sect and Islam alone.

The possibility of the main Jewish influence on Muhammad having been that of a heretical Jewish sect was first put forward by S. D. Goitein in 1933,[2] and elaborated in 1953,[3] when he specified this sect as one 'strongly influenced by Christianity'. In his Columbia University lectures of the same year,[4] he suggested that Muhammad was in his debate with the Jews of Medina merely carrying on an internal Jewish controversy, being supplied with arguments by his heretical teachers,[5] and also seriously weighed the possibility of these teachers coming from 'an offshoot of the community of the Dead Sea Scrolls',[6] but rejected this, 'because if it were so, it would not have had such close affinities with the Talmudic literature to which the Koran bears such eloquent testimony'.

By stressing the close affinities of the Qumran sect with Rabbinic Judaism, the preceding pages have endeavoured to remove just that objection. I may now set out in detail the similarities which I have so far encountered, and then try to assess their significance.

1. Like the Qumran literature, the Koran makes extensive use of the symbolism of light and darkness to distinguish between the realms of God and Satan, e.g. 'Allah is the light of heavens and earth . . . Allah guides to His light whom He wills . . . as to those

[1] Cf. B. Reicke, *N.T. Studies*, i (1954) 137–41.
[2] In a lecture delivered at Tel-Aviv.
[3] *Gotthold Weil Jubilee Volume* (1952), pp. 10–23 (in Hebrew).
[4] Published in the *Jewish Observer*, 1953–4; now as *Jews and Arabs* (New York, 1955).
[5] *Jewish Observer* of 5 Dec. 1952, p. 12.
[6] Ibid., 28 Nov. 1952, p. 12; *Jews and Arabs*, pp. 57–58.

who disbelieve, their deeds are like . . . darkness upon a vast abysmal sea, layer upon layer of darkness . . . and he for whom Allah has not appointed light, for him there is no light' (24. 35–40). This symbolism, of course, also exists in the N.T., which even has the Qumran term 'children of light',[1] missing in the Koran, but does not, like Qumran literature and the Koran, link 'light' with the idea of absolute predestination (cf. Eph. v. 8, 'ye were darkness before, but now ye are light in the Lord'). The Koran also frequently repeats the idea that Allah misleads the sinners, for which cf. CDC ii. 13, 'but those whom He hated, He misled'.

2. The leader of the sons of light is the 'prince of lights',[2] and it is he by whose hand Moses and Aaron were raised, while Belial raised Jannes and Mambres (CDC v. 18). Similarly, Muhammad's career is guided by Gabriel, called 'the holy spirit' in 16. 104; 26. 193. Gabriel is the 'herald of light'[3] in the apocryphal *Story of Joseph the Carpenter*.[4] In DSW, on the other hand, Michael is the special angel appointed over Israel. Yadin[2] argues from this and other sources that in fact Michael was the prince of lights; however, the very passage he adduces, DSW xvii. 6–8, can also be taken as an argument against it. If, as is said there, 'God made mighty (*he'ĕdhir*) the office of Michael with light of eternities . . . so as to raise amongst the angels the office of Michael and the authority of Israel amongst all flesh', this implies that Michael's power—like that of Israel—is for the time being in eclipse, and that the 'light' will only be bestowed upon him at the final battle. A certain rivalry between Michael and Gabriel is implied by the tradition, preserved in the Ethiopic poem *Ṭabība Ṭabībān*,[5] that 'Gabriel was raised like Michael' after the fall of Lucifer. However, it must be noted that the name of Gabriel for the guiding angel appears only at Medina, and that an Islamic tradition[6] tells us that the Jews of Medina held Gabriel to be the angel of divine wrath. The name may thus be secondary and polemical,[7] and the

[1] Luke xvi. 8; John xii. 36; Eph. v. 8; 1 Thess. v. 5.

[2] Cf. Yadin, ch. 9, para. 5. [3] For 'herald' = teacher, cf. pp. 55, 98.

[4] Ch. xxii. This apocryphal Gospel exists in Arabic.

[5] Dillmann, *Chrestomathia Aethiopica*, p. 108, vs. 3, line 2.

[6] See Katsh, op. cit., pp. 68–69.

[7] Cf. also O'Shaughnessy, *The Development of the Meaning of Spirit in the Qur'an* (1953), pp. 48–49.

connexion with Qumran thought, while attractive, remains obscure.

3. Like the Qumran sect and the N.T., Muhammad held the entire O.T., prophets and all, to be books of prediction.[1] They were indeed thought also in Rabbinic literature to predict details of the Messianic coming, so that the difference lies not so much in the attitude to the O.T. as in the evaluation of one's own time, which the former three identified with that preceding the Coming. Muhammad did not get his belief, that his coming and actions were foretold in the 'Torah', from Christian sources, since he tells us himself: 'And lo, it is in the scriptures of the men of old. Is it not a sign for them that the learned ones of the children of Israel know it?' (26. 197). Moses is made to say: 'I shall write down my mercy for those that believe in my verses, that follow the gentile prophet whom they shall find written down for them in the Torah and the Gospel'[2] (7. 156–7). Details of his ministry were foretold, as, for example, the change of the direction of prayer: 'Those unto whom we gave the scripture know this as they know their sons, but a party of them knowingly conceal the truth' (2. 146).

This kind of prediction was expected from Jews. Ṭabarī[3] tells how Kaʿb al-Aḥbār informed ʿOmar I that he had read in the Torah of his impending death. To the latter's question, 'Did you really find ʿOmar b. al-Khaṭṭāb in the Torah?', he replies, 'Not your name, but your description and appearance'. Similarly, Kaʿb's son predicted the death of ʿAmr b. Saʿīd, and later an exilarch the death of Ḥusain.[4] We are reminded of Josephus' statement about the Essenes (*BJ* II. viii. 12): 'There are some among them who profess to foretell the future, being versed from their early years in holy books, &c.'[5] It is hardly an activity typical of Rabbinic Jewry, but this kind of lower prophecy must have been widespread amongst the Qumran sect, to judge from the treatise on physiognomy preserved amongst the fragments from Cave IV.

[1] Cf. below, p. 128, on the *Pesher* to Psalms.

[2] Since Waraqa also had a 'gospel' in Hebrew, it is not impossible that the 'gospel' (*injīl*) in this connexion refers to a sectarian writing rather than the N.T.

[3] Leiden edn., i. 5, pp. 2722–3.

[4] Cf. Van Vloten, *Recherches sur la domination arabe* (1894), pp. 55–56.

[5] See also Thackeray's note in the Loeb edn., and cf. the instance in *Ant.* XV. x. 5.

3. The use of the O.T. for prognosis is, of course, called *pesher* by the Qumran sect, with the verb *pashar* Qal (לפשור, DSH ii. 8). The noun occurs Eccles. viii. 1, not in any technical sense, and both noun and verb in Bibl. Aram., in Samar., and in Syr. for the interpretation of dreams. For the technical sense of interpretation Bacher[1] has no Tannaitic example and only one from the *Pesiqta*. Otherwise, Rabbinic Hebrew uses *prsh* Piʿel. The use of *pshr* seems ultimately to be derived from Accadian *pašāru*, 'to interpret a dream', *pišīru*, 'interpretation', but the application to the interpretation of texts seems to have arisen in the special circumstances of the Qumran sect, where such interpretation was a form of inspiration. It is therefore significant when we find in Koran 25. 32 (second Meccan period) the verbal noun *tafsīr* in a context referring to sacred books,[2] and in Islamic usage *fassara* as the normal word for Koran interpretation.

4. We learn from various sources about the pre-Islamic *ḥanīfs*, men who had accepted monotheism without becoming Jews or Christians[3] and practised asceticism. The Koran uses this term six times of Abraham, twice of Muhammad (10. 105; 30. 29), and twice of the Muslim community (22. 32; 98. 4). The word has so far defied interpretation.[4] It is different in form from Syr. *ḥanpā*, 'heathen', with which it is most frequently connected, but fairly close to Heb. *ḥānēf*, which in MH means one who is insincere in his faith.[5] By connecting it either with the Syriac or the MH word, we imply that it was a name given to these men by Jews or Christians and misunderstood by them as a name of honour.

It is, however, possible to suggest an explanation which makes *ḥanīf* a straightforward descriptive word. The Qumran sect had proselytes among its ranks (*gerim*, CDC xiv. 6); in DSD v. 6 these are called *ha-nilwim ʿălehem*, 'they that join themselves unto them'.[6] Arabic *ḥanafa*, 'to incline, turn', is a synonym of Arab.

[1] *Die exegetische Terminologie* (1905), ii. 174.

[2] See also Jeffery, *The Foreign Vocabulary of the Qur'an* (Baroda, 1938), p. 92.

[3] There were also full proselytes to Judaism; cf. Nöldeke, *ZDMG* xli (1887), 720.

[4] The various suggestions are summarized in Hirschberg, *Jüdische und christliche Lehren im vor- und frühislamischen Arabien* (Krakow, 1939), p. 33, n. 1.

[5] Gen. Rabba 25. 1: 'Enoch was a *ḥanef*, being at times righteous, at others wicked'; cf. also *ḥănefē Torah*, B.T. Soṭ. 42a.

[6] Used for 'proselyte' in Isa. xiv. 1; lvi. 3, 6; Zech. ii. 15.

lawā; the Hebrew word may thus, not unreasonably, have been understood from its Arabic homonym as 'those who incline', viz. towards the teaching of the sect.

Since the Qumran sect daily expected the Messianic coming, there was not much point in proselytizing unless the heathen proselytes played some role in its plan of salvation. The connexion of the hanif movement with the sect thus gains ground from what we shall learn later of the attitude to the 'gentile prophet'.

5. Wellhausen's chief objection[1] to a Jewish origin of Islam was its intense preoccupation with the end of the world, which is absent in Talmudic Judaism, and, as Wellhausen admits, also from seventh-century Christianity. It remained a preoccupation of Muslims until *c.* A.D. 750, when those interested in learning in Egypt are said to have studied nothing but eschatological prophecies.[2] All its eschatological terminology must therefore be early.[3] It is mostly attached to the name of Ka'b al-Aḥbār. Kuthayyir 'Azza (d. A.D. 723) says:

That is the Mahdī of whom Ka'b the fellow of the *aḥbār* told us in times past.[4]

As we know, intense Messianism was also one of the characteristics of the Qumran sect. It is important that precisely in the field of eschatological terminology connexions exist.

6. The generic Muslim name for Messianic events is *malḥama*, pl. *malāḥim*.[5] This is obviously the Hebrew word *milḥamah*, 'war', but in Rabbinic parlance these events are called *ḥevlē ha-Mashiaḥ*, 'birth pangs of the Messiah', and the only place, to my knowledge, where *milḥamah* occurs in this sense is in a report about the finding of an old Messianic scroll, B.T. San. 97b. In DSW the word occurs in the Messianic sense in the title, and again in 'the epochs of the wars of Thine hands', xi. 8. While the Messianic wars in Rabbinic eschatology are fought out by the heathen nations, the war of DSW is fought by Israel, begins in the 'desert of Jerusalem', and ends

[1] *Reste arabischen Heidentums*, 2nd edn. (1927), pp. 240–2.

[2] Nawawī, *Tahdhīb*, xi. 319; cf. Goldziher, *Muhammedanische Studien*, ii. 73.

[3] Cf. Casanova, *Mohammed et la fin du monde* (1911), *passim*.

[4] Mas'ūdī, *Prairies d'Or*, v. 181.

[5] On which see Steinschneider, *ZDMG* xxviii (1874), 627–59; Goldziher, *Muhammedanische Studien*, ii. 73, 127.

forty years later with the conquest of Ham and Japheth.[1] The Muslim *malḥama* begins at Medina and ends with the destruction of 'Rome' (Constantinople),[2] according to one version by 70,000 'sons' of Isaac'.[3] Probably the final event of the sectarian war also was the conquest of Rome.

It is interesting to note, in this connexion, that Saadiah renders *ish milḥamah* in Exod. xv. 3 as *dhū 'l-malāḥim*, apparently following the eschatological interpretation of the song hinted at in B.T. San. 91b.

7. One of the stages of the *malḥama* is called *al-harj*, a word without any meaning in Arabic,[4] but evidently the Hebrew *heregh*, 'slaughter'. This occurs in DST xv. 17, *yom hăreghah*. The latter is borrowed from Jer. xii. 3, but the Arabic form reminds one more of *heregh* in Isa. xxx. 25, 'on the day of the great slaughter, when the towers fall'.

8. The word *ḥashr* occurs twice in the Koran, once in the early Sura 55. 44, in an eschatological setting, and again in the Medinean 59. 2, in connexion with the destruction of the Jewish Banū Naḍīr. There is, of course, the common Koranic verb *ḥashara*, 'to gather',[5] and the sense 'gathering' fits the context in the first passage. In the second there is no 'gathering', and Muslim commentators find much difficulty in accounting for the word. It is just possible that we may have here, perhaps used sneeringly, the word *naḥshīr* which describes the final battle in DSW i. 9, 10, 13. This word, ultimately from Persian *nakhchīr*, 'hunt', occurs also in Syriac and in the derivation *naḥshīrkhān*, 'hunter', in Targumic Aramaic.[6] In Syriac it appears once as *ḥashīrā*,[7] which

[1] The Banū Qantūrā', a Turkish people, play a part in Muslim eschatology; cf. Attema, *De mohammedaansche opvattingen omtrent het tijdstip van den jongsten dag en zijn voorteekenen* (1942), p. 57. In DSW ii. 13 the Benē Qĕṭurah are the last Semitic people to be conquered.

[2] Cf. Attema, op. cit., pp. 89 seq. (Ibn Ḥanbal, ii. 174; vi. 27, &c.).

[3] Ibid., pp. 92–93 (Muslim 52. 79). For the number, cf. in DSW: seven skirmishing standards, seven heavy infantry formations, &c., and the 'myriad' as the largest military unit.

[4] For occurrences, see Attema, pp. 63–66. Ibn Ḥanbal, v. 389, says the word is Ethiopic: there is no such word in Ethiopic, but it is used in South-Arabian.

[5] South-Arabian *ḥśr* (note the sibilant), 'to collect produce', perhaps MH *ḥshr*, 'to distil (?)'.

[6] See Yadin ad. loc.

[7] Cf. Brockelmann, *Lexicon*, 2nd edn., p. 263b.

is possibly not a scribal error, but due to the *na-* being taken as a nominal prefix.[1] The matter, however, is rather uncertain.

9. The name of the Muslim Messiah, *mahdī*, literally 'the rightly guided one', is strange.[2] It is 'written of him in the *Malāḥim* books that he will fill the earth with justice'.[3] The preoccupation with justice which dominates Hebrew prophecy is alien to Islam, and its appearance in this connexion unusual. Perhaps we have here some attempt at translating *moreh ha-ẓedheq*. We instinctively take this as an active participle, but it is not at all impossible to read *mureh ha-ẓedheq*, 'he that is taught righteousness', stressing the inspirational side of his character.[4]

10. We are on safer ground with the Arabic name for the Antichrist (and also occasionally for the devil), *dajjāl*. This is said to be a loan from Syriac *daggālā*, which (like the corresponding Chr. Pal. Aram. word) means indeed 'liar', but not 'Antichrist', which is *mĕshīḥā dĕ-dhaggālūthā*. In the scrolls the opponent of the Teacher of Righteousness is called the teacher (or man) of lies,[5] the latter form borrowed from Prov. xix. 22. Now the root *dgl*, 'to lie', appears only in the Syriacizing Targum to Proverbs (mostly corrupted to *rgl*). In xix. 22 we have, indeed, *gavrā kaddāvā* (though Pesh. has *gavrā da-mdaggel*), but a few verses farther on we get *daggalā* as translation of *bĕliyaʿal* (in 'a false witness', Pesh. *ʿāwālā*). The transition from 'liar' to 'Antichrist' thus seems to have taken place in a Jewish milieu rather than in a Christian one, and it might at least be surmised that it served as an Aramaic rendering for *ish kazav*. Incidentally, *dajjāl* also appears in Muslim eschatology simply as 'false teacher', as in the tradition of the thirty *dajjālūn*, where another version has thirty *kadhdhābūn*.[6]

11. The other name for the devil, *Iblīs*, is generally derived

[1] As, e.g., in *nabrīḥā*=*barḥā*, 'he-goat'. [2] Cf. Casanova, op. cit., pp. 66–67.
[3] Bīrūnī, tr. Sachau, p. 19. The idea also in traditions (B. Ḥanbal, iii. 36; A. Dā'ūd, 35:1, No. 3), cf. Attema, p. 101.
[4] Since the name is based on Hos. x. 12, where the subject of 'will teach' is God, a passive sense is perhaps more faithful to Scripture. Pesh. and Vulg., however, have the active participle.
[5] See above, p. 55.
[6] Attema, p. 53. Muhammad is said to have called a Jew in Medina *dajjāl* (Van Vloten, op. cit., p. 59): does this perhaps mean that Muhammad's Jewish friends called that man 'teacher of lies'?

from διάβολος, and it has been suggested that the *d*- was dropped owing to its being taken as the Syriac genitive particle. Jeffery[1] rightly points out that the name was not current in Syriac. We might therefore draw attention to the theory of Künstlinger[2] and J. Finkel,[3] according to which the name was corrupted from a hypothetical *Belias*; cf. the *Beliar* of some Greek pseudepigrapha. This would establish a further connexion with the scrolls, where Belial frequently occurs as the name of the 'prince of darkness'.

12. The sinners, who hide the proofs and the revelation received by them, shall be cursed by Allah and 'those who curse' (2. 159); those who die in unbelief have upon them the curse of 'Allah and the angels and all men'. Similarly, in CDC xx. 8 the backslider will be cursed by 'all the holy ones (= angels) of the highmost'.[4]

13. Aḥmad b. Muḥammad ath-Thaʿlabī (d. A.D. 1035) in his *Stories of the Prophets*[5] says that the name of Muhammad was created 2,000 years before the creation of the world and inscribed on the throne of glory. This is remarkably like the midrashic statement about the name of the Messiah having been created before the world (Gen. Rabba 1. 4); even closer is the version in the late Midr. Psalms on Ps. xc, in which all the pre-existing things were created 2,000 years[6] before the world and the name of the Messiah is engraved on the altar of the heavenly sanctuary. In CDC the names of the elect are fixed from all eternity (CDC ii. 13; iv. 5). Similarly, Koran 30. 56 states: 'And to those to whom knowledge and faith have been given, say, you are permanently inscribed in the book of Allah until the day of the resurrection.'[7] The Shiʿite messiah must bear the same pre-created name as Muhammad.[8]

[1] *The Foreign Vocabulary of the Qur'an*, p. 48.

[2] *Rocznik Orient.* iv (1928), 238–47.

[3] *D. B. Macdonald Presentation Volume*, p. 156.

[4] Perhaps the 'cursers' are none but the 'angels of destruction'; CDC ii. 6; DSW xiii. 12.

[5] Cairo edn., p. 181.

[6] The number is in the midrash based on *yom yom* in Prov. viii. 31 (one day of God = 1,000 years), hence no doubt the Jewish version is the original one.

[7] Jeffery, *The Qur'an as Scripture* (1952), p. 10, rightly takes this to mean that the names were inscribed; the interpretation of the Muslim commentators is different.

[8] Casanova, op. cit., p. 64.

14. An important difference between the Scrolls and Rabbinic Judaism is that the latter knows of an evil force within man, the 'evil inclination',[1] while the Qumran sect, like Christianity, the Mandaeans, and some late midrashim (*Pirqe R. Eliezer*, *Midrash ha-Gadol*),[2] know only of an external Satan who misleads men into sin. This, of course, is the position of Islam, too. Possibly a polemic against the doctrine of the internal duality in man is reflected in the statement, Koran 33. 4, in the wake of a rather obscure reference to divorce and adoption, 'Allah has not given man two hearts.'

The above items are not all of the same value; on the other hand, it seems not unlikely that the number of correspondences could be increased. Their importance, as I have said before, rests precisely on their comparative unimportance, which makes independent creation in most of the cases rather improbable. We must now attempt to trace the way in which they may have reached Muhammad.

His contemporaries were aware that he had informants, and called his teachings 'ancient fables which he has written from dictation in the morning and in the evening' (25. 4). The prophet admitted this indirectly when he said: 'the speech of him at whom they hint is barbaric,[3] but this Koran is clear Arabic speech' (16. 103). Tradition tells us that Muhammad did not understand the meaning and nature of his visions, and had to be enlightened by the Judaizing cousin of his wife, Waraqa;[4] the latter was in possession of a 'gospel' which he had copied in Hebrew.[5] The presence of informants is also indicated by the fact that Biblical examples are completely missing from the earliest Suras[6] and during the first Meccan period are stated with cryptic brevity smacking of unfamiliarity.[7] But these teachers did not only tell

[1] Although the story of the slaughtering of the 'evil inclination' (B.T. Suk. 52a) suggests that it could also be imagined as a person.

[2] Hirschberg, op. cit., p. 52.

[3] This may either mean foreign, or Arabic badly pronounced.

[4] Blachère, *Le problème de Mahomet* (1952), p. 41.

[5] Bukhārī, ed. Krehl, i. 5.

[6] In fact, historical examples are not used at all before Sura 105; cf. Attema, op. cit., p. 9, n. 8.

[7] e.g. (in the order of Suras as in Nöldeke) 87. 19; 95. 2; 85. 18; 73. 15; 53. 52. The earliest of these, 87. 19, refers to the 'scrolls of Abraham and Moses';

him Biblical stories: like Waraqa, they also enlightened him about his own mission.

Muhammad uses of himself the phrase *an-nabī al-ummī*,[1] which has long been recognized to mean 'the gentile prophet', derived from the MH *ummoth ha-ʿolam*, 'gentes mundi',[2] and not, as the Muslim commentators say, 'the illiterate prophet'. In 62. 2 this is expressed even more clearly as 'the prophet raised up from the midst of the gentiles (*ummiyyūna*)'. The word occurs only in connexion with prophecy: it is therefore likely that he received the whole phrase from a Jewish source. What does 'gentile prophet' mean?

The Byzantine chronicler, Theophanes,[3] writing about A.D. 815, relates that certain prominent Jews believed Muhammad to be the Messiah they expected. They went to him, but soon realized their hopes were false, nevertheless they stayed on and managed to turn him against the Christians. The same story is also preserved in a Jewish account from the Genizah.[4] This claims that their conversion was feigned, and their plan was to prevent him from turning against the Jews. Also some of their names are given. The most important one is the famous Kaʿb al-Aḥbār,[5] to whom so many of the Biblical and eschatological items in Arabic tradition are traced back. B. Chapira[6] has made it probable that writings by him continued to circulate amongst orthodox Jews. His title is suggestive: although later Muslim writers say *aḥbār* is a singular and means 'Rabbi', its form is obviously a plural of *ḥaber*, and he is called 'Kaʿb of the *ḥaberim*'; this was still clear to Kuthayyir ʿAzza[7] when he called him 'the fellow of the *aḥbār*'. However, *ḥaber* was not a common title of a Rabbi in the seventh century, and it may show him to have belonged to a group where the title was still typical.

Whether the story of these converts is true or not—and it is

this almost gives the impression as if this was written under the impetus of some new source with which he had just become acquainted.

[1] 7. 157–8.

[2] Jeffery, *Foreign Vocabulary*, p. 69, recognizes *umma* as a loan-word, but does not discuss *ummī*.

[3] i. 333; cf. Schwabe, *Tarbiẓ*, ii (1930–1), 74 seq.

[4] Ed. Leveen, *JQR* xvi (1925–6), 399–406; cf. Baneth, *Tarbiẓ*, iii (1931–2), 112–16.

[5] On him, cf. M. Perlmann, *Joshua Starr Memorial Volume* (1953), pp. 85–99; *JQR* xlv (1954), 48–58.

[6] *RÉJ* lxix (1919), 86–107.

[7] In the verse quoted above, p. 118.

difficult to see why Jews should have circulated it—the conversion of Ka'b is undoubtedly an historical fact. What could have caused a man of such learning to become a convert and Muslim propagandist? I think the answer can be found in Sura 7. 156–8 (Medinean): 'the gentile prophet whom ye find written in the Torah . . . and who will remove from them their burden and the fetters that are upon them'. The Jews of Arabia were free and prosperous; the 'fetters' clearly point to a Byzantine origin of the idea. Whoever communicated the thought to Muhammad must have seen in him a possible liberator of Jewry from the yoke of the 'kingdoms', a figure in the Messianic drama.

This view is put unequivocally in the 'Secrets revealed to R. Simeon bar Yoḥai',[1] which date, as has been shown by B. Lewis,[2] from the end of the Omayyad dynasty *c.* A.D. 750 and probably contain a nucleus written at the very beginning of the Islamic conquests. We read there: 'Metatron answered and said, God only raises the kingdom of Ishmael to save you from this wicked power,[3] and He will establish over them a prophet according to His desire (*navi ki-rĕẓono*).'[4] Ibn Hishām, indeed, tells us[5] that the Jews of Medina expected such a prophet just before Muhammad appeared on the scene. There seems to have been some Messianic ferment leading to difficulties. Balādhurī[6] has preserved the information that at the time some Jewish merchants lived at Ṭā'if, who had been banished (*ṭuridū*) from Yemen and Yathrib (i.e. Medina). While Yemenites might, as Lammens suggested,[7] have come there after the destruction of the Jewish kingdom in Yemen, Jews from Medina can have been 'banished' only as a result of internal quarrels. It is suggestive that Ṭā'if was the home town of the Ḥanīf poet Umayya ibn Abī 'ṣ-Ṣalt, whose work exhibits such curious similarity with the Koran.[8]

[1] Publ. Jellinek, *Beth ha-Midrasch*, iii (1855), 78–82.

[2] 'An Apocalyptic Vision of Islamic History', *BSOAS* xiii (1950), 308–38.

[3] The common appellation of the Roman Empire, both in the Scrolls and in Rabbinic literature. Cf. CDC vi. 10; DSW i. 13; B.T. Shab. 15a: '180 years before the Temple was destroyed, the wicked kingdom atacked Israel.'

[4] The phrase 'according to His desire' for God's cosmic plan occurs also DSD v. 1, as well as in the *Kaddish* prayer (*ki-rĕ'utheh*).

[5] i. 286, 373; cf. Pautz, *Muhammed's Lehre von der Offenbarung* (1898), p. 130.

[6] *Futūḥ*, Leiden edn., p. 56.

[7] *Ta'if*, p. 88.

[8] On him, see Hirschberg, op. cit.

The attitude of certain Jews to Muhammad's revelations is shown by two passages in Suras from the end of the Meccan period: 'when the Koran is being recited to them they say, We believe in it, it is the truth from our Lord' (28. 53); 'those unto whom we gave the scriptures rejoice in what has been revealed to thee, but of the (Arab) tribes there are who deny some of it' (13. 36). Yet when Muhammad came to Medina he met with the undisguised hostility and ridicule of the Jewish community there. This becomes much easier to understand if we assume that the teachings he brought were not unfamiliar to the Medinean Jews, being those of heretics they had but recently expelled. But above all, the theory of heretical Jewish mentors explains the remarkable knowledge Muhammad soon displays of inner-Jewish controversies and his use of subtle points of Jewish theology, and even of Hebrew phrases, in his debate with the Medinean Jews.

Thus he attacks them for being insufficiently concerned with the impending judgement day: 'if the abode of the world-to-come with God were reserved to you to the exclusion of all other men, then, if ye were speaking the truth, ye should long for death' (2. 94). This is aimed at the doctrine of M. San. 10. 1, 'All Israel have a share in the world-to-come.'[1] Even more specific: the *ummiyyūna* among the Jews[2] believe that 'hell-fire will not touch us save for some days' (2. 79)—a reference to the teaching of R. Akiba, who limits a Jew's stay in Gehenna to twelve months, and of his contemporary Johanan b. Nuri, who thought it to be seven days only (M. Edu. 2. 10).

After having repeated the midrashic statement that the Jews accepted the Torah only after Mount Sinai had been held threateningly over their heads,[3] he goes on to say (2. 93) that instead of the expected 'we hear and obey' they said *samiʿnā wa-ʿaṣīnā*, thus 'changing the words from their proper places'. As Obermann[4] has shown, these words, in Arabic 'we hear and disobey', are in fact

[1] Except heretics. It is a piquant thought that Muhammad's mentors made him here argue their own private cause.

[2] Here *ummiyyūna* probably = Am-Haareẓ; cf. Horovitz, *HUCA* ii (1925), 191.

[3] Cf. Ginzberg, *Legends*, iii. 92.

[4] 'Koran and Aggada: The Events at Mount Sinai', *AJSLL* lviii (1941), 23–48, especially 41–44.

the *shamaʿnu wĕ-ʿaśinu* of Deut. v. 24, as against the *naʿăśeh wĕ-nishmaʿ* of Exod. xxiv. 7. We have Talmudic authority that this difference in Scripture was the subject of sectarian attacks against the Rabbis.[1]

We can now understand why so many of Muhammad's attacks against the Jews of Medina can be paralleled from the New Testament:[2] both the N.T. and he drew from the same sectarian arsenal. Thus the Jews are frequently accused of slaying the prophets wrongfully.[3] This, of course, also occurs in the N.T. (Matt. v. 12; xxiii. 31), but CDC vii. 18 already accuses the Jews of despising the words of the prophets; cf. also Test. Levi xvi. 2. We may thus have a development of the Qumran view. Indeed, such arguments in both N.T. and Koran may have preserved much which by accident has not been preserved amongst the fragments of the Qumran literature available to us.

In a number of passages Muhammad holds up his own Jewish partisans as an example to the Medinean Jews. We may expect to learn from these something of their identity. That they were Jews is evident from 3. 110: 'Ye were the best community that has been put forth to mankind, enjoining right conduct and forbidding what is wrong and believing in Allah. If the people of the book believed, it would be better for them, but some of them are believers and most are evildoers.' We thus learn that the 'believers' were few in comparison with the mass of the Jews, and that the difference was not merely in whether they believed in Muhammad or not, but was halakhic. What it was, we learn further from 10. 93; 45. 17: the Jews 'did not differ until the knowledge came to them'. While other groups always claimed to preserve the pristine purity of Judaism, the Qumran sect ascribed its halakhah to the new revelation of 'hidden things concerning which all Israel had gone astray' (CDC iii. 13). It is those Jews who 'have the knowledge' who accept Muhammad's claims (17. 108), saying, 'the promise of our

[1] B.T. Shab. 88a; Ket. 112a; in most copies 'Sadducee' replaces 'Min', because of the censorship (which always insisted that 'Min' meant a Christian).

[2] Cf. Ahrens, *ZDMG* lxxxiv (1930), 156–9; Andrae, *Der Ursprung des Islam und das Christentum*, pp. 198 seq.

[3] 2. 58, 81, 85; 3. 20, 112, 177, 180; 4. 154; 5. 74. For 'wrongfully' (*bi-ghairi ḥaqqin*), cf. *ăsher lo bĕ-mishpaṭ*, DSD vii. 13.

Lord is indeed carried out'—i.e. Muhammad is the 'gentile prophet' expected. The 'differing' is about the interpretation of scripture (11. 110; 41. 45); only a 'group' (*farīq*) distorts scripture (3. 78; 4. 45). The distorters of scripture in CDC i. 18–19 are chided in words based on Isa. xxx. 10 for speaking *ḥălaqoth*, 'smooth things', which is an abbreviation of the idiom exhibited in *maḥăliq lĕshono*, Prov. xxviii. 43, where Saadiah translates *al-mulayyinu lahu lisānahu.* The way of speaking of the wicked *farīq* is in Koran 3. 78 expressed by the words *yalwūna* (written يلون) *alsinatahum bil-kitābi*, 'they make their tongues involved concerning the book': possibly we have here an Arabic popular etymology (or merely a misreading?) of the Hebrew phrase.

As against these, there is 'among you a community (*umma*) that calls to that which is right' (3. 107); 'and of the people of Moses there is a community who guide rightly (or are rightly guided) with truth and thereby become just' (7. 159); 'They are not the same as a community among the people of the book who stand and read the verses of God part of the night, while prostrating themselves, who believe in God and in the last day . . . they are the upright' (3. 113). In the last quotation we may well have an allusion to the practice of studying one third of all the nights,[1] according to DSD vi. 7 combined with communal prayer. The name, 'the upright' (*aṣ-ṣāliḥūna*), reminds one that the Hebrew equivalent, *yĕsharim*, appears practically as a name of the Qumran sect.[2]

It may well be that sectarian writings account for the 'scrolls of Abraham and Moses', from which Muhammad quotes in the early Sura 53. 36–54, for Waraqa's 'gospel', and for the 'book of the Jews' which Zaid, at Muhammad's order, 'studied within two weeks'.[3] From such books may have come the lists of moral precepts (2. 176) or the rewritings of the Decalogue in 17. 23–40 (second Meccan period) and 6. 152 seq. (third Meccan period). Finally, this may account for the curious information of Thaʿlabī[4]

[1] Cf. p. 43.

[2] CDC xx. 2; DSD iii. 1; iv. 22. Ibn Quṭaiba relates that before Muhammad's mission *zindīqs* were making proselytes at Mecca (cf. Obermann, in *The Arab Heritage*, Princeton, 1944, p. 60). In later Arabic *zindīq* means Gnostic. It probably comes from Syriac *zaddīqā*, 'upright', hence it is just possible we have here another reference to the *yĕsharim*. [3] A. Dā'ūd, ii. 34; Balādhurī, *Futūḥ*, p. 477.

[4] *Qiṣaṣ al-anbiyā'*, Cairo edn., p. 244.

that of the Psalms 50 dealt with ethical matters, 50 were prophecies concerning the first exile, and 50 dealt with the Roman oppression. Did his informants know about a *Pesher* on Psalms?

To sum up, there can be little doubt that Muhammad had Jewish contacts before coming to Medina; it is highly probable that they were heretical, anti-Rabbinic Jews; and a number of terminological and ideological details suggest the Qumran sect.

Arabia was the obvious place for a group from the neighbourhood of the Dead Sea to flee to. The desert regions of Transjordan and the northern Hijaz were the home of several Judaeo-Christian sects, and 'Arabia' was known to the Church Fathers to be *ferax haereseon.* With the Qumran sect, the exodus into the desert may have been part of their Messianic plan. DSD viii. 13 speaks of the going into the desert as an event of the Messianic future; DSW i. 2–3 envisages the return of the 'exiles of the desert' 'from the desert of the nations'. As Khirbet Qumran lies within the confines of the Promised Land, the very term 'desert of the nations' suggests an exodus into Arabia. On the other hand, they were not the only Jews in the Peninsula. There was the large community of the Yemen, and the village dwellers of the Wādī 'l-Qurā, as well as the prominently Aaronid[1] city of Medina. These were Rabbinic Jews, and relations could hardly have been good. Or possibly the main body stayed in eastern Transjordan, the region through which Muhammad travelled as a young man, and where he is said to have met the 'monk'[2] Baḥīra,[3] who recognized him from a mark on his body as the future prophet; again a method reminding us of the Qumran fragments on physiognomy.

If our theory is right, it will go a long way towards explaining how certain ideas of the Qumran sect could have percolated into Palestinian Judaism during the Arab period. To a very large

[1] Goitein, *Jews and Arabs*, p. 49.

[2] The word 'monk', *rāhib*, though commonly used for the Christian monks, is still unexplained. Geiger's derivation from Syr. *rabbā*, *rabbānā*, '*doctor*, abbot', fails not only on the meaning, but mainly on the intrusive *h*. Possibly the word is simply Arabic and means 'fearing' (also in Syr. *rahīb*, 'fearful'); it may then be originally a translation of a phrase like *yir'ē el*, CDC xix. 20, or the Rabbinic *yĕrē shamayim*, 'pious'; cf. also *ḥăredhim bĕ-mizwoth*, Ezra x. 3.

[3] In the Genizah story of Muhammad's Jewish companions (above, p. 123), Baḥīra appears as if he belonged to them, though his residence 'on a pillar in Balqīn' smacks more of a Christian Stylite.

extent the Muslim conquest meant to the Jews of the Middle East that liberation from 'their burden and the fetters that are upon them' which the Prophet had promised—at least for several centuries. The sectarians who came—as I suggest—in the wake of the victorious Muslim armies were thus proved right, and the 'Secrets of R. Simeon bar Yohai' go to show that they did what they could in order to bring this home to the widest circles. Being close to the ruling power, their prestige must have been tremendous. On the other hand, the first-century controversies had been forgotten by the Jews outside Arabia, and the struggle against Minim and Gnosticism had long ceased. The new-comers could thus be received without hesitation, and their ideas were absorbed to some extent in works like *Pirqe R. Eliezer*, while some of their halakhic tenets found acceptance in certain circles. Even their writings—as far as they still possessed any—could circulate, and so the two copies of CDC ultimately reached the Cairo Genizah. On the other hand, this percolation of ideas explains the very selective nature of the whole process. It is natural that their teachings should have found readiest acceptance in circles dissatisfied with the existing state of things. This explains their influence upon the emergent Karaite movement, in which perhaps the last remnants of the group were finally absorbed. The above account assumes, of course, that not all members of the group went as far as joining the Muslim community, as Ka'b had done.

There is nothing inherently improbable in the survival of a small religious community for centuries. We need only mention the Mandaeans and the Samaritans. While such communities in general tend to lose their vitality and militancy, they experience revivals. Moreover, where the existence of a closely related yet hostile group keeps such a community on the alert, the original militancy may last for a long time. The theory enounced in this chapter does therefore not favour any particular dating of the original Qumran community, though of course a later date makes the supposed period of survival shorter, and thereby more probable. This theory would also explain why contemporary Jewish sources are silent about the sect: during the Talmudic period it was outside the field of interest, and for the fifth–seventh centuries our sources

INDEX OF PASSAGES FROM THE DEAD SEA SCROLLS

ZADOKITE DOCUMENTS

Abbreviations

AJSLL	American Journal of Semitic Languages and Literatures
Ant.	*Antiquitates Judaeorum*
BJ	*Bellum Judaicum*
BSOAS	*Bulletin of the School of Oriental and African Studies*
B.T.	Babylonian Talmud
CDC	The Zadokite or Damascus Document
DSD	The Discipline Scroll
DSH	Pesher Habakkuk
DST	The Thanksgiving Scroll
DSW	The War of the Sons of Light and the Sons of Darkness
Edu.	Eduyoth
Enc. Isl.	*Encyclopaedia of Islam, first edition*
Ginzberg, *Legends*	*Legends of the Jews*, 1909
Heb.	Hebrew
HUCA	*Hebrew Union College Annual*
JQR	*Jewish Quarterly Review*
Ket	Kethubboth
M.	Mishnah
MH	Mishnaic Hebrew
Midr	Midrash
N.T.	New Testament
O.T.	Old Testament
PAAJR	*Proceedings of the American Academy for Jewish Research*
Pesh.	Peshitta
RÉJ	*Revue des études juives*
San.	Sanhedrin
Shab.	Shabbath
Soṭ	Soṭah
Suk.	Sukkah
Vulg.	Vulgate
Yadin	*Megilath Milhemeth bene or bi-vene hoshekh*, Jerusalem 1955
ZDMG	*Zeitschrift der Deutschen Morgenländischen Gesellschaft*

2

JESUS AND MARY IN THE QUR'ĀN: SOME NEGLECTED AFFINITIES

Neal Robinson

After briefly describing the principal non-Muslim and Muslim approaches to the Qur'anic material about Jesus and Mary, the author explores four aspects of this material which have been relatively neglected. In the first section he shows how the representation of Jesus and Mary is integrated in the structure of the Qur'anic discourse. In the second section he lists the similarities between Muhammad and the Qur'anic Jesus. In the third and fourth sections he draws on the Qur'ān and on Islamic tradition in order to show that both 'Aisha and Muhammad had a number of things in common with Mary. In the concluding discussion he states that the Qur'anic story of Jesus and Mary serves to authenticate the prophetic ministry of Muhammad and then makes some more specific remarks about the observations listed in the four main sections.

The Qur'ān narrates a number of episodes from the lives of Jesus and Mary. It acknowledges that Jesus was a prophet who worked miracles but it emphatically denies that he was the Son of God. It also seems to deny that he was crucified. Although the material about Jesus' adult life is somewhat sparse there is a wealth of detail concerning the events surrounding his nativity. The virgin birth is apparently affirmed and God is said to have chosen Mary above all the women of the worlds.

Needless to say the Qur'anic representation of Jesus and Mary has attracted the attention of countless Christian writers. Most studies of the subject by Christians have had a distinctively polemical, apologetic or historical orientation. Anti-Muslim polemicists have argued that the Qur'ān gives a garbled and heretical version of the Christian tradition. Christian apologists have tried to show that the Qur'ān does not explicitly deny the divinity of Christ or the crucifixion and that its statements about Jesus and Mary provide stepping stones towards full-blown Christian faith. Historians have endeavoured to throw light on the Qur'anic material by investigating the penetration of Christianity into pre-Islamic Arabia, by noting apocryphal parallels and by sifting the evidence concerning Muhammad's encounters with Christians. Understandably the work of these Christian scholars has been predominantly Christocentric. That is to say they have usually taken orthodox or heretical Christian representations of Jesus and Mary as the basis for elucidating the Qur'anic material about them. Of course some of the more astute Christian scholars have recognised that this material has been moulded by Muhammad's religious experience and adapted to serve the theological purposes of the Qur'an as a whole[1] but they have not, in my opinion, realised the full extent of the moulding and adaptation that has taken place.

Muslims have also produced a wealth of literature concerning the Qur'anic representation of Jesus and Mary. Much of this is incorporated in encyclopaedic commentaries on the Qur'ān. The predominant form of Muslim exegesis is traditional. It purports to retail authoritative interpretations which can be traced back to the Prophet Muhammad, his Companions or their Followers. The Prophetic *ḥadîth* provide convenient defence against Christian polemic and apologetic by explaining away an apparent error in the Qur'ān[2] and by relativising its extravagant statement about God's choice of Mary above all the women of the worlds.[3] They also incorporate an Islamicised form of the Christian belief in Jesus' future return, an attenuated version of the immaculate conception and a few statements about the occasions on which the Qur'anic material was revealed. The traditions attributed to the Companions and Followers are too numerous to be summarised. They include haggadic expansions of the Qur'anic narratives which make it clear that Jesus was indeed born of a virgin and equally clear that a look-alike substitute was crucified in his place. In theory Muslims hold that the interpretation of the Qur'ān by the Qur'ān is even more authoritative than interpretation based on received tradition. In practice however, the commentators only comb the Qur'ān for parallels when they are faced with a rare word or grammatical construction or when there is a need to respond to Muslim heresy or Christian apologetic. A good example of the latter is their marshalling of evidence to show that neither the virgin birth nor the miracles differentiate Jesus from other human messengers of God.[4]

In this article I wish to explore certain features of the Qur'anic representation of Jesus and Mary which have been relatively neglected by Christian and Muslim scholars alike. I shall begin by discussing the way in which the material which concerns us is mediated by the structure of the Qur'anic discourse. The structure itself has been analysed by Mohammed Arkoun[5] but its relevance to an assessment of the material about Jesus and Mary is rarely appreciated, least of all by Christian apologists. In the second section I shall highlight the affinity of Muhammad and Jesus as portrayed in the Qur'ān. That such an affinity exists is universally acknowledged but its extent is not well known. In the third and fourth sections I shall break entirely new ground by pointing out that in important respects there is also an affinity between 'A'isha and Mary and between Muhammad and Mary.

JESUS AND MARY IN RELATION TO THE QUR'ANIC DISCOURSE

Muslims believe that the Qur'ān is the word of God which was brought down by the angel Gabriel. They further believe that although the revelations were addressed in the first place to the Prophet Muhammad they were destined for a wider audience: the people of Mecca and Medina and ultimately all mankind. Whether or not these beliefs are well grounded theologically and historically they are consonant with the structure of the Qur'anic discourse. The Qur'anic discourse implies an Omniscient Magisterial Speaker (God) who addresses a privileged individual (Muhammad) and requires him to relay the message to others.

One of the striking features of this discourse is that the Omniscient Magisterial Speaker employs the first person singular (I, Me, My), the first person plural (We, Us, Our) and the third person singular (He, Him, His) when speaking of Himself.[6] Moreover, He sometimes shifts quite unexpectedly from one self-designation to another. For instance in the following passage where He employs all three modes of speaking:

> God's are the fairest names. Invoke Him by them. Leave the company of those who blaspheme His names. They will be requited what they do. Of those whom We created there is a nation who guide with the truth and establish justice with it. And those who deny Our signs—step by step We lead them on whence they know not. I give them rein. Behold! My scheme is strong. (7:180–183)[7]

The Omniscient Magisterial Speaker knows the intimate details of events that took place in the remote past and speaks as though they were the result of His activity. A striking instance of this is the account of the young men who took refuge in a cave to avoid persecution and were made to sleep for many years until the persecution was over:

> We narrate their story to you in its true form. . . . You would have believed them awake though they were asleep, and We caused them to turn over to the right and to the left, whereas their dog stretched out his paws on the threshold. If you had observed them you would certainly have fled from them, you would have been filled with terror. (18:13,18)

The Omniscient Magisterial Speaker also knows the innermost thoughts of the privileged individual whom He addresses:

> We know that the things they say cause you grief . . . (6:33)
> Your Lord has not forsaken you nor does He hate you. (93:3)

Despite the fact that the revelations are always vouchsafed to the privileged individual, the Omniscient Magisterial Speaker sometimes addresses the wider audience directly and refers to the privileged individual as 'him':

> If he had invented false sayings concerning Us, We would have siezed him by the right hand. Then We would surely have severed his artery and not one of you would have been able to defend him. (69:44–7)

Moreover, although the privileged individual is frequently in the forefront of the message he himself never makes intrusions into the discourse to provide elements of prophetic autobiography. Thus from start to finish it is implied that the Qur'anic discourse is the utterance of the Omniscient Magisterial Speaker.

Turning now to the material about Jesus and Mary, we should first note that this too is the utterance of the Omniscient Magisterial Speaker who designates Himself He, We and I:

> The Messiah Jesus Son of Mary was only a messenger of God and His word which He conveyed unto Mary. . . . (4:171)
> And We caused Jesus Son of Mary to follow in their footsteps . . . (5:46)
> And when God said 'O Jesus Son of Mary remember My favour unto you and unto your mother; how I strengthened you with the Holy Spirit . . .' (5:110)

In this material there is one striking instance where the Omnipresent Magisterial Speaker emphasises that the privileged individual addressed did not witness the events narrated:

> This is the tidings of the Unseen which We reveal to you. You were not with them when they cast their reeds [to decide] which of them should have charge of Mary. You were not with them when they disputed. (3:44)

This oblique reference to the casting of lots to decide who should be Mary's guardian occurs like a cinematographic flash-back in the course of the narration of the annunciation. It has the effect of enhancing the verisimilitude of the story and of giving the impression that the narrator—the Omniscient Magisterial Speaker—observed the events in question.

It is also implied that the Omniscient Magisterial Speaker knows the innermost thoughts of Jesus for He is able to report in advance what Jesus will say when challenged:

> And when God says 'O Jesus son of Mary, did you say to mankind "Take me and my mother for two gods beside God."?' Jesus says 'Glory be to You! It is not for me to say what I have no right to say. If I had said it You would know it. You know what is in my inner self but I do not know what is in Your inner self.' (5:116)

Like everything else in the Qur'ān this authoritative revelation of the story of Jesus and Mary is addressed in the first place to a privileged individual but is destined for a wider audience. There are three âyas which are of particular interest because they mention Jesus in lists of prophets which also include the privileged individual addressed. Two of these âyas are couched exclusively in We–you discourse directed at the individual:

> We have revealed to you as We revealed to Noah and the prophets after him and We revealed to Abraham, Ishmael, Isaac, Jacob and the Tribes, Jesus and Job,

> Jonah and Aaron. . . . (4:163)
> And when We exacted a covenant from the prophets and from you and from Noah and Abraham and Moses and Jesus Son of Mary . . . (33:7)

The third âya is more complex. It combines We–you discourse addressed to the privileged individual with He–you discourse addressed directly to the wider audience. This is quite clear in Arabic but it is difficult to represent in modern English where 'you' can be either singular or plural. I have therefore included explanatory glosses in square brackets:

> He has appointed for you [Muslims] as religion what He enjoined on Noah and what We have revealed to you [O Prophet] and what We enjoined on Abraham, Moses and Jesus . . . (42:13)

All three âyas indicate quite clearly that in the Qur'ān the story of Jesus serves, like the stories of the other prophets, to authenticate the prophetic ministry of Muhammad and to emphasise the authority of the message of which he is the mediator.

MUHAMMAD AND JESUS

It is well known that the Qur'ān depicts Jesus as one of a series of prophets sent by God, a series beginning with Adam and culminating in Muhammad the privileged individual to whom the Qur'ān itself is addressed. It is hardly surprising, therefore, that the Qur'ān depicts Muhammad and Jesus as having a number of things in common. Nevertheless the extent of their affinity is not generally appreciated.

Like Muhammad, the Qur'anic Jesus is called a 'prophet' (*nabī*), a 'messenger' (*rasūl*) and a 'servant' (*'abd*) of God. Like him too he is said to have been sent as a 'mercy' (*raḥma*). He received a revelation called 'the Gospel' just as Muhammad subsequently received the Qur'ān. Jesus' teaching and the teaching of the Gospel are referred to as 'wisdom', 'right path', 'guidance', 'light' and 'admonition'—terms that recur as descriptions of the Qur'anic message. Jesus declared licit some of the things that were forbidden to the Jews (3:50) just as Muhammad did, for some of the more detailed food laws were a punishment imposed on the Jews because of their disobedience and thus were relaxed for Muslims (6:146f). Nevertheless, the Gospel, like the Qur'ān, was a confirmation of previous Scriptures (3:3). Its central thrust was identical with the central thrust of the Qur'an—the summons to serve and worship God. Jesus is said to have threatened idolaters with hellfire (5:72) and to have promised paradise to those who died fighting in God's cause (9:111)—threats and promises which correspond to those made in the Qur'ān. Moreover Jesus is said to have practised ritual prayer (*ṣalāt*) and almsgiving (*zakāt*) (19:31), and two fundamental religious obligations of Islam. In view of all this it should come as no surprise that the Qur'ān also states that the revelation addressed to Jesus' disciples urged them to believe in God and His messenger and that they declared that they were 'submitted' (*muslimūn*, i.e. Muslims? 5:111) and wished to be enrolled 'with those who bear witness' (*ma'a al-shāhidīn*, i.e. 'with those who recite the shahâda'? 3:53).

From what has been said so far it should be clear that the Qur'anic representation of Jesus serves to legitimise Muhammad by giving the impression that he was doing what Jesus had done before him. In one very striking instance this becomes quite explicit:

> O you believers! Be God's helpers as when Jesus Son of Mary said to the disciples 'Who will be my helpers in God's way?' The disciples said, 'We are God's helpers.' A group of the Children of Israel believed and a group disbelieved. We upheld those who believed against their enemies and they gained the victory. (61:14)

Although this passage is very condensed its purport is clear enough. The believers are urged to fight at Muhammad's side on the grounds that in so doing they will be following the example of Jesus' disciples and that like them they will prove victorious.[8] The word 'helpers' (*anṣār*) is pregnant with meaning. It is the official title given to the people of Medina who rallied to Muhammad's cause (9:100,107). It also puns with *naṣārā*, the Qur'anic name for Christian.

There would have been no need for a promise of victory if Muhammad and Jesus had not met with mockery and opposition. Muhammad's critics mocked him for needing to eat food (25:7). Yet Jesus and his mother had had similar needs (5:75). The 'signs' which Muhammad brought as proof of his authority —the inimitable revelations of the Qur'ān—led to allegations of sorcery (21:3, 38:4f., 43:31). Yet although Jesus' miraculous 'signs' had been rather different they too had provoked this response (5:110).[9] So was Muhammad to expect the same fate as Jesus? There can be no simple answer to this question because the Qur'ān's statements about Jesus' death are themselves so notoriously ambiguous and controversial.[10] Nevertheless, even here there are some tantalising similarities between what is said about Muhammad and what is said about Jesus:

(1) Muhammad's status as a messenger of God was no guarantee that he would not die or be killed:

> Muhammad [is] only a messenger. Messengers have passed away before him. If he dies or is killed will you turn upon your heels . . . ? (3:144)

The phrase 'have passed away before' (*qad khalat min qabli*) occurs a number of times with reference to past generations and vanished peoples but the closest parallel to this particular āya is a statement about Jesus:

> The Messiah Jesus son of Mary [was] only a messenger. Messengers have passed away before him. (5:75)

(2) Muhammad's opponents schemed against him but God was also scheming:

> When those who disbelieve plot to keep you in bonds or kill you or drive you out, they are plotting and God is plotting. God is the best of plotters. (8:30)

Similar things are said about the opposition to other prophets including Abraham (14:47) and Sālih (27:50) but the phrase 'God is the best of plotters' occurs elsewhere only in connection with Jesus:

> They plotted and God plotted. God is the best of plotters. (3:54)

(3) The verb *tawaffā* ('cause to die' or 'receive alive') occurs three times with Muhammad as the object of the action. As the meaning of the verb is disputed I shall translate it as 'receive' to preserve the ambiguity:

> Whether We cause you to see something of what We have promised them or whether We receive you (*natawaffayanna-ka*), on you is incumbent only the preaching and on Us the reckoning. (13:40)
> Whether We cause you to see something of what We have promised them or whether We receive you (*natawaffayanna-ka*), unto Us is their return (*marji'u-hum*) and God is witness (*shahîd*[un]) over what they do. (10:46)
> Whether We cause you to see something of what We have promised them or whether We receive you (*natawaffayanna-ka*), unto Us they will be returned (*yurja'ūn*) (40:77)

There are only two other âyas where this verb is used in the active voice with God as the subject and with one of his prophets as the object. In both instances the prophet is Jesus. Moreover there is a similar emphasis on God's witnessing man's actions and man's return to Him for Judgement:

> [Remember] when God said 'O Jesus I am about to receive you (*mutawaffī-ka*) and raise you to myself and purify you from those who disbelieve. I am setting those who follow you above those who disbelieve until the day of resurrection. Then to Me shall be your return (*marji'u-kum*) [all of you] . . . (3:55)
> [Jesus said] I was a witness against them as long as I remained with them. Then when You received me (*tawaffayta-nī*) it is You who were the watcher over them, You are witness (*shahid*[un]) of everything (5:117).

'A'ISHA AND MARY

There is one instance in which Mary is cited for an explicitly hortatory purpose. This occurs at the end of the sixty-sixth sura. The passage states that God has proposed the wife of Pharaoh together with 'Mary daughter of Imrān who guarded her chastity' as examples for the believers (66:13–14). This is directly related to the first part of the sura which is concerned with a domestic problem occasioned by Muhammad's wives. The details of that problem need not detain us and in any case they cannot be deduced directly from the text. Suffice it to note that the trouble was caused by two wives (66:3f) and that it was suggested that unless they had a change of heart they might be divorced and replaced with women who were better Muslims, either women who had already been married (i.e. like Pharaoh's wife?) or virgins (i.e. like Mary?) (66:4f). According to the most plausible tradition the two wives who caused the trouble were Hafsa and 'A'isha. They would certainly fit the bill admirably for Muhammad married Hafsa after she was widowed whereas 'A'isha was his only virgin bride.[11]

Taking our lead from this passage we may enquire whether any of the other things that the Qur'ān says about Mary were relevant to Muhammad's *ménage.* If the Qur'anic information about the Prophet's wives is supplemented with details derived from early Muslim tradition, and if attention is focused on 'A'isha some quite remarkable parallels emerge.

When the Prophet moved to Medina he was about fifty years old and had only one wife, Sawda, who was at least thirty. The residence which was built for him also served as the first mosque.[12] It consisted principally of an enclosed courtyard in which he conducted business, addressed his followers and led communal prayers. In the pre-Islamic period marriage was uxorilocal, that is to say wives used to remain in their family homes where they were visited by their husbands. Muhammad departed from this custom and established virilocal marriage as the norm. Thus Sawda lived with him in the mosque or rather in her own apartment which opened onto the courtyard. Muhammad soon contracted a further marriage with 'A'isha. His relationship with her must to begin with have been more that of a guardian than a husband for she was only nine and was allowed to keep her toys. Nevertheless, 'A'isha had to leave her family and live at the Prophet's residence.[13] Quarters were built for her resembling those of Sawda and opening onto the *eastern* side of the courtyard. In addition to being separated from her folk, 'A'isha was screened off from them because of a revelation instructing Muslims to speak to the Prophet's wives from behind a 'curtain' (*ḥijâb* 33:53). There are various traditions as to why the *ḥijâb* was introduced but the underlying reason was that the mosque was frequented by large numbers of people and it was undignified for the women to be exposed to all and sundry. God wished to 'purify' them (33:33) and give them unique status as mothers of the believers (33:12).

Many of these details tally with what the Qur'ān says about Mary. The two principal versions of her story associate her with Zechariah. He was a prophet, advanced in years and married to a woman who was barren. He is mentioned in connection with an important place of worship. While Mary was still only a girl she was put in the care of Zechariah because her mother had dedicated her to God. In one version of the story it is implied that Mary lived in the *miḥrāb* (3:37) which was either the place of worship itself or a chamber adjoining it. In the other version she is said to have withdrawn from her folk to an 'easterly' place and screened herself from them with a 'curtain' (*ḥijâb* 19:16).[14] Moreover, she was told by the angels that God had 'purified' her and preferred her above all the women of creation (3:42).

There is a further important resemblance between 'A'isha and Mary: both were accused of sexual immorality.[15] When the Muslims were returning from a campaign 'A'isha was accidentally left behind at the camp site. Apparently her howda had been loaded onto the camel while she was in the privy and because she was so light no one had realised that the howda was empty. Tongues began to wag when she returned to Medina accompanied by a handsome young man who had also fallen behind for some reason and had not spent the night with the troops. The accusations provoked a serious crisis which was only resolved when Muhammad received a revelation declaring her innocence. Tradition identifies this revelation as 24:11ff. The passage does not name 'A'isha but it clearly refers to a false accusation of unchastity made against an eminent Muslim woman. The accusers are lambasted for speaking lies and not bringing four witnesses. The believers are reprimanded for listening to scandal-mongering and not dismissing it as slander; they should have realised that it was 'a tremendous calumny' (*buhtān 'aẓîm* 24:16). The case of Mary is of course different in as far as she was visited by God's Spirit and returned to her people with a child. There are, however, a number of similarities. In the first place, the encounter with the Spirit took place when she was alone and he presented himself to her in the form of a perfect mortal (19:17), that is to say, as a handsome young man. Second, her people suspected her of unchastity and her virtue had to be defended by revelation (19:27–33). Finally, the Qur'ān criticises the People of the Book for having spoken 'a tremendous calumny' against Mary (4:156).[16]

MUHAMMAD AND MARY

In addition to having to deal with the slanderous suggestions about 'A'isha, the Prophet had to face accusations that were even more damaging. His enemies alleged that he himself was deluded or a fraud and had not really received revelations. Once again there are similarities to the story of Mary and Jesus. This time, however, the parallels are between Muhammad and Mary rather than 'A'isha and Mary. For the sake of clarity I shall list them one by one together with relevant quotations:

(1) God's agent who brought the revelations to Muhammad was the angel Gabriel who is sometimes referred to as the Spirit:

> Say, 'Who is the enemy of Gabriel when it is he who sent it down on your heart by God's permission . . . ?' (2:97)
> Say, 'The Holy Spirit sent it down from your Lord in truth and to confirm those who believe and to be a guidance and good news for the Muslims.' (16:102)

170

Mary also received angelic visitations (3:42) and God's agent at the annunciation/conception is referred to as the Spirit (19:17).

(2) The Spirit or Gabriel sometimes appeared to Muhammad in human form. According to a well-known hadith the Prophet said:

> At times the angel presented himself to me (*tamaththala l-ī*) as a man (*rajul*^{an}) and spoke to me.[17]

Moreover the Qur'ān itself mentions that Muhammad's critics once hinted that his so-called revelations came from a fellow human being:

> And We know very well that they say, 'It is only a mortal (*bashar*) who is instructing him.' (16:103)[18]

The Spirit also looked like a man on the occasion when he was sent to Mary:

> And We sent unto her Our Spirit who presented himself to her in the form of a perfect mortal (*tamaththala la-ha bashar*^{an} *sawiyy*^{an} 19:17).[19]

Moreover, Mary's folk evidently thought that a man had made her pregnant (19:27f).

(3) Satan seeks to impart false revelations but Muhammad was protected from his wiles by a simple expedient:

> When you recite the Qur'ān [O Prophet] seek God's protection against the accursed Satan. He has no authority over those who believe and trust in their Lord . . . (16: 98f)

Satan also seeks to tempt human beings to engage in sexual immorality (24:21) but Mary would not have succumbed to such temptations because at her birth her mother supplicated God with the words:

> 'I seek your protection for her and her offspring against the accursed Satan.' (3:36)

And when the Spirit presented himself to Mary she herself said:

> 'I seek the protection of the Compassionate against you if you are God-fearing' (19:18)

(4) Many of Muhammad's revelations were first uttered in his sermons at Medina. According to tradition, to begin with the mosque did not have a *minbar* for Muhammad to preach from:

> It was on the trunk of a palm tree that the Prophet used at first to lean.[20]

According to the Qur'ān Mary gave birth to Jesus in a similar setting:

> The labour pains drove her to the trunk of the palm tree. (19:22)

(5) Muhammad's critics desired firmer evidence of his inspiration. We should perhaps infer from the following passage that they expected to see God

address him directly:

> It is not for any mortal that God should speak to him, except by inspired communication (*waḥy^{an}*), or from behind a curtain (*min warā'ā^{i} ḥijāb^{in}*) or that He should send (*yursila*) an [angelic] messenger (*rasūl*) who would then communicate (*yūḥiya*) by His permission what He wishes. (42:51).

The interpretation of this is much disputed. Muslim theologians assume that the noun *waḥy* and verb *awḥā* denote Gabriel's recitation of the words of the Qur'ān to Muhammad. On the other hand, Watt makes out a good case for thinking that the fundamental sense is 'the communication of an idea by some quick suggestion or prompting'.[21] Fakhr al-Dīn al-Rāzi argues that the reference to a curtain must be metaphorical and that what is meant is that when a man hears speech without seeing the speaker it is as though the speaker were behind a veil or curtain.[22] Note that we have already met with the expression 'from behind a curtain' for it occurred in its literal sense in connection with the Prophet's wives.[23] Should we infer that Muhammad often presented revelations which he claimed he had received when he was behind the curtain in his wives' quarters?

It can hardly be fortuitous that terms 'communicate', 'curtain', 'send' and '[angelic] messenger' occur in close succession in one of the accounts of the annunciation and conception. Zechariah was alone when he received a revelation and was struck dumb. The rest of mankind neither saw nor heard anything but:

> He came out of the mihrab to his people and communicated (*awḥâ*) to them . . . (19:11)

Mary was in seclusion when the Spirit came to her:

> She took apart from them a curtain (*ḥijāb^{an}*) and we sent (*arsalnā*) to her Our Spirit . . . (19:18f)
> He said 'I am only an [angelic] messenger (*rasūl^{u}*) of your Lord . . .' (19:19)

Thus the mystery of Mary's conception of Jesus like the mystery of Muhammad's reception of the Qur'ān was hidden from profane eyes.

CONCLUDING DISCUSSION

What are the implications of these observations? I have already stated that the Qur'anic story of Jesus serves to authenticate the prophetic ministry of Muhammad and to emphasise the authority of the message of which he is the mediator. I will now attempt to draw some more specific conclusions from each of the four main sections of this paper.

In the first section we saw that the image of Jesus is mediated by the structure of the Qur'anic discourse and is inseparable from it. It follows that any attempt to translate what the Qur'ān says about Jesus into a series of propositions is likely to reduce the impact of the Qur'anic version of the story and thus to seriously misrepresent it. This is equally true of the Gospels, although there the structure of the discourse is very different for there is an implied human narrator who tends to recede behind the story which he is telling and to leave Jesus at the centre of the stage.

Let us next consider the resemblance between what the Qur'ān says about Muhammad and what it says about Jesus. Michaud, who was aware of some of the parallels which I have listed, thought it unnecessary to postulate that Muhammad had deliberately contrived to produce them. His own explanation had two parts to it. First, following Harnack and Schoeps, he assumed that Muhammad was influenced by Jewish Christianity and that consequently he initially believed that the religion which he preached closely resembled that of Jesus.[24] Second, Michaud suggested that later on the traditional data about Jesus, which did not fit the image of him as a model prophet, were partially harmonised with it by a slow and profound spiritual travail which took place within Muhammad.[25] I accept the likelihood of both the Jewish Christian influence and the long-term spiritual travail but I question whether they are sufficient to explain all the similarities that we have observed. Take, for instance, the three sets of āyas in which similar statements are made about the fate of Muhammad and that of Jesus. Michaud does not mention these. Yet the similarities are striking. Moreover, in all three cases the statements about Jesus were revealed shortly after the statements about Muhammad.[26] Are we really to believe that this degree of harmonisation was brought about entirely unconsciously?

My account of the similarity between 'A'isha and Mary depends partly on details drawn from tradition. I suggest that here we must almost certainly reckon with Muhammad's deliberate attempt to indicate that such a similarity existed. His domestic arrangements in the mosque at Medina were, I think, consciously made with that end in mind. His primary motive was probably the desire to compensate for the aura surrounding Mary and the virginal conception—features of the traditional Christian story which were hard to reconcile with the belief that Jesus was merely a model prophet. In the process, however, he also blazed the trail for the establishment of virilocal marriage.[27] The Qur'anic āya exonerating 'A'isha from the charge of unchastity came later. It would have made sense to the Muslims who were by then long familiar with the story of how Mary's innocence had likewise been defended by revelation. Just in case they failed to see the similarity, the charge against 'A'isha was referred to as 'a tremendous calumny'.

The parallels between Muhammad and Mary are more difficult to interpret. It is impossible to be certain of the degree to which Muhammad was conscious of them. They are, however, undeniably there. They have a twofold effect. First, they relativise the miracle of Mary's *conception* of Jesus by making it an analogue of Muhammad's *reception* of the Qur'ān. Second, they provide a precedent for the mysterious circumstances that led to Muhammad being suspected of fraud.

NOTES

1 For example, Henri Michaud, *Jésus selon le Coran*, Delachaux et Niestlé, Neuchatel, 1960 and Claus Schedl, *Muhammad und Jesus*, Vienna, Herder, 1978.

2 According to ḥadīth the reference to Mary as 'Sister of Aaron' (19:28) does not imply that she has been confused with the Old Testament Miriam. It was customary in Mary's time to name people after pious individuals of former ages.

3 By stating that she was the most excellent woman *of her time*.

4 See Neal Robinson, 'Creating Birds from Clay: a Miracle of Jesus in the Qur'ān and Classical Muslim Commentaries', *Muslim World*, vol. LXXIX/1, 1989, pp. 1–13.

5 Mohammad Arkoun, *La pensée arabe*, Paris, P.U.F., 1979, pp. 10–13.

6 For a discussion of the significance of this see Neal Robinson 'The Qur'ān as the Word of God' in A. Linzey & P. Wexler (eds), *Heaven and Earth: Essex Essays in Theology and Ethics*, Worthing, Churchman, 1986, pp. 38–54.

7 Translations of the Qur'ān are made by the author from the standard Egyptian edition of the Arabic text. The first figure refers to the sura, the second to the āyas.

8 It is possible that as a result of typological exegesis or confusion Jesus is here portrayed as the Old Testament figure of Joshua. The whole passage seems odd to us but would have made sense to Muhammad's audience because of the Byzantine Christians' conquest of Palestine. See John Bowman, 'The Debt of Islam to Monophysite Syrian Christianity', *Nederlands Theologisch Tijdschrift* 19 (1964–5), pp. 177–201.

9 Jesus' miracles are referred to as a sign (*āya*) at 3:49. Passages of the Qur'ān are referred to as signs at 2:106. There are challenges to unbelievers to bring a sura or ten suras like the Qur'ān at 2:23, 10:38 and 11:13. This is the basis of the doctrine that every prophet is given a miracle as proof of his mission and that the chief miracle given to Muhammad was the inimitable Qur'ān itself. In this connection it is worth noting that Muhammad's revelations (e.g. 2:97) and Jesus' miracles (3:49 and 5:110) occur 'by permission' of God. Note also that one of Jesus' miracles involves God's 'sending down' of something (5:114f), a word frequently used of the 'sending down' of the Qur'anic revelations.

10 Traditional Muslim exegesis interprets all the relevant Qur'anic texts in the light of 4:157 which is taken to imply that a substitute was crucified in Jesus' place. Many Christians and some Muslims think that Jesus' death is implied at 19:33, 3:55 and 5:117 and argue that 4:157 could simply be a denial of the Jews' claim that *they* crucified Jesus.

11 The various traditions are summarised in N. Abbott, *Aisha The Beloved Of Muhammed*, London, Al-Saqi Books, 1985 pp. 44f. where references to the original sources are given. For Hafsa's former marriage see W. M. Watt, *Muhammad at Medina*, Oxford, O.U.P., 1956, p. 396. For 'A'isha's vaunting the fact that she was Muhammad's only virgin bride see N. Abbot, *op. cit.*, p. 65.

12 For the description of the mosque see Maxime Rodinson, *Mohammed*, E. T. Harmondsworth, Penguin, 1971, pp. 149f.

13 For the change to virilocal marriage see W. M. Watt, *op. cit.*, pp. 272–277. The information about 'A'isha is conveniently set out by W. M. Watt, "A'isha bint Abî Bakr', in *The Encyclopaedia of Islam*, New Edition, vol. 1, pp. 307f.

174

14 According to Muslim tradition this passage was revealed at Mecca, i.e. before the *ḥijāb* was introduced for Muhammad's wives. Christian historians argue that the Qur'anic reference to Mary adopting a veil is based indirectly on *The Protoevangelium of James* 10:1 which states that she was engaged in making a veil for the temple.

15 For the accusation against 'A'isha and the incident that provoked it see N. Abbott, *op. cit.*, pp. 29–38.

16 N.B. The expression 'a tremendous calumny' (*buhtân 'aẓīm*) occurs only twice in the Qur'ān—at 4:156 in connection with Mary and at 24:16 in connection with 'A'isha.

17 Bukhâri *sahīh* ed., *Ahmad Muhammad Shākir*, 9 parts bound in 3 volumes, Beirut, 'Alam al-Kutub n.d., part 1 pp. 2f.

18 The second half of the āya states that the speech of the person to whom they blasphemously alluded was *a'jamiyy* whereas the revelations were in clear Arabic. The word *a'jamiyy* could simply mean 'indistinct' but Muslim exegesis usually takes it to mean 'foreign'. The traditions traced to the early generations of Muslims disagree as to who the person was; see Ibn Kathīr, *tafsīr al-qur'ān al-'aẓīm*, 7 volumes, Beirut, dâr al-andalus, 1385 H., vol. 4, p. 226. N.B. Muslim exegesis does not link the Qur'anic passage wth the hadith in the way that I have done. On the contrary they are kept apart because of other hadith which state that Gabriel at times looked like Muhammad's companion Dihyā; see Abdul Hamid Siddiqi, *Sahih Muslim*, New Delhi, Kitab Bhavan, 1977, vol. 1, p. 108 & vol. 4, p. 1308. Dihyā's speech was neither foreign nor indistinct because he was an Arab and was used by Muhammad for ambassadorial purposes: see A. Guillaume, *The life of Muhammad: a translation of Ibn Ishaq's Sirat Rasul Allah*, Oxford, O.U.P., 1955, pp. 655f.

19 Mary at first mistook him for a human being. It is interesting to note that there was another occasion when the contrary happened and a human being was mistaken for an angel. The human being was the patriarch Joseph who successfully resisted the governor's wife's attempt to seduce him. When she subsequently brought him out to be viewed by the women who were gossiping about her they cried, 'God help us! This is not a mortal (*bashar^{an}*). It can only be a noble angel'. (12:31)

For Muslim exegesis of 19:17 see Neal Robinson, 'Fakhr al-Dīn al-Rāzī on the Virginal conception', *Islamochristiana* 14 (1988), pp. 1–16.

20 Bukhārī, *op. cit.*, part 2, p. 11.

21 R. Bell & W. M. Watt, *Introduction to the Qur'an*, Edinburgh, Edinburgh University Press, 1970, pp. 20–22.

22 See Michael L. Fitzgerald, 'The Manner of Revelation: The Commentary of Al-Rāzī on Qur'ān 42, 51–53', *Islamochristiana* 4 (1978), pp. 115–125.

23 The expression 'from behind a curtain' (*min warā'i ḥijāb^{in}*) occurs only twice in the Qur'ān—at 42:51 in connection with the manner of revelation and at 33:53 in connection with the Prophet's wives.

24 Michaud, *op. cit.*, p. 42.

25 Ibid., p. 91.

26 One cannot of course be dogmatic about the precise chronological order of the suras but in this instance both Nöldeke's chronology and the traditional Muslim one lend support to my claim. See the tables in Bell & Watt, *op. cit.*, pp. 206–213.

27 There is another feature of the story of Mary which probably served to reinforce Muhammad's social reforms. Mary's mother was distressed at giving birth to a daughter rather than a son but God accepted the child and miraculously fed her (3:6f). This fits in well with Muhammad's eradication of the pre-Islamic practice of burying girl children alive because of the shortage of food (cp. 16:58).

NEAL ROBINSON is Senior Lecturer in Religious Studies at the College of St Paul and St Mary, Cheltenham. He is a graduate of Oxford University and gained a Birmingham Ph.D. for work on the New Testament. He is currently completing a book on the representation of Jesus in the Qur'ān and the classical Muslim commentaries which will be published by the Macmillan Press under the title *Christ in Islam and Christianity*.

3

THE THEOLOGY OF SEPARATION AND THE THEOLOGY OF COMMUNITY: A STUDY OF THE PROPHETIC CAREER OF MOSES ACCORDINGTO THE QUR'ĀN

M. Causse

A study on the prophetic vocation of Moses according to the Qur'ān

A most enticing little book by F.-J. Leenhardt[1] has recently analysed the religious types of Abraham and Moses in the Bible. Meditating on these great figures will lead us along one of two theological ways. One of these we will call "theology of severance" in order to keep it separate from Biblical terminology. Basing his argument on the significance of Abraham for St Paul in particular, Leenhardt recognises this in Protestant spirituality. The figure of Moses, on the other hand, dominates a "theology of community", which he recognises in Catholic spirituality.

Leenhardt further elaborates the slight distinction between spiritual types in a note:[2] it may originate partly from a projection of the theological tendency of the source onto particular persons. Perhaps, however, one ought to bear in mind the possibility that every historical person may well have his own spiritual development.

The object of this study is not this discussion, which would raise many questions simultaneously. We have undertaken it within the bounds of the Qur'ān where it is significantly simplified owing to the fact that Muḥammad is the only bringer of Qur'ānic revelation, and that there are many texts which allow us to follow its development without adding the preliminary difficulties inherent in a discussion of the sources.

Thus we are intending to study the development in the Qur'ān which moves from a "theology of severance" to a "theology of community". We will disregard every Biblical parallel because it is evident that we have already been guided by the similarity of the difficulties within dogma which arise in the Islamic and in the Biblical context as well as in the various Christian traditions. We have also been influenced by concerns similar to those of Leenhardt.

---

[1] F.-J. Leenhardt, *La Parole et le Buisson de Feu,* Neuchâtel, Delachaux et Niestlé.

[2] *Ibid.*, pp. 49–50

2

In *La Philosophie du Moyen Age* M.E. Gilson offers the following penetrating observation as "a kind of law": [61] "For to a thinker of the Middle Ages, the State is to the Church what philosophy is to theology and nature is to grace".[3]

Just as the Church is defined outside the state, in opposition to a civil society, to the "world", theology objects to knowledge through reason, and the grace of God is incomprehensible and outside the mechanisms of nature – three aspects of one and the same "theology of severance". If these options were reversed, we would automatically have a sketch of the "theology of community".

While for Gilson certainly this is a logical observation, it is also, above all, a statistical one. Every theologian, and for Leenhardt every spiritual type as well, develops within a set framework. The Qur'ān adds a new dimension here in that it allows passage from one setting to the other. From the theology of severance, which is expressed in the beginnings in Mecca, the Prophet of Medina moved on to a theology of community.

This theological development is recognised by all Islamic scholars. Moubarac terms it a *natural development*[4] and also, with good reason, emphasises "the priority of religious over political matters" in this development.[5] We wish to examine, to some extent, in what respect a theological development can be characterised as being "natural", i.e. in what respect it can be said to obey "natural laws", which would spread into a precise historical and theological framework.

If, consequently, there is a logical natural element immanent to the human spirit in this development, every believer who adheres to the absolute truth of their faith will not doubt that the area which requires the most meditation is just that which eludes this human logic. However, as E. Mounier pointed out, mystery loves light.

As far as the Qur'ān is concerned we can approach the question from an oblique angle. Throughout the twenty-odd years of the Revelation the figure of Moses plays an essential role as a type and an example for Muḥammad. Gaudefroy-Demombynes has written that Muḥammad's taking Moses as an example took place in Medina.[6] We will see that, in a way, the opposite is true: Moses' position as an example is much less firmly and deeply rooted in Medina than in Mecca.

---

[3] *La Philosophie du Moyen Age*, p. 254.

[4] 'Moise dans le Coran' in *Moise, l'homme de l'Alliance*, p. 380, Paris, Desclée et Cie, 1955. This expression appears twice. See also *Abraham dans le Coran*, p. 18.

[5] *Abraham dans le Coran*, p. 55.

[6] Gaudefroy Demombynes, *Mahomet*, p. 109.

3

We will study the way in which the Prophet understood Moses' vocation, and its development during the three Meccan periods and the last Medinan one, thus gaining an insight into his understanding of his own mission. We will follow Blachère's classification [62] and criticism in this study.[7] The results may be only approximations for certain suras, but then we are only trying to emphasise a general development.

The other prophets, especially Abraham, but also Noah, might serve as examples just as well. Referring to them, however, is not necessary for most of the time, for two reasons:

1. In the Qur'ān, prophets appear as incarnations of a uniform type of men who succeed each other and intervene in God's name in a human situation which is also fairly uniform. This Jewish and Jewish-Christian doctrine is taken up explicitly on several occasions in the Qur'ān. Thus, for instance, in sura 26 (no. 58), following the stories of Moses and Abraham:

> "Noah's people denied their apostles, when their brother Noah said to them: "Do you have no piety? I am a true apostle for you. Fear God and follow me. I do not ask a reward from you, for only the Lord of Creation can reward me" ...
> This is truly a sign. The majority of them did not become believers. Your Lord is indeed the Mighty One, the Merciful."[8]

The complete quotation is repeated word for word in the contexts of Hūd, Ṣāliḥ, Lot, the Men of the Thicket, and the last two verses also appear in the context of Moses and Abraham. The repetition indicates that there is not only a permanent spiritual significance in prophecy, but also an identical role for its messengers. While the nature of the prophecy may change throughout the development of the Qur'ān, except in details it will develop in a similar way for the different prophets.[9]

2. Despite Abraham's important role, Moses remains the person who is most closely associated with Muḥammad by the Qur'ān and the tradition. Moses is, in total, mentioned about one and a half times more frequently than Abraham;[10] moreover, Abraham appears as a model believer, whereas Moses is the model prophet, Muḥammad's personal model.[11] Tradition quotes the Prophet as having said:

[7] *Le Coran* (translated by Blachère), Paris, Ed. Maisonneuve, 1949–51.
[8] (26:105–9; 121–2)
[9] See Gaudefroy-Demombynes, *Mahomet*, p. 390.
[10] See the precise study by Moubarac: 'Moise dans le Coran', p. 374; *Abraham dans le Coran*, p. 27.
[11] See Gaudefroy-Demombynes, *Mahomet*, p. 390.

4

> "Do not assign to me pre-eminence over Moses: on the day of the resurrection, all men will faint with fear, I as well as the others, but I will be the first one to regain my senses. At that moment Moses will be clinging to the throne. I do not know whether he will have fainted like the others and regained [63] his senses before me, or whether he will be an exception, according to God's will."[12]

In another tradition Mohammed has the advantage over Moses for the latter will cry during the Last Judgment because the number of his disciples will be fewer than Muḥammad's.[13]

FIRST MECCAN PERIOD (NO. 1–48, BLACHÈRE)

The first thing which strikes the reader is that Moses' preaching is not directed at the Jews but at Pharaoh and that it is in this form that its relation with Muḥammad's message is asserted:

> "In truth, we have sent to you an apostle to testify against you (*shāhidan 'alaykum*), as we sent an apostle to Pharaoh before. Pharaoh disobeyed that apostle, and we have punished him terribly. If you are unbelievers, how will you defend yourselves on the day which will make your children's hair go grey?"[14]
>
> This is an action directed against one of the mighty, the "Master of the Stakes"[15] and a rebel, as are all great men.
>
> "Go to Pharaoh, he is rebelling. Ask him: "Do you have it in you to purify yourself and fear the Lord if I lead you to him? Moses showed Pharaoh the greatest of miracles, but Pharaoh did not believe and rebelled. Then he went away and called his men together and said to them "I am your supreme Lord." God punished him with the scourge of this life and the life to come."[16]

Opposite Pharaoh, who declares himself God, Moses is entrusted with divine power, the greatest of miracles. Before the test it is established that Pharaoh *is* a rebel (*tagha*, in the past tense); furthermore the sign of the warning is also the sign of the Last Judgment which immediately

[12] Bokhari, 44, 4, 1; 60, 31, 2; 60, 35, 3.
[13] *Ibid.*, 62, 1, 2.
[14] 73 (no. 34):15–17
[15] 89 (no. 42):9
[16] 79 (no. 20):17–25

5

follows Pharaoh's refusal. Moses the prophet is thus given a part in the fulfilment of the Last Judgment, the part of *shāhid*, the witness for the prosecution of this supreme trial.

The individual character of this warning and the punishment, as well as their instantaneous realisation, has to be stressed. In this context the required – and intended – conversion is that of the individual who is fully responsible for his actions and who changes abruptly and purifies himself. The motive for the change will have been the fear of the Judgment.

What exactly comprises this purification as far as Moses is concerned is not stated. All that is said, after the "pages about Abraham and Moses", is that praying to God is necessary[17] and the assurance [64] is given that "no sinful soul shall bear another's burden, that a man will be judged only according to his own labours, that the result of his efforts will be observed and that he will be fully rewarded."[18]

All the traits connected with Muḥammad and his prophetic witness pointed out so far can be found in the texts from the same period. The Prophet "has seen one of the greatest signs of his Lord"[19] and he has been commissioned to relate them as the preliminaries of the Judgment.

"Those who have not believed our signs will be on God's left, and a great fire will come upon them."[20]

Besides, everything has in fact already been decided: it is not for man to purify himself "unless God, the Lord of the worlds, wills it".[21]

Henceforth the Prophet is the witness for the Last Judgment.[22]

Throughout this period Muḥammad is surrounded by a group of believers to whom he recommends piety. The practice is directly inspired by Jewish or Jewish-Christian practice, but that in itself would not prove the affinity between the Prophet and Moses. The form of the conversion appears to be more important by virtue of its instantaneous and total character. On the one hand we see the condemned rebels, on the other the pure, the servants of the Lord who "give food to the poor, the orphan, the captive, all for the love of God".[23] This conversion is modelled on the instantaneous conversion of the prophet during his vision, be it Moses' or Muḥammad's.[24]

---

[17] 87 (no. 16):15
[18] 53 (no. 30):38–41
[19] 53 (no. 30):18
[20] 40 (no. 40):19–20
[21] 81 (no. 18):29; 76 (no. 34A):30; 74 (no. 36):56 etc.
[22] 85 (no. 43):3
[23] 76 (no. 34A):8; see also 2 (no. 93):30
[24] 78 (no. 20):16; 53 (no. 30)

6

More important still is the use of the root *dh k r*, "to remind, to admonish, to remember", to describe the preaching. The first Qur'ānic texts on this subject are:

> "Admonish them (*dhakkir*), if admonishing (*dhikra*) them would be any use"[25]
>
> "He might mend his ways, and then the admonition (*dhikra*) would have been useful...
>
> This is an admonition (*tadhkira*) – let him who wishes remember (*dhakara*) it – this admonition is contained in honoured pages, exalted and purified, out of the hands of noble and pure scribes."[26]

The text used in sura 87 (no. 16) refers explicitly to the "pages about Abraham and Moses"; the contexts are identical in that the initial sermon, seen [65] as a whole by the Prophet, is itself modelled on all that precedes it and is essentially connected to Moses. As regards Abraham, he is only mentioned twice in this whole first Meccan period, both times in this phrase.

It would obviously be very interesting to know the contents of these "pages", but it seems that, from the very beginning, this knowledge has been reserved for the initiated. They are "secret scripture only to be touched by the purified"[27] which announces and describes the Last Judgment.[28] The vision of the Lord on his throne,[29] with the chosen on his right side and the damned on his left – in one text a group of the chosen is set apart as those of the first order[30] – who commends the former for having fed the poor, the orphan and the *captive*,[31] who invites them to enter into paradise[32] and sends the damned to the eternal fire and to Gehenna,[33] recalls Chapter 25 of the gospel according to St Matthew.

It is possible that this is a more or less direct reference. There are others of the same type in later texts of the Qur'ān, and also in the tradition literature.

For the aim of the present study it is particularly important that these "pages" are connected with the authority of Abraham and Moses. From here onwards there is unity in the history of Qur'ānic revelation.

---

[25] 87 (no. 16):9
[26] 80 (no. 17):4, 11–16
[27] 56 (no. 23):78
[28] 52 (no. 22):2-7
[29] 81 (no. 18):20; 85 (no. 43):15
[30] 56 (no. 23); 40 (no. 40):18; 74 (no. 36):39
[31] See footnote 23.
[32] 89 (no. 42):30; see also 50 (no. 56):34 and Matthew 25:22, etc.
[33] There are fifteen instances of this.

7

With a few exceptions the warning is directed at rebels, who are being threatened and condemned. In general, as with the example of Pharaoh, the rebels are the rich and powerful:

> "Disaster will befall those who have amassed a fortune and counted it again and again. They believe that it will make them immortal."[34]

It is obvious that this social vision, where riches as well as family influence are actual obstacles to accepting the prophecy, dominates the individual idea of bearing witness and of the Judgment:

> "He did not believe and he did not pray, but he denied the truth and turned his back. Then he went to his kinsfolk, striding proudly."[35]
>
> "On that day (of the Judgment) each man will forsake his brother and his mother, his consort and his children.[36] He will try to give them up in his place."[37]

[66] One can see that, from that time onwards, God's revelation begins to take place in a personal context. He has chosen a poor and orphaned man[38] who "has no ties in this town'[39] to bring it to the people; the Prophet's personal history is the element that enables him to understand God's will:

> "Did he not find you an orphan and give you shelter?
> Did he not find you in error and guide you?
> Did he not find you poor and enrich you?
> Therefore, do not wrong the orphan.
> Therefore, do not send the beggar away.
> Proclaim the goodness of the Lord."[40]

Thus the Prophet is set apart from human society and he calls on those who believe to do the same. He has passed to the side of God and into the life to come, leaving this life behind him; the Day of the Judgment will see a complete reversal of the situation; indeed, the outcome of the Judgment is already arranged for everyone with certainty. No intercession will be accepted for the damned,[41] and their fate does not concern

---

[34] 109 (no. 39):1-3; see also 69 (no. 24):28; 89 (no. 42):20; etc.
[35] 75 (no. 27):33
[36] 80 (no. 17):34
[37] 70 (no. 33):11
[38] 93 (no. 4)
[39] 40 (no. 40):2
[40] 93 (no. 4)
[41] 74 (no. 36):48, etc.

8

the Prophet. God says to him: "Leave me alone with them."[42] It is more an execution than a judgment:

> "There will be a single blast from the trumpets, the earth and the mountains will be raised high and shattered to dust in a single blow."[43]

The theology of the first Meccan period is, in its pure state, a theology of *severance.* It is not a revolutionary mystical theology in that it does not, or nearly does not, comprise the organisation of a new society. The Great Day, and the Great Night are the completion, and the action comes from above. It is a call to conversion, but the real convert is he who does not believe that it was all his own choice. This vivid reality expresses the slightly paradoxical doctrine of "double predestination" which asserts at the same time the total responsibility of the adult human towards God:

> "Whosoever wants will remember;
> They shall not remember anything unless God should have willed it."[44]

Thus the *severance* on the social, moral and doctrinal levels appears simultaneously as a sign and as a submission. As submission it feeds the hope of salvation; as a sign it gives the assurance that this salvation is now and henceforth realised. He who has believed "has been saved by his hope", as St Paul said.

[67] The social severance on the other hand is first of all a severance from normal ties, from normal hierarchies, from the family and from all that is great, rich, respectable and wise in society. Discussion is impossible under these circumstances; therefore God's motives cannot be known and everything is decided.

If taken to its utmost logical limits, the austerity of such an attitude might take on a mechanical character and lose the sensibility by which souls become attached to it.

But God is at the same time awesome and a loving friend (*udud*).[45]

Finally, while it is stated explicitly that no intercession will be possible whatsoever, the angel who has given this benevolent revelation to the Prophet possesses all the same "great power with the Lord of the throne".[46]

---

[42] 73 (no. 34):11; 74:11
[43] 69 (no. 24):13
[44] 111 (no. 37):54–6, see also 81 (no. 18):28
[45] 85 (no. 43):14
[46] 81 (no. 18):20

9

SECOND MECCAN PERIOD (NO. 49–70, BLACHÈRE)

The peculiar relationship between Moses' and Muḥammad's prophetic witness is always asserted, either by explicit comparisons[47] or by the sheer number of instances, of which there are almost twice as many as those related to Abraham.

Moses' mission is still addressed to Pharaoh, but with important modifications. Firstly, Moses is not alone anymore and neither is Muḥammad.[48] Aaron appears as Moses' vizier[49] and the call is sometimes even addressed to the team of the two brothers;[50] furthermore, as a child, Moses has received help from his mother and sister[51] and finally he is given a family.[52]

On the other hand while this mission, being directed at Pharaoh, frequently keeps its individual character, from now on it is also a mission to an unjust people.[53] As well, not everything is absolutely determined: "Go to the unjust people, the people of Pharaoh. Are they not going to show fear of me?".[54] And if everything is not absolutely determined, the prophet has a special responsibility towards the people he is sent to warn. "Go to Pharaoh, for he is rebelling. Speak to him with gentle words; maybe he will take heed and show fear of me."[55] Besides, Pharaoh's magicians are convinced by Moses' signs and become believers, finding martyrdom and salvation.[56]

[68] As not all believers are dead, they form a new people of servants to God and Moses has the new mission of leading them: "Leave in the night, at the head of My servants. You will be persecuted. ... And Moses and all those who were with him were saved."[57]

At this point in the revelation the mission to the believing people introduces a considerable change in what might be called the history of the Last Judgment. The practical fact that the saved people are perfect no more bursts forth from the evidence. Still, from now on there is a bond, an alliance between God and Moses and also between God and his chosen people on earth.[58] The function of the alliance between God and

[47] 44 (no. 55):17; 43 (no. 63):45
[48] 20 (no. 57):132
[49] 20:30
[50] 37 (no. 52):114
[51] 20:37 ff.
[52] 27 (no. 69):7; see also 20:10
[53] 26 (no. 58):11; 25 (no. 68):36
[54] 26:11; 23 (no. 66):49
[55] 20:44
[56] 20:70 ff.; 26:46 ff.
[57] 26 (no. 58):52; see also 20:77; 44 (no. 55):23
[58] 43 (no. 63):49; 44 (no. 55):32; 20 (no. 57):86

10

Moses is in fact to ensure that the alliance between God and his people remains steadfast. Moses must never leave his people, God says, not even in order to get closer to him, because the people are weak and not able to resist temptation in Moses' absence.[59]

The logical link established by rabbinical theology between the oneness of the chosen people and that of God (together with the oneness of the Temple) is known. Therefore it is not surprising to see, as a correlative of this alliance, the sin of association in the episode of the golden calf.[60] On the other side, the divisions between various Christian sects are a sign that their doctrine about God has fallen into the sin of association.[61]

This double correlation, of the unity of the group of servants and the unity of God on the one hand and of the links between God and his prophet, between the prophet and the chosen people and between God and the people on the other, is already a *knowledge of God* which goes beyond fear of the Judgment. The revelation becomes "a salvation and a clarity"[62] and one of its material signs is now "the scripture, full of clear evidence"[63] which leads Moses and Aaron on the straight path (*ibid.*) in order that they may lead converted sinners along it.[64]

It is obvious that the fact that the Judgment has been part of the divine plan ever since the beginning of the revelation invests the prophecy with a historical function rather than a passing role in a momentary episode. The link between God and his people is put in a hierarchy: "I have lavished my love on you, so that you might be brought up under my eyes."[65]

However, the greatness of the mission only enhances the weakness of the messenger. He was a sinner,[66] he is despicable and [69] cannot express himself clearly,[67] he is afraid of Pharaoh's wrath[68] and he lacks intelligence and patience in his understanding of God's actions.[69]

But the love of God is absolute and demands absolute and unconditional faith: "Do not let someone who does not believe and who follows

---

[59] 44:33; 20:85

[60] 20:88 ff.

[61] 43 (no. 63): compare verses 59, 64, 65; similarly 23 (no. 66):50, 52, 53, 59; also 21 (no. 67):91, 92, 93

[62] 21 (no. 67):48

[63] 37 (no. 52):117

[64] 23 (no. 66):49

[65] 20 (no. 57):39

[66] 26 (no. 58):20

[67] 43 (no. 63):52

[68] 20 (no. 57):45

[69] 18 (no. 70):59–81

11

his whims turn your heart away from the Hour (of Doom), lest you perish."[70] In return, he will accompany the prophet and follow him in his work which is at the same time human and divine: "Fear not. I shall truly be with you, and I will hear and see."[71] He will hear the prophet's prayer and grant his wishes.[72]

Thus the link with God for as long as one is conscious of its existence, comprises, a commitment on God's part.

Within Muḫammad's own particular vision, different lines separated by the analysis of Moses' mission remain:

> "Do not pray to any other deity beside God, lest you become one of the punished. Admonish your kin and be kind to those among the believers who follow you."[73]

Muḫammad is not isolated anymore, either in his faith or in relation to his people. During this time the name "Muslim" appears and many texts mention the Prophet's responsibility towards the obedient people. The scripture is revealed, "descended through the faithful spirit, in pure Arabic, as was foretold in the scripture of the ancients."[74] This revelation conforms to a *law* of the actions and the Judgment of God: "We have never destroyed the inhabitants of a city whose fate was not preordained in their scripture."[75]

To put it differently, while the revelation is directed at the Prophet it is meant for his people to whom, in fact, it belongs.

This new alliance could allow for intercession on Judgment Day.[76]

The community thus formed is One (see footnote 61); during this period the sin of association, which is at least a secondary issue at the beginning of the revelation, is formulated more precisely.[77]

Thus there is a mutual commitment, by the people and also by God.[78] While disaster is always possible on Judgment Day, [70] perhaps even for the Prophet,[79] the faithful are united in their hope as well as their piety:

"Who but a sinner would despair of God's mercy?"[80]

---

[70] 20:16
[71] 20:46
[72] 20:36
[73] 26:213
[74] 26:193
[75] 15 (no. 59):4
[76] 19 (no. 60):87
[77] 59 (no. 30):19
[78] 51 (no. 49):22; 50 (no. 56):31
[79] 67 (no. 65):28
[80] 15 (no. 59):56

12

The parallel which has been shown between the vocations of Muḥammad and Moses within this period of the Qur'ān is all the more remarkable, despite a few slight differences, because the actual facts of the lives of the two prophets are not as similar as their situations:

Moses' "hegira", which is mentioned in suras 20 and 26, precedes Muḥammad's hegira in the Qur'ānic revelation. The context, from then on, only shows the relationship more clearly. The Muslim hegira will be explicitly connected to the Jewish hegira in the Medinian suras. Therefore one may conclude that the comparison has its origin not so much in the similarity of events but rather in the profound similarity Muḥammad himself felt where prophecy was concerned. What we said above about the "pages about Abraham and Moses" goes in the same direction in showing that this similarity is a primary fact. Muḥammad is the Moses of the Arabs.

The comparison between the two hegiras expresses a similar dynamism of action: the Muslim hegira, whatever its political import, was above all a prophetic action. Moubarac reaches the same conclusion when he assigns the principal role to Abraham's hegira (see footnote 5). This comparison seems to us to be less precise than that between Moses and Muḥammad, but the spiritual demands are the same: the hegira is one of the laws of prophetic action and the work of God.

THIRD MECCAN PERIOD (NO. 71–92, BLACHÈRE)

This is the period during which the earthly contents of the alliance are defined. Moses' essential mission is henceforth the Book, sign of the people's election, which will cause part of the promise to come true.

> "We have truly given the scripture and the enlightenment and the prophecy to the children of Israel. We have given them good nourishment and elevated them above the world. We have given them proof of the order."[81]
>
> "Indeed, we have given the scripture to Moses and made it a guide for the children of Israel. And we have appointed [71] leaders from among them who guided them according to our orders, as a reward because they were steadfast and believed in our signs."[82]

Finally part of the eschatological expectation is found on earth: "Maybe God will give you the earth at last."[83]

---

[81] 41 (no. 73):16
[82] 32 (no. 71):23
[83] 7 (no. 89):129

13

It is obvious that this realisation presupposes an organisation, if not a certain spiritual hierarchy, among the people. This organisation would spread across the whole world through the collective election of the people: "It is our will to favour those who were oppressed in the land, to make them leaders and to give them noble heritage and to give them power in the land."[84]

The main consequence of this transformation is that God's will (and not only his immediate moral demands, but also an idea of his plan of the Judgment and his way of acting) becomes *intelligible* to the mind of a "people who knows",[85] a "people who reasons"[86] etc.

> "We sent Moses forth with our signs and said: "Lead your people out of the darkness into the light"."[87]

Sura 18 (no. 70) clearly shows the transition from the second to the third Meccan period. The story of Moses and his mysterious companion conveys God's commitment towards his prophet; as well, it conveys the consciousness of this mutual commitment in which knowledge is discernible. However, God's actions can only be understood after the event through an individual initiation for everyone.

At the moment: "Moses, says the Lord, I have chosen you of all men to make known my message and my word. Take what I give you and be thankful. We inscribed for him on the tablets a precept for everything and *an understandable account of everything.* Take these tablets wholeheartedly and order your people to observe what is best in them."[88]

The unity between Moses' and Muḥammad's missions is always asserted clearly. They are both expressed in identical terms,[89] the scripture they are commissioned to make known is fundamentally the same[90] and nowadays, as in Moses' time, it allows the believer to understand God's action within history and even to discern certain normative rules.

Misfortune may be a sign of blessing: "We have never sent a prophet to a city without first afflicting [72] the people with calamity and misfortune in the hope that they might become humble. Afterwards, we always replaced adversity with good fortune, and they would forget (what we had done for them)."[91]

---

[84] 28 (no. 81):5
[85] 41 (no. 72):2
[86] 45 (no. 73):5
[87] 14 (no. 78):5
[88] 7 (no. 89):144; 6 (no. 91):154
[89] 14 (no. 78):1 (=5)
[90] 11 (no. 77):17; 29 (no. 83):50 etc°
[91] 7 (no. 89):93

14

> "Your Lord did not destroy these cities until he had sent an apostle to their capital cities who proclaimed our signs among them. We have not destroyed any city unless its inhabitants were sinful."[92]
>
> "*It was not possible (wa mā kāna)* that your Lord should have destroyed a city unjustly, a city whose inhabitants were just people."[93]
>
> "We take vengeance on the guilty, and *it was our duty (wa kāna ḥaqqan 'alaynā)* to succour the believers."[94]

At the reckoning, *God reveals something about his being as he dictates his will.*

Within the framework of the alliance the weakness of the believers is no longer an incredible disaster; on the contrary, it is foreseen and God's promise reaches beyond the punishment. The punishment does not destroy the alliance, at least not "for this time".[95] The greatest of sinners, even Pharaoh himself, can still convert and save themselves at the hour of death.[96] Finally, the prophet is qualified to beg God's forgiveness for repentant sinners or for his near relations in prayer. The term "intercession" (*shafā"a*) cannot be used here, as its Qur'ānic meaning is clear: it is an intervention at the Last Judgment in favour of the damned. As this was an attribute of pagan deities,[97] it is denied in the Qur'ān "unless it is by God's special permission".[98] Besides, this was not an innovation of this particular period.

However, as the existence of a believing community called to salvation imposes the notion of history onto salvation and Judgment, a new term, *istighfār*, indicates the praying for forgiveness by a living person for third persons. This testifies to a greater spiritual responsibility, e.g. in Moses' prayer:

> "Lord... would you destroy us because of what fools among us did? This was a temptation from you, to guide and to mislead whom you willed. You are our guardian. Forgive us and have mercy on us, for you are the noblest of those who forgive."[99]

---

[92] 28 (no. 81):59
[93] 11 (no. 77):117
[94] 30 (no. 76):47
[95] 17 (no. 74):4–8
[96] 10 (no. 86):90–92
[97] 10:18 etc.
[98] 10:3; 34 (no. 87):22, etc.
[99] 7:155

15

This prayer does indeed have the character of an intervention with the aim, and the result, of changing God's will in pursuance of a [73] more essential will which He had expressed through the alliance and the mission entrusted to his prophet for him to be its guardian.

The same spiritual function is found in connection with other ancients. Jacob's sons say to their father:

> "Father, ask God's forgiveness for us for our sins. We have been sinners. – I will ask my Lord's forgiveness, for he is forgiving and merciful."[100]

Joseph is formal when he says to his brothers: "No one shall reproach you today. God will forgive you."[101]

As for Muḥammad himself, he is even more formal: "Your Lord has vowed to be merciful."[102] And he recommends every believer to intercede for his father and mother.[103]

It should also be stated that Jacob, and also Joseph, show their faith as much by their understanding (and literally their divination) of God's plan as by their faithful observation of his commandments. This is what gives them strength.

It is easy to see that any contemplation of these topics from the point of view of doctrine would quickly become dangerous in Muslim eyes. It would be difficult to transfer the intensity of feeling about God's presence, and the certainty based on the rights of prayer, to the level of dogma, or even to simply express it.... As we have already seen in the previous period, the guarantee of absolute divine transcendence is found in the human weakness of the prophet. Despite his superior vocation, he is constantly in need of God's help.

> "When you see those who deride our signs, keep away from them until they direct their derision at something else. Satan will certainly make you forget this."[104]
>
> "If we had not given you strength, you could not have helped to move towards them a little..."[105]

[100] 12 (no. 79): 97
[101] 12 (no. 79):92
[102] 6 (no 91):54
[103] 17 (no. 74):24
[104] 6:67; see also 7:200
[105] 17:76

16

FOURTH PERIOD: SURAS FROM MEDINA (NO. 93-116, BLACHÈRE)

The new topic in this period is holy war which completes God's commitment to his people. This is also connected to the example of Moses:

> "(Moses says:) "O my people, enter the holy land which God has assigned for you. Do not turn back, for if you do you will be lost."
>
> [74] "O Moses, they replied, there is a people of giants in this land. We will not enter until they have left it. Should they leave, then we shall enter it." Two god-fearing men who had been favoured by God said: "Go in to these giants through the gate. Once you have passed this, you shall be victorious. Put your trust in God, if you are believers."
>
> But they cried: "O Moses, we will not enter this land as long as these giants are there. You go, you and your Lord, and you can fight them. We will stay here and not fight.""
>
> And as punishment for this unfaithfulness the Promised Land will be forbidden to them for forty years.[106]
>
> Subsequent to Moses, (the council of the children of Israel) said to a prophet they had: "Appoint us a King and we will fight for the cause of God." – "What if you should refuse to fight when ordered to do so?" – "Why should we refuse to fight for God's cause, now that we and our children have been expelled from our dwellings?"
>
> However, when they were ordered to fight, they would turn their backs, except for a small number among them.[107]

Here again we find the same elements in Muḥammad's appeals to the faithful: the aversion to war, its justification in closely related terms[108] and especially the support and finally order of God. And again, independent of Muḥammad's political and strategic understanding, holy war has a theological origin.

This is a translation of God's total commitment to men. The men who have waged holy war have fulfilled their commitment to God.[109]

> "Not you have killed these infidels, it is God who killed them. You did not smite them: it was God who did it so that he might richly reward the faithful."[110]

---

[106] 5 (no. 116):24–27
[107] 2 (no. 93):246
[108] 4 (no. 102):75
[109] 33 (no. 105):23
[110] 8 (no. 97):17

17

In return, the presence of the faithful and their literally superhuman efforts were necessary for God to be able to accomplish one of his own tasks:

> "If God had not fought certain men with other men, hermits' cells would have been destroyed, and synagogues, chapels and mosques where God's name is frequently invoked."[111]

Finally, holy war is the realisation of part of the Last Judgment: [75] martyrs are "accomplishing their fate"[112] and will be "living in paradise";[113] the infidels will go to hell.[114]

In a certain sense, holy war *is* the Last Judgment. It introduces the concepts of time and history into the knowledge of God, for his judgment.[115]

An essential difference appears here in connection with Moses. There is no doubt that the essential significance of holy war can also be found in the holy texts of the Israelites. Thus, forbidding them the Promised Land for *forty years* represents the enforcement of the judgment for one whole generation, in accordance with the Biblical significance of that period in other instances, such as in the books of Joshua and Judges.

However, Moses failed in his mission to lead Israel into holy war, while Muḥammad succeeded, and won. Certainly, Moses and his brother are saved, but that was not the aim of his life. In the Meccan suras Moses accomplished his mission both to Pharaoh and in other respects, and Muḥammad could make him his absolute example. Now, on the other hand, it appears that a prophet's mission is not so much to acquire salvation for himself but rather to lead a whole people to the faith. The image of Moses crying at the Last Judgment because his own people are less numerous than Muḥammad's is an illustration of this failure.[116]

There is nevertheless a resemblance if we consider the two prophets not in the context of their two peoples and their respective missions, but in the context of only the Jews, who resists:

> "O children of Israel, remember (...) when you say: "O Moses, we will not believe in you until we see God with our own eyes"."[117]

Still, this resemblance, which is in effect a defeat both prophets have in common, is not prophetic and missionary because it does not bear on

[111] 22 (109):23
[112] 33 (no. 105):24
[113] 2 (no. 93):154; 3 (no. 99):169
[114] 66 (no. 111):9 etc. ...
[115] 3:142; 57 (no. 101):25
[116] See footnote 10.
[117] 2:55; see also 61 (no. 100):5 and 4 (no. 102):153

18

the prophetic mission anymore. On the contrary, it is a result of the similarity of the two situations.

Furthermore it has to be mentioned that holy war does not have a missionary character because its primary aim is not to convey that salvation which is the possession of the believers; its objective is to render perfect the relation between God and the believer, not to convert the heathen. The supreme ideal is to be killed in the course of the war, as the prophetic function is not extended from the prophet to the faithful. The following example allows us to specify this non-missionary character of prophecy and of piety at that time:

> "Thus they are described in the Torah and in the [76] Gospel: they are like grains which have put forth their shoots and strengthen them, so that they rise and stand firmly on their stems, delighting the sowers."[118]

This image appears in a number of different guises in the gospels, but it always has a specifically missionary intent through evoking the ripened grains. Here, the image is that of the strength and purity of the straight stem. There is more: the image of the ripened grains is found in other instances in the Qur'ān.[119] But there again, it appears in a completely different context, foreseeing the future fortune of those who have spent their possessions in the path of God.

Moses and his defeat can thus explain how holy war could have restrained the spirit of spiritual conquest in Muḥammad's prophetic consciousness.

Thus, while Moses is not the model of prophecy any more, his role is not exhausted. He is the precursor and rejoins the ranks of the prophets from among whom, most importantly, Abraham and Jesus have come. One might say, specifically, that the image of Moses rejoins that of Abraham.

The figure of Abraham has followed a slightly different itinerary, because Abraham did not have initial success with his people. However, as soon as the revelation becomes more precise, his son joins him in his faith before the sacrifice:[120] henceforth the people of Abraham are his descendants.

Here we find again the development described in the case of Moses, transferred onto the mystical level. Moubarac is justified in insisting on Abraham's "spiritual hegira".[121] In the spiritual history of this prophet,

---

[118] 48 (no. 110):29
[119] 2:261
[120] 37 (no. 52):102
[121] *Abraham dans le Coran*, pp. 108 ff.

19

the *rupture* occurs in one *moment.* To persist in this state of *rupture*, however, would exclude any works, any participation in the realisation of God's plan. God's plan presupposes a theology of community. In Abraham's case, the spatial community, which would be the ideal of government, is replaced by a community in time. And the characteristics of the "theology of community" can be found in the piety of the "children of Abraham": consciousness, security, and finally participation in the kingdom of the heavens (see footnote 121).

Thus we have two theologies of community whose characteristics are transposable. There is a continuity from the faith of the children of the community to the serenity of the just one; from belonging [77] to the community to participating in the "cloud of witnesses" in the kingdom of the Heavens; from the apostolate to the education of children; from the mission of the leader to that of the father.

Furthermore, it is in continuity with Abraham's spiritual heritage that Moses leaves the heritage of the divine presence to the *descendants of his people*[122] and that he remains the one "to whom God speaks clearly".[123]

However, we are left with the fact that, while the faithful can still profit from Moses' meditation, his vision is no longer Muḥammad's model and constant reference, as it had been in Mecca.

There is another reason which contributes to removing the image of Moses from the Prophet's mission. The scripture no longer belongs to Moses or the Jews exclusively. It belongs to the Christians, in its general shape as well as in the form of the Gospel, which is integrated into it. It is as such that Muḥammad recognises it and inserts his own revelation. Even holy war appears as a commandment from the Gospel.[124] Between Muḥammad and Moses there is now Jesus.

The point of reference for the Muslim community is no longer the people of Moses, not even when faithful, but Jesus' disciples, the first *anṣār* and the first Muslim community.[125] At least they support Jesus in his struggle, which is an explicit model of holy war, and he will emerge victorious.[126] Thus we can see how the Medinian community could have been based on a certain Christian tradition. However, the prophetic problem remains, as in no place is Muhammad's mission, in its origin or its spirit, compared to that of Jesus as it was to that of Moses.

---

[122] 2:248
[123] 4:142
[124] 9 (no. 115):111
[125] 3 (no. 99):52
[126] 3:52; 61 (no. 100):6–14

20

Muḥammad received God's word through the faithful spirit; Jesus *was* this word and a spirit coming from God incarnated in a man.[127] Finally, Jesus was gifted with a unique power over sickness and death. The last of the suras says:

> "(O Jesus, son of Mary, remember) how I instructed you in the scriptures, the wisdom, the Torah and the Gospel; how you created from clay the form of birds by my leave and breathed into it so that they became living birds by my leave; how you healed the dumb man and the leper by my leave; and how you raised the dead (from their tombs) by my leave..."[128]

[78] These last words can even be compared to another verse of the same sura:

> "Because of Cain's crime we decreed for the children of Israel that whoever kills a human being, except for murder and for wicked crimes, should be judged as if he had killed all mankind, and whoever revives a human being should be judged as if he had revived all mankind."[129]

It is not impossible that, while Muḥammad's prophetic consciousness is not questioned, he felt some hesitation concerning the exact significance of his own ministry in the history of the revelation. This hesitation might furthermore correspond to the difficulty we have in specifying the doctrinal nature of the various sects which the Qur'ān names "Jews" or "Christians". The idea appears that the Christians (and to a lesser degree the Jews)[130] would have had a part in the truth, if they had been faithful to the Gospel in their actions.[131] But their community was unfaithful to its own revelation, and we find, concomitant with the division of people into sects, the sin of association.[132]

If they had been faithful... one might wonder what would have been the sense in a third revelation.

As they were not faithful, it is now Muḥammad's mission to form finally, in accordance with the earlier revelations, the faithful people of the Muslims, the "obedient ones".

There is also the idea that the Qur'ān is the third panel of a revelation in triptych, constituted by the Torah, the Gospel, and the Qur'ān,[133] with

[127] 4 (no. 102):171
[128] 5 (no. 116):110
[129] 5:32
[130] 5:45
[131] 2 (no. 93):253; 5:48, 66, 68
[132] 5:14–17
[133] 3:2; 9 (no. 115):11

Abraham as a prelude.[134] Through Moses, God reveals the extent of prophecy and election, through Jesus, the extent of his beneficent power on earth. Islam, finally, realises a harmonious synthesis of the two previous revelations.

Whichever of these, or another, is the better interpretation, it seems to us that Muḥammad's autonomous mission is henceforth directed towards practical organisation of the perfect community and that he is conscious of having succeeded.

> "This day I have perfected your religion for you and completed my favour to you. I have chosen Islam to be your faith."[135]
>
> "You are the noblest community that has ever been raised up for mankind."[136]

The believers have passed from death to life.[137]

[79] In this Muslim expression of "God's Kingdom on Earth", what is the Prophet's role?

His authority is the same as God's: "Whoever obeys the apostle obeys God."[138] "It is not for true believers, men or women, to make their own choice in a matter once this matter has been decided by God and his apostle."[139]

And the expression which recurs constantly in the Medinian period is "God and his apostle".

Muḥammad is no longer only the man who brings a message to the people; he *is* a light to them,[140] a good example for whoever puts his hope in God;[141] he is the witness, the protecting friend who is linked closer to the believer than they are among themselves. *His wives are their mothers.*[142]

A major transformation has taken place since the beginnings in Mecca. We have arrived at a *theology of community.*

At the time when conversion is experienced as a collective action or as participation, and life in the community makes the believers sure of the option they have taken regarding salvation, this conversion ceases to be

---

134 3:65
135 5:3
136 3:110
137 6 (no. 91):122; 2:28, 56, the latter verses refer to Moses.
138 4:80
139 33 (no. 105):36
140 33:46
141 33:21
142 33:6

22

totally within salvation. It is the beginning, the initiatory act. The believers cease to be responsible adults who have taken an independent decision; instead they become children, children of one and the same father. Their father is the leader of the community, around him they are without fear and life is theirs. To repeat Gilson's formula (see footnote 3), the grace of God is inserted into the natural course of things, the "Church" has been inserted into the state; and theology has become a true political philosophy.

The theology of *severance* is that of the orphan, the persecuted man; the theology of community is a theology of the family, and especially the father. All religious teachings are normally situated in a similar theological context. The theology of *severance*, on the other hand, cannot know anything about teaching... because it corresponds exactly to those grains of sand which God occasionally drops into our well-regulated spiritual and social mechanisms.

> "God has promised to those among you who believe and who do good works to make them rulers over the land, as he had made their ancestors before them. He has promised to strengthen their faith which he chose for them and to change their fear to safety."[143]
>
> [80] "We have sent among you an apostle from your midst who will make known to you our signs, who will purify you and instruct you in the scripture, in the wisdom and in that of which you can have no knowledge. Invoke my name and I will remember you. Be thankful towards me always."[144]

The comparison of the following two texts shows clearly, in our view, this development in the field of piety:

> The pious (*abrār*) keep their vow, *fear* a day when sorrow will be universal. For the love of God they give food to the poor, the orphan, the captive: "We will feed you for our Lord's sake, not asking any reward or gratitude from you. We fear a day of terror and disaster from our Lord, but God has protected them from that terrible day..."[145]
>
> Pious goodness (*birr*) does not consist in turning your face East or West. But the pious man (*birr*) is he who believes in God and in the Last Judgment, in the angels, in the scripture and in the prophets, who, for the love of God, gives to his

---

[143] 24 (no. 107):55

[144] 2:151

[145] See footnotes 20 and 28.

> neighbour, to the orphans, to travellers, to beggars, towards the freeing of slaves and who prays and gives alms. Those who keep alliances when they have committed themselves, who are steadfast in adversity, in evil and dangerous situations, they are the pious.[146]

This text can also be compared to 2:83, where the same advice is placed in Moses' mouth.

All the variants go in the same direction: fear has passed to the second level; the moral attitude remains strictly the same and the permanence of Moses' authority may be the reason for that, but faithfulness has become the essential virtue, the obedience to a recognised authority.

Faithfulness to the religion of the fathers used to comprise a temptation – that of riches.[147] Now it has become the virtue of the children in the community.[148]

God's presence has come so close as to be in the hearts of the believers,[149] as he was in the past to the children of Israel.[150] Thus God himself becomes the model for the community: "If you overlook their offences and forgive them, it will be good, for God is forgiving and merciful."[151]

[81] Once we have reached this point in the development of the revelation, the faithful cannot commit a greater sin than apostasy:

> "Those who believe and then renounce the faith, and then believe again and renounce again, their unbelief will only grow, and God will never forgive them."[152]
>
> "Where they are concerned it is all the same whether you ask forgiveness for them or not. God will not forgive them."[153]

And as revelation is now perfect, prophecy has come to an end. The Qur'ān is "the seal of prophecy";[154] only God can, at the Judgment and the resurrection, add anything (*yunabbi'uhum allāhu*).[155]

And by obeying God's laws, the Muslim community will finally extend the prophetic witness in the world to a certain extent.

---

146 2:177
147 43 (no. 63):23
148 2:132
149 48 (no. 110):4
150 2:248
151 64 (no. 95):14
152 4:137
153 63 (no. 106):6; 9:80
154 33:40
155 5:14

24

> "We have made you a moderate nation, so that you may testify against mankind and that your apostle may testify against you."[156]

This might seem contradictory to what we have said above regarding holy war, to wit that its spiritual contents for the believer were not of a missionary nature.

We have shown a profound development between the beginnings of the preaching in Mecca and the Medinan period: from a theology of *severance* we have passed to a theology of community; but at this precise point in time the Muslim community is breaking the bridges linking it to the Jews and also to the Christians, thus the verse quoted (footnote 156) has to be seen in this context. One could also speak of a kind of community prophecy similar to the prophecy of the first Meccan period and its meaning for Muḥammad or for Moses. In this sense, even holy war assumes a prophetic and missionary character for the community taken as a whole.

One might also say that the *severance* with the non-Muslim communities creates in the Muslim conception of the testimony a discontinuity between that which restores the piety of the believers in its being and the testimony of *severance* to which the community is vowed. The study of this discontinuity in other communities does not enter into the present discussion.

Finally we can ask whether the image of Moses and its specific Islamic character could not explain these distinctive traits and perhaps also certain problems which have troubled his story. The Qur'ānic Moses [82] is elevated above the sinful Israel by means of his particular election by God who, in His justice, shields him from general punishment. The Biblical Moses has participated in the sin of his people who were afraid to enter the Holy Land[157] and his punishment is to die before crossing the Jordan. However, in his closeness to God, this punishment is fully accepted. In this way, Moses' death is an integral part of his prophecy whose testimony cannot be extinguished by any living man.

For, in death which is put into the service of God's work, in the grain of wheat which dies in the ground,[158] *severance* and breaking away can become presence and faithfulness, seeds of the community. Furthermore, through faith and the support of the community and through *wisdom*, man will find valid preparation for breaks and *severances* to come.

---

[156] 2:143

[157] Deuteronomy 1:32-37. See also the study by H. Cazelles in *Moise, l'homme de l'Alliance*, pp. 24–25.

[158] John 12:24

4

"AND BECOME YE ACCURSED APES"

Ilse Lichtenstaedter

The Prophet Muḥammad proudly proclaimed his Revelation to be *Qur'ānun 'arabiyyun, qur'ānun mubīn* "an Arabic Koran, a clear, intelligible Koran." [1] Whether this phrase simply meant that his Meccan audience could readily understand it without any further interpretation because it was revealed in their native tongue, or whether it was a revelation that could not be contradicted, it did not take long before the Prophet's followers, after his death, were in need of further implementation and explanation of even the obvious meanings of its *Sūrahs* and *Āyās.* Even the next generation, the so-called *Ṭābi'ūn*, began to ask the *Aṣḥāb*, Muḥammad's surviving contemporaries, for further elucidation on the connections of Koranic verses with specific events in Muḥammad's own life, their origins and their meanings.[2] This search led to the scholarly commentaries on the Koran, culminating in *Tafsīr*, "The Commentary," by al-Ṭabarī (d. 390 A.H./922 A.D.). This work became the leading, authoritative work on which most, if not all, later Muslim attempts at explanation were based, not excluding late interpretations based on different approaches, such as that of Sufism.

Ṭabarī's *Tafsīr* remains to this day the traditional orthodox commentary even for modern liberal Muslim movements such as that built upon the school of 'Abduh, in Egypt; the commentary of Maulana 'Abd al-Kalam Azad in India (d. 1958); and the edition published, with translations and notes, by 'Abd Allāh Yūsuf 'Alī of Saudi Arabia.[3]

Modern Western Orientalists, too, have continued to depend to a certain extent on Ṭabarī's comments on the *Sūrahs* and *Āyās* of the Koran. However, they differ essentially from the ancient commentators

---

1 Koran, *Sūrah* XII verse 2. Or, as R.A. Nicholson called it, "perspicuous."

2 See J. Horovitz, "The Earliest Biographies of the Prophet and their Authors," in: *Islamic Culture*, vols. I & II, Hyderabad, 1927.

3 New York 1946, 2 vols. Nor is the commentary by the Ahmadiya sect an exception, published by the Oriental and Religious Publishing Corp. Ltd., Rabwah, Pakistan, 1964 (4 vols., 2nd ed.); cp. vol. I, p. 131.

in not acknowledging the divine origin of the revelations; they tried to gain deeper insight by searching for similar ideas in earlier kindred religions and cultures in Muḥammad's environment, mainly in Judaism, Christianity and its various sects, as well as Zoroastrianism. To Nöldeke's and Horovitz's studies along these lines, those of Ditlev Nielsen added a new dimension. He pointed to South Arabian religious[4] ideas and their influence on Muḥammad's North Arabian religiosity. The studies of these leading Western authorities laid the foundation for all ensuing research and they will probably remain fundamental reference works for a long time to come. However, they also encouraged a somewhat sterile and stereotyped search for further new parallels to Koranic tenets in Jewish or Christian sources as additional examples of "Judeo-Christian" influence on Muḥammad's thought.

For quite some time I have felt that a new approach was needed. As long ago as the colloquium held in connection with the bicentennial celebration of Princeton University in 1947,[5] I pointed out the need for archaeological exploration in North Arabia, and the great gap in our knowledge of Muḥammad's native milieu resulting from the lack of such exploration -- a circumstance attributable to the sacred nature of his North Arabian sphere of activity, especially of Meccah and Medinah. I began, therefore, to search for an approach that steered away from the mere juxtaposition of Koranic stories, personalities and phrases with analogous elements in Jewish or Christian traditions, since these correspondences, however valuable when first examined,[6] have tended to degenerate into an accumulation of an ever-increasing number of "parallels" between Jewish or Christian, or for that matter, pre-Islamic Persian, literatures and

---

4 Ditlev Nielsen, *Handbuch der Altarabischen Altertumskunde*, Copenhagen, 1927.

5 *Near Eastern Culture and Society. The Arab and Muslim World: Studies and Problems*, Princeton University Bicentennial Conferences, Series 2, Conference 6, p. 12. Princeton, 1946.

6 Abraham Geiger, *Was hat Muhammad aus dem Judentum angenommen?* 1833, Christian Gerok, *Die Christologie des Korans*.

Koranic counterparts.[7] I felt deeply dissatisfied with this rather mechanical effort, which seemed to me incapable of contributing to a deeper understanding of the workings of Muḥammad's mind and of the message he tried to convey. This statement is not intended to belittle the valuable research done into many facets of the Koran and specific problems by many Jewish and Christian scholars.[8] Only when the search *ends* in such juxtapositions of ever more parallels, does it become mechanical and sterile.

For a number of years I have been intrigued by this problem, and I have searched for a wider range of cultural influences on Muḥammad's thinking. I took at its face value Muḥammad's own statement that he was a *nabī ummī* "an unlettered prophet," that is, a man who drew his inspiration from the cultural atmosphere in which he lived, from the air he breathed, so to speak. This led me to examine religious ideas in his wider environment, and to consider myths of ancient peoples that may have been current in his own time.

The first step away from the mere compilation of Koranic passages together with their parallels in Judeo-Christian literature was taken by A.J. Wensinck in his seminal studies.[9] He prepared the way for the investigation of Koranic legends by tracing them back to similar ones in more ancient religions, which still appeared to him to be closely related to the Koranic myths. In these studies, however, Wensinck restricted himself mainly to the realm of North Semitic cultures. I was deeply stirred by his studies and felt the urge to search even further for what I called "the origins of Koranic symbolism," in

7 The most striking example of this is A.I. Katsh, *Judaism in Islam*, New York, 1954, which is mostly an enumeration of parallel versions in Jewish/Aramaic works and a Koranic phrase used in relation to one single personality, i.e. Abraham, and based almost exclusively on one *Sūrah*.

8 E.g., S.D. Goitein, *Prayer in the Koran* [unpublished doctoral thesis, University of Frankfurt a.M., ca. 1928], J. Horovitz, *Koranische Untersuchungen*, Berlin-Leipzig, 1926; Heinrich Speyer, *Die Biblischen Erzählungen im Koran*, Hildesheim, 1971, pp. 313, 314. (1st printing, 1931).

9 E.g., "Tree and Bird as Cosmological Symbols in Western Asia," Amsterdam, 1921, and "The Ocean in the Literature of the Western Semites," Amsterdam, 1918 (Verh. d. Koninkl. Akad. van Wetschap., Afd. Letterk. N.R., deel XVII, 1; XI, 2; XXII, 1.)

response to the great Dutch Orientalist's own suggestion that other students should follow up his own research by further pursuing the path and methods that he had shown.[10]

In a number of articles I have proposed solutions to several of these "symbols."[11] In these studies I ventured beyond the strictly Semitic sphere and also drew on Egyptian mythology[12] and folklore,[13] using them in my attempt to solve several problems which had previously only cursorily caught the attention of scholars and, at least in the case of the *gharānīq*, had escaped the comprehension of even Theodor Nöldeke, the dean of Koran studies.[14] By exploring these methods I have been able to suggest what I believe to be solutions to these select puzzles and to show, at the very least, one more feasible approach to the task of tracing their origins and hitting upon satisfactory solutions for them and for similar ones.

In the present article, I propose to extend this attempt by drawing attention to certain other well-known *āyāt* presenting problems that have hitherto even been completely overlooked. I have used the same method in tackling these Koranic passages and establishing their meaning. The passages selected are concerned with "a people who sinned by violating the Sabbath," and with the punishment meted out to them: their transformation into apes. In the order of the traditional ʿUthmanic Koranic count, the passages under discussion are the following:

1. *Sūrah* II (*al-Baqarah*) verse 65: "Ye know too of those among you who transgressed upon the Sabbath and We said:

---

10 See Wensinck, *loc. cit*

11 See "Origins and Interpretations of Some Qur'ānic Symbols" [I]; in *Studi Orientalistici in onore di Giorgio Levi Della Vida*, vol. II, pp. 58ff.; [II] in *Arabic and Islamic Studies, in Honor of Hamilton A.R. Gibb*, pp. 426ff.; "A Note on the Gharānīq and Related Qur'ānic Problems," in *Israel Oriental Studies*, vol. V, Tel Aviv, 1975, pp. 54ff.

12 See especially in LDV and Gibb Festschrifts.

13 See especially "Folklore and Fairytale Motifs in Early Arabic Literature" in *Folklore*, vol. LI, Edinburgh, 1940.

14 Nöldeke-Schwally, *Geschichte des Korans*, part 1, Leipzig, 1909, p. 101, note 4.

Become ye apes, despised and spurned."

2. *Sūrah* V (*al-Mā'idah*) verse 65: "Say, can I declare unto you something worse than retribution from God? Whomsoever God has cursed and been wroth with — and he has made of them apes and swine — and who worship Tāghūt, they are in a worse plight and more erring from the level path."

3. *Sūrah* VII (*al-A'rāf*) verses 163ff.: "Ask them about the city which stood by the sea, when they transgressed upon the Sabbath, when their fish came to them sailing straight up to them, but on the day when they kept not the Sabbath they came not to them — thus did We try them for the abomination that they wrought . . . evil was the abomination that they did, but when they rebelled against what they were forbidden We said to them: become ye apes despised and spurned."

In addition to these verses, the following *āyāt* must be considered for they proscribe swine, as does *Sūrah* V above, though not jointly with apes. There are also many other references to the Sabbath, but these deal with other aspects of Sabbath observance.

4. *Sūrah* II (*al-Baqarah*) verse 168 [Flügel]: "He has only forbidden for you what is dead, and blood, and flesh of swine, and whatsoever has been consecrated to other than God."

5. *Sūrah* V (*al-Mā'idah*) verse 4: "Forbidden to you is that which dies of itself and blood and the flesh of swine, and that which is devoted to other than God." (see also V, 93).

6. *Sūrah* VI (*al-An'ām*) verse 146: ". . . unless it be dead (of itself) or blood that has been shed or the flesh of swine — for that is a horror -- or an abomination that is consecrated to other than God."

7. *Sūrah* XVI (*al-Naḥl*) verse 116: "He has only forbidden you that which dies of itself, and blood and the flesh of swine and that which is devoted to other than God."

The first three *āyāt* quoted were part of Muḥammad's attempt at gradually gaining the support of Meccan Jews, reinforced with thinly veiled threats as to what might befall them if they persisted in their refusal to join him. Nöldeke-Schwally assign these verses to the third Meccan and early Medinian periods, but make no further comments regarding their contents. However, as long ago as the ancient Muslims, scholars were intrigued by them, and wondered who these people were that had violated the Sabbath and were so severely punished. The Koran itself does not provide any clue as to their identity. Therefore some answer had to be invented. The one that Ṭabarī gives in his commentary to *Sūrah* II verses 63ff. gives full rein to his imagination and speculation. At the same time, several of the items woven into this tapestry were obviously reminiscent of folkloristic motifs which can be found in many cultures world-wide.

> He (Ṭabarī) said: Thus also did God speak to Mūsa when the Jews talked to him about the institution [lit. affairs] of the Sabbath namely, that they should not "hunt" for fish nor any other animal nor should they do any other work on that day. He (Ṭabarī) said: However, when fish appeared on a Sabbath in (*'alà*) the water -- as He (God) said in the Qur'ān: "When their fish came to them on the day of their rest straight up to them (*shurra'an*)" [Surah VII, 163] that is, visible on the water — referring to their rebellion against Mūsà. But on any other day but Sabbath, the Jews went fishing as usual -- that is the meaning of Allah's word 'and on the day when they did not rest, the fish did not come to them.' The fish acted that way for as long as Allah willed. When the people saw the fish coming in droves (lit. like that), they yearned to catch them, but feared the punishment; yet others caught some of them [on the Sabbath] and did not abstain from it, disregarding the punishment from Allah about which Mūsà had warned them. When they saw that no punishment befell them, they did it again and told each other that they had caught fish and nothing had happened to them. So they did it again and again and thought, Mūsà's order was vain (*bāṭil*). That is the meaning of Allah's word 'Know those of you who violated the Sabbath. We said to them: be like apes driven by stones.' He said that to those who had caught fish —

> and Allah transformed them into apes on account of their transgression . . . Allah had created the apes and the swines and all other creatures in the six days Allah mentions in His Book, and He transformed those people into the shapes of apes. Thus will He do with whomever He wants, how He wants, and transforms as He wants. [Ṭab. *Tafsīr*, vol. II, pp. 167ff., edition *Dā'irat al-Ma'ārif*, Cairo 1374 H., 2nd ed.]

In this attempt at clarification, Ṭabarī is using a motif familiar to anyone versed in Jewish lore. In particular, two motifs of Jewish folklore occur, even today, to those brought up with Jewish traditions: the myth of the primordial Fish, called Leviathan, and that of the river *Sambatyon,* which is thought to flow with water over rolling rocks and sand on every weekday, but to rest on the Sabbath.[15] Neither is mentioned by name in any of the Koranic verses; but Louis Ginzberg and, most recently, Heinrich Speyer,[16] have drawn attention to this fact and have assembled references from both Rabbinic and Midrashic literature.

In the Koranic *āyāt* there is no indication of the exact nature of the Sabbath violation; the commentators, however, could easily have heard stories told by Jews about the *Sambatyon.* Ginzberg's notes deserve to be quoted more extensively.

[On *Sambatyon*] vol. IV, p. 317 and note 56 in vol. VI, p. 407ff.:

> [When the Jews were led to captivity by Nebuchadnezzar and forced to sing a song of Zion] at the fall of night a cloud descended and enveloped the Sons of Moses and all who belonged to them. [A pillar of fire descended as well; these vanished at daybreak]. Before the Sons of Moses lay a tract of land bordered by the sea on three sides. For their complete protection God made the river *Sambatyon* to flow on the fourth side. This river is full of sand and stones, and on the six working days they tumble over each other with such vehemence that the crash and the roar are heard far and wide. But on the Sabbath [Ginzberg, note 56, see below] the tumultuous river subsides into quiet. As a guard against trespassing on that day a column of cloud stretches along the whole length of the river,

15 But see below, note 56 in the quotation from L. Ginzberg's *Legends of the Jews.*

16 Louis Ginzberg, *Legends of the Jews*, vol. IV, p. 317:VI, p. 407ff. Heinrich Speyer, *loc. cit.*

160 "And become ye accursed apes"

and none can approach the *Sambatyon* within three miles.

[Ginzberg, note 56, see above]

> **Pliny *Hist. Nat.* 31.2 agrees with the Rabbis (*Sanhedrin* 65a, in conversation between R. Akiba and the Roman general Tineius [Turnu?] Rufus etc.) that this river rests on the Sabbath, whereas Josephus Bell. VII, 5.1 maintains just the opposite, that it rests on week-days and flows on the Sabbath. Josephus and the Rabbis differ also as to the location of this river. The former maintains that it is situated in SYRIA [my caps; see below for the importance of this location] between Acre and Raphanea, whereas the latter implicitly assume that it is in a country very far from Palestine. [Ginzberg adds here references to *Sambatyon* in Christian, Mohammedan and Samaritan writings, in Nöldeke, *Alexanderroman*, Masʿūdī, *Murūj*, and others.] . . . The holiness of the Sabbath is "attested" by the river *Sambatyon* and also by a certain fish which spends the Sabbath resting on the banks of the river and by a mountain from which silver is taken every day in the week with the exception of the Sabbath, when no silver can be found there.**

The name of the river *Sambatyon* is not mentioned in any book of the Old Testament; it has been identified by some authors with the river Gozan, mentioned in 2 Kings 17:6, across which the Ten Tribes were led into exile.[17]

The contrasting statement by Josephus, quoted above, also seems to have been the version that led to Ṭabarī's commentary repeatedly emphasizing the fact that the fish came on the Sabbath, but not on workdays. According to this interpretation, the violation of the Sabbath consisted in fishing in a river that teemed with fish on the day of rest, while none were seen during the rest of the week. The Muslim commentators, in their customary manner, embroidered this simple fact by enlarging their account with details about digging a channel on the Sabbath into which they lured the fish so that they could be caught, prepared and eaten on a weekday; the smell of fried fish lured more and more men to join

17 Thus Pseudo-Jonathan *Targum* to Ex. 34:10.

the Sabbath breakers.[18]

A very interesting passage is found in a discussion of hell and the damned in E. A. W. Budge's *The Gods of the Egyptians or Studies in Egyptian Mythology*.[19] It reads:

> In this place were several other terrible serpents, and to one of these which had teeth like iron stakes, the poor soul was given to be devoured. This monster crushed the soul for five days of each week, but on Saturday and Sunday, it had respite. This last sentence seems to suggest that the serpent respected the Sabbath of the Jews and the Sunday of the Christians.

The Jewish myths about the Leviathan, the sea monster, may have influenced the role that fish played in the Islamic tales, often elaborated as in the passage of Ṭabarī's commentary quoted above. The word "Leviathan" occurs several times in the Old Testament,[20] i.e., in Ps. 104:26,[21] Isa. 27:1 (twice), Ps. 74:14, and Job 40:25ff. (King James Version, 41:1ff.). All of these passages speak of a sea monster or serpent used by God to smite the enemies of His people. The later commentators embroidered these verses with allegorical exegeses.[22] One of these is relevant to the Koranic *āyāt* under discussion: the Talmud *Baba Batra* 746 tells us that the sea monster Leviathan is slain by the Lord to provide sustenance for the righteous in the world to come.

In his *Tafsīr*, Ṭabarī presents another problem. He maintains that the violators of the Sabbath were people who lived in a city called Madyan[23] situated between Ailah and Mount Sinai.

---

18 For further comments on the river *Sambatyon*, see the *Jewish Encyclopedia* and *Encyclopedia Judaica*, *s.v.*

19 Vol. I, p. 269, New York (1964).

20 See Wm. G. Braude, *Pesikta Rabbati* (Yale 1968), p. 480 and note 29, and Gerald Friedlander, (trans.) *Pirke de Rabbi Eliezer*, p. 63f. New York (Hermon Press), 1965.

21 See E.R. Goodenough, *Jewish Symbols in the Graeco-Roman Period*, p. 99. New York, N.Y. 1965.

22 For references see the *Jewish Encyclopedia*, *s.v.*

23 Compare the article "Sambatyon" in *Encyclopedia Judaica*: "These passages give no indication as to the supposed location of the river or of the origin

The preceding remarks and references to scholars' comments on possible sources for/or parallels to Koranic verses about violators of the Sabbath, though not exhaustive, will suffice to establish their dependence and that of post-Muḥammad interpretations on them.

However, none of the above-quoted comments pays any attention whatsoever to a striking, if not the most striking, part of the *āyāt*, namely, the punishment meted out to the Sabbath violators of being transformed into "accursed apes." A fleeting reference to this fact was made by H. Speyer,[24] yet none of the other authorities seems to have given any thought to this rather strange motif or paid any attention to it. Nöldeke-Schwally, in the long discussion of *Sūrah* II,[25] do not even mention the crucial verse 65.

It seems that neither Muslim nor Western scholars ever considered this transmutation of sinners into apes worthy of special examination, let alone wondered whether it might not be more than an expression for "apt punishment" of evil-doers. However, it seemed to me that it was more than a skillful turn of phrase for "severely punished," and that its origin therefore deserved a thorough investigation. The more I studied this curious problem together with the *āyāt* and commentary referring to it, the more intriguing the ramifications and possible solution became. In the following discussion I shall try to unravel the intricate skein of the underlying ideas.

Examples of transmutation of human beings into animals of all kinds abound in the folklore and mythology of practically all races and peoples of the world. Such transmutations occur in a variety of circumstances, e.g., saving someone from persecution; as just punishment for a misdeed or for a breach of promise; in consequence of a curse by an enemy, and many more. Frequently, the opposite also occurs: the release of people from the animal

---

of its name. The only inference that can be drawn from them is that it was located in Media." (Media=Midyan?)

24 *Loc. cit.*, p. 313.

25 Nöldeke-Schwally, vol. I, p. 175f.

form into which they had been changed. There are many animals that serve as figures of bewitched human beings.[26]

The starting point for my deliberations was the above-quoted *āyāh* (*Sūrah* V, v. 65) in which the sinners were changed into *apes* and *swine* while also being accused of worshipping the idol Tāghūt. In this and the other *āyāh* quoted above, swine are called "an abomination," and their flesh is among the things forbidden by Koran *Sūrah* VI v. 146; XVI, 116, since swine are associated with idol worship and idolatrous sacrifice, and thus are consecrated to deities other than Allāh. The same reason accounts for the prohibition of the *maisir* game and the drinking of *khamr* (wine), along with the consumption of pork. The fact that swine were sacrificed to idols is mentioned in Plutarch,[27] *De Iside et Osiride*, and in Lucian,[28] *De Dea Syria*. These passages also describe how cows were put into sacks and thrown down from a height. Earlier the author mentioned that young maidens were sometimes used for this sacrifice, and that they were later called "pigs." This "sacrifice and eating of pigs at the time of the full moon" is connected with Typhoon and the story of Osiris.

The fact that apes were linked with swine in Koran V, 62 led me to search for a cult in which an ape played a role. Two ancient religions come to mind in which an ape holds a place in myth or ritual: in India the ape god Hanumān and in Egypt, Thoth, the Baboon god. In fact, in the aforementioned passage in Plutarch's *De Iside et Osiride*, the pig, an unclean animal, is connected with Typhoon, who plays a role in the Osiris myth and the quarrel between Seth and Horus.[29] Typhoon, in turn, is identified as Seth[30]

26 E.g., the bird, snake, ram, cat, deer, elephant, lizard, frog, toad, and ass; for our present purposes I wish to call attention to a man changed into an ape and swine (Grimm, *Anmerkungen zu den Kinder- und Hausmärchen der Gebrüder Grimm*, neu bearbeitet von J. Bolte and G. Polivka, Leipzig 1913–18, II, 240; I, 375; for swine, see *Grimm*, index).

27 Loeb Classical Library, *De Iside et Osiride*, p. 21.

28 Loeb Classical Library, *De Dea Syria*, pp. 404, note 3 and 405.

29 See my article in Gibb volume, p. 430, note 2.

30 Plutarch, *loc. cit.*, pp. 101, 121, 147.

in the Egyptian myth. Thoth plays the role of mediator in that quarrel. But in the Pyramid texts, "our earliest authorities, the functions of Thoth are of a purely *funeral* [italics mine] character, that is to say he appears only as a god who is willing to act as helper to the deceased king."[31] This action will be shown to be a decisive clue to the solution of the problem posed by the Koranic verses.[32]

Thoth himself is often described as a

> dog-headed ape[33] . . . this ape was associate and companion of the god Thoth . . . The ape seated on the pillar of the Scales belonged to a species which is now only found in the Sudan[34] but which in pre-historic times might have been found all over Egypt. The dog-headed ape is very clever . . . the high esteem in which it was held by the ancient Egyptians is proved by the fact that the god Thoth was held to be incarnated in him.[35]

It was the epithet "dog-headed ape" that led me to an astonishing series of references, which initially seemed somewhat far-fetched. But by following them step by step, I was led to what appears to me to be an incontrovertible solution of the Koranic problem. The

---

31 See Budge, *loc. cit.*, I, p. 400.

32 Typhoon is held by the Pythagoreans to be "a demoniac power," see Plutarch, *loc. cit.*, p. 75.

33 Among the animals assigned to Typhoon, Plutarch (*De Iside*, p. 171) mentions *cynocephalus*, see also Greek text, p. 170. See also Janson, *Apes and Ape Lore*, p. 25, note 30.

34 I beg to add here a few remarks, which my colleague and friend Professor Dr. Ingeborg Leister, Professor of Historical Geography at Marburg University, sent me (letter of Sept. 11, 1983): "Zum natürlichen Verbreitungsgebiet der Affen, siehe Brockhaus, unter A. Karte, Seite 146. . . . Mecca lag/liegt ziemlich nahe der natürlichen Nordgrenze der Affen." Furthermore, in connection with our many oral discussions of the Koranic problem, she suggests the following: "Ich habe den Verdacht, dass Südarabien und Oman in der Koranforschung bisher zu kurz gekommen sind. Ist es denn nicht auffällig, dass ausgerechnet *tubba* vorkommt und sonst kein Titel eines Königs? Könnte in Südarabien der Schlüssel liegen, der über Ihre drei Aufsätze hinaus Ihren Vortrag zum "Vermächtnismacht?" [see supra, note 11]

35 Budge, *loc. cit.*, vol. 1, p. 20f.

first indication of a possible solution came from Professor Stanley Marrow, S.J. Upon hearing about my research concerning a possible connection between "the accursed apes" and the Egyptian Thoth, interpreted as being the baboon, he drew my attention to the fact that St. Christopher, who suffered martyrdom under Decius, was represented in Christian legend by a dog's head. Professor Marrow referred to a discussion in an article on an Irish Litany of Pilgrim saints.[36] Professor Brian Daley, S.J. followed up this suggestion and provided me with further references in Christian Martyrologies and *Acta Sanctorum*. In addition to indicating these references to me, he sent me the following résumé of his search, an essay which he has kindly allowed me to incorporate, at my request, as his contribution to my attempt at solving the Koranic problem. Professor Daley's stress on the Christopher legend in the following statement is due to the fact that Professor Marrow's spontaneous reaction to my question concerning men changed into apes was to refer to that legend. To anticipate the end result: the circle led from Christian Syriac sources back to Egypt, and in fact, back to Thoth. A second influence, that of Hanumān, the ape-god of the Ramayana epos of India, may have reached the Arabian Peninsula via South Arabia and the spice trade.

The following are Professor Daley's findings:

> I've done some searching in various source books this week, to see if I could come up with anything more about monkey-like people in the ancient Christian Near East, particularly in connection with the St. Christopher legend and Syria. I've found some interesting things, I think, but no clear instance of any Syrian or Palestinian witness to such a legend - except for a reference to Christopher as a "Canaanite" in some medieval Western versions of the legend, which seems to rest on a textual error. But let me explain what I've found in detail.
>
> 1) The one point of contact between monkeys, strange people, and St. Christopher seems to be the term *kynokephaloi* (Lat. *cynocephali*, "dog-heads"). Aristole, *Historia Animalium* 2.8, in describing the kinds of ape then known, distinguishes three types: the ordinary ape (*pithēkos*), the "dog-head" (*kynokephalos*), which modern scholars identify as the *baboon*, and the "long-tailed monkey" (*kēbos*). Apparently, the baboon is only found today on the Arabian peninsula and in Ethiopia; in antiquity,

36 In *Analecta Bollandiana*, 77 (1959), pp. 328-331, the question of the dogheads is discussed in an appendix.

according to Diodorus Siculus (*Hist.* 1.33.4), it was also found in abundance in the Nile delta. In any case, some references to *kynokephaloi* in ancient literature seem quite clearly to be to this kind of monkey and nothing more. So Pliny, *Nat. Hist.* 7.23.31, says the Ethiopian nomads along the River Astragus "live on the milk of the animals we call *cynocephali*, herds of which they keep in pastures." Strabo (*Geographia* 16.774) refers to a place on the Somali coast, near the "Southern Horn" (i.e., the Horn of Ethiopia), called "the watering-place of the *Kynokephaloi*." This could refer to some legendary tribe, of course, but more probably refers to baboons.

2) Another set of ancient references to *kynokephaloi* clearly present them as a curious tribe of human-like creatures, usually in Northern India. Strabo (*Geog.* 1.43; 7.299) refers to allusions to such people in the plays of Aeschylus, but those references are apparently now lost. The fullest description we have of this tribe is in the summary of Ctesias of Onidos's *Indika* (5th cent. B.C.), included in Photius's *Biblioteca* 72. Ctesias tells us that a tribe known as "dog-heads" lived in India along the River Hyparchus, a tributary of the Indus flowing down from the Himalayas. They were some 120,000 strong, he says, and had heads, teeth, claws and voices like dogs, but otherwise resembled humans. They couldn't speak, but rather barked; however, they were able to understand the speech of neighboring Indian tribes. They were black-skinned, and each had a tail; they mated as dogs do, washed seldom or not at all, and lived in caves, sleeping on straw – to an age of 170–200 years! They lived, he says, from hunting and from the cattle they raised, and ate the fruit of the Siptachora tree (whatever that is). They know how to tan hides, he says, and wear simple clothes made from them; the richest among them wear clothes of linen. In general, they were a just, harmless and peaceable lot. All of this may be a somewhat garbled version of Indian accounts of an aboriginal, black-skinned tribe; there are, apparently, references in Indian literature (in the *Prabhasa-Khanda*) to an aboriginal tribe called the *Suna-mukha*, which means "dog-face."

This same account, in somewhat abbreviated form, appears in Aelian, *De Animalibus* (2nd cent. A.D.) – Ctesias is 5th cent. B.C.) 2.1; also in Aulus Gellius' *Noctes Atticae* 9.4 (2nd cent. a.d.), where the author says he found in an old Greek book a report that "there are in the mountains of the land of India men with dog-like heads, who bark and who feed upon birds and wild animals which they have taken in the chase." Philostratus, in the *Life of Apollonius of Tyana* 6.1 (3rd cent. A.D.), says that in Ethiopia (!) and India there are "black people, who are not found elsewhere, and pygmies, and people who bark in various ways, and other marvels . . ."

3) The legend of St. Christopher seems to exist in different versions, all of

them quite bizarre. He seems to have been honored in northeastern Asia Minor, especially in Chalcedon, the town across the Bosporus from Constantinople, from the second half of the *fifth* century. His relics (his head!) were honored in Constantinople in the 11th century, at least, and his cult had spread westwards at least by Carolingian times. The critical notes on his life in the *Acta Sanctorum* (by Joannes Pinius) conclude that nothing can be known for certain about his real name, origin, date and place of death, but that he *may* have been *executed* in *Lycia* (*SW corner of Asia Minor*) at the beginning of the *fourth* century. [Italics added. I.L.]

In any case, the Greek form of his life (represented in a Latin version in the *AS*) says that he "came from an island, from the race of dog-heads" (*Canineorum: kynokephaloi* in Greek) and was *originally a cannibal.* His original name was *Reprobus,* but after being strangely converted to Christianity he took the name Christopher. He is then supposed to have become a missionary and to have acquired the gift of human speech - before this, presumably, he could only bark. Whether his features also changed from dog-like to human is unclear. He then is supposed to have become a missionary, and to have settled in Samos in Lycia; later legends make him a soldier, and say he acquired human speech through eating some kind of heavenly fruit. In any case, he is supposed to have been executed for his faith by a local king named Dagnus (which may be a corruption of Decius, the *third-century* Roman emperor connected with many of the acts of the martyrs). The usual succession of unsuccessful attempts to kill him by burning, torture, etc., the conversion of prostitutes sent to seduce him in prison, etc., is concluded by a successful beheading.

In Western medieval versions of the legend, he is not a dog-head or cannibal, but rather *a giant.* As a young man (named Offerus) he decided to give his service to the strongest king in the world, wandered around trying out various masters, and is finally convinced by a monk that Christ is that "strongest master." So he settles by a river to be a monk, and exercises his service by carrying travellers across the river in flood-time. Then the familiar story happens: a child comes, asks to be taken across, and Christopher finds as they go that he becomes heavier and heavier, until he can hardly make the far bank. When he does arrive, the child reveals himself as Christ, the lord he has been serving. From then on, he is called Christopher.

The only possible connection between Christopher and the Syro-Palestinian area comes in a textual variant in the Latin versions of the Eastern legend. The text that appears in the *Acta Sanctorum* says that he "*venit de insula, genere Canineorum,*" which corresponds to the detail in the Greek menologia that he came from the land of the cannibals and had a dog-face (*kynoprosopon*). The Bollandists note, however, that other Latin versions have "*Chananaeorum*" or "*Cananaeorum*" for "*Canineorum,*" and Peter Damiani, in an 11th-century sermon, calls him "a rose from

168 "And become ye accursed apes"

Canaanite thorns." This seems to rest on a simple textual alteration, however, which corresponds to a tendency in the Latin versions to downplay Christopher's monstrous origins. There is no evidence of a cult of Christopher in Syria or Palestine, or of an association with these "dog-headed" people with the Eastern Mediterranean.

One interesting set of reflections on the "dog-heads" is contained in a letter of Ratramnus of Corbie, the learned 9th-century monk, to a presbyter named Rimbertus, on the question of whether the dog-heads of Greek legend are human and have souls. Ratramnus concedes that it is the opinion of "learned men" that they are beasts rather than human, because they look at the ground instead of upwards, and because they bark rather than speak. On the other hand, the reports attribute to them distinctly human characteristics: living in society, observing custom, practicing agriculture, and wearing clothing. On the basis of these four traits - social living, law, crafts and a sense of modesty - Ratramnus concludes that they must be human, have souls, and be descendants of Adam and Eve. And the legend of St. Christopher confirms this conclusion, he says; also, Isidore of Seville included *Cynocephali* along with giants and cyclopes, as monsters of human origin - deformed members of the human race.

Neither Ratramnus nor the legend of St. Christopher mention *apes (pithekoi; simiae)*. The only connection that I have found is the common attribution of the name *"dog-heads"* to a variety of apes (Aristotle and others), and to a legendary tribe of people (Ctesias; the Christopher material and Ratramnus). The tribe are mainly connected with India, and I have found no evidence of anyone knowing of their existence in the Eastern Mediterranean.

There are a few secondary works that might be useful on this:

Reese, *Die griechischen Nachrichten über Indien zum Feldzuge Alexanders des Grossen* 10-14, 24-28.
T.H. White, *The Book of Beasts* (London 1954), 34ff;
W.C. McDermott, *The Ape in Antiquity* (Baltimore 1938);
H.W. Janson, *Apes and Ape Lore in the Middle Ages and Renaissance* (London 1952).

Professor Daley has some doubt as to whether the discussions of the dogheaded apes in the ancient medieval works would shed any light on the Koranic passages. Yet they contain a fairly large number of important leads. It is necessary, however, to keep in mind a characteristic facet of folklore and mythology alike: the combining of actual data with imagination and embroidery that become as closely connected to the reality as do barnacles to a ship.

In searching for the correct answer to our problem, these barnacles have to be scraped off so that the underlying reality can emerge.

There are obviously three strains of myth and traditions: one comes from India (Daley's no. 2), i.e. Hanumān — a monkey-god from Hindu mythology, the leader of a host of monkeys — via the spice trade to South Arabia; a second starts in Egypt and wanders, as does the third strain, via the Christopher legend into Asia Minor, and is found (Daley's no. 3) in various regions adjacent to Arabia, including the "Syrio-Palestinian area." Daley's doubts about their influence on the Koran will not affect any scholar familiar with the techniques of modern *Koranforschung*.

In all three strains there is an abundant mixture of facts and myths, of scientific observation and folkloristic interpretation and fantasy. Indian influence has prevailed in South Arabia since pre-Christian days. In his paragraph on India, Daley gives a list of dog-headed creatures in Indian legend. He obviously aimed at answering my question on this problem. But he makes no mention of Hanumān, who plays a central role in the *Ramayana*.

Hanumān "was a child of a nymph by the god of the wind . . . He is the leader of a host of monkeys who aid in these exploits [told in the Ramayana epos]."[37] Hanumān is also described as "a quaint figure in the pantheon of the heroic age, the deified chief of the monkeys -- probably meant to represent the aboriginal tribes of southern India."[38]

In addition, he is "benign to the virtuous and smites evildoers." In battle "he was a fierce and valiant fighter," and "he shattered all opponents and demons with a fierce roar."[39] As K.C. Aryan points out, "it is interesting to note that in some paintings, ten severed heads of Ravana are shown hanging from Hanumān's

---

37 *Encyclopedia Britannica* (11th ed.) vol. 12, p. 932. See also K.C. Aryan and Subhashin Aryan, *Hanumān in Art and Mythology*, Delhi, [1974?] pp. 15, 16, 22ff., 75, 76. Ananda K. Koomaraswamy, *The Sister Nivedita*; Margaret E. Noble, *Myths of the Hindus & Buddhists* (Dover Pub.) New York, pp. 20–23. See especially p. 21, lines 2ff.

38 See *Encyclopedia Britannica* (11th ed.) vol. 13, p. 103.

39 See K.C. Aryan, *Hanumān in Art and Mythology*, pp. 15, 16.

tail. In such portrayals, the emphasis is on the heroic (*Vira*) and fierce (*Raudra*) aspects of Hanumān."[40] In the present context his "fierce and valiant" aspects and his "shattering of all opponents" — not his benign sides — are relevant to the problem.

An echo to this fierce aspect of Hanumān might be found in Ṭabarī's speculation about the "city."[41]

> [This city] was divided by a wall with two gates, one leading to the part inhabited by Muslims, the other to that of the evildoers (*kuffār*). One day, the Muslims climbed the wall [into the quarters] of the evildoers, and behold, they were monkeys who were attacking [lit. jumping against] each other. [The Muslims] were victorious over them [the apes] who dispersed into the land. To this refers Allāh's word, "and when they rebelled against what they were forbidden, We said: become ye apes, despised and spurned." (Sūrah VII, 166)[42]

This interpretation in turn underlies the story told by Adolph von Wrede in the diary of his travels in Hadramawt.[43] Indeed, it is

40 See *Ibid.*, p. 33.

41 Ṭabarī, *Tafsīr*, vol. VII, p. 166.

42 In this edition of the *Tafsīr* a note is added on the word *khāsi'īn*, explaining it as "dog," when you say to him "scram" (lit. be chased away), with a reference to *Lisān al-'arab*, which quotes the very *āyāh* under discussion. This explanation reminds one of the "pelted devil" of *Sūrah* III verse 31, and it was perhaps influenced by a reminiscence of the rite of "stoning the devil" at Mina. However, the Arabic words used in that *Sūrah* are *al-shayṭān al-rajīm*.

43 *Adolph von Wrede's Reise in Hadramaut, Beled Beny 'Yssà und Beled el Hadschar*. Hersg . . . von Freiherr Heinrich von Maltzan, Braunschweig, 1870, pp. 151ff. "Während ich mit dieser Arbeit beschäftigt war, vernahm ich einen Lärm, als wenn sich mehrere Persone zankten . . . . Jetzt entdeckten wir erst auf der anderen Seite der Schlucht die Ruhestörer, nämlich eine Truppe von einigen 60 Affe die herabgekommen ware, um ihren Durst mit dem auf dem Boden der Schlucht stehenden Wasser zu löschen. In seinem Ärger schleudert mein Schaych unter allen möglichen Verwünschungen Steine gegen sie, welche aber keine andere Wirkung hervorbrachte, als das die ganze Gesellschaft in einer grösseren Entfernung niederkauerte. Schaych SSalym sah ihnen nach und rief dann aus: Nun wie werdet ihr mir gehorchen, da ihr nicht einmal auf die Ermahnung Hud's, des Propheten Gottes, geachtet habt?" There follows a legend about King Shaddad, from the legendary tribe of 'Ād, which ends, in Wrede's account, as

remarkable that it is precisely in South Arabia that an echo of the Indian legend, though in a strongly Islamicized form, can be found.

Even weightier is the second strain originating in Egypt in the person of the dog-headed ape, the associate and companion of Thoth, who was incarnate in him. This dog-headed *cynephalos* ape is the baboon.[44] The sources mentioning dogheads in some of the data quoted by Professor Daley lead us to the third, fourth and fifth centuries A.D. For the purposes of this essay, we may disregard the various changes and additions the legends of the *kynokephaloi* underwent through the interpretations of the Christian hagiographers in connection with the Christopher legend, and cull out of Professor Daley's report a few statements within those sources that are relevant to the Koranic problem and its solution. In doing so, I shall mention only such items as are connected with the dog-face characteristics. The Christopher myth as such developed out of the legendary existence of such dog-headed creatures, identified even at an early time with the baboon, and enlarged in ever-growing measure in terms of Christian hagiography and martyrologies (as pointed out in Professor Daley's contribution).

The relevant items to be considered (as taken from his statement) are:

References to the third, fourth, and fifth centuries A.D:

TIME: 3rd c. the local king Dagnus, possibly a corruption of the name of the 3rd century Roman emperor Decius [Rome-Byzantium]

---

follows (p. 153): "Bildest Du Dir ein, dass der Gegenstand, mit dem jetzt Dein Geist beschäftigt ist . . . Dich vor den Streichen des Todes schützen wird?' — Mit diesen Worten öffnet der Tod (denn dies war der geharnischte Ritter) die Erde unter seinen Füssen — und der König Schaddad verschwindet. — Sein Volk aber wurde in Affen verwandelt und ihre Stadt Iram-Dsat-el'Issnad [sic] . . . verschwand."

44 A discussion of the identification of the *cynocephali* ("dogheaded ones") with *simia* (apes) and in particular with the baboon, referring principally to the sacred baboon of Egypt, is found in H.W. Janson, *Apes and Ape Lore in the Middle Ages and the Renaissance*, London, 1952, pp. 16, 18 (The Warburg Institute, University of London).

4th c.	*may* have been executed in Lycia (SW corner of Asia Minor) at the beginning of the 4th century
5th c.	may have been honored in northeastern Asia Minor, especially in Chalcedon, across the Bosporus from Constantinople
LOCALITIES:	Samos, in Lycia; Constantinople (Asia Minor); Syria: (*Acta Sanctorum*, July VI p. 146 D: *"et ingressus ipse Sanctus intra Syriam")*

All the foregoing dates and localities fall within the sphere of interest, contacts and mutual relationships with the Arabian Peninsula before and during the Prophet's lifetime. Though not always documented in historical or literary records, they may be postulated, or even *assumed*, to have existed. Indian influence on South Arabia has been proven to have existed since earliest times. Trade -- especially the spice trade -- goes back to pre-Christian times, while Syrian/Christian culture was well established in the various Christian groups found in the areas adjacent to Arabia (e.g. Syria) and in North Arabia itself. Proof for this assertion is found in indigenous sources, as e.g. the *Sīrah* (biography) of the Prophet, and in pre-Islamic poetry and literature, with their references to monks and Christian tribes (e.g. the Tanūkh), to the Ghassanid kings, to Christian settlements like al-Ḥīra, and to its famous poet ʿAdi b. Zayd. These enable us to understand how the tales about the legendary animal-headed men could reach the Prophet and stimulate his imagination. It is imperative, however, to relinquish the prejudice that any influence from one culture upon another must necessarily rest on "literary" and/or written documents. Much of it is transmitted by word of mouth, by travellers and storytellers, and, last but not least, through icons, statues and other representations, though they may exaggerate or otherwise distort real events by their imagined features.

There remains one important point to be discussed: the demoniac and devilish elements, and the underlying emotional association of the apes with punishment, death and destruction. Thoth is characterized as "a purely *funeral* character" and as "a demoniac power."[45]

From very ancient times these dog-faced creatures were the object of great curiosity, which resulted often in rather fanciful description of details, and identification with legendary or mythological peoples and animals. Professor Daley has discussed references to these ancient identifications in detail in his contribution to this paper. For me, however, there remains one essential aspect which he has not sufficiently considered in his discussion, namely, the relevance of his findings to the Koranic *āyāt*, especially the ape as a demonic and satanic figure. However, when I read the text of the passages he discusses, this lack became immediately evident to me. In some of his sources, the *kynokephaloi* were identified (by ancient as well as by modern scholars) with baboons. The baboon, as we have seen, is clearly connected with the Egyptian god Thoth (or Typhoon-Seth), the "purely funeral," who in turn is characterized by the Pythagoreans as "being a demoniac power."

In his essay *Ape and Ape Lore in the Middle East,*[46] H.W. Janson shows us the way to solving the problem of the present study, so that we can supply the answer to the crucial question of why the violators of the Sabbath were punished by being transformed into apes. According to Janson's sources, primitive man explained the existence of creatures "being human and bestial at the same time" by assuming that "they must have descended from men who had failed to heed some Divine injunction and *in punishment* [italics added] for their *hybris* had been debased to the infra-human level."[47] For the ancients, "the ape was *turpissima bestia*," and became "the prototype of the trickster, the sycophant,

45 See above.

46 H.W. Janson, *Apes and Ape Lore, passim.*

47 *Loc. cit.*, p. 14f. In the discussion that follows, Janson refers, inter alia, to "the legend of Hercules and the Ceropes, according to which the latter (dwarfed comic humans with tails) were turned into apes by Zeus because they had tricked the hero" (p. 14). He also refers to Aristotle and Galen, who, "in their detailed accounts of simian anatomy, tend to exaggerate its human features" (p. 14).

the hypocrite."[48] Janson lists among the nomenclature for apes "such designations as *cynocephalis*"; he adds that the various classical terms apply "to one or more of the following three types:[49] 1) The tailless ape . . . 2) The baboon *(cynocephalus) referring principally to the sacred baboon of Egypt* [italics added] . . . 3) Tailed simians, such as . . . the macaques and langurs of India." Early scholars used the term *cynocephalus* for ape (= simius), and stressed that it represents the devil, e.g. Solinus (3rd c. A.D.) and Isidore of Seville (6th c. A.D.). The Physiologus[50] makes this identification explicit: "Auch der Affe ist ein Bild des Teufels: Wie er einen Kopf hat, aber keinen Schwanz, so hatte der Satan einen herrlichen Anfang im Himmel als oberster Engel, aber er fiel und seine Verdammnis wird kein Ende haben." Lauchert adds: "Dieser Abschnitt ist Ägyptischen Ursprungs, . . . wahrschenlich erst in alexandrinischer Zeit von den Griechen übernommen."

For the corresponding date concerning the ape, Lauscher cites a number of sources which he declares to be late. However, for the purposes of this study, they fall within the period before Muḥammad's time. A Latin version of the Physiologus[51] discussing the same incident confirms the identity of the ape with the devil: *"Similiter et simia figuram habet diaboli."*

In Christian iconography, the ape was increasingly used as a symbol for evil, demons and the devil. For the present essay -- which seeks a solution of the Koranic problem — Janson provides a convincing argument for considering Egypt the ultimate source of the transmogrification of evildoers into apes, though transmitted through Christian legends about dog/ape-headed creatures, and via the Christopher legend as it was told by Syrian Christians:

> All this, to be sure, does not explain how the ape came to play the role of the devil; nevertheless it suggests that our problem may have some special connection with Egypt, and thus provide us with a valuable

---

48 *Loc. cit.*, p. 14.

49 *Loc. cit.*, p. 15, and see note 16 to this passage on p. 24.

50 *Geschichte des Physiologus*, Herausgegeben von Friedrich Bauchert. Original edition Strassburg, 1889, Slatkine Reprints Geneva, 1974, p. 36.

51 *Physiologus Latinus Francis J. Carmody*, Paris 1939, p. 38.

> clue. In the eyes of Early Christian authors, Egypt carried a twofold connotation of evil. Branded by the Old Testament as the "land of darkness" . . . it became synonymous with the dark and sinful temporal life from which mankind was to be saved by Christ. In a more specific sense, Egypt also provided the most horrifying example of idolatry. Even pagan writers had at times felt compelled to ridicule the boundless number and variety of Nilotic *numina* . . . Significantly enough, such attacks usually single out the worship of apes as the most revolting of these practices. The same attitude is strikingly revealed by an incident that is reported to have occurred during the anti-pagan riots at Alexandria in 391 A.D. The Christians, led by Bishop Theophilus, drove away the pagan priests and destroyed the pagan temples and idols, with one exception: Theophilus commanded them to preserve a statue of an ape and to set it up in a public place, as a monument to heathen depravity.[52]

On the basis of the above-quoted material we can assert with a great deal of confidence that the ape/baboon represented at the time of Muḥammad's activity, and the religious atmosphere that surrounded him, the very emblem of depravity and turpitude. Thus, the punishment meted out to the Sabbath violators was indeed a very severe one. They were not just changed into animals -- punishment enough -- but as apes or baboons they were expelled from human society and thrust into the sphere of Satan, the very antithesis of Allāh.

52 H.W. Janson, *loc. cit.*, p. 17.

5

WHAT DID MUḤAMMAD MEAN WHEN HE CALLED HIS RELIGION "ISLAM"?: THE ORIGINAL MEANING OF ASLAMA AND ITS DERIVATIVES

D.Z.H. Baneth

Dedicated to Prof. R. WALZER

Professor Helmer Ringgren[1] has already discussed sufficiently the existing explanations of *islām*, including the rather far-fetched theories of Margoliouth, Lidzbarski, Künstlinger and Bravmann. The first of these connects the word with Musailima, the so-called false prophet, the second with *salām* in the supposed meaning of salvation, the third with Hebrew *šālōm* and cognate Arabic words, assuming a signification "covenant between God and man", and the fourth interprets *islām* as "defiance of death, self-sacrifice [for the sake of God and his prophet]" or "readiness for defiance of death". Therefore I may be allowed to dispense with analysing these theories.

Moreover, Professor Ringgren has very thoroughly examined the occurrence of the root *s l m* in its various forms not only in the Koran, but also in the Hadith, in Old Arabic poetry and other ancient Arabic sources. So, owing to his painstaking work, practically all the basic material lies before us in a lucid and well-ordered form. The present writer would hardly have been able to perform this very difficult task. Consequently, if there is any merit in my suggestion, most of the credit belongs to Professor Ringgren.

As we shall see later on, Professor Ringgren's comprehensive and very careful investigation marks a large step towards the interpretation of *islām* that is here attempted. However, in the concluding part of his booklet, that which deals with the verb *aslama* (in the 4th form) and its derivatives, he stands by the most widely accepted explanation, viz. "to submit, to surrender, to resign [to God]". Strangely enough, among the numerous verses from pre-Islamic and Islamic poetry he quotes, there seems to be none for which this meaning must *necessarily* be admitted, nor does, I venture to say, his fairly complete survey of koranic passages where *aslama*, *muslim* or *islām* occurs, include any passage that must *needs* be understood this way and no other. This is not the author's fault but is due to the nature of the material, which

[1] In his monograph, *Islām, Aslama and Muslim* (Uppsala 1949).

is often rather vague, as he himself states (p. 24 at the bottom). Under such circumstances it is impossible to prove more than that the word *can* have a certain meaning everywhere or practically everywhere; and that Professor Ringgren has very ably done.

Notwithstanding, I dare to raise a few objections to the usual interpretation of *aslama* and *islām*, which seems to be chiefly derived from the best-known mediaeval Arabic dictionaries and is also found in mediaeval Arabic Koran commentaries, though not exclusively,

Is not a word expressing "surrender", "submission", "resignation" as a name for the new religion far too spiritual for the social environment in which Muḥammad had to preach? Such a name might well fit the aims of a pietistic community in a highly developed society but not the demands that could be directed to Muḥammad's countrymen. Here we cannot take into account the Prophet's own high spiritual level; it is well known that, side by side with his religious enthusiasm, he was gifted with a rare sense for reality, and Islam rightly prides itself on the fact that, more than other religions, it has found the way to the heart and understanding of the *simple* man.

Of course, our point of departure must not be the verbal noun *islām*, which appears rather late in the Koran, but the verb *aslama*, which denotes an action. Now imagine the Prophet addressing the slaves and other poor people who were among his early converts, or bedouin tribesmen at a later time, with such words as "surrender ye [or submit, or resign] to God", what would this have meant to them? What were they supposed to change in their religious life? Did not their former (polytheistic) religion also demand submission to the gods including even submission to Allāh?

The answer is clear. The fundamental change required by Muḥammad was the abandonment of polytheism, to serve one god only, the same god which they had already previously known under the name Allāh. Does not the idea suggest itself to seek this very meaning of adopting monotheism in the words *aslama*, *islām?*

I have hinted before that Professor Ringgren has already gone a good deal of the way in this direction. When concluding his investigation into the various forms of the root *s l m* with the exception of the 4th form of the verb, he says (p. 13):

> If we now sum up our results and try to find what is common for the various words that are formed out of the root سلم, it appears that the common idea is that of wholeness, entirety, or totality. The words in question express that something is whole, unbroken and undivided and therefore sound and healthy, or peaceful and harmonious. The same idea of entirety is behind the words in the cases we have met with when

> they denote a total surrender or submission. *The stress lies on totality, not on submission* (emphasis mine).

Also in dealing with *aslama* itself Professor Ringgren often emphasizes the totality of the surrender as an essential point.

Now I wish to go one small, almost invisible step further. According to Professor Ringgren *aslama* means approximately "to give oneself entirely to God". Now, when you give something to somebody *entirely*, you give it to him *exclusively*. "To give exclusively" instead of "to give entirely" is certainly a trifling modification of meaning from the semasiological point of view, but its existence in actual language has to be proven or at least to be made probable, the more so, since from the theological viewpoint the difference is rather great.

Before dealing with this matter it will be well to remember just what is the Mohammedan conception of, and terminology for, polytheism. It was not with idolatry, in the exact sense of the word, that Muḥammad charged his countrymen mainly, nor with adoring other gods *instead* of Allāh, but his most repeated reproach was that they served other gods *in addition* to Allāh and acknowledged them as *partners* to him. This conception of polytheism as establishing *partnership* between Allāh and false gods finds its expression in the terms *ašraka*, *širk*, *mušrik*. So we may expect for the word *islām* a signification that expresses the opposite idea.

There is substantial support for the suggested meaning of *aslama* and its derivatives in the Koran, as I hope to show later on; but, as I have mentioned, the word is nowhere absolutely unequivocal. Fortunately, the existence of the postulated meaning can be proved, if not for the *fourth* form of the verb, at least for its *first* form, as well as for a noun belonging to the same root.

It is sufficient to look this root up in Lane's dictionary to find there, under the first form, an explanation that fits our idea exactly, viz.:

> One says also سلمت له الضيعة, meaning [The landed estate] was, or became, free from participation to him; syn. خلصت.

Lane's authorities are *Tāj al-ʿArūs* and al-Muṭarrizī's *Mughrib*, a twelfth century special dictionary for lawyers, but the same explanation is also given in Zamakhsharī's Koran commentary and, a little less expressly, in that of Ṭabarī, in connexion with the verse immediately to be quoted.

However, our best evidence is to be found in the Koran itself. In Surah XXXIX (*sūrat az-zumar*), verse 29[2] (or, in Flügel's edition, 30) we read:

ضَرَبَ اللهُ مَثَلا رَجُلا فيهِ شُرَكاء مُتَشاكِسونَ وَرَجُلا سَلَماً لِرَجُلٍ هَل يَستَوِيانِ مَثَلاً.

[2] Koran verses are numbered here according to the King Fu'ād edition.

In the late Richard Bell's very good translation:

> Allah hath coined a similitude — a man who belongs to [several] partners at variance with each other, and a man wholly belonging to one man, are they to be compared to the same thing? [Lit. Are they equal to a similitude?]

The parable speaks of two kinds of slaves, one, who (by inheritance or otherwise) is the property of several owners at one and the same time, a very common case in ancient and mediaeval law; the other the property of one man exclusively. These two kinds of slaves are obviously compared to the adherents of two different kinds of religion: polytheists, *mušrikūn*, who acknowledge *šurakā'*, partners to God in his domination over themselves and the world, and monotheists, who serve one God, Allāh, only.

We have here, in a late Meccan or early Medinan passage, a word from the root *s l m*, which has undoubtedly and unequivocally the meaning "belonging to one only" or "exclusive property of one" (it may be an adjective or a substantive), in contradistinction to a thing or a man that belongs to several partners, perhaps a juridical term. Ṭabarī's commentary quotes old interpretations as رجل خالص لرجل or الذي لا يملكه الا واحد. Ṭabarī himself speaks of خلوصه لواحد لا شريك له. From this noun — about whose vocalization tradition is not unanimous (*salam*, *sālim*, *salm*, *silm*) — quite easily, according to grammatical rule — a denominative verb in the 4th conjugation (*aslama*) may be derived[3] in the meaning of "he was, or became, a *salam* (etc.), i.e. exclusive property of one". So the problem why *aslama* usually appears as an intransitive verb, though in the fourth form, finds a simple solution.

The verb *aslama* in the aforementioned sense is likely to have existed before Muḥammad, although it seems not to have left traces outside the Koran. How did this come about? Most probably because both the noun *salam* and the verb derived from it were peculiar to the dialect of Mecca or the Hedjaz, or, as Professor Chaim Rabin[4] might put it, to Western Arabian, at all events to an Arabic idiom that vanished soon after the great Islamic conquests, at least from written Arabic. The fact that the original vocalization of the noun was no more known to later generations seems to prove this.

I do not think we have means to decide whether the verb *aslama* was first transferred into the religious sphere by the Prophet of Islam himself or was already used in a similar way before him as Professor Charles Cutler Torrey has shown to be probable for some koranic terms originally connected with commerce. However this may be, certainly the verb *aslama* in its religious

[3] See Wright's *Grammar*[3] vol. I, § 45, Rem. c (pp. 34–36).

[4] See his book, *Ancient West-Arabian* (London 1951).

sense originally wants a complement as *lillāhi* or the like, to produce the meaning "to belong to, or to serve, Allāh alone". Indeed it is quite often thus used in the Koran, though in most cases just with a suffix referring to Allāh or in the form *li rabbi'l-'ālamīna*. However, if, as I suppose, the verb is derived from the noun *salam*, that denotes "exclusive property (of one person)", it could be used absolutely, too, without a nominal complement, in the meaning "to become one's alone", "to serve one alone"; and that absolute use is by far the prevailing one in the Koran.

Various scholars, at least from Zamakhsharī down to our own times, have been inclined to regard *aslama* as an abridgement of the expression *aslama wağhahu ilā 'llāhi* or *lillāhi*, which occurs four times in the Koran. I do not deny this possibility, though I do not agree to the interpretation that is usually connected with it. It is said that *wağh* is synonymous with *nafs* and means "self"; accordingly *aslama wağhahu lillāhi* is understood as "to surrender oneself to God". Now *wağh* is certainly nowhere else in the Koran used in the sense of "self", and I doubt whether it has precisely this meaning anywhere in ancient Arabic literature. Ṭabarī, in his Koran commentary, gives two ancient verses, one by al-A'shā[5], the other by Dhu'r-Rumma[6], as proof, but neither is at all convincing. Sir Charles Lyall, followed by Professor Ringgren, has adduced just one verse:

وأبذُلُ في الهيجاء وجهيَ وإنني   له في سِوَى الهيجاء غَيرُ بذولِ

which is thus translated by Professor Ringgren (I omit two redundant words):

> And I give my face [i.e. myself] freely in the fight, but I give it not in anything else than fight.

Though I am most reticent to contradict such a great authority on Arabic poetry as Sir Charles Lyall, I venture to contend that *wağh* in this verse really means "face", in the first half quite literally, in the second hemistich the face as the symbol of man's honour; بذل وجهه "to risk one's honour" is a common expression, noted also by Dozy. A verse of the *Ḥamāsah* contains the same idea in rather plain words:

نُعَرِّضُ للسيوف إذا التقينــــا   وجوهــاً لا تُعَرَّضُ لِلّطــام

> When we meet in battle we expose to the sword faces that are never exposed to slapping.

This should leave no doubt that real faces are intended.

[5] Ed. Geyer, No. 18, verse 32, p. 106.
[6] Ed. Macartney, No. 70, verse 55, p. 560.

In my own opinion *aslama wağhahu lillāhi* means "to direct one's face to Allāh *exclusively*", and should not be separated from *wağğaha wağhahu*, which occurs in Surah VI, verse 79.

إنّي وجّهت وجهي للذي فَطَرَ السموات والأرض حنيفاً وما انا من المشركين

I turn my face to the Creator of Heaven and Earth as a *Ḥanīf*, and I am not of those who acknowledge partners to God.

The connexion between the turning of the face towards the Creator and monotheism is obvious here; in the phrase *aslama wağhahu lillāhi* (and the like) the mention of monotheism is compressed into one word. I need not remind the reader how important a part the direction of the face plays in Oriental religions; just think of the *qiblah*.

As to *aslama* as an intransitive verb, I have found in the Koran one passage only, where it apparently does not have the proposed meaning. It is Surah XXXVII, verse 103, where of Abraham and his son, after the latter's consent to be sacrified, it is said — ولما أسلما وتله للجبين. There are different readings (*sallamā* and *istaslamā*) and diverging interpretations (e.g. Professor Blachère's: they pronounced the *salām*).[7] The translation "when they were resigned" may be correct; but, it seems, only in the sense of a despairing state of mind, not in the religious sense of "submitting to the will of God"; for this should have been expressed by a principal sentence, not by a temporal clause.

It may be argued that *aslama* is occasionally used in opposition to Judaism and Christianity, though these are monotheistic religions. But, as is well-known, Muḥammad, from a certain time on, used to accuse the Jews and Christians of his day for not sticking to pure monotheism, which had been the religion of their prophets. The unimpaired monotheism of the prophets, however, is always identified with *islām*. Besides, *aslama* gradually received the new signification "to become a follower of Muḥammad".

There are a considerable number of verses in the Koran in which *islām* is either expressly opposed to polytheism, or at least monotheism is stressed, as e.g. XXI:108 (second Meccan period):

قل إنما يوحى الي أنما إلهكم إله واحد فهل انتم مسلمون

VI: 14 (third period):

قل اغير الله أتخذ ولياً فاطر السموات والأرض وهو يطعم ولا يطعم
قل إني أمرت ان أكون اول من اسلم ولا تكونن من المشركين

VI: 162–163:

قل ان صلاتي ونسكي ومحياي ومماتي لله رب العالمين ،
لا شريك له وبذلك أمرت وأنا أول المسلمين

[7] One may also suggest as a possible meaning: after they professed their creed in Allāh's unity, or: after they recited a confession to the same (similar to the Hebrew *Šema ʿYisrāʾēl*).

The Original Meaning of Aslama

III: 67 (at Medinah):

ما كان ابراهيم يهودياً ولا نصرانياً ولكن
كان حنيفاً مسلماً وما كان من المشركين

XXII: 34 (at Medinah):

فالهكم إله واحد فله أسلموا

Many more verses could be adduced; but since the word occurs still more frequently in other connexions, it cannot be said that its use in the Koran yields conclusive evidence by itself.

The best-known Koran commentaries, e.g. those of Ṭabarī, Zamakhsharī and Baiḍāwī, frequently explain أسلم, both the transitive and the intransitive verb, by أخلص, which may mean and sometimes undoubtedly means "to devote [or be devoted] exclusively" to...; but more often they give other explanations, chiefly أذعن ، انقاد "to obey", تذلل "to humiliate oneself", استسلم "to give oneself over entirely"; and in many passages they mix up different interpretations, as if they were identical.

In fine, I wish to stress once more that this is a suggestion for further research, not a fully proved theory. Yet, I am inclined to believe that it has certain advantages over other explanations that have been brought forth, including the most accepted one. In the following lines I wish to summarize these advantages, bearing in mind that not all of them pertain to all the interpretations at once.

The word *islām* would have a meaning that was easily comprehensible to the simple people whom the Prophet wanted to convert .

It would be distinctive, immediately conveying to the people of Arabia what was the difference between their pagan faith and that preached by Muḥammad.

The word *islām*, if it means "serving one alone", could imperceptibly shift into a name for the new religion; there was no need for a solemn proclamation, which, if it had taken place, would probably have been commemorated.

The word would be the exact counterpart to *širk*, the koranic expression for polytheism.

It would become easy to understand why the religion of the ancient monotheists and Muḥammad's religion are called by the same name.

The fact that in Surah XLIX, verse 14 *īmān* represents a much higher degree than *islām*, would cause no difficulty.

Derived from the noun *salam*, which in the Koran itself denotes "exclusive property of one person", *aslama* could be used as an intransitive verb according to a grammatical rule; we need not suppose an omission.

Both the construction of *aslama* with *lillāhi* and the like, and the absolute use would seem justified.

The phrase *aslama waǧhahu lillāhi* would have an appropriate meaning.

It is, in my opinion, one of the glories of the Mohammedan religion that, as soon as polytheism ceased to be the enemy number one to pure religion in its

confines, it generally preferred to substitute an even deeper meaning (that of complete surrender to God) to the original signification of its name, which vigorously expressed the lofty idea of pure monotheism.

The above is in the main the text of a paper read by the author at the 23rd International Congress of Orientalists, Cambridge 1954, with some slight changes and a few omissions.

6

TOWARDS A PERIODIZATION OF EARLIEST ISLAM ACCORDING TO ITS RELATIONS WITH OTHER RELIGIONS

Jacques Waarenburg

Since the periodization of Islamic history is one of the main themes of this congress, it is worthwhile to look at earliest Islam with the aim of discovering how it may be divided into periods. Is it possible to distinguish certain phases in the growth of the new religious movement which correspond with its successive interactions with existing religious communities? The problem is an old one and well-known. Nearly a hundred years ago, for instance, C. Snouck Hurgronje connected the occurrence of the Ibrāhīm cycle in the Qur'ān with Muḥammad's conflict with the Jews in Medina.[1] Moreover, numerous studies have been made over the last hundred years of Jewish, Christian and other influences on Muḥammad's preaching and practice [2] and on the institutional

---

[1] C. Snouck Hurgronje, *Het Mekkaansche Feest*, Leiden 1880, repr. in *Verzamelde Geschriften—Gesammelte Schriften*, Vol. I (Bonn-Leipzig: Kurt Schroeder, 1923), pp. 1-124, especially pp. 23-27. Partial French translation of this book as "Le pèlerinage à la Mekke" by G.-H. Bousquet in *Oeuvres Choisis-Selected Works* de C. Snouck Hurgronje, présentées en français et en anglais par G.-H. Bousquet et J. Schacht (Leiden: E. J. Brill, 1957, pp. 171-213; see especially pp. 186-190. Compare also C. Snouck Hurgronje, "Une nouvelle biographie de Mohammed", (first published in *RHR*, 15e année, t. 30, 1894), reprinted in *Verzamelde Geschriften*, Vol. I, pp. 319-362 (esp. pp. 334-336) and in *Oeuvres Choisis-Selected Works*, pp. 109-149 (esp. pp. 122-125). It becomes clear here that Snouck Hurgronje, in his interpretation of the Ibrāhīm story, wanted to refute the idea that the *millat Ibrāhīm* would have been the religion of the ancient *ḥanīfs* before Muḥammad's public activity. Snouck Hurgronje's theory was influenced by A. Sprenger; see his *Das Leben und die Lehre des Moḥammad* . . . (Berlin 1861-65), Vol. 2, pp. 276ff.

[2] For the literature on the various kinds of historical influences on Muḥammad see Maxime Rodinson, "Bilan des études mohammadiennes", *Revue historique*, Vol. 229, fasc. 465 (January-March 1963), pp. 169-220. Studies on such influences continue to appear; see for instance lately Erwin Gräf, "Zu den christlichen Einflüssen im Koran" in *Al-Bahit, Festschrift Joseph Henninger* . . . (Studia Instituti Anthropos 28). St Augustin bei Bonn: Anthropos Institut, 1976, pp. 111-144. Attention is here given to the liturgical use of the Qur'ān in relation to Christian Syriac liturgical sources. The present approach presupposes such studies of historical influences but also assumes that Muḥammad was not a passive receptacle of them. Just like the author of the first chapters of Genesis, the Hebrew prophets, Jesus and Paul,

development of early Islam.[3] During the last twenty-five years, however, Snouck Hurgronje's theory has been criticized,[4] new biographical studies of Muḥammad have been made, placing him in the social and political situation of his time,[5] and considerable progress has been made in Qur'anic studies.[6] As a consequence, it would seem to be appropriate to look now again into the problem of the rise of Islam as a historical religion and the different phases of that rise, from the point of view of history of religions.[7]

Muḥammad too should be seen primarily according to his response to and "digestion" of the values, norms and rules which he encountered or was confronted with. This, of course, is also part of historical research. An analysis of the different roles taken by Muḥammad throughout his career after the model of earlier prophets is given in Jan Hjärpe, "Rollernas Muhammad", *Religion och Bibel* (Uppsala), XXXVI (1977), pp. 63-72.

[3] "Institutional development" means here largely the development of institutionalization, "institutions" being taken in the broader sense of the word. See for instance S. D. Goitein, *Studies in Islamic History and Institutions* (Leiden: E. J. Brill, 1966), pp. 73-134.

[4] So Y. Moubarac, *Abraham dans le Coran. L'histoire d'Abraham dans le Coran et la naissance de l'Islam. Etude critique des textes coraniques suivie d'un essai sur la représentation qu'ils donnent de la Religion et de l'Histoire* (Etudes musulmanes V). Paris: Vrin, 1958, esp. pp. 51-95. Also W. A. Bijlefeld, *De Islam als na-christelijke religie. Een onderzoek naar de theologische beoordeling van de Islam, in het bijzonder in de twintigste eeuw* (with a summary in English). Den Haag: Van Keulen, 1959, esp. pp. 124-136.

[5] We think in the first place of the two studies by W. Montgomery Watt, *Muhammad at Mecca* and *Muhammad at Medina*. Oxford: Clarendon Press, 1953 and 1956. We used these studies for the factual data of this paper, as well as Rudi Paret, *Mohammed und der Koran. Geschichte und Verkündigung des arabischen Propheten*. Stuttgart: W. Kohlhammer, 1957, 1966[2]. Compare also Maxime Rodinson, *Mahomet*. Paris: Club français du livre, 1961; revised edition Paris: Seuil, 1968. English translation at the Penguin Press 1971 (Pelican Book 1973).

[6] One may think of the semantic studies carried out on the Qur'ān, for instance by Toshihiko Izutsu, *God and Man in the Koran. Semantics of the Koranic Weltanschauung* (Tokyo: The Keio Institute of Cultural and Linguistic Studies, 1964) and *Ethico-Religious Concepts in the Qur'ān* (Montreal: McGill University Institute of Islamic Studies, McGill University Press, 1966). On the progress in research on the Qur'ān see for instance Rudi Paret, ed. *Der Koran* (Wege der Forschung, Vol. 326). Darmstadt: Wissenschaftliche Buchgesellschaft, 1975. A precise translation of the Qur'ān with commentary has been given by Rudi Paret (Stuttgart: W. Kohlhammer, 1961 and 1971).

[7] On this approach see the Conclusion of this paper, which, while not claiming originality in the facts brought together here, seeks to offer a new formulation and treatment of the problem of the gradual growth of a religious purification movement to a reform movement to a religion and its connection and interaction with the religious communities it met in the course of its development.

Even if one assumes that certain ideas and practices of the new religious movement had been in the air, so to speak, before Muḥammad started his prophetic activity, and that there were certain social, economic and political problems and corresponding needs and latent expectations among the Arabs at the time, which made them sensitive to Muḥammad's message, the problem remains: how did this lead to a particular religious movement which developed an autonomous set of ideas and practices held by an independent community? And how subsequently did this religious movement become a religion on a par with the great religions which existed in the Middle East at the time? Our hypothesis is that the key to solving this problem lies in the interaction which took place between the prophetic leader with his community on the one hand, and the existing communities on the other. In this interaction the encounter between Muḥammad's basic inspiration as expressed in the Qur'ān and the religious beliefs and practices surrounding him has a particular relevance for a periodization of earliest Islam. Attention is paid here to Muḥammad's relations with the polytheists in Mecca, the Jews in Medina and the Christians in Arabia.

1. *The Meccan Polytheists*

The sheer fact that Muḥammad started preaching in Mecca implies that he explicitly set himself apart from the world in which he had grown up and with whose assumptions and rules he had been familiar. His message was directed primarily to the *mushrikūn*, in particular the Meccans whom he identified as such, and even apart from the further political consequences his interaction with the Meccan milieu was extremely important from a religious point of view.[8]

As has been demonstrated by W. Montgomery Watt,[9] Allāh was

[8] See for instance J. Waardenburg, "Un débat coranique contre les polythéistes" in *Ex Orbe Religionum. Studia Geo Widengren . . . dedicata*, Vol. 2. Leiden: E. J. Brill, 1972, pp. 143-154. This is an abridged form of an originally more extensive paper. The author is indebted to Dr. G. H. A. Juynboll for kindly drawing attention to some mistakes which occurred in this paper. The historical facts of Muḥammad's interaction with the Meccans have received much attention already. Compare also Charles Wendell, "The pre-Islamic period of Sīrat al-Nabī", *MW*, Vol. 62 (1972), 1, pp. 12-41.

[9] W. Montgomery Watt, *Muhammad at Mecca*, esp. pp. 23-29, and "Belief in a 'High God' in pre-Islamic Mecca", *Journal of Semitic Studies*, Vol. 16 (1971), pp. 35-40. See also the same author's "The Qur'ān and belief in a 'High God' " in the present volume and in *Der Islam*, Vol. 56 (1979), Nr. 2, pp. 205-211.

a god recognized by the Meccans as *rabb al-bait* and lord of the town, but not as the only divine being. To Muḥammad Allāh became *rabb al-ʿālamīn*, a universal god—creator, sustainer and judge—outside whom there was nothing divine. This message, together with the theme of resurrection, judgment and afterlife, led to violent debates between Muḥammad and the Meccans whom he reproached for not being able to recognize the oneness of God and draw the consequences of such a recognition. Instead of powers like Fate and Time, it was this almighty *al-ilāh* who decided on the major determinants of life. Over against a current confidence in a good life on earth and material well-being, Muḥammad preached man's quality of being a creature and his dependence on God; he preached a morality of divine commands instead of tribal tradition, a sanction of eschatological reward and punishment instead of tribal honor, religion as a basis for human solidarity instead of tribal and other factional interests. These notions of divine commands, judgment and religious community were probably new to the Meccans, and ideas and practices which may have been half-known from other religions were presented now in a new "arabicized" form.

In response to disbelief in his prophethood Muḥammad elaborated a more historical dimension of his activity—in fact of a rather mythical nature—by means of the stories of the prophets of the past, which contained both Arabic elements like the seven *mathānī* and figures from the patriarchal time of the Judeo-Christian tradition. Such prophets of the past in whose line Muḥammad stood could serve as an argument in sermon and debate and they also made a link between the prophet and both the Arab and the patriarchal past.

The religious bases of the new movement, and in particular the authority of its prophet, were elaborated in different terms, the most important being that Muḥammad's prophetic words or *qurʾāns* were due to divine revelation through an angel. Although there was a link with the past through the notion that earlier prophets like Mūsā and ʿĪsā had brought revelation by means of similarly a revealed scripture, the stress must have been laid by Muḥammad on the prophet's own *āyāt*. There are many aspects to this particular belief in revelation, with regard to its form, content, roots, and so on,[10] but the most important aspect as far as our

[10] On Muḥammad's concept of revelation the classical study is Otto Pautz, *Muhammeds Lehre von der Offenbarung, quellenmässig untersucht*,

theme is concerned is that Muḥammad assumed prophetic authority not only in his words, like the typical Old Testament prophets, but also in his deeds, like Moses and the patriarchs. His claim that his message was basically the same as that of the prophets before him had many implications. It gave to his activity a supplementary charismatic quality, it provided a link with the Judeo-Christian religious tradition, and it gave his message a particular kind of universality. Those who joined the movement entered the group of the believers of the one universal monotheistic religion, so to say in its Arab branch. The Arabs would have their own religion while sharing in the universal one.

The refusal of the majority of the Meccans, and certainly their leaders, to drop their religious tradition and abjure divine powers besides Allāh, whose veneration was part of the tradition, led to intense debates with the prophet, who raised his demands on this point. He finally rejected any compromise, arrived at a position of absolute monotheism and separated the movement rigorously from the *mushrikūn* with their basic sin of *shirk* or *ishrāk*, from which they had to be purified. At this point, significantly, the earlier openness and receptivity on the part of the prophet stopped, and the fight against idolatry in any form became one of the striking features of the religion which developed. Paradoxically enough, the Meccan opposition caused the new religion to develop and stress the stories of the prophets and the continuity of the prophetic message, the claim of divine revelation and absolute truth, the need for repentance with a view to the Judgment to come, and the fight for the unity of God as a defense of God's honor. It also forced Muḥammad to give the necessary historical, theological and social weight to the message he conveyed.

When Mecca finally fell in 629 A.D./7 A.H., once it had been purified a number of ancient practices and ideas were retained, provided they did not constitute *shirk*. The religious purification movement, having become a reform movement, became a "complete" religion precisely when the *ḥajj*, slightly modified, was incorporated. The transfer of such traditional Arab practices,

Leipzig, 1898. Tor Andrae hinted at Manichaean influences in his *Mohammed, sein Leben und Glaube* (Göttingen, 1932), pp. 77-92 (English translation *Mohammed, the Man and his Faith*, New York, Harper Torchbook TB 62, 1960, pp. 94-113). Compare also Thomas O'Shaughnessy, S.J., *The Koranic Concept of the Word of God* (Biblica et Orientalia, Vol. 11), Roma: Pontificio Istituto Biblico, 1948.

though with a change of meaning, into the new setting not only made the movement into a religion which Muḥammad held to be complete. It was also the last important contribution which Meccan polytheism, or rather polydaimonism, made, in a singular kind of interaction, to the formation of Islam. In various ways the interaction between Muḥammad and the polytheists in Mecca clearly and decisively shaped the new religion.[11]

2. *The Jews in Medina*

Although hardly any Jews appear to have been living permanently in Mecca itself, elements of Jewish religious ideas and practices cannot have been unknown, and such elements must have reached Muḥammad both before and after the beginning of his prophetic activity. Well-known elements are the notion of a universal religion with the worship of one god only, the existence of sacred scriptures in languages other than Arabic, the connection between divine revelation and scripture. Already in the early sūra's we find eschatological representations, certain cult practices, references to biblical stories, and so on, these last containing Judaic elements which may have reached Muḥammad via Christian channels or directly. Since the prophet was convinced that his inspirations had the same origin as those of former prophets, there was no harm in looking for further information, as is referred to in S. 25:4-6/5-7 and S. 16:103/105. As W. Montgomery Watt has correctly observed,[12] this does not detract from the fact that it was Muḥammad who, facing particular problems, gave a definite Arabic formulation to truths held in Christian and Judaic religion as he had an immediate experience of such truths himself. And with their new formulation they obtained their proper meaning within the whole of the message conveyed by the prophet in word and deed.[13]

---

[11] Muḥammad's interaction with Bedouin *mushrikūn* played a role too, but this has been left out of account here.

[12] W. Montgomery Watt, *Muhammad at Mecca*, pp. 80-85. The originality of the Qur'ān, strictly speaking, is given precisely with its Arabic presentation.

[13] In history of religions attention should be given both to establishing historical facts and to discerning the meaning of these facts in the given historical context for particular groups and persons. In the absorption of facts within a particular religious tradition there nearly always occurs a change of meaning which needs careful analysis. Even the most direct factual influences often imply considerable changes in meaning and interpretation.

310

Precisely such notions of the nature of revelation and the unity of revealed religion made it possible and legitimate for Muḥammad to adjust his cultic regulations in certain respects to Judaic ones when the prospect of going to Yathrib presented itself. One could speak of an "ecumenical" effort in matters of ritual: Friday (the preparatory day for Shabbāt) as the day for public worship, Jerusalem as the *qibla*, the fast of ʿĀshūrā parallel to that of 10 Tishrī, the adding of the midday *ṣalāt* so that there would be three daily prayers in Islam too, permission to eat the food of the people of the Book and to marry their women. Although there must have been an implicit hope on Muḥammad's part that he would be recognized by the Jews as a prophet—if not for them, then at least for the Arabs—, his open attitude can be seen not only as a result of tactical policy making but also as a logical consequence ot the universalist assumptions underlying his own religious notions as a prophet. It would seem that we have also to see in this light Muḥammad's appeal to the Jews for reconciliation on the basis of the common faith in one God.[14] It was through his contact with Medinan Jews, some of whom converted, that Muḥammad received further religious information. So he learnt, for instance, that the Jews had their *tawrāt* and the Christians their *injīl*, that Mūsā had been the founder of Judaism and had preceded ʿĪsā who, as the last prophet, came from the Jews, and that Ibrāhīm had preceded both of them. Apparently, Muḥammad held that the Jews and Christians of his time were two branches of the ancient Banū Isrāʾīl. He must have learnt more about Judaism too and become aware of the weight of a particular religious tradition and history, and the importance of historical action.

When the Jews did not cooperate and in fact were able to undermine his authority by denying the divine origin of his revelations—which was possible precisely because Muḥammad held that his inspiration was in essence identical with the revelation given to the Jews—Muḥammad oriented himself completely according to the religion of Ibrāhīm as he saw it and made some changes in ritual practice away from that of Judaism. The use of the Ibrāhīm materials clearly made Muḥammad's movement more acceptable to the Arabs while retaining a universal monotheistic framework.

[14] S. 29: 46/45: . . . *wa-ilāhunā wa-ilāhukum wāḥidun* . . . The nature of this appeal, and its later interpretation, deserves further study as well as the responses to it on the part of Jews and Christians then and in later times.

The results, in polemic and action, of the confrontation of the Jewish claim to be God's chosen people with Muḥammad's claim to be God's chosen prophet are well-known.[15]

Muḥammad's interaction with the Jewish tribes in Medina had profound consequences for the further development of his religious movement. Besides the halachic-biblical elements absorbed earlier in Mecca, certain Jewish ritual regulations provided a model for ritual innovations made by Muḥammad in the period of assimilation which started shortly before the Hijra. In the period of opposition, starting about a year and a half after the Hijra, this model was abandoned however. In the long run it seems to have been more important that his negative experience with the Jews caused Muḥammad to be disillusioned in his assumption of the unity of the "revealed religions", so that he seems to have maintained instead rather the idea of the unity of "revelations" by the same God than that of "revealed religions". The one given revelation would have been distorted subsequently by the Jews and of course also by the Christians.

This conclusion could not but result in Muḥammad distancing himself from the empirical religion of the Jews, and all the arguments which could be brought together against it and all possible evidence for Jewish sins were hammered out in Qur'anic prophecies. Apart from what he learnt from Judaism and partly incorporated into his own religious movement, Muḥammad's "Jewish experience" must have reinforced his prophetic selfconsciousness considerably and forced him to reconsider the meaning of both his preaching and acting and the significance of his movement in terms not only of history but also of the future. He now moved toward identifying his movement completely with the religion of Ibrāhīm, the *millat Ibrāhīm*, the *ḥanīfiyya*. Although through the figure of Ismā'īl and the idea of the *millat Ibrāhīm* something of the notion of a chosen people and its historical role was transferred and applied to the Arabs, paradoxically enough it was precisely the particularism of Judaism which stimulated Muḥammad's elaboration of a universalistic orientation. Significantly, the movement took the name of the Ḥanīfiyya now, before becoming known as "Islam". Just as the resistance of the Meccans had induced a strict monotheistic

[15] See for instance J. Waardenburg, "Koranisches Religionsgespräch", in *Liber Amicorum. Studies in Honour of Prof. Dr. C. J. Bleeker* . . . Leiden: E. J. Brill, 1969, pp. 208-253.

stand, so the resistance of the Jews in Medina induced not only a greater precision but also a universalization of this stand.

3. *The Christians in Arabia*

Among the elements of Christianity which must have been in the air in the Mecca where Muḥammad grew up and along the caravan routes where he travelled, were—besides the notion of one almighty God and certain biblical stories—the idea of Judgment and the Day of Judgment, representations of the Hereafter, certain practices of worship and particular religious-ethical values and virtues. Materials of this kind can be found in the Qur'ān already in the early Meccan periods, with patriarchal figures from the Old Testament, apocryphical stories about Mary and Jesus, the notion of angels and more abstract spiritual entities. As in the case of Judaism, data from Christian communities could be assimilated in principle on the assumption of the unity of revealed religions.

Although there is some probability that Muḥammad was already making open or implied statements against Christianity—when he saw infringements of his strictly monotheistic stand—in the Meccan period, the attitude of the prophet on the whole was open and favorable with regard to the devotional attitudes and moral virtues which struck him among the Christians as expressed for instance in S. 57:27, 5:82-84/85-87. Before the Hijra, for security reasons adherents of the community were sent to Christian Ethiopia and apparently approaches were made to Christian tribes before the decision was taken to go to Yathrib. In the first Medinan years, in his conflict with the Jews, Muḥammad compared the Christians most favorably with the Jews and used stories about ʿĪsā as part of his ideological attack on the latter. After his victory, first over the Jews and then over the Meccans in 629/7 there was a remarkable change in his attitude toward the Christians and Christianity and this ended in the command to make war against them in the well-known passage of S. 9: 29-33.[16]

A first explanation of this change is the fact that Muḥammad, when expanding to the North, was confronted with tribes which were mostly Christian and linked to what may be called the By-

---

[16] W. Montgomery Watt, "The Christianity criticized in the Qur'ān", *The Muslim World*, Vol. 57 (1967), pp. 197-201. Compare the article mentioned in Note 15. For the historical facts see the studies by W. Montgomery Watt and R. Paret quoted in Note 5.

zantine defense system. Muḥammad's attack on Christianity would have been primarily of a political nature, so as to loosen these tribes from their Christian overlords by making an ideological attack on their religion as part of an overall war. It is questionable, however, whether there may not have been better political means to get these tribes on the prophet's side than by attacking their religion. So we have to look for another explanation, without denying that Muḥammad made a political use of his religion in his struggle against the Christian tribes.

A singular aspect of the Qur'anic texts directed against the Christians and Christianity is their doctrinal interest, which had hardly been present in Muḥammad's refutation of the polytheists and the Jews. Another particularity is that only certain Christian doctrines are mentioned in order to be refuted subsequently, so that the question may be raised why Muḥammad was so badly informed about Christianity.[17] A third striking fact is that, contrary to the Qur'anic texts directed against the polytheists and the Jews, which seem to reflect real debates in which Muḥammad used any argument he could find in the arsenal of the beliefs of the other party, the Qur'anic texts against the Christians are rather wishy-washy and give the impression of a man shouting at an enemy who is far away.

It would seem, indeed, that the new attitude which the prophet was taking against the Christians was due to several factors. It was in part due to his disillusionment with the idea of the unity of the revealed religions through the experience with the Jews in Medina, and it was in part the immediate consequence of his new conceptualization of what his religion was like, as expressed and elaborated in the *millat Ibrāhīm* idea. The old name of the movement, the *ḥanīfiyya*, suggests, besides the originally Meccan religious purification movement against polytheism, a kind of "reform movement" with regard to the *ahl al-kitāb*. Once this monotheistic religious reform movement had become "established"

---

[17] The lapidary information which is given in the Qur'ān about Christianity and Judaism is not only a scholarly problem but has also caused religious concern among Christians and Jews, especially when they set out to pursue a dialogue with Muslims. The Qur'ānic view of other religions and other scriptures needs further analysis. Compare "The Qur'ānic view of other Scriptures: a translation of sections from writings by ʿAfīf ʿAbd al-Fattāḥ Ṭabbāra and al-Ustādh al-Ḥaddād", tr. by A. J. Powell, *MW*, Vol. 59 (1969), 2, pp. 95-105.

314

after the victories over the Jews and the Meccans, Muḥammad could simply draw the consequences. So when he attacked what he held to be the doctrines of the Christians it was not because he had studied Christianity, but because he had been struck by those doctrines held by the Christians which were contrary to the religion of Ibrāhīm, the *ḥanīfiyya*, Islām as he conceived it.

In Medina Muḥammad had got to know the Jews from nearby, just as he had known the Meccans from his childhood. We must assume that he was less immediately familiar with the life of the Christians and rather saw their religion always from a distance, first respecting and even admiring what he saw of their devotions and virtues, later combatting what he thought to be their doctrinal errors.

The interpretation suggested here does not preclude the view that Muḥammad used the true religion against the Christians in warfare, just as he could very well use the Ibrāhīm story against the Jews in political conflict. Our contention, however, is that Muḥammad's view of Ibrāhīm and the true religion *represents an autonomous religious structure beyond the political use made of it*, and precedes it. The key to the problem of why Muḥammad provides so little information about Christianity, and information which does not represent orthodox Christianity at that, is simply that Muḥammad was not interested in it, since he already had his own religion as a religious purification and reform movement. Muḥammad was not a scholar of religion or a theologian but a prophetical reformer. *As a reformer he only saw* of the religion of the Christians *what was objectionable in his view* and what should be reformed, and this concerned doctrine. In a similar way he had been struck by the idolatry of the Meccans and the pretenses of the Jews, and he had directed his reform activities against these elements which were the ones he found objectionable.

Muḥammad's change of policy in his actual dealings with Christian tribes in the North can be interpreted along these lines. The earlier treaty with Judhām suggests that the prophet was first prepared to enter into alliances with Christian tribes, as he had made them from time to time also with other tribes and groups without making specific religious demands. Then, between the defeat at Mu'tah (Sept. 629) and the expedition to Tabūk (starting Oct. 630) he changed his policy, at least in the North. Alliances were concluded now only on the basis of acceptance of Islam so that the Christian tribes, if they wanted to avoid war, had only the alternative either to accept Islam or to submit to it with the payment of an annual tribute. But whereas in the South Christian tribes who refused to become Muslims preferred a treaty settlement like the Christians of Najrān, in the North they opposed Muḥammad's troops with armed resistance. It is important to keep in mind that the command of war as contained in the Qur'ān was almost certainly not directed against the Christians as Christians but against political enemies who happened to be Christians. In this war Muḥammad *used the religious ideal* which was at the basis of his monotheistic reform movement *as a war ideology*, just as he had used the idea of the Ibrāhim religion against the Medinan Jews a few years earlier, but the monotheistic idea and the idea of Ibrāhīm's religion as such had been conceived already before the political and military conflicts with the Jews and the Christians.

It should be noticed in this connection that the command of war against the Christians as contained in S. 9:1-37 is linked immediately with a similar command against the Jews—with the argument that neither of them were true monotheists—and also with the general command of war proclaimed in March 631 against all Arabs who had remained pagan. The unbelief of the *ahl al-kitāb* is equated here with the unbelief of the pagan Arabs, which is an obvious conclusion from the standpoint of a reform movement. In other words, the new attitude taken to the Christian tribes is *also* one of the consequences of Muḥammad's general decision *to impose the dīn which had been destined for the Arabs on all Arabs without exception*. Christians and Jews were not forced to adopt Islam themselves but they had to recognize the dominance of this *dīn* as the religious basis of society, and they had to pay tribute accordingly. The religious movement which had started in Mecca as a purification movement and which had become a religious reform movement and potential religion in Medina, had now become a religion in the full sense of the word, according to what was understood by a "religion" at the time.

When trying to sum up the consequences of the interaction between Muḥammad and his movement on the one hand, and the Christians in Arabia on the other hand, the first thing we must notice is the fact that the Christians whom Muḥammad had to deal with were not a given community with which the prophet lived, like the polytheists in Mecca and the Jewish tribes in Medina.

They were scattered, they had different political allegiances, they belonged to different churches and sects, and they had different forms of piety. Partly as a consequence of this state of affairs, there was much less real interaction possible between Muḥammad and the Christians than with the polytheists in Mecca or the Jews in Medina. The new religious movement owed in particular to the Christians certain aspects of a creating, sustaining and judging God, a large part of its eschatology and certain devotional practices, while a particular Christian ascetic life style could provide a model for the pious. It has been observed that such elements were "in the air" in Mecca and at other places in Arabia and that this made for an open attitude on Muḥammad's part towards the way of life and religious practice of the Christians. During the Medinan conflict Muḥammad compared the Christians favorably with the Jews, notwithstanding the fact that neither group recognized him as a prophet. But the Christians were less dangerous politically then and he was attracted by their virtuous life.

The prophet refuted Christian doctrines with regard to the relationship between God and man as a logical consequence of an absolute monotheism as he conceived it and on the basis of the way in which his religion had developed through the conflicts with the Meccans and the Medinan Jews. Politically, Christian tribes had to choose now between adopting the new religion and making a treaty with payment of tribute, if they wanted to avoid war. Although the very resistance of the Christian Arab tribes in the North may have accelerated the ideological use of monotheistic reform doctrine against them, the refutation itself—of all that seemed to be contrary to strict monotheism—was in fact a logical consequence of the proclaimed monotheistic *millat Ibrāhīm* with which the prophet had identified his religious movement.

The movement presented itself at this time in at least two different ways: as a religious reform movement of polytheism, Judaism and Christianity, and as the religion destined for the Arabs. Both were of consequence for Muḥammad's attitude to the Christians he encountered in the North, as was the fact that Muḥammad's religious movement had established itself and was becoming a religion in its own right. The resistance of the Christian tribes may indeed have been one of the many factors which contributed to the transition of Islam from a religious reform movement to a universal religion, defined as the *dīn al-ḥaqq* and opposed to empirical

Judaism and Christianity. The Christianity of the northern Arab tribes, paradoxically, may thus indirectly have contributed to the full development of the new religion of the Arabs and to the sense of competition which this religion developed with Christianity in general.

Looking back at the interaction of the Islamic religious movement with the existing religious communities, we are struck by the importance of socio-political factors. Yet on closer analysis one has to recognize another dimension as well, and here the interactions just described take on all their significance and weight. Muḥammad at the same time acted on earth and pronounced a series of *āyāt* held to be inspired and consequently having religious authority. In his actions he behaved as a statesman; by his inspirations he was a prophet. *Each encounter with another community, consequently, took place on two levels*: a settling of affairs in the realm of socio-political action, and an interaction of religious ideas and practices due or leading to particular religious inspirations of the prophet. If Muḥammad had not considered himself to be a prophet nor been considered by his followers as such, he would have been obliged to deal with the Meccans, the people of Yathrib and the Bedouin tribes without this second—religious—dimension. It was precisely his prophethood which made his interactions take place on two levels at the same time.

In the foregoing a sketch has been given of the main phases of the development of the religious movement, through successive interactions with existing religious communities, into a religion. Now it is worthwile to pay attention for a moment to an aspect of its internal development and see to what extent there is a parallelism between the attitudes taken towards other religions and the progressive self-definition of Islam as a religion. What does the Qur'ān say about the religion which Muḥammad brought, both as *millat Ibrāhīm* and as *dīn*?

4. *Millat Ibrāhīm*

After the fundamental studies by C. Snouck Hurgronje and A. J. Wensinck on the patriarchal figure of Ibrāhīm and his religion in the Qur'ān, further inquiries by Y. Moubarac and W. A. Bijlefeld have brought some corrections to Snouck Hurgronje's stress on the political aspects of the Ibrāhīm story.[18] They

[18] On the Ibrāhīm problem, see besides the literature quoted in Notes 1

have also given a more precise dating of some verses of the Qur'ān which Snouck Hurgronje held to be Medinan,[19] and as a result they have been able to show that already in the Meccan period of the Qur'ān Ibrāhīm had a special link with the Ka'ba and the Meccans, even though Muḥammad apparently did not know in his Meccan period that Ismā'īl was a son of Ibrāhīm. These inquiries have shown that there is a continuous development of the Ibrāhīm conception in the Qur'ān, and that the basic notions of it were already present in the third Meccan period. R. Paret summarizes the significance of Ibrāhīm in the Qur'ān as: [20]

(1) the founder or purifier of the Ka'ba;
(2) the prototype of all *muslimūn* as his spiritual descendants;
(3) a patriarchal figure who preceded Mūsā and 'Īsā with their revelations, and to whom Muḥammad could appeal as a *ḥanīf*, not a *mushrik*, without him being a Jew or a Christian.

In the Qur'anic Ibrāhīm story, Ibrāhīm is the prototype of Muḥammad and all spiritual descendants of Ibrāhīm participate in the privileges of the *millat Ibrāhīm*. Through the Qur'ān the community of Muslims has received the definite revelation and has become *ahl al-kitāb* and part of the millat Ibrāhīm in a purer sense than the Jews and Christians.

It may be contended that this appeal to the *millat Ibrāhīm* gave to Muḥammad's movement a universal dimension. The claim could now be made that the movement was not only a purification of polytheism and a reform of Judaism and Christianity but that it was also a religion in its own right, apart from the fact that such a universalist outlook could lead to the envisaging of a *Pax Islamica* throughout the Arabian peninsula. On the one hand, by recognizing the value of the revelation given to Jews and Christians, Islamic religion has a particular relationship to Judaism and Christianity *beyond the empirical forms of these religions*. It can accept, for

and 4 also A. J. Wensinck, *Mohammed en de Joden te Medina* (Leiden: E. J. Brill, 1908), pp. 131-133 and the same, art. "Ibrāhīm" in EI^1, Vol. 2, pp. 431-2, and E. Beck, "Die Gestalt des Abraham am Wendepunkt der Entwicklung Muhammeds; Analyse von S. 2.118 (124)-135 (141)", *Le Muséon*, Vol. 65 (1952), pp. 73-94.

[19] S. 14: 39/41b should be considered as a Medinan interpolation within a Meccan text S. 14: 35-41/38-42. S. 2: 126/120 ff. is a later Medinan elaboration of the Meccan S. 14: 35-40/38-42, and verse 127a/121a may be a later interpolation in the whole of v. 125-129/119-123. See Bijlefeld, *op. cit.*, pp. 127-132.

[20] Rudi Paret, *Mohammed und der Koran* (Stuttgart, 1966^2), pp. 108-110.

instance, on the basis of its particular assumptions, the presence of spiritual *ḥanīf* monotheists within the Jewish and Christian communities. In this way the idea of a *millat Ibrāhīm* is of paramount importance for the relations between Islam and other religions.

On the other hand, by claiming to offer a universal monotheism as *millat Ibrāhīm* Islamic religion revealed a characteristic dialectic in its history between its particularistic tendencies which are linked to particular historical developments on the one hand, and the universality of its prototype, the *millat Ibrāhīm*, on the other. So the idea of a *millat Ibrāhīm* is also of major importance for the very selfview of Islam. The *ḥanīfiyya* of Ibrāhīm as an interior spiritual experience which demands a break with manifest as well as hidden forms of idolatry, has played for instance a major role in the history of Muslim spirituality.

The fact that Muḥammad had a model of his religion in the *millat Ibrāhīm*, an ideal and pure religion according to his conception of it, must have been one of the reasons for his success in bringing about and "perfecting" his religion with its own kind of monotheistic faith in many variations—over against other forms of monotheism—and with its own kind of basic structure of society in many variations—over against other socio-political structures. A number of sayings and actions of Muḥammad as a prophet become more understandable against the background of this notion of a universal religion which he formulated, in good Semitic tradition, in terms of a patriarchal genealogy.

Was there perhaps in the back of Muḥammad's mind from the very beginning of his prophethood the notion of a kind of *Urreligion*, a notion which crystallized at the end of the Meccan period into the conception of a *millat Ibrāhīm* and which received its definite shape in Medina? This leads to another question which must be left open here. What kind of relationship may the prophet have envisaged between the *dīn al-islām* which he brought on earth and that basic and universal *Urreligion* of the *millat Ibrāhīm* which seems to have provided the model for it?

5. *Dīn in the Qur'ān*

If we leave aside the use of *dīn* in the sense of "judgment" as being less relevant for the present inquiry, a survey of the use of the concept of *dīn* in its meaning of "religion" in chronological order in the Qur'ān leads to the following result: [21]

In the Meccan period *dīn* occurs as the religion of an individual (109:6, 10:104) or a people—including a people of unbelievers, though their religion can be changed (40:26/27). There should be no factions and divisions within the *dīn* (30:32/31, 42:13/11). *Dīn* implies possession of religious prescriptions, right ones (42:13/11) or wrong ones (42:21/20); it is the right monotheistic worship of God (*lahu al-dīnu wāṣiban*, 16:52/54) for which man has been created and to which he is called as a *ḥanīf* (10:105, 12:40, 30:30/29, 43/42); the worship (*dīn*) should be directed to God alone and completely 7:29/28, 10:22/23, 29:65, 31:32/31, 39:11/14 and 14/16, 40:14 and 65/67; the pure worship (*al-dīnu'l-khāliṣu*) is toward God (39:3). The right *dīn* is the *milla* of Ibrāhīm the *ḥanīf* (6:161/162). Unbelievers have *milla*'s which are bad (14:13/16, 38:7/6), as opposed to the good *milla* of Ibrāhīm, Isḥāq and Ya'qūb (12:37, 38).

In the Medinan period *dīn* is used much more often and in many more different contexts, and it is illuminating to observe a clear development in its use, according to the chronological order of Medinan sūra's proposed by Th. Nöldeke. At the beginning of the Medinan period, for instance, a well-known text (2:256/257) affirms that there is no enforcement (*ikrāh*) in religion (*dīn*).[22] After a text from the next sūra (98:5/4) which summarizes the right religion (*dīn al-qayyimati*) as consisting of monotheistic worship (as performed by *ḥanīfs*), *ṣalat* and *zakāt*, Sūra 8:39/40 then commands fighting until there is no more *fitna* and the religion or worship is monotheistic only (. . . *ḥattā lā takūna fitnatun wa-yakūna al-dīnu kulluhu li-'llāhi* . . .). The command to fight for the right religion will come back now again and again.

Next, in Sūra 3, three verses speak of *dīn*. For the first time *islām*

---

[21] On the concept of *dīn*, see for instance Josef Horovitz, *Koranische Untersuchungen* (Berlin-Leipzig, 1926), p. 62 (also compared with *milla*); Toshihiku Izutsu, *God and Man in the Koran* . . . (Tokyo, 1964), pp. 228-229; Louis Gardet, art. "dīn" in *EI*^{2}, Vol. 2, pp. 293 f. (also compared with *milla*); M. M. Bravmann, *The Spiritual Background of Early Islam*: *Studies in Ancient Arab Concepts* (Leiden: E. J. Brill, 1972), pp. 1-6, 34. When preparing this paper we did not know Y. Y. Haddad's article "The conception of the term *dīn* in the Qur'ān", *MW*, Vol. 64 (1974), pp. 114-123, which analyzes the term *dīn* basically in terms of "God Action" and "Man's Action".

[22] Compare Rudi Paret, "Sure 2, 256: lā ikrāha fī d-dīni. Toleranz oder Resignation", *Der Islam*, Vol. 45 (1969), pp. 299-300.

—presumably the maṣdar aspect is here predominant—is connected with *dīn* in the famous saying *Al-dīn 'inda 'llāh al-islām* (3:19/17). The verses 83/77 and 85/79 reject anything else except the *dīn Allāh* and *islām* as *dīn* (... *a-fa-ghaira dīni 'llāhi yabghūna* ... (83/77), ... *wa-man yabtaghi ghaira 'l-islāmi dīnan* ... (85/79). Like verse 19/17, these verses 83/77 and 85/79 imply that there is no alternative for man as far as true religion is concerned but "to surrender" (*islām*), verse 83/77 adding that in its being the whole creation has "surrendered" (*aslama*).

Subsequently (61:9) for the first time the expression *dīn al-ḥaqq* is used as the religion which will be made triumphant over every religion (... *'alā 'l-dīni kullihi* ...), a statement repeated in S. 48:28 with a slight nuance, and also in S. 9:33 (*Huwa 'lladhī arsala rasūlahu bi-'l-hudā wa-dīni'l-ḥaqqi li-yuẓhirahu 'alā 'l-dīni kullihi* ...). *Dīn al-ḥaqq*, "the true, real religion", is a stronger expression than *al-dīn al-qayyim*, literally "the immutable, stable religion". Although Islam is not identified explicitly with the *dīn al-ḥaqq*, such an identification is implied. There is here not only a command to fight but also a promise of victory over any other religions, in other words an ascertainment of the mundane superiority of Islam.

After a text with a monotheistic tendency such as had occurred already in the Meccan period with regard to *dīn* (4:146/145), Sūra 24 contains some interesting statements. In verse 2 it is said that the *dīn Allāh* has no place for pity if a major delict has been committed, which suggests a puritanical rigidity in religion. In verse 24 it is said that at Judgment Day Allāh will requite the people according to ... *dīnahum al-ḥaqqa* ..., while Allāh himself will be recognized as the clear truth (... *huwa al-ḥaqqu 'l-mubīnu* ...). These two verses having referred to an ethical command and to man's conscience, verse 55/54 again promises that Allāh will make powerful the religion which he has thought right for his believers (... *wa-la-yumakkinanna lahum dīnahum* ...), which is a well-known theme.

Sūra 60:8-9, next in chronological order, refers to a rule of war; when people do not fight against the faithful "in religion" (*qātala fī 'l-dīn*) they should be treated kindly, for instance by treaty, but as soon as there has been such "fighting in religion" such a treaty is impossible. After a text in which an allusion is made to the powerlessness of unbelievers if they want to justify their religion before

322

Allāh (49:16) we have arrived at the well-known last two sūras.

Sūra 9 has four verses in which *dīn* occurs. In case of conversion the people become "brethren in religion" (. . . *fa-ikhwānukum fī 'l-dīn* . . ., verse 11) if they also perform *ṣalāt* and pay *zakāt*. Verse 29 is the famous command to make war against: (a) unbelievers; (b) those who do what is forbidden; and (c) those among the people who received the Book who do not adhere to the true religion: . . . *wa-lā yadīnūna dīna 'l-ḥaqqi mina 'lladhīna ūtū 'l-kitāba* . . . and in all three cases the war should continue until they pay tribute. According to verse 36 the *ḥarām* character of four months in a year is right religion (*al-dīn al-qayyim*). And verse 122/123 exhorts people from each army-group to receive instruction in religion (. . . *li-yatafaqqahū fī 'l-dīni* . . .), in order to "warn" the others when they return home.

An important verse occurs in the chronologically last sūra (5:3/4, 5): ". . . *al-yawma ya'isa 'lladhīna kafarū min dīnikum fa-lā takhshawhum wa-'khshawnī 'l-yawma akmaltu lakum dīnakum wa-atmamtu 'alaikum ni'matī wa-raḍītu lakumu 'l-islāma dīnan* . . ." The unbelievers are radically separated from "your" religion and have nothing to hope for; God has perfected his grace toward the community; he is satisfied that the faithful have *islām* as religion. Whether or not *islām* is used here as a proper name remains open to discussion. Verse 57/62 of the same Sūra 5 forbids making a treaty with those among the people who received the Book who had made a mockery of the new religion: ". . . *lā tattakhidhū 'lladhīna 'ttakhadhū dīnakum huzuwan wa-la'iban mina 'lladhīna ūtū 'l-kitāba min qablikum wa-'l-kuffāra awliyā'a*."

Some texts of the Medinan period which use *dīn* in connection with the *millat Ibrāhīm* are particularly interesting in the context of our inquiry. Thus, the early text S. 2: 130-132/124-126 states that only a fool can reject the *millat Ibrāhīm*, that Ibrāhīm surrendered (*aslama*) to God, and that Ibrāhīm like Ya'qūb said to his sons: . . . *inna 'llāha 'ṣṭafā lakumu 'l-dīn* . . . (". . . Allah has chosen your religion for you . . ."), and that they should not die without being *muslim* (with a strong verbal aspect: "surrendering to God"). They key words *millat Ibrāhīm*, *aslama* and *dīn* which occur in these three verses are united here into one whole.

Sūra 22:78/77 equally combines a statement about *al-dīn* (namely, that there is nothing in it which "burdens" man: . . . *wa-mā ja'ala 'alaikum fī 'l-dīn min ḥarajin millata abīkum Ibrāhīma* . . .) with the expression *millat Ibrāhīm*, "your father", indicating the nature of this religion. Here again, as a third term, *muslim* is added as the name which Ibrāhīm gave to the faithful of his *milla*: "... He called you *muslims (huwa sammākumu 'l-muslimīna)* ..." *Millat Ibrāhīm*, *aslama* and *dīn* apparently belong together.

The development of the use of *dīn* as a concept in the Qur'ān apparently *reflects the development of earliest Islam from a purifying religious movement to a reform movement and then to a new independent religion.* Corresponding with the latter phase we find *dīn* in a reified sense, for instance in S. 3: 73/66, and as synonymous with *millat Ibrāhīm* in S. 6: 161/162; we find it used as a kind of "war ideology" in the commands to war, for instance in S. 8: 39/40, and as indicating an all encompassing religious, social and political system in S. 5: 3/5. The *dīn* of Muḥammad's movement is opposed to the *dīn* of the unbelieving polytheists; contrary to the Jews and Christians, the adherents of *dīn al-islām* are part of the *millat Ibrāhīm*. The relationship between these two appears to be of crucial importance.

The connections between the use in the Qur'ān of *dīn* on the one hand and *islām* [23] and *imān* [24] on the other demand further at-

---

[23] On the concepts of *islām*, *aslama* etc., see for instance Dawid Künstlinger, " 'Islām', 'muslim', 'aslama' im Ḳurān", *Rocznik Orjentalistyczny*, Vol. 11 (1935), pp. 128-137; Helmer Ringgren, *Islam, 'aslama, and Muslim* (Uppsala, 1949); D. H. Baneth, "What did Muḥammad mean when he called his religion 'Islam'? The original meaning of *aslama* and its derivatives", *Israel Oriental Studies*, Vol. I (1971), pp. 183-190; Abdul Khaliq Kazi, "The meaning of Īmān and Islām in the Qur'ān", *Islamic Studies*, Vol. 5 (1966), pp. 227-237; Toshihiko Izutsu, *Ethico-Religious Concepts in the Qur'an* (Montreal, 1966), pp. 189-191; Muhammad Abdul Rauf, "Some Notes on the Qur'anic use of the terms Islām and Imān", *MW*, Vol. 57 (1967), pp. 94-102; S. McDonough, "Imān and Islām in the Qur'ān", *Iqbal Review*, Vol. 12 (1971), 1, pp. 81-88; M. M. Bravmann, *The Spiritual Background of Early Islam* ... (Leiden, 1972), pp. 7-26.

[24] On the concept of *īmān*, see besides the articles by A. K. Kazi, M. A. Rauf and S. McDonough mentioned in Note 22, for instance Helmer Ringgren, "The conception of faith in the Koran", *Oriens*, Vol. 4 (1951), pp. 1-20; Toshihiko Izutsu, *The Structure of the Ethical Terms in the Koran, a Study in Semantics* (Tokyo, 1959), pp. 118-122, 173-175; the same, *God and Man in the Koran* ... (Tokyo, 1964), pp. 198-204, 216-219; the same, *Ethico-Religious Concepts in the Qur'ān* (Montreal, 1966), pp. 184-188; M. M. Bravmann, *The Spiritual Background of Early Islam* ... (Leiden, 1972), pp. 26-31. Compare R. Caspar, "La foi selon le Coran. Etude de thèmes et perspectives théologiques", *Proche Orient chrétien*, Vol. 18 (1968), pp. 7-28, 140-166, and Vol. 19 (1969), pp. 162-193.

tention and a few remarks must suffice here. For a long time, deep into the Medinan period, *islām* is the act of self-surrender to the divine will, stepping out of the status of a *jāhil* into that of a *muslim*, which remains for a long time an active participle before being used as a substantive. According to S. 51: 36 there were also *muslimūn* before the historical religion of Islam. Only much later does *islām* become a full substantive and the name for the new religion, but even then it retains to some extent its maṣdar aspect. Later *aslama* too acquires the technical meaning of joining the community in an external way (S. 49: 14) without certainty about the inner conviction of the convert, which is indicated by *īmān*, the inner religious attitude before God. Just as in Mecca *dīn* stands for religious attitude and worship, so *īmān* stands for the pure, monotheistic faith in God. *Mu'min* at the beginning of the Medinan period can still be used for the faithful among the *ahl al-kitāb* too. The opposite of *islām* (and *īmān*) is *Kufr*.[25]

Aslama "to surrender oneself") is near to *'abada* ("to serve") and *akhlaṣa* [26] ("to make pure, to free from admixture"), all being part of the good *dīn* according to the Qur'ān.

Conclusion

The problem dealt with in this paper has been to trace the way in which, in the course of Muḥammad's public activity, a prophetical message developed into a fully-fledged religion, both as a social and historical reality and according to the inspirations of its prophet himself. In order to treat this problem we have distinguished several phases in the development of earliest Islam, basing our argument on two assumptions. The first assumption has been that the interaction which took place between the new religious movement with its prophetic leader and the three major existing religious communities was of paramount importance for this process, and that a periodization could be established accordingly. Our second assumption has been that the two main conceptualizations of the notion of religion in the Qur'ān, *millat Ibrāhīm* and

---

[25] Compare M. R. Waldman, "The development of the concept of kufr in the Qur'ān", *JAOS*, Vol. 88 (1968), pp. 442-455.

[26] Compare Helmer Ringgren, "The pure religion", *Oriens*, Vol. 15 (1962), pp. 93-96. The concept of *akhlaṣa* needs further investigation, as do other Qur'anic terms used in connection with *dīn* and left aside here (see for instance Rudi Paret, *Mohammed und der Koran* (Stuttgart, 1957, 1966²), pp. 72-74).

dīn, as they developed in the course of the successive Qur'anic revelations, furnish a particular key to understanding not only the external forms which this religion took in combining mundane action with religious inspiration and thought, but also the particular notion which Muḥammad himself had of what a true religion—his religion—should be.

Our problem is what "islām" with a small i was before it became "Islam" with a capital I, that is to say as a religion in history. It is a search, beyond written history, for the beginnings of historical Islam which interests Muslims and Islamicists alike. The very fact, however, that "Islam" has become the name of a historical religion makes it difficult to grasp what *islām* in the course of Muḥammad's lifetime meant and implied. At present the latter term refers to something different which is now largely an ideal of Muslims and a subject of research of Islamicists who, unfortunately, have tended sometimes to interpret this "Islam" in terms of western ideas of religion. Notwithstanding the difficulties involved, it is a scholarly necessity to try to push backward into history beyond the moment at which Islam became an established religion and to reach the stage at which it was still the fluid "religion of Surrender" in becoming.

As has been observed earlier, the *millat Ibrāhīm* represented for Muḥammad the *Urreligion*, some kind of basic, original religion of universal validity. A problem which deserves further research is whether Muḥammad still continued to recognize the priority of this basic original religion over his own religion established in Medina, or whether he finally arrived at a straight identification of his "Islamic" religion with the Abrahamitic "basic" religion. In the last analysis this problem concerns the Islamic claim of universality. Whereas "universality" for us is mostly expressed in terms of a generally valid idea, in Muḥammad's time it was first of all expressed in terms of a common origin. Ibrāhīm being the *ḥanīf* or monotheist *par excellence*, he is considered to be the "father" of all monotheistic "surrenderers" and of the one universal and basic religion. While Ibrāhīm had instituted monotheism over against idolatry, Muḥammad had "rediscovered" it and proclaimed its essential truth over against the Arab idolaters in the first place and the Jews and Christians of his time in the second place. The "surrendered ones" or *muslims* follow the religion of Ibrāhīm which remains the norm for their own empirical religion. Although the question whether, throughout the history of Islam, Islamic religion has been seen as *the only* or as *one possible* realization of the basic religion—the *ḥanīfiyya*, the true universal religion of the one God on earth—is a vital one, the problem of what constituted "universal religion" for Muḥammad and how he saw his own religion in relation to it should be treated, however, *independently of what happened after his death*, and without consideration of what has later been understood by "Islam"[27] or by a natural monotheism given as *fiṭra* within each human being.

Many interpretations have already been given of these delicate but decisive years of the beginning of Islam and none of them has proved to be exhaustive.[28] An impartial history of religions can certainly make a contribution by throwing more light on these crucial phases of earliest Islam.[29]

---

[27] See for the later use of this term for instance Jane I. Smith, *An Historical and Semantic Study of the Term Islam as Seen in a Sequence of Quran Commentaries* (Harvard Dissertations in Religion 1). Missoula, Mont.: Scholars Press, 1975. Compare the same author's "Continuity and change in the understanding of 'Islam'", *The Islamic Quarterly*, Vol. 16, Nrs. 3/4, pp. 121-139. Since this paper was written, the underlying assumption that the Qur'anic texts date from Muḥammad's lifetime has been fundamentally questioned by J. Wansbrough, *Quranic Studies. Sources and Methods of Scriptural Interpretation* (London Oriental Series Vol. 31). Oxford etc.: Oxford University Press, 1977; and his *The Sectarian Milieu. Content and Composition of Islamic Salvation History* (London Oriental Series Vol. 34). Oxford etc.: O.U.P., 1978. Discussion of Wansborough's work should take into account Angelika Neuwirth, *Studien zur Komposition der mekkanischen Suren* (Studien zur Sprache, Geschichte und Kultur des islamischen Orients, N.F., Band 10). Berlin-New York: Walter de Gruyter, 1981.

[28] A history of "religions" also needs to take into account data which had a religious connotation or significance at the time in which they occurred. In Islamic studies social and political realities, for instance, should always be taken into account. With regard to our theme the observation of Tor Andrae about the connection of the development of Islam and the growing awareness of Arab identity within the framework of a universal monotheistic religion deserves attention: "Hence we must assume that the struggle for religious independence, and the belief in a general monotheistic religion, revealed to all peoples, which came from the Manichaean and Syrian *hanpe*, did not, in Mohammed's time, so far as he was aware, originate in direct connection with these sects, but rather as a feeling after a new independent religion, free from the idol-worship of heathenism, and not bound by any Jewish or Christian rites or laws—and thus a religion to which one could swear allegiance without having to sacrifice national distinctiveness and independence, such as one would have to do on joining a foreign religious community (*umma*)" (*Mohammed, the Man and his Faith*, Harper Torchbook 1960, p. 110). The original German text appeared in 1932 (See Note 10).

[29] I.e. those of religious purification, of reform, and of the development of *islām* into a religion (*dīn*).

7

QUR'ĀNIC *SIĞĞĪL* AND ARAMAIC *SGYL**

Fred Leemhuis

Although it is clear that the Qur'anic word *siğğīl* indicates a material of which stones may be made, its exact meaning has been the subject of a discussion which is by now some fourteen centuries old. The reason for this is a simple one that may be stated in the words of Ibn Zaid, as recorded by Ṭabarī: *wa-asmā'u-l-ašyā'i lā tudraku illā min luġatin sā'iratin aw ḫabarin min allāhi ta'āla ḏikruhu*[1] "one cannot know the names of things except from a generally known language or from a piece of information from God". God's only information in the case of *siğğīl* was contained in the context wherein this word occurs in the Qur'ān:

XI,82: ... *wa-amṭarnā 'alaihā ḥiğāratan min siğğīlin (manḍūḍin musawwamatan 'inda rabbika* ...) "... and [we] rained on it stones of *siğğīl*, (one on another, marked with thy Lord ...)"[2]

XV,74: ... *wa-amṭarnā 'alaihim ḥiğāratan min siğğīlin.* "... and [we] rained upon them stones of *siğğīl*".

CV,4: *(wa-arsala 'alaihim ṭairan abābīla) tarmīhim biḥiğāratin min siğğīlin.* "(and He loosed upon them birds in flights), hurling against them stones of *siğğīl*".

And that was about all, although scholars in the past and the present have argued on the basis of LI,33, where we find *li-nursila 'alaihim ḥiğāratan min ṭīn (musawwamatan 'inda rabbika ...)* "[in order] to loose upon them stones of clay, (one on another, marked with thy Lord ...)", that the two words *ṭīn* and

* I am very grateful to my colleagues G.J.H. van Gelder and H.L.J. Vanstiphout, who contributed many valuable suggestions and references from the fields of Arabic poetry and cuneiform studies respectively.

[1] *Tafsīr aṭ-Ṭabarī, ad* CV,3, in connection with the discussion about the meaning of *abābīl* and *siğğīl*.

[2] Except for *siğğīl*, Arberry's translation is adopted for the rendering in English of quotations from the Qur'ān.

siğğīl must be approximately synonymous. A corresponding etymology was found by suggesting that *siğğīl* was a compound of the two Persian words *säng* "stone" and *gil* "clay" or "mud". Following this, Jeffery thus simply states that its meaning is "lumps of baked clay", and adds that the two words entered Arabic via Middle Persian.[3] Paret in his translation agrees with the meaning, but is more cautions in his commentary,[4] in that he also quotes Horovitz, who, at least partially, agrees with the equivalence of *siğğīl* and *ṭīn*, but who also states "Die schon von den Arabern gegebene Herleitung aus säng und gil befriedigt nicht".[5] The trouble with this derivation, of course, is that it reeks as it were, of having been constructed after the conclusion was reached that *siğğīl* must mean more or less the same as *ṭīn*. Indeed, one wonders why such a loanword from Persian (in which language it did not apparently occur as such) did not retain the /n/, which in other loanwords from Persian into Arabic seems to be quite normal.[6] Ibn Hišām, possibly implying that this "loanword" was concocted later on by the commentators themselves, rather bluntly states: "some of the commentators mentioned that it is [composed of] two words in Persian, of which the Arabs made one word".[7]

Certainly, other interpretations have also been put forward. Ṭabarī registers the following, in addition to the one just mentioned:[8]

2. *as-samā' ad-dunyā* "the nearest heaven".
3. *aṣ-ṣulb* "something very hard" which is used of stones and of beating.
4. a *fi''īl* form of *asğala* (= *arsala*) which should mean "discharged on them".
5. a *fi''īl* form of *sağala* "to draw water", which can also mean "to give".

[3] A. Jeffery, *The foreign vocabulary of the Qur'ān* (Baroda 1938), 164-5.

[4] R. Paret. *Der Koran, Kommentar und Konkordanz* (Stuttgart 1971), 240-1, *ad* XI, 82 f.

[5] J. Horovitz, *Koranische Untersuchungen* (Berlin 1926), 11.

[6] E.g. *ḫandaq*, *singāb*, *sundus*, *ṭunbūr*, *zindīq*.

[7] ذكر بعض المفسرين أنهما كلمتان بالفارسية جعلتهما العرب كلمة واحدة وإنما هو سَنْج وجِلّ... Ibn Hišām, *as-Sīra an-Nabawiyya*, ed. Muṣṭafā as-Saqā, Ibrāhīm al-Ibyārī and 'Abd al-Ḥafīẓ Šalabī (Cairo 1955[2]), I, 55. Ṭabarī also mentions that the Persian explanation is the one given by the *mufassirūn*.

[8] *Tafsīr aṭ-Ṭabarī*, *ad* XI, 82.

QUR'ANIC *SIĞĞĪL* AND ARAMAIC *SGYL*

6. [a derivation] of *siğill*, because there were signs on it as on a book.
7. *ṭīn yuṭbaḫ* "baked clay", like *āğurr* "baked brick".

It may be clear that most of these simply represent *testimonia ignorantiae* or more or less clever attempts to solve the enigma, thereby underlining the arbitrariness of the above-mentioned putative equivalence of *siğğīl* and *ṭīn*. In my opinion, only one of these interpretations deserves consideration as an alternative to this equivalence together with its Persian etymology. In fact, it merits very serious consideration, as will become clear in what follows.

Although Ṭabarī does not mention him by name, it is in fact Abū 'Ubaida who is quoted from his *Mağāz al-Qur'ān* as having stated the above mentioned third interpretation.[9] However, the wording of the quotation is somewhat ambiguous. When we look at Sezgin's edition of the *Mağāz* we find Abū 'Ubaida's wording to be somewhat different, in that he writes: "stones of *siğğīl*, that is to say, hardness; and it is used of solid stones and of beating".[10] *Ad* CV,4, he simply mentions that it is "every hard thing".[11] In both cases, he records as a *šāhid* the second hemistich of the following verse of Ibn Muqbil,[12] which apparently later on became more or less standard in the discussion of the meaning of *siğğīl*, as may be gathered from Ibn Qutaiba, Buḫārī, Ṭabarī, Zamaḫšarī, the *Lisān* and Ibn Kaṯīr:[13]

[9] وكان بعض أهل العلم بكلام العرب من البصريين يقول السجيل هو من الحجارة الصلب الشديد ومن الضرب

[10] حجارة من سجيل وهو الشديد من الحجارة الصلب ومن الضرب. Abū 'Ubaida b. al-Muṯannā, *Mağāz al-Qur'ān*, ed. Muḥammad Fu'ād Sazgīn, I (Cairo 1954[1]), 296.

[11] Abū 'Ubaida, *op. cit.*, II (Cairo 1962[1]), 312. It is noteworthy that Ibn Hišām, *op. cit.*, 55, before mentioning the Persian interpretation, states "As for *as-siğğīl*, Yūnus an-Naḥwī and Abū 'Ubaida related to me that, amongst the Arabs, it means "a hard and solid thing (*aš-šadīd aṣ-ṣulb*)".

[12] Born before Islam, died after 35/656 or even 70/690. See Sezgin, *GAS*, II, 248-9, and *EI*[2] Suppl., s.v.

[13] See Abū 'Ubaida, *loc. cit.*, nn. 10-11; Ibn Qutaiba, *Kitāb al-ma'ānī al-kabīr* (Hyderabad 1949), 991, who also quotes Abū 'Ubaida as having stated that the Persian explanation is of no significance; *Ṣaḥīḥ al-Buḫārī*, *kitāb at-Tafsīr*, *ad* sūra XI (in the Cairo ed. of Muḥammad 'Alī Ṣubaiḥ, VI, 92): سِجِّيلٌ الشَّدِيدُ الْكَبِيرُ followed by Ibn Muqbil's verse, but *ad* sūra CV (ed. Ṣubaiḥ, VI, 218): مِنْ سِجِّيلٍ هِيَ سَنْكْ وكِل on Ibn 'Abbās's authority; *Tafsīr aṭ-Ṭabarī*, *ad*

QUR'ANIC *SIĞĞĪL* AND ARAMAIC *SGYL*

wa-rağlatin yaḍribūna-l-baiḍa ʿan ʿuruḍin / *ḍarban ṭawāṣā bihi-l-'abṭālu siğğīlan*[14]

"And men [there are among us] that strike the helmets from the side / with a blow that heroes would recommend among themselves, stone-hard". Of course, Abū ʿUbaida knew that the word is a rhyme-word in a *qaṣīda nūniyya* and that Ibn Muqbil uses the word as *siğğīnan*, but he remarks that some people substituted an /n/ for the /l/ and he pointedly quotes a line from an-Nābiġa where *rafinni* is sustituted for *rafilli*. From the *Lisān* we are informed that the line is by an-Nābiġa al-Ğaʿdī.[15] Apart from the fact that this substitution of /n/ for /l/ appears to have indeed been fairly common,[16] Abū ʿUbaida's statement gains in strength and credibility when we realise that both Ibn Muqbil and an-Nābiġa al-Ğaʿdī[17] were members of the tribe of ʿĀmir b. Ṣaʿṣaʿa,[18] which had its habitat in Central Arabia;[19] the mutation may well have been a tribal peculiarity.

There is something else that must be taken into consideration. We possess indirect evidence that Abū ʿUbaida's interpretation must in fact be quite near to the mark. Ibn Hišām in his recension of Ibn Isḥāq's *Life of the Prophet* records a few lines from a *qaṣīda* of the Quraishite poet ʿUbaidallāh b. Qais ar-Ruqayyāt[20] which deal with the episode of the Elephant. One of the lines goes as follows:

wa-stahallat ʿalaihimu-ṭ-ṭairu bi-l-ğandali ḥattā ka'annahu marğūmu

"The birds poured down on them solid rock till it was as if stoned"[21]

The identification of *siğğīl* with *ğandal* "stone, rock" which is suggested by this line is especially plausible when we take into consideration that the poet was not forced by the metre (*ḫafīf*) to choose the word *ğandal*. Had he wanted to convey the meaning

xi, 82; az-Zamaḫšarī, *al-Kaššāf*, *ad* cv, 4; *Lisān al-ʿArab*, s.v. √ *s ğ l*; *Tafsīr Ibn Kaṯīr*, *ad* xi, 82.

[14] The first hemistich is not quoted by Abū ʿUbaida and is here taken from *LA*, *loc. cit*. For different versions, see *inter alia*, *LA*, s.v. √ *s ğ n* and Buḫārī, *loc. cit*.

[15] *LA*, s.v. √ *r f n*.

[16] See H. Fleisch, *Traité de philologie arabe*, i (Beirut 1961), 75-6.

[17] Born before Islam, died after 60/680; see *GAS*, ii, 245-7.

[18] See *GAS*, *loc. cit*., nn. 12 and 17, and also Ibn Ḥazm, *Ğamharat ansāb al-ʿArab*, ed. ʿAbd as-Salām Muḥammad Hārūn (Cairo n.d.), 288-9.

[19] See *EI*², *s.v.* "ʿĀmir b. Ṣaʿṣaʿa".

[20] Born after 10/631 in Mecca, died after 63/683; see *GAS*, ii, 418-19

[21] Ibn Hišām, *op. cit*., i, 61.

"baked brick" he might as well have used the not uncommon word *āğurr*,[22] which expresses precisely that. There is another aspect to the solution of the problem with which we are dealing and which I would like to put forward. It is again provided by Ṭabarī. After he has made clear (*ad* XI,82) that he thinks the Persian connection to be right, he nevertheless records, almost as an afterthought and without further commentary, on the authority of 'Atā' b. as-Sā'ib that Sa'īd b. Ğubair thought the word to be of mixed Persian and Nabataean origin. In the *Tafsīr Warqā'* we find the same opinion attributed to 'Ikrima (*ad* CV,4), also *'an* 'Atā' b. as-Sā'ib.[23] It is probable that the recensor of the *Tafsīr Warqā'*, Ādam b. Iyās, who found this opinion included by Warqā', thought fit to counterbalance it by a tradition which he found in a *Tafsīr* collection of Ḥammād b. Salma *'an* Ayyūb as-Siğistānī and Ḥumaid aṭ-Ṭawīl *'an* 'Ikrima that stated the Persian connection, which after all also was faithfully recorded by Warqā' *'an* Ibn Abī Nağīḥ *'an* Muğāhid, but, however, only in connection with XI,82.[24] Ṭabarī also records the reasoning of Ibn Ğubair. The word consists of the Persian *sig* and the Nabataean *īl*, because if it were wholly Persian, the second part should be *ğil*. But what does Ibn Ğubair's reasoning imply for the meaning of the word? Ṭabarī does not record explicitly what Ibn Ğubair's interpretation was, but it is apparently implicit in his etymology. It does not seem far-fetched to suppose that Ibn Ğubair viewed the element *īl* as being the same as the *īl* in such

[22] The word was already known before Islam, as appears from the *Diwān* of an-Nābiġa aḏ-Ḏubyāni, who died after 604 (*GAS*, II, 110-13). See Derenbourg's edition of the *Diwān*, poem 14, l. 16 in *JA*, 6e série, tome XII (1868), 282. It is also found in a poem by Badr b. 'Āmir, who took part in the conquest of Egypt (*GAS*, II, 263): J. G. L. Kosegarten, *The Hudsailian poems*, I (London 1854), poem 66, l. 10 on p. 125, listed in B. Lewin, *A vocabulary of the Huḏailian poems*, Acta Regiae Soc. Scient. et Litt. Gothoburgensis, Humaniora 13 (Goteborg 1978), 3. Another witness to the early occurrence of this loanword is Mālik b. Asmā' b. Ḫāriğa al-Fazārī, who died *ca.* 100/719 (*GAS*, II, 331-2), in *Kitāb al-Aġānī*, ed. Dār al-Kutub (Cairo 1927-73), XVII, 234; Ibn Qutaiba, *aš-Ši'r wa-š-Šu'arā*, ed. Aḥmad Muḥammad Šākir (Cairo 1966), 783; *idem*, 'Uyūn al-Aḫbār (Cairo 1343/1925), I, 314; *LA*, s.v. *ḫ ṣ ṣ*.

[23] *Kitāb at-Tafsīr*, *'an* Warqā b. 'Umar *'an* Ibn Abī Nağīḥ *'an* Muğāhid, Ms. Cairo, Dār al-Kutub, *tafsīr* 1075, fol. 93 verso. In the edition of 'Abd ar-Raḥmān aṭ-Ṭāhir b. Muḥammad as-Sūratī, which is called *Tafsīr Muğāhid* (Islāmābād n.d.), II, 782-3.

[24] *Op. cit.*, fol. 32 verso; as-Sūratī's ed., I, 306-7.

names as Ğibrīl;[25] in other words, that *siğğīl* should mean "stone of God".

Until not too long ago, this did not bring us much further on, although it was known, as Nöldeke had already pointed out, that the Arabs used the term "Nabataean" for the Aramaic speakers of the countryside of Syria and especially, in the case of grammarians and philologists, of Mesopotamia also.[26] In Aramaic, however, a word *siğğīl* or something like it with a meaning that would fit the Qur'anic contexts of the Arabic word was not known. Of course, the Aramaic word *sgīla*, a variant form of *sīgla*,[27] probably denoting a kind of bulrush, was known, as well as its Syriac cognate *segla*,[28] which probably is the kind of sedge that is scientifically known as *cyperus rotundus* and which is still called *siğal*[29] among the so-called Marsh Arabs of Southern Iraq. Obviously, a connection with the Qur'anic *siğğīl* was out of the question.

Fortunately, however, a new Aramaic word *sgyl* has turned up. In 1968 Fu'ād Ṣafar published inscriptions which have been found on the south wall of the great northern *īwān* of the Central Temple complex at Hatra.[30] Some of these inscriptions, numbers 240, 244, 245 and 246, immortalise the names of people

[25] Cf. *Tafsīr aṭ-Ṭabarī, ad* II, 97, where he records a number of traditions concerning the meaning of the names Ğibrīl and Mīkā'īl, all stating the equivalence *īl* = *allāh*. Among these appears, for instance, "Abū Kuraib related to us. He said, Ğābir b. Nūḥ al-Ḥimmānī related to us from al-A'maš, from al-Minhāl, from Sa'īd b. Ğubair, that Ibn 'Abbās said, 'Ğibrīl and Mīkā'īl are like the expression 'Abd Allāh'".

[26] Th. Nöldeke, "Die Namen der aramäischen Nation und Sprache", *ZDMG*, XXV (1871), 113-31, cf. 122-8.

[27] J. Levy, *Chaldäisches Wörterbuch über die Targumim*, etc. (repr. Cologne 1951), II, 144, "סִיגְלָא *m.* (syr. ܣܶܓܠܳܐ) eine Art Binsen, Gerte, juncus palustris, scirpus..." In his *Wörterbuch über die Talmudim und Midraschim* (Berlin 1924²), III, 475, Levy mentions the variant form סְגִילָא.

[28] R. Payne Smith, *Thesaurus syriacus* (Oxford 1901), II, col. 2525, "ܣܶܓܠ emph. ܣܶܓܠܳܐ, f. cyperus rotundus...". I. Löw, *Aramäische Pflanzennamen* (Leipzig 1881), 269 (no. 208), apparently considers סיגלא and ܣܓܠܐ to be the same plant = Cl. Ar. *su'd*.

[29] W. Thesiger, *The Marsh Arabs* (New York 1964), 62 (= Penguin ed., 70): "I learnt that, when they were grazing, they fed on *qat* ..., as well as *sijal*, a kind of sedge (*Cyperus rotundus*)...". It is to be noted that Thesiger's transcription apparently does not denote vowel length.

[30] Fu'ād Ṣafar, "Kitābāt al-Ḥaḍar", *Sumer*, XXIV (1968), 12-18 (Arabic part).

who contributed something (probably gold or silver) to *sgyl*. Ṣafar himself supposed that the word denotes the stately altar that filled the central part of the *īwān*. He used the word altar (*maḏbaḥ*) as a translation for *sgyl*, in analogy with Christian usage for what could be perhaps more precisely defined as an impressive sacrarium, where the treasures of the temple and its liturgic vessels and utensils were kept.[31] He further pointed out that the word was actually already known from a previously-found stone altar, albeit in a defective spelling. On this altar, described by Teixidor in 1965, the short line *sgl dšmš* was inscribed. Teixidor connected the word *sgl* with the Hebrew root *sgl* "to acquire property" and the Aramaic *sgula* "acquisition" or "property", and proposed the translation "(altar) property of Shamash".[32] Ṣafar himself gave the additional connection with the Akkadian *sikiltu* "hoard".[33] In fact, Teixidor used some legerdemain by supplying the word "altar" between brackets; he apparently realised that the obvious interpretation would be simply "altar of Shamash". After the four above-mentioned inscriptions were published, it was quickly found out that a puzzle in line 6 of inscription no. 107 could be solved, in that the line should be re-read in order to contain the word *sgyl*. Thus we find mentioned ... *byt ḥdy' 'ly' dy sgyl hykl' rb' dy bn' brmryn lšmš* ... "... the elevated house of joy of the SGYL of the great temple, which Barmaren has built for Shamash ...", Many proposals for the precise meaning of *sgyl* have since been brought forward, ranging from the cautious "part of the building" to a suggestion that it may be the name of the great temple itself, and as such a reminescence of Esangila, the great temple of Marduk at Babylon.[34] However,

[31] *Op. cit.*, 13: "wa-nuraǧǧiḥu anna kalimata 'sǧīl' al-wāridata fī hāḏihi-l-kitābāt ta'nī-l-maḏbaḥa-l-faḫma-llāḏī kāna yamla'u ṣadra hāḏa-l-'īwāni ..." and also: "wa-'aẓunnu annahā musta'malatun fi-l-ḥaḍari bi-ma'na kunūzi-l-ma'badi wa-l-binā'i-llāḏī tūḍa'u fīhi tilka-l-kunūzu wa-hāḏa-l-binā'u aṭlaqnā 'alaihi kalimata-l-maḏbaḥi muqtabisīna ḏālika mina-l-kanā'izi-l-masīḥiyyati wa-lākinnahu fi-l-ḥaḍari 'ibāratun 'an ma'badin mušayyadin fī ṣadri-l-'īwāni ..."

[32] J. Teixidor, "The altars found at Hatra", *Sumer*, XXI (1965), 85-92 (European part), see p. 87.

[33] *Op. cit.*, 13. Fu'ād Ṣafar also supposes that there may be a connection with the Arabic *siǧǧīl* or the Latin *sigillum*. For the connection of the Akkadian *sikiltu* and the Aramaic *sgula*, see also S.A. Kaufman, *The Akkadian influence on Aramaic* (Chicago 1974), 93, s.v. *suk/gallu*.

to me there seems to be no conclusive argument why Fu'ād Ṣafar's original proposal should not be retained, sc. that here also it means the "sacrarium of the great temple".

By now it should be clear what my suggestion about the development of the Hatran Aramaic word *sgyl* will be: smooth hard stone →altar stone → altar → sacrarium. The plausibility of such a development of meaning is enhanced by the abovementioned interpretation of Sa'īd b. Ğubair for the Arabic word. Moreover, perhaps Ibn Ğubair's etymology may be seen as an indication whence the word *siğğīl* was borrowed by the Arabs; the region where both a Persian and an Aramaic influence was felt, i.e. the Ğazīra, where the ancient Hatra was located. But there is more. The above suggestion is not based on a mere wish to provide us with an acceptable etymology for the Arabic word; I agree with Fu'ād Ṣafar that there is an Akkadian connection too.

If we take into consideration what Abū 'Ubaida stated about the meaning of *siğğīl* as illustrated by the line of Ibn Muqbil, it does not astonish us to establish that there must be a connection with the Sumerian loanword in middle and late Akkadian *sikillu*, or *śigillu* in its Ugaritic spelling, which denotes a kind of stone; to be more precise, it is as *abnu barīḫu* "a smooth, shiny stone" or *aban elli*, *aban telilti* "stone of purity" that we find it defined in bilingual glossaries.[35] It does not seem too bold to suppose that the Aramaic *sgyl* may be a direct or indirect loan from the Akkadian and that it passed from Aramaic into Arabic in the form *siğğīl*. After all, the example of the Arabic loanword *āğurr* "baked brick", which is the same as the Syriac *agūrrā* and which was almost certainly borrowed from the Akkadian *agurru*, may sufficiently show the plausibility of such an ety-

[34] See H. J. W. Drijvers, "Mithra at Hatra?", *Acta Iranica, Ser. 3, Textes et Mémoires, IV, Études Mithriaques* (Tehran-Liège 1978), 151-86. On pp. 160-1, inscr. no. 107 is discussed, and in n. 45 the word *sgyl* is commented upon and bibliographical references are given. The occurrence of the term *esangila* in an Aramaic inscription from the Teima oasis (KAI 228a) seems rather questionable.In l. 16, the name SNGL' or ŠNGL' occurs in a series of three gods. To me, it seems more likely to suppose that we have here a combination of Sin and his wife Ningal (= Sinniggal?) than to suppose that the name of a temple was taken as the name of a God, especially as no other examples of such a use of the name Esangila are known.

[35] W. von Soden, *Akkadisches Handwörterbuch*, II (Wiesbaden 1972), 1041, s.v. *sikillu*: "(2) ein Halbedelstein?".

mology.[36] Incidentally, the Akkadian homonym *sikillu*, also a Sumerian loanword,[37] probably followed a similar course; it denotes a kind of plant, which after all may be the same as the Syriac *segla* and the Aramaic *sigla/sgīla* and which is still known by the Marsh Arabs as *siğal*.[38]

In view of the existence in Arabic of such pairs as *laqafa* and *lağafa* "to break into the side of a well" or *ba'q* and *ba'ğ* "fissure, crack, split" (to be connected with the Hebrew √ *b q '* "to split, cleave"), it is tempting to connect also *saqala*, which is an old dialect variant of *ṣaqala* "to smooth, to polish".[39] Similarly, in view of such correspondences as Hebr. √ *p s q* D with Arabic *fašağa* (and also *fasağa*) G and D "to sprawl one's legs", and Hebr. √ *ẓ ' q* "to utter a plaintive cry, to call to aid" with Arab. *ẓa'aqa*, but also *ẓa'ağa*, I think there may be a connection too with the well-known Hebrew √ *s q l*.[40] This root, which is only used as a verb (with or without bā'ᵃvānīm), means in G and D "to stone" and in D also privatively "to free from stones"; and this seems especially likely, because there is no well-established etymology of this Hebrew root. Yet it may be that this would carry us too far into the field of speculation.

To summarise my suggestion for the etymology and meaning of the Qur'anic *siğğīl*. A non-Semitic word, Sumerian or what was already a loanword in Sumerian, attested in Akkadian as *sikillu* or *šigillu* and denoting a smooth kind of stone, entered Aramaic (via Akkadian or otherwise)[41] as *sgyl* or *sgl* (probably for **sigil*), denoting the same or a similar kind of stone. In Hatran Aramaic, it had acquired the specialised meaning of

[36] D. Cohen, *Dictionnaire des racines sémitiques*, fasc. 1 (Paris-The Hague 1970), 7, s.v. √ *' g r*; S. Fraenkel, *Die Aramäischen Fremdwörter im Arabischen* (Leiden 1886, repr. Hildesheim 1962), 5.

[37] Von Soden, *op. cit.*, 1041, s.v. *sikillu* (1).

[38] See above, nn. 27-9.

[39] See *LA* under the respective roots.

[40] See for the Hebrew roots, L. Koehler and W. Baumgartner, *Lexicon in Veteris Testamenti libros* (Leiden 1958), and for the Arabic roots *LA*. Cf. also the name of the river Tigris: Hebrew *hiddäqäl*; Aramaic *diqlat* and *diglat*; and Arabic *diğla*.

[41] A direct loanword into Aramaic (at least via Assyrian) would make a form written with a *šīn* more likely. See Kaufman, *op. cit.*, 140-2. Because the word *sikillu* may be considered as a so-called "culture word", the caveat of Kaufman, *op. cit.*, 18-19, is not out of place here: "In such cases, not only is the ultimate origin of the name in doubt, but even the direction and process of its spread from one language to another is less than certain".

"altar stone",[42] and from there "altar" or "sacrarium". Quite early this word had entered the Arabic dialects of the neighbouring desert, and had spread southwards with a probable meaning of "smooth, hard stone". The verse of Ibn Muqbil may be seen as additional proof that, at least shortly after the death of the Prophet, the word was known as such in Central Arabia. All this would suggest that the Qur'anic expression *ḥiǧāra min siǧǧīl* should best be translated by something like "stones of flint", and this after all is no great surprise.

[42] Such a specialised meaning may well have been expressed by a special form like **saggīl* for "altarstone", of which the Arabic equivalent form would be *siǧǧīl* (cf. Aramaic *ṣaddīq* and *sakkīn*, Arabic *ṣiddīq* and *sikkīn*). on the other hand, an Aramaic **sgīl* could also produce Cl. Ar. *siǧǧīl* (with secondary gemination) because a form **siǧīl* would be considered dialectal. However, *saǧīl* would also be a possible Cl. Ar. rendering of a dialectal **siǧīl*; cf. W. Wright, *A grammar of the Arabic language*[3] (repr. Cambridge 1964), I, 136, and, indeed, this form is also recorded in the *LA*, s.v. √ *s ǧ l*: *wa-s-saǧīl aṣ-ṣulb aš-šadīd*.

TWO NOTES

Michael B. Schub

1. An Eternal Question ?

Although everyone agrees that too much has already been written about the "outside influences"[1] on the Prophet, we note here that one of the foremost scholars of the Arabic language of all time, ĞALĀL AD-DĪN AS-SUYŪṬĪ[2] (1443-1505), believed that the word *'aḫlada* in Qur'ān 7.176/175 is of Hebrew origin[3,4].

The root √*ḫld* in its various forms, all with the basic meaning "to be eternal", occurs over 80 times in the Qur'ān, excluding our verse. But here, we have: *wa-law šī'nā la-rafa^cnāhu bi-hā wa-lakinnahū 'aḫlada 'ilā l-'arḍi wa-ttaba^ca hawāhu* "And had We willed We could have raised him by their means, but he clung to the earth and followed his own lust."[5]

As noted, AS-SUYŪṬĪ accepts AL-WĀSIṬĪ's contention that *'aḫlada* in conjunction with *'ilā l-'arḍi* here is the Hebrew equivalent to the Arabic *raka/ina* "to lean to, incline to". Thus we seem to have here a *hapax legomenon* (according to these two above-mentioned authorities): that is, the root √*ḫld* has a unique signification here, quite different from its other 80+ Qur'ānic occurences.

But is this attributable to Hebrew?!

The standard modern work in this area is ARTHUR JEFFERY's *The Foreign Vocabulary of the Qur'an*[6], which if anything, is *too* thoroughly extensive. But in this work JEFFERY does not mention the root √*ḫld*: his answer to our question is a resounding no.

In early Hebrew, this root occurs in Psalms 49,2: Give ear, all you inhabitants of *ḥeled* (that is "the world" = Ar. *al-'arḍ*)". By the process of semantic extension, this term came to signify "man's limited span of life on earth" somewhat paralleling the Ar. *ad-dunyā* "this *lower* existence"[7] for "the world" (or, even in some modern dialects now, "the weather"). So in Psalms 39, 6: "Look, you have made my days but a few hand-breadths, and my *ḥeled* 'lifetime' is nothing before you".

In later Hebrew, under Aramaic influence, this root came to mean "to dig in or under the earth". Cf. Heb. *ḥōled* = Ar. *ḫuld* "mole".

That Muḥammad was acquainted, at least indirectly, with the Psalter, is irrefragable:

1 Specifically, too much *ḥibr* has been spilled about the alleged influence of the *'aḥbār*.

2 For his beautifully edited autobiography, cf. SARTAIN, E.M., *Jalāl al-dīn al-Suyūṭī*, (2 vols.), Cambridge 1975. V. p. vii: "The proper assessment of al-Suyūṭī's contribution as a scholar is a task which must be left to specialists in each of the fields in which al-Suyūṭī worked."

3 *al-'Itqān fī ^culūm al-Qur'ān*. Cairo, 1951. p. 137, *in medio*, quoting AL-WĀSIṬĪ's *'Iršād*: *qāla l-wāsiṭiyyu fī l-'iršādi 'aḫlada 'ilā l-arḍi raka/ina bi-l-^cibriyyati*.

4 This root presents difficulties in Ethiopic, too. Cf. DILLMANN, A., *Lexicon Linguae Aethiopicae*, 1865 (=Reprint Osnabrück 1970), p. 579, col. 2, *in initio*: "rad., cujus significatio plane incerta est ... sed hoc scholion ad explanandum locum sequentum nihil efficit."

5 PICKTHALL, M., *The Meaning of the Glorious Koran*. Mentor, NY. 1953, p. 135, *in initio*.

6 Baroda 1938.

7 Indeed, AL-BAYḌĀWĪ, following AZ-ZAMAḪŠARĪ, paraphrases *'aḫlada 'ilā l-arḍi* as: *māla 'ilā d-dunyā 'aw 'ilā s-safālati* "he inclines to the *dunyā*, or to baseness." (*Beidhawii Commentarius in Coranum*, ed. H.O. FLEISCHER, 1846-1848 (=Repr. 1968), Vol. I, p. 352, *in initio*.

96

he uses the term for it, *zābūr*, three times in the Qur'ān[8]. The close connection in the Psalms between the root √*ḫld* and the concepts of "the earth" or "the mundane, lowly life of man contrasted to the sublimity of the heights to which, if any[9] man chooses, God is ready to elevate him", supports the contention of AL-WĀSIṬĪ and AS-SUYŪṬĪ.

Namely, that *'aḫlada 'ilā l-'arḍi* in Qur'an 7.176/175 represents an Arabic assimilation of an originally Hebrew Concept.

2. The Deconstruction of the Deconstruction: A New Translation of and Tafsir on Sūra 109

Sūra 109: (1) *qul yā 'ayyuhā l-kāfirūna* (2) *lā 'aᶜbudu mā taᶜbudūna* (3) *wa-lā 'antum ᶜābidūna mā 'aᶜbudu* (4) *wa-lā 'anā ᶜābidun mā ᶜabadtum* (5) *wa-lā 'antum ᶜābidūna mā 'aᶜbudu* (6) *lakum dīnukum wa-liya dīni.*

(1) Say: O Unbelievers! (2) I don't worship what you worship (3) And you don't worship what I worship (4) And I don't worship what you always worshipped (and always will worship) (5) And you don't worship what I worship (6) You have your religion and I have mine. (My translation)

The most striking feature of this text is its jingle-like cadence, what PARET calls "Schmucklosigkeit ihres Stils"[1]. The Prophet Muḥammad himself testified[2] to its soporific monotony by saying (to Farwa b. Nawfal al-'Ašǧaᶜī's father): "If you begin to recite Sūrat al-Kāfirīna on lying down in bed, you'll be asleep by the time you get to the end of the sixth verse (i.e. by the time your head hits the pillow)". This Ḥadīṯ is related to us by ABŪ ᶜALĪ AL-FAḌL B. AL-ḤASAN AṬ-ṬABARSĪ (d. ca. 1153, and thus a contemporary of AZ-ZAMAḪŠARĪ), the Šīᶜite Qur'ān exegete, in his edifying commentary *Maǧmaᶜ al-Bayān li-Tafsīr* (or, *li-ᶜUlūm*) *al-Qur'ān*; he transmits this Ḥadīṯ as a testimony of this Sūra's excellence (*faḍluhā*). He claims also that recitation of this Sūra is worth the recitation of fully one-quarter of the entire Qur'ān[3].

In this apologetic mode, AṬ-ṬABARSĪ reminds us that one of the rhetorical devices used by Arabs for emphasis and teaching (*'ifhām*) is repetition[4]. Thus an Arab may answer a question with "yes, yes" or "no, no". True true.

Structure of the Sūra

Firstly, Muḥammad has the last word, namely "My religion". About the final and sixth verse, PARET aptly states: "Sie klingt wie ein Kampfruf"[5].

The first verse is a command to the Prophet to address the unbelievers; a tone of warning may be inferred.

Verses 2 - 5 all begin with a negative *lā* in the first part, and with a nominalizing *mā* in the second. These particles are followed by the imperfect tense (of root √*ᶜbd* four (4) times; the active participle of the same root three (3) times; and, in what PARET refers to as "Störung des Parallelismus membrorum"[6] the perfect tense once.

PARET considers that this disturbing appearance of the perfect tense in the second part of v. 4, *without the corresponding change to the perfect tense in the first part of that verse*, was adequately interpreted by the Qur'ān exegete AL-BAYḌĀWĪ (d. 1286); he explained that in the recent past the unbelievers had worshipped idols, *but the*

8 At Q 4.161; Q 17.57; and Q 21.105

9 The commentators agree that probably no specific person, but rather every person, is referred to in Q 7.176/175.

1 PARET, R., *"Sure 109."* Der Islam 39 (1964) 197-200

2 ṬABARSĪ, *Maǧmaᶜ* ... Repr. of 1339-1379 ed. (ca. 1965), (GAL I 405). Vol. 9+10, p. 551

3 ṬABARSĪ, loc. cit.

4 ṬABARSĪ, loc. cit.

5 PARET, loc. cit.

6 PARET, loc. cit.

Prophet had not yet found God. Hence PARET's translation: "4. Und ich verehre nicht, was ihr (bisher immer) verehrt habt"[7].

Pace PARET (and AL-BAYḌĀWĪ), I see the key to the problem in the perfect tense form *ᶜabadtum*, by Pan! The actual function of this form is not to limit action in time, but just the opposite! It *identifies* the unbelievers (as if *by definition*) as past, present, and future idolaters: this is their quintessence. *'antum 'antum 'ay ᶜalā ḥālikum* "You are you; that's the way you are", as IBN ᶜARABĪ's disciple AL-QAŠĀNĪ put it in his mystical *tafsīr*[8].

This use of the perfect tense (and sometimes the imperfect[9]), I have termed PANCHRONIC (cf. JSS 27, 1982). It is the failure to recognize the panchronic function of *ᶜabadtum* here that has resulted in frantic attempts at interpretation and the jangle and discord of the marvelously chaotic (mis)translations into European (and non-European) languages of this tantalyzingly trenchant text.

أنا أبو النجم وشعرى شعرى

7 PARET, loc. cit.

8 IBN ᶜARABĪ, M. *Tafsīr al-Qur'ān al-Karīm*. Beirut 1968, Vol. 2, p. 863, *in medio*.

9 Cf. Exodus 3:14 *ehyeh-asher-ehyeh* ≙ *'akūnu llāḏī 'akūnu*.

9

A PROPHET AND MORE THAN A PROPHET?: SOME OBSERVATIONS ON THE QUR'ĀNIC USE OF THE TERMS "PROPHET" AND "APOSTLE"

W.A. Bijlefeld

The choice of this topic is far from original. Besides numerous shorter references to this subject in many general surveys of Islam,[1] some widely-known Islamic scholars have discussed this issue at considerable length. To this latter group belong, among others, Pautz (1898),[2] Caetani (1905),[3] Wensinck (1924),[4] Horovitz (1926),[5] Ahrens (1935),[6] Jeffery (1950),[7] and Bell (1953).[8]

Whereas the only way of attempting to answer the criticism of staleness—and the suspicion of a mere repetition of what has been

---

[1] In most 'introductions' the two words are not distinguished (see below pp. 12 f.). This is true not only for the older surveys (such as e.g., Gibb, Guillaume, Massé, Sourdel), but also for such a recent publication as Caesar E. Farah's *Islam. Beliefs and Observances* (Woodbury, N.Y.: Barron's Educational Series, 1968), pp. 70-72. Of the exceptions to this rule I mention A. S. Tritton's *Islam. Belief and Practices* (London: Hutchinson University Library, 1951; 4th impression 1962), p. 49 (see below note 63) and Louis Gardet's *L'Islam, Religion et Communauté* (Paris: Desclée de Brouwer, 1967), esp. pp. 69 ff. (see below note 61).

[2] Otto Pautz, *Muhammed's Lehre von der Offenbarung quellenmässig untersucht* (Leipzig: J. C. Hinrichs'sche Buchhandlung, 1898), esp. pp. 220-264.

[3] Leone Caetani, *Annali dell 'Islām,* I (Milano: Libraio della Real Casa, 1905), 192-215.

[4] A. J. Wensinck, "Muhammed und die Propheten," *Acta Orientalia,* II (1924), 168-198.

[5] Josef Horovitz, *Koranische Untersuchungen* (Berlin-Leipzig: W. de Gruyter and Co., 1926), esp. pp. 44-47. Cf. also his *Jewish Proper Names and Derivatives in the Koran* (Ohio, 1925; reprint, Hildesheim: Georg Olms Verlagsbuchhandlung, 1964), pp. 78 f.

[6] Karl Ahrens, *Muhammed als Religionsstifter* (Leipzig, 1935; reprint, Nendeln, Liechtenstein: Kraus Reprint Ltd., 1966), esp. pp. 127-139.

[7] Arthur Jeffery, *The Qur'ān as Scripture* (New York: Russell F. Moore Co., 1952), esp. pp. 18-46. (This edition does not acknowledge the fact that all but the last fourteen pages are a photomechanical reprint of the series of four articles published, under the same title, in *The Muslim World,* XL [1950], 41-55, 106-134, 185-206, 257-275. In this article the reference to the book edition is followed by a reference to the *M.W.* articles.)

[8] Richard Bell, *Introduction to the Qur'ān* (Edinburgh: The University Press, 1953), pp. 145-148.

2

said before [9]—is through the following article itself, we need to deal explicitly with another, maybe even more important objection: why do we turn once again to a (at least here on earth) more than 1300-year-old literary document rather than directing our attention to the reality of the daily life of contemporary Muslims?

There is certainly every reason to note gratefully the growing awareness among historians of religions that they cannot conceive their task exclusively in terms of the study of religious systems—and that there is no justification at all for an *a priori* dealing with these systems as static, 'time-less' entities. [10] Yet the question arises whether the thesis that "the study of religion is the study of persons" [11] is not a somewhat reactionary move to another almost equally one-sided position. [12] Caution is needed also with regard to some other ideas implicit not infrequently in the plea to focus attention on the question of what the various religious traditions mean to those who live in them. First of all, history forbids us to overemphasize the newness of this approach. Tiele pointed seventy years ago to the inadequacy of a purely descriptive-historical approach and to the need to understand 'man's inmost being,' "that religious spirit which is the true essence of religion," and Benjamin Constant remarked in 1824 that until that time the interest had been in 'the exterior side of religion' and that the history of 'the interior sentiment' was still to be written. [13] Secondly, there is no reason for the History of Religions to consider the reactions and convictions, beliefs and practices of contemporary men in any way as a more proper object of study than 'the living faith' of men who died hundreds or thousands of years ago. Some

---

[9] Especially in this case, since I summarized and discussed the main conclusions of the authors just mentioned in my *De Islam als na-Christelijke Religie* (Islam as a Post-Christian Religion) (Den Haag: van Keulen, 1959), pp. 136-148.

[10] This is not to deny that many believers look upon the fundamentals of their religious tradition as unchangeable and valid for all times because they see them as 'anchored in eternity' (see p. 3); the issue here is simply that one can not describe any 'religious tradition' adequately without relating it to a certain period in history, to specific geographical areas and to particular cultural and socio-economic conditions.

[11] W. Cantwell Smith, "Comparative Religion: Whither—and Why?", in *The History of Religions, Essays in Methodology,* ed. by M. Eliade and J. M. Kitagawa (Chicago: The University of Chicago Press, 1959), pp. 34 ff. Cf. also the same author's *The Meaning and End of Religion* (New York: Macmillan, 1962, 1963).

[12] I referred briefly to some of the issues raised in this paragraph in a bibliographical note "Trend in the contemporary discussion on 'Christians and Men of other Faiths'" in *The Hartford Quarterly,* VIII, 3 (1968), 50 ff., and deal with it more explicitly in a forthcoming article, mentioned in note 29.

[13] The references are given in *The Hartford Quarterly,* VIII, 3, pp. 51, 56, notes 12 and 13. For a contemporary statement in which a similar terminology is used cf. Smith in *History of Religions,* pp. 34 f. ("a study not only of tangible externals but of human hopes and aspirations and interpretations of those externals." "The externals of religion can be examined separately; and this is largely what in fact was happening until quite recently, perhaps particularly in European scholarship.")

historians of religions may be able to make an important contribution to the inter-religious dialogue of our days [14]—but we should be careful not to define the discipline itself in terms related to the urgent questions of the religiously pluriform world-society which, according to many, is emerging at this time. [15] Finally, historians of religions are not asked to evaluate the validity of the claim of millions of believers that 'the classical foundation' of their religious tradition remains the most meaningful issue to discuss. Even if we would limit ourselves to the contemporary Muslim world, the choice of a Qur'anic subject would still be fully justified on the basis that millions of now living Muslims continue to look upon the Qur'ān as being immediately relevant to our time and situation.

In a way this means reintroducing the notion of the 'others'. [16] Whatever our own conviction may be with regard to the challenge of the contemporary situation to religious traditions, notions and formulations, as historians of religions we do not question the conviction of those who expect the solution to every problem from a return to the classical formulations of their faith. This is not a lack of concern for others, but a respect for their conviction coupled with a concern about the proper limitations of the discipline with which we are dealing. Reacting against the emphasis on 'systems of thought' rather than on 'living people', as much as reacting against the attitude of those who saw in the people of other religions primarily potential converts to Christianity, some scholars come dangerously close to the point that their 'religious inclusivism' [17] begins to shape their work in the field of History of Religions.

The issue at stake is not disagreement with the theological position of those who wish to work towards the coming into being of one great,

---

[14] See the remarks of Smith, in *History of Religions*, pp. 47 ff. (with the controversial 'disqualification' of Kraemer as far as the role of chairman in an inter-religious dialogue is concerned, p. 50, and an important reference to the potential role of 'departments of comparative religion' for such a dialogue, p. 51; as far as the latter point is concerned, we think especially of the tremendous possibilities of the 'Departments of Religion' at some universities in Africa and Asia).

[15] A well-known representative of this interpretation of the History of Religions is Friedrich Heiler; cf. his "The History of Religions as a Preparation for the Co-operation of Religions," in *History of Religions*, pp. 132-160.

[16] Notwithstanding—and to a large extent in agreement with—Cantwell Smith's penetrating remarks on this habit of thinking of 'some of us' as 'others'; cf. *History of Religions*, pp. 34, 57f.

[17] An example of this 'imperialistic inclusivism' at the Christian side is, in my opinion, the vision of (all—many—some?) Muslims, Hindus, Buddhists, etc., as 'anonymous Christians', and that acknowledgment of 'truth' in all religions which 'explains' this fact and justifies this thesis with a reference to 'the latent Christ.' Whatever the validity of such statements may be in the perspective of Christian theology, this kind of openness for the truth of 'other religions' must be offensive to all those persons of other faiths who can not but interpret these expressions as a refusal to take the 'other religions' seriously on their own terms.

4

unified 'world religion';[18] who try to show the 'religious' implications of the conviction that "the human community is the only real community there is, and who, rejecting the last remnants of a 'parochial' theology, are open to a "new approach to universality."[19] Kenneth Cragg—to give one more example—has made it clear, in a most impressive way, that in the perspective of his theology there are no aliens and outsiders as far as God and faith are concerned: "Our discussions of God are not domestic matters. Indeed it is fair to say that where theology is the concern there are no outsiders."[20]

All of these statements are absolutely valid for those who share the (theological or philosophical) presuppositions on which they are based. But they are clearly invalid for those Muslims for whom theology *is,* in a certain sense, a domestic affair; who *do* divide mankind into people who accept and the people who reject the message of 'the Seal of the Prophets'; who link the notion of the 'Finality of Prophethood' with the idea of Islam as 'the final and perfect religion'.[21]

In this connection we wish to point also to Adams' significant reference to the fact that Islamicists of our time "cannot avoid affecting our Muslim contemporaries in quite vital ways" through their work.[22] The fact itself cannot be denied; some Islamicists unmistakably affect many Muslims nowadays—a few times perhaps by inspiring and stimulating them; much more frequently, it seems, by antagonizing them. Is it not better, the author then asks in a rhetorical question, "that we should become self-conscious about what we are

---

[18] That such a 'religion of mankind' will not arise out of conferences and discussions where representatives of various religious 'institutions' meet, but that a new 'charismatic leader' is needed, is emphasized by W. Montgomery Watt in his thought-provoking *Truth in the Religions* (Edinburgh: The University Press, 1963), p. 175: "To emphasize the central ideas of the one religion, and to express them in such a form that men become enthusiastic and physical energy is liberated requires, if not a new prophet, at least a creative individual or a series of such men."

[19] Wilfred Cantwell Smith challenges "the practitioner of comparative religion" to become "a participant in the multiform religious history of the only community there is, humanity"; *History of Religions,* p. 55. An example of the last mentioned approach can be found e.g. in the writings of Father Robley Edward Whitson. The specific reference here is to his "Religious Convergence and Commitment," *The Hartford Quarterly,* VIII (1968), 31-47.

[20] "Islamic Reflections on Contemporary Theology," *The Duke Divinity School Review,* XXXI (1966), 103.

[21] The reference is to the idea of Muḥammad as "the Seal of the Prophets," S. 33 : 40, and the concept of Islam as the 'completed', perfect religion, S. 5 : 3/5, the true religion which triumphs over whatever else is considered and accepted as religion, S. 61 : 9; 48 : 28; 9 : 33. The interpretation of Islam as *the* religion in the double sense of the (historical) fulfilment of original religions of the Jews and the Christians as well as the natural, original, 'primal' religion is the subject of my article "Islam's forstaelse af sig self," *Nordisk Mission Tidsskrift,* LXXIV, 2 (1963), 37-46; LXXIV, 3 (1963), 25-37.

[22] Charles J. Adams, "The History of Religions and the Study of Islām," in *The History of Religions. Essays on the Problem of Understanding,* ed. by J. M. Kitagawa (Essays in Divinity, I; Chicago-London: The University of Chicago Press, 1967), p. 193.

doing? And is not also an aspect of our very scholarship that we should seek this self-consciousness?" My reaction is that we should indeed be conscious of this dimension of the study of another religious tradition than our own — but that we should not look upon our work in the History of Religions as a means by which we *seek* to affect and influence in any way those who are living in the tradition which we are studying. For reasons which are valid seen from our theological-philosophical perspective we may feel it as our task and responsibility to exert influence on and bring about a change in that religious community—but this conviction and desire should not become one of the determining factors in our work in the History of Religions. Van der Leeuw's warning that the phenomenology of religion has no place for the question of the origin of religion [23] (with regard to any particular religious tradition we do not seek any other 'explanation' for its origin than that — or those — found in the tradition itself) [24] needs to be complemented by the warning that the subject of the future development of any religious tradition, the questions of modernization, rethinking and restructuring, can within the context of History of Religions come up only in as far as and in the way in which these questions are raised within that religious community itself. This point needs to be emphasized. Rather than accepting and enjoying the position of guests who, grateful for the opportunity to cross at least the threshold of the House of Islam, enter primarily to become acquainted and to understand, some non-Muslim historians of religions behave as if they have been called by the Muslims as counselors and advisers to restructure and redirect that household of faith which they themselves have decided not to join.

---

[23] I think of the passage on "the religion of Adam," in which he deals with the distinct tasks of theology, psychology and history of religions, as well as the following statement in his Preface: "In accordance with the view of Jaspers, I have tried to avoid, above all else, any imperiously dominating theory, and in this volume there will be found neither evolutionary, nor so-called anti-evolutionary, nor indeed any other theories. *More specifically, those which attempt to reveal the 'primary origin' of Religion have from the outset been excluded.*" [ital. mine]; *Phänomenologie der Religion* (Tübingen: J. C. B. Mohr, 1933, 2nd ed., 1956), pp. 669 and VI; in the English translation *Religion in Essence and Manifestation* (London: Allen and Unwin Ltd., 1938; reprint with additions as Harper Torchbook, New York-Evanston: Harper and Row, 1963; reprint Gloucester, Mass.: Peter Smith, 1967), pp. 591 and VI.

[24] It is for this reason that the well-known volumes of Joseph Campbell's *The Masks of God* (New York: The Viking Press; *Primitive Mythology*, 1959, 4th print 1968; *Oriental Mythology*, 1962; *Occidental Mythology*, 1964, 2nd print 1965; *Creative Mythology*, 1968) can, in my opinion, definitely not be classified as studies in the field of History of Religions. A science which is concerned with "a natural history of the gods" (*Primitive Mythology*, pp. 3-18) has its legitimate place among the academic disciplines, but needs to be distinguished very clearly from the History of Religions. Campbell is working on "a natural history of the gods and heroes, such as in its final form should include in its purview all divine beings, not regarding any as sacrosanct or beyond its scientific domain" (*op. cit.*, p. 5). For the History of Religions, too, no God or hero is "beyond its domain," but every God and every hero is sacred to it.

6

This notion of 'decision' leads us to the last point which has to come up in these introductory remarks. The question which still needs to be faced is whether we do take Islam itself seriously if our concern is exclusively to describe, know and understand what it means to *others* to belong to this community. Kenneth Cragg's warning remains with us:

> But for all its painstaking service to the understanding of Islam, scholarship in Islamics is not a final response to the muezzin. The mosque does not exist to be admired; nor the minaret to dominate a landscape. Nor does the Holy Book expect the devotion only of calligraphers. A purely artistic or academic interest in historical religion fails to do it justice. If Islam speaks of God and for God imperiously, God cannot be greeted with a mere agreement to study Him.
>
> This truth does not invalidate the scholarly duty to understand, to analyze, to explore Islam. It does affirm that such a duty remains partial, even when it is perfectly discharged. [25]

Taking Islam, the Prophet and his Message seriously, means — I wholeheartedly agree with Kenneth Cragg — that we cannot confine ourselves to studying the message which Muḥammad brought, but that we also have to respond to his call to conversion. That unavoidable decision leads us, however, once more outside the boundaries of the History of Religions. We can not live with History of Religions alone; [26] that would be as irresponsible as trying to live on bread alone. But in our academic disciplines we can and should distinguish clearly between these different types of concerns and responses. The Hartford Seminary Foundation will, I fully trust, in many ways continue to express its deep interest in the Church's answer to *The Call of the Minaret* [27] and in general in the significant issue of Christian presence in a religiously pluralistic world. But we do divide our tasks. The History of Religions program accepts with joy and pride its limitations. In this discipline we simply seek to know and understand, in as personal and as passionate a way as possible, what it means to live in the Muslim, the Hindu and the Buddhist tradition.

[25] Kenneth Cragg, *The Call of the Minaret* (New York: Oxford University Press, 1956), p. 174.

[26] Cf. Hendrik Kraemer's remark: "... these value-judgments are unavoidable because, without these, how could one classify religion? How could one Live?"; *Religion and the Christian Faith* (London: Lutterworth; Philadelphia: The Westminster Press, 1956), p. 139. If one sees within the framework of History of Religions a place for a classification as well as for a typology of religions, it is obvious that both subjects should be approached in such a way that the issue of value-judgments plays no part in this discussion. The thesis of an 'unavoidable' choice and response is, as stated above, valid, but raises an issue that falls outside the History of Religions.

[27] Cragg's epoch-making and in many ways unsurpassable study referred to in note 25, published while he was on the faculty of The Hartford Seminary Foundation.

In this discipline we try not to ask our own questions, let alone to impose our own answers on others; we attempt to let the 'others' speak to us (and this is true with regard to the text of the Qur'ān as much as with regard to a contemporary Muslim scholar), so that we may catch the questions which 'they' ask and hopefully begin to understand some of the answers which 'they' give or receive.

One additional qualification needs to be made. Taking Islam seriously in its claim to bring God's ultimate truth to mankind implies the necessity to answer the 'Call of the Minaret' as it sounds in the Muslim World, and not as 'rearranged' by us. A reference to Montgomery Watt can illustrate this point. At the end of his *Muḥammad, Prophet and Statesman*, the author introduces a section "Was Muḥammad a Prophet?" with the following remark:

> So far Muḥammad has been described from the point of view of the historian. Yet as the founder of a world-religion he also demands a theological judgment. [28]

And one of the next paragraphs contains what comes close to a definition of 'prophethood':

> Prophets . . . share in (what may be called) 'creative imagination'. They proclaim ideas connected with what is deepest and most central in human experience, with special reference to the particular needs of their day and generation. The mark of the great prophet is the profound attraction of his ideas for those to whom they are addressed.

In the context of our present discussion it is only a side-issue whether the History of Religions is that section of the discipline of History which is concerned with the religious traditions of mankind. My own conviction is that it is not. It is the combination of the 'historical' and the 'phenomenological' approach which makes the History of Religions an autonomous discipline with a character of its own. [29] Historians deal with the man Muḥammad, the son of ʿAbd Allāh, who claimed to be a prophet; historians of religions are concerned with the Prophet Muḥammad, studying the Qur'anic data, the relevant statements in later Muslim literature, [30] Muslim devotional life, the celebration of *mawlid al-nabī*, etc. But whether we distinguish between the historical and the religio-historical approach or not, Watt's second remark falls indeed outside the scope of our discipline. The issue at stake, then, is that we are in my opinion not responding to the Qur'anic appeal to believe in and to obey God and

---

[28] (London: Oxford University Press, 1961), pp. 237 f.

[29] Cf. my forthcoming article, "History of Religions as an Autonomous Discipline and its Relevance for Christian Theological Study," to be published in *Perspectives,* Journal of Pittsburgh Theological Seminary.

[30] Especially the literature on the *shamā'il* and *dalā'il al-nubuwwa* and the *Qiṣaṣ al-anbiyā'*.

8

His Prophet-Apostle if we base our answer on a concept of prophethood which is essentially non-Qurʾanic.[31] Only if at any time the Muslim community would reinterpret the Qurʾanic data on revelation so as to be in line with Montgomery Watt's concept of 'creative imagination'—as far as the Muslim *community* is concerned this may seem a purely hypothetical statement, but we have no right to exclude this possibility—could an answer to that appeal be given in terms of the recognition of Muḥammad as "a man in whom creative imagination worked at deep levels and produced ideas relevant to the central questions of human existence."[32]

These preliminary remarks were an attempt to answer the question of what it means to do justice to Islam. The answer is basically simple, elementary and obvious: that we take Islam seriously on its own terms. That implies, as stated, a decision with regard to its call to 'hear and obey'—and I am fully aware of the fact that for many Muslims a positive answer is the only way of really 'doing justice' to Islam[33]—a decision which lies outside the scope of the History of Religions. It also implies an honest attempt to describe, interpret and understand the Muslim tradition as far as possible[34] in its own categories and its own perspective. With regard to our particular subject this means that we do not approach the Qurʾanic data on prophets and apostles with a theory or doctrine of prophethood derived from other sources: Jewish,[35] Christian,[36] Mandaean or Manichaean.[37] One can rightly raise the question whether a com-

---

[31] An issue of which Montgomery Watt is obviously aware himself; cf. his remarks *op cit.*, pp. 239 f.

[32] *Op. cit.*, p. 240.

[33] A good example is Sharafuddīn's remark about the contribution which 'Western Orientalists' (can) make to the study of Islam: "No discussion is possible until this principle is recognized [the principle "that the Qurʾān is the undisputed Word of God revealed to Muḥammad the Apostle, and not the word of Muḥammad himself"], just as it is impossible to understand Islam without it" ʿAbduṣ-Ṣamad Sharafuddīn (ed.), *Majmūʿat Tafsīr Ibn Taimiyya* (Bombay: ad-Darul-Qayyimah, 1347/1954), p. 7.

[34] Many have discussed this question whether it is possible really to understand 'from within' any other religious tradition than one's own. In a sense we need to commit ourselves to a religious tradition in order to 'know its truth'.That issue has been raised frequently in another discipline, in connection with a new Testament statement, John 7:17, but it arises evidently with regard to any 'proclamation'.

The words "as far as possible" express therefore an extremely significant restriction. To be fully aware of this limitation does not mean, however, that one would give up the attempt to approach this ideal as closely as possible.

[35] Cf. Jeffery's survey of O.T. references to the prophets as an introduction to his discussion of the Qurʾanic material; *The Qurʾān*, pp. 22-26 (= *M.W.*, XL, 110-114).

[36] Cf. Wensinck, *Acta Orientalia*, II (1924), 170 f., 173 ff.; Horovitz, *Untersuchungen*, p. 49 f. (with a reference to Tor Andrae); Geo. Widengren, *Muḥammad, the Apostle of God, and his Ascension* (Wiesbaden: Otto Harrassowitz, 1955), pp. 7 ff., 65 ff., 170 ff. and *passim*.

[37] Cf. Ahrens, *Muhammed*, pp. 130-132, 154; Horovitz, *Untersuchungen*, p. 46; Widengren, *Muḥammad*, pp. 13, 55 ff., 127 ff.

parative study of various notions of prophethood contributes to our understanding of the Muslim (Qur'anic) data. My objection is to the practice of placing the Qur'anic material at the very outset of the investigation in the light of non-Muslim concepts and to interpret the Qur'anic data on the basis and in the context of these 'alien' notions. This is particularly harmful and confusing when the non-Muslim concept becomes a normative value-judgment. To give only one example, I refer to Ahren's *Muhammed als Religionsstifter*. One of the merits of this book is that the author in his discussion of the Qur'anic words 'prophet' and 'apostle' pays careful attention to the chronological order of the chapters of the Qur'ān. In this connection he observes—an issue with which we shall deal below—that the word *nabī* (prophet) is not applied to Muḥammad in any Meccan passage.[38] But rather surprisingly his book is divided into three main chapters of which the first one—dealing with the early Meccan period—describes Muḥammad as 'Prophet', the second and third ones as 'Teacher' and 'Lawgiver'. In other words, according to the author, Muḥammad can best be described as a Prophet for that early period during which the Qur'ān does not apply this title to him at all, whereas this title is less appropriate for the period after 622, when the Qur'ān emphatically refers to Muḥammad as such. In his preface Ahrens stated that he would let the Qur'ān speak rather than the later Muslim tradition.[39] It is obvious that he allows the Qur'ān to speak only within the normative context of the Christian tradition.

The subtitle of this paper speaks about the *Qur'anic use* of the words 'prophet' and 'apostle'. This implies that I do not intend to define a Qur'anic 'theory' or 'doctrine' of prophethood.[40] We simply study the various contexts in which the words 'prophet' and 'apostle' are used, and try along this way to reach a fuller understanding of what these words meant to Muḥammad and those whom he addressed.[41]

The terms we want to discuss are *nabī* and *rasūl*. The first one, usually translated as 'prophet', occurs in the singular and in two plural forms seventy-five times.[42] There is no need to discuss here

[38] *Op. cit.*, pp. 127 f., 154 f.

[39] *Op cit.*, p. VII.

[40] Notwithstanding the many inacceptable statements in H. Th. Obbink's article "Denker of Profeet," *Theologische Studiën*, XXI (1903), 35-59 (reprinted in a volume of essays by H. Th. Obbink, Amsterdam: H. J. Paris, 1939, pp. 1-28), this contribution remains important as one of the early warnings in "the West" not to see Muḥammad as 'a systematic thinker', but as an enthusiastic preacher-prophet, and therefore to be extremely careful with a definition of 'the Qur'anic doctrine' on any point.

[41] The reason is obvious I hope, why the formulation "what these words meant to Muḥammad" is used instead of the still more common but totally inacceptable expression "what Muḥammad meant with these words."

[42] The two plural forms are *nabiyūn* (sixteen times, of which three Meccan) and *anbiyā'* (five times, all Medinan: 2:91/85; 3:112/108, 181/177; 4:155/154—in all

10

in detail the various etymological interpretations, of which two interestingly different surveys are easily accessible in Jeffery's *The Foreign Vocabulary of the Qurʾān* [43] and in the article *"nabī"* in Lane's *Lexicon.* [44] It is striking to see how easily an etymological problem can become a theological issue. The main point in discussion is that of the relation between the genuine Arabic word *naba'a* and the noun *nabī*, which, according to Jeffery and many other Western scholars, "in the meaning of 'prophet' is a borrowing into Arabic from the Judaeo-Christian tradition." [45] None of the major Western studies of the concept of prophethood in the Qurʾān mentioned in the beginning of this article deals in any detail with the verb, in some cases apparently because the author is convinced that the verb is irrelevant for our understanding of the noun *nabī.* [46] A study of the use of *naba'a* in the Qurʾān (forty-six times in the IInd, four times in the IVth and once in the Xth form) makes it evident that in several cases it is indeed not related to the notion of prophethood. [47] It is worth noticing,

---

four cases in the statement: "they killed the prophets," see below note 97—and S. 5:20/23.

[43] (Baroda: Oriental Institute, 1938), p. 276.

[44] I, 8 (London: Williams and Norgate, 1893), 2752 f. (Cf. also note 46 below.)

[45] *The Qurʾān*, p. 20 (= *M.W.*, XL, 108).

[46] The issue of the etymology of the noun *nabī* can and in my opinion needs to be distinguished from the question as to what this word meant to Muḥammad. As far as the etymology is concerned, *nabī* has been seen as derived from نبا in its meaning: to be high, elevated (cf. Jeffery, *Vocabulary*, p. 276, note 3, and Lane's *Lexicon*, I, 8, 2753 end second and beginning third column: نَبْوَةٌ as 'conspicuous, evident' or 'elevated') or from *nabaʾa* in the IInd and IVth form (see note 47). An important point in the discussion is the absence of a hamza in نَبِيّ (Lane's note on the Meccan dialect form نَبِيْءٌ is of interest here). It is most likely for this reason that Hans Wehr's *Dictionary of Modern Written Arabic* (English translation ed. by J. Milton Cowan; Ithaca: Cornell University Press, 2nd printing, 1966) lists نبى and نبوّة under نبا (to be far off, distant, to move away; p. 941) and نبأ and نبوءة under نبأ (p. 937). A. de Biberstein Kazimirski's *Dictionaire Arabe-Français*, II (nouvelle éd., Paris: G.-P. Maisonneuve) lists نبىّ (as "chemin—terraine élevé—prophète") and نبوّة under نبا (p. 1190), نبىء and نبوّة under نبأ (p. 1179), both times with a cross reference to the other root. Confusing and misleading is Muḥammad Alī's remark that the 'dropping' of the hamza is the reason that "some authorities are of opinion that *nabī* is derived from *nubuwwat* meaning *the state of being exalted"*; *The Religion of Islam* (Lahore: The Aḥmadiyyah Anjuman Ishāʿat Islām, 1950), p. 219. No matter what the etymology of *nabī* is, it seems justified to study the use of the verb *nabaʾa* in the Qurʾān in order to see whether the words have anything in common in their meaning and usage.

[47] The verses in which the IVth and Xth forms are used are unrelated to the concept of 'prophethood' (2 : 31/29, 33/31 twice; 66 : 3; Xth form 10 : 53/54).

however, that the IInd form is used approximately ten times in the same context: on judgment day God will 'inform' men of all that they have done. The word has in these verses certainly the connotation of absolutely truthful, accurate and reliable information, while there is also the idea of a knowledge of what was kept hidden. [48] The same form occurs, with Muḥammad as subject, in the sense of proclaiming, informing men of what they do not know, of the judgment day, etc., nine times. [49] Of special interest in our context are also S. 3:49/43 (Jesus 'informs' the Jews of some of their actions of which he, humanly speaking, could not have any knowledge), and S. 9:64/65 (the *munāfiqūn* fear that a *sura* will be sent down which will inform them with regard to that which they conceal in their hearts). Moreover, the derivative *nabaʾ* (plural: *anbāʾ*; possible translations include news, rumor, story, history, information), occurring twenty-nine times, is found rather frequently in a context which is not unrelated to the ministry and the preaching of the prophets. From the fifteen cases where it is used in the singular, ten texts use it in the sense of the story (or history) of long past, religiously significant events, while in two or possibly three other texts 78:2; 38:67 and 6:67/66 it comes close to 'proclamation'. [50] The plural is used nine times for such histories of the past, and in three of these references we find the significant formula: *dhalika min anbāʾi ʾl-ghaybi*: "this belongs to the histories of what is hidden," obviously meaning that these events were not known in a natural way to anyone present. [51]

Before we discuss the word *nabī* any further we turn to some basic information on the second term, *rasūl.* It occurs two hundred and thirty-six times in the singular (in forty-nine suras) and ninety-five times in the plural (in thirty-six suras), a total of three hundred and thirty-one occurrences. [52] Another derivative of the same root *r s l,*

Pautz's remark (*Muhammads Lehre*, p. 222, note 4) that the Qurʾān uses the IVth form with the meaning of 'proclaiming' ("Verkündigen") is almost as surprising as his suggestion that the IInd form is identical with the Hebrew נִבָּא

Besides the verses listed in the two following notes as well as in the text above, the IInd form is used in S. 53:36/37; 54:28; 18:78/77; 12:15, 36, 37, 45; 10:18/19; 6:143/144; 13:33; 66:3.

[48] S. 41:50; 39:7/9; 35:14/15 (?); 6:60, 164; 62:8; 9:94/95 twice, 105/106; 5:48/53, 105/104.

[49] Four times in Suras of the middle Meccan period: S. 26:221; 15:49, 51; 18:103; once in the late Meccan Sura 34:7; and four times in Medinan passages: S. 3:15/13; 22:72/71; 66:3; 5:60/65.

[50] The ten texts referred to are: S. 26:69; 38:21/20 (middle Meccan); S. 14:9; 28:3/2; 10:71/72; 7:175/174; 6:34 (late Meccan); S. 64:5; 9:70/71; 5:27/30 (Medinan). Sura 78—early Meccan—has this word *al-nabāʾ* as title; the two other texts belong to the second and third Meccan period. The two former are used for the message which Muḥammad brings; the last one is used in a general sense.

[51] S. 54:4; 20:99; 18:13/12; 7:101/99; 11:100/102, 120/121 (all of them Meccan). The three specifically referred to are S. 11:49/51; 12:102/103; 3:44/39.

[52] A complete listing of these texts is unnecessary. Several of them are men-

mursal, is used thirty-six times, of which only twice in the singular. [53]

The rendering of *rasūl* as 'apostle' seems to commend itself because the verb *arsala* (IV) is a rather exact equivalent of the Greek ἀποστελλω; ἀπόστολος would be the obvious Greek translation for *rasūl,* [54] and therefore we render it in most cases in English as 'apostle', although in a small number of texts the more general 'messenger' is the only acceptable translation. [55] The verb *arsala* is used one hundred and thirty-five times, of which approximately eighty times in connection with the sending of apostles and prophets. [56] Finally the word *risāla* is used ten times. [57]

This brief survey of occurrences is more than just a matter of statistics. The striking difference in frequency of these words (75 contrasting with 331) raises questions with regard to the still widely

---

tioned later on in this article in the discussion of their usage. The division over the various periods is:

	singular	plural	total
early Meccan	7	1	8
middle Meccan	31	9	40
late Meccan	24	48	72
Medinan	174	37	211

The singular and plural being used frequently in the same chapters, we find both forms or either one of them in a total of sixty-one suras.

[53] The singular is found in S. 7:75/73; 13:43 (both late Meccan). The plural is used

early Meccan:	1
middle Meccan:	26
late Meccan:	6
Medinan:	1

[54] This is not to deny the evident fact which Wensinck, Horovitz and Widengren have stressed, that "although رَسُول corresponds to the Christian terms ἀπόστολος and שליחא, the designations of 'apostle', the Ḳur'ān *never* uses رَسُول of the 'apostle' in the New Testament Christian meaning of the word"; Widengren, *Muḥammad,* p. 15.

[55] Generally speaking *mursal* makes the impression of being somewhat less a *terminus technicus* than *rasūl*; the verses in which *mursal* is used in an entirely different way are S. 27:35 (the queen's messengers); S. 15:57 and 51:31 (angelic messengers to Ibrāhīm); S. 15:61 (angelic messengers to Lūṭ). In S. 77:1 it is used in the plural feminine, perhaps referring to winds (early Meccan).

Rasūl is used for the king's messengers in S. 12:50 and for angels in S. 42:51 (mediators of revelation); 35:1 (as messengers); 11:69/72; 29:31/30 (messengers to Ibrāhīm); 11:77/79, 81/83; 29:33/32 (messengers to Lūṭ); 6:61; 7:37/35 (angels of death); 43:80; 10:21/22 (angels responsible for the Heavenly Record of man's deeds); 19:19 (God's *Rūḥ,* the archangel, to Mary).

[56] In connection with God's sending of (human) messengers it is used for Muḥammad twenty-one times, for Nūḥ six times, for both Ibrāhīm and Yūnus once, for Mūsā eight times, for both Ṣāliḥ and for Hūd twice, in general (or especially: among the Children of Israel) thirty-seven times.

Almost 80 per cent of the verses in which the verb is used belong to the middle and late Meccan period.

[57] Twice in middle Meccan, six times in late Meccan and twice in Medinan passages. It is used in general S. 72:28; 6:123/124; 33:39; in connection with Muḥammad S. 72:23/24; 5:67/71; for Nūḥ, Hūd, Ṣāliḥ, Shuᶜayb and Mūsā in S. 7:62/60, 68/66, 79/77, 93/91, 144/141.

spread opinion that the words *nabī* and *rasūl* are used interchangeably in the Qurʾān. How common this tendency is not to distinguish the two words is clear not only from the usual rendering of the *shahāda,* as if it would be the confession that "there is no God but Allāh and that Muḥammad is His Prophet" (whereas the Arabic speaks about him as God's *rasūl*), but also in many listings of the doctrines of Islam in the series Allāh, Angels, Books, Apostles, Last Day and Predestination, where frequently—one of the remarkable instances is such an excellent text as Jeffery's *Islam* [58]— the 'Apostles' are replaced by the 'Prophets'. [59]

There are, however, in Muslim as well as in non-Muslim literature, many exceptions to this practice of treating the two words as being interchangeable. A very significant case is the widely accepted opinion that Sura 96 forms the beginning of Muḥammad's ministry as a prophet, while the task of being an apostle began with the revelation of Sura 74:

> *fa kāna fī nuzūl sūrat IQRA nubuwwatuhu*
> *wa fī nuzūl surat AL-MUDDATHTHIR risālatuhu.* [60]

The implicit interpretation of the words *nabī* and *rasūl* clearly is that a prophet is a person who receives a revelation from God and that only when he is called to proclaim that message publicly is he also called an apostle. This is indeed the way in which many Muslim scholars have defined these two words explicitly. In his catechism Jazā'irī answers the question of what the meaning of 'prophet' is in the following way:

> The prophet is a person to whom a Law (*Sharᶜ*) has been revealed, even if he is not instructed to proclaim it. And if he is instructed to proclaim it, he is also called an apostle. Therefore is every apostle a prophet, but not every prophet an apostle. [61]

---

[58] Arthur Jeffery, *Islam-Muḥammad and his Religion* (New York: The Liberal Arts Press, 1958), pp. 130 ff. Another author who does not distinguish between the two words is C. C. Torrey, *The Jewish Foundation of Islam* (New York: Jewish Institute of Religion Press, 1933), pp. 64 ff.

[59] For the expression "God and His apostles" see note 91; "God-Angels-Apostles" is used in S. 2:98/92; "God-Angels-Scriptures-Apostles" in S. 2:285 and 4:136/135 (the last one with the addition: "the Last Day"). S. 2:177/172 has the 'unusual' form: God-Last Day-Angels-Book-Prophets. The traditions and creeds have—without exception?—God-Angels-Books-*Apostles*-Last Day; cf. A. J. Wensinck, *The Muslim Creed* (Cambridge: The University Press, 1932, reprint 1965), pp. 23, 35, 188, etc.

[60] Ḥusayn b. Muḥammad b. al-Ḥasan al-Diyārbakrī, *Taʾrīkh al-khamīs fī aḥwāl anfas nafīs,* I (Cairo, 1302), 319. In the quotation by Th. Nöldeke-F. Schwally, *Geschichte des Qorāns,* I (Leipzig: Dieterich'sche Buchhandung, 1909), 86 f., the word نزول prior to اقرأ has been omitted.

[61] Ṭāhir b. Ṣāliḥ al-Jazāʾirī, *al-Jawāhir al-Kalāmiyya, fī īḍāḥ al-ᶜaqīda al-islamiyya* (Cairo, 1919), p. 29. This interpretation is accepted by Gardet, *L'Islam,* p. 69.

14

Nabī is seen as the wider notion, the more general one (*aᶜammu*), and the apostles are prophets with a special assignment.

This Muslim definition has been discussed by several Orientalists. Wensinck defended in 1924 the thesis that the distinction between 'prophet' and 'apostle' was not a post-Qur'anic development, and that already in the Qur'ān itself the category of the apostles relates to the larger group of prophets as "the great heroes of history to their epigons." [62]

> According to Muḥammad's view the Apostle stands as founder and leader at the beginning of a series formed by his representatives, the prophets. [63]

Horovitz, agreeing with Wensinck in so far that he, too, believes that the two words have distinctive meanings in the Qur'ān, rejects Wensinck's definition of this relationship. [64] Before we discuss their interpretations, two other authors must be mentioned who expressed themselves on this question whether the words *nabī* and *rasūl* are synonyms or not. Bell seems to affirm this question. He writes (referring to the *rasūl* as 'messenger'):

> Under the influence of Jewish and Christian ideas, ... and especially the story of Moses, the messenger or prophet, *nabīy*, as in early Medinan times he came to be called, assumed higher status. [65]

Somewhat confusing is the paragraph which Jeffery devoted to this issue:

> Apparently he [Muḥammad] made no special distinction between the two names *rasūl* and *nabī*. The later theologians made a definite distinction between them, taking *nabī* to be a word of wider significance than *rasūl*... The Qur'ān does not support such a distinction. If anything the Qur'anic evidence would seem to point the other way and suggest that the *nabī* was the narrower term, the prophet being a special class among the messengers. [66]

Muḥammad 'made no special distinction' ... but the Qur'ān 'seems to point to' a certain distinction. Whatever that means, even after Wensinck and Horovitz, Bell and Jeffery, it still seems an open question: are these two words interchangeable—and if not, is the prophet 'more' than an apostle or the apostle 'more' than a prophet?

---

[62] *Acta Orientalia*, II, 172.
[63] *Ibidem*, 175. Tritton, too, sees the prophets as those who only repeat the message brought by the apostles; *Islam*, p. 49. Cf. also below note 85.
[64] *Untersuchungen*, p. 48.
[65] *Introduction*, p. 147.
[66] *The Qur'ān*, pp. 27 f. (= *M.W.*, XL, 115 f.).

In an attempt to survey and summarize the main arguments used and the most important Qur᾿anic data which are relevant to this discussion, I would like to deal with three issues: first of all, with the chronological order of the *nabī* and *rasūl* texts, secondly, with the question to whom these titles are applied in the Qur᾿ān, and finally, with some contextual material which in my opinion contributes greatly to a better understanding of the meaning of these two notions.

Chronological Order

We have already quoted some statements dealing with this subject: Ahrens' and Bell's remarks that the word *nabī* is not applied to Muḥammad in any Meccan passage. It is important to note that this does not mean that *nabī* is not used at all prior to 622. Al least twelve texts in which this word occurs are Meccan (middle Meccan: 37:112; 19:30/31, 41/42, 49/50, 51/52, 54/55; 43:6/5, 7/6; late Meccan: 17:55/57; 39:69; 7:94/92; 6:112. Moreover, we find the word 'prophethood', *nubuwwa,* in three very important late Meccan verses: S. 45:16/15; 29:27/26 and 6:89.[67]

The issue to which Ahrens and Bell referred deserves further consideration. The only Meccan sura in which there is a direct reference to Muḥammad as prophet is Sura 7. But many 'Western' scholars agree that this passage, verses 157-158/156-158, is a Medinan interpolation,[68] and their arguments seem rather convincing. We should be careful, however, not to draw any too radical and definite conclusions from this. If S. 25:31/33 is not a later interpolation—a point which is difficult to decide—we would have here at least an indirect reference to Muḥammad as prophet: "The apostle says, 'O my Lord, see, my people has looked upon this Qur᾿ān as a thing to be avoided.' And so have We appointed for every Prophet enemies from among the sinners." In addition, there are, as we have seen (note 49), two Meccan texts in which the verb *naba'a* (II), used with Muḥammad as subject, comes close to an indication of a prophetic ministry: "Tell (announce, proclaim to) My servant that I am the all-forgiving; the all-compassionate, and that my punishment is the painful punishment," S. 15:49. And in S. 34:7, "The unbelievers say, 'Shall we lead you to a man who tells you that when you have been totally destroyed, you will be created anew?' "

Irrespective of whether one holds that there is no mentioning of Muḥammad as a prophet in any Meccan passage or whether one accepts one or two direct or indirect references, the scarcity of these data contrast both with the use of *nabī* for other persons in the Meccan

[67] The other verses in which this word occurs are S. 3:79/73 and 57:26.

[68] Cf. especially Nöldeke-Schwally, *Geschichte*, I, 159 f. This view is shared by Richard Bell and Régis Blachère (cf. their Qur᾿ān translations at S. 7:156-158) as it had been accepted earlier by Horovitz (*Untersuchungen*, p. 38; *Proper Names*, pp. 78 f.), Ahrens (cf. note 38) and others. See also below notes 77 and 92.

16

period and with its use for Muḥammad in Medinan suras, approximately thirty times. When we, moreover, realize that in the Meccan period the *rasūl* title is applied to Muḥammad fourteen times, [69] it becomes indeed very difficult to accept the view that the terms 'prophet' and 'apostle' are fully interchangeable.

Two observations need to be added to this preliminary conclusion. Pautz' study, still significant for many reasons, is in a final analysis inadequate because it does not take into consideration the chronological order of the suras. That may be understandable for a publication of 1898—but it is inexcusable when even in recent years some authors ignore this issue altogether. In the light of what we have just seen with regard to the 'late' use of the term *nabī* for Muḥammad, it is astonishing to read in Jeffery's article that "Muḥammad as he took up his mission claimed to be both a *rasūl* and *nabī*." [70] One blindfolds oneself in this way for one of the intriguing questions in Qur'anic studies: why do we not find Muḥammad designated as *nabī* in the whole period till 622—or at least: why are the references so unclear and so scarce?

The second observation is with regard to Caetani. In the first volume of his masterwork on the early history of Islam he pays, in his discussion of *nabī* and *rasūl,* careful attention to the question of the chronological order, but reaches some untenable conclusions because he does not distinguish between these words and treats them as synonyms. [71] After a thorough study of each word separately one may come to the conclusion that they are interchangeable, but one is methodologically not allowed to base one's investigation of their meaning on the assumption that they are practically identical.

Persons for whom the terms *nabī* and *rasūl* are used

Nūḥ, Ibrāhīm, Ismāᶜīl, Isḥāq, Yaᶜqūb, Mūsa, Hārūn, Dāwūd, Sulaymān, Idrīs, Ayyūb, Yūnus, Yaḥyā, ᶜĪsā and Muḥammad are the persons to whom in the Qurᵓān the *nabī* title is directly applied.

If we want to include indirect references as well, Ilyās, al-Yasaᶜ, Lūṭ, Yūsuf and Zakāriyyāᵓ can be added, because a passage which

[69] Early Meccan: S. 81:19; 69:40; 73:15. Middle Meccan: 4:13/12; 43:29/28; 72:23/24; 23:69/71; 25:7/8, 27/29, 30/32, 41/43 (cf. *mursal* in S. 36:3/2). Late Meccan: 17:93 f./95 f.; 46:9/8.

[70] *The Qurᵓān,* p. 22 (= *M.W.*, XL, 110).

[71] Cf. note 3. Caetani's main thesis in this section is that the very frequent designation of Muḥammad as an apostle-prophet in the Medinan suras is in sharp contrast with the 'modesty' of his role as described in Mecca, and that this development reflects the change of a religious into a 'political' mission; the crucial issue is now who will be the absolute ruler in Arabia. *Annali,* I, 211 f. The question whether the emphasis on Muḥammad's authority as *apostle* is in conflict with his recognition of the other *prophets* needs, in my opinion, to be answered in the negative. Caetani comes to the conclusion of a sharp contrast between the Meccan and Medinan data on this point because he fails to distinguish clearly between *nabī* and *rasūl.*

lists them and several of the prophets mentioned before concludes with the statement: "Those are they to whom We gave the Scripture, the Judgment and Prophethood" (S. 6:83-89).

It has been suggested that there is also some Qurʾanic justification for the inclusion of Adam among the prophets, a practice common in later Islam. One of the most important texts in this connection is said to be S. 3:33/30, where Adam, Nūḥ, Ibrāhīm's family and ʿImrān's family are mentioned together. Because of the significant role of the latter ones in the history of prophethood, some scholars are inclined to accept as at least 'implicity Qurʾanic' the functioning of Adam at the beginning of the 'chain of prophets'. [72]

We shall return to these data in our next section, and want at this moment to add immediately the list of apostles: Nūḥ, Lūṭ, Ismāʿīl, Mūsā (twice with Hārūn), ʿĪsā, Hūd, Ṣāliḥ Shuʿayb and Muḥammad. If we include those referred to as *mursalūn* we can add Ilyās and Yūnus.

Again some preliminary conclusions can be drawn. The impression of a distinction between *nabī* and *rasūl* is confirmed by these lists of prophets and apostles. The prophets are exclusively among the descendants of Ibrāhīm, while the list of apostles includes three names of messengers of God apparently sent to other communities. Horovitz drew attention to this point more than forty years ago, [73] and emphasized that the characterization of the apostles as the great heroes and the prophets as their successors was invalid, because in that case one should definitely expect to see Ibrāhīm described as a *rasūl,* whereas the Qurʾān does 'only' use the *nabī* title for him. [74]

It is an undeniable fact, however, that not all of the prophets receive the apostle-title. "Not every prophet is an apostle" is indeed a thesis which has full Qurʾanic support. But this statement should not be interpreted as if it means that the apostles constitute a nucleus within the larger community of prophets. For, as we have seen, the Qurʾān does not refer to every apostle as a prophet either: Hūd, Ṣāliḥ and Shuʿayb do not receive the latter title at all. Even more significant is the notion, explicitly expressed in a few texts, [75] that there have been many more apostles than those whose names have been revealed to Muḥammad.

Is the apostle 'more than' a prophet? Studying the persons to whom the Qurʾān applies the titles a positive answer seems question-

[72] Jeffery, *The Qurʾān,* p. 29 (= *M.W.*, XL, 117), where the expressions that God taught Adam, guided him and chose him are also quoted as "terms which have a special use in connection with Allah's calling of messengers." Wensinck bases his statement that it is only "by accident" that Adam is not included in the list of apostles (*Acta Orientalia,* II, 175) on S. 3: 59/52, where Adam and ʿIsā are closely linked.

[73] *Untersuchungen,* pp. 48 f.

[74] See below notes 109, 110.

[75] S. 40:78; 4:164/162. Cf. also S. 14:9 and note 85.

able, although there is the significant issue that only some among the thirteen or eighteen prophets sent to the Children of Israel are also listed as apostles. At the end of the next section we shall have to return to this issue.

The *nabī* and *rasūl*-References in their Qur'ānic context

Although we referred already to some context-issues in the preceding paragraphs, we wish to deal in this final section explicitly with some notions, concepts and expressions which are linked with references to the prophets and apostles and are therefore meaningful for a fuller understanding of the connotations of these two words.

No one studying this subject can overlook the fact that 'prophethood' is linked—as we have seen—in a very special way with Ibrāhīm and his descendants and that there seems to be a close association between prophethood and Scripture:

> And We gave him (Ibrāhīm) Isḥāq and Yaʿqūb and We established Prophethood and Scripture within his descendants. S. 29 : 27/26

Ibrāhīm's place at the beginning of the list of prophets is, according to many, presupposed in the statement of S. 4: 54/57:

> We have bestowed upon the descendants of Ibrāhīm the Scripture and Wisdom.

The combination Prophethood-Scripture-Wisdom is also found in S. 3 : 79/73, 81/75; 6 : 89; 45 : 16/15. Moreover, we know that several prophets are linked with a specific sacred text: Ibrāhīm with the *ṣuḥūf* (pages),[76] Mūsā with the Tawrāt,[77] Dāwūd with the Zabur,[78] ʿĪsā with the Injīl[79] and Muḥammad with the Qur'ān.[80] There are some more texts which associate—directly or indirectly—prophets and Sacred Scripture.[81]

---

[76] S. 87:19; 53:36 f./37 f. Cf. for the notes 76-79 Horovitz, *Untersuchungen*, pp. 68 ff. and especially Jeffery, *The Qur'ān*, pp. 63-67 (*M.W.*, XL, 201-205). Torrey, *Foundation*, p. 89 emphasizes the role of Ibrāhīm as "the father of the written revelation of God to mankind."

[77] S. 5:43 f./47 f. Cf. 62:5; 3:50/44, 93/87; 61:6. It is very frequently referred to as the Book of Mūsā (S. 11:17/20; 46:12/11 and passim). The *Taurāt* and *Injīl* both are mentioned in: S. 3:3/2, 65/58; 48:29; 9:111/112; 5:46/50, 66/70, 68/72, 110 (all Medinan) and S. 7:157/156 (see note 68).

[78] S. 17:55/57; 4:163/161.

[79] S. 3:48/43; 57:27. Cf. also the end of note 77.

[80] Although the word *Qur'ān* obviously is used frequently in the sense of recitation, reciting, preaching—see Bell, *Introduction*, pp. 128-136 and Jeffery, *The Qur'ān*, p. 67 f., 70 ff. (= *M.W.*, XL, 205 f., 258 ff.)—the notion that Muḥammad has received a Book is also expressed in many Meccan suras (cf. S. 44:1, 19:16, 41/42, 51/52, 54/55, 56/57; 38:29/28; 18:1; 16:64/66; 39:1f.; 29:47/46; 42:17/16; 7:2/1; 46:12/11, 30/29; 6:92, 114. If 'Book' and 'Prophethood' belong so closely together as Horovitz and others suggest, it is rather surprising that Muḥammad is not designated more clearly as a Prophet in the Meccan period; cf. below p. 24.

[81] Among the other texts S. 19:30/31; 2: 213/209; 57:26.

In the light of these statements it is surprising to read in Bayḍāwī's classical Qur'ān commentary a definition of the *rasūl* as the person who combines a (revealed) Book with a miracle confirming his ministry, whereas the *nabī* who is not a *rasūl* has no Book. [82] One wonders whether this same idea is behind a statement of al-Taftāzānī in his Commentary on al-Nasafī's Creed:

> A *rasūl* is a man whom God sends to creatures in order to announce His judgments; he may be commissioned with a Book; in contrast to a prophet, for 'prophet' is a more general term. [83]

One does not have to interpret this statement as if it says that the bringing of a Book is the distinction between an apostle and a prophet, but Bayḍāwī's remark leaves open the possibility of this interpretation.

These post-Qur'anic data as well as many texts in the Qur'ān which bring the apostles and the Scripture together [84] must make us careful not to overstate the significance of the prophet-scripture combination, as many authors seem to do.

Directing our attention primarily to the apostles, a number of significant connotations arise out of the context in which the word *rasūl* is used. First of all there is the idea that "every community (*umma*) has its (own) *rasūl*." S. 10:47/48; 16:36/38; 17:15/16; 23:44/46; 30:47/46. [85] A similar expression is used in connection with other

---

[82] Bayḍāwī, *Anwār al-tanzīl wa asrār al-ta'wīl*, I (ed. H. O. Fleischer, Lipsiae, 1846), 636, *ad* S. 22:52/51 (والنبىّ غيرُ الرسول من لا كتاب له).

[83] al-Taftāzānī, *Sharḥ ʿAqāʾid al-Nasafī* (Istanbul, A. H. 1313 [Cairo, A. H. 1335]), pp. 35 f. [pp. 31 f.].

[84] Late Meccan: S. 40:70/72; 35:25/23. Medinan: S. 2:87/81 (?), 101/95, 129/123, 151/146; 98:2 f.; 62:2; 3:101/96, 164/158, 184/181; 57:25; 4:136/135; 65:11; 5:15/18. In ten of these texts the reference is directly to Muḥammad. It is interesing to note that none of the texts listed here seems fully comparable to the statements quoted above which mention *nubuwwa* and *kitāb* (and *ḥukm*). In four of the texts listed in this note we find the word *bayyināt* "proofs," which is used frequently and it almost seems more characteristically in connection with the apostles and—except for those already referred to, S. 35:25/23; 98:2 f.; 3:184/181 and 57:25—without mentioning of a Scripture or Books: (late Meccan) S. 30:9/8, 47/46; 14:9/10; 40:22/23, 34/36, 50/53, 83; 10:74/75; 7:101/99; (Medinan) 64:6; 3:183/180; 9:70/71; 5:32/36 (in none of these thirteen texts specifically used in connection with Muḥammad, which may be a not insignificant difference between this list and the one at the beginning of this note).

[85] It may be that the word *umma* must be understood as a community in a specific period of history (note the use of this word in the sense of a certain period of time in S. 11:8/11), which would make it possible to reconcile the notion of more than one *rasūl* to the same tribal community with the idea of the 'exclusive' character of the relationship between an *umma* and its apostle. This idea of a 'series' of *rusul* does, according to some, apply to the community of the Children of Israel. Leaving Nūḥ, Lūṭ, Ismāʿīl, Yūnus, Hūd, Ṣāliḥ and Shuʿayb out of consideration, we still have Mūsa, Hārūn and ʿĪsā, and if we include the indirect references, Ilyās (see p. 16). Definitely the emphasis in the case of Mūsā (and Hārūn) is on his functioning with regard to the people of Pharaoh, but he is also seen, it seems, as a *rasūl* to the Children of Israel, a title which is applied explicitly to ʿĪsā (cf. note 107). Of interest is also S. 5:19/22, which speaks about the coming of Muḥammad during an interval (*fatra*) in the series of

20

nouns which seem to describe the apostle's function: every city has its 'warner' (*nadhīr*; S. 26:208; 35:24/22 and possibly 25:51/53; cf. also note 85) and its 'leader' (*hādin*; S. 13: 7/8); and on judgment day every community will have its 'witness' (*shāhid*; cf. note 89).

Once it is said that each city receives a prophet before calamity strikes it (S. 7:94/92). The fact that there is only one text with this last word combination fully justifies seeing this notion of a very close relation between an apostle and 'his' community as indeed an important aspect of the work and the function of the *rasūl*. [86]

This notion of a close relationship is also reflected in such texts as S. 2:143/137; 5:109/108; 10:74/75; 22:78; 40:5; 77:11 (only once the plural occurs: "your apostles," S. 40:50/53). [87] The *rasūl* is a

---

apostles. His coming makes it impossible for the People of the Book—who had already received Scripture and Prophets—to complain: "no messenger of good tidings and no warner has come to us." Is, then, the apostle in this case the one who reminds the people of what they have received from the Prophets? That can hardly be described as a clear line in the Qur'anic use of the word 'apostle', and the apostle's confirming of previous revelation in S. 3:81/75 must be interpreted differently. The idea of Ibrāhīm's link with the Arabs and the testimony that Muḥammad is the one sent to a community to which no warner had come before him should neither be interpreted as a contradiction, nor should it be used as an argument for this thesis of more than one apostle to the same community (cf. my *De Islam*, pp. 132 ff., p. 26 and notes 109 f. below and the Qurʾanic references S. 33:3/2; 34:44/43; 28:46; 36:6/5). The idea of a series of *prophets* is generally accepted, although it is explained in various ways. My understanding is that it is an indication of a 'progressive revelation' and that it should not be interpreted as if the prophets repeat and 'diffuse' the message of the apostles (the interpretation of Wensinck, Tritton [note 63] and others, whose remarks are fully in line with those of Bayḍāwī in his comment on S. 22:52/51 [*Anwār al-Tanzīl*, I, 636]: God sent the *rasūl* with a *sharīʿa mujaddad* and the *nabī* comes to spread this message and to confirm the previous revelation, *li taqrīr sharʿ sābiqa.*). It is evident that an implication of the latter view is that the number of prophets is much larger than that of the apostles. In the passage referred to above Bayḍāwī gives the figures 124 (prophets) and 313 (apostles); see also note 75 above.

A few remarks on the words *nadhīr* and *bashīr*—used in 5:19/22 may be appropriate here. It is obvious throughout the Qurʾān how closely the notions *rasūl* and *nadhīr* (warner) are related. *Nadhīr, mundhir* and the verb *nadhara* occur one hundred and twenty-six times: seventy-three times in connection with Muḥammad; seven times as God's warning, in the context of Nūḥ's story six times, of Lūṭ's story four times, for Hūd twice, for Ṣāliḥ once and with the jinn as subject once: twenty-seven times in general and in the other cases unrelated to the notion of God's warning to men through His messengers.

Much less frequent is the use of *bashīr* (and *mubashshir*; messenger of good tidings) and the verb *bashara.* These words are used forty-eight times, in thirty-two cases with reference to Muḥammad, six times with God and four times with the Qurʾān as subject, four times in general and twice in another context than that of the proclamation of God's good tidings.

[86] See also texts as S. 2:108/102; 23:69/71. Cf. Horovitz's definition (*Untersuchungen*, p. 49) that the *rusul* are those messengers sent to a specific community, and Wensinck's conclusion (*Acta Orientalia*, II, 172) that every *rasūl* represents one specific community.

[87] This point is particularly emphasized by Horovitz. "Für Muhammad stand es fest, dasz jedes Volk seinen Boten oder Warner habe." [As far as the *rasūl*-concept is concerned:] "nur die Sendung an ein bestimmtes Volk ist wesentlich." *Untersuchungen*, pp. 46, 49.

witness and warner to his own people, who therefore will have no excuse on judgment day (S. 4:165/163; 20:134; 28:47, 59; 39:71). His message is fully understandable, for he speaks their language, [88] he is from among their midst: S. 2:129/123, 151/146; 3:164/158; 6:130; 7:35/33; 9:128/129; 16:113/114; 23:32/33; 39:71; 62:2 (the same expression *minhum*, from among them, is used with *nadhīr*, warner, in S. 7:63/61, 69/67; 38:4/3; 50:2; and as "a man from among them" in S. 10:2).

It has been noted before that one aspect of the function of the *rasūl* is that he acts in a way as his community's representative with God. [89] But the Qur'ān emphasizes much more the other side: he is God's 'representative' to his people, and as such he has a great responsibility [90] as well as a tremendous authority. "God and His apostles" is an expression used three times; [91] "God and His apostle" (i.e., Muḥammad) occurs not less than eighty-five times: men are called to listen to, believe in and obey God and His apostle. [92]

---

[88] Cf. S. 14:4; 19:97 (44:58). In this connection it should be noted that all the passages which refer to the fact that Muḥammad brings a message in *Arabic* are of the Meccan period, when he is described (primarily) as a *rasūl:* S. 20:113/112; 26:195; 43:3/2 (middle Meccan); 41:3/2; 16:103/105; 12:2; 39:28/29; 42:7/5; 46:12/11; 13:37. The message of all *rusul* is identical—the difference is in the language in which they bring it. It is, therefore, surprising that Julian Obermann, discussing the change from a Meccan "Islamism" to a Medinan "Arabism," states as one of his 'arguments': "His revelation, he *now* constantly emphasizes, is an Arabic Koran, and not a foreign one"; "Early Islam" in *The Idea of History in the Ancient Near East* (New Haven: Yale University Press, 1955), p. 274.

[89] Cf. Wensinck, *Muslim Creed*, p. 203 (the apostle is "representative of a community or people to which God has sent him") and the same author's remarks in *Acta Orientalia,* II, 172. Important in this context are the references to the role of the apostles on judgment day, when all men will have to account for their response to the apostles (S. 28:65, 75; 16:84/86, 89/91; 4:41/45) as much as the apostles will have to account for the fulfilment of the task assigned to them (S. 7:6/5; 39:71—note the difference between the apostles in verse 71 and the prophets in verse 69—and 77:11).

[90] The responsibility is primarily that of a faithful proclamation of the message received from God; S. 5:67/71, 109/108; 7:62/60, 68/66, 79/77; 37:171; 72:27 f. They are not responsible for the 'success' of their ministry (S. 11:88/90; 36:17/16; 64:12; 72:23/24) and if they are obedient to their calling they will not be held accountable for those in hell fire (S. 2:119/113; 3:272/274; 7:188).

"Yours is the proclamation—Ours it is to call them to account." This expression as applied to Muḥammad has been seen by many non-Muslim scholars as a typical 'Meccan-expression' and has been used to illustrate what they saw as the radical contrast between the suffering preacher-prophet in Mecca and the shrewd lawgiver-statesman in Medina (some examples of this thesis of a sharp contrast between 'the pre-and the post-Hijra Muḥammad' are listed in my *De Islam*, pp. 119 ff., where an attempt is made to show the great measure of continuity in the Apostle-Prophet's career). This statement, *innamā ʿalayka ʾl-balāghu wa ʿalaynā ʾl-ḥisāb,* is at any rate an invalid argument in this discussion. For it is used not only in late Meccan suras (S. 16:35/37, 82/84; 29:18/17; 42:48/47; 13:40) but also in Medinan suras, including the very last one: S. 3:19/20; 24:54/53; 5:92/93, 99.

[91] S. 4:150/149, 152/151, 171/169. "I and My apostle" (ʿĪsā) occurs once, S. 5:111.

[92] The expression occurs eighty-three times in a total of seventeen out of the

22

This latter expression leads to an observation which illustrates the distinctive use of *rasūl* and *nabī* in the Qur^ʾān: the words obey-obedience, disobey-disobedience are used twenty-eight times in connection with *rasūl*, not one single time combined with *nabī*. [93]

Noteworthy is also the clear assurance that God will protect and rescue His *rasūl* (which is not to deny that He also helps the prophets and all believers), [94] because the defeat of His representative would be a victory over Him—and that is evidently impossible. No matter how strong the resistance is, [95] the ultimate victory is not with men but with God, at the moment that the Jews try to crucify ᶜĪsā as much as in any other crisis-situation of any one of His apostles. [96] Prophets have been killed, [97] but the Apostle must triumph in order to manifest on earth the triumph of God.

---

twenty-four suras listed as Medinan by Blachère (most frequently in S. 8, 24, 33, 9). The two other occurrences are in S. 7: 158/157 f. (almost certainly a Medinan passage, see notes 68 and 77) and in S. 72: 23/24—which would then be the only Meccan text containing this expression.

[93] "Obey Allāh and obey His apostle "is used eighteen times. In addition to this formula we find: "whosoever obeyeth the apostle obeyeth Allāh," S. 4: 80/82; "whosoever obeyeth Allāh and the (His) apostle," 4: 13/17, 69/71; 24: 52/51; 33: 71; 48:17; cf. also 49: 14 and 9: 71/72; "obey the apostle," 24: 55 f.; "We sent no apostle but to be obeyed by Allāh's permission," S. 4: 64/67; "be reverent unto Allāh and obey me," occurring eight times in the stories of Nūḥ, Hūd, Ṣāliḥ, Shuᶜayb and Lūṭ, preceded five times by the sentence: "Behold, I am unto you a faithful apostle."

In line with the foregoing, we see that the word 'disobey' is used nine times with *rasūl*, and never with *nabī* (S. 60: 12 is no exception). The expressions are 'disobedience towards Allāh and His apostle' (S. 72: 23/24; 4: 14/8; 33: 36) and 'disobedience towards the (an) apostle' (S. 69: 10; 73: 16; 11: 59/62; 4: 42/46; 58: 8 f./9 f.).

[94] The most important passage in this connection is probably S. 30: 47/46. That is is 'incumbent upon God to help the believers' (*wa kāna ḥaqqan ᶜalaynā naṣru ʾl-muʾminīn*) is the final statement of a verse which deals with the sending of apostles to each and every community.

[95] The rejection of the apostles and their message is mentioned so frequently that we can list only a few of these references: (middle Meccan) S. 51: 52; 54: 25; 50: 14/13; 15: 11; 38: 14/13; 36: 14/13, 30/29; 43: 7/6; 23: 44/46; 21: 41/42; 27: 48 ff./49 ff.; 18: 56/54, 106; (late Meccan) S. 41: 14/13; 30: 9/8, 47/46; 11: 38 f./40 f.; 14: 13/16; 40: 5, 22/23, 26/27, 70/72; 29: 18/17; 10: 39/40; 34: 45/44; 35: 4, 25/23; 6: 10, 34; (Medinan) S. 2: 101/95; 8: 13; 47: 32/34; 4: 42/45; 65: 8; 22: 72/71. Cf. also note 97.

[96] It is the well-known pattern of the punishment-stories; see e.g., Bell, *Introduction*, pp. 119 ff.

[97] In addition to the four texts listed in note 42, the two references to the killing of (the) prophets are S. 2: 61/58 and 3: 21/20. It makes indeed sense to distinguish also on this point between prophets and apostles and not to suggest —as many have done—that the Qurʾān contradicts itself frequently with regard to this issue. Only one text speaks clearly about the killing of apostles (S. 3: 183/180) a fact which would be an important argument if we were thinking in terms of a systematic 'doctrine' of prophethood and apostleship in the Qurʾān, but which does not really affect our present thesis about the primary associations of the words *nabī* and *rasūl* in their Qurʾanic context. A most interesting expression is found in S. 2: 87/81 and S. 5: 70/74: the Jews declared a group [of the apostles] to be liars, and a group they kill (*fa farīqan kadhdhabtum wa farīqan taqtulūn; farīqan kadhdhabū wa farīqan yaqtulūn)*. The perfect tense of the first verb (and throughout the text) in contrast to the imperfect tense of

We have not exhausted the Qurʾanic data. Some interesting word combinations remained undiscussed altogether, others have been treated insufficiently. But we have reached the point that we must try to bring together the preliminary results of the various sections and come to some final conclusions on the Qurʾanic use of the words 'prophet' and 'apostle'.

It seems preferable to move, in this case, from the use of these two titles for Muḥammad to a more general characteristic of these notions *rasūl* and *nabī*.

As far as the 'apostle' title is concerned, its application to Muḥammad in Meccan suras is as significant as its remarkably frequent use in Medinan chapters.

In the pre-Hijra period the connotation is primarily that of a messenger sent by God to bring to his own community in its own language the very same message which other apostles and communities had received before them. Caetani's interpretation of the Medinan use of the *rasūl*-title for Muḥammad is one-sided and distorts the Qurʾanic emphasis.[98] The 'uniqueness' of Muḥammad is not to be understood as an exclusivism with regard to and a denial of earlier prophets and apostles, but as following the pattern which makes every *rasūl* unique

---

the second attracted the attention of many interpreters. Some suggested that it is only because of the rhyme or to make the description more vivid (so e.g., Bayḍāwī, *Anwār al-Tanzīl, ad* S. 2:87/81); others have interpreted the second verb in the sense of 'trying' or 'intending' to kill (cf. among others, Abdullah Yusuf Ali, *The Holy Qurʾān* (Lahore: Muḥammad Ashraf, 1934; reprint New York: Hafner Publ. Co., 1946), I, 40, note 91, and Muḥammad Asad, *The Message of the Qurʾān* (Mecca: Muslim World League, 1964), p. 26, note 72, with a reference to *Manār* I, 377). Bayḍāwī's comment that the verb *kdhdhb* refers to such persons as Mūsā and ʿIsā, and that *qtl* is used with a view to such persons as Yaḥyā and Zakāriyyāʾ (comment on S. 2: 87/81) clearly reflects his conviction that the killing can not possibly refer to Mūsa and ʿIsā mentioned specifically in this passage of S. 2 (and the latter one also in the context of S. 5: 70 ff./74 ff.). It is one of those questions on which Islamic scholars ought to be so fully aware of and sensitive to the traditional Muslim interpretation that they should carefully and precisely formulate their arguments if they wish to defend the interpretation that S. 2: 87/81 refers to the death of ʿIsā. For this reason Montgomery Watt's note on this verse seems very inadequate ("the primary reference may be to Jesus"); *Companion to the Qurʾan* (London: George Allen and Unwin Ltd., 1967), p. 24. The interpretation 'intend, try, wish' to kill seems to make good sense, especially when we realize how much the apostle-stories function as an *encouragement* to the Prophet Muḥammad, obviously assuming the ultimate delivery and triumph of the *rasūl*; cf. especially S. 11: 120/121: "And We relate to you [such, these] histories of apostles in order to strengthen your heart therewith." Although it leads us outside the field of Qurʾanic studies, it is of interest to note that the attempt to kill the Prophet by poisoning him at Khaybar failed *at that moment*, that he lived another three years to complete his mission, and that when his death is seen as a consequence of the eating of the poisoned sheep and therefore as martyrdom (*shahāda*), the words linked specifically are *prophet* and *martyr*, so at least in the significant text of Imām Abū ʾl-Fidāʾ Ismāʿil b. Kathīr, *al-Bidāya wa'l-Nihāya*, of which a section was edited by Muṣṭafā ʿAbd al-Wāḥid, entitled *al-Sīra al-Nabawiyya*, 4 vols. (Cairo: ʿIsā al-Bābī al-Ḥatabī Press, 1964-1966), III, 400; IV, 449.

[98] Cf. note 71.

and absolute with regard to his own community.[99] In the case of Muḥammad there is, according to some, one new dimension in so far that he is seen as a *rasūl* not only to his particular *umma,* the people in and around Mecca, but to the whole world (S. 4:79/81; 34:28/27).[100]

With regard to the 'prophet' title, the main question obviously is why this name is not applied to Muḥammad clearly and explicitly—or at least with greater emphasis—in the period prior to 622. My suggestion is that the emphatic use of this title coincides with[101] a greater emphasis on the Arabs' descendance from Ibrāhīm and with the first clear references to Ismāᶜīl's functioning in the line Ibrāhīm-Ismāᶜīl-Arabs.[102] To this interpretation of the word *nabī* we shall return below in a more general context.

If we accept this interpretation—rather than the one which links the notion of 'prophet' primarily with that of 'Book-Revelation'— the fact that Meccan suras which scarcely refer to Muḥammad as prophet contain clear indications of his vocation to bring a (new) Scripture does not raise any problem.[103] Moreover, since there are a few references to a link between Ibrāhīm and the Meccans (Arabs) already in Meccan suras,[104] the above interpretation of *nabī* leaves open the

---

[99] The issue of Medinan statements about the relation to 'those to whom (a portion of) the Scripture had come' previously must, as far as the words *nabī* and *rasūl* are concerned, be studied primarily in the light of the use of the former one. These data lead to the same conclusion as the study of the Medinan references to Ibrāhīm (—Ismāᶜīl—Arabs): we should speak of a Medinan 'inclusivism' rather than of an 'exclusivism'. Cf. my *De Islam,* pp. 147 f.

[100] While many Muslims are of the opinion that Muḥammad was aware of the universal dimension of his vocation and saw Islam definitely as more than an 'Arab' religion, many Western Islamic scholars expressed disagreement with this interpretation. A rather recent discussion—including references to Frants Buhl's well-known statements on this point—is found in W. Montgomery Watt, *Muḥammad at Medina* (Oxford: Clarendon Press, 1956), pp. 345-347.

[101] I wish to emphasize the choice of this term, which should not be misconstrued as if it suggests that this new emphasis was due to changing conditions or that it was an answer arising out of a deep 'disappointment' in the Jewish reactions to the new leader in Medina. For a discussion of this latter interpretation cf. my *De Islam,* pp. 125 ff.

[102] The Meccan references to Ismāᶜīl are S. 19:54 f./55 f. (Ibrāhīm, Mūsā, Ismāᶜīl, Idrīs); 6:83 ff. (Ibrāhīm, Isḥāq, Yaᶜqūb, Nūḥ, Dāwūd, Sulaymān, Ayyūb, Yūsuf, Mūsā, Hārūn, Zakāriyyāʾ, Yaḥyā, ᶜIsā, Ilyās, Ismāᶜīl, al-Yasaᶜ, Yūnus, Lūṭ); 21:85 (after Ayyūb, and listed with Idrīs and Dhū 'l-Kifl); 33:48 (Ibrāhīm, Isḥāq, Yaᶜqūb are mentioned in verse 46; 48 lists: Ismāᶜīl, al-Yasaᶜ, Dhū 'l-Kifl). As Medinan references I see not only S. 2: 127/121, but also S. 14:39/41 (arguments for interpreting verses 38^{b}, $39/41^{b}$, ^{c} as Medinan verses in a Meccan sura are given in my *De Islam,* pp. 126-132, with references to the very significant studies of Y. Moubarac, *Abraham dans le Coran,* Paris: J. Vrin, 1958 and E. Beck, "Die Gestalt des Abraham am Wendepunkt der Entwicklung Muhammeds," *Le Muséon,* LXV (1952), 73-94.

[103] Cf. above note 80.

[104] Especially S. 14:35 ff./38 ff. (see note 102) and S. 43:26 ff./25 ff., a passage to which Blachère in his Qurʾān translation rightly gives the subtitle "Oubli de l'enseignement d'Abraham, chez les Mekkois." S. 11:73/76 may well be understood as speaking of Ibrāhīm's family as 'the people of the Kaᶜba,'

possibility that there are also some Meccan references to the 'prophetic' calling of Muḥammad and suggests, therefore, a change in emphasis rather than any radical contrast between Meccan and Medinan data on this point.

When we turn now to the Qurʾanic use of the terms *nabī* and *rasūl* in general, only a very few additional remarks are required. The foregoing discussion of the use of the *nabī* title for Muḥammad makes it clear that I see 'belonging to the seed of (Nūḥ-) Ibrāhīm' as the main characteristic of the notion 'prophet' rather than the latter person's involvement in the history of the written revelation. In one of the previous sections we referred to the texts which clearly link the *nabī* with the notion of (revelation through) Scripture, but noted at the same time that the combination *rasūl*-Book also occurs so often that this functioning in the history of the Book-revelation can hardly be seen as the primary distinction between the prophet and the apostle. If, moreover, the prophet-Scripture relation would be so essential, it is difficult to see why Nūḥ 'opens' the series of Prophets when he is never specifically connected with a Book-revelation.[105] In my opinion, the link *nabī-kitāb* is of secondary significance only, and results from the special attention given to the Scriptures granted to Ibrāhīm's family.[106] Prophethood must be understood first of all as a special gift to that part of mankind which can be indicated with the names (Adam-) Nūḥ-Ibrāhīm-Ibrāhīm's descendants (through Isḥāq-Yaʿqūb as well as through Ismāʿīl), with a clear emphasis on the Ibrāhīm and post-Ibrāhīm section of this line.

All the elements which constitute the notion of *rasūl* have been

---

which would be another Meccan reference to a link between Ibrāhīm and the Meccans.

[105] A total of 132 texts, divided over twenty-eight suras—of which twenty-one are Meccan—deal with Nūḥ. It is remarkable that in these twenty-one Meccan passages only one refers (indirectly) to him as prophet, S. 6:84, 89. This passage, moreover, places no emphasis on him at all, and Blachère's subtitle (in his Qurʾān translation) seems fully justified: "Chaîne des prophètes depuis Abraham jusqu'à Mahomet." In the Medinan period we find four relevant statements. Scripture and Prophethood have been given to the descendants of Nūḥ and Ibrāhīm, S. 57:26. Revelation has been sent down on Nūḥ and the prophets after him, S. 4:163/161. S. 19:58/59 (in a Medinan section of a middle Meccan sura) speaks about the prophets among the seed of Adam, Nūḥ, Ibrāhīm and Ismāʿīl. And finally there is the significant series: Nūḥ, Ibrāhīm, Mūsā and ʿIsā in S. 33:7. At least in the Meccan passages (the overwhelming majority) Nūḥ functions as a *rasūl* and *nadhīr* in a punishment-story much more than as a *nabī*. Cf. the grouping together of the Nūḥ, Hūd and Ṣāliḥ stories in S. 69:4-12; 53:50/51-52/53; 51:41-46; 54:9-32; 50:12 f.; 26:105-159; 38:12 f./11 f.; 25:39 f.; 11:25/27-68/71, 89/91; 40:31/32; 7:59/57-79/77; 22:42/43; 9:70/71.

[106] Cf. above p. 18. The question needs to be faced whether Prophethood and Scripture are two distinctive gifts to Ibrāhīm's family, and, if so, whether not only the first one (cf. S. 5:20/23) but also the second one is a gift exclusively granted to this community. The reference to Ibrāhīm's descendants, Jews and Christians, as *ahl al-kitāb,* seems to suggest a positive answer to the latter question. Even so, I maintain the thesis stated above, i.e., that the *primary* connotation of the word *nabī* in the Qurʾān is not 'Book-revelation' but 'Children of Ibrāhīm'.

26

referred to already in the discussion of the use of this title for Muḥammad. The 'apostle' is a messenger from among his own people to bring to them in their own language the Warning of God: he speaks for God and is so closely linked with God that obedience to the Almighty coincides with obedience to the messenger. He represents in (a particular phase of) the history of his community the great moment to decide: his coming forces a split into two opposing factions,[107] one rejecting him and his message, the other one accepting him in faith and obedience.

Is then, after all, an 'apostle' more than a 'prophet'? The interpretation of the two notions suggested above makes it clear that the question is illegitimate: the words have such different and distinctive connotations that one cannot be expressed in terms of being more and greater than the other one. This argument for denying the preeminence of the apostles is clearly different from Horovitz's reasoning, who saw in the fact that Ibrāhīm does not receive the *rasūl*-title in the Qurʾān sufficient ground for rejecting Wensinck's characteristic of the apostle-group.[108] Obviously it would make no sense to suggest that the Qurʾanic apostles Hūd, Ṣāliḥ and Shuʿayb are greater and more than Ibrāhīm. But it seems unsatisfactory to base an argument on the non-occurrence of a text using *rasūl* for Ibrāhīm when his function—not with regard to the Arabs,[109] but with regard to his father's community—comes very close to the role of an apostle.[110]

The statement that only some among the prophets are also called *rusul* is invalid as a generalization, as we have seen; it applies only to the messengers sent to the 'Children of Israel.' These *rusul* are persons who—at different phases in the history of his community;

[107] This is a part of the pattern of each punishment-story; cf. e.g., S. 27: 45/46. The coming of ʿIsā leads to a split of the one *umma* of the Children of Israel into factions which oppose each other; S. 19: 37/38 and 23: 52/54. While Mūsā is primarily the *rasūl* to the people of Pharaoh (only exceptionally do we find him referred to as 'apostle' in connection with his functioning in the history of the Children of Israel, esp. S. 61:5), ʿIsā is explicitly described as the *rasūl* to the Children of Israel in S. 3: 49/43; 61: 6. The fact that fourteen out of the fifteen texts in which the word 'Christians' occurs contain also a reference to the 'Jews' (S. 2: 62/59, 111/105, 113/107 twice, 120/114, 135/129, 140/134; 3: 63/60; 22: 17; 9: 30; 5: 18/21, 51/56, 69/73, 82/85. The only exception is S. 5: 14/17) justifies seeing the 'Jews' and the 'Christians' as the two parties into which the one community of the Children of Israel became divided.

[108] Cf. above notes 73-74.

[109] Cf. Moubarac, *Abraham*, p. 61: "Comment Abraham peut être l'avertisseur' des Arabes, s'il est leur père?"

[110] The idea of opposition to the man sent by God, the attempt to kill him and God's act of rescuing him—all typical parts of a *rasūl*-story—are found in S. 37: 98/96; 21: 68-71; 22: 42 f./43 f. One could say that the title *rasūl* is implicitly used for Ibrāhīm in S. 29: 18/17 ("the only task of the apostle is the proclamation") and S. 9: 70/71 (the stories of the people of Nūḥ, ʿĀd, Thamūd, Ibrāhīm ... their *rusul* came to them ...) This is not to deny that the Ibrāhīm story contains very significant elements which set it apart from the punishment-stories: the emphasis on his conversion, preaching, intercession for his father, etc. Cf. my *De Islam*, pp. 132 f.

cf. note 85—fulfilled the same task as the apostles sent to all other communities on earth, and carried out this task with the same authority and ultimate success as they did.

As far as the post-Qurʾanic development is concerned, it should be noted that the 'classical' Muslim definition quoted above has basically preserved the Qurʾanic connotation of the *rasūl*-term, but has reinterpreted and 'generalized' the specific meaning of the word *nabī*, considering as a prophet every person who receives a special 'communication' from God. While the reasons for this reinterpretation are not too difficult to discern when we accept the above interpretation (i.e., that the primary association of the word *nabī* is a recognition of the special place of Ibrāhīm's family, including the Isḥāq-Yaʿqūb line, in the history of God's dealing with mankind) it is much more difficult to understand why there would have been among Muslims such uncertainty as we noted with regard to the crucial link between a prophet and a Book if the functioning in the history of the Scriptural Revelation was the primary contextual meaning of the word 'prophet' in the Qurʾān.

Going finally for one moment beyond our proper subject, and leaving aside the distinction between prophet and apostle, it is of interest to realize that the Muslim and Christian traditions, which both place such an emphasis on the notion of prophetic revelation, reflect also an awareness of the relativity of the significance of this particular ministry. Jesus' recognition of John the Baptist as a prophet "and far more than a prophet" was followed by the astounding remark, "and yet the least in the kingdom of Heaven is greater than he" (Matth. 11 : 9, 11). And the Muslim tradition—pointing not without valid reasons to a text as S. 30:30/29—knows of a "natural knowledge of God" and sees Islam not only as the religion based upon the Book and the Sunna of the Prophet but also as "the natural religion of man," the religion in which every child on earth is born.[111] This last paragraph makes it clear that even when dealing with Qurʾanic and in general Muslim key-words as 'prophet' and 'apostle' caution is needed not to interpret the whole theological structure of Islam as exclusively based upon and consistently elaborated along the line of these two notions.

We are, in the History of Religions, involved in a modest enterprise. We do not let 'the light of eternity' shine upon historical data, and are content when we begin to see religious phenomena somewhat more clearly in their own light. Our constructions are constantly open to revision—and we can never afford ourselves the luxury of forgetting about the facts:

---

[111] On this famous tradition and its use in the controversy with the Kharijites see Wensinck, *Creed*, pp. 42, 214.

28

> In his own work, then, the phenomenologist is bound up with the object; he cannot proceed without repeatedly confronting the chaos of the given, and without submitting again and again to correction by the facts.[112]

The chaos of the given has been illustrated in this paper, and there is no doubt concerning the ongoing need to be corrected by the facts, again and again. The present paper tried to lay a few bricks in the right place so that we have them at hand in our common effort to build up a more adequate "phenomenology of Muḥammad." This formulation is our last reference to Van der Leeuw who by his statement that there is "not only a phenomenology of the saint, but also a phenomenology of Francis of Assissi"[113] has made it abundantly clear that phenomenology of religion is not only 'comparative religion.'

Many may and actually do doubt the academic validity of a discipline which intentionally limits itself to an attempt at congenial interpretation and empathic understanding of the religious traditions of mankind. No one denies that many people have their own 'ulterior motives' for their interest in this study and accept its 'partial' character only because they intend to use it ultimately in a normative context. But those who have no other intention than to know and understand may feel encouraged by a word of the tradition:

> Seeking knowledge without an intention is an intention in itself.[114]

I simply interpret and comment: a good and valuable intention.

---

112 *Religion in Essence and Manifestations,* p. 685 (Ch. 109, section 2).
113 *Ibidem,* p. 596 (Ch. 88, section 4).
114 al-Dārimī, *Musnad,* Intr., b. 46.

10

THE EARLIEST MEANING OF "QUR'ĀN"*

William A. Graham

Students of Islam as well as Muslims themselves customarily think of and use the Arabic word *qur'ān* primarily as a proper noun with the definite article: "al-Qur'ān", *The* Qur'ān.[1] With this they refer to the collected and written corpus of Muḥammad's revelations from God as assembled and arranged in essentially its present form by the most respected original "reciters" (*qurrā'*) or "transmitters of the recitation" (*ḥamalat al-qur'ān*) who were still alive in the reign of the third Caliph, 'Uthmān (23/644-35/656).[2] As a codified whole, the revelations have

* This article is a revised version of a paper presented at a conference honoring Wilfred Cantwell Smith, held at Harvard University in June 1979. It was presented in roughly its present form as a portion of a longer paper on the oral aspects of scripture at a conference on "Islam and the History of Religions", held at Arizona State University in January 1980. A revised and expanded version of the latter paper, which includes small portions and a summary of the arguments of the present article, will be published late in 1984 in R. Martin, ed., *Islam and the History of Religions* (Tempe, Az.: Arizona State University Press). The present article was written before the publication of Angelika Neuwirth's impressive study, *Studien zur Komposition der mekkanischen Suren* (Berlin: de Gruyter, 1981) [Cf. also her article "Zur Structur der Yūsuf-Sure", in W. Diem and S. Wild, edd., *Studien aus Arabistik und Semitistik. Anton Spitaler zum siebzigsten Geburtstag* (Wiesbaden: Harrassowitz, 1980), pp. 123-152]. Her insistence on the primary character of the Qur'ān as a "Rezitationstext" and her formal and structural approach to the text and its traditional units argue convincingly for the need to recognize more clearly the inherently oral and recitative function of the Qur'ān. The present article seems worth presenting in its original form if only as a complementary argument for the centrality of this oral and recitative function not only in later, but even in earliest Islam.

[1] An exception to this is the title "Qur'ān karīm" that appears on many editions (rather than "al-Qur'ān al-karīm"), apparently as a quotation from Surah 56:77.

[2] This interpretation of the history of the creation of the Qur'ānic *textus receptus* is that generally subscribed to in modern non-Muslim scholarship as well as among Muslim scholars. It has recently been radically, if less than wholly convincingly, attacked by several scholars, most notably John Wansbrough: *Quranic Studies: Sources and Methods of Scriptural Interpretation* (Oxford, 1977); and John Burton: *The Collection of the Qur'ān* (Cambridge, 1977).

been known and thought of since that time both as "al-Qur'ān" and simply as "the Book" or (better) "the Scripture" (*al-Kitāb*). This is expressed in traditional usage as "that which is between the two boards" (*mā bayn al-daffatayn*)[3] and understood in Islam theologically as "the Speech of God" (*Kalām Allāh*) preserved in the eternal Scripture of God (*al-Kitāb* or *Umm al-Kitāb*) and written down for human use in earthly exemplars (*maṣāḥif*; sing. *muṣḥaf*). As such, the Qur'ān is held by Muslims to be God's final Word to humankind, the scriptural revelation that corrects and supersedes God's earlier "scriptures" (*kutub*) which have been only faultily preserved by those previously given the Divine Word, especially Christians and Jews.

It is obvious that "al-Qur'ān" in the later, fixed meaning of God's Word as written down in the *maṣāḥif* is necessarily a post-ʿUthmānic, or certainly a post-Muḥammadan, usage. Until the codification of what has since served as the *textus receptus*—or at least until active revelation ceased with Muḥammad's death—there could have been no use of *al-qur'ān* to refer to the complete body of "collected revelations in written form".[4] This is not to deny that even in the Qur'ān there are hints of a developing notion of the collective Revelation in the use of the words *qur'ān* and *kitāb*, but rather to emphasize the fallacy involved in "reading back" the later, concretized meaning of these terms into the qur'ānic or other traditional-text usages. As will be seen below, the term *qur'ān* did not originally designate the full range of God's communications to Muḥammad, nor did it denote "the Scripture" as a single, fixed whole.

The first important consideration in understanding the earliest meaning of *qur'ān* for Muslims is that God's revelatory process was apparently understood by the Prophet and Companions and by the next several generations of Muslims in a relatively dynamic rather than static fashion. Whereas individual revelations were apparently called *āyah* ("sign") or *qur'ān* ("recitation"), given a special status, and distinguished from Muḥammad's own words from the outset, there were other revelatory words of God in circulation from early on. Further, even the revelatory process by which *qur'āns* were given to the Prophet seems to

---

[3] Muḥammad b. Ismāʿīl al-Bukhārī, *al-Ṣaḥīḥ*, (9 voll. Beirut, n.d.), 66:16; Aḥmad b. Ḥanbal, *al-Musnad*, (6 voll. Cairo, 1313/1895), I, 415.

[4] F. Buhl, "Koran", *EI*, II, 1063b. His discussion of this point is the clearest in the literature; but see Th. Nöldeke, *Geschichte des Qorāns* (2 voll. rev. by F. Schwally. Leipzig, 1909-19) [Hereafter "Nöldeke-Schwally"], I, 31-34.

have been a diverse one and a much more "internal" or "psychological" one than later theological interpretation (in its concern for the "immaculate", verbatim accuracy of the Divine Word in the collected Qur'ān) could accept. Muḥammad was in touch with God, and thus Divine guidance would hardly stop with the formal recitations known as "qur'ān" alone. This picture of revelation in early Islam is an important backdrop for the specific consideration of the earliest signification of the term *qur'ān*.[5]

What then was the hallmark of a *qur'ān* as opposed to the Prophet's words or even other non-qur'ānic, divine words? The key may lie in a later Muslim statement about the most important genre of non-qur'ānic words of God, the so-called "Divine Saying" (*ḥadīth qudsī*).[6] This statement occurs in the earliest extant work on the Qur'ānic sciences,[7] and is an attempt to distinguish the Divine Saying, which is unequivocally called "revelation" (*waḥy* and *tanzīl*), from the Qur'ānic revelation *per se*. The Divine saying is said to be

> a prescript that [God] ordained and revealed and sent down. It is not permissible to recite any of it in the *ṣalāt*, for it was not sent down in the same arrangement (*naẓm*) in which all of the Qur'ān was sent down—which [Qur'ān] has been given us to recite, which is written in the *maṣāḥif*, and the transmission of which has come to us as generally attested from one generation to the next.[8]

Later discussions of the same issue add the external distinction that a *qur'ān* is verbatim word (*lafẓ*) of God, while a Divine Saying is Muḥammad's report of God's word according to sense (*ma'nā*) only—i.e. only the Qur'ān has *i'jāz*, the miraculous character of being the inimitable Divine Speech itself.[9] The statement quoted is, however, less theologically than functionally oriented, and it is in this latter direction that I would seek a clearer understanding of the original meaning of *qur'ān* in Muslim usage. It is the Qur'ān's character as revelation with *a particular form (naẓm) intended for recitative use in worship* that distinguishes it from other texts. Theologically, of course, it came to be

[5] For a detailed presentation of these ideas, see William A. Graham, *Divine Word and Prophetic Word in Early Islam* (The Hague, 1977), esp. Part I.

[6] Concerning these sayings, see *ibid.*, esp. Part II, "The Divine Saying".

[7] The anonymous *Kitāb al-Mabānī* [written 425/1033], ed. Arthur Jeffery, in *Two Muqaddimas to the Qur'anic Sciences* (Cairo, 1954), pp. 5-250.

[8] *Ibid.*, p. 89.

[9] See W. Graham, *Divine Word and Prophetic Word*, pp. 56-62, for description of these later discussions, including that of Ibn Khaldūn.

distinguished in a variety of ways (e.g. by its "inimitability" and its "uncreatedness") from all other speech, but the tendency both in medieval Muslim and modern Western scholarship (under the influence in both cases of a Greek philosophical bias?) to give precedence to its ontological or "essential" status as God's Speech over its functional or "accidental" character as scripture used in worship leads away from what I perceive to have been the active force of *Qur'ān* in early (and indeed in later) Muslim life apart from speculation.

The Arabic word *qur'ān* is not attested to prior to the Qur'ān itself.[10] Muslim sources give various original meanings and derivations, seeing it as either (1) a special formation without a root, used for the Arabic Scripture as *Tawrāt* is used for the Jewish and *Injīl* for the Christian;[11] (2) a verbal noun (without *hamzah*), *qurān*, derived from *qarana*, "to tie, draw, bring together";[12] or (3) a verbal noun (with *hamzah*, *qur'ān*) derived from *qara'a*, meaning either "to collect, draw together" [13] or "to proclaim, recite, read [aloud]".[14] Modern scholarship has identified the last derivation as the correct one linguistically and has rightly stressed the primacy of the meaning "to proclaim, recite, read aloud" over any more literal sense of "to read" in a silent or purely cognitive sense.[15]

---

[10] A. Jeffery, *The Foreign Vocabulary of the Qur'ān* (Baroda, 1938), p. 233.

[11] Jalāl al-Dīn al-Suyūṭī, *al-Itqān fī 'ulūm al-qur'ān*, (2 voll. Cairo, 1951/1370), I, 50-51, citing al-Bayhaqī and al-Khaṭīb as two main sources. Cf. Jeffery, *For. Vocabulary*, p. 234, n. 1.

[12] Suyūṭī, *Itqān*, I, 51, citing al-Ash'arī as one of those giving this derivation. Cf. Jeffery, *For. Vocabulary*, p. 233.

[13] Muḥammad b. Jarīr al-Ṭabarī, *Tafsir*, voll. I-XVI [incomplete], edd. M. M. Shākir and A. M. Shākir (Cairo, n.d.), I, 95-96; E. W. Lane, *An Arabic Lexicon*, 8 voll. (London, 1863-93), VII, 2502; Nöldeke-Schwally, I, 31-32. It is from this meaning of the root, in the sense of "to contract [the womb]" (= to conceive) that the word *qurū'* (S. 2:228) derives; cf. below, n. 28.

[14] Ṭabarī, *Tafsir*, I, 94, glosses it with *tilāwah* and *qirā'ah*; cf. Lane, *Lexicon, VII, 2502.* Note also, as my colleague Wolfhart Heinrichs has called to my attention, that it is at least plausible that the "read" sense of *qara'a* could have developed from the "collect" sense without any outside influences: cf. Lat. *legere*, Ger. *lesen*, which have both senses [personal communication, September 1979].

[15] The best authorities are all in accord on this. The view of E. Meyer (*Ursprung und Geschichte der Mormonen* [1912]) and K. Dyroff ("Zu Sure 96, 1-5", *MVAG*, XXII [1917], 178-180) that the primary rather than the secondary meaning of *qara'a* is "to read [something written]" only is most convincingly refuted by J. Pedersen, *Der Islam*, V, 110-115. See also Nöldeke-Schwally, I, 31-34, 78-82; Jeffery, *For. Vocabulary*, p. 233; Josef Horovitz, *Koranische Untersuchungen* (Berlin and Leipzig, 1926), pp. 74-76; and C. Snouck Hurgronje, *Mekka*, vol. II (The Hague, 1889), p. 225, n. 1, and "Une nouvelle biographie de Mohammed", *RHR*, XXX, 61-62, 154-155.

This reading of *qara'a* is strengthened by the probable influence on the semantic field of this verb and its derivatives from Syriac Christian usage. In Syriac, *Q-R-'* has the sense "to call, call out" and then "to recite, read aloud [scriptural texts especially]".[16] Most crucial is the use of the substantive form *qeryānā* specifically for the oral, liturgical "reading" from holy writ (= *lectio*, ἀνάγνωσις) and for the passage of scripture that is read (= *lectio*, *periocha*, *locus leganda*, ἀνάγνωσμα, περιοχή).[17] The linking of the verbal-noun (*maṣdar*) form *quran* to the Syriac *qeryānā* has been stressed by virtually all major Western Qur'an scholars, even though all have done so without specific reference to even one historical attestation of the Christian liturgical usage in a pre-Islamic Syriac source.[18] Such attestation can apparently now be confirmed in Syriac liturgical manuscripts of the 6th and 7th centuries C.E.,[19] which strengthens the argument for an historical influence here upon Arabic usage and for the vocal, oral sense of the Arabic. It should be stressed, however, that the use of the form *qur'ān* (a perfectly good and not infrequent *maṣdar* form) indicates that one has here a possible Syriac Christian *influence* upon the total richness of meaning of the Arabic, certainly not a direct "borrowing" (which would have yielded a *maṣdar* form such as *qiryān*, presumably).[20]

---

[16] Cf. R. Payne Smith, *Thesaurus Syriacus*, 2 voll. (Oxford, 1883-1901), II, 3715f.

[17] *Ibid.*, II, 3716b, citing several occurrences in the first sense in pre-Islamic Christian sources, beginning with I Tim. 4:13, and several in the second sense in sources as early as St. Cyril's commentary on Luke. A spot check of these occurrences does not, however, yield clear attestation of the word as a technical term in the liturgical context.

[18] All generally cite one another or other secondary-literature references as authority or else give this opinion strictly on grounds of linguistic affiliation. E.g., A. Mingana, "Syriac Influence on the Style of the Kur'ān", *Bull. J. Rylands Lib.*, XI (1927), 88, n. 1; Nöldeke-Schwally, I, 33-34; Julius Wellhausen, "Zum Koran", *ZDMG*, LXVII (1913), 634; F. Buhl, *EI*, II, 1063b; Tor Andrae, *Mohammed. Sein Leben und sein Glaube* (Göttingen, 1932), p. 79; Horovitz, *Der Islam*, XIII, 66-67; Richard Bell, *The Origin of Islam in Its Christian Environment* (London, 1926), pp. 90-91; Rudi Paret, *Mohammed und der Koran*, 2nd ed. (Stuttgart, 1957), pp. 53-54; and Jeffery, *For Vocabulary*, p. 234.

[19] Personal communication from Alford T. Welch, 26 March 1980. In this, he informs me that Sebastian Brock at Oxford has cited to him specific occurrences of *qeryānā* in 6th and 7th century mss. of liturgical texts, e.g. the *Qeryānā d-yōm bā'awātā* ("Reading for the Day of Supplications") and *Qeryānā d-sulāqeh d-māran* ("Reading for Ascension Day"). I have since (October, 1982) confirmed this personally with Professor Brock.

[20] The *maṣdar* form *fi'lān* is, as a personal communication from my colleague W. Heinrichs reminds me, certainly common enough that one would have every reason to expect *qiryān* as the directly borrowed form. Cf. *maṣdars* such as *riḍwān*, *ḥirmān*, or *nisyān*.

Mention should also be made of a second, more neglected possible influence upon the specific meaning and connotations of *qur'ān* in the original Islamic usage, namely that of related Hebrew forms of the root *Q-R-'*. Rabbinic Jewish use of *q'rī'ā* and *miqrā'* parallels the two uses of *qeryānā* among Syriac Christians noted above.[21] *Miqrā'* is also used as a Talmudic term for the whole Bible,[22] one which "serves to underline both the vocal manner of study and the central role that the public reading of the Scriptures played in the liturgy of the Jews".[23] While here again the difference in the specific form of *qur'ān* from either Hebrew term argues against direct "borrowing" from the Hebrew, these two Jewish usages may well have served along with the Christian terminology to influence the meaning of *qur'ān* in Arabic usage.

Whichever derivation one prefers, the implication of the evidence is clear in one regard: *qur'ān* must have been understood as referring to *scripture reading* or *recitation* such as Jews and Christians in the Arabian environment would have also had.[24] Whatever its linguistic history, "qur'ān" in this situation would have signalled to everyone that these words were being presented as God's holy word to be recited in worship. In the seventh-century Arabian milieu, where these older scriptural traditions (and probably that of the Zoroastrians) were very much in evidence, a "book" used in liturgy and devotions would not have been a silently-read document but a sacred word that one proclaimed aloud and to which one listened with reverence.

---

[21] J. Horovitz, "Qur'ān", *Der Islam*, XIII (1923), 67, does not distinguish between the two, calling both "Schriftverlesung"; Nöldeke-Schwally, I, 32, notes that *miqrā'* can be used for parts as well as the whole of Scripture. Jeffery, *For. Vocabulary*, p. 234, notes that Marracci and Geiger had earlier argued for the Hebrew derivation of *qur'ān*, but he prefers the Syriac. I have become more convinced of the importance of these two Jewish usages for an understanding of the historical background against which *qur'ān* must be seen after seeing part of an unpublished paper by Ms. Judith Wegner, a researcher at Harvard Law School, and discussing both her paper and the present one with her (Nov. 1979). Her position is to presume Jewish influence something that remains to be demonstrated, however.

[22] D. Künstlinger, "Kitāb und Ahlu-l-kitāb", *RO*, IV (1928), 239, and "Die Namen der 'Gottes-Schriften' im Qorān", *RO*, XIII (1937), 76, n. 2. Cf. Nöldeke-Schwally, I, 32; *EJ*, IV, 816.

[23] *Ency. Judaica*, IV, 816; I. Elbogen, *Der jüdische Gottesdienst in seiner geschichtlichen Entwicklung* (3rd ed. rev. Frankfurt a./M., 1931), pp. 155-205.

[24] This view is substantially the same as that advanced by Tor Andrae, *Mohammed*, pp. 78-79 (= p. 96 of Eng. trans. by Th. Menzel [rev. ed. New York, 1960], which is wholly inadequate on this particular passage), in somewhat more deterministic fashion, but with Andrae's particular brilliance.

This becomes more obvious when one remembers, wholly apart from the natural association of oral recitation with sacred word, that "books" as such were until relatively recent times basically texts to be read aloud from or learned by heart and recited. (This was *a fortiori* true of sacred books.) The Gutenberg revolution in the West gradually changed this,[25] until especially in the past two to three centuries, first in the West and then worldwide, the explosion of "book-culture" fixed the notion of text inextricably to the printed rather than the spoken word. (Only in recent decades, under the impact of newer communications technologies is the written word's hegemony perhaps waning.[26]) This was never previously the case, for until latter times in a few European countries, the majority of any given cultural or religious group was illiterate and hence dependent upon reading aloud or reciting for the communication of texts of any kind. Indeed, even the literate minority in most societies would only very late have practiced "silent reading"; for most of human history reading was done with moving lips, aloud, even when alone.[27]

Returning to the Qur'ān, one finds that its internal evidence corroborates this idea that *qur'ān* meant originally "reciting [aloud]". The recurring imperative "Qul!" ("Say!"; over 300 occurrences) that introduces so many Qur'ānic passages is itself a striking reminder that these texts are intended to be recited aloud. What has not, however, been adequately stressed, is the equally striking coherence of meaning that results when one insists upon the basic sense throughout the Qur'ān of "to proclaim aloud, recite orally" [= German *vorlesen, vortragen*,

---

[25] Cf. Elizabeth Eisenstein, *The Printing Press as an Agent of Change* (Cambridge, 1979), which gives greater causal centrality to printing as a revolutionary force in the Reformation and all subsequent European history than seems credible. But that a revolution in communication did occur as a result of the invention of the press can hardly be denied.

[26] I.e., under the influence of video and computer technology, which have already begun to change radically today's communications and "storage" of information.

[27] Cf. J. Balogh, "Voces Paginarum. Beiträge zur Geschichte des lauten Lesens und Schreibens", *Philologus*, LXXXII (1926-27), 83-109, 202-240; J. Leclercq, *L'Amour des lettres et le désir de Dieu* (Paris, 1957), pp. 20-23; Walter J. Ong, *The Presence of the Word* (New Haven, 1967; 2nd ed. Minneapolis, 1981), pp. 58-65; and Marshall McLuhan, *The Gutenberg Galaxy: The Making of Typographic Man* (Toronto, 1962), pp. 82-95; also pp. 18-21, 26-28, 45-50, 74-79. Cf. the famous passage in Augustine's *Confessions* in which he is so amazed that when Ambrose would read a book, "his eyes glided over the pages, and his heart searched out the sense, but his voice and tongue were at rest", that he cannot help but comment on the novelty of this (tr. E. Pusey [New York, 1949], p. 98; Latin orig., edd. J. Gibb and W. Montgomery [2nd ed. Cambridge, 1927], p. 141, lines 10-11).

368

verlesen] for all eighty-seven occurrences of the root *Q-R-'*,[28] and in particular when one retains the verbal quality of "reciting" for the most frequent form (seventy of the eighty-seven instances) of the root, the verbal noun *qur'ān* itself.

There are a few occurrences of the finite verb *qara'a* in conjunction with the word *kitāb* where a simple meaning of "to read" seems indicated:[29] S. 17:93, "... until you send down to us *a scripture that we may read* (*kitāban naqra'uhu*)";[30] 10:94, "... ask *those who* [*have*] *read the Scripture* (*alladhīna yaqra'ūna l-kitāb*) before you";[31] and the three passages (17:14, 71; 69:19) in which *qara'a* is used with *kitāb* as object to refer to the "reading" of each person's "book" of good and evil deeds at the Last Judgment.[32] In all of these cases, however, the vocal sense of "to read" gives the best sense. Reading here is, in good part for the aforementioned historical reasons, but also from the internal context, "reading aloud". Certainly each passage contains a clear link between oral reading or reciting and a "Book" or "Scripture"—either a heavenly one from which revelation comes or a heavenly, but individual, one in which one's personal fate is inscribed.[33]

---

[28] There is in fact an eighty-eighth occurrence (S. 2:228), but in the form of *qurū'*, a plural substantive meaning "menstrual cycles" and derived from *qara'a* as indicated above, n. 13; this word is not otherwise linked to any other forms of the root in the Qur'ān.

[29] The following and all subsequent Qur'ān-translations are my own. I have consulted throughout several European translations: R. Paret, *Der Koran* (Stuttgart, 1962); R. Blachère, *Le Coran*, 2 voll. (Paris, 1949-51); R. Bell, *The Qur'an*, 2 voll. (Edinburgh, 1937-39); and (to a lesser extent) A. J. Arberry, *The Koran Interpreted*, 2 voll. (London and New York, 1955). All Qur'ān references are to the standard Cairo text.

[30] Buhl, *EI*, II, 1063a, cites this as the place where *qara'a* "certainly stands for 'to read'"; Blachère translates it with *lire*, Bell and Arberry with *read*, and Paret with *lesen*.

[31] Unaccountably, when compared with the similar context of S. 17:93 treated above, only Paret translates *qara'a* here with *lesen*; Bell and Arberry have *recite*, and Blachère *réciter*, which support my own rendering below. Of course the German "lesen" here can, like the French and English equivalents, be taken to mean "to read aloud" (i.e. = *verlesen, vorlesen*).

[32] Blachère, Bell, and Arberry all translate *qara'a* here as in 17:93 (cf. n. 30 above). Paret, however, renders it more felicitously in two instances (17:71; 69:19) with *verlesen*, "to read aloud, forth", and only in 17:14 with *lesen*.

[33] On the link between these two different notions of a heavenly *Kitāb*, see F. Buhl, "Die Schrift und was damit zusammenhängt", in *Oriental Studies* (P. Haupt Festschrift), edd. C. Adler and A. Ember (Baltimore and Leipzig, 1926), pp. 370-73, cf. 364-69; G. Widengren, *The Ascension of the Apostle and the Heavenly Book* (Uppsala and Leipzig, 1950), *passim*, esp. ch. I; and J. Horovitz, *Kor. Untersuchungen*, pp. 65-68. Cf. also J. Pedersen's review of E. Meyer, *Ursprung und Geschichte der Mormonen* (1912), in *Der Islam*, V (1914), 110-115; D. Künstlinger, "Kitāb und Ahlu-l-kitāb", *RO*, IV (1928), 238-

Otherwise, the remaining twelve instances of the finite verb are all clearly best translated as "to recite, read loud" or "to proclaim" (e.g. 96:1: "*Proclaim* [or 'Recite': *iqra'*] in the name of your Lord..."; [34] 26:198-199: "Had We sent it [the Revelation] down to some of the non-Arabs, *and had he* [the Prophet] *then recited it for them* [*fa-qara'ahu 'alayhim*], they would not have accepted it [him?]"; and 87:6, "*We shall cause you to recite* [*sa-nuqri'uka*], and then you will not forget").

With the oral sense of *qara'a* firmly in mind, the verbal noun *qur'ān* can be properly understood in the Qur'ān. The word occurs in all seventy instances in only three basic senses: (1) as *the act of reciting* God's words (also *dhikr*, "reminding"; *tilāwah*, "reciting"), (2) as *the whole Revelation* that God is giving to be proclaimed/recited (also *Dhikr*, "Reminding"; *Nudhur*, "Warning; *Furqān*, "Salvation" or "Discrimination"),[35] and (3) as *any particular revelation* given to be recited (also *āyah*, a "sign", then a "verse"; *sūrah*, a "scripture portion" or "line" [?].[36] It is often possible to read *qur'ān* in any one of these three senses in a given passage. Scholars have tended to prefer the second, "collective" sense in all but a few cases where this is clearly impossible (e.g. S. 75:17-18 and 17:78, where it describes an action, and in 72:1, 12:3, and 10:16, where it refers to a single revelation). This tendency is the result of the aforementioned "reading back" of the later, reified sense of *al-Qur'ān* as "what is between the two boards" (i.e. the complete and collected "Scripture") onto the "recitations" that only later came to be the collected Qur'ān. If this proclivity is resisted, however, and the verbal force of the word kept in mind, the reading of *qur'ān* as *the act of reciting* (sense no. 1, above) clearly predominates.

In at least half of the seventy total occurrences, this active sense is preferable to or at least as good as either of the other two readings. Nowhere is this clearer than in the two passages about whose translation there is no dispute:

247; and Geo Widengren, *Muhammad, the Apostle of God, and His Ascension* (Uppsala and Wiesbaden, 1955), esp. pp. 115-139.

[34] Traditionally, the first *qur'ān* revealed to Muḥammad.

[35] On *furqān*, see the fine summary article by R. Paret, *EI*², II, 949-950, and the further references given there.

[36] The derivation and original meaning of *sūrah* are uncertain; cf. Jeffery, *For. Vocabulary*, pp. 180-181 (with further references), and Bell, *Origin*, p. 52.

370

Observe the *ṣalāt* at the sinking of the sun until the darkening of night, and *the dawn recital (qur'ān al-fajr)*; truly, *the dawn recital (qur'ān al-fajr)* is *well-attested (mashhūd)*. (17:78)

Do not move your tongue with it so that you hurry too much! Ours it is to collect it and *to recite it (qur'ānahu)*, and when We recite it, *follow its recitation (fa-ttabi' qur'ānahu)*. (75:16-18)

Almost equally undebatable is the refrain in S. 54 in which God says that He has "made the reciting manageable/accessible" (*yassara l-qur'ān*) "for [the purpose of] reminding/making mention" (*li-l-dhikr*) (S. 54:17, 22, 32, 40).

Surah 20:114 warns Muḥammad not to "hurry" in "reciting" (*wa-lā ta'jal bi-l-qur'ān*) before the revealing (or "suggesting": *awḥā*)[37] to him is completed. Surah 73:4 orders him to "perform the recitation carefully/distinctly" (*rattil al-qur'ān tartīlan*). God is referred to in 28:85 as "He who *made reciting your* [Muḥammad's] *duty*" (*faraḍa 'alayka al-qur'ān*). Three further passages refer also to this reciting or proclaiming of the divine Word by the Prophet:

Those who ungratefully deny [God] said: "*Do not listen to this reciting (lā tasma'ū li-hādhā l-qur'ān); confuse it* [by interrupting it with?] *babbling (wa-lghaw fīhi)* – perhaps you will gain the upper hand." (41:26)

When We turned aside to you a band of Jinn to listen to *the reciting (al-qur'ān)*, and when they witnessed it, they said [to one another?]: "Keep still" ... (46:29)

... and *when you* [Muḥammad] *were mindful/made mention of your Lord in reciting (idhā dhakarta rabbaka fī l-qur'ān)*, they turned their backs in aversion. (17:46)

The "shunning" of the prophetic reciting (*al-qur'ān*) by some is also mentioned in S. 25:30, and 4:82 (= 47:24): "... Do they then pay no attention to the recital ...?" (*a-fa-lā yatadabbarūna l-qur'ān*). That the act of oral recitation of God's word is not to be scoffed at is made vivid in 13:31, where a rhetorical question is posed: "If, through a[n act of] recitation (*qur'ān*), the mountains were moved, or the earth cleft ... [would people then have faith]?" Those persons with understanding will of course fear the retribution promised in the recitation (50:45: "Warn by reciting [*dhakkir bi-l-qur'ān*] those who fear my threat"), but some

[37] The argument for the translation "suggesting" by R. Bell (W. M. Watt, ed., *Bell's Introduction to the Qur'ān* [Edinburgh, 1970], pp. 20-22) is persuasive even if not conclusive.

people are still so perverse as to "call the reciting lies" (*ja'alū l-qur'ān 'iḍīna*, 15:91). They *hear* the Scripture recited, but they do not *listen*.

A substantial number of the occurrences of *qur'ān* are with the demonstrative *hādhā*.[38] In these instances it would be possible to interpret "this recitation" either as the act or as the whole or part of the Recitation; however, in at least eight of these cases,[39] reading *qur'ān* as the *act* of reciting recalls an historical context in which the passages would have been recited for all to hear. Two examples (one found in two places) suffice:

Were men and jinn to join forces *to produce reciting like this (an ya'tū bi-mithl hādhā l-qur'ān)*, they would not match it... (17:88)

We have coined for people *in this reciting (fī hādhā l-qur'ān)* all kinds of similitudes. (30:58; 39:27)

Still other instances in which *qur'ān* can be read as either the act of reciting or what is recited are the following:

...a group of jinn listened and said: "*Truly we have heard a wondrous recital* [or "reciting that was wondrous"] (*innā sami'nā qur'ānan 'ajaban*) (72:1)

The All-Merciful—He taught reciting [or "the Recitation"] (*'allama l-qur'ān*); He created man; He taught him the clear explanation. (55:2)

We have not taught him [Muḥammad] [the art of] poetry, nor would it become him. Truly, it is naught but *a recollecting and a clear reciting* [or "a reminder and a clear recited text"] (*dhikr wa-qur'ān mubīn*). (36:69)

To these should be added the six verses that speak of revelation "for reciting in Arabic" [or "in the form of an Arabic recitation"] (*qur'ānan 'arabiyyan*)[40] and the one instance in which "a foreign recitation" is mentioned.[41] In two of the "Arabic *qur'ān*" passages (41:3; 43:3), the

[38] In addition to the eight treated in this paragraph, *hādhā l-qur'ān* occurs in 25:30; 34:31; 41:26; 43:31; and 59:21.

[39] S. 17:9, 41, 88, 89; 18:54; 27:76; 30:58; and 39:27.

[40] S. 12:2; 20:113; 39:28; 41:3; 42:7; 43:3. It is significant that this phrase is translated by Snouck Hurgronje, *RHR*, XXX, 154, as a "texte à réciter arabe"! Other passages in which *qur'ān* should be read either as the act of reading or as the passage recited are those which begin with an oath, "by the *qur'ān*": *wa-l-qur'ān al-ḥakīm* (36:2); *wa-l-qur'ān dhī l-dhikr* (38:1); *wa-l-qur'ān al-majīd* (50:1). Likewise, with "the tree cursed in the *qur'ān*" (referring to the Zaqqūm tree mentioned in 37:62? [So Ibn Kathīr, *Tafsīr* (4 voll. Cairo, n.d.), III, 48-49]), the phrase could mean "in reciting" or "in the recitation [in which it is mentioned]", or "in the Recitation [as a whole]."

[41] S. 41:44: *Wa-law ja'alnāhu qur'ānan a'jamiyyan*, which I translate as "Had we caused it to be recited in a non-Arab tongue [they would have said, 'Why are its signs (verses) not made distinct...?']".

act of reciting is linked to the notion of *kitāb*: "something ordained or written, a scripture". Similarly, "reciting" (*qur'ān*) is in six other passages associated with a written scripture or tablet, apparently a heavenly one from which what is to be recited is taken.[42] Compare two of these: "... These are *the 'signs' of the Scripture and of a clear recitation (āyāt al-kitāb wa-qur'ānin mubīnin)* (15:1),[43] and "... Truly it is *a clear recitation in a written Scripture (qur'ānun mubīnun fī kitābin maktūbin)* (56:77). This kind of juxtaposition of the act of reciting with a written text points to the kind of understanding of scripture already suggested: *Scripture is something to be recited.* The presence in the text of the collected Qur'ān of both the idea of a heavenly *Kitāb* and the concept of divine Word as something intended for oral repetition is only an apparent contradiction; each belongs to the larger revelatory process.

In the light of the preceding, the latter passages above and those others that speak of "reciting the recitation" (*qara'a l-qur'ān*[44] or *talā l-qur'ān*[45] are seen to reflect the way in which the Prophet's reciting of individual revelations led to use of *qur'ān* as the "proper-noun" title of the (Arabic) Recitation from the heavenly Book containing God's Word. "Al-Qur'ān" is a Recitation given by God to Muḥammad just as previous scriptures had been given to other prophets to recite. "Reciting the recitation" means (knowing by heart—memorizing—and) declaiming the divine prescript (*al-Kitāb*) or a portion of it.[46]

Thus, in the one passage (9:111) that speaks explicitly of "a promise binding upon" God "in the Torah, the Evangel, and the Qur'ān" (*fī l-tawrāt wa-l-injīl wa-l-qur'ān*), *qur'ān* should be understood as "the Recitation" (i.e. "the Scripture") that God is giving to the Arabs. As such it parallels and fulfills the previous scriptures that He gave to Jews

---

[42] *Kitāb* is the word used in five instances (cf. the linking of *qara'a* and *kitāb* noted above, p. 368); 10:37, 61; 15:1; 27:1; 56:77.

[43] S. 27:1 reverses these and their grammatical definition: "These are signs of *al-qur'ān* and of a *kitāb mubīn*."

[44] S. 7:204; 16:98; 17:45; 84:21. Similar to these are 73:20, "Recite of the Recitation [or, of the particular passage in question? *min al-qur'ān*] what you can manage [lit. 'what is easy for you']," and 17:106, "a recitation (*qur'ān*) that We have divided [made clear? *faraqnā*] that you might recite it (*la-taqra'ahu*) to the people ..."

[45] S. 27:92. *Talā* occurs throughout the Qur'ān in the sense of "recite". Cf. M. F. 'Abd al-Bāqī, *al-Mu'jam al-mufahras li-alfāẓ al-Qur'ān al-karīm* (numerous editions), *s.v.*

[46] This sense of *qur'ān* as scripture is especially evident in a further passage, 34:31: "Those who have ungratefully denied [God] say: 'We have no faith in this Recitation' (*lan nu'mina bi-hādhā l-qur'ān*)." *Qur'ān* could refer here to the act of recitation, but the *āmana bi* usage suggests "scripture", i.e. God's very Word, as the preferable translation.

and Christians and others in *their* own languages. Similarly, in the cases in which *al-qur'ān* (or *hādhā l-qur'ān*) is spoken of as being "sent down" (*N-Z-L* in one of its finite verbal forms: eight occurrences,[47]) "given" (*ātā*, 15:87), "received" (*laqqā*, 27:6), or "revealed [suggested]" (*awḥā*, 6:19, 12:3),[48] the concept of the whole Revelation or a particular segment of it being communicated by God from on high to Muḥammad as "scripture" for Arabic speakers seems to be what is intended. The process, however, like the product, is first and foremost an oral one; the "proper-noun" sense of *qur'ān* in the Qur'ān is that of a fundamentally oral and certainly an active, ongoing reality, rather than that of a written and "closed" codex such as is later represented by the *maṣāḥif*.[49]

There is considerable evidence outside the Qur'ānic text to support this interpretation of the denotation and connotation of *qur'ān* in the earliest period. While a thorough examination of the extra-qur'ānic sources is a subject for a separate inquiry, it is important to note here at least some of the material that supports the foregoing argument.[50]

Early poetic references to verbal use would be a logical place to start, but the Muslim sources themselves quote only one such instance of *qur'ān* in their discussions of the word's meaning. This is in a verse generally ascribed to Ḥassān b. Thābit, the most famous of the poets associated with the rise of Islam and an older contemporary of Muḥammad.[51] Ḥassān speaks here of one who "breaks the night[52] by

---

[47] S. 2:185; 5:101; 17:82, 106; 20:2; 43:31; 59:21; and 76:23.

[48] Cf. also S. 10:15, where those who deny the resurrection-preaching are quoted as saying: "Recite something other than this, or change it! (*i'ti bi-qur'ānin ghayr hādhā aw baddilhu*)." Here "a *qur'ān*" is best understood as referring to one particular "recitation", but could also apply to the Revelation as a whole.

[49] Other materials in the Qur'ān itself remain to be examined for the additional light they might shed on this aspect of the earliest understanding of *qur'ān*. In particular, the *numerous (63) occurrences of the root T-L-W*, "to dictate, recite", and the less frequent but important use (16 times) of *Ḥ-F-Ẓ*, "to preserve, guard, have by heart". Similarly, *J-M-'*, "to collect, learn by heart" also bears scrutiny.

[50] Evidence of what has been argued here to be a later (at least post-'Uthmānic) phenomenon—namely the understanding of *qur'ān* primarily as the fixed, written record of revelation to Muḥammad, "al-Qur'ān"—is of course amply available. Dozens of examples of the more concretized or reified use can be seen even by scanning the entries in A. J. Wensinck *et al.*, *Concordance et indices de la tradition musulmane*, 7 voll. (Leiden, 1936-69), *s.v.* "qur'ān".

[51] W. 'Arafat, "Ḥassān b. Thābit", *EI²*, III, 271-73.

[52] I.e. gets up in the night [lit. "interrupts, breaks up the night (constantly)"] to perform his devotions. This has of course been a common devotional practice in Islam: cf. A. J. Wensinck, "Tahadjdjud", *SEI*, p. 559.

praising [God] and reciting" (*yuqaṭṭi' al-layl tasbīḥan wa-qur'ānan*),[53] a clear adverbial (*ḥāl*) use of the *maṣdar* form to denote the *act* of reciting.

The Ḥadīth literature provides a rich fund of examples, especially of *qur'ān* as the act of reciting. Ibn Ḥanbal cites a tradition in which it is said that whoever recites Sūrahs 2 and 3 "has recited a great deal" (*qad qara'a qur'ānan kathīran*).[54] Another account describes how Muḥammad, when he performed the *Ṣalāt*, "raised his voice with the recitation" (*rafa'a ṣawtahu bi-l-qur'ān*),[55] and Muḥammad is said to have spoken highly of a man who "was constantly mindful of God in/during [his] reciting" (*kāna rajulan kathīr al-dhikr li-llāh fī l-qur'ān*).[56] "In every *Ṣalāt* there is a recitation (*qur'ānun*)," [57] and several *ḥadīths* speak of "the one of you [or 'them'—in either case, the Muslims] who can recite the most (*aktharukum/hum qur'ānan*)" [58] as the person most qualified to lead the *ṣalāt*. Repeatedly in the Ḥadīth, recitation of God's Word is linked in similar fashion to formal worship or to private devotion. Two further examples deserve particular mention. The first is a Divine Saying in which the Prophet is quoted as saying that

> ... the Lord says: "Whosoever is kept from petitioning Me [for help, favors] because of preoccupation with *reciting and constant mindfulness of Me (al-qur'ān wa-dhikri)*, him shall I give far better than what I give to those who ask things of Me ..."[59]

The second example is an account of how one night one of the Companions was reciting a *qur'ān* (in some versions, specifically Sūrah 18, "Kahf"), and suddenly one of his animals in the courtyard tried to break loose and run away. He looked to see what had frightened the

---

[53] *Kitāb al-Mabānī*, p. 58; Ṭabarī, *Tafsir*, I, 97 (where *qur'ān* is glossed as *qirā'ah*, which is the common *maṣdar* form of *qara'a*, at least since *qur'ān* took on its "proper-noun" sense; Ṭabarī also gives the passive participle, *maqrū'*, in this discussion. Also cited by Horovitz, *Kor. Untersuchungen*, p. 74, n. 1, and Nöldeke-Schwally, I, 34.

[54] *Musnad*, III, 245.

[55] Muslim b. al-Ḥajjāj, *aṣ-Ṣaḥīḥ*, ed. M. F. 'Abd al-Bāqī, 5 voll. (Cairo, 1374/1955-1375/1956), 4:145.

[56] Ibn Ḥanbal, *Musnad*, IV, 159.

[57] *Ibid.*, II, 285.

[58] Bukhārī, 10:54 (= *Musnad*, V, 71); Bukhārī, 64:53:3 (= *Musnad*, V, 30, and Aḥmad al-Nasā'ī, *Sunan*, 8 voll. [Cairo, n.d.], 7:8); Muḥammad b. 'Īsā al-Tirmidhī, *Ṣaḥīḥ* (13 voll., Cairo, 1350/1931-1353/1934), 8:31.

[59] Tirmidhī, 46:25; also 'Abdallāh al-Dārimī, *Sunan*, ed. 'Abdallāh al-Yamanī al-Madanī, 2 voll. (Cairo, 1386/1966), 23:6. [Note that this Divine Saying is not included in, and should be added to, the ninety dealt with in W. Graham, *Divine Word and Prophetic Word*.]

beast, but could find nothing. When he related this to Muḥammad the next day, the Prophet said, "That was the power of the Divine Presence that descended with the reciting [that you were doing]" (*tilka al-sakīnah tanazzalat bi-l-qur'ān*).[60]

There are also numerous instances in the Ḥadīth where *qur'ān* refers clearly to a single revelation/recitation.[61] The Companions seem to have had a fear of doing something that might cause "a *qur'ān* to be sent down about that".[62] Particular *qur'āns* were revealed on particular occasions, as several traditions show;[63] Ibn 'Umar tells how a man came from Muḥammad to say that "a *qur'ān* was sent down to him last night" (*inna ... qad unzila 'alayhi al-laylata qur'ān*).[64] Muslims asked for and gave *qur'ān*s on numerous particular issues,[65] but the need for knowing such *qur'ān*s to deal with specific problems was less important—at least in terms of the widespread and frequent use of *qur'ān*s among all the Muslims—than the need to know them in order to perform the *ṣalāt*. A performance of the formal act of worship without a *qur'ān* in it is "deficient",[66] although in Muḥammad's instructions to a bedouin who asks how to perform the *ṣalāt*, he says: "if you 'have' a *qur'ān*, recite it; if not, then praise and magnify God."[67] In any case, the reciting of God's word is something that, according to one *ḥadīth*, is "to be returned" to God as "the very best" of all that He has given man.[68]

---

[60] Bukhārī, 66:11; Tirmidhī, 46:25. On *sakīnah*, see W. Graham, *Divine Word and Prophetic Word*, p. 21, n. 13.

[61] This usage also continues to appear in later sources, e.g., al-Qushayrī (d. 466/1074), *al-Fuṣūl fī l-uṣūl* (ed. and tr. Richard Frank, forthcoming in *MIDEO*, 1980/81), article 45 [concerning God's Word]: "And what is recited is called 'a recitation' (*wa-yusammā al-maqrū' qur'ānan*), just as what is drunk is called 'a drink'"; or the story [ref. provided by Wolfhart Heinrichs] cited by Ibn Manẓūr, *Lisān al-'Arab* (Beirut ed.), VII, 183ab, of how the wife of the poet 'Abdallāh b. Rawāḥah suspects him of having just had intercourse with a slave girl. Since he had earlier sworn never to recite the Qur'ān unless ritually pure, his wife cleverly asks him to recite from scripture in order to catch him out. Thereupon the poet recites a poetic *shahādah* of three lines, which satisfies his wife as to his innocence because "she thought this to be a *qur'ān*" (*ḥasibat hādhā qur'ānan*).

[62] *Musnad*, II, 252.

[63] *Musnad*, I, 237; II, 307, 337; III, 255 (= Muslim, 5:297).

[64] Bukhārī, *Tafsīr* S. 2, *ḥadīth* 14 (also in 15, 16).

[65] Ibn 'Abbās answers another man's question with "I shall recite for you a *qur'ān* about that" (*sa-atlū 'alayka bi-dhālika qur'ānan*): Tirmidhī, *Tafsīr* S. 63, ḥadīth 5. Cf. *Musnad*, V, 30.

[66] *Musnad*, III, 215.

[67] Tirmidhī, 2:110.

[68] *Ibid.*, 46:17:2.

376

The Ḥadīth reports confirm what the Qur'ānic evidence suggests: that the Muslim concept of scripture was originally—perhaps for generations, and for many Muslims, still today—one of an oral Recitation of God's Word. The later merging of the *idea* of the divine Scripture/Prescript (*al-Kitāb*) with the *fact* of the collected Qur'ān of the *maṣāḥif* tended to overwhelm the earlier, more active, aural apprehension of God's Word made present in recitation. Yet the Muslim community did manage to hold on in remarkable fashion to the fundamentally recitative quality of their scripture. Both in the *ṣalāt* and in the widely practiced night vigils, *dhikr*-exercises, festive Qur'ān recitations [e.g. in Ramaḍān], personal prayer (*du'ā'*) and other supererogatory devotional exercises, Muslims early and late have raised the recitation of Holy Writ to an art and to a constant and ever-present reality in their personal and communal life. In this way they have kept alive the original sense of *qur'ān* as recitation even while revering it as a book. In other words, they have retained with considerable vigor their sense of Qur'ān as *scripture* in both its oral and written dimensions.

It is the active oral participation in the scriptural reality that the preceding evidence from Qur'ān and Ḥadīth reflects most vividly. The recitation, memorization, and "mindfulness" (*dhikr*)[69] of the Qur'ān in liturgical and devotional life are keys to understanding the basic character of this scriptural reality in earliest Islam and, in significant degree, throughout Islamic history. The theological concept of an impeccably revealed divine Word is posterior to the concept of God's Word as that which God wants His servants to hear and to recite in worship of Him. The reciting of *qur'āns* and the prostrating of the body—whatever their original form and regulation[70]—were the fundamental devotional acts urged on the individual and the community of Muslims. It is in liturgy (and recitation *is* the liturgy effectively in Islam) and in devotional life that one has to seek the distinctive character of *qur'ān* as scripture; what bound Muhammad's community together

---

[69] Cf. P. Nwyia, *Exégèse coranique et langage mystique* (Beirut, 1970), pp. 36-37, where the author points out how, in Muqātil's *Tafsir*, the word *dhikr* is closely linked to recitation in the *ṣalāt* and is often interpreted as *qur'ān* in particular.

[70] On the development of the cultus, see J. Horovitz, "Bemerkungen zur Geschichte und Terminologie des islamischen Kultus", *Der Islam*, XVI (1927), 249-263; E. Mittwoch, "Zur Entstehungsgeschichte des islamischen Gebets und Kultus", *Abhl. d. Pr. Ak. d. Wiss.* (1913), n. 2; and C.H. Becker, "Zur Geschichte des islamischen Kultus", *Der Islam*, III (1912), 374-99.

was the faith that through the revelation to him they too, like the Jews and Christians before them, had been given God's Word for guidance and comfort—which are realized in the acts of committing to heart and reciting that Word at every opportunity, thereby living that Word and confirming its status as scripture.

11

THE QUR'ĀNIC VIEW OF YOUTH AND OLD AGE

Thomas J. O'Shaughnessy

To some extent youth and old age are relative concepts. In examining attitudes towards them in an Arabic document dating from the six hundreds many physical and cultural adjustments have to be made to changed situations. Today's First World societies have an infant mortality rate of eight to sixteen per thousand live births; in primitive societies the rate fluctuates from three hundred to over five hundred per thousand.[1] Life expectancy at birth now runs from seventy to seventy-five in developed countries, but in some retarded areas it falls to forty years or less.[2] Leviticus 27: 7 makes sixty the dividing line between the mature and the aged, and even today people judge a person over sixty or sixty-five to be old, a statistic that is realized even more commonly in less developed nations. In extremely primitive groups most of the population dies before forty and a man of sixty is usually decrepit.[3]

Classical Arabic usage, describing ideal conditions, divides man's life span as follows: Before eighteen one is classed as a child; from eighteen to forty one enjoys full vigor in body and mind; and from fifty to eighty one experiences old age.[4] Muḥammad lived to be sixty-three but, orphaned at the age of six, his early years were not marked by affluence.[5] Though the physical conditions in which he matured probab-

[1] In Gambia in 1953 it was a high as five hundred and twenty-five per thousand in some areas. See Sripati Chandrasekhar: *Infant Mortality in India 1901–55*. London: Allen and Unwin 1959, p. 87.

[2] Between 1900 and 1960 life expectancy has grown worldwide by twenty years. Around 1000 B.C. in Greece it is estimated to have been less than twenty years. It was twenty-three years in Rome in Christ's time and thirty years in Europe throughout the Middle Ages. See E. Carwile Le Roy, M. D.: *Life, Expectation of*. In: *New Age Encyclopedia*. 20 vols. New York: Lexicon Publ. 1981, vol. 10, p. 555–56. See also Clark Tibbitts [ed.]: *Handbook of Social Gerontology*. Chicago: Univ. of Chicago Pr. 1960, p. 67.

[3] Tibbitts. *Handbook*, ibid.

[4] See Edward William Lane: *Arabic-English Lexicon*. 2 vols.; a lithogr. reprod. of the 1863 original. Cambridge: The Islamic Texts Soc. Trust 1984, 1, 1477–78; 2, 1519, col. 2; and 2, 1629, col. 1.

[5] Sura 93: 6–8 seems to refer to Muḥammad's early years: "Did He not find you an orphan and give (you) a home? and find you misled, and guide you? and

34

ly did not fall to an extremely primitive level, still the men of his time and place would have aged more rapidly than people of the 1990's living in similar situations. SCHIMMEL's judgment about today's Bedouin could in all likelihood apply to the Arab townsmen of Mecca in the six hundreds: "By the age of 40, particularly among the women, old age has begun."[6]

Comments on the young in the First Meccan Period, that is, in the very early suras of the *Qurʾān* dating approximately from 610 to 615, deal with four topics: (1) killing infants out of shame or poverty is reprehensible; (2) being served by young men and women is one of the rewards of Paradise; (3) Muslims should show concern for fatherless children; and (4) wealth and children can make people forget God. According to BLACHÈRE's chronological arrangement of the suras the earliest text on any of these themes develops the first of the four.

> (18th)[7]81:8f (On Judgment Day) . . . the girl-child who was buried alive will be asked for what sin she was killed.

Muslims usually understand these two verses as condemning the pre-Islamic Arabs for burying unwanted female infants alive partly to control population growth where resources were scarce. The above translation gives the common interpretation but the Arabic text can also apply to evil-doers who on Judgment Day will have to answer for their mur-

---

find you destitute, and free you from want?" RICHARD BELL: *The Qurʾān Translated, with a Critical Arrangement of the Surahs.* Edinburgh: Clark 1937–39, p. 663, n., and RUDI PARET: *Der Koran: Kommentar und Konkordanz.* Stuttgart: Kohlhammer 1971, p. 513, believe that this passage is literally true.

[6] ANNEMARIE SCHIMMEL: *Cultures of the Mashriq.* In: *Encyclopaedia Britannica.* 15th ed. 1978 *Macropaedia,* 11, 574.

[7] The present order of suras in the *Qurʾān* is not chronological. Here the ordinal preceding the number of the sura gives the approximate sequence of the sura according to the calculation of RÉGIS BLACHÈRE, based on the work of the Muslim commentators and that of several European Islamists. Verse numbers preceding the diagonal are those of the standard Egyptian edition of the *Qurʾān*; those following are the numbers of FLÜGEL's edition.

1st–48th	First Meccan Period	610–11 and 615–16
49th–70th	Second Meccan Period	619–19
71st–92nd	Third Meccan Period	619–22
93rd–116th	Medinan Period	622–32

The *Qurʾān* has 114 suras, but BLACHÈRE numbers 116. He comes to this figure by making Suras 74 and 96 into four suras, numbering Suras 73 and 76 as 34 and 34 bis, and omitting the 54th place in his ordering. See RÉGIS BLACHÈRE: *Le Coran: Traduction selon un essai de reclassement des sourates.* Paris: Maisonneuve 1947–51, 2, xv.

derous misdeeds.[8] In (70th) 18: 74–80/73–79, a text dating from the end of the Second Meccan Period, the *Qur'ān* recounts a rabbinic legend telling how al-Khiḍr, corresponding perhaps to Elijah, kills a young man, apparently without any justification but really to protect the Islamic faith of the youth's parents. This passage is followed by a series of texts which warn parents against killing their children, either male or female,[9] out of fear of disgrace or impoverishment. Most often the warning concerns "children" without distinction of sex[10] but in 16: 58f/60f it speaks of a female child, as in 81: 8f. This kind of warning occurs in texts of all Periods.

In contrast to the long span of almost two decades over which the first topic occurs, the descriptions of beautiful lads and maids of Paradise are confined to less than three years late in the First Meccan and early in the Second Meccan Periods. In five suras of the First Meccan Period[11] and in one of the early Second Meccan (44: 54) beautiful young men and women entertain the faithful in Paradise. Individuals of both sexes are compared to pearls in descriptions using a Christian vocabulary[12] and are probably inspired by depictions of angels in Christian paintings or mosaics.[13]

A topic that receives much attention in the *Qur'ān* over a period of about twelve years – from late in the First Meccan to the mid-Medinan Periods – is the just treatment of the orphan, not in the usual English meaning of a child bereft of both parents, but of the fatherless child *(yatīm)*.[14] The Arabic term for parentless *(latīm)* never occurs in the *Qur'ān*. When used in the Medinan Period "orphan" usually refers to children whose fathers had lost their lives fighting to defend or promote Islam. Nineteen texts[15] make mention of orphans, seven in suras classed as Meccan by Blachère and the rest in Medinan passages.

The earliest of the nineteen speaks of God's providential care of Muḥammad, deprived of his father before his birth and motherless by

[8] Blachère: *Le Coran*, pp. 37–38, n.

[9] Ibid., p. 382, n. and 695 n., in connection with 17: 31/33 and 6: 137/138.

[10] E.g., 6: 137/138. 140/141. and 151/152; 17: 31/33; and 60: 12.

[11] Namely 52: 20. 24; 55: 72; 56: 17. 22. 35ff./34ff.; 76: 19 and 78: 33.

[12] Arthur Jeffery: *The Foreign Vocabulary of the Quran*. Repr. Lahore: Al-Biruni 1967, p. 120.

[13] Ibid.

[14] This is also the sense of the noun *yathōm* in the Hebrew Bible.

[15] Namely 2: 83/77. 177/172. 215/211. 220/218; 4: 2. 3. 6/5. 8/9. 10/11. 36/40; 6: 152/153; 8: 41/42; 59: 7; 76: 8; 89: 17/18; 90: 15; 93: 6. 9; and 107: 2.

36

the age of six. The rest forbid harsh and oppressive treatment of fatherless children and urge kindness and justice towards them, above all in the matter of property rights. The Hebrew Bible and especially Aphraates, the Syriac Christian writer, treat the subject in much the same way. But both also recommend as objects of mercy the poor, the oppressed, the stranger, and the widow.[16] The *Qur'ān* too commends the first three[17] to the charity of Muslims but not the widow. The word for widow (or widower), *ayyim*, occurs only once in the *Qur'ān* (in 24: 32) and there in the plural and not in context with orphan. Even in this one occurrence the word means any person now unmarried, whether previously married or not. Marriageable women, single, widowed or divorced, are normally not expected to remain unmarried in Islam.

If the Qur'ānic references to orphans are listed in BLACHÈRE's chronological order, they show the following sequence.

(4th)	93: 6	(91st)	6: 152/153	(102nd)	4: 2
(4th)	93: 9	(93rd)	2: 83/77	(102nd)	4: 3
(8th)	107: 2	(93rd)	2: 177/172	(102nd)	4: 6/5
- - - - - - -	- - - - - - -	(93rd)	2: 215/211	(102nd)	4: 8/9
(34th bis)	76: 8	(93rd)	2: 220/218	(102nd)	4: 10/11
(40th)	90: 15	(97th)	8: 41/42	(102nd)	4: 36/40
(42nd)	89: 17/18			(104th)	59: 7
- - - - - - -	- - - - - - -				

The first three passages, originating early in the First Meccan Period, celebrate God's providence towards the orphan Muḥammad and repudiate oppression of orphans as a class. Then, after an interval of twenty-six suras, three passages from suras of the late First Meccan Period[18] speak of feeding the orphan and the poor, all three using "feed" *(aṭʿama)*, "orphan" *(yatīm)*, and "poor" *(miskīn)*, in close proximity. The time at which these three suras originated saw the beginnings of active opposition to Muḥammad's preaching on the part of the Meccans. Around this time too, a number of his followers emigrated to Abyssinia,

[16] Aphraatis Demonstratio 4, *De Oratione*, 18 (*Patrologia Syriaca*, R. GRAFFIN and I. PARISOT [edd.] Paris: Didot 1894–1926, 1, 179–80; Demonstratio 15, *De Distinctione Ciborum*, 7 (*P. S.*, 1, 751–52); Demonstratio 20, *De Sustentatione Egenorum*, 2 (*P. S.*, 1, 895–96); ibid., 4 (*P. S.*, 1, 897–98); ibid., 15 (*P. S.*, 1, 917–18).

[17] The orphan and also the poor (76: 8), the oppressed (90: 15f.), and the stranger (2: 215/211).

[18] 76: 8; 90: 15; and 89: 17/18.

either to escape persecution or, as WATT surmises,[19] more probably because of rising dissension in the Muslim community. These three exhortations to deeds of beneficence could well have been aimed at strengthening unity among the Muslim converts in the face of a growing threat from outside as well as from within the group. In any case the orphan theme is abandoned abruptly after the third of these passages (89: 17/18, BLACHÈRE's 42nd) and is not resumed until the end of the Third Meccan Period, after an interval of forty-eight suras, in 6: 152/153, BLACHÈRE's 91st.

The resumption begins with 6: 152/153 and continues with a number of recommendations about orphans in twelve other texts, four of them in Sura Two,[20] six in Sura Four,[21] and one each in Suras Eight[22] and Fifty-nine.[23] BELL and WATT date most of these from the second and third year after Muḥammad's arrival in Medina and link them with two important battles, Badr and Uḥud, between the Muslims and Muḥammad's Meccan opponents.[24] The fatherless children mentioned in these passages are now in great part those of Muḥammad's followers who fell in battle in the early years at Medina. The new exhortations go beyond mere kindness to the orphan and look to respect for their property rights and provision for their security by marrying them off — even into the polygamous unions permitted by the *Qur'ān*.[25]

Notable too about almost all these Medinan texts is the occurrence of "relatives" *(al-qurbā)* in close or immediate context with orphans. In Mecca the *Qur'ān* frowned on help founded on ties of kinship, because the Meccan basis for social solidarity was not tribal but religious. Men were to be judged as individuals in isolation from relatives (35: 18/19). But in Medina, where the Muslim community is now firmly established,

[19] W. MONTGOMERY WATT: *Muhammad at Mecca.* Oxford: Clarendon Pr. 1953, p. 115.

[20] Verses 83/77; 177/172; 215/211; and 220/218.

[21] Verse 2, 3, 6/5, 8/9, 10/11, and 36/40.

[22] Verse 41/42.

[23] Verse 7.

[24] See BELL: *The Qur'ān,* in the introductions to Suras Two, Four, and Eight, pp. 2, 66 f., and 159 f. WATT: *Muhammad at Medina.* Oxford 1956, p. 232, n. 2, and p. 255, n. 4, refers 8: 41/42 and 59: 7 to Badr. W. MONTGOMERY WATT: *Bell's Introduction to the Qur'ān.* Edinburgh: Edinburgh Univ. Pr. 1970. (Islamic Surveys. 8.), p. 76, also connects 4: 3 with Uḥud and 8: 41/42 with Badr.

[25] See BELL: *The Qur'ān,* p. 66, and W. MONTGOMERY WATT: *Companion to the Qur'ān.* London: Allen and Unwin 1967, p. 61.

:38

blood ties and the duties they impose are again emphasized (2: 177/172).[26]

Some of these orphan texts are in the form of maxims introduced by "Say" and devised for public use in answer to problems proposed or criticisms directed to Muḥammad. Such criticisms apparently awakened concern among his followers and Muḥammad, after seeking guidance from above, received an answer telling him what to say.[27] Examples are:

(93rd) 2: 215/217 They will ask you what they should contribute. Say: The wealth you bestow is for parents, relatives, orphans, the poor, and the stranger.

(93rd) 2: 220/218 They will ask you about orphans. Say: To deal justly with them is best. . . .

(91st) 6: 148–152/149–153 The polytheists will say: If God had so willed, we should not have committed idolatry. . . . Say: Come, I will tell you what your Lord has forbidden you. . . . Do not meddle with the property of the orphan. . . .

But by far the greatest emphasis on the young occurs in association with possessions and children. In various ways the *Qur'ān* in all four Periods of its promulgation proposes both of them as a temptation, not only to disbelievers, but also to the believers themselves. Possessions *(māl* or *amwāl)* are understood in the widest sense as gold and silver, cattle, horses, garments, weapons, land (3: 14/12), or even wives (64: 14) and relatives (60: 3). Children *(banūn, aulād)* include both sons and daughters, although the Arab preference is for sons.[28] Excessive preoccupation with wealth and children is an obstacle to disbelievers because it makes them indifferent to moral values and to God's invitation to Islam. Even to believers such concern is a "temptation" (8: 28 and 64: 15) causing them to forget God and the life to come (57: 20/19 and 63: 9).

BLACHÈRE lists the passages that warn against over-reliance on wealth and children as follows:

[26] See WATT: *Muhammad at Mecca*, pp. 73–74, and *Companion*, p. 35, on 35: 18/19.

[27] See WATT: *Bell's Introduction*, p. 76.

[28] For these details of usage see also LANE: *Arabic-English Lexicon*, 1, 262, col. 3; 2, 2966, col. 2; and 2, 3026, col. 1. Noteworthy too is the insistence of the Syriac Christian writer Aphraates on wealth and children as obstacles to spiritual progress in Demonstratio 5, *De Bellis*, 7 (*P. S.*, 1, 195–96): "facultates tuae . . . filiis tuis"; Demonstratio 22, *De Morte et Novissimis*, 9 (*P. S.*, 1, 1012, 4): "possessiones . . . liberos"; and Demonstratio 23, *De Acino*, 67 (*P. S.*, 2, 143–46): "divitias . . . filios." See also Bardesanes: *Liber Legum Regionum*, 19 (*P. S.*, 2, 570–71): "divitiae . . . pueri."

First Meccan Period:
(36th) 74: 13

Second Meccan Period:
(51st) 68: 14
(53rd) 71: 12/11
(53rd) 71: 21/20
(58th) 26: 88
(58th) 26: 133
(60th) 19: 77/80
(66th) 23: 55/57
(70th) 18: 39/37
(70th) 18: 46/44

Third Meccan Period:
(74th) 17: 6
(74th) 17: 64/66
(87th) 34: 35/34
(87th) 34: 37/36

Medinan Period
(99th) 3: 10/8
(99th) 3: 14/12
(99th) 3: 116/112
(108th) 58: 17/18
(95th) 64: 14
(95th) 64: 15
(97th) 8: 28
(101st) 57: 20/19
(106th) 63: 9
(112th) 60: 3
(115th) 9: 55
(115th) 9: 69/70
(115th) 9: 85/86

In the above list four texts are placed out of sequence, three in Sura Three (99th) and one in Sura Fifty-eight (108th). The reason for the displacement is their close connection with the Battle of Uḥud in March 625. Bell dates the first three from before this Battle and the last one after it.[29] All four continue the theme of the fourteen texts preceding them in the list, from 74: 13 (36th) to 34: 37/36 (87th): a warning to disbelievers for their excessive reliance on wēalth and children. Bell dates the six passages immediately following the eighteen, that is, from 64: 14 (95th) to 60: 3 (112th), from after Uḥud. These six direct the same warning to Muslim believers: excessive attachment to wealth and children poses a temptation to their faith. The last three texts, all from Sura Nine, hold up as a warning to believers the punishment of disbelievers who abounded in this world's goods.

Sixteen passages speak of certain young people endowed with special virtues worthy of esteem, for example, faith (4: 25/29; 18: 13/12; 21: 60/61; and 52: 21), wisdom (51: 28; 15: 53; and 19: 12/13), mild temper (37: 101/99), integrity (21: 72 and 18: 10/9), devoutness (19: 7ff.), purity (19: 9), and the gift of miraculous speech (19: 29/30). Nearly all these texts were promulgated during the Second Meccan Period (616–619) amid growing opposition from the Meccan leaders who saw their established position and their material interests threatened. During these years too Christian influences appear more prominently. Many in the series of prophets appearing in the suras of the Second Meccan Period are not from the Hebrew Bible but are found in primitive Christian literature more or less heretical.[30] This Christian in-

[29] Blachère: *Le Coran*, pp. 857, 886 n., and 1022, partly confirms this dating by locating 3: 10/8 after the Battle of Badr in February 624 and 3: 116/112 and 58: 17/18 after Uḥud.

[30] See Fr. Buhl: *Muḥammad.* In: EI[1] 3, 690. A positive and kindly concern for the young seems to coincide with periods of stress in Muḥammad's life; e.g.,

40

fluence also appears in many words of Christian origin occurring for the first time in suras of the Second Meccan Period, for example: *ḥanān*, grace (Syriac); *ḥizb*, group (Ethiopic); *tābūt*, ark (Ethiopic); *salwā*, quail (Syriac); *khardal*, mustard seed (Syriac); *aswāq*, streets (Christian Aramaic); *tafsīr*, explanation (Syriac); *baʿl*, Baal (Syriac); *zukhruf*, ornamental work (Syriac), and many others.[31] Six of these sixteen passages also speak of persons mentioned in the Gospels: Zechariah (19: 7), John the Baptist (19: 7 and 19: 12/13), Jesus (19: 19, 20, and 29/30; and 3: 45ff./40ff.), and the Virgin Mary (19: 19, 20; and 3: 45ff./40ff.). Moreover, much of the legendary material introduced in this Period (for example, the stories of the Seven Sleepers of Ephesus, of Alexander the Great, and of Moses and al-Khiḍr), while never associated with the Bible, was well known in Christian Syriac literature.

These texts are listed below in the order assigned to them by Blachère, with one exception: Blachère and Bell both agree that 52: 21 is an addition[32] to a sura of the First Meccan Period made rather late in the Medinan Period by Muḥammad himself. It will be noted too that the terms for boy or youth tend to fall together in passages closely succeeding one another. *Ghulām*, said of male offspring from birth until young manhood,[33] has been translated as "child" and also as "young man," according to the context. *Ghulām* is more common in the earlier texts, *ṣabīy* (a youth) in those around the middle of the Period, and *fatan* (a youth) and its derivitives together with *walad* (child) towards the end. *Dhurrīya* occurs twice in a Medinan passage in the general sense of offspring or young persons, but here old enough to make an act of faith and, as the text implies, to carry it out in action.

(49th) 51: 28 They gave him (Abraham) good news of a wise child *(ghulāmin)* (Ismael)

(52nd) 37: 101f./99–102 We gave him (Abraham) good news of a mild-tempered child *(ghulāmin)* (Ismael)

615–16, the emigration of some of his adherents to Ethiopia; 618, during the boycott by the clan of Hāshim; 621, during the year before Muḥammad's departure for Medina; 624–25, during the battles that made orphans of many children of his companions.

[31] See Jeffery: *Foreign Vocabulary* under the words cited. *Ḥanān* is first found in 19: 13–14, *ḥizb* in 19: 37/38, *tābūt* in 20: 39, *salwā* in 20: 80/82, *khardal* in 21: 47/48, *aswāq* in 25: 7/8, *tafsīr* in 25: 33/35, *baʿl* in 37: 125, and *zukhruf* in 43: 35/34.

[32] Blachère: *Le Coran*, p. 48 n., and Bell: *The Qurʾān*, pp. 535ff.

[33] Lane: *Arabic-English Lexicon*, 2, 2287, col. 1.

(59th) 15: 53 We give you (Abraham) good news of a wise child *(ghulāmin)* (Isaac).
(60th) 19: 7 We give you (Zechariah) good news of a child *(ghulāmin)* whose name is John.
(60th) 19: 12/13 We gave him (John the Baptist) wisdom when a boy *(ṣabīyan)*.
(60th) 19: 19 That I may bestow on you (Mary) a pure child *(ghulāman)* (Jesus).
(60th) 19: 20 How shall I (Mary) have a child *(ghulāmun)*?
(60th) 19: 29/30 One (Jesus) who is in the cradle, a boy *(ṣabīyan)*.
(67th) 21: 60/61 We heard a youth *(fatan)* (Abraham) mention them.
(67th) 21: 72 We bestowed on him (Abraham) . . . Jacob as a grandson *(nāfilatan*-gift).
(70th) 18: 10/9 The youths *(fityatu)* retired to the cave.
(70th) 18: 13/12 They were youths *(fityatun)* who believed in their Lord.
(79th) 12: 19–22 O good news! here is a young man *(ghulāmun* – Joseph*)*
(22nd) 52: 21 Their offspring *(dhurrīyatuhum)* have followed them . . . We have caused their offspring *(dhurriyatuhum)* to join them.
(99th) 3: 45–47/40–42 How shall I (Mary) have a child *(waladun)*
(102nd) 4: 25/29 From among your young women *(fatayātikum)* who are believers.

A shorter series of eleven texts, dating mostly from the Third Meccan or the Medinan Periods, manifests either an attitude of indifference towards youth or of positive repugnance towards certain qualities of the young. The passages occur in the following approximate chronological sequence:

Second Meccan Period
(53rd) 71: 26f./27f. They (disbelievers) beget only vicious ingrates.
(70th) 18: 60ff./59ff. Moses said to his slave boy *(fatā)*.

Third Meccan Period
(76th) 30: 54/53 God created you in weakness (as infants).
(79th) 12: 30 The wife of the nobleman (Pharaoh) has solicited her slave boy *(fatā)*.
(79th) 12: 36 Two slave boys *(fatayān)* entered the prison with him (Joseph).
(79th) 12: 62 He (Joseph) said to his slave boys *(fityān)*: Put their goods in their packs.
(80th) 40: 67/69 He (God) brings you forth as infants *(ṭiflan)*.

Medinan Period
(102nd) 4: 9f./10f. If they left behind them weak offspring *(dhurrīya)*. . . .
(102nd) 4: 75/77 Why do you not fight for the cause of God and of the miserable ones from among men, women, and slave born children *(wildān)*?
(102nd) 4: 97f./99f. Their abode is Hell, except the miserable ones from among men, women, and slave born children *(wildān)*.

42

(102nd) 4: 127/126 God tells you clearly (what to do) concerning . . . the miserable ones from among . . . the slave born children *(wildān)*.

These passages tend to employ pejorative terms for children. *Fatan* and its derivitives are associated with male and female slaves. *Wildān* in classical usage is used of children born in servitude. The neutral words *ṭifl* and *dhurrīya* in all these texts are used with radicals denoting weakness and misery. The over-all view of the young in passages originating in these years is that of offspring who are wicked, skeptical in religious matters, born in slavery, weak, miserable, and oppressed. The contexts of the passages indicated describe servile situations, solicitation to evil, and imprisonment. The joyful images of youth, so common in the Second Meccan Period, have now given way to a rather depressing portrayal of young people surrounded by evil and oppression.

Seven texts, most of them located in the Third Meccan Period, stress, usually by implication, the strong love of parents for their children. Some of these praise the gratitude that good children have towards their parents; some regard the child as a precious gift to be tenderly cared for; others see in children a consolation and a support to their parents. Five of the texts are Meccan and two are Medinan.

Second Meccan Period

(58th) 26: 18/17 Said Pharaoh: Did we not bring you up among us as a child *(walīdan)?*

Third Meccan Period

(74th) 17: 24/25 My Lord, have mercy on both (parents) since they brought me up when I was small *(ṣaghīran)*

(79th) 12: 21 He who bought him (Joseph) . . . said to his wife: Give him honorable lodging. He may be of service to us or we may adopt him as our child *(waladan)*.

(81st) 28: 9/8 Pharaoh's wife said: (Joseph will be) a comfort to me and to you. Don't kill him. He may be of service to us or we may adopt him as our child *(waladan)*.

(84th) 31: 33/32 . . . Fear a day on which a father will not make satisfaction for his son *(walad)* and a son *(maulūdun)* will not make satisfaction for his father at all.

Medinan Period

(93rd) 2: 233 Mothers shall breast feed their children *(aulād)* for two full years.

(99th) 3: 35/31 . . . Imran's wife said: My Lord, I have vowed to You what is in my womb as a dedicated (offering).

Nine passages, five of them also dated by Bell from around 624, express admiration at the strength and full vigor *(ashudd)* of young adulthood.

(70th) 18: 82/81 Your Lord wished that they both should attain full vigor *(ashudd)*.
(76th) 30: 54/53 After weakness (of infancy) He appointed strength *(qūwa)* (of adulthood) and after strength He appointed weakness (of old age) and gray hairs.
(79th) 12: 22 When he (Joseph) reached full vigor *(ashudd)*, We gave him judiciousness and knowledge.
(80th) 40: 67/69 He gave you birth as an infant that you might reach full vigor *(ashudd)*.
(74th) 17: 34/36 Do not approach the orphan's property except to improve it, until he reaches his full vigor *(ashudd)*.
(81st) 28: 14/13 When he (Moses) reached full vigor *(ashudd)* and became full grown, We gave him judiciousness and knowledge.
(90th) 46: 15/14 When he attains full vigor *(ashudd)* and reaches forty years . . . .
(91st) 6: 152/153 Do not approach the orphan's property except to improve it, until he reaches his full vigor *(ashudd)*.
(109th) 22: 5 (We sustain you through youth) that you may reach full vigor *(ashudd)*.

The use of a noun like *ashudd*, indicating a state of strength rather than the quality itself, brings out the sentiment of admiration expressed in these passages. The weaker term, strength *(qūwa)*, could express the quality and is actually used in 30: 54/53 (76th) to contrast the weakness of infancy with the strength of adulthood. Three of the above passages (30: 54/53; 46: 15/14; and 22: 5) describe the course of human life by enumerating its stages. In these three full vigor *(ashudd)* is seen as the ideal stage worthy of admiration. Two passages (46: 15/14 and 28: 14/13) define the sense in which the *Qur'ān* understands *ashudd* by linking it with an equivalent. In 28: 14/13 the equivalent is *istawā*, to become of full vigor in body and intellect, that is, from twenty-eight to forty years of age.[34]

The extreme limit of maturity in 46: 15/14 is set at forty years. Here no starting point is given, but the lexicons place it variously at seventeen, eighteen or thirty years of age.[35] Only one of the passages (22: 5) cited here occurs in a sura which BLACHÈRE regards as Medinan. But BELL makes four other texts of this set (i.e., 17: 34/36; 28: 14/13; 46: 15/14; and 6: 152/153) Medinan additions to Meccan suras. BLACHÈRE regards Sura Seventeen as of uncertain date; MUIR and HIRSCHFELD[36] put it almost immediately before the Hijra. The chrono-

[34] Ibid., 1, 1477–78.
[35] Ibid., 2, 1519, col. 2.
[36] BLACHÈRE: *Le Coran*, p. 375, and HARTWIG HIRSCHFELD: *New Researches into the Composition and Exegesis of the Qoran*. London: Royal Asiatic Soc. 1902, pp. 36 and 143–44.

logical arrangement of ʿUmar b. Muḥammad b. ʿAbdalkāfī[37] confirms Bell's Medinan date for 6: 152/153 and 46: 15/14.

A large number of passages deny that God has offspring *(waladun)*.[38] *Waladun* has a broad meaning and is variously translated as "a son," "a child," "children" or "offspring." Unless there is explicit mention of Jesus in the context,[39] these denials should be understood as opposing the pagan Arab belief that the angels were God's offspring or that God had begotten "daughters" – a term applied to the pre-Islamic deities.[40] "Child" or "children" in such texts generally has a neutral sense, but in one passage, 43: 81, at least by implication, there appears a positive attitude of respect for a son (similar to the honor shown to his father):

> 43: 81 If the Merciful One had a son, then I would be the first of the worshippers. (See also 39: 4/6.)

Blachère regards 43: 81 and 39: 4/6 as texts of the Second and Third Meccan Periods respectively.

Several legal texts ruling on inheritance (4: 11 ff./12 ff. and 4: 175) understand *waladun* as children, descendants or heirs. Implicit in these Medinan texts is a positive attitude towards children, especially males, both as deserving of just treatment and as capable of supporting parents or others who depend on them. If a man should die without issue, Qur'ānic law divides his property among other relatives.

Four Medinan passages from Sura Twenty-four (107th in Blachère's sequence), aimed at keeping the young innocent, seem to have been occasioned by an incident involving ʿĀ'isha, the youngest wife of Muḥammad. Around the beginning of the year 627 on a night march she was accidentally left behind in the desert. A young soldier brought her back to Medina on the following day. This gave rise to gossip and Muḥammad promulgated Sura Twenty-four to legislate punishment for unsubstantiated accusations of adultery and, incidentally, to lay down rules for domestic life. Several passages in this Sura make significant mention of the young, three explicitly and one implicitly.

> 24: 31 Tell believing women . . . not to show their ornaments (to anyone) except to their husbands . . . or to children not distinguishing women's nakedness.

[37] Cited in the sura headings (except in Suras 110 and 114) of the standard Egyptian edition of the *Qurʾān*.

[38] Paret: *Kommentar*, p. 27, on 2: 116/110, gives fourteen direct references.

[39] E.g., as in 4: 171 f./169 f. and 19: 35/36.

[40] Watt: *Muhammad at Medina*, p. 318.

24: 33 . . . Do not force your slave girls into prostitution for your own chance gain of (this present) life, if they (themselves) wish to live chastely. . . .

24: 59/58 When your children reach puberty, let them ask leave (before coming into your presence), as those before them asked leave. . . . (See also 24: 58/57.)

24: 60/59 As for women past (the age of) child-bearing and without hope of (further) marriage, it is no sin for them to lay aside their (outer) garments, as long as they do not show off their ornaments; but to avoid (taking this liberty) is better for them.

Two of these texts (24: 31 and 24: 59/58) recognize the innocence of very young children, the second adding a rule to prevent their exposure to immodest sights. The word "prostitution" in 24: 33 probably means some form of temporary union not necessarily against pre-Islamic custom.[41] But in any case the sentiment expressed would imply regard for the rights of young female slaves. Also by implication in 24: 60/59 it is expected that younger women should observe proper modesty. All four passages show a positive attitude towards innocence and modesty in the young.

In summary, then, the Qur'ānic attitude towards youth progresses over the years at Mecca from an attitude of concern for the young themselves to concern lest their parents become too possessive in their regard. This sentiment at a later stage gradually verges towards indifference. Then it shifts to admiration for young adulthood and concern for the rights of the young towards the end of Muḥammad's years at Mecca and early in the Medinan Period.

* * *

In the Qur'ān the elderly receive far less attention than the young. The earliest reference to them is in 73: 17 (34th), a Sura of the First Meccan Period dating from about 615. The reference is indirect and looks only to a condition usually found in the old — their gray hair.

How then will you protect yourselves, if you are disbelievers, from a day which will make children gray-headed?

The reference is to the Day of Judgment when fear[42] will cause the hair even of children to turn white. The attitude towards old age itself could

[41] Ibid., pp. 384–85.

[42] Instead of fear Zamakhsharī gives another possible interpretation, namely duration.

46

be interpreted as neutral. But it could also be one of revulsion or dislike from its association with terror as a cause of graying, even in the very young. Two other texts, both dating from the Second Meccan Period, also portray old age as neutral or slightly undesirable. Both associate old age with a punishment from God like that inflicted on Lot's wife.[43]

(58th) 26: 171 f. . . . We delivered him (Lot) and all his family except an old woman, one among those who remained behind.[44] (See also [52nd] 37: 134 f.)

Another group of seven texts of a slightly later date associate old age with traits that arouse aversion or disgust. BLACHÈRE locates these passages in the Second and early Third Meccan Periods, from around the years 617 to 621 when Muḥammad was in his late forties or early fifties. Their rather depressing content appears in the following citations in their approximate chronological order.

(59th) 15: 54 He (Abraham) said: Do you give me good tidings (of a son), despite the fact that old age has overtaken me?
(60th) 19: 4 f./3 ff. He (Zechariah) said: O my Lord, my bones are weak and my head has become hoary with white hair . . . I fear my relatives . . . and my wife is barren. . . .
(60th) 19: 8/9 He (Zechariah) said: O my Lord, how shall I have a son when my wife is barren and I have come to the stiffness of old age?[45]
(62nd) 36: 68 We make stooped in stature[46] him to whom We give long life.

[43] The earliest text (54: 33–38) to mention the deliverance of Lot's family describes all its members as being delivered. Another (21: 74 f.) says Lot himself was saved. These two make one exception, an unidentified old woman. All other passages about the escape of Lot and his family – 7: 83/81; 11: 81/83; 15: 60; 27: 57/58; and 29: 32/31 – are of a later date and identify the one exception as Lot's wife. WATT: *Muhammad at Mecca*, p. 159, attributes this development to Muḥammad's growth in knowledge of the Hebrew Bible.

[44] According to another interpretation of the term "those remaining behind" *(al-ghābirīna)* Lot's aged wife was guilty of a transgression of God's law and was punished for this. See HEINRICH SPEYER: *Die biblischen Erzählungen im Qoran.* Hildesheim: Olms 1971, p. 157 n. 2, citing AL. SPRENGER: *Das Leben und die Lehre des Mohammad.* 2nd ed. 3 vols. Berlin: Nicolai 1869, 1, 493, n. 1.

[45] LANE: *Arabic-English Lexicon*, 2, 1951, cols. 1–2, also explains *ʿitīyan* as implying stiffness or rigidity in the joints and bones. See also PARET: *Kommentar*, p. 322 on 19: 8/9.

[46] LANE, ibid., 2, 2851, col. 1, translates *nakasa* or *nakkasa* as "inverts." Most translations of the *Qurʾān* make *nunakkis* refer to the stooped posture of old age, but the Muslim commentators interpret it by 16: 70/72 and 22: 5 and understand it as the enfeeblement to which God subjects the aged.

(74th) 17: 23/24 Your Lord has commanded . . . (that you show) kindness to (your) parents. If one or both of them attain old age (while living) with you, do not say to them, "Shame on you," . . . but . . . behave humbly towards them out of pity. . . .

(76th) 30: 54/53 God it is who created you weak. Then after weakness He gave you strength, then after strength He reduced you to weakness and gray hairs. . . .

(79th) 12: 78 They (Joseph's brothers) said: O mighty (one), he has a father, a very old man. So take one of us in his place. We see that you are a kind person.

These texts, departing from the neutral or slightly biased attitude of the three earlier passages (73: 17; 26: 171 f.; and 37: 134 f.) now see old age as something altogether repulsive. Three (15: 54; 19: 4 f./3 ff.; and 19: 8/9) speak of the aged as unable to have children; three (19: 4 f./3 ff.; 36: 68; and 30: 54/53) point out their physical weakness, and two (17: 23/24 and 12: 78) regard their condition as pitiable. Other limitations mentioned in these passages are the gray hair, the stiff joints, the stooped posture, the timidity, and the fear of having to bear the contempt of their own children that are the lot of many people in their declining years.

This view of old age as positively undesirable in texts promulgated around 617 to 621 gives way to a view even more extreme found in a series of seven texts dating from the last years at Mecca and the first few years at Medina. These texts, taken as a whole, see old age as pitiable and even disgusting.

(75th) 16: 70/72 God created you; then He will cause you to die. Among you is he who is reduced to the most contemptible stage of life, so that after knowing something he may know nothing.

(79th) 12: 94 f. Indeed I perceive the smell of Joseph although you (Jacob's sons) think that I'm in my dotage. They answer: By God, your mind really is wandering, as before.

(80th) 40: 67/69 It is He who . . . brings you forth as infants, then (makes) you attain your full vigor, then become old men – though some of you die before that – and reach a term determined. . . .

(81st) 28: 23 He (Moses) found, apart from them (the people watering their flocks), two women holding back (their flocks). He said: What is the matter with you? They said: We do not water (our flocks) until the shepherds drive away (their flocks), for our father is a very old man.

(88th) 35: 11/12 . . . Nothing is added to the age of him whose life is prolonged and nothing is cut off from his lifetime except what is (written) in a book. That is easy for God.

(93rd) 2: 266/268 Would any of you like to have a garden of palm trees and vines with rivers flowing through it and with all kinds of fruits? Old age has smitten him and he has an offspring of weaklings. Then a strong, fiery wind strikes it and it is burned up.

48

(109th) 22: 5 ... We bring you forth as infants; then (We make) you attain your full vigor; and some of you die (young); and among you is he who is reduced to the most contemptible stage of life, so that after knowing something he may know nothing.

The first of the above passages, 16: 70/72, belongs to a sura dating from early in the Third Meccan Period – from about the year 619 when Muḥammad was forty-nine years old. It pronounces old age as the vilest stage of human life, contemptible because it reduces mentally competent persons to senility. The second text ridicules Jacob (although in fact he is right) by having his sons rebuke him for yielding to the illusions of dotage, as they see it.[47]

In seeming contrast to this dark picture the next text, 40: 67/69, appears tolerant towards old age. But closer inspection shows how sharply full strength and old age are contrasted. Here too, strong emphasis is put on God's action of determining the individual's life span, the implication being that it is His decree that imposes the burden of old age on some. Moreover, the words, "God makes you become old men, though some of you die before that" would seem to carry some such meaning as, "If you are fortunate, you may escape these changes and the tragedy of decrepitude by dying young." In fact, say the commentators Zamakhsharī and Rāzī, you may die extremely young: Some of you may be born as miscarried fetuses.

In 28: 23 Moses finds two women unable to water their flock until others have gone before them. They take last place, they say, because their father is a very old man – the implication being that he is too old to water the animals himself[48] or to help his daughters defend their rights against the shepherds. Either explanation stresses the helplessness and the pitiable state to which old age reduces human beings.

In saying that it is God's decree alone that gives long or short life, 35: 11/12 like 40: 67/69 seems to maintain a neutral attitude towards old age. But, because of the view taken of old age in the other suras promulgated in this Third Meccan Period, it would seem only right to conclude that it is God's decree alone that imposes on mankind either of the two unpleasant alternatives here mentioned, the sad spectacle of a young life cut off in its prime or the pitiable burden of advanced years.

[47] See A. F. L. Beeston: *Baiḍāwī's Commentary on Surah 12 of the Qur'ān*, Oxford: Clarendon Pr. 1963, pp. 47–48, and also his note 160 (p. 73) translating Zamakhsharī's comment on this passage. See also Lane: *Arabic-English Lexicon*, 2, 2448, col. 2, on *fannada*.

[48] *Tafsīr al-Jalālain*,

The use of the verb *aṣāba*, to smite, with old age in 2: 266/268 makes it clear that the *Qur'ān* at this stage of its promulgation regards this period of life as a misfortune. Worse still, their physical weakness appears in the progeny generated by old men. The comment of the Jalāls on this passage, "Old age makes one too weak to earn a living," stresses the incapacity of the elderly in still another way.

Chronologically the last passage of this set, 22: 5 is a combination and a recasting of several other passages, especially of 16: 70/72 and 40: 67/69 with many phrases textually identical with parts of these. Like 16: 70/72, it represents old age as the most contemptible stage of man's life. In it he enters on a period of intellectual emptiness and physical infirmity.

Ten displaced texts, all attributed by BELL to the Medinan Period, return to a more tolerant view of advanced years. Four of these, classed as early Medinan, portray the barrenness of old age as overcome by God's power (3: 40/35; 11: 72/75; 14: 39/41; and 51: 29). The context of these passages shows that this divine intervention is a sign of God's special mercy and beneficence. Two other early Medinan passages (2: 96/90 and 35: 37/34) see long life as a gift from God, of which those now suffering punishment in the hereafter did not take advantage in their lifetime. One similar text (21: 44/45) regards prolonged life with the enjoyment of prosperity as desirable.

Finally, three verses, revised according to BELL in Medina, make length of years a neutral concept. In 10: 16/17 the *Qur'ān* speaks of Muḥammad's having remained a lifetime – perhaps forty years – among those to whom he preached before beginning his mission. Sura 28: 45 represents another neutral expression of duration similar to ways of speaking occurring elsewhere in the *Qur'ān*.[49] In a late passage (24: 31) which BELL dates from around the year 627, "old age" is implicitly referred to in a neutral sense as a circumstance of legislation on proper conduct for women: women may display their ornaments to men who no longer desire carnal union – presumably because of old age.[50]

* * *

[49] PARET: *Kommentar*, p. 380, refers to a parallel text in 21: 44/45 and to less exact equivalents in 20: 86/89 and 57: 16/15.

[50] Others understand "men without sexual desire" here not only as "old men" but also those classed with them, viz., eunuchs and the insane. See BLACHÈRE: *Le Coran*, 1009f.

50

If Bell's dating of individual passages is accepted, forty-five texts out of approximately one hundred and eleven dealing with the young occur around the years 624 to 625, that is, in the third and fourth years after the Hijra. Only one of these forty-five (4: 9/10) mentions a negative quality – weakness – in children. Within this same period Fāṭima, Muḥammad's daughter, married 'Alī ibn Abī Ṭālib, and their union was blessed with two male children, Ḥasan and Ḥusain. At no other period during the promulgation of the *Qur'ān* are the young mentioned so often. Such a concentration on this theme would seem to reflect Muḥammad's tender feelings towards children in general and towards his own descendants in particular.[51]

In general, then, in regard to the young, the attitude expressed in the *Qur'ān* over the twenty years of its promulgation first shifts from neutrality to mild concern lest children impede the spiritual development of their parents. Towards the later years in Mecca and during the Medinan Period this attitude softens to admiration mingled with regret for adverse situations that might threaten the young. The mood finally yields to one of admiration for the young and concern for their welfare.

As the attitude towards the young mellows over these two decades so, on the contrary, feelings seem to harden towards old age. Early in Mecca, when Muḥammad was still in his early forties, the attitude is one of neutrality or tolerance. In the mid-Meccan years, when he was approaching his fifties, there is a gradual shift towards aversion. Late in Mecca and throughout most of the Medinan Period old age is seen as pitiable and repulsive.

This double development fits in with the changes that advanced years bring to the average person. In the earlier stages one is respected for his experience and wisdom. But with the passage of time come declining strength, a narrowing circle of family and friends, a loss of status, and to many a diminishing sense of worth and self-esteem. These changes can lead to moodiness, self-pity, and a demanding possessiveness. Negative attitudes of this kind seem to have led Muḥammad, when he was fifty-seven years old, at the time of the crisis in his harem, to promulgate a group of Qur'ānic ordinances concerning the conduct of his own wives and curtailing the liberties of women in general. At this same time or a little later, when his advancing years and lessening energies led some of his companions to consider marriage with his wives after his death, he promulgated a verse forbidding them to remarry if they survived him.

[51] Watt: *Muhammad at Medina*, p. 322, remarks on this tenderness and cites H. A. R. Gibb in support of it.

(105th) 33: 53 . . . You (O believers) must not annoy the Prophet and you must not marry his wives after him — ever! That would be a great (offense) to God.

The Muslim commentator Rāzī says that this verse was occasioned by Ṭalḥah ibn 'Ubaydallāh's remark that he would marry Muḥammad's youngest wife 'Ā'ishah if he outlived Muḥammad.[52] Another commentator, Ṭabarī, gives the Muslim explanation for this prohibition in a Tradition from 'Ā'ishah passed on by Abū Ayyūb, Muḥammad's standard-bearer: It would not be right for others to marry Muḥammad's wives because Muḥammad had conferred on them the title of "Mothers of the Believers" and it is not lawful for a man to marry his mother,[53] WATT with more probability explains the prohibition as a means of averting division in the Muslim community.[54]

[52] Fakhr ad-Dīn ar-Rāzī: *At-Tafsīr al-kabīr.* 1st ed. 16 vols. Cairo: al-Maṭba'a al bahīya al-miṣrīya 1357/1938, vol. 13, part 25, 225. On this whole matter see NABIA ABBOTT: *Aishah the Beloved of Mohammed.* Chicago: Univ. of Chicago Pr. 1942, pp. 21 and 57f.

[53] aṭ-Ṭabarī: *Jāmi' al-bayān fī tafsīr al-Qur'ān.* 12 vols. Beirut: Dār al-Ma'rifa 1400/1980, vol. 10, part 22, 29, on 33: 53.

[54] WATT: *Muhammad at Medina,* p. 287.

12

THE DIVINE NAME "AL-RAḤMĀN" IN THE QUR'ĀN

Jacques Jomier

[361] THE DIVINE NAME *al-Raḥmān* occurs frequently in the Qur'ān. It figures primarily in the ritual formula with which all the *sūra*s begin. In the body of the *sūra*s, it is found 56 additional times (sixteen times in *Sūra* XIX alone). At first glance the sense of the term seems clear; it is connected to the root *r–ḥ–m*, which expresses the idea of mercy. Grammatically it has been understood by the commentators as an adjectival *fa'lān*, a classical type in Arabic; it expresses the intensity of the character of mercy. In order to distinguish it from another adjective derived from the same root, *al-Raḥīm*, the Merciful, it has been rendered in French as a special word: *le Clément* ("the Clement One", used quite frequently), *le Bienfaiteur* ("the Benefactor", used by Blachère) and by a superlative, *le Très Miséricordieux* ("the Most Merciful", used by Montet). Such a solution is satisfactory if one sees it exclusively from the point of view of the religious values perceived in the Qur'ān. It enhances the profound Qur'ānic (and Biblical) idea of the immense divine goodness; the presence, together, of these two quasi-synonymous adjectives suggests a means of expressing their mutual reinforcement. All things considered, it would be something like the Latin version of the Bible, where one finds the expression *Misericors et Miserator Dominus*.[1] [362] Most Muslims adhere to this religious interpretation.

However, a closer examination reveals a difficulty which has drawn the attention of certain Orientalists, especially Blachère. Is the parallelism of the two adjectives *al-Raḥmān al-Raḥīm* really as clear as has been suggested? *Al-Raḥmān* was the most important name under which God was invoked by certain Arabian groups at the time of the birth of Islām; the evidence for this is clear with respect to certain religious groups in Yemen.[2] In this

[1]Cf. Vulgate, Psalms 111:4, 145:8. Note that the comparison extends only as far as the religious sentiment expressed and not to textual criticism. The two Latin adjectives, derived from the same root, translate two Hebrew words from entirely different Hebrew roots: *ḥannon we-raḥōm*, the Merciful and Compassionate.

[2]The inscriptions discovered in South Arabia show that before Islam *RAḤMANAN* served to designate God in Jewish texts and the Father in trinitarian Christian inscriptions. Cf. G. Ryckmans, *Les religions arabes préislamiques* (Louvain, 1951), 47–48.

2

environment the phrase seems to have had the sense which was given in the second and third centuries to the expression "Dieu bon" or the sense which is given in France today to the expression "le Bon Dieu". The believers know that God can be called Great, Good, Omnipotent, and so forth, but the word "Good" in this case is not only an adjective: it forms a part of the expression which the believers, in preference to all other terms, use to designate God in His being. They attempt to express the Being of God, the mysterious totality, when they add to His name the word which best suggests the reasons for the immense confidence that He inspires.

In the Qur'ān, the difference between the grammatical roles played by *al-Raḥmān* and *al-Raḥīm* is evident:

1. *Al-Raḥmān* is always used with the article whereas *al-Raḥīm* occurs sometimes with the article, other times without it.

2. If *al-Raḥmān* acts as an adjective in the typically Muslim doublet *al-Raḥmān al-Raḥīm* (seven cases out of the 56 instances of *al-Raḥmān* within the various *sūras*), it is never constructed elsewhere in the same manner as other adjectives which describe God. *Al-Raḥmān* always appears alone in these other cases, whereas the other divine names are **[363]** very frequently associated with a certain diversity. *Raḥīm*, for example, is found alone only four times (without the definite article) out of 115 cases. It is coupled with *Ghafūr* (more than 70 times, with or without the article), *Tawwāb* (nine times, with or without the article), *Ra'ūf* (nine times, without the article), *al-'Azīz* (thirteen times with the article), etc.

3. Finally, the adjectives which serve as names of God within the Qur'ān are used sometimes in a profane manner, in reference to a created being: *raḥīm*, for example, characterizes Muḥammad (Qur'ān IX, 129/128) whereas *al-Raḥmān* designates only God.[3]

[3] A fourth difference is evident, but it is very difficult to construct a convincing argument for it; this concerns the use of the divine names in Medina and in the late Meccan *sūras* which do not contain the name *al-Raḥmān*. In these passages, the mention of the divine names is linked harmoniously to the style. The Qur'ān enunciates a proposition, an order or a deed with its habitual conciseness; next, the phrase is completed by an invocation of an attribute of God in keeping with the context. In this one has a sort of short and sonorous story which echoes and lifts the spirit of the audience above the concrete situation, occasionally prosaically. One is taken from the particular not to the general, but directly to God, remaining then in the domain of existence which delights the ancient Arabian spirit, which is little inclined to the abstract realm. See, for example, Qur'ān VIII, 71–72/70–71, where, after a promise of restitution and grace made to the captives, the text

The Divine Name "al-Raḥmān" in the Qur'ān 3

[364] Moving beyond strictly grammatical points, the differences are cast into still sharper contrast. Whereas the ordinary attributes signify just one aspect of the divine majesty, His power or His knowledge for example, *al-Raḥmān* most often designates God himself. Without a doubt, *al-Raḥmān* occurs in verses where the context speaks explicitly of mercy and where it seems natural to call God "the Most Merciful" (cf. Qur'ān XLIII, 31–32/32–33); without a doubt, it is possible to say that God always acts with mercy and that *al-Raḥmān* is a term that is always suitable. It is no less true, however, that these explanations are insufficient. Although in most cases the fine balance of the Qur'ānic phrases will change if one replaces a divine name with that of Allāh, in virtually every case Allāh can substitute for *al-Raḥmān* without changing the sense. The commentators were well acquainted with this equivalence; they employed the two names as equals in order to designate God when they glossed passages where there was a question of *al-Raḥmān*.

Occupying a totally unique place in the Qur'ān, the word *al-Raḥmān* deserves to be studied apart, independent of the other divine attributes.

For a long time, Orientalists have remarked that *al-Raḥmān* is the most characteristic signal of Mecca; they have used its presence as a sign of the texts of the second Meccan period. Without going over all of this question again, we would like to see only how the Qur'ān uses the word *al-Raḥmān* in order to designate God himself. We will ask if one can reconstruct a precise cycle of beliefs associated with this name. We will attempt finally to raise once again the points which will allow us to determine the areas of Arabia in which God was worshipped under this name.[4]

*

* *

adds: "God pardons, He is merciful", and after an invocation on possible treason: "God is all-knowing and wise". It is clear that each of these attributes is in direct relationship with an element of the preceding phrase. See also Qur'ān IV, 36–38/32–34, where a series of orders is punctuated by clauses such as: "God of all things is all-knowing", "God of all things sees all things", "God is majestic and great". The idea that God sees all and watches all is certainly there to incite the hearers not to disobey the received commandments. One can present other examples by the dozen. The word *al-Raḥmān* is never used as an adjective to secure this sort of harmony of thought and style.

[4]We will not investigate here the question of *RAḤMANAN* in South Arabia, nor the question of its connection with *al-Raḥmān* in the Qur'ān. Y. Moubarac treats this in his "Les noms, titres et attributs de Dieu dans le Coran et leurs correspondants en épigraphie sud-sémitique", *Le Muséon* 68 (1955), 93–135, 326–68. As the present article risked encroaching on the work of Moubarac, we made our intentions clear to him; he had the courtesy and the grace to forgo his rights of priority, for which we are grateful to him.

4

[365] For the study of a problem such as this, we only have Muslim documents at our disposal. The first of these is the Qur'ān. The others are the different traditions collected by the exegetes, the jurists and the historians. For our present concerns the Qur'ān offers us two types of texts. There are doctrinal texts where *al-Raḥmān* is spoken of dogmatically, and there are apologetic-type texts. The latter contain the objections made by the pagan Meccans to the teachings of the Prophet as well as the arguments destined to refute those objections; they are of special interest because they throw a certain light on the psychology of the opposition. Despite all this, the situation remains obscure and it is not possible to maintain today—as certain nineteenth-century Orientalists did a little too quickly—that Islam was born in the clear light of history and that the life of its apostle was as well known as the lives of the Christian reformers of the Renaissance. Historians have a need to know the background to the events which they are studying, and, in the case of Islam, that background is still a great mystery. The impossibility of making excavations in central Arabia deprives us of epigraphical and archeological evidence which, in the absence of other texts, would allow us to have some knowledge of the faith and customs of the Arabs of the past—be they pagans, Jews, Christians or Sabeans—and of how the distribution of their beliefs followed geographic considerations.

As a result, one is reduced to building up research hypotheses, then discussing them without having any illusions about their provisional character. In the case of Allāh and *al-Raḥmān*, it seems that one may advance the following assertions. The name Allāh designated the creator God known by the Meccans, but His cult, before Islam, allowed for the worship of other secondary divinities. *Al-Raḥmān*, on the other hand, was a name of the unique God in certain portions of Arabia (at least in al-Yamāma and Yemen), but the [366] Meccans felt an aversion to its use. The name was a stranger to them.[5]

The Qur'ān contains traces of the opposition that the Meccans manifested toward the preaching of the name *al-Raḥmān*, the One God. The texts are well-known and are frequently cited:

[5]The fact that Islam prefers Allāh as the principle name of the unique God agrees with what we know from elsewhere about the spirit of the Qur'ān. As the pre-Islamic cult of the Kaʿba was preserved with a completely changed spirit, so the cult of Allāh persisted with a rejuvenated doctrine. This solution had the advantage of not provoking the aversion of the Meccans to the name of *al-Raḥmān*, while not totally giving up on the doctrine. The attempt at preaching the name of *al-Raḥmān* had so outraged the Meccans that its continuation would have been quite a disadvantage. It should be noted that the *ḥadīth* reflecting the Ḥijāzī Muslim attitude only uses this divine name on a few occasions (only two references in Wensinck's *Index*).

The Divine Name "al-Raḥmān" in the Qur'ān 5

1. "When the unbelievers behold thee [Muḥammad], they take thee only for mockery: 'Ha, is this the one who makes mention of your gods?', [they say]. Yet they in the Remembrance of *al-Raḥmān* are unbelievers". (Qur'ān XXI, 37/36).
2. "But when they are told: 'Bow yourselves to *al-Raḥmān*,' they say: 'And what is *al-Raḥmān*? Shall we bow ourselves to what thou biddest?' And it increases them in adversion." (Qur'ān XXV, 61/60).
3. "Say: 'Call upon Allāh, or call upon *al-Raḥmān*; whichsoever you call upon, to Him belong the Names Most Beautiful." (Qur'ān, XVII, 110).
4. "Thus We have sent thee among a nation before which other nations have passed away, to recite to them that we have revealed to thee; and yet they disbelieve in *al-Raḥmān*." (Qur'ān XIII, 29/30).

The commentators often speak of *al-Raḥmān* when dealing with these four texts. According to one of their explanations, having heard Muḥammad invoking God saying: "Oh Allāh! Oh our Father *al-Raḥmān*", the Meccans murmured and added: "He pretends only to praise one God; in fact, he praises them two by two".[6] Whatever the circumstances were precisely, it is clear that for the transmitters of the traditions, the pagan Meccans saw a divinity distinct from Allāh in *al-Raḥmān*.

[367] Regarding the fourth text, the commentators speak of the incident of its revelation at the time of the treaty of al-Ḥudaybīya (AD 628). The Muslims wrote the formula *bi'smillāh al-Raḥmān al-Raḥīm* at the beginning of the agreement; the Meccan pagans opposed it and put in its place, following Meccan custom, *bi'smika Allāhumma*. This only recognizes the name of Allāh. One of the reports states that Quraysh had said at the time: "*Al-Raḥmān*, we know him not."[7]

Classical Qur'ānic exegesis directed its attention in a third way. It is true to say, however, that the appraisal of these traditions is very difficult. The Meccans opposed the Prophet on the pretext that he demanded their allegiance to al-Raḥmān of al-Yamāma.[8] The commentary adds that they meant by that Musaylima, the future enemy of Islam who presented himself

[6] Al-Ṭabarī, *Tafsīr* (Cairo, AH 1321), XV, 113, on Qur'ān XVII, 110. Perhaps here we also have a very general allusion to the fact that the Qur'ān often mentions the divine attributes in pairs.

[7] Al-Ṭabarī, *Tafsīr*, XIII, 88–89, on Qur'ān XIII, 29/30; cf. al-Bukhārī, *Ṣaḥīḥ* (Leiden, 1864), II, 180; trans. Houdas (Paris, 1896), II, 253.

[8] Al-Ṭabarī, *Tafsīr*, XV, 113 (on Qur'ān XVII, 110); XIX, 17–18 (on Qur'ān XXV, 61/60).

6

as a prophet and incited al-Yamāma[9] to revolt in Arabia (632–34). This exegesis is difficult to accept. The texts of the Qur'ān with which it is concerned date from before the *hijra*, and Musaylima seems to have come out of obscurity at the end of the Medinan period about ten years later.[10] Why *al-Raḥmān* is mentioned in connection with this area, then, is a question to which we shall return later.

An additional argument can be drawn from people's proper names. Here, in the absence other documents, one can often discover the **[368]** beliefs of people. The examination of names confirms the impression that in the pre-Islamic Ḥijāz, *al-Raḥmān* figures as a name of a foreign God only. Only very seldom does one find the name 'Abd al-Raḥmān (that is to say, the slave or worshipper of *al-Raḥmān*) among the pagans of the Ḥijāz at the beginning of the seventh century. This rarity contrasts sharply with its appearance and frequency of use among the second generation of Muslims.[11] Some use of the name existed among the very first Muslims; however, there it is a question of whether they were called such since their birth or, rather, due to a change of name brought about by their conversion. In certain cases it is difficult to know.[12] A change of name appears clearly in the case of at least three people. The first, Ibn 'Abd Allāh ibn 'Awf, one of the oldest and most influential Companions, was named 'Abd al-Raḥmān by the Prophet himself when he converted. This was in Mecca, before the first group of Muslims settled in the house of al-Arqām and also before the emigration to Abyssinia. This detail, if it is authentic, shows the importance accorded by the Prophet to this divine name from the moment the Qur'ān first used it.[13] The second, Abū 'Aqīl al-Ishārī was known as 'Abd al-

[9] Al-Yamāma is situated in the center of Arabia, on the routes between Iraq and Yemen opposite al-Baḥrayn. It was located in the region of present-day Riyadh, capital of Saudi Arabia. At the time of the Prophet the tribes of Banū Ḥanīfa lived there. One tradition speaks of grain being cultivated there and says that some of this crop was exported to Mecca. Cf. al-Bukhārī, *Ṣaḥīḥ*, III, 166; trans. Houdas, III, 214.

[10] Cf. Leone Caetani, *Annali dell'Islam* (Milan, 1905–26), II.1, 332–37.

[11] Note, however, that in a very small number of cases these second-generation Muslims named 'Abd al-Raḥmān traced their origin to the Ḥimyar. Cf. Ibn Sa'd, *Ṭabaqāt* (Leiden, 1904–40), III.1, 23 (the assassination of 'Alī); IV.1, 42. The rarity of 'Abd al-Raḥmān before Islām cannot serve to establish that the name *al-Raḥmān* had been one of the important divine names. One does not find *'Abd al-Raḥīm*, etc., either. But if it were known by other means that *al-Raḥmān* was one of the important divine names, we could try to determine the regions in which it was employed.

[12] *Ibid.*, IV.1, 77, 180. When a man who carried a theophoric pagan name converted to Islam, the divine name was replaced by a monotheistic name like 'Abd Allāh, 'Abd al-Raḥmān. Cf. *ibid.*, IV.2, 52, 68, among other examples.

[13] *Ibid.*, III.1, 57.

'Uzza in the time of paganism; when he embraced Islam **[369]**the Prophet replaced the pagan theophoric name by the mention of the One God and he was named 'Abd al-Raḥmān, the enemy of the idols.[14] The third is 'Abd al-Raḥmān ibn Samura ibn Ḥabīb; he also received his name from the Prophet.[15] We do know, however, of some very rare cases in which the name was used before Islam in the Ḥijāz. One of the first Muslims traced his descent to a maternal grandfather 'Abd al-Raḥmān, who lived, it seems, in al-Ṭā'if. Note here that a brother (by the mother) of this Muslim was called Ḥabīb, a name which we will find connected quite often to the use of *al-Raḥmān*.[16] Another Muslim of the first generation had a maternal grandfather 'Abd al-Raḥmān, and he was attached to Banū Lawdhān.[17]

The rarity of 'Abd al-Raḥmān in the Ḥijāz before Islam contrasts strikingly with the frequency of 'Abd Allāh or theophoric pagan names. The Qur'ān itself confirms this impression and shows that the name Allāh was familiar to the Meccans. The Meccans admitted that Allāh was the Creator of the world and the ruler of natural phenomena.[18] He was their Lord and the Lord of their ancestors. The pagans of Mecca took shelter behind His authority in order to allow certain acts which the Qur'ān describes as abominable. "God has commanded us to do it", they declare.[19] Moreover, they went so far as to oppose Muḥammad on **[370]** the basis of the traditional ideas of their environment and held that the resurrection of the body was a lie forged "against Allāh".[20] It is clear, then, that for the Meccan pagans, the use of the name *al-Raḥmān* was entirely new. The name of Allāh was well known to them, but the Muslim teaching disrupted more than one point of their traditional theology.

---

[14] *Ibid.*, III.2, 41. The reader will note the connection made between the divine name and hostility towards idols.

[15] *Ibid.*, VII.2, 100–101.

[16] *Ibid.*, III.2, 107.

[17] *Ibid.*, IV.2, 87. On 'Abd al-Raḥmān before Islam see Josef Horovitz, *Koranische Untersuchungen* (Berlin, 1926), 162. His work on the subject, ["Jewish Proper Names and Derivatives in the Koran",] published in *Hebrew Union College Annual*, 2 (1925), 201–203, was not accessible to us.

[18] Qur'ān XXIX, 61/63; XXXI, 24/25; XXXIX, 39/38.

[19] Qur'ān, VII, 27/28.

[20] Qur'ān XXXIV, 8. It is possible that this old text makes an allusion to a retort of the Meccans before the transformation undergone by their traditional beliefs in a new situation. Cf. equally Qur'ān XLII, 23/24, where the accusation of forging a lie against Allāh is made in an interrogative phrase. Cf. Qur'ān XXIII, 40/38, regarding the contemporaries of Noah and the situation of this Patriarch.

8

*

* *

Our next task is to determine if it is possible to discern within the Qur'ān a special cycle of religious ideas which are placed in relation to the preaching of the name *al-Raḥmān*. At the outset it must be stated that it is difficult to give a categorical reply. The Qur'ān preaches, above all, the One God; Allāh and *al-Raḥmān* are only two of His names. The particular union of them as shown in the formula *bi'smillāh al-Raḥmān al-Raḥīm* is distinctive in Islam.[21] In the Qur'ān all that is said of *al-Raḥmān* is said also of Allāh, and no teaching is presented uniquely related to the name of *al-Raḥmān*. However, without forcing the data and staying within the domain of suggestion, it is possible to make some remarks.

1. Among the ancient prophets that are spoken of in the Qur'ān, one group clearly detaches itself from others. This is formed of figures from pre-Islamic Arabia, unknown in the Bible: Hūd, Ṣāliḥ, and Shu'ayb, **[371]** with whom are coupled Noah, Lot,[22] and Moses until the time he is sent to Pharaoh.[23] Most of the time the Qur'ān mentions the prophets side by side. Their respective histories are variations on the same theme; they form a veritable literary cycle within the Qur'ān. Charged with warning their people, these men of God only encountered stubbornness and incredulity. All the stories are terminated by the destruction of the guilty. The prophets' names appear from the first Meccan period onward. It is interesting to note that from the beginning, the cycle of prophets is put in relation with the name of Allāh.[24] Later, long pieces of the *sūra*s dwell **[372]** on their

[21] Qur'ān, at the beginning of all the *sūras* except *Sūra* IX, and at the beginning of the letter sent by Solomon to the Queen of Sheba (XXVII, 30).

[22] Note that the Biblical announcement that a son is given to Abraham is attached to the cycle of Lot, although it does not appear every time Sodom is discussed. As in the Bible, the announcement takes place at the moment the mysterious Host calls on the Patriarch before going to destroy the tainted city. See, for example, Qur'ān LI, 24–46; XV, 49–75; XI, 72–84/69–83.

[23] Much later Moses appears in another context. Attached to the Biblical accounts, his history is enriched by a number of well-known events. In the prophetic accounts of the destruction, the figure of Pharaoh sometimes has more importance than that of Moses: see Qur'ān VIII, 56/54.

[24] Qur'ān XCI, 13 (concerning the camel of Allāh in relation to the people of Thamūd of Ṣāliḥ); LXXXIX, 12/13; LXXXV, 8–20; LIII, 51–62. On the other hand, LXIX, 4–12, on the same group of prophets, uses only *Lord*.

It cannot be stressed too highly that from the debut of the Qur'ānic teaching, the names of these prophets have been put together with the name of Allāh.

During this time, in effect, the use of the name of Allāh was always relatively infrequent. God speaks in the first person (always in the plural) or is designated by the word

story; the name of Allāh always figures there, and never that of *al-Raḥmān*. Additionally, except for rare exceptions, the cycle does not appear even in the vicinity of passages which call God *al-Raḥmān*. It seems that these passages are related to traditions which were known and admitted by all in the Ḥijāz. Three traditions explain the origins of the ruins along the routes which were used by the caravans, and two other traditions are linked to an exact place. When the Qur'ān mentions them for the last time in Medina, the context shows that it is attempting to motivate the Arabs of the region. Therefore its objective is, in the first case, to underline the futility of the Meccan pagans' conduct with regard to the Prophet (Qur'ān XXII, 43); in the second case, it is to bring the hypocrites back to more admirable sentiments (Qur'ān IX, 71/70). The Qur'ān, of course, would not base itself on stories that would be questioned by its hearers.

2. *Eschatology*. In a large number of Qur'ānic passages where the discussion centers around the last things and the Last Judgment, God is designated, at first, by the word Lord, or he speaks in the first person (ancient Meccan *sūras*). Very quickly, however, the name of Allāh acquires a prominent position; the name *al-Raḥmān* also appears. A close examination shows that these rare instances of *al-Raḥmān* are found in passages most closely related to apocalyptic literature of the same type known in **[373]** Jewish and Christian heterodoxy and orthodoxy.[25] The trumpet of the Last Judgment

---

Rabb (Lord). It seems that the accent is to be placed on the personal relations between Muḥammad and God and, thus, the very tone of the style. According to the concordance of 'Abd al-Bāqī, the name Allāh figures 2,697 times in the Qur'ān. But in the first Meccan period (of Blachère) it only appears 35 times if one does not take into account v. 20 of *Sūra* LXXIII (a Medinan addition) in which Allāh is employed seven times. If one also considers *Sūra* LXXVII to be chronologically later, as is the advice of many (and we tend to agree), five additional uses of Allāh are removed. That then leaves a maximum of 30 usages. Calculating the average according to the number of Arabic lines in the Qur'ān of the Cairo edition (9,500 approx.), one arrives at the following results. Whereas for the whole of the Qur'ān, the number of uses of Allāh compared to the number of lines is in the proportion of 28 to 100, in the first Meccan period it is at most 4.5 per cent. Furthermore, if one examines the text closely, it appears that even this percentage could be diminished, because the name of Allāh figures only in the verses which many estimate to be later. Among the 30 uses, there are five in which the name of Allāh is directly related with the group of prophets of ancient Arabia and two in which it appears in their vicinity. Certain French versions of the Qur'ān can deceive the reader because, for the clarity of style, the translation replaces a pronoun by Allāh whereas the context requires Lord.

[25]The numerous Qur'ānic passages on the last events and the Last Judgment should be compared to traditional apocalyptic literature. Many Qur'ānic passages represent images well known within this genre of literature: the cosmic disruption at the end of time, the role of Gog and Magog, the animals, the trumpets, the angels, the books of human actions,

10

is mentioned once beside the name of *al-Raḥmān*[26] and twice in the *sūras* where this name is **[374]** employed.[27] The garden of Eden is "promised" by *al-Raḥmān*.[28] These are only details, but a more characteristic text presents the appearance of a theophany, which is very rare in the Qur'ān. One finds it in the context of the idea of storm clouds (*ghamām*), which are so characteristic of apocalyptic literature: "Upon the day that heaven is split asunder with the clouds and the angels are sent down in majesty, the Kingdom that day, the true Kingdom, shall belong to *al-Raḥmān*" (Qur'ān XXV, 27–28/25–26).

A tradition transmitted by Mujāhid brings this text[29] together with a later text where the theophany is expressed very clearly and the way of God

---

fire, chains, rank liquids, sombre and radiant faces, gardens, springs, fruits, right and left as symbols of good and evil, terrors which turn the hair of little children white, the new earth and the new heaven, the earth sparkling in the light of God. Despite this, the spirit of the apocalypses and the spirit of the Qur'ān are quite different. The majority of Qur'ānic passages insist on retribution and on works which merit heaven or hell. The discussions between the chosen people and the damned are numerous (as are discussions between members of the same group). These discussions provide the occasion for saying to the one group, and to the others, that their lot is the result of their previous attitude to Islam. The apocalyptic visions (and it is their proper character) describe, in advance and in a symbolic way, the titanic struggle in the last moments of history, a struggle which pits the forces of good against the powers of evil. The justice which, unceasingly, is counteracted on earth, finally establishes itself after the advent of the Reign of God. This advent is alone or is accompanied by a messianic manifestation. However, the apocalyptic battle does not appear in the Qur'ān. The symbolism which is a trait of the final history of the world, with ciphers or animals designating the terrestrial realities, is not found in the Qur'ān. One only finds the incessant polemic between Muḥammad and the liars. One also finds the struggle that, on an individual basis, Satan conducts against man. In the Qur'ān, the Last Judgment is the triumph for Muslims; Satan and the impious are the hosts of Hell. The analogy of the situation explains the repetition of numerous images. But the apocalyptic blast is only heard in short outbursts. There is no more than *one* dramatic history of the world, centred on the elected people, but the *many* short histories of communities go on only by the pleasure of God. The apocalyptic worries are totally overshadowed, and the stress is laid on the description of what awaits the Muslims and the others.

[26]Over and above this passage (Qur'ān XXXVI, 51–52), the trumpet *al-Ṣūr* is mentioned nine times in the Qur'ān. In these other *sūras*, God speaks either in the first-person plural (LXXVIII, 18) or is designated by the title Lord (LXIX, 13) or, more often, the name Allāh is used (XXXIX, 68, etc.).

[27]Qur'ān L, 19/20; XX, 102.

[28]Qur'ān XIX, 62 (where the text goes on after this with a mention of the prophets after Idrīs). Eden is found eleven times in the Qur'ān; this text is the only one which explicitly employs the word "promise" for Eden. For the promise of Paradise (*janna*) for whoever fears *al-Raḥmān*, see L, 32/33.

[29]Al-Ṭabarī, *Tafsīr*, XIX, 5 (on Qur'ān XXV, 27–28/25–26.

(Allāh) is clearly indicated.[30] The rarity of Qur'ānic passages where it is a question of the "coming" of God on the Last Day gives an exceptional importance to the mention of *al-Raḥmān*.[31] The same impression is given in Qur'ān LXXVIII 37–38, where a mention of the Last Judgment, of *al-Raḥmān* and of his assistants, the Spirit and the angels, is found. The text evokes, moreover, the silence and the order which hangs over the assembly.[32] One may note additionally **[375]** that at the time of the final appearance of God, no Messiah appears to play a role in the first plan.

3. The idea that God is above all the Creator, the Master of the world, is developed quite fully in the Qur'ān. It is almost impossible to count the number of passages in which the name of Allāh is put together with the phenomena of nature. The pagans of Mecca were familiar with this idea. We should not attach, therefore, much significance to the fact that the name *al-Raḥmān* figures, itself, in this context.[33] It is more striking to find it beside the classical notions of Jewish, Biblical or later tradition, such as the Creation in six days,[34] the seven heavens,[35] and the divine throne that symbolizes the omnipotence of God, as well as from the time of the Creation to the day of the Last Judgment.[36] After one of these instances a phrase adds: "Ask he who is informed about him (*al-Raḥmān*)". Certain commentaries propose here, beside other explanations: "Ask the people of the Book".[37] This proves that this divine name is seen as a part of the Jewish–Christian vocabulary.

---

[30] Qur'ān II, 206/210. This passage clearly appears to be addressed to the Jews of Medina. It expresses the beliefs of the speakers by means of the Qur'ān calling them in these terms: "What do they look for but that God shall come to them in the cloud-shadows, and the angels?" The word (storm) cloud, *ghamām*, is only found four times in the Qur'ān, in the two apocalyptic passages cited here and twice regarding the Israelites in the desert at the time of the Exodus.

[31] In addition to these two texts on the "coming" of God, there exist two other very old references: Qur'ān LXIX, 16–17, where God is designated as the Lord; and the same in LXXXIX, 23/22, but more briefly. Another text on the "coming" (Qur'ān XI, 107/105) is very enigmatic, but for the most part the exegetes do not understand it as a divine "coming".

[32] Cf. equally Qur'ān XX, 107/108, with *al-Raḥmān*.

[33] Lord of the heavens and the earth (Qur'ān LXXVIII, 37), who counts all individuals and will return them one by one on the day of resurrection (XIX, 94–95/93–95), who supports the birds in their flight (LXVII, 19).

[34] Qur'ān XXV, 60/59, and another time, although that comes four verses after the mention of *al-Raḥmān*, in L, 37/38. The stock phrase of six days is found only seven times in the Qur'ān.

[35] Qur'ān LXVII, 3. The mention of seven heavens is frequent with the name Allāh.

[36] Qur'ān XX, 4/5; XXV, 60/59. Mention is frequently made with the name Allāh.

[37] Qur'ān XXV, 60/59. See al-Bayḍāwī; there is nothing in al-Ṭabarī on this passage.

12

4. The name of *al-Raḥmān* appears no less than six times connected to the idea of revelation; four times it is connected to the revelation of the Qur'ān and once to the Prophets of the Old Testament.[38]

[376] 5. The name *al-Raḥmān* designates a unique God. He has no sons or daughters. The Qur'ān is opposed to the pagans and considers the false gods as angels wrongfully deified.[39] This is a matter, then, of opposing the faith of the unique God designated by His name *al-Raḥmān* to the pretensions of the pagans. While it may be suggested that the divinity of Jesus is visible in these passages, it does not seem that way to us, although the argument in *Sūra* XIX includes the case of Jesus from the Muslim point of view.[40] Three texts insist on the fact that other divinities can protect man against *al-Raḥmān*.[41] However, these lessons are also found frequently with the name of Allāh.

6. The name *al-Raḥmān* appears in passages where it is a question either of the Old Testament prophets, or of Mary, mother of Jesus, or of an anonymous saint in the Qur'ān whom the commentators identify with Ḥabīb, venerated in Antioch. Ḥabīb was put to death for having supported the preaching of two disciples of Jesus. Quite clearly, we are dealing with Judeo-Christian traditions on the matter. However, in four of these passages the Qur'ān presents selections directly related to monotheism. The clearest texts are the following. One is put in the mouth of Aaron, who said to the Hebrews: "Your Lord is *al-Raḥmān*".[42] This is in the context of the affair of the golden calf. Another bears traces of the ancient Apostles: "Ask those of our Messengers we sent before thee: Have we appointed, **[377]** apart from *al-Raḥmān*, gods to be served?"[43] The *sūra* which contains this verse speaks only of Abraham, Moses and Jesus.

Additionally, one sees Abraham urge his father to practise monotheism; twice he uses the name of Allāh and once that of *al-Raḥmān*, against whom

---

[38] Qur'ān LV, 1; XXVI, 4/5; XXXVI, 10/11, 14/15; XLI, 1. See as well XIX, 59/58; XLIII, 35.

[39] Qur'ān XLIII, 14–18/15–19, where the name Allāh is likewise mentioned; cf. XIX, 91–95/88–95; XXI, 26; XLIII, 81. A lesson on monotheism which rests on this divine name is given in XLIII, 44/45.

[40] The Meccan pagans knew that men existed who believed in the divinity of Jesus. Cf. Qur'ān XLIII, 57–58. Since certain Christians in Arabia called God *al-Raḥmān*, it is possible that the pagans may have argued this fact in response to Muḥammad. Several times when this is mentioned in the Qur'ān it is a matter of *al-Raḥmān*.

[41] Qur'ān XXXVI, 22/23; LXVII, 20; XXI, 43/42.

[42] Qur'ān XX, 92/90.

[43] Qur'ān XLIII, 44/45.

Satan rebelled.[44] Immediately after, the text mentions Isaac, Moses, Aaron, Ishmael, and Idris, and adds: "When the signs of *al-Raḥmān* were recited to them, they fell down, prostrate, weeping."[45]

Mary employs the same divine name twice, referring to her vow of silence.[46] Finally, there is the piece which, following the commentators, is connected to Ḥabīb; it contains both the divine name and the preaching of monotheism.[47] The word for a pact of alliance, *'ahd*, is used many times in the Qur'ān, especially in Medina, in the context of the covenant between Israel and God; one also finds it in Meccan passages, and it is often tied to the name *al-Raḥmān*. On the Day of Judgment, only those who have been received into the covenant with *al-Raḥmān* will be able to intercede on behalf of others.[48] One does not have to force the text here to see a Judeo-Christian atmosphere.

7. Although the notion of love is found clearly in the Qur'ān, the idea of giving love is rare. One does find, however, the latter explicitly tied to the name *al-Raḥmān*: **[378]** "Surely those who believe and do deeds of righteousness, unto them *al-Raḥmān* shall assign love."

The position of this verse does not allow one to say if it is linked with the preceding context (see Montet, Blachère) or if it is independent and absolute, thus applying equally to this life (see al-Ṭabarī, numerous traditions, and al-Bayḍāwī, who also mentions the first solution in passing). This is an idea with a Judeo-Christian allure.[49]

8. We have seen above that the Meccans opposed the preaching of the name *al-Raḥmān*; it is significant to note also that, at the same time, the Qur'ān presents, on one occasion, the first Muslims as the "slaves of *al-Raḥmān*". The importance of this text is underlined by the fact that it is

[44] Qur'ān XIX, 45/44.

[45] Qur'ān XIX, 50–59/49–58. The presence of the name of Idrīs in this list reminds one of the book of Enoch, which is so celebrated in apocalyptic literature.

[46] Qur'ān XIX, 18, 27/26. These texts are found in the oldest lengthy piece of the Qur'ān where the question of Mary arises.

[47] Cf. *EI*, "Ḥabīb"; Qur'ān XXXVI, 14–32/15–32. Only this passage of the Qur'ān has a trace of this personage.

[48] Qur'ān XIX, 90/87, 81/78. However, the power of intercession is subordinate to the permission of *al-Raḥmān* (XX, 108/109). This second idea is expressed very frequently with the name of Allāh; the first idea, on the other hand, is hardly ever expressed using that name.

[49] Qur'ān XIX, 96. The solution of the other life would announce an idea developed in later *sūras*. In Paradise, God removes from the hearts of the chosen the remainder of their malice (see Qur'ān concordance under *ghill*). The most general solution explains that God loves the believers and loves them through the angels, the creatures and the other believers. He makes them love their brothers in the faith.

not a question of a word in passing but a kind of manifesto. The program of the new community is given these great lines and the model Muslim is described there in all his qualities: he walks the earth modestly, is friendly to all, stays up all night praying, fears Gehenna etc.[50] Elsewhere Muḥammad affirms, on the command of the Qur'ān, that "Our Lord is *al-Raḥmān*".[51] Muslims have confidence in *al-Raḥmān*;[52] they know that *al-Raḥmān* grants the impious a respite before chastizing them when the Hour comes.[53] All will be **[379]** re-assembled for the judgment.[54] Those who are the most arrogant toward *al-Raḥmān* will be withdrawn from each group and destined to Hell.[55]

*

* *

The attention of Orientalists was for long drawn to the scattered references in the Qur'ān to the divine name which we have just examined. The Orientalists remarked that the use of *al-Raḥmān* corresponds to a certain Meccan period of the Qur'ānic preaching; the first Muslims, then, would have been drawn closer to the poorly known Judeo-Christian milieu. Examination of the texts has shown that the name seems to be tied to the preaching of specific themes; *al-Raḥmān* seems to be connected to a new teaching for the Meccan environment. One final question poses itself, and it is on this point that our study will end; unfortunately, we are unable to draw definitive conclusions. Is the cycle of *al-Raḥmān* in the Qur'ān characteristic of a faith which was professed by a group of believers in pre-Islamic Arabia? There is a chance that communities of Jews or Christians, orthodox or heterodox, preached this religious doctrine. However, a veil of mystery still covers the past of Arabia and archeological digs are not possible there, so we cannot make a categorical assertion. It seems that the ancient zone of al-Yamāma could be, in the future, the theater of interesting discoveries. In the years following the death of the Prophet (632–34), it is in this region that the resistance of the rebels was the most unyielding. The chief of the Banū Ḥanīfa,

---

[50] Qur'ān XXV, 64/63ff. Note that here Hell is called *Jahannam*, a word derived from Hebrew, which figures 77 times in the Qur'ān and many times together with *al-Raḥmān*. A Muslim tradition reports that at Medina, the war cry of the Emigrants was: "O Banū 'Abd al-Raḥmān", while the Anṣār had other war cries, Cf. al-Māwardī, *Al-Aḥkām al-sulṭānīya*, trans. Ostrorog, II, in the chapter on holy war.

[51] Qur'ān XXI, 112.

[52] Qur'ān LXVII, 29.

[53] Qur'ān XIX, 76/75. This idea is expressed very frequently with Allāh.

[54] Qur'ān XIX, 88–89/85–86.

[55] Qur'ān XIX, 70–71/69–70.

Musaylima, had rallied the opposition around the name of *al-Raḥmān*.[56] This new alliance of tribes would have been difficult if God **[380]** had not been worshipped under this name for a long time; the example of the reluctant Ḥijāzīs several years earlier is the best proof of this. Perhaps one day we will be able to locate documents which will reveal the faith of the servants of *al-Raḥmān* in this area. The little that we do know from the works of Muslim traditionists, who are very hostile to Musaylima, makes one envisage doctrines of eschatology, prayer, purity, fasting and sexual restraint.[57]

The Qur'ānic texts mentioned in the course of this article are applicable neither to orthodox Jews (because of the virginity of Mary) nor to orthodox Christians (because of a Messiah-less eschatology).[58] Muslims themselves know this, **[381]** since they accuse Jews and Christians of using sacred texts that are falsified or badly interpreted. This opposition leads to a search for other communities of servants of *al-Raḥmān*, close to the first Muslims. Perhaps we should think in terms of descendants of Judeo-Christians separated from the Great Church, as sought by Harnack and Schoeps.[59] Alternatively,

[56]The Muslim tradition insists Musaylima called himself *Raḥmān*, without an article; cf. al-Ṭabarī, XIX, 17, on Qur'ān XXV, 61/60. However, one finds other important texts that no falsifier would have profited to forge. Musaylima says himself that he received revelation from *al-Raḥmān* (al-Ṭabarī, *Annales*, I, 1937; Cairo ed., III, 246). In an oracle which is attributed to him, he preaches the alliance with Banū Tamīm and adds: "If we die, their fate will be in the hands of al-Raḥmān" (al-Ṭabarī, *Annales*, I, 1933; Cairo ed., III, 245).

[57]Al-Ṭabarī does not say that Musaylima was a Christian, whereas he affirms it expressly about Sajāḥ, the prophetess who, at the same time, directed her followers, who originated in the neighboring zones of al-Yamāma, in their revolt against the Muslims. She had been instructed in the faith by Banū Taghlib. After the defeat of the movement she sought refuge with Musaylima, whom she married. Musaylima, as far as is known, preached "salvation" on the Day of Judgment (this expression of "salvation", rarely used in the Qur'ān for the Last Judgement, is found connected to *al-Raḥmān* in Qur'ān XIX, 72/71). He worshipped the King of the Heavens and the Ruler of the Storm Clouds (*ghamām*), apocalyptic terms which the context forces down to the level of meteorology by adding "and of the rain". He speaks of the role of the righteous on the Last Day; his disciples are pure (*abrār*). At one time, he proscribed for them a fast one day out of every two and to pray at night; he spoke, likewise, about continence and abstention from wine. The law promulgated by Musaylima forbade sexual relations between a married couple after the birth of a son, and another son was not permitted if the first son died (al-Ṭabarī, *Annales*, I, 1915). The hours of prayer at dawn and on the fall of night did not exist in his community (*ibid.*, I, 1919). Musaylima also spoke about sons and grandsons of Ḥabīb, a name that commentators find in *Sūra* XXXVI together with *al-Raḥmān*. See "Musaylima", *EI*.

[58]At the time these texts were preached, the Qur'ān used neither the word *Injīl* nor *Tawrā* and only spoke of books and pages. The Gospels and the Torah are only mentioned in Medina, with the exception of one late Meccan text.

[59]H.J. Schoeps, *Theologie und Geschichte des Judenchristentums* (Tübingen, 1949),

16

we could investigate the case of the mysterious Sabaeans, a type of Baptist sect,[60] to whom the pagan Meccans somewhat ironically compared the first Muslims.[61] The question remains open; it is impossible to settle it given the present state of our knowledge.

334–42. The Jews of Medina seem to have ignored the name *al-Raḥmān*, as far as the argument from silence permits this affirmation.

[60]One of the results of the recent discoveries of Khirbat Qumrān, near the Dead Sea, shows that at the time of Christ the Baptist Essenes united the concern for purification with apocalyptic literature. The presence of a great library in their desert made them one of the people of the Book. Perhaps this tendency persisted with the Sabaeans for several centuries. Wellhausen, in his *Reste arabischen Heidentums*, in the final chapter on the Muslims, gives a series of references to texts which mention the identification of the new Muslims with the Sabaeans. This list is not exhaustive. Wellhausen, however, judges this identification very oddly; he thinks that the Sabaeans are, above all, Baptists, and he does not see the possible apocalyptic element in their doctrine.

[61][On this point, see now Şinasi Gündüz, *The Knowledge of Life: the Origins and Early History of the Mandaeans and their Relation to the Sabians of the Qur'ān and to the Harranians* (Oxford, 1994).]

13

SAJ' IN THE QUR'ĀN: PROSODY AND STUCTURE

Devin J. Stewart

From pre-Islamic times until the twentieth century, *saj*ᶜ has continuously occupied an important place in Arabic literature and in Arab society. It has been used in the sayings of the pre-Islamic *kuhhān*, in sermons and prayers, proverbs and aphorisms, epistles, *maqāmāt*, biographies, and histories. From the tenth until the twentieth century, book titles were almost invariably written in *saj*ᶜ. Introductions to works of many genres were often written entitely in *saj*ᶜ. In short, *saj*ᶜ constitutes an extremely important feature of Arabic writing, including both elite and popular literature. It seems strange that a literary phenomenon of this dimension has received so little attention on the part of medieval and modern Arab literary critics.

What is *saj*ᶜ? The common English translation of the term is "rhymed prose", but is *saj*ᶜ simply that: prose which rhymes? A cursory reading of examples of *saj*ᶜ reveals that there are certain basic rules governing its composition, yet Arab critics wrote very little about these rules in contrast to their monumental efforts to record the rules of poetry. In his *Miftāḥ al-ᶜulūm*, which has been perhaps the most widely used text book of rhetoric for centuries, al-Sakkākī (d. 626/1228) devotes only two sentences to the topic of *saj*ᶜ. However, not all Arab critics ignored *saj*ᶜ to this degree. Abū Hilāl al-ᶜAskarī (d. after 395/1005) discusses *saj*ᶜ in some detail in his *Kitāb al-ṣināᶜatayn*, as does Ḍiyāʾ al-Dīn ibn al-Athīr (d. 637/1239) in his *al-Mathal al-sāʾir fī adab al-kātib wa-ʾl-shāᶜir* and al-Qalqashandī (d. 821/1418) in his *Ṣubḥ al-aᶜshā fī ṣināᶜat al-inshā*. Many other medieval works on rhetoric and *iᶜjāz al-Qurʾān* treat the subject, but have received little attention from Western scholars. Modern Arab scholars appear to be more aware of medieval criticism of *saj*ᶜ, but do little more than report the opinions of their predecessors without criticizing or building on these ideas. These medieval sources ought to be examined in order to reach a satisfactory definition of *saj*ᶜ and to establish norms for the criticism of *saj*ᶜ.

This study will not include a detailed historical analysis of the development of *saj*ᶜ criticism, nor will it attempt to treat important topics such as the development of *saj*ᶜ in the *jāhiliyyah*, the relationship of Qurʾānic *saj*ᶜ to pre-Islamic *saj*ᶜ, or the influence of Qurʾānic *saj*ᶜ on later writers of *saj*ᶜ. It will rather apply rules derived from medieval critical works to the Qurʾān in an attempt to analyze the structure of Qurʾānic *saj*ᶜ, and thereby reach a better understanding of the formal rules governing this type of composition.

*The Question of Saj*ᶜ *in the Qur*ʾ*ān*

The most enduring examples of *saj*ᶜ in Arabic are to be found in the Qurʾān. Much ink has been spilled over the question of whether or not the Qurʾān contains *saj*ᶜ. According to Goldziher, *saj*ᶜ is the oldest type of poetic speech in Arabic, pre-dating *rajaz* and the *qaṣīdah*.[1] It was one of the prevalent types of eloquent speech in pre-Islamic Arabia, and was used specifically in orations and in statements with religious or metaphysical content. Muslim scholars concede that the Qurʾān was revealed in language consistent with that which was considered eloquent in the speech of the Arabs; as Ibn Sinān al-Khafājī (d. 466/1074) states, *inna* ʾ*l-qur*ʾ*āna unzila bi-lughati* ʾ*l-*ᶜ*arabi wa-*ᶜ*alā* ᶜ*urfihim wa-*ᶜ*ādatihim*; "The Qurʾān was revealed in the language of the Arabs, in accordance with their usage and custom".[2] Goldziher goes so far as to state that no Arab would have acknowledged utterances as coming from a divine source had they not been presented in *saj*ᶜ.[3] It seems logical, therefore, that the Qurʾān would contain *saj*ᶜ.

Diametrically opposed to this view is the doctrine of *i*ᶜ*jaz al-Qur*ʾ*ān*, the "inimitability" of the Qurʾān. For example, in his work entitled *I*ᶜ*jaz al-Qur*ʾ*ān*, al-Bāqillānī (d. 403/1013) goes to great lengths to show that the Qurʾān does not contain *saj*ᶜ, and he even attributes this opinion to al-Ashᶜarī.[4] The doctrine of inimitability holds that the Qurʾān may not be compared to any type of sublunary composition, since the Qurʾān represents one of God's attributes—His speech. To call the Qurʾān *saj*ᶜ would be to impute a mundane attribute to God.[5] Denial that the Qurʾān contained *saj*ᶜ was part of a more general insistence that the Qurʾān was God's speech, not Muḥammad's. Enemies of Muḥammad tried to detract from the validity of his messages by labelling them the inventions of a poet or soothsayer.[6] To counter such attacks, many scholars chose to deny that the Qurʾān was a document of *saj*ᶜ or that it contained *saj*ᶜ, just as they denied that it contained poetry. It would appear that the rigidity of this doctrine left no room for the critic to exercise his skill, yet

[1] Ignaz Goldziher, *Abhandlungen zur arabischen Philologie*, (Leiden: E. J. Brill, 1896), 2: 59.

[2] Ibn Sinān al-Khafājī, ᶜAbd Allāh b. Muhammad, *Sirr al-faṣāḥah*, ed. ᶜAbd al-Mutaᶜāl al-Ṣaᶜīdī (Cairo: Maṭbaᶜat Muḥammad ᶜAlī Ṣubayḥ, 1969), 167.

[3] *Introduction to Islamic Theology and Law*, trans. Andras and Ruth Hamori, ed. Bernard Lewis (Princeton: Princeton University Press, 1981), 11.

[4] See *I*ᶜ*jāz al-Qur*ʾ*ān*, ed. Aḥmad Ṣaqr (Cairo: Dār al-maᶜārif, 1954), 86-100. For the statement about al-Ashᶜarī, see 86.

[5] Jalāl al-Dīn al-Suyūṭī, *al-Itqān fī* ᶜ*ulum al-Qur*ʾ*ān*, (Cairo: al-Bābī ʾl-Ḥalabī, 1951), 2: 97.

[6] On this subject, see Qurʾān 37:36, 52:30, 69:41.

it is telling of the method of the Islamic sciences that the greatest advances in literary criticism and the study of rhetoric were made in the course of discussions of *iᶜjāz al-Qurʾān*, and it was possible for Muslim scholars to hold a wide range of opinions on the issue of *saj*ᶜ without being judged heretical.

In the time of the Prophet, *saj*ᶜ was associated not only with eloquent speech in general, but also with the pronouncements of diviners and soothsayers.[7] The Arab critics report some of their often cryptic messages: *al-samāʾu wa-ʾl-ard/ wa-ʾl-qardu wa-ʾl-fard/ wa-ʾl-ghamru wa-ʾl-bard* "The sky and the earth, the loan and the debt, the flood and the trickle..."[8] These soothsayers were frequently thought to be in contact with the *jinn* or familiar spirits and have magical powers. They used *saj*ᶜ to perform pagan functions such as foretelling the future, cursing enemies and warding off evil. To Muslims, the soothsayer's statements were necessarily ridiculous, false, or even heretical. As al-Bāqillānī states, "Soothsaying contradicts the prophecies" (*al-kihānatu tunāfī ʾl-nubuwwāt*).[9] The danger which the *kuhhān* could pose to the religion is demonstrated by the career of Musaylimah the Liar, a *kāhin* from the Banū Ḥanīfah tribe in Yamāmah contemporary to the Prophet Muḥammad, who held a rival claim to prophecy and formed his own community of believers. Their conflict with the Muslims, which began shortly after Muḥammad's death, culminated in the battle of ᶜAqrabāʾ in year 12 of the *hijrah*, in which Musaylimah was killed and his forces defeated.[10]

Much discussion of *saj*ᶜ in the Qurʾān revolves around a *ḥadīth* known as the *ḥadīth* of the fetus. Abū Dāwūd (d. 275/889) gives three versions of this *ḥadīth* in *al-Sunan*. Though there are slight differences between the versions, the general context is as follows. Two women of the Hudhayl tribe quarreled, and one struck the other, who happened to be pregnant, in the belly with a staff or, according to another version, a stone. The wounded woman had a miscarriage before dying herself. She had been very close to giving birth, for the fetus, a male, had already begun to grow hair. The guardians of the two women disputed as to whether blood money should be paid for the fetus in addition to that paid for the mother. The dispute was brought before the Prophet, and when the Prophet gave the verdict that blood money should be paid for the fetus also, the guardian of the attacker remonstrated:

[7] On soothsaying (*al-kihānah*) and the association of *saj*ᶜ with it, see Ibn Khaldūn, *al-Muqaddimah*, ed. M. Quatremère (Paris: Institut impériale de France, 1858), 1:181-5; Rosenthal translation, (New York: Pantheon, 1958), 1:202-7.

[8] Abū Hilāl al-ᶜAskarī, *Kitāb al-ṣināᶜatayn*, ed. ᶜAlī Maḥmūd al-Bajāwī and Muḥammad Abū ʾl-Faḍl Ibrāhīm (Cairo: Dār iḥyāʾ al-kutub al-ᶜarabiyyah, 1952), 261.

[9] *Iᶜjāz al-Qurʾān*, 87.

[10] See Frantz Buhl in *The Encyclopaedia of Islam*, 1st edition, s.v. "Musailima".

"Oh Prophet of God! How can I pay blood money for him who has not yet drunk nor eaten, nor uttered a sound nor cried? Is blood money to be paid for such as this?"
(*kayfa aghramu diyata man lā shariba wa-lā akall wa-lā naṭaqa wa ʾstahal(l)/ fa-mithlu dhālika yuṭal(l)?/*)

The Prophet replied, "This man is of the ilk of the *kuhhān* because of the *sajᶜ* he has spoken".[11]

[Other versions give as the Prophet's reply, "Is this *sajᶜ* like the *sajᶜ* of the *jāhiliyyah wa-kahānatihim*?"[12] "Is this *sajᶜ* like the *sajᶜ* of the *aᶜrāb*?"[13] Is this *sajᶜ* like the *sajᶜ* of the *jāhiliyyah*?"[14] "Is this *sajᶜ* like the *sajᶜ* of the soothsayers (*kuhhān*)?"[15]]

The unwilling guardian phrased his question in *sajᶜ*, and the Prophet expressed disapproval of this man's *sajᶜ*, asking if it was like the *sajᶜ* of the pre-Islamic soothsayers. Many critics have taken this *ḥadīth* as proof that the Prophet disapproved of *sajᶜ* as such. Several critics refute this interpretation, on a variety of grounds. Both Abū Hilāl al-ᶜAskarī and Ḍiyāʾ al-Dīn ibn al-Athīr state that if the Prophet meant to criticize *sajᶜ* per se, he would have said simply, "*a-sajᶜan*?" ("Is this *sajᶜ*?") in his reply rather than "*a-sajᶜan ka-sajᶜi ʾl-kuhhān*?" Al-ᶜAskarī's view is that the Prophet was not expressing a negative view of *sajᶜ* in general, but of the *sajᶜ* of the *kuhhān* in particular, because their *sajᶜ* was very stilted or unnatural; *li-ʾanna ʾl-takullufa fī sajᶜihim fāshin.*[16] Isḥāq Ibn Wahb (d. ?) states that the Prophet criticized the questioner because he spoke completely in *sajᶜ*—for according to him *sajᶜ* is not good if over-used—and because this particular example of *sajᶜ* was unnatural and stilted, like that of the soothsayers: *wa takallafa fī ʾl-sajᶜi takallufa ʾl-kuhhān.*[17] Ibn al-Athīr states that the Prophet intended to criticize the man's argument itself.[18] According to him, the Prophet's statement meant *a-ḥukman ka-ḥukmi ʾl-kuhhān*; "Is this a pronouncement like those of the soothsayers?"[19] ᶜAbd al-Ṣamad Ibn al-Faḍl al-Riqāshī, as cited by al-Jāḥiẓ (d. 255/868),

---

[11] *al-Sunan*, ed. M. Muḥyī ʾl-Dīn ᶜAbd al-Ḥamīd (Cairo: Dār iḥyāʾ al-sunnah al-nabawiyyah, 1970), 4: 192-3.

[12] *Ibid.*, 4: 192.

[13] *Ibid.*, 4: 190-1.

[14] al-Jāḥiẓ, *al-Bayān wa-l-tabyīn*, ed. ᶜAbd al-Salām Muḥammad Hārūn (Cairo: Maktabat al-Khānjī, 1960), 1: 287-91.

[15] *al-Mathal al-sāʾir fī adab al-kātib wa-ʾl-shāᶜir*, (Cairo, Maktabaṭ nahḍat Miṣr, 1959-62), 1: 274. It is interesting to note that this exact wording, that commonly found in works on rhetoric, is not given in the most popular *ḥadīth* collections. See A. J. Wensinck, *Concordances et indices de la tradition musulmane*, (Leiden: E.J. Brill, 1936-88), 2: 431.

[16] *Kitab al-sinaᶜatayn*, 261.

[17] Isḥāq b. Ibrāhīm b. Sulaymān b. Wahb al-Kātib, *al-Burhan fī wujūh al-bayān*, ed. Aḥmad Maṭlūb and Khadījah al-Ḥadīthī (Baghdad, 1967), 208-9.

[18] *al-Mathal al-sāʾir*, 1: 275.

[19] *Ibid.*, 1: 275

states that the Prophet's censure of his questioner is not because he had used *saj*ᶜ, but rather because he resorted to casuistry to avoid payment:

> *law anna hādha ʾl-mutakallima lam yurid illā iqāmata ʾl-wazni lamā kāna ᶜalayhi baʾsun lākinnahu ᶜasā an yakūna arāda ibṭālan li-ḥaqqin fa-tashādaqa fī kalāmih.*
>
> If the speaker had only wanted to maintain a *wazn*,[20] he would not have been subject to reproach, but it seems that he wished to deny a right, and so spoke in an affected manner.[21]

Some critics used the issue of form and meaning to argue that the Qurʾān was not *saj*ᶜ. In doing so, they were thinking primarily of the ridiculous or incomprehensible statements attributed to the diviners. One of the early critics who argued this way is al-Rummānī (d. 384/994) in his *al-Nukat fī iᶜjāz al-Qurʾān*:

> *al-fawāṣilu ḥurūfun mutashākilatun fī ʾl-maqāṭiᶜi tūjibu ḥusna ifhāmi ʾl-maᶜānī, wa-ʾl-fawāṣilu balāghatun, wa-ʾl-asjāᶜu ᶜaybun, wa-dhālika anna ʾl-fawāṣila tābiᶜatun li-ʾl-maᶜānī wa-amma ʾl-asjāᶜu fa-ʾl-maᶜānī tābiᶜatun lahā.*
>
> *Fawāṣil* are similar letters which occur at the ends of phrases and cause the content to be conveyed well. *Fawāṣil* are [an element of] eloquence, but *asjā*ᶜ are a defect. The reason for this is that *fawāṣil* are dependent on the content, whereas [in *saj*ᶜ] the content is dependent on the *asjā*ᶜ.[22]

He states that using *saj*ᶜ in order to be eloquent is a waste of effort, like making a necklace for a dog.[23] He thought of *saj*ᶜ as being, by definition, a poetic mold for a worthless message. He gives an example attributed to Musaylimah the Liar:

> *yā ḍifdaᶜu niqqī kam taniqqīn lā ʾl-māʾa tukaddirīn wa-lā ʾn-nahra tufāriqīn.*
>
> *O frog, croak away! You croak so much, but you don't muddy the water, and you don't leave the river.*[24]

Al-Rummānī attempts to justify the idea that in *saj*ᶜ the content is necessarily inane with his interpretation of the etymology of *saj*ᶜ. The term *saj*ᶜ, lexicographers agree, is derived from the cooing of doves. Al-Rummānī states that this is because they repeat sounds which are similar but have no meaning. Therefore, he holds that the original and true meaning of *saj*ᶜ is any nonsense which rhymes.[25]

---

[20] By *wazn* here, he means not meter as in poetry but the morphological pattern of the final words in the phrases of *saj*ᶜ. This point will be discussed below.

[21] *al-Bayān wa-ʾl-tabyīn*, 1: 288.

[22] *al-Nukat fī iᶜjāz al-Qurʾān*. In *Thalāth rasāʾil fī iᶜjāz al-Qurʾān*, ed., Muḥammad Khalaf Allāh and Muḥammad Zaghlūl Salām (Cairo: al-Maṭbaᶜah al-taymūriyya, 1969), 97.

[23] *Ibid.*, 97.

[24] *Ibid.*, 97-98.

[25] *Ibid.*, 98.

Al-Rummānī's example evinces a biased view of the possibilities for the content of *sajᶜ* to say the least, but his work was nevertheless influential. Al-Bāqillānī, who drew on al-Rummānī, argues similarly but syllogistically. In the Qurᵓān, the form is subordinate to the meaning. In *sajᶜ* the meaning is subordinate to the form. Therefore, the Qurᵓān cannot be *sajᶜ*.[26] The conclusion here follows logically from the two premises, but the premises are faulty. It is easy for a non-Muslim to say the first premise might be wrong, since there are many examples of the use of formal devices in the Qurᵓān where the meaning is somewhat subordinated for aesthetic or rhetorical reasons. On the other hand, if we take the Qurᵓān to be literally the word of God, could not God have the ability to express the desired meaning and mold it in an artistic form like *sajᶜ* or poetry at the same time? Al-Bāqillānī, however, would probably have seen any attempt to say that God followed specific formal rules in the Qurᵓān as an attempt to limit His power. The second premise is a disputed idea, and medieval critics pointed out that it was not necessarily true. In fact, Ibn al-Athīr turns al-Rummānī's idea on its head, stating that in order for *sajᶜ* to be good, the form *must* be subordinate to the meaning and not vice-versa. If not, the *sajᶜ* is like a gold scabbard enclosing a wooden blade (*ka-ghimdin min dhahabl ᶜalā naṣlin min khashabl*).[27] Al-ᶜAskarī insists that *sajᶜ* is meritorious if it is not stilted,[28] and further states that Qurᵓānic *sajᶜ* is unlike human discourse for the very reason that it captures the fullest meaning and achieves elegance while adopting formal constraints.

> *wa-kadhālika mā fī ᵓl-Qurᵓāni mimmā yajrī ᶜala ᵓl-tasjīᶜi wa-ᵓl-izdiwāji mukhālifun fī tamkīni ᵓl-maᶜnā wa-ṣafāᵓi ᵓl-lafẓi wa-taḍammuni ᵓl-ṭalāwati wa-ᵓl-māᵓi li-mā yajrī majrāhu min kalāmi ᵓl-khalq.*
>
> Qurᵓānic discourse which assumes the form of *sajᶜ* and *izdiwāj*[29] is contrary to human discourse which assumes this form in its ability to convey the meaning, its clarity of expression, its sweetness and musicality.[30]

Many critics object to the use of the word *sajᶜ* to refer to Qurᵓānic discourse, while admitting that it is often *sajᶜ*-like. Al-Suyūṭī states that the majority of scholars do not allow the use of the term *sajᶜ* in the context of the Qurᵓān.[31] In such scholars' view, the final words of Qurᵓānic verses should be called *fawāṣil* (literally "dividers") rather than *asjāᶜ*.

---

[26] *Iᶜjāz al-Qurᵓān*, 88.
[27] *al-Mathal al-sāᵓir*, 1: 276.
[28] *Ibid.*, 261.
[29] *Izdiwāj* will be discussed below.
[30] *Kitāb al-ṣināᵓatayn*, 260.
[31] *al-Itqān*, 2: 97.

Many critics, however, make this statement while at the same time using verses from the Qurʾān as examples of the various types of *sajᶜ*.[32] They claim to derive the term *fawāṣil* from *sūrat fuṣṣilat* (41:3):

> *kitābun fuṣṣilat āyātuhu Qurʾānan ᶜarabiyyan li-qawmin yaᶜlamūn*
>
> A book, the verses of which have been divided into sections;[33] a Qurʾān in Arabic, for a people who understand.

Al-Taftazānī (d. 791/1389) states that one does not use the word *sajᶜ* to refer to the Qurʾān, not because it is not *sajᶜ*, but out of respect and veneration (*riᶜayatan li-l-adabi wa-taᶜẓīman lahu*), since the term *sajᶜ* originally denotes the cooing of pigeons, a rather humble epithet for Qurʾānic discourse.[34] Al-Suyūṭī makes a similar statement about the term *sajᶜ*: *li-anna aṣlahu min sajᶜi l-ṭayri fa sharufa ʾl-Qurʾānu an yustaᶜāra li-shayʾin minhu lafẓun aṣluhu muhmal*; "Because it derives from the cooing of birds, and the Qurʾān is above having an expression the origin of which is trifling used metaphorically to refer to any part of it".[35]

The problem of *sajᶜ* in the Qurʾān has not been settled. The recent *Cambridge History of Arabic Literature* contains two statements on the issue which could not be farther apart. Paret baldly states; "The Qurʾān is written throughout in rhyming proze (*sajᶜ*)".[36] On the other hand, Abdulla el Tayib states.

> The rhythmic deviation by which it (the Qurʾān) departs from *sajᶜ*, *rajaz*, and verse eludes all probing because it is a fundamental tenet of Islam that the Qurʾān is by nature miraculous.[37]

The first statement takes a preconception to its furthest limit, forcing the text into a pre-determined mold through insensitive examination, and the second attempts to deny the value of investigation. This contradiction points to a serious problem. In investigating the problem of *sajᶜ* in the Qurʾān and in trying to define *sajᶜ* itself, it is wrong to impose existing

---

[32] See, for example, Muḥammad b. Abī Bakr al-Rāzī, *Rawḍat al-faṣāhah*, ed. Aḥmad al-Nādī Shuᶜlah (Cairo: Dār al-ṭibāᶜah al-muḥammadiyyah, 1982), 210.

[33] Abdullah Yusuf Ali translates this as "A Book, whereof the verses are explained in detail". *The Meaning of the Glorious Qurʾān* (Cairo: Dār al-kitāb al-miṣrī, n.d.), 1287. The critics obviously interpret the verb *fuṣṣilat* differently.

[34] *al-Sharḥ al-mukhtaṣar li-talkhīṣ al-miftāḥ*, printed with Muḥammad al-Karamī's *al-Wishāh ᶜalā al-sharḥ al-mukhtaṣar*, (Qum: Maṭbaᶜat Qum, 1375 a.h.), 3: 175. ᶜAbd al-Mutaᶜāl al-Ṣaᶜīdī makes this point without mentioning the source in *Bughyat al-Īḍāḥ*, 96, n. 2.

[35] al-*Itqān*, 2: 97.

[36] "The Qurʾān - I", in *Cambridge History of Arabic Literature. Arabic Literature to the End of the Ummayyad Period*, ed. A.F.L. Beeston et. al. (Cambridge: Cambridge Univ. Press, 1983), 196.

[37] "Pre-Islamic Poetry", *Ibid.*, 34.

conventions on the material, whether they be Arabic-Muslim or Western Orientalist, for this can only advance our understanding in a limited fashion. It is more important to understand the conventions within the tradition of criticism of the Qurʾān and of *sajᶜ*. Abdulla el Tayib's statement, in my view, reflects a lack of awareness of the variety of opinions held on the issue within the Arabic-Muslim tradition; he is not aware of the conventions, but rather is trapped by them. Is it not more fruitful to take the doctrine of *iᶜjāz* as a challenge to investigation and comparison rather than a declaration of the futility of independent thinking? Did not the greatest Muslim literary critics do just that?

One such critic, at the opposite end of the spectrum from critics like al-Rummānī, is Ḍiyāʾ al-Dīn ibn al-Athīr, who, placing formal examination of the Qurʾānic text itself before doctrinal considerations, affirms that the greater part of the Qurʾān is *sajᶜ*. He states that almost every *sūrah* in the Qurʾān contains some *sajᶜ*, and that many *sūrahs*, including *sūrat al-qamar* (54) and *sūrat al-raḥmān* (55), are entirely in *sajᶜ*.[38] Al-Qalqashandī adds *sūrat al-najm* (53) to the list of *sūrahs* entirely in *sajᶜ*.[39] It is not surprising that the medieval critics who so plainly recognize Qurʾānic *sajᶜ* as such are those who have produced the best analyses of *sajᶜ* that have come down to us. It is with their analyses that my own begins.

Rhyme in Qurʾānic Sajᶜ

An important though admittedly preliminary step in determining the percentage of *sajᶜ* in the Qurʾān is to determine the number of rhyming *āyāt*. I have examined the final words of the *āyāt* of the entire Qurʾān and have recorded the numbers of rhyming *āyāt* separately for each *sūrah* in Appendix 1; 85.9% of the *āyāt* in the Qurʾān rhyme. These numbers are not final or definitive; they are at best a close approximation.[40] It is also an error to assume that everything which rhymes is *sajᶜ*. Nevertheless, of the one hundred and fourteen *sūrahs* in the Qurʾān, only two, *sūrat quraysh* (106) and *sūrat al-naṣr* (110), have no rhyme. Thirty-three *sūrahs* rhyme

---

38 *al-Mathal al-sāʾir*, 1: 271.

39 Aḥmad b. ᶜAlī ʾl-Qalqashandī, *Ṣubḥ al-aᶜshā fī ṣināᶜat al-inshā*, (Cairo: al-Muʾassasah al-miṣriyyah al-ᶜāmmah li-ʾl-taʾlīf wa-ʾl-tarjamah wa-ʾl-ṭibāᶜah wa-ʾl-nashr, 1964), 2: 280.

40 There are a number of difficulties involved in deciding exactly what constitutes a rhyme, or whether or not internal rhymes should be considered. On rhyme in the *qāṣīdah*, see Saᶜīd b. Masᶜadah al-Akhfash, *al-Qawāfī* (Damascus: Maṭbūᶜāt mudīriyyat iḥyāʾ al-turrāth al-qadīm, 1970); S. A. Bonebakker, *The Encyclopaedia of Islam*, 2nd edition, *s.v.* "*Kafiya*".

completely. The results tend to indicate that the Qurʾān contains a great deal of *sajᶜ*, and is probably more *sajᶜ* than not.

A word about rhyme in the Qurʾān is necessary.[41] *Sajᶜ*, like *rajaz*, and unlike the *qaṣīdah*, does not require mono-rhyme.[42] Qurʾānic *sajᶜ*, while it does include examples of several rhymes being used in a single *sūrah*, has a tendency towards mono-rhyme. For instance, the seventy-eight verses of *sūrat al-raḥmān* (55) all rhyme in *ān/ām*. In this, Qurʾānic *sajᶜ* is quite unlike other common forms of *sajᶜ*, such as that of the *maqāmāt* and the epistles of later centuries, where a single rhyme is not so persistent, and rarely reaches eight or ten consecutive rhymes.

I have listed the main rhymes for each *sūrah* in Appendix 1. The most common rhyme in the Qurʾān is the *īn/ūn/īm/ūm* rhyme; other common rhymes include *īl/ūl* and *īr/ūr*. Many of the longer *sūrah*s, including *sūrat al-baqarah*, are written almost entirely in the *īn/ūn/īm/ūm* rhyme. Altogether, this rhyme appears in fifty-five *sūrah*s of the Qurʾān. It is one example of inexact rhyme which is also allowed in poetry, since the long vowel *ū* may rhyme with *ī*, and *n* may rhyme with *m*. There are, however, other inexact rhymes in the Qurʾān which are less often recognized as such. The common presence of *d*, *b*, and *q* in environments where rhyme is on the whole quite regular or expected tends to show that these letters often rhyme, as do *l* and *r*. For example, these rhyme consonants are found in conjunction in *sūrat abī lahab* (111) with the rhyme words *wa-tab/kasab/lahab/ḥaṭab/masad/*, *sūrat al-falaq* (113) with the rhyme words *falaq/khalaq/waqab/ᶜuqad/ḥasad*, and many other passages. These rhymes are not allowed in poetry and, to the best of my knowledge, are not used by later writers of *sajᶜ*. Al-Rummānī terms the exact rhymes *ḥurūf mutajānisah* and the inexact rhymes *ḥurūf mutaqāribah.*[43] Al-Suyūṭī and other critics use the term *ḥurūf mutamāthilah* instead of *ḥurūf mutajānizah.*[44] Al-Suyūṭī reports some critics' claim that all *fawāṣil* in the Qurʾān are either *ḥurūf mutamāthilah* or *ḥurūf mutaqāribah.*[45] The evidence does not support this claim: the *fawāṣil* in *sūrat al-naṣr* (110), for instance, are *allāh/afwājan/tawwāban*.

The rules governing the rhyme word in *sajᶜ* are different from those in poetry. One main difference is that the writer of *sajᶜ* should observe *taskīn*: i.e., the last words of the *sajᶜ* phrases should be in "pausal form". In his *Talkhīṣ*, al-Qazwīnī (d. 739/1338) states, *al-asjāᶜu mabniyyatun ᶜalā*

[41] On rhyme in the Qurʾān, see Theodor Nöldeke, *Geschichte des Qorāns*, revised by Friedrich Schwally (New York: Georg Olms Verlag, 1970), 1: 37-42.

[42] al-Suyūṭī, *al-Itqān*, 2: 97.

[43] *al-Nukat*, 98-99.

[44] *al-Itqān*, 2: 105.

[45] *Ibid.*

sukūni ʾl-aʿjāz: "*asjāʿ* end regularly in *sukūn*".[46] Al-Suyūṭī makes a similar statement: *mabnā ʾl-fawāṣili ʿalā ʾl-waqf*.[47] Al-Qazwīnī explains that to complete the *iʿrāb* would ruin the rhyme, as is the case in the example he provides, the proverb *mā abʿada mā fāt// wa-mā aqraba mā huwa āt//*. If one were to include the final vowels, *fāta* would be made to rhyme with *ātin*, or, according to the rules for rhymes in poetry, *ābī*. A similar example from the Qurʾān is *sūrat al-ikhlāṣ* (112):

qul huwa ʾllāhu aḥad//
allāhu ʾṣ-ṣamad//
lam yalid wa-lam yūlad//
wa-lam yakun lahu kufuʾan aḥad//

If this were read with full declension, the resulting final words, *aḥadun, ʾṣ-ṣamadu, yūlad*, and *aḥadun*, would no longer rhyme.

Al-Suyūṭi states that some rhymes which are considered defective in poetry are permissible in *sajʿ*: *wa-mā yudhkaru min ʿuyūbi ʾl-qāfiyati min ikhtilāfi ʾl-ḥarakati wa-ʾl-ishbāʿi wa-ʾl-tawjīh fa-laysa bi-ʿaybin fī ʾl-fāṣilah*.[48] *Ikhtilāf al-ḥarakah* refers to variation of vowels in the final syllables of the rhyme words. For example, a genitive may rhyme with a nominative. This, in most cases, does not usually affect the rhyme since the rhyme words are read in pause form, as mentioned above. *Ikhtilāf al-ishbāʿ* and *ikhtilāf al-tawjīh* are defined as variation in the short vowels immediately preceding the *rawiyy*, the rhyme letter, *al-ishbāʿ* denoting specifically the vowel before a voweled *rawiyy*, and *al-tawjīh* the vowel before a quiescent *rawiyy*. An example of this is *sūrat al-qamar* (54), which includes rhyme words such as *qamar*, *mustamir(r)*, and *nudhur*.

Al-Suyūṭī also notes that the Qurʾān often exhibits *luzūm mā lā yalzam* ("adhering to that which is not obligatory"), where the rhyme consists of more than one letter.[49] The following Qurʾānic examples demonstrate this.

fa-amma ʾl-yatīma fa-lā taqhar/
fa-amma ʾl-sāʾila fa-lā tanhar/

(93:9-10. Here the two rhyme letters are *h* and *r*).

tadhakkarū fa-idhā hum mubṣirūn/
wa-ikhwānuhum yamuddūna fī ʾl-ghayyi thumma lā yuqṣirūn/

(7:201-2. Here the three rhyme letters are *ṣ*, *r*, and *n*).

---

[46] Jalāl al-Dīn Muḥammad al-Qazwīnī, *al-Talkhīṣ fī ʿulūm al-balāghah*, ed. ʿAbd al-Raḥmān al-Barqūqī (Cairo: Dār al-Fikr al-ʿArabī, 1904), 400.

[47] *al-Itqān*, 2: 105.

[48] *Ibid.*, 2: 97.

[49] *Ibid.*, 2: 104-5.

Western poetics would tend to describe this in terms of syllables rather than letters. The rhyme in Qurʾānic *sajᶜ* is often one syllable, as *ā* in *sūrat al-ᶜalaq* (96), verses, 6-14, but may embrace as many three syllables, as in *sūrat al-zalzalah* (99), which has the rhyme words *zilzālaha*, *athqālahā*, *mā-lahā*, *akhbārahā*, and *awḥālahā*.

Inquiry into the Prosody of Sajᶜ

Traditional definitions of *sajᶜ* start with the statement that it is "prose", *nathr* or *manthūr*, divided into phrases or clauses which end in a common rhyme. For this reason, Western scholars first translated the term *sajᶜ* as "rhymed prose". Medieval rhetoricians tried to impose the prose/poetry dichotomy on a triad of composition styles—ordinary prose, *sajᶜ*, and quantitative poetry—with the result that *sajᶜ* was somewhat unfairly shoved into the prose category because it lacked quantitative meter. Many medieval critics realized that these categories were in some ways inadequate. Ibn Khaldūn (d. 808/1406), for example, states that prose (*nathr*) falls into two categories: *mursal*, free or ordinary prose, and *musajjaᶜ*,[50] but adds that recent authors have used "poetic modes and methods" in their prose, including, among others, *asjāᶜ* and rhyme: *wa-qad istaᶜmala ʾl-mutaʾakhkhirūna asāliba ʾl-shiᶜri wa-manāziᶜihi fī ʾl-manthūri min kathrati ʾl-asjāᶜi wa-ʾltizāmi ʾl-taqfiyah*...[51]

Rhyme, however, is not the only poetic characteristic of *sajᶜ*. There are constraints on the relative lengths of the rhyming phrases, and though *sajᶜ* does not have quantitative meter, it does have meter of a sort. How, does, then, one determine the length of the rhyming phrases?

Scholars have long recognized that *sajᶜ* has metrical qualities. In 1896, Goldziher stated that *sajᶜ* was the earliest form of poetic speech in Arabic, and proposed the theory that *rajaz* developed as a form of metrically regular *sajᶜ*.[52] Research in this area, as is the case with the study of *sajᶜ* in general, has been quite slow, and has been particularly characterized by a failure to combine textual analysis with examination of the medieval critical works on *sajᶜ*. It is telling that Krenkow's article on *sajᶜ* in the first edition of the *The Encyclopaedia of Islam* does not cite any medieval Arabic critical works.[53] Zakī Mubārak's *al-Nathr al-fannī fī ʾl-qarn al-rābiᶜ* gives a good overview of the history of *sajᶜ* and its uses in the first four Islamic

50 *al-Muqaddimah*, 3: 322; Rosenthal translation, 3: 368.

51 *Ibid.*, 3: 323; Rosenthal translation, 3: 369.

52 *Abhandlungen zur arabischen Philologie*, 1: 59, 76. On p. 76, he states: "Die älteste metrische Schema der arabischen Poesie ist das sogenannte *Regez*. Dasselbe ist im Grunde nichts Anderes als *rhythmisch disciplinirtes Sagᶜ*".

53 *The Encyclopaedia of Islam*, 1st edition, *s.v.* "Sadjᶜ".

centuries and draws on a number of the available critical works.[54] He is not interested in the questions of form and prosody of *saj*ᶜ but rather the topics and genres in which it was used, to what extent it was used in the composition of various authors, and to what degree it was enhanced with other rhetorical devices. Régis Blachère improved the translation of the term *saj*ᶜ to "rhymed and rhythmic prose" and produced the best definition of *saj*ᶜ to date, probably as a result of his studies of the Qurʾān.

> Cette prose est caractérisée par l'emploi d'unités rhythmiques, en général assez courtes, allant de quatres à huit ou dix syllabes, parfois davantage, terminées par une clausule. Ces unités rhythmiques sont groupées par séries sur une même rime. Dans ces groupes, chaque unité rhythmique ne comporte pas obligatoirement le même nombre de syllabes et, en dernière analyse, l'élément essentiel est constitué par la clausule rimée. Par approximation, on traduira le mot *saj*ᶜ par prose rimée et rhythmée.[55]

In 1974, Scheindlin included some remarks on metrical analysis of *saj*ᶜ in his book *Form and Structure in the Poetry of al-Muᶜtamid Ibn ᶜAbbād*, stating that the medieval rhetoricians recommended maintaining rhythmical equality between rhyming phrases. He cites two of the most important medieval works on the subject, al-ᶜAskarī's *Kitāb al-ṣināᶜatayn* and Ḍiyāʾ al-Dīn Ibn al-Athīr's *al-Mathal al-sāʾir*.[56] In 1976, Abd al-Fattah Kilito alluded to medieval Arab critics' statements on this topic: "Le *saj*ᶜ suppose un schéma métrique certes moins rigide que celui de la poésie, mais obéissant néanmoins à certaines regles que les rhétoriciens n'on pas manqué de codifier".[57] In 1981, Pierre Crapon de Caprona published a work entitled *Le Coran: aux sources de la parole oraculaire*, in which he performed a rhythmical analysis of a number of Meccan *sūrah*s without recourse to any medieval sources on *saj*ᶜ.[58] While undertaking a prosodic analysis of selected *maqāmāt* by al-Hamadhānī and al-Ḥarīrī in 1982, Hayim Y.

---

[54] Zaki Mubārak, *La Prose Arabe au IVe siècle de l'Hégire* (Paris: Maisonneuve, 1931), 78-94; *al-Nathr al-fannī fī ʾl-qarn al-rābi*ᶜ, (Cairo: Dār al-kātib al-ᶜarabī, 1934), 1: 75-123, 137-53.

[55] Régis Blachère, *Histoire de la Littérature Arabe des origines à la fin du XVe siècle de J.-C.* (Paris: Adrien-Maisonneuve, 1964), 189.

[56] (Leiden: Brill, 1974), 58. See n. 88. However, he incorrectly states that Ibn al-Athir recommended composing *saj*ᶜ phrases of roughly the same number of syllables, and that he "stresses this requirement rather more forcefully than does ᶜAskarī". Ibn al-Athīr states that *saj*ᶜ phrases should have roughly the same number of words (*lafẓah*), but does not mention syllables. This will be discussed below.

[57] "Le Genre séance: une introduction", *Studia Islamica* 43 (1976), 29. Kilito did use some medieval works which deal with *saj*ᶜ in writing this article, including Ibn Rashīq al-Qayrawānī's *al-ᶜUmdah*, ᶜAbd al-Qāhir al-Jurjānī's *Asrār al-balāghah*, and al-Bāqillānī's *Iᶜjāz al-Qurʾān*, but to the best of my knowledge, he could not have derived the above statement from these works.

[58] (Publications Orientalistes de France, 1981) It was the author's thesis at the University of Geneva.

Sheynin found Kilito's statement unsupported by his sources and tried, independently, to locate earlier scholarship on the issue. He examined medieval works on rhetoric—he does not say which—but failed to find anything related to questions of prosody, and concluded, "Surprisingly, no work has been done on the study of the prosodic structure of *saj*ᶜ".[59] In his *Introduction à la poétique arabe*, published in 1985, Adonis emphasized the importance of *saj*ᶜ in the development of the notion of meter in Arabic poetry and presented different types of *saj*ᶜ as defined by Arab rhetoricians, drawing on al-ᶜAskarī's *Kitāb al-ṣināᶜatayn* and other works.[60] In short, a number of modern scholars have shown interest in exploring the poetic qualities and prosody of *saj*ᶜ. Unfortunately, Western scholars, though they have expended great effort on examining *saj*ᶜ texts, have been largely unaware of medieval Arab critics' work on the subject. Modern Arab scholars, while more aware of medieval criticism of *saj*ᶜ, have not yet applied their understanding of these critical works to original *saj*ᶜ texts in order to advance scholarship in this area.

*The Accent-Based Meter of Saj*ᶜ

Ḍiyāʾ al-Dīn ibn al-Athīr is one of the earliest rhetoricians to discuss the length of *saj*ᶜ phrases in detail and one of the few to do so in numerical terms.[61] Many later critics drew heavily on his work in this regard. The following discussion of his work requires the introduction of some important terms. In Arabic, the single clause or phrase of *saj*ᶜ is termed *sajᶜah*, pl. *sajaᶜāt*, *faṣl*, pl. *fuṣūl*, *fiqrah*, pl. *fiqar*, or *qarīnah*, pl. *qarāʾin*.[62] Ibn al-Athīr, in analyzing the prosody of *saj*ᶜ, gives examples showing how the length of one *sajᶜah* is very close, if not exactly equal, to the length of its partner *sajᶜah*. He terms this effect *iᶜtidāl*, "balance".[63] But how does he determine the length of the *sajᶜah*? He describes the length of the *sajᶜah* in terms of "words", Arabic *lafẓah*, pl. *lafaẓāt*. Nowhere does he mention syllables or the *tafāᶜīl* of al-Khalīl. This indicates that, at least according to him, the basic unit of the meter is the word. Each word represents one foot, or one beat, in the meter, without much regard to the length of each

[59] "A Prosodic Study of *Saj*ᶜ in Classical *Maqāmāt*", parts I and II. (Unpublished papers, Univ. of Pennsylvania, 1982), Part I, p. 5.

[60] Adonis, *Introduction à la poétique arabe*, trans. Bassam Tahhan and Anne Wade Minkowski. (Paris: Éditions Sindbad, 1985), 23.

[61] On *saj*ᶜ in general see *al-Mathal al-Sāʾir*, 1: 271-337. On length of *saj*ᶜ phrases in particular see 1: 333-37.

[62] Ibn al-Athīr most often uses the term *faṣl*, but the term *sajᶜah* will be used throughout this study.

[63] *al-Mathal al-sāʾir*, 1: 333.

word, or the length of its syllables. His analysis implies that *sajᶜ* has an accent-based meter, where the word stress accents provide the beats. In other words, in *sajᶜ*, the *lafẓah* corresponds to the *tafᶜīlah* in poetry.

The recent work of Hayim Sheynin shows remarkable agreement with the system of Ibn al-Athīr, although Sheynin was unaware of Ibn al-Athīr's treatment of *sajᶜ*. A detailed prosodic analysis of a number of the *maqāmāt* of al-Hamadhānī and al-Ḥarīrī convinced Sheynin that *sajᶜ* conformed to an accentual system of metrics. He writes, "The metrics of *sajᶜ* is accentual, i.e. all the RS [rhyme syntagmata = *sajaᶜāt*] of one RU [rhyme unit = group of *sajaᶜāt* united by common rhyme] usually have the same number of syntagmatic stresses".[64]

It might be objected that the number of words may not correspond exactly to the number of syntagmatic beats in a particular *sajᶜah*, since there are certain lexical items which are written as separate words but do not have their own accent, such as *fī* when followed by *hamzat al-waṣl*. Although Ibn al-Athīr's examples are not numerous enough to work out a complete system, they provide help with problems such as the status of proclitics, propositions, particles, attached pronouns. For instance, he states that the following Qurʾānic verse contains eight "words":

> *bal*/1*kadhdhabū*/2*biʾl-sāᶜati*/3*waᶜtadna*/4*li-man*/5*kadhdhaba*/6*biʾl-sāᶜati*/7*saᶜīran*//8 (24:11).[65]

Here we see that attached prepositions such as *bi-* and *li-* are not considered separate: *biʾl-sāᶜati* is one foot, as is *li-man*. Proclitics such as *wāw* are not considered separate: *waᶜtadna* is one foot. Finally, particles such as *bal* are considered separate feet. He states that the following verse contains nine "words":

> *idhā*/1*raʾathum*/2*min*/3*makānin*/4*baᶜīdin*/5*samiᶜū*/6*lahā*/7*taghayyuẓan*/8*wa-zafīran*//9 (25:12).[66]

Here the preposition *min* counts as a separate foot. This shows that proclitics such as attached prepositions *bi-* and *li-*; and *wa-*, *fa-*, *a-*, etc., together with suffixes, are considered to be part of the word to which they are joined. Since they have no word accent of their own, they will not be considered separate words here. Other particles and unattached prepositions, such as *hal, in, lam, min, ᶜan*, are assumed to carry a word stress of their own and count as separate words. This shows that the system of Ibn al-Athīr and that of Sheynin are virtually identical.

---

[64] "A Prosodic Study of *Sajᶜ* in Classical *Maqāmāt*", Part II, 115. Sheynin, having not located Arabic sources treating this aspect of *sajᶜ*, terms the *fuṣūl* "rhyme syntagmata" (RS).

[65] *al-Mathal al-sāʾir*, 1: 333-4.

[66] *Ibid.*, 1: 333-4.

More difficult to define are words such as *fī* and *mā*, which may be construed as being either long or short, depending on their placement and use. For example, *fi'l-sā^cati* is no different from *bi'l-sā^cati*, the *fī* being shortened to *fi-* when followed by an elidable hamzah. The *fi-* has no stress of its own, and acts like a proclitic. Therefore, when *fī* is shortened to *fi-* as in *fi'l-sā^cati*, it must be considered one word. Similarly, *mā* when followed by an elidable *hamzah* must be considered part of the following word, as in *sūrat al-qāri^cah*:

wa-mā/ adrāka/ mā'l-qāri^cah// (101:3)

In my opinion, the first of them should be considered a separate word, and the second one should be considered part of the following word.

There is some leeway in determining whether or not something should be considered one "word" using Ibn al-Athīr's terminology, or as having one "beat", to use Sheynin's. The rhyme-words at the ends of the *āyāt* in *sūrat al-zalzalah* (99:1-5) provide an interesting example:

zilzā`lahā
athqā`lahā
mā`lahā
akhbā`rahā
awḥā`-lahā

The two phrases *mā-lahā* and *awḥā-lahā* are each composed of two separate words, each of which would normally have its own word accent. However, it is obvious that for the rhyme, these phrases should be treated as one-word or one-beat units, and this dictates how one should read them. Here is a similar example:

fa-ummuhu/ hā`wiyah//
wa-mā/ adrāka/ mā`hiyah//
nārun/ ḥā`miyah// (101:9-11)

The phrase *mā` hi`ya* "what it is", consisting of two words, *mā* and *hiya*, is rendered as one word, *mā`hiyah*, to preserve the balance of the *saj^c*.

Many points remain to be studied, but the essential conclusion, reached recently by Sheynin, and by Ibn al-Athīr over seven hundred years ago, is that the word, not the syllable, is the basis of *saj^c* prosody. To describe the length of *saj^cahs* in terms of syllables, as Blachère does—in the statement cited above, he states that the *saj^c* phrase is generally between four and ten syllables—is to misunderstand the metrical essentials of *saj^c*. It is surprising that Scheindlin, having read the section on *saj^c* in *al-Mathal al-sā'ir*, incorrectly states that Ibn al-Athīr recommended composing *saj^c* phrases of roughly the same number of syllables, and that he "stresses this requirement rather more forcefully than does ᶜAskarī''. Scheindlin read the mention of syllables into the text; preconception got the better of him. Obsession with the syllable is presumably a consequence of the ingrained habit of syllable counting in quantitative poetry, an exaggerated reverence for the system of al-Khalīl, and a lack of attention to word accent in traditional Arabic prosody.[67]

*The Introductory Phrase in Saj*ᶜ

One of Ibn al-Athīr's examples allows us to define a property of *saj*ᶜ which is extremely important in the formal analysis of *saj*ᶜ texts. Of the following piece of *saj*ᶜ, which he wrote himself,

> *al-ṣadīqu man lam yaᶜtaḏ ᶜanka bi-khālif,*
> *wa-lam yuᶜāmilka muᶜamalata ḥālif,*

he states that each phrase contains four words, because the first *faṣl* is *lam*/$_1$*yaᶜtaḍ*/$_2$*ᶜanka*/$_3$*bi-khālif*//$_4$.[68] This implies that the words *al-ṣadīqu man* are not part of the *faṣl*. They form an introductory phrase, falling outside the ordinary structure of the *saj*ᶜ. This type of introductory phrase, although not obligatory, is very common in *saj*ᶜ, including Qurʾānic *saj*ᶜ. For example, in the following *āyāt*, the introductory phrase has been placed in parentheses:

> *(al-ḥamdu lil-lāhi) rabbi ʾl-ᶜālamin*
> *al-raḥmāni ʾl-raḥī*
> *māliki yawmi ʾl-dīn...* (1:1-3)

Al-ᶜAskarī failed to comprehend the use of the introductory phrase. He cites the following *saj*ᶜ passage describing locusts, attributing it to Bedouins (*aᶜrāb*):

> *(fa-subḥāna man yuhliku) ʾl-qawiyya*/ *ʾl-akūl*//
> *bi-ʾl-ḍaᶜīfi*/ *ʾl-maʾkūl*//

Al-ᶜAskarī states that in this *saj*ᶜ, the phrase *fa-subḥāna man yuhliku ʾl-qawiyya ʾl-akūl* is longer than the following phrase, and thus breaks the rule that the phrases should be of equal length. He goes on to say that since this was only a small part of the *saj*ᶜ passage, it was forgivable and not objectionable.[69] Actually, the *saj*ᶜ phrases are of equal length, a fact emphasized by the *ṭibāq* and formal parallelism between the two phrases *al-qawiyya ʾl-akūl* and *bi-ʾl-daᶜīfi ʾl-maʾkūl*. Al-Taftazānī failed to under-

---

[67] One notable exception to this last statement is Kamāl Abū Dīb's work, *Fī ʾl-bunyah al-īqāᶜiyyah fī ʾl-shiᶜr al-ᶜarabī* (Beirut: Dār l-ᶜilm li-ʾl-malāyīn, 1974), which contains a detailed discussion of word stress or accent (*nabrah*).

[68] *Ibid.*, 1: 334.

[69] *Kitāb al-ṣināᶜatayn*, 262-3. See 264 for other similar examples from the *ḥadīth*.

stand the nature of the introductory phrase in interpreting a passage of al-Qazwīnī's *Talkhīṣ*, although al-Qazwīnī in all likelihood did not share this confusion. Al-Qazwīnī, following Ibn al-Athīr and al-ᶜAskarī, states *wa-lā yaḥsunu an tu'tā qarīnatun aqṣaru minhā qaṣran kathīran* "It is not proper that a much shorter *qarīnah* be made to follow [the previous *qarīnah*]". Al-Taftazānī explains that al-Qazwīnī said *qaṣran kathīran* "much shorter" to avoid criticizing examples of Qurʾānic *saj*ᶜ such as *sūrat al-fīl*, in which the first *saj*ᶜ*ah* is longer than the following ones:

> *(a-lam tara) kayfa/ faᶜala/ rabbuka/ bi-aṣḥābi/ ʾl-fīl//*
> *a-lam/ yajᶜal/ kaydahum/ fī/ taḍlīl//* (105:1-2)[70]

Although there are examples of Qurʾānic *saj*ᶜ in which a short *saj*ᶜ*ah* follows a longer one, this example should not be analyzed as such; it is clear that *a-lam tara* is an introductory phrase, and that the two *saj*ᶜ*ah*s are five words each.

Sheynin partially understood the phenomenon of the introductory phrase, but explained it differently:

> The vast majority of the *saj*ᶜ are RU[rhyme unit = group of *saj*ᶜ*ah*s united by common rhyme] consisting of two RS[rhyme syntagmata = *saj*ᶜ*ah*s]. When the first RS is much longer than the second, it can be divided into two parts, from which the second is equal to the following RS. The length of the first RS in such is prosodically irrelevant. Therefore it can vary in relatively wide limits.[71]

Sheynin's analysis is very close to that of Ibn al-Athīr; when Sheynin divides the RS into two parts, the first part is the introductory phrase, and the second is the *saj*ᶜ*ah* proper. It makes more sense to consider the introductory phrase a separate entity, and state that the *saj*ᶜ*ah* proper begins after that phrase. I have chosen to give this introductory phrase an Arabic term to be used for future reference: *maṭla*ᶜ, an introduction.[72] It is one feature which distinguishes *saj*ᶜ from poetry, because in poetry, nothing falls outside the metrical scheme of the poem, whereas the *maṭla*ᶜ falls outside the prosodic framework of the *saj*ᶜ.

The limits within which *maṭla*ᶜs in the Qurʾān can vary are not so wide. They are often very short, being, in some instances, only one or two words. In the following example from *sūrat al-zilzāl* (99), the *maṭla*ᶜ is only one word, and the following *saj*ᶜ*ah* three:

---

70 *al-Sharḥ al-mukhtaṣar*, 3: 174.

71 Sheynin, Part II, 115.

72 cf. the use of the term *maṭla*ᶜ in the Andalusian poetic tradition, where it indicates an optional *simṭ* before the first full strophe of a *muwashshahah*. See James T. Monroe, *Hispano-Arabic Poetry* (Berkeley: Univ. of California Press, 1974), 392.

(idhā/) zulzilati/ ʾl-arḍu/ zilzālahā//
wa-akhrajati/ ʾl-arḍu/ athqālahā//
wa-qāla/ ʾl-insānu/ mā lahā//... (99:1-3)

In the example by Ibn al-Athīr mentioned above, the *maṭlaᶜ* is two words (*al-ṣadīqu man*), and the following *sajᶜahs* four (*lam yaᶜtaḍ ᶜanka bi-khālif// wa-lam yuᶜāmilka muᶜāmalata ḥālif//*). Sometimes, the *maṭlaᶜ* is as long as the following *sajᶜah*, as in the example from *sūrat al-fātiḥah* given above, or in *sūrat al-ikhlāṣ*:

(qul/ huwa/) ʾllāhu/ aḥad//
allāhu/ ʾl-ṣamad//... (112:1-2)

Here, the *sajᶜahs* are composed of two words each, as is the *maṭlaᶜ*. In an example from *sūrat al-ᶜādiyāt*,

(a-fa-lam/ yaᶜlam/ idhā/) buᶜthira/ mā/ fiʾl-qubūr//
wa-ḥuṣṣila/ mā/ fiʾl-ṣudūr// (100:9-10)

both the *maṭlaᶜ* and the following *sajᶜahs* have a length of three words. It seems that the most effective length for the *maṭlaᶜ* is less than or equal to that of the following *sajᶜah*. The longest examples I have found in the Qurʾān are just equal in length to the following *sajᶜah*. A *maṭlaᶜ* any longer than this would upset the metrical balance between itself and the following phrases. In the second part of his study on *maqāmāt*, Sheynin, sensing the shortcomings of his previous analysis, considered the *maṭlaᶜ*s separated rhyme syntagmata (= *sajᶜahs*).[73] I think he erred in doing so, first because they do not rhyme, and secondly because they may be extremely short in comparison with the following *sajᶜahs*.

Number of Words or Feet in a Sajᶜah.

One way Ibn al-Athīr classifies *sajᶜ* is by length of *sajᶜah*.[74] He gives two major categories, short *sajᶜ* (*sajᶜ qaṣīr*) and long *sajᶜ* (*sajᶜ ṭawīl*), and sets numerical definitions of these. Again, he determines length only in terms of words, rather than syllables or *tafāᶜīl*. Short *sajᶜ* is that in which the phrases are made up of from two[75] to ten words each, and long *sajᶜ* is that in which the *sajᶜahs* have eleven or more words. There is no specific limit

[73] *Ibid.*, i-ii.
[74] *al-Mathal al-sāʾir*, 1: 335-7.
[75] We should note here that although Ibn al-Athīr states that the shortest possibile *sajᶜ* is to have *sajᶜahs* of two words, it is possible to have a *sajᶜah* of only one word as part of a more complete structure, as in the first *āyah* of *sūrat al-raḥman* (55: 1-3): *al-raḥmān // khalaqa ʾl-insān// ᶜallamahu ʾl-bayān//*. It appears that in discussing the length of the individual *sajᶜah*, the critics limited their thinking to cases where all *sajᶜahs* are of equal length.

to the length of *saj*ᶜ phrases; according to Ibn al-Athīr, long *saj*ᶜ is without set limit (*ghayr maḍbūṭ*).[76] The longest example he gives, from *sūrat al-anfāl*, has nineteen (he states "about twenty") words in each *saj*ᶜ*ah*:

idh/ yurīkahumu/ ʾllāhu/ fī/ manāmika/ qalīlan/ wa-law/ arākahum/ kathīran/ la-fashiltum/ wa-la-tanāzaᶜtum/ fiʾl-amri/ walākinna/ ʾllāha/ sallama/ innahu/ ᶜalīmun/bi-dhāti/ ʾl-ṣudūr//

wa-idh/ yurīkumūhum/ idh/ iltaqaytum/ fī/ aᶜyunikum/ qalīlan/ wa-yuqallilukum/ fī/ aᶜyunihim/ li-yaqḍiya/ ʾllāhu/ amran/ kāna/ mafᶜūlan/ wa-ilā/ ʾllāhi/ turjiᶜu/ ʾl-umūr//[77] (8:43-4)

In *al-Īḍāḥ*, al-Qazwīnī divides *saj*ᶜ by length into three groups: short, medium, and long.[78] He does not, however, give specific numerical indices. He gives a Qurʾānic example of short *saj*ᶜ which has *saj*ᶜ*ahs* of two words:

wa ʾl-mursalāti/ ᶜurfan//
wa ʾl-ᶜāṣifāti/ ᶜaṣfan// (77:1-2)

The example of medium *saj*ᶜ, from *sūrat al-qamar*, has *saj*ᶜ*ahs* of 4 and 7 words:

iqtarabati/ ʾl-sāᶜatu/ waʾnshaqqa/ ʾl-qamar//
wa-in/yaraw/ āyatan/ yuᶜriḍū/ wa-yaqūlū/ siḥrun/ mustamir(r)// (54:1-2)

The example of long *saj*ᶜ he gives is that given by Ibn al-Athīr. Al-Qalqashandī also gives the same example of long *saj*ᶜ, but he states this is the greatest length *saj*ᶜ reaches in the Qurʾān, disagreeing with Ibn al-Athīr's statement that there is no limit to the length of the *saj*ᶜ*ah*.[79] This provides another criterion, in addition to rhyme, for the determination of the quantity of *saj*ᶜ in the Qurᶜān. Al-Qalqashandī seems to think that all *āyahs* longer than this are not *saj*ᶜ, presumably because they do not preserve the balance and parallelism evident in this example. The Qurʾān contains many *āyahs* which, although they rhyme with the surrounding *āyahs*, are far longer than nineteen words and also of uneven length. For example, the three *āyahs* 2: 281-3 rhyme in *ūm* or *īm*, yet their lengths are 15, 127, and 32 words, respectively. They are clearly not *saj*ᶜ as al-Qalqashandī understands it.

Al-Qalqashandī adds that since the Qurʾān represents the epitome of eloquence, writers of *saj*ᶜ should not write *saj*ᶜ*ahs* any longer than the limit

---

[76] *al-Mathal al-sāʾir*, 1: 337.
[77] *Ibid.*, 1: 337.
[78] *al-Īḍāḥ fī ᶜulūm al-balāghah*, ed. Muḥammad ᶜAbd al-Munᶜim al-Khafājī (Beirut: Dār al-kutub al-lubnānī, 1949), 2: 548-9.
[79] *Ṣubḥ al-aᶜshā*, 2: 287.

found in the Qurʾān.[80] Thus, not only does he see that the Qurʾān contains a great deal of *sajᶜ* and claim to have examined the entire Qurʾān for *sajʾ*, but he also considers the Qurʾān the appropriate model for all writers of *sajᶜ*. He goes on to give some practical advice for secretaries concerning length of *sajᶜahs*, stating that the first *sajᶜah* of the body of an official letter should not carry over on to the second line, so that the content of the letter may be known at a glance. In this case, the acceptable length of the *sajᶜah* depends on the size of the paper used.[81]

The medieval critics show a marked preference for short *sajᶜahs*. Ibn al-Athīr insists, as did al-ᶜAskarī before him, that shorter is better, because the end-rhymes are closer to each other and therefore more pleasing to the listener. The best type of *sajᶜ*, as far as length of *sajᶜah* is concerned, is that with two word *sajᶜahs*. Ibn al-Athīr gives the following example from *sūrat al-muddaththir*:

(yā) ayyuhā/ ʾl-muddaththir//
qum/ fa ʾndhir//
wa-rabbaka/ fa-kabbir//
wa-thiyābaka/ fa-ṭahhir//
wa ʾr-rujza/ fa ʾhjur// (74:1-5)

The rules governing *sajᶜ* are less rigid with regard to length than those governing poetry. The critics make it clear that the shorter the *sajᶜah*, the better. However, some allow *sajᶜ* to be of any length, while al-Qalqashandī insists that the limit is nineteen words per *sajᶜah*, in keeping with that found in the Qurʾān. This is much longer than any line of quantitative poetry. It is rare, however, to find *sajᶜ* of anywhere near this length in the compositions of later writers. At the other extreme, *sajᶜ* may maintain a series of *sajᶜahs* of only two words, shorter than any hemistich in quantitative poetry. Both in the Qurʾān and in later *sajᶜ* we see that shorter *sajᶜ* is much more common, but the range in the Qurʾān is greater.

Number of Sajaᶜāt in a Sajᶜ Unit

It is a norm in poetry that a *qaṣīdah* should maintain the same rhyme and meter throughout, but the *sūrah* is much more flexible than the *qaṣīdah* with regard to rhyme, it being allowable or even desirable to change rhyme in *sajᶜ*. Al-Suyūṭī emphasizes this distinction: *wa jāʾa ʾl-intiqālu fī ʾl-fāṣilati wa-ʾl-qarīnati wa-qāfiyati ʾl-urjūzati min nawᶜin ilā ākhara bi-khilāfi qāfiyati ʾl-qaṣīdah* "It occurs that the *fāṣilah* (the last word of

[80] *Ibid.*
[81] *Ibid.*

an *āyah* in the Qurʾān), the *qarīnah* (the last word in a non-Qurʾānic *sajʾah*), and the rhyme word of the *urjūzah* (a poem in *rajaz* meter where the two hemistichs of each line rhyme) may change from one rhyme to another, in contradistinction to the rhyme of the *qaṣīdah*''.[82] Ibn Sinān al-Khafāji states that mono-rhyme has been used in sermons, correspondence, and other writings, but adds that it is a fault to compose an entire letter of *saj*ʿ with one rhyme because it tends to be repetitive and stilted: *li-ʾanna dhālika yaqaʿu taʿarruḍan li-ʾl-takrāri wa-maylan ilā ʾl-takalluf.*[83] Although some *sūrah*s include many rhymes, the tendency to maintain mono-rhyme is quite strong in the Qurʾān. *Sūrat al-aʿrāf* (7) has 206 *āyāt*, of which 203 rhyme in *ūn*, *ūm*, *īn*, or *īm*. *Sūrat al-muʾminūn* (23), with 118 *āyāt*, *sūrat al-naml* (27), with 93 *āyāt*, *sūrat yā sīn*, (36) with 83 *āyāt*, and *sūrat al-raḥmān* (55), with 78 *āyāt*, all maintain complete mono-rhyme. However, as will be discussed below, various devices are used to create divisions in the *sūrah* while maintaining mono-rhyme. At the other extreme, some short *sūrah*s have several different rhymes. *Sūrat al-ʿādiyāt* (100) has four distinct rhymes in only eleven *āyāt*.

What, then, is the basic unit of *saj*ʿ? In poetry, the basic unit is the line. A single line may be considered an independent whole, but is the basic unit of *saj*ʿ one *sajʿah*? Ibn al-Athīr answers this question when he tells us that *taṣrī*ʿ in poetry is like *saj*ʿ in prose.[84] *Taṣrī*ʿ requires that the first hemistich (*miṣrā*ʿ) of a line of poetry rhyme with the second. This comparison shows that each *sajʿah* corresponds roughly to the hemistich in a line of poetry. In fact, al-Bāqillānī uses the term *miṣrā*ʿ (pl. *maṣārī*ʿ) to refer to the *sajʿah* on several occasions.[85] Therefore, the basic unit of *saj*ʿ is two *sajʿah*s, corresponding to one line of poetry. When discussing how *saj*ʿ phrases are combined to form *saj*ʿ units, Ibn al-Athār only gives examples containing two or three *sajʿah*s.[86] Although a series of three, four, or more *sajʿah*s may form a unit, the method of the critics shows that they felt the most common sort of *saj*ʿ, *or ''echt''* *saj*ʿ, was that which comes in paired phrases. According to Abū Hilāl al-ʿAskarī, the basis of *saj*ʿ is two *sajʿahs*.[87]

What are the rules governing the lengths of mono-rhyme sections of *saj*ʿ? Al-ʿAskarī's statement about the number of *sajʿah*s in a unit is the most explicit of those made by the critics consulted. He believes that it is best to have two, but acceptable to have three or four *sajʿah*s constitute

---

[82] *al-Itqān*, 2: 97.
[83] *Sirr al-faṣāhah*, 171.
[84] *al-Mathal al-sāʾir*, 1: 338.
[85] *Iʿjāz al-Qurʾān*, 90, 99.
[86] *al-Mathal al-sāʾir*, 1: 333-5.

a unit.[88] A *saj'* unit with any more than four *saj'ahs* tends to be strained: *fa-in jāwaza dhālika nusiba ilā 'l-takalluf.*[89] While many writers of the fourth Islamic century wrote paired *saj'ahs* as a rule,[90] this was not the case in the Qur'ān. Scheindlin notes that the Qur'ān has little pairing, but that the *maqāmāt* of al-Hamadhānī contain a great deal of pairing, and the *maqāmāt* of a al-Harīrī are made up almost exclusively of paired phrases.[91] Sheynin finds that the vast majority of rhyme units in the *maqāmāt* of al-Harīrī and al-Hamadhānī which he analyzed are composed of two paired phrases.[92] These two writers seem to follow the prescription al-'Askarī mentions. Sheynin's statistics, based on an analysis of three long *maqāmat* of each author, show that for al-Hamadhānī, two-phrase *saj'* units make up 48.97%, three-phrase units 29.83%, four-phrase units 11.04%, and all longer units 10.16%; that for al-Harīrī, two-phrase units make up 42.02%, three-phrase units 29%, four-phrase units 17.53%, and all longer units 11.45%. These results are skewed upwards, because, as mentioned above, in Part II of his study, he treated introductory phrases as additional *saj'ahs*.

The following are Qur'ānic *saj'* units of various lengths containing *saj'* phrases of equal length.

> Of 2:
> *fa-atharna/ bihi/ naq'an//*
> *fa-wasatna/ bihi/ jam'an//*   (100:4-5)
>
> Of 3:
> *wa-l-'ādiyāt/ dabhan//*
> *fa-l-mūriyāti/ qadhan//*
> *fa-l-mughīrāti/ subhan//*   (100:1-3)
>
> Of 4:
> *(a-lam) nashrah/ laka/ sadrak//*
>   *wa-wada'nā/ 'anka/ wizrak//*
>   *al-ladhi/anqada/ zahrak//*
>   *wa-rafa'nā/ laka/ dhikrak//*   (94:1-5)
>
> Of 5:
> *tabbat/ yadā/ abī/ lahabin/ wa-tab//*
> *mā/ aghnā/ 'anhu/ māluhu/ wa-mā/kasab//*

---

[87] *Kitāb al-sinā'atayn*, 260.
[88] *Ibid.*, 263.
[89] *Ibid.*, 263.
[90] Zaki Mubarak, *al-Nathr al-fannī fī 'l-qarn al-rābi'*, 1: 137. Mubarak describes these writers as those who write almost completely in *saj'* and only abandon *saj'* when using pairing without rhyme. They include al-Hamadhānī, al-Sāhib Ibn 'Abbād, al-Tha'ālibī, al-Sābī, and others.
[91] Scheindlin, *op. cit.*, 57.
[92] Sheynin, part II, p. 115.

sa-yaṣlā/ nāran/ dhāta/ lahab//
wa'mra'atuhu ḥammālata 'l-ḥatab//
fī/ jīdihā/ ḥablun/ min/ masad// (111)

Short *saj*^{c} units such as these, especially those of three and five *saj*^{c}*ah*s to a unit, are quite common in the Qur'ān. However, how can one reconcile al-^{c}Askari's disapproval of having more than four *saj*^{c} phrases in a *saj*^{c} unit with the following Qur'ānic text from *sūrat al-takwīr*?

idhā/ 'sh-shamsu/ kuwwirat//
wa-idhā/ 'n-nujūmu/ 'nkdarat//
wa-idhā/ 'l-jibālu/ suyyirat//
wa-idhā/ 'l-^{c}ishāru/^{c}uṭṭilat//
wa-idhā/ 'l-wuḥūshu/ ḥushirat//
wa-idhā/ 'l-biḥāru/ sujjirat//
wa-idhā/'l-nufūsu/ zuwwijat//
wa-idhā/ 'l-ma'ūdatu/ su'ilat//
bi-'ayyi/ dhanbin/ qutilat//
wa-idhā/ 'l-ṣuḥufu/ nushirat//
wa-idhā/ 'l-samā'u/ kushiṭat//
wa-idhā/ 'l-jaḥīmu/su^{cc}irat//
wa-idhā/ 'l-jannatu/ uzlifat//
^{c}alimat/ nafsun/ mā/ aḥḍarat// (81:1-14)

Here, fourteen *saj*^{c} phrases form a cohesive *saj*^{c} unit without any clear subdivisions. The rhyme remains constant, and there is a high degree of parallelism between the phrases. One particular syntactic pattern persists throughout the unit.

The Saj^c *Unit*

How are *saja*^{c}*āt* grouped together? Ibn al-Athīr only treats cases where two or three phrases form a unit, and gives no indication of the maximum number of *saja*^{c}*āt* to form a unit. But first it is necessary to define the unit. Sheynin speaks of a rhyme unit (RU), but this term is insufficient, for the reason that in *saj*^{c} two or more consecutive but clearly distinct groups of *saja*^{c}*āt* might have the same rhyme. The Qur'ān often presents large numbers of consecutive lines ending in the same rhyme, as many as fifty or more, but it is clear from their structure that the lines fall into smaller blocks. Thus, rhyme is not the only grouping principle in *saj*^{c}, as Sheynin assumes and as Blachère's statement "Ces unités rhythmiques sont groupées par séries sur une même rime" implies. Insertion of a *maṭla*^{c} automatically begins a new unit, as do, in most cases, changes in *saj*^{c}*ah* length. For instance, three *saj*^{c}*ah*s of two words might be followed by two *saj*^{c}*ah*s of three words. Change in length is essentially a change in meter. Even if all five *saj*^{c}*ah*s had the same rhyme, they would obviously form two distinct units. Ibn al-Athīr does not use a specific term for these larger units. He refers to units consisting of two *saj'ahs* as *al-faṣlān* or *al-saj'atān*, and units consisting of three *saj'ahs* as *al-saja'āt al-thalāth* or *saj' 'alā thalāth fiqar*.[93] While not ruling out the possibility of discovering an Arabic term in other critical works, I will term this grouping the "*saj'* unit" to distinguish it from the *saj'* phrase = *saj'ah*.

As stated above, Ibn al-Athīr treats only the cases where two or three *saj'* phrases form a *saj'* unit. Within this context, he discusses four major patterns.[94] The first pattern has *saj'ahs* of equal length. It appears in both two and three-phrase *saj'* units. Ibn al-Athīr's examples include the following passages from the Qur'ān:

> fa'amma/ 'l-yatīma/ fa lā/ taqhar//
> wa'amma/ 'l-sā'ila/ fa lā/ tanhar//   (93:9-10)

> wa'l-'ādiyāti/ ḍabḥan//
> fa'l-mūriyāti/ qadḥan//
> fa'l-mughīrāti/ ṣubḥan//   (100:1-3)

Ibn al-Athīr states that this is the best type of *saj'* because of the balance (*i'tidāl*) created. The examples given earlier show that this type of *saj'* unit may be extended to include more than three *saj'ahs* of equal length, reaching, in the case of the Qur'ān, fourteen or more *saj'ahs*.

The second pattern has the second *saj'ah* in a two-phrase unit slightly longer than the first. Al-'Askarī makes a similar statement meant to apply primarily to two-phrase units. He states that if the two *saj'ahs* are not of the same length, the second must be longer than the first.[95] According to Ibn al-Athīr, this is acceptable as long as the second *saj'ah* is not so long as to upset the effect of balance: *an yakūna 'l-faṣlu 'l-thānī aṭwala min al-awwali lā ṭūlan yakhruju 'an il-i'tidāl*.[96] If it is much longer, it is considered defective. As an example of this, Ibn al-Athīr cites:

> bal/1 kadhdhabū/2 bi'l-sā'ati/3 wa'tadna/4 li-man/5 kadhdhaba/6 bi'l-sā'ati/7 sa'īrā//8
> idhā/1 ra'athum/2 min/3 makānin/4 ba'īdin/5 sami'ū/6 lahā/7 taghayyuẓan/8 wa-zafīrā//9
> wa-idhā/1 ulqūw/2 minhā/3 makānan/4 ḍayyiqan/5 muqarranīna/6 da'aw/7 hunālika/8 thubūrā//9

(25:11-13)

[93] *al-Mathal al-sā'ir*, 1: 333-5.
[94] *Ibid*. He calls them three types, but presents another construction as a sub-category of the second type.
[95] *Kitāb al-ṣinā'atayn*, 263.
[96] *al-Mathal al-sā'ir*, 1: 333.

He then states that these *āyāt* contain eight, nine, and nine words respectively. This shows that his previous statement was meant to apply not only to two-phrase units, but also to three-phrase and probably longer units as well. The general rule implied is that in *saj*ᶜ units of several phrases, where all the phrases are of roughly equal length, it is acceptable to have the longer phrases following the shorter ones, but not vice versa. A familiar example of this is from *sūrat al-fātiḥah*:

(al-ḥamdu li-llāhi) rabbi/ ʾl-ᶜālamīn//
al-raḥmāni/ ʾl-raḥīm//
māliki/ yawmi/ ʾl-dīn// (1:1-3)

Here the three *saj*ᶜ*ah*s consist of two, two, and three words respectively. In numerical terms, it may be inferred from Ibn al-Athīr's statements that acceptable differences in length are those of only one or two words. In the examples above, the differences in length are only one word, and Ibn al-Athīr gives another example of two *saj*ᶜ*ah*s where the first is eleven words and the second is thirteen.

A third type, which Ibn al-Athīr criticizes as being severely flawed (*ᶜayb fāḥish*),[97] has the second *saj*ᶜ*ah* shorter than the first. The logical extension of this rule is that it is not acceptable to have any *saj*ᶜ*ah* shorter than a previous *saj*ᶜ*ah* within a unit where all *saj*ᶜ*ah*s are of roughly equal length length. Ibn al-Athīr does not provide any examples of this third type, and one wonders how he would analyze *sūrat al-nās* (114):

(qul aᶜūdhu) bi-rabbi/ ʾl-nās//
māliki/ ʾl-nās//
ilāhi/ ʾl-nās//

---

min/ sharri/ l-waswāsi/ ʾl-khannās//
al ladhi/ yuwaswisu/ fī/ ṣudūri/ ʾl-nās/
mina/ ʾl-jinnati/ (wa ʾl-nās)//

The first three *āyāt* form a unit conforming to the first pattern above, as all three *saj*ᶜ*ah*s are of two words. The last three *āyāt* present a problem, because it is obvious that the last *āyah* is much shorter than the two preceding lines—three words as opposed to four and five.

The fourth and most complex pattern is to have two *saj*ᶜ*ah*s of equal length followed by a third about twice as long as the previous *saj*ᶜ*ah*s. As an example of this, Ibn al-Athīr cites the passage of his own composition:

(al-ṣadīqu man) lam/ yaᶜtaḍl/ ᶜanka/ bi-khālif//
wa-lam/ yuᶜāmilka/ muᶜāmalata/ ḥālif//
wa-idha/ ballaghat-hu/ udhnuhu/ wishāyatan/ aqāma/ ᶜalayhā/ ḥadda/ sāriqin/ aw/qādhif//[98]

[97] *Ibid.*, 1: 335.
[98] *Ibid.*, 1: 334.

As he explains, the first two *sajʿahs* contain four words and the third *sajʿah* contains ten. If we extend the analogy of *sajʿ* to poetry, we see that this formation is equivalent to one line with rhyming hemistichs—that is, with *taṣrīʿ*—followed by one line without *taṣrīʿ*. This type of formation is commonly found in the *rubāʿī* or "quatrain", consisting of four hemistichs of which the first, second, and fourth rhyme.[99] Al-Qazwīnī gives an example of this type, but merely states that here the third *sajʿah* is longer than the first two:

khudhūhu// fa ghullūhu//
thummal ʾl-jaḥīmal ṣallūhu//[100] (69:30-31)

This example shows that often in this type of construction, a single *āyah* may contain two *sajʿahs*. A similar example is included in *sūrat al-ikhlāṣ*:

lam yalid// wa lam yūlad//
wa lam yakun lahu kufuʾan aḥad// (112:3-4)

This does not happen very often, but it shows that calculations of the number of *sajʿahs* in the Qurʾān based merely on the number of *āyāt* will not be exact.

Ibn al-Athīr indicates that the third *sajʿah* must be longer than the first and second *sajʿahs* combined. When speaking of the Qurʾānic example,

(fī) ṣadrin/ makhḍūd//
wa ṭalḥin/ manḍūd//
wa ẓillin/ mamdūd// (56:28-30)

he states that these three *sajʿahs* are two words each, but that if one made the third *sajʿah five* or *six* words, it would not be bad. He also states that if the first and second *sajʿahs* are each four words, as in his own passage cited above, then the third must be ten or eleven words. He then says that if the first two are made longer or shorter, one must increase or decrease the third accordingly. Thus it appears that the third *sajʿah* may be from one to three words longer than the first two *sajʿahs* combined.

Al-Qazwīnī describes an extension of the *rubāʿī* form. In this type, there are three *sajʿahs*, the second of which is longer than the first, and the third longer than the second.[101] The example he gives is *sūrat al-ʿaṣr* (103):

waʾl-ʿaṣri// 1
innal ʾl-insānal la fīl khusrin// 4

[99] I have discussed this construction in an unpublished paper, "Quickies: Form and Closure in the Limerick, *Rubāʿī*, *Taṣrīʿ*, and Koranic *Sajʿ*" (University of Pennsylvania, 1988).

[100] *al-Talkhīṣ*, 399; *al-Īḍāḥ*, 2:548.

[101] *al-Īḍāḥ*, 2:548.

*illā/ ʾl ladhīna/ āmanū/ wa ᶜamilū/ ʾl-ṣāliḥāti/ wa tawāṣaw/ bi ʾl-ḥaqqi/ wa tawāṣaw/ bi ʾl-ṣabri//*9

Al-Qazwīnī gives no particular name to this construction, and unlike Ibn al-Athīr, he does not differentiate clearly between cases where a *sajᶜah* is slightly longer than the preceding *sajᶜah* and cases like this. This will be referred to as the pyramidal construction. In the Qurʾān, it usually appears in *sajᶜ* units of three *sajᶜahs*, and especially at the beginning of *sūrahs*. The opening lines of *sūrat al-ḍuḥā* provide another example:

wa ʾl-ḍuḥā/
wa ʾl-layli/ idhā/ sajā//
mā/ waddaᶜaka/ rabbuka/ wa mā/ qalā// (93:1-3)

This type of construction seems to be extremely rare in non-Qurʾānic *sajᶜ*.

The Grouping of Sajᶜ Units

Sheynin believes that the only way to begin a new *sajᶜ* unit is to change the rhyme, hence his term Rhyme Unit (RU) for the *sajᶜ* unit. This definition may work for the analysis of *maqāmāt*, but fails to provide an adequate analysis of Qurʾānic *sajᶜ*. In the case of the Qurʾān, many other devices, as well as rhyme change, are used to set apart *sajᶜ* units.

Change in rhyme is used quite often. *Sūrat al-ᶜādiyāt* (100) is a good example of this type of structure:

wa ʾl-ᶜādiyāti/ ḍabḥan//
fa ʾl-mūriyāti/ qadḥan//
fa ʾl-mughīrāti/ ṣubḥan//

---

fa-atharna/ bihi/ naqᶜan//
fa-wasaṭna/ bihi/ jamᶜan//

---

inna/ ʾl-insāna/ li rabbihi/ la kanūd//
wa-innahu/ ᶜalā/ dhālika/ la shadhid//
wa-innahu/ li ḥubbi/ ʾl-khayri/ la shadīd//

(a-fa-lam/ yaᶜlam/ idhā/) buᶜthira/ mā/ fi ʾl-qubūr//
wa ḥuṣṣila/ mā/ fi ʾl-ṣudūr//
inna/ rabbahum/ bihim/ yawmaʾidhin/ la khabīr//

This *sūrah* divides into four *sajᶜ* units, each with a different rhyme. The *sajᶜ* units are also distinguished by length of *sajᶜah*, the first unit having *sajᶜahs* of two word length, the second unit *sajᶜahs* of three word length, the third unit *sajᶜahs* of four word length, and the fourth unit *sajᶜahs* of three word length, except for the final *sajᶜah* of five words.

Another extremely common device for separating *sajᶜ* units is change in the length of the *sajᶜahs* without change in the rhyme. That this is much more common in the Qurʾān than in other *sajᶜ* compositions such as *maqāmāt* is another aspect of the tendency to maintain mono-rhyme. An example of this is *sūrat al-nās* (114):

(qul/ aᶜūdhu/) bi rabbi/ ʾl-nās//
māliki/ ʾl-nās//
ilāhi/ ʾl-nās//

---

min/ sharri/ ʾl-waswāsi/ ʾl-khannās//
al ladhi/ yuwawisu/ fī/ ṣudūri/ ʾl-nās//
min/ al-jinnati/ wa ʾl-nās//

This *sūrah*, though maintaining the same rhyme throughout, breaks up into two *sajᶜ* units of three *sajᶜahs* each. The first *sajᶜ* unit has *sajᶜahs* of two words each, but the second *sajᶜ* unit has longer *sajᶜahs*: four, five, and three words.

A structural device which does not appear often is the use of a refrain *āyah*, as found in *sūrat al-raḥmān* (55) and *sūrat al-qamar* (54). In the 78 verses of *sūrat al-raḥmān*, the verse *fa-bi-ayyi ālāʾi rabbikumā tukadhdhibān*? is repeated 31 times, marking off 28 couplets and 3 tercets within the *sūrah*. Ibn Abī al-Iṣbaᶜ (d. 654/1256), referring to the couplets in particular, calls this type of figure a *tawʾam* "twin".[102] In doing so, he refers to the fact that the two *āyahs*, though they rhyme with each other, are generally of unequal length, so that the first *āyah* of each couplet rhymes not with the second *āyah* of the same couplet, but with the first *āyah* of the next couplet, just as the second *āyah* of the couplet rhymes with the second *āyah* of the next couplet, producing something like the rhyme scheme *abab*. Ibn Abī al-Iṣbaᶜ gives the four *āyāt* 55:33-6 as an example:

> *yā maᶜshara ʾl-jinni waʾl-insi in istaṭaᶜtum an tanfudhū min aqṭāri ʾl-samawāti waʾl-arḍi faʾnfudhū lā tanfudhūna illā bi sulṭān// fa bi ayyi ālāʾi rabbikumā tukadhdhibān//*

> *yursalu ᶜalaykumā shuwāẓun min nārin wa nuḥāsun fa lā tantaṣirān//fa bi ayyi ālāʾi rabbikumā tukadhdhibān//*

According to his interpretation, each couplet here is like one line of poetry with an internal rhyme placed after the hemistich division, creating the effect of having two meters simultaneously.

In *sūrat al-qamar*, refrain phrases create five parallel strophes, describing how five groups of the past rejected the warnings of God and were consequently punished. The first line of each strophe begins with the

---

[102] *Taḥrīr al-taḥbīr* (Cairo: Lajnat iḥyāʾ al-turāth al-islāmī, 1963), 522-3.

verb *kadhdhabat*, followed by the name of the particular group whose story is related in the strophe—Qawm Nūḥ, ᶜĀd, Thamūd, Qawm Lūṭ, and Qawm Firᶜawn—as the agent of the verb. The last line of each strophe ends with the rhetorical question: *fa-hal min muddakir* "Then is there any that will receive admonition?"[103] The variation in the number of lines in each strophe is considerable (5-11 lines), as is the number of words in each line (4-10 words), but the first and last lines of each strophe provide a closed framework and set off an independent unit.

Wazn, or Quantitative Meter at the End of a Sajᶜah

Critics pay a great deal of attention to the last word of the *sajᶜah*. They use several terms for this word, including *fāṣilah* (pl. *fawāṣil*), *maqṭa*ᶜ (pl. *maqāṭi*ᶜ), and, perhaps to our confusion, *qarīnah* (pl. qarāʾin) and *saj*ᶜ (pl. *asjā*ᶜ).[104] Not only is it important for the word to have rhyme (*qāfiyah*), it is also considered important that the *fāṣilah* be of the same morphological pattern (*wazn*) as those of neighboring *sajᶜahs*. Medieval critics classify *saj*ᶜ according to the presence or absence of this property.

*Saj*ᶜ *muṭarraf* "lop-sided" or "skewed" *saj*ᶜ is that in which the *fawāṣil* rhyme without having the same pattern. The Qurʾānic example given by al-Qalqashandī and many other critics is the following:

(mā lakum lā) tarjūna/ liʾllāhi/ waqāran//
wa qad/ khalaqakum/ aṭwāran// (71:13-4)[105]

Although *waqāran* and *aṭwāran* rhyme, they are not of the same morphological pattern. As regards syllabic quantity, *waqāran* scans short-long-long, but *aṭwāran* scans long-long-long. The critics consider this type of *saj*ᶜ inferior to *saj*ᶜ *mutawāzī* "parallel *saj*ᶜ", which has both rhyme and identical pattern in the final words of the *sajᶜahs*. Examples from the Qurʾān include the following,

(fīhā) sururun/ marfūᶜah//
wa akwābun/ mawḍūᶜah// (88:13-14)[106]

Not all critics use the term *saj*ᶜ *mutawāzī*. Al-Qalqashandī, for example,

---

[103] The translation is from Abullah Yusuf Ali, *The Meaning of the Glorious Qurʾān*, 1456.

[104] See al-Suyūṭī, *al-Itqān*, 2: 97, where he refers to the the last word of a *saj*ᶜ-phrase as *qarīnat al-sajᶜah*; also al-Taftazānī, *al-Sharḥ al-Mukhtaṣar*, 3: 173, where he states: *fa-ʾl-ḥāṣilu anna ʾl-sajᶜa qad yuṭlaqu ᶜala ʾl-kalimati ʾl-akhīrati mina ʾl-fiqrah*.

[105] *Subḥ al-aᶜshā*, 2: 282; Zayn al-Din Muhammad b. Abī Bakr al-Rāzī (d. end of 7th/13th c.), *Rawḍat al-faṣāḥah*, 207; Shihāb al-Dīn Aḥmad b. ᶜAbd al-Wahhāb al-Nuwayrī (d. 733/1332), *Nihāyat al-arab fī funūn al-adab*, (Cairo: al-Muʾassasah al-miṣriyyah al-ᶜāmmah li-ʾl-taʾlīf, 1964), 7: 105.

[106] al-Qazwīnī, *al-Talkhīṣ*, 398; *al-Iḍāh*, 2: 547; al-Rāzī, *Rawḍat al-faṣāḥah*, 206.

uses no special term for this type of *saj^c*, a fact which indicates that he considered it the norm from which *saj^c muṭarraf* deviates.[107]

The importance of the effect of *wazn* is illustrated by the existence of a type of composition which conforms to all the characteristics of *saj^c* except that of rhyme. It is called *izdiwāj*[108] or *muwāzanah.*[109] Al-Qalqashandī defines this as follows: ...*an yakhtalifa ḥarfu ʾl-rawiyyi fī ākhiri ʾl-fiqratayn*, "...that the rhyme letter at the end of the two *fiqrah*s differs."[110] In this type of composition, the *fawāṣil* either do not rhyme or rhyme inexactly, but have identical pattern. Some critics consider *muwāzanah* a type of *saj^c* itself, especially if it has inexact rhymes, and they term it *saj^c mutawāzin.*[111] Others, such as al-^cAskarī, do not consider it *saj^c*, but deem it slightly inferior *saj^c* in literary merit.[112] Al-Qalqashandī and others give the following Qurʾānic example:

wa namāriqul maṣfūfah//
wa zarābiyyul mabthūthah// (88:15-16)[113]

The words *maṣfūfah* and *mabthūthah* are of the same morphological pattern, yet they do not rhyme.

An understanding of *muwāzanah* may help clarify some confusing terminology. When speaking of poetry, the word *wazn* is used to refer to the quantitative meter used throughout the verse; thus the use of *mawzūn* in Qudāmah b. Ja^cfar's famous definition of poetry: "*kalāmun mawzūnun muqaffan maqṣūd*". Here it means conforming to one of the established quantitative meters of al-Khalīl. When speaking of *saj^c*, however, *wazn* refers to the morphological pattern of the *fawāṣil*. The word *mawzūn* indicates that the *fawāṣil* are of the same morphological form without necessarily implying that they rhyme. It is in this latter sense that al-Jāḥiẓ uses the word. He reports an anecdote about ^cAbd al-Ṣamad Ibn al-Faḍl al-Riqāshī, who spoke continually in *saj^c*. Someone asked al-Riqāshī why he preferred to speak in *saj^c*, maintaining *qāfiyah* and *wazn*. He replied, "The good prose (*manthūr*) which the Arabs have spoken is more than the good *mawzūn* which they have spoken, but not a tenth of the prose has been saved, and not a tenth of the *mawzūn* has been lost".[114] Ibn Rashīq

[107] *Ṣubḥ al-a^cshā*, 2: 282-3.
[108] *Ibid.*, 2: 283.
[109] Ibn al-Athīr, *al-Mathal al-sāʾir*, 1: 377-80.
[110] *Ṣubḥ al-a^cshā*, 2: 283.
[111] al-Nuwayrī, *Nihāyat al-arab*, 7: 104; al-Suyūṭī, *al-Itqān*, 2: 104.
[112] *Kitāb al-ṣinā^catayn*, 263.
[113] *Ṣubḥ al-a^cshā*, 2: 283; al-Nuwayrī, *Nihāyat al-arab*, 7: 15; al-Rāzī, *Rawḍat al-faṣāḥah*, 208. Al-Rāzī makes the distinction that in prose this is called *tawāzun*, but in poetry it is called *muwāzanah*, as in this line by al-Buḥturī:
fa-kun mus^cadan fī-hinna in kunta ghādiran wa-sir mub^cadan ^can-hunna in kunta lāʾimā.
[114] *al-Bayān wa-ʾl-tabyīn*, 1: 158.

al-Qayrawānī (d. 456/1064) denies that *sajʿ* is *mawzūn*, saying that of the two distinguishing characteristics of poetry, *qāfiyah* "rhyme" and *wazn* "meter", *sajʿ* has taken over the rhyme, leaving only meter as the exclusive distinguishing mark of poetry.[115] It is clear that he uses the word *wazn* here in the restricted sense of conformation to a quantitative poetic meter. Al-Subkī (d. 773/1372) differentiates between the two meanings of *wazn* by calling one *wazn taṣrīfī* and the other *wazn shiʿrī*.[116]

Conformity to an identical quantitative pattern at the ends of *sajʿ* phrases, although not absolutely necessary, is considered a standard feature of *sajʿ*. This effect is termed *muwāzanah* and was important enough for medieval critics to classify types of *sajʿ* on this basis. Indeed, *muwāzanah* is so effective that some critics consider it a type of *sajʿ* even if not accompanied by rhyme. The desired effect is to enhance the accentual meter with quantitative regularity when approaching the end of the *sajʿah*, producing matching cadences. These cadences are closely parallel to the *clausulae* of Latin oratory: cadences of quantitative meter used to end prose sentences.[117] Blachère must have been thinking of the *clausulae* when he stated that phrases of *sajʿ* ended in a "*clausule*", and he showed insight in stating." ... en dernière analyse, l'élément essentiel est constitué par la clausule rimée". Again, it is important to note that the length of the matching cadences is described in terms of words rather than syllables, and that the standard length of the cadence is one word.

Complete or Near-Complete Quantitative Parallelism

In *muwāzanah*, discussed above, quantitative parallelism is restricted to the last word in a *sajʿ* phrase. However, critics prized more complete parallelism, and considered *sajʿ* of even higher merit if it had this property. Al-Qalqashandī and others call this type *tarṣīʿ* or *sajʿ muraṣṣaʿ*, "proportioned" *sajʿ*.[118] Al-ʿAskarī calls it *sajʿ fī sajʿ* "*sajʿ* within *sajʿ*", adding that it is the best type of *sajʿ*.[119] It is defined as *sajʿ* where most or all of the words in one *qarīnah* are similar in form (*wazn*) to the corresponding words in its partner *sajʿah*. Qurʾānic examples include:

---

[115] Ibn Rashīq al-Qayrawānī, *al-ʿUmdah fī ṣināʿat al-shiʿr wa-naqdih*, ed. Muḥammad Badr al-Dīn al-Naʿsānī al-Ḥalabī (Cairo: Maṭbaʿat al-Khānjī, 1907), 1: 137.

[116] al-Subkī, Bahāʾ al-Dīn Aḥmad b. Taqiyy al-Dīn, *ʿArūs al-afrāḥ fī sharḥ talkhīṣ al-miftāḥ*, printed with al-Taftazānī's *al-Mukhtaṣar*, (Cairo: Būlāq Press, 1317/1899-1900), 4. 456.

[117] On the *clausulae*, see Henri Bornecque, *Les Clausules métriques latines* (Lille, 1907).

[118] *Ṣubḥ al-aʿshā*, 2: 282. al-Rāzī, *Rawḍat al-faṣaḥah*, 200.

[119] *Kitāb al-ṣināʿatayn*, 263.

innal ilaynā/ iyābuhum//
thummal innal ʿalaynā/ ḥisābuhum// (88:25-6)

and

innal ʾl-abrāral la fī/ naʿīm//
wa innal ʾl-fujjāral la fī/ jaḥīm// (82:13-14)

In these examples, the words both rhyme and follow the same pattern, except for the difference of pattern of *abrār/fujjār* in the second example. Syllable lengths are exactly the same, if *thumma* in the second *sajʿah* of the first example and *wa-* in the second *sajʿah* of the second example are discounted.

Tarṣīʿ often involves multiple parallel rhymes as well as quantitative parallelism. Al-ʿAskarī gives an example of this by al-Baṣīr:

(ḥattā ʿāda) taʿrīḍukal taṣrīḥan//
wa tamrīḍukal taṣḥīḥan//

and others by al-Ṣāḥib Ibn ʿAbbād, including the following:

(lākinnahu ʿamada liʾl-shawqi) fa ajrāl jiyādahul ghurranl wa qurḥan//
wa awrāl zinādahul qadḥanl fa qadḥan//

This example of *sajʿ muraṣṣaʿ* by al-Ḥarīrī takes parallelism to its extreme:

(fa-huwa) yaṭbaʿul ʾl-asjāʿal bi jawāhiril lafẓih//
wa yaqraʿul ʾl-asmāʿal bi zawājiril waʿẓih//[120]

Not only do the words in these two *sajʿah*s exhibit exact quantitative and morphological parallelism, they each rhyme with the corresponding word in the partner *sajʿah*. Scheindlin states that al-Ḥarīrī especially endeavored to write phrases of *sajʿ* of this type, with rhythmical equality.[121] Scheindlin believes that this type of *sajʿ*, as used by al-Hamadhānī and al-Ḥarīrī, is the most advanced stage of *sajʿ* in the history of Arabic literature.[122] It is clear that many medieval rhetoricians and writers of *sajʿ* shared his opinion.

Conclusion

Analysis of medieval criticism on *sajʿ* and formal examination of the Qurʾān make possible a more complete definition of *sajʿ*. *Sajʿ*, though generally considered a sub-category of prose (*nathr*), is a type of composi-

[120] *al-Īḍāḥ*, 2: 547; also al-Rāzī, 201. The phrase is from al-Ḥarīrī's *al-maqāmah al-ūlā al-ṣanʿāʾiyyah.*

[121] *Form and Structure in the Poetry of al-Muʿtamid Ibn ʿAbbād*, p. 58.

[122] *Ibid.*

tion distinct from both free prose (*nathr mursal*) and syllabic verse (*naẓm*). It consists of rhyming phrases termed *sajaʿāt* (sing *sajʿah*). The rules governing the rhyme in *sajʿ* are slightly different from those governing the rhyme in the *qaṣīdah*, the most noticeable difference being that the rhyme-words in *sajʿ* generally end in *sukūn*. *Sajʿ* conforms to an accentual meter: each *sajʿah* tends to have the same number of word-accents as its partner *sajʿahs*. Therefore, the fundamental unit of *sajʿ* prosody is the word, *lafẓah* (pl. *lafaẓāt*), and not the syllable or the *tafʿīlah*.

The *maṭlaʿ* is an important structural element in *sajʿ* unit, yet lies outside the prosodic structure of the *sajʿahs* themselves. Although it is common, it is not a necessary feature of *sajʿ*, many *sūrahs* of the Qurʾān and other passages of *sajʿ* being without it. Nevertheless, it functions within certain constraints, namely that it should be no longer than the following *sajʿah*.

Quantitatively parallel cadences at the ends of *sajʿahs* are a standard although not absolutely necessary feature of *sajʿ*. Quantitative parallelism is achieved by requiring the words in question to have the same *wazn* or morphological pattern. It is the norm for these cadences to be restricted to the *fawāṣil*, the final word of *sajʿahs*, although some *sajʿahs* maintain complete or near-complete parallelism.

I have chosen to term groups of *sajʿahs* which may be formally distinguished from surrounding *sajʿahs* "*sajʿ* units". Mono-rhyme is not required in *sajʿ*, though it is possible. *Sajʿahs* form groups with common rhyme, but rhyme is not the only grouping principle in *sajʿ* compositions. A significant change in the length of a *sajʿah* marks a new *sajʿ* unit as clearly as does a change in rhyme. Insertion of a *maṭlaʿ* also marks the beginning of a new *sajʿ* unit. Most *sajʿ* units contain a series of *sajʿahs* of equal or nearly equal length, but there exist more complex formations including the type of *sajʿ* unit which I have termed the *rubāʿī* figure, formally similar to a couplet with *aaba* rhyme-scheme, and that which I have termed the pyramid figure.

Nothwithstanding considerable reluctance to use the term *sajʿ* in reference to the Qurʾān, most medieval rhetoricians realize that the Qurʾān contains a great deal of *sajʿ*. The analysis undertaken in this study makes possible some preliminary observations on the formal differences between Qurʾānic and later *sajʿ*, especially that of the epistles of al-Ṣāḥib ibn ʿAbbād and Ibn al-ʿAmīd and the *maqāmāt* of al-Hamadhānī and al-Ḥarīrī. Qurʾānic *sajʿ* has a much greater tendency to mono-rhyme than does later *sajʿ*. A small number of rhymes, including *ūn/īn/ūm/īm* and *īl/īr*, are predominant in the Qurʾān whereas rhyme in later *sajʿ* shows greater variation. The Qurʾān allows inexact rhymes which are not found in later *sajʿ*. The *sajʿahs* in Qurʾānic *sajʿ* are in many cases much longer than those found in later *saj*ʿ, though the shorter Meccan *sūrah*s tend to have fairly short *saj*ʿ*ah*s. *Saj*ʿ units in the Qurʾān reach much greater lengths than those found in later *saj*ʿ. The formation of *saj*ʿ units in Qurʾānic *saj*ʿ also exhibits a greater degree of variety, *saj*ʿ units of two rather short *saj*ʿ*ah*s. Finally, quantitative *saj*ʿ units of the *rubā*ʿ*ī* type and the pyramid type being much more common. Later *saj*ʿ tends to consist primarily of parallelism and multiple rhymes become much more important effects in later *saj*ʿ than they are in the Qurʾān.

What does this imply about our translation of the term *saj*ʿ? Our traditional English rendering, "rhymed prose", leaves much to be desired, especially since it completely ignores the metrical qualities and constraints of *saj*ʿ. Blachère's translation, "rhymed and rhythmic prose", begins to make up for this defect, but retains the main source of misunderstanding, the very word "prose". The phrase "rhymed prose" seems, in every-day English at any rate, to be a contradiction in terms. This contradiction is only resolved when we realize that in the classical Arabic literary tradition, convention has somewhat arbitrarily established compliance with the quantitative meters of al-Khalīl as the fundamental criterion of division between poetry and prose. A modern view of poetry as any text which aspires to be seen as a poem, or a view such as that of Jakobson, according to which a poem is a text in which the paradigmatic function of language supercedes the syntagmatic, would allow us to include *saj*ʿ in the realm of poetry with relative ease. This, however, is not the important issue. The point is rather that within traditional Arabic poetics, there was an awareness of the deeper "poetic" nature of *saj*ʿ which many critics found difficult to state outright because of the force of conventions such as the doctrine of *i*ʿ*jāz al-Qur*ʾ*ān* and that of the supremacy of quantitative poetry, but which, with critics such as Ibn al-Athīr, led to an analysis of *saj*ʿ as a type of accent poetry. It is this awareness which allows us to see *saj*ʿ as a complex interplay of accentual meter, rhyme, and morphological pattern, and it is this same awareness which allowed the poet Aḥmad Shawqī to assert: "*Saj*ʿ is Arabic's second poetry" (*al-saj*ʿ*u shi*ʿ*ru* ʾ*l-arabiyyati* ʾ*l-thānī*).[123]

[123] Aḥmad Shawqī (d. 1932), *Aswāq al-dhahab* (Cairo: al-Maktabah al-tijāriyah al-kubrā, 1970), 115.

APPENDIX 1: RHYME IN THE QURʾĀN

no.	*sūrah*	*āyāt*	rhyming	all/none	main rhymes
1	*al-Fātiḥah*	7	7	all	*ūn*
2	*al-Baqarah*	286	264		*ūn/āb-ād/īr-īl*
3	*Āl ʿImrān*	200	183		*ūn/ān-ām/āb-ād-ār*
4	*al-Nisāʾ*	176	143		*īrā-īmā/īdā/ūn*
5	*al-Māʾidah*	123	108		*ūn/īd/īr*
6	*al-Anʿām*	165	159		*ūn*
7	*al-Aʿrāf*	206	203		*ūn*
8	*al-Anfāl*	75	64		*ūn*
9	*al-Tawbah*	129	124		*ūn*
10	*Yūnus*	109	107		*ūn*
11	*Hūd*	123	101		*ūn/īr/īẓ/īd-īb*
12	*Yūsuf*	111	107		*ūn*
13	*al-Raʿd*	43	37		*ūn/āb-ād-āq/ār-āl*
14	*Ibrāhīm*	52	28		*īd/ūn/ār-āl/*
15	*al-Ḥijr*	99	97		*ūn*
16	*al-Naḥl*	128	126		*ūn*
17	*al-Isrāʾ*	111	99		*īlā-īrā-īmā-īnā/īdā-ībā*
18	*al-Kahf*	110	110		*a(n)*
19	*Maryam*	98	89		*iyya/ūn/dā*
20	*Ṭāhā*	135	134		*ā/ī*
21	*al-Anbiyāʾ*	112	111		*ūn*
22	*al-Ḥajj*	78	36		*īd/īr/ūn*
23	*al-Muʾminūn*	118	118	all	*ūn*
24	*al-Nūr*	64	59		*ūn/āl-ār/āb*
25	*al-Furqān*	77	77	all	*īlā-īrā/āmā-ānā*
26	*al-Shuʿarāʾ*	227	223		*ūn*
27	*al-Naml*	93	93	all	*ūn*
28	*al-Qaṣaṣ*	88	87		*ūn/ī-īl*
29	*al-ʿAnkabūt*	69	68		*ūn/īr*
30	*al-Rūm*	60	58		*ūn*
31	*Luqmān*	34	30		*ūn/īr*
32	*al-Sajdah*	30	29		*ūn*
33	*al-Aḥzāb*	73	60		*īlā-īrā-īmā-īnā*
34	*Sabaʾ*	54	52		*īr/īd-īb*
35	*al-Fāṭir*	45	42		*īr/ūn/īd*
36	*Yā-Sīn*	83	83	all	*ūn*
37	*al-Ṣāffāt*	182	180		*rā/āCīd/ūn**
38	*Ṣād*	88	83		*āb-ād-āq/ār/ūn*

* *C* represents a variable consonant.

no.	sūrah	āyāt	rhyming	all/none	main rhymes
39	*al-Zumar*	75	70		*ār/āb-ād/ūn*
40	*Ghāfur*	85	76		*īm-īn/īr/īd-īb*
41	*Fuṣṣilat*	54	46		*īm-īn/īr/īd-īb*
42	*al-Shūrā*	53	47		*īm/īr/īl/īm*
43	*al-Zukhruf*	89	88		*ūn*
44	*al-Dukhān*	59	59	all	*ūn*
45	*al-Jāthiyah*	30	30	all	*ūn*
46	*al-Aḥqāf*	35	35	all	*ūn*
47	*Muḥammad*	38	35		*ālahum*
48	*al-Fatḥ*	29	28		*īmā-īnā*
49	*al-Ḥujurāt*	18	17		*ūn*
50	*Qāf*	45	38		*īd/īb*
51	*al-Dhāriyāt*	60	55		*rā/ūn*
52	*al-Ṭūr*	49	47		*ūr/iʿ/awrā/ūn*
53	*al-Najm*	62	61		*ā/ifah/ūn*
54	*al-Qamar*	55	55	all	*ir-ur-ar*
55	*al-Raḥmān*	78	78	all	*ān-ām*
56	*al-Wāqiʿah*	96	90		*iʿah/ūn*
57	*al-Ḥadīd*	29	19		*īm-īr/īd/ūn*
58	*al-Mujādilah*	22	16		*īr-īm/ūn*
59	*al-Ḥashr*	24	17		*īr-īm/ūn*
60	*al-Mumtaḥanah*	13	8		*īl-īr-īm*
61	*al-Ṣaff*	14	13		*ūn*
62	*al-Jumuʿah*	11	11	all	*ūn*
63	*al-Munāfiqūn*	11	11	all	*ūn*
64	*al-Taghābun*	18	13		*īr-īm*
65	*al-Ṭalāq*	12	10		*rā*
66	*al-Taḥrīm*	12	11		*īr-īm-ūn*
67	*al-Mulk*	30	30	all	*īr/ūn*
68	*al-Qalam*	52	52	all	*ūn*
69	*al-Ḥāqqah*	52	49		*āqqah/iyah/ūhū/ūn*
70	*al-Maʿārij*	44	36		*āCiʿ/īdā/īhī/ā/ʿā/ūn*
71	*Nūḥ*	28	22		*ūn/ārā*
72	*al-Jinn*	28	17		*abā-adā*
73	*al-Muzzammil*	20	17		*īlā/īmā*
74	*al-Muddaththir*	56	54		*ir/ūr/īdā/ar/ūn/rah*
75	*al-Qiyāmah*	40	39		*āmah-ānah/ar/īrah /irah-ilah/āq/ā*
76	*al-Insān*	31	30	all	*īrā-īlā-īmā*
77	*al-Mursalāt*	50	46		*rā/at/li/ūn/ātā/ab*
78	*al-Nabāʾ*	40	31		*ūn/ādā-ābā-āqā*

no.	*sūrah*	*āyāt*	rhyming	all/none	main rhymes
79	*al-Nāzi^c^āt*	46	38		*an/ifah/irah/ā/āhā*
80	*^cAbasa*	42	35		*ā/rah/bā-qā/īhī/rah*
81	*al-Takwīr*	29	25		*rat/as/ūn*
82	*al-Infiṭār*	19	17		*rat/ak/ūn*
83	*al-Muṭaffifīn*	36	36	all	*ūn*
84	*al-Inshiqāq*	25	23		*al/ak/ūn*
85	*al-Burūj*	22	17		*aqqat/īhū/ūrā/aCaq/ūn*
86	*al-Ṭāriq*	17	14		*iq-ib/ir/^ci/aydā*
87	*al-A^clā*	19	19	all	*ā*
88	*al-Ghāshiyah*	26	21		*āCiyah/ī^c/ū^cah/at/ir /ābahum*
89	*al-Fajr*	30	28		*rī/ād/ani/īm/ammā/ad/ī*
90	*al-Balad*	20	20	all	*ad/īn/ab(d,m)ah*
91	*al-Shams*	15	15	all	*āhā*
92	*al-Layl*	21	21	all	*ā*
93	*al-Ḍuḥā*	11	10		*ā/ar*
94	*A-lam nashraḥ*	8	8	all	*rak/rā/ab*
95	*al-Tīn*	8	8	all	*ūn*
96	*al-^cAlaq*	19	18		*aq/am/ā/āCiyah*
97	*al-Qadr*	5	5	all	*ri*
98	*al-Bayyinah*	8	6		*ayyinah-ayyimah/iyyah*
99	*al-Zalzalah*	8	6		*ārahā-ālahā/arah*
100	*al-^cĀdiyāt*	11	11	all	*ḥa/^cā/īd/īr*
101	*al-Qāri^cah*	11	6		*āCi^cah/āCiyah*
102	*al-Takāthur*	8	8	all	*ir-ur/ūn*
103	*al-^cAṣr*	3	3	all	*ri*
104	*al-Humazah*	9	8		*dah*
105	*al-Fil*	5	5	all	*īl*
106	*Qurayash*	4	0	none	——
107	*al-Mā^cūn*	7	7	all	*ūn*
108	*al-Kawthar*	3	3	all	*ar*
109	*al-Kāfirūn*	6	2		*ūn*
110	*al-Naṣr*	3	0	none	——
111	*al-Lahab*	5	5	all	*ab-ad*
112	*al-Ikhlāṣ*	4	4	all	*ad*
113	*al-Falaq*	5	5	all	*aq-ab-ad*
114	*al-Nās*	6	6	all	*ās*

Total *āyāt*: 6,236
Totah rhyming *āyāt*: 5,355
Percentage: 85.9%

APPENDIX 2: *SAJ^c* TERMINOLOGY

faṣl (pl. *fuṣūl*)—a single phrase of *saj^c* ending in a rhyme-word, also termed *saj^cah*.

fāṣilah (pl. *fawāṣil*)—the final word of a *saj^cah*. Some critics maintain that only this term should be used to refer to the final words of *āyāt* in the Qur'ān.

fiqrah (pl. *fiqar*)— = *saj^cah*.

ḥarf (pl. *ḥurūf*)—the rhyme letter or rhyme in *saj^c* phrases.

ḥurūf mutajānisah/mutamāthilah—exact rhymes.

ḥurūf mutaqāribah—inexact or near rhymes.

i^ctidāl—"balance", the basic principle of *saj^c* metrics, according to which adjacent *saj^cah*s should be of equal length (i.e. number of words).

izdiwāj—A type of composition similar to *saj^c*, in which clauses do not rhyme but end in words having the same morphological pattern.

kalimah (pl. *kalimāt*)—the word, the foot or *taf^cīlah* of *saj^c* prosody.

lafẓah (pl. *lafaẓāt*)— = *kalimah*.

manthūr—opposed to *manẓūm*. Any type of composition which does not conform to quantitative meter.

manẓūm—poetry conforming to quantitative meter.

masjū^c— = *saj^c* (1).

maqṭa^c (pl. *maqāṭi^c*)— = *fāṣilah*.

mawzūn—any type of composition in which the last words of phrases have the same morphological pattern whether they rhyme or not.

miṣrā^c—(1) a hemistich in poetry; (2) a *saj^cah* (al-Bāqillānī).

mumāthalah—a type of composition in which paired clauses exhibit complete or near complete syllabic parallelism, but do not rhyme.

mursal—ordinary or free prose.

musajja^c— = *saj^c* (1).

muwāzanah—a type of composition in which the final words of the phrases do not rhyme, but are of the same morphological pattern. Also termed *izdiwāj*.

nathr— = *manthūr*.

naẓm— = *manẓūm*.

qarīnah (pl. *qarā'in*)—(1) same as *saj^cah*. (2) the final word of a *saj^cah*.

saj^c—(1) traditionally, prose (*nathr*) which has rhyme; in my view, a type of rhyming poetry with accentual meter.

saj^c (pl. *asjā^c*)—(2) the rhyme words in *saj^c* occurring at the end of *saj^c* phrases.

sajjā^c—a writer of *saj^c*.

saj^cah (pl. *saja^cāt*)—a phrase of *saj^c* associated with one end rhyme.

saj^c fī saj^c—(1) *saj^c* in which *saj^cah*s exhibit complete or near complete syllabic parallelism and sustained parallel rhymes (al-ʿAskarī); (2) the inclusion of two (or more) *sajʿah*s within a longer *sajʿah*, producing the rhyme scheme *aab ccb* (al-Qalqashandī).

sajʿ muraṣṣaʿ— = *sajʿ fī sajʿ* (1).

sajʿ mutamāthil— = *mumāthalah*.

sajʿ muṭarraf—*sajʿ* in which the last words in the *sajʿah*s rhyme but are not of the same morphological pattern.

sajʿ mutawāzī—*sajʿ* in which the last words in the *sajʿah*s rhyme and are also of the same morphological pattern.

sajʿ mutawāzin—for those critics who consider this *sajʿ* (many do not and refer to it as *izdiwāj* or *muwāzanah*), a type of *sajʿ* in which the final words of the phrase do not rhyme, but are of the same morphological pattern.

sajʿ qaṣīr—*sajʿ* in which the *sajʿah*s are between two and ten words in length (Ibn al-Athīr).

sajʿ ṭawīl—*sajʿ* in which the *sajʿah*s are eleven or more words in length (Ibn al-Athīr); *sajʿ* in which the *sajʿah*s are between eleven and nineteen words in length (al-Qalqashandī).

tarṣīʿ—(1) the use of internal rhyme in poetry. (2) = *sajʾ fī sajʿ*.

taṣrīʿ—in a line of poetry, making the end of the first hemistich rhyme with the end rhyme, usually at the beginning of a *qaṣīdah*.

tashṭīr—the use of internal rhyme in poetry so that the line contains exactly four rhymes and each hemistich is divided in two.

tasjīʿ—the use of internal rhyme in poetry, usually two, three, or four rhymes in one line.

tawāzun—(1) = *sajʿ mutawāzin*; (2) = *sajʿ mutamāthil*.

wazn—(1 = *wazn shiʿrī*) one of the traditional quantitative meters of Arabic poetry. (2 = *wazn taṣrīfī*) the morphological pattern of a word.

14

SOME REMARKS ON THE SPECIAL LINGUISTIC AND LITERARY CHARACTER OF THE QUR'ĀN

Angelika Neuwirth

[736] IN WESTERN RESEARCH, the Qur'ān has had a fate similar to that of ancient Arabic poetry, in the sense that as a document of religious history and as evidence for matters of history and grammatical and linguistic studies, it has been made the object of so vast a literature that it can hardly any longer be comprehended. However, it has rarely been honored with an academic examination in terms of what it essentially is, and as what it was originally conceived to be: a liturgical oration, as a text for recitation.

A literary study of the Qur'ān on the basis of its essential function is all the more pressing as the attempts up until now have misclassified the character of the Qur'ān and have applied criteria of judgment that produce a false image of its literary form. The Qur'ān evades the usual terms of classification on the grounds of its claims to be a text for recitation, which is clear from the self-testimony of the oldest *sūras*. It is neither to be classified as spiritual poetry nor as prophetic oration in the sense of the ancient Hebrew genre. Above all, it is not to be understood by the term "sermon" in the precise sense of rhetoric that expresses a truth that has already been announced and attempts to urge that truth upon the listener.[1] The Qur'ān may contain some elements of homily along with its many other elements, but it yields just as few examples of these as it yields of the catch-all categories of hymns, narratives or legislation. For the Qur'ān as a whole we are left with its own self-designation "text for recitation" until a description of the form can be devised that makes a more exact designation possible.

[1]On the concept of sermon, see Leo Baeck, "Griechische und jüdische Predigt", in *Aus drei Jahrtausenden. Wissenschaftliche Untersuchungen und Abhandlungen zur Geschichte des jüdischen Glaubens* (Tübingen, 1958), 142: "Very early on, clarifications had to be given of the classical religious literature. Admonitions and edifying lectures were added. A special kind of instruction and discourse develops which no longer announces a new truth, but which seeks instead to depict and spread the already announced truth. Behind the seekers who saw godly faces and received voices from on high there now follow the speakers who possess their book and the seers and companions of the seers follow the preachers. For the term sermon, properly understood, cannot be used to refer to the prophetic word, but rather only to this eloquent imitation."

2

However, the subject of an examination of form cannot be the collection of texts entitled "al-Qur'ān", but rather must be the unit which was intended by the Prophet as the formal medium for his proclamation. I would like to point to the *sūra* as this medium. For although smaller thematic units may have come into being on the occasion of a specific "occasion of revelation" (*sabab al-nuzūl*), for the purposes of literary study it is not the external cause of a theme but rather the formation of the theme and its ordering in the total composition that is of interest. Therefore I would like to emphasize the unit of the *sūra* as a heuristic basis, a unit that is also ignored in the tendency towards atomization that predominates in recent investigation. It is the individual *sūra* that will serve as the textual foundation for literary study.

Fortunately, Mr. Gregor Schoeler will deal extensively in the following presentation with the application of the methods of modern literary study in Arabic studies.[2] Therefore I will only delve into a few of the specific demands of examination of the Qur'ān. The specific circumstances of the **[737]** stratified genesis of various *sūra*s on the one hand, and the collection and arrangement of the *sūra*s by later redactors on the other, raise methodological problems that under normal circumstances do not arise in a literary work. This situation has its closest parallels in certain parts of the literature of the Old Testament, such as the prophetic books and some of the Psalms. Old Testament studies has therefore developed a series of methodological steps which also prove to be extremely useful for study of the Qur'ān. The most recent reflections on methods for the literary study of the Old Testament is offered by Wolfgang Richter in his *Exegese als Literaturwissenschaft. Entwurf einer alttestamentlichen Literaturtheorie und Methodologie* (Göttingen, 1971). Richter suggests the following methodological steps: literary investigation, investigation of form, investigation of genre, investigation of redaction. The literary investigation examines the text, in our case the *sūra*, as an isolated unit: that is, in terms of its secondary composition. The investigation of form analyzes the exterior form, thereby yielding a description on the levels of sentence, word and individual phoneme. It then examines the collective structure of the individual text (*sūra*). Following this, the investigation of genre elaborates a typology of the structures of the individual text described in the previous two steps. The investigation of redaction examines the secondary composition of the text in

[2][Gregor Schoeler, "Die Anwendung neuer literaturwissenschaftlicher Methoden in der Arabistik", the article following that of Angelika Neuwirth in the proceedings of the XIX. Deutscher Orientalistentag.]

terms of its literary compilation. In our case this would entail an analysis, on one hand, of those *sūra*s that were not composed by the Prophet himself but were rather assembled during the process of redaction, and on the other hand, of the collection entitled "al-Qur'ān."

If one takes the term *sūra* not only as a proper name, a chapter heading reserved for a particular book, but rather as the name of a genre, then a quick glance at the literature to date shows that the genre of the *sūra* has almost never been recognized. In the works of Richard Bell[3] and Régis Blachère,[4] who have in recent times studied the composition of the Qur'ān, the *sūra* as a whole does not fall within the scope of study, which rather concerns the smaller components from which the *sūra* is composed. For them, the composition of a *sūra*, as a rule, is a later work undertaken by the Prophet himself or even by later redactors. In contrast to Bell and Blachère, Theodor Nöldeke, in his work of 1860, *Geschichte des Qorâns*, takes the *sūra* as a whole under consideration. He says that the relative chronology that he constructed is based on examination of the *sūra* in its entirety. And yet Nöldeke does not advance the term *sūra* as a genre. This is not because an interest in the "smallest components of revelation" draws his gaze away from the whole. Rather, his position of brusque rejection of the Islamic tradition makes it impossible for him to recognize the unique rules of Qur'ānic discourse. For in stark contrast to the strong tendency found in Islamic treatments of the Qur'ān as high above profane literature on the basis of the dogma of inimitability (*i'jāz*), Nöldeke refuses to consider the formal elements of the Qur'ān outside of a relation to the corresponding forms in poetry and rhymed prose. Nöldeke recognizes and describes numerous stylistic features of the Qur'ān with the utmost exactness. **[738]** Nonetheless, the technical and compositional function of these elements does not come into his field of observation because they possess no such function outside of the Qur'ān. Aside from a few examples with especially conspicuous composition, the *sūra*s remain for him an amorphous construct and his few observations regarding form remain unutilized in terms of a concept of genre.

The fact that the treatments of the form of the Qur'ān to date have not been able to see the *sūra* as anything more than an external designation for the consequence of a more or less accidental division of the text has to do

[3]Richard Bell, *The Qur'ān: Translated with a Critical Re-arrangement of the Sūras* (Edinburgh, 1937–39); *idem*, *Introduction to the Qur'ān* (Edinburgh, 1953).

[4]Régis Balchère, *Introduction au Coran* (Paris, 1947); *idem*, *Le Coran. Traduction selon un essai de reclassement des sourates* (Paris, 1949–51); *idem*, *Histoire de la littérature arabe*, II (Paris, 1964), 187–230.

4

with the variety of the elements of the *sūra*. The *sūra* is a "mixed composition", that is to say, a complex later stage, coming after a longer process of religious and historical development. It is not a historical homogeneity but rather a secondary genre composed of elements that originally came from a variety of sources.

A comparison with the Hebrew Psalms serves to illuminate the subject. In the Psalter, along with longer and shorter pieces that belong to a single identifiable genre, there are also more complex compositions. Each of the individual Psalm genres, such as the hymn, proverb, oracle of salvation, eschatological song, and song of sacrifice among others, has, in itself, a different origin, a different context or Sitz im Leben and a different style, vocabulary and set of conventions. These complex compositions in the Psalms, referred to in Old Testament studies as "Mischgedichte", join together several of these originally separate genres into a larger unity. A portion of these Psalms can be called "liturgies" because they have to be understood as excerpts from liturgies if not as complete liturgies.[5] Of course, this typological comparison is not meant to suggest any direct influence of these Psalms on the Prophet. The aim is merely to compare the results of religio-historical developments that are in many ways parallel in order to cast light on phenomena in the Qur'ān, which are still poorly understood, through comparison with a better understood parallel.

The development of the Psalms took place within the same cult. The Arabian prophet, who stands on a much later stage of religio-historical development, found various religious groups already in existence. All of them have in common that their religious services are composed of various elements such as pericopes, songs that introduce or come between segments of the services and prayers among others. At this time, a variety of forms within a common framework is already a normal phenomenon. The prophet's awareness of form must have oriented itself according to such phenomena, if it developed at all in terms of liturgical form. This process by which a composition of elements that do not directly cohere thematically came into being could more naturally have been realized in this way than by way of that representative type of contemporary profane poetry, the *qaṣīda*. The compound genre that we encounter in the case of the *sūra* becomes much more understandable when one takes into consideration that the com-

[5]S. Hermann Gunkel, *Die Psalmen* (Göttingen, 1926), *passim*; Hermann Gunkel and Joachim Begrich, *Einleitung in die Psalmen*, I (Neukirchen, 1961), lvvi: "One not infrequently has the impression that singers or poets, either arbitrarily or with a very definite tendency, put together individual elements from a 'liturgy' in the Psalms. A particular 'selection' is found, for example, in Psalm 132 or in Psalm 110."

plex form of liturgical discourse was "something natural" in the time of the Prophet.

Our methodological approach of taking the *sūra* to be a legitimate unit, and of seeing in individual *sūra*s—as they now stand—various realizations of a single definable genre, can be proven **[739]** if distinct categories of *sūra*s can be demonstrated. Such categories do in fact exist. With the exception of a few examples that are still not entirely clear to me, all of the *sūra*s of the middle and last Meccan period can be categorized according to distinct compositional schemes. Compared to this phase of development, the *sūra*s of the first Meccan period vary too drastically for one to be able to speak of distinct schemata. Nonetheless, even the early *sūra*s show themselves to be distinct forms through their clearly proportioned composition. To demonstrate the division of the early Meccan *sūra*s from the earlier-mentioned distinct compositional schemes of the middle and late Meccan *sūra*s is not possible in the framework of this paper. However, this much can already be said: It is not only the study of the Qur'ān that stands to be greatly enriched through the use of the methods of general literary study. In the process, general literary study can also gain, in the *sūra*, a genre that cannot be found in such clear expression in other literatures.

15

THE BEGINNINGS OF MUḤAMMAD'S RELIGIOUS ACTIVITY

Richard Bell

For nearly half a century the view has prevailed that Muhammad began his mission as a preacher of the Judgment. In the excitement, the terror and anxiety for himself and his people which the idea of the near approach of the Day of Judgment awoke in his soul, has been found the impulse which drove Muhammad to the recitation of the Qur'ān and the assumption of the rôle of a prophet. On general grounds that view seems questionable. It is difficult to reconcile the man who lost his balance and began to recite confused descriptions of the coming judgment, with the man who afterwards fought his way to success in Arabia, and showed himself so level-headed amid the varying fortunes of his later years. While there is no denying the prominence of ideas of Judgment in certain portions of the Qur'ān, it may be doubted whether the impression left on an unprejudiced reader of the book as a whole would be that these were the fundamental thing in it.

I have elsewhere[1] developed certain lines of argument which point to a different conclusion. (1) Criticism of the traditions as to Muhammad's call leads to the rejection of them as without historical foundation. In any case these traditions do not imply that it was a vision of Judgment which initiated his mission, and the passage of the Qur'ān most commonly stated in these traditions to have been the earliest does not refer to the Judgment, but sets forth Allah as having bestowed certain blessings upon man.

(2) Examination of the visions described in the Qur'ān (Sūrah liii) shows that, while they may be accepted as genuine experiences, Muhammad himself was a little doubtful as to their interpretation. Originally set out as visions of Allah, they were afterwards modified and finally interpreted as visions of an angel. But the descriptions given of them do not suggest that they had any relation to the Judgment.

(3) A third line of argument dealt with the accounts of previous messengers given in the Qur'ān. It is generally admitted that Muhammad found in the sending of messengers to other peoples something analogous to his own mission in Mecca. But even a cursory reading of these accounts gives the impression that as described in the Qur'ān these messengers were all preachers of Monotheism. This is confirmed by an attempt to unravel the earliest strands in the narratives. The Last Day is seldom mentioned in these stories, and only in the later forms of them.

In this paper I mean to examine some of the "sign"-passages of the Qur'ān and sum up the results. There are in the Qur'ān a great many passages in which natural phenomena are referred to, and ascribed to Allah as the creator. The creation of the heavens and the earth, the sun, the moon, the stars, the alternation of night and day, the production of men and animals, the growth of seed, the production of food, the sending of rain, the revival of dead (parched) land, the sailing of ships upon the sea—these and other things are often referred to in the Qur'ān as "signs." Some of them are occasionally used as proofs or confirmations of the doctrine of the resurrection. But on the whole the impression a reader gets from the use made of these signs is that they are indications of Allah's power and bounty. One of the signs mentioned above is peculiarly apt as an illustration of the resurrection, viz., that of the rain reviving dead land. It is often used without any reference to that doctrine; but in a few passages it is used to enforce it. Sūrah vii, 55, 56, reads as follows:—

"He it is who sends the winds as heralds in front of His mercy (*i.e.* the rain), until when they have lightened heavy clouds, We (note the change of pronoun) drive it to dead soil, and send down water thereby, and bring forth therein all kinds of fruits; thus do We bring forth the dead, mayhap ye will be reminded.

[1] "Moslem World," 1934

18

The vegetation of good land comes forth by the permission of its Lord, but of that which is bad it comes forth only scantily; thus do We turn the signs about for a people who show thankfulness."

That is the close of a passage recommending Allah as Lord, citing other signs and inviting to His worship. As it stands, it is an example of the maundering style with which the Qur'ān is often credited, wandering from clouds and rain to the resurrection and then without apparent reason bringing in vegetation a second time. But if we follow the hint of the sudden change of pronoun, and leave out the latter half of v. 55, what we get is the following :—

"He it is who sends the winds as heralds in front of his mercy until when they have lightened heavy clouds, the vegetation of good land comes forth by the permission of its Lord, but of that which is bad it comes forth only scantily."

That is a perfectly intelligible statement, in fact a very good sermon-illustration, implying that lack of response to Allah's bounty is due to poverty of soul. Evidently, the reference to the resurrection has been worked into a passage which originally had nothing to do with it. The rhyme-phrase of v. 56 might even be interpreted as telling us that that had actually been done. We may note in passing that the rhyme-phrase is not essential to the meaning of the passage.

A similar change of pronoun occurs in xxxv, 10. The passage reads as follows :—

"10. Allah it is who hath sent forth the winds, which then stir up cloud, and We drive it to dead ground, and revive the earth thereby after it has become dead; so is the arousing (*i.e.*, the resurrection).

"11. If anyone desires honour, honour belongs to Allah entirely; to Him goodly speech ascends, and upright acting He exalts, but for those who plot evil deeds is punishment severe; the plotting of such shall come to nought.

"12. Allah it is who hath created you of dust, then from seed, and then made you pairs.

"13. No female conceives or brings forth but He knows it; not one is given long life, nor is any one cut short in his life but it is in a book; verily for Allah that is easy."

V. 11 is out of connection, and in v. 10 there is a sudden change from speaking of Allah in the third person, to the We—presumably Allah Himself speaking. The most natural explanation seems to be that the second part of v. 10 has been inserted into an older passage, and that in making the insertion a scrap of paper (or whatever the material was) has been used, on the back of which stood v. 11. If we remove this, and also disregard the tag at the end, "verily for Allah that is easy," which is merely a clause added to supply the rhyme in *-īr*, we are left with a passage setting forth the power and knowledge of Allah, and already rhymed in syllables containing a long *ā* followed by a consonant—*saḥāb*, *turāb*, *azwāj*, *kitāb*.

Other passages in which this illustration of the resurrection is used show similar evidences of being secondary. It is used in xxx, 49, but in the immediately preceding verses reference has been made to the rain for quite a different purpose, viz. to set forth the beneficence of Allah in sending rain which brings joy to men. In xli, 39, there is a change of pronoun similar to what occurs in the two passages cited above. In xliii, 8 ff., we find the same abrupt change of pronoun, and the reference to the resurrection occurs merely in the rhyme-phrase. In Sūrah l, v. 11 comes at the end of a passage in which a group of "signs" are apparently used as an argument for the resurrection. In v. 2 the unbelievers are introduced as saying, "This is a strange thing, When we are dead and turned to dust? That is a return far-off." Then in v. 6 begins the citation of the signs, "Have they not looked at the sky above them? . . ." But the reference to the resurrection in v. 11 is evidently an after-thought, for the beneficent results of rain have been already recounted in vv. 9, 10. It looks as if a previously existing "sign"-passage had been simply fitted in here and adapted to enforce the doctrine of the resurrection.

It is not of course suggested that the "signs" were not used to support the doctrine of the resurrection, or that these "sign"-passages are all earlier than the resurrection and judgment passages. As a matter of fact, these "signs" are a standing part of Muhammad's stock-in-trade as a preacher, and were used by him at all stages of the composition of the Qur'ān, so long as it was necessary for him to argue for the acceptance of his doctrines. But the passages cited above point to the fact that when Muhammad became a preacher of the resurrection and judgment, there were already in existence a number of "sign"-passages which had had originally no reference to those doctrines, but which he could and did adapt to support them. In his teaching there must then have been, prior to the resurrection and judgment, a stratum of natural religion based upon the evidences of God in creation. In short, it is amongst these "sign"-passages and not amongst the passages dealing with the resurrection, the Last Day and the Judgment, that we have to look for the earliest portions of the Qur'ān. There are of course a great number of these passages which even in the Qur'ān as it stands have no reference to eschatology, and even the particular "sign" of the rain reviving dead land, apt illustration as it is, is quite ordinarily used without any reference to the resurrection, *e.g.*, xvi, 67; xlv, 2 ff.; xxix, 67.

To complete the argument, I may perhaps quote the beginning of an address which is found scattered in surah ii, 19b, 20, 26, 27:—

"19b. O ye people, serve your Lord who hath created you and those who were before you—mayhap ye will act piously.

"20. Who hath made for you the earth a carpet, the heaven a dome; who hath sent down water from the heaven, and thereby produced fruits as a provision for you; so do not set up peers to Allah, when ye know (better).

20

"26. How will ye disbelieve in Allah, seeing that ye were dead and He gave you life; then He causes you to die and brings you to life again, after which to Him do ye return.

"27. He it is who created for you what is in the earth, all of it; and who then set about the heaven and formed them seven heavens; He every thing doth know."

That is almost certainly Medinan, and it shows Muhammad beginning there as I hold that he began in Mecca, by appealing for the acceptance of Allah on the basis of His power and bounty. The rain appears amongst the "signs" as one of Allah's bounties, not as illustrating by its reviving effect the resurrection. The resurrection is no longer a doctrine to be argued for. It has become a certainty, itself a "sign" of Allah's power on the same footing as the rain or any other physically evident fact. The line of development has apparently been (1) signs as evidence of Allah's power, (2) signs adapted as support for the doctrine of the resurrection, (3) signs, including the resurrection, as evidence of Allah's power.

The "signs" are put to other uses. They are employed, as in the Medinan passage just quoted, and in several Meccan ones, to demonstrate the superiority of Allah over other gods. There are indications too that this was not their earliest use. For instance, in xvi, 3-16 we find a fairly long list of the benefits which Allah has bestowed on man. This leads up to the question—

"Is then one who creates like one who creates not? . . . But those upon whom they call apart from Allah create nothing, being themselves created; dead not alive, they are not aware."

But the passage is not in its original form. It does not read smoothly. The rhyme-phrases can be detached throughout without much damage to the sense. In the latter part of it when we discard the present rhyme-phrases, we can detect the presence of another rhyme or assonance in *-ā(t)*. It looks as if an earlier "sign"-passage, or perhaps two, had been revised and adapted for this argument. This is not quite an isolated case; but the matter is not so clear as the adaptation of "signs" to support the resurrection. The point is, however, of some interest, for there is a tradition given by Ibn Hishām (p. 166) that for some time after Muhammad began his work his people showed no aversion to him, and did not oppose him until he began to speak against their gods. The Qur'ān also contains an admonition to the believers not to speak against the (false) gods, lest they should thereby provoke the unbelievers to speak foolishly against Allah. So that I incline to believe that Muhammad did not, to begin with, speak against the other gods, but simply set forth the claims of Allah to gratitude and worship. That is the nature of the great majority of the "sign"-passages taken by themselves. They are simply lists of the bounties of Allah, setting Him forth as a beneficent Being who has dealt generously with man and who has claims upon man's gratitude and worship.

In analysing some of the passages in which "signs" have been adapted to enforce the resurrection the rhyme-phrases have been discarded. Something further may now be said on that point. In the Qur'ān, as it stands, rhyme is essential. It was evidently intended that each verse of a surah should rhyme with the others. So much so, that when within a surah there is a break in the rhyme, we may almost assume that some confusion has happened. But there are a great many passages in which the phrases which carry the rhyme are very loosely attached. They are not woven into the texture of the verses, and sometimes even interrupt the sense. Occasionally when we detach them we get back to another rhyme — a pretty clear indication that an older passage has been fitted into a new surah. But in quite a number of passages, when we detach these loose rhyme-phrases, we are left with no rhyme at all. It is as if an originally unrhymed passage has been fitted out with rhymes to suit the surah into which it is inserted. That does not apply only to "sign"-passages, but it does apply to a good number of them. As an example we may take vi, 95 ff. :—

"95. Allah is the one who causeth the grain and the date stone to burst, producing the living from the dead, and producing the dead from the living; that is Allah, how then are ye beguiled?

"96. Who causeth the dawning to break forth, and hath appointed the night as a rest and the sun and the moon as a reckoning;

"that is the disposition of the Sublime, the Knowing.

"97. He it is who hath appointed for you the stars that ye may guide yourselves thereby in the darknesses of land and sea;

"We have made the signs distinct for a people who have knowledge.

"98. He it is who hath caused you to spring from one person, and there is a gathering-place and a place of deposit;

"We have made the signs distinct for a people who understand.

"99. He it is who hath sent down the water from the heaven; and thereby have We produced vegetation of every kind, and from it have We produced green shoots, from which We produce close-packed grain, and palm-trees from the fruit stalks of which come close-hanging bunches of dates, and gardens of vines and olives and pomegranates, like and unlike; look at its bearing and ripening when it produces fruit;

"surely in that are signs for a people who believe."

The rhyme-phrases in that passage come in quite parenthetically. They can be left out, not only without damage, but with advantage to the sense. Three of them are simply variations one of the other. In fact, I am not sure but that in two of them we are told in so many words what is being done; that the "making of the signs distinct" simply means that they are being separated out, each into a verse, by the insertion of these rhyme-phrases.

The inference is that these "sign"-passages were in many cases originally unrhymed. They therefore did not belong to what Muhammad regarded as Qur'ān. The presumption is that they belonged to a period prior to his beginning to deliver a Qur'ān. (It may be recalled that Sir William Muir came to a similar conclusion on quite other grounds.) Of course it might be that they were composed for some other purpose,

22

say for an ordinary address, during the Qur'ān period, and were afterwards worked up for inclusion in the Qur'ān. There are Medinan passages which have been so treated, and the same may have happened in Mecca. But the balance of probability seems to me to lie on the side of some of these passages having been composed before he began to deliver a Qur'ān. There is in fact one little surah included in our present Qur'ān which remains unrhymed, viz., cvi :—

"1. For the bringing together by Quraish,
"2. For their bringing together the winter and the summer caravan,
"3. Let them serve the Lord of this House (*i.e.*, the Ka'ba)
"4. Who hath given them provision against famine,
"5. And made them secure against fear."

That is of the nature of what the sign "-passages have been described as being. It is an appeal to the Quraish on the ground of blessings received to worship and show their gratitude to God. Now it is possible to hold that it is late, after Muhammad had conquered Mecca, and definitely made Allah its Lord. But I do not think that Muhammad at that stage of his career would have made an appeal of that kind. The only feasible alternative is to take it as being very early, as in fact an example of his earliest appeals. If so, then his design was to stimulate the religious sense of gratitude to God. The little passage has remained unrhymed, and therefore only by accident included in the Qur'ān, because it was not an appeal on behalf of the great Allah, but on behalf of the Lord of the Ka'ba, *i.e.*, it was an attempt to make real and effective the religion which the Quraish already had;—a further confirmation of the tradition already cited, that Muhammad did not at first offend his people by attacking the native gods.

Another point worth noting about these "sign"-passages is that the great majority of them speak of Allah in the third person. Not all of them; some of them are spoken ostensibly in the name of Allah. But a great many of them begin, "Allah it is who . . .," and continue, "He it is who . . ." The Moslem view, of course, is that the whole Qur'ān is in the words of Allah. But it is hardly likely that Muhammad thus made Allah sing His own praises, speaking of Himself in the third person. It is more natural to think that these passages were originally spoken by Muhammad himself; and the conclusion, I think, is that he did not begin his work as a prophet, but simply as the advocate of revived religion, speaking as one man to another; not as the mouthpiece of Allah, but as a preacher, a messenger of Allah.

One last point may be recalled. There is a tradition, given by Ibn Hishām (pp. 157, 161), that Muhammad began his work privately, speaking to those nearly related to him and to those in whom he had confidence. That is so much at variance with what we should expect from the prevailing tradition of the appearance to him of the angel on Mt. Ḥirā and the command to recite then given to him, that I think we may accept it as genuine. It is confirmed by the passage in surah lxxi, which is perhaps Muhammad's own account of his early activity, but which as it stands is made to refer to Noah. Noah is there represented as first calling his people night and day, then calling them publicly, then combining the two methods of public proclamation and private exhortation, on the basis of Allah's beneficence and bounty.

We are now in a position to sum up. Muhammad's religion had not its origin in Apocalyptic, or in any half-crazy notions as to the immanence of the Last Day. It was based upon natural religion. It was his personal response to nature as he knew it, to life as it thrust itself upon him. Himself impressed by the dependence of man upon divine bounty for all the blessings of life, even for life itself, impressed also no doubt by the decay of religion, and the neglect by the Quraish, rendered proud and arrogant by the influx of new wealth, of the kindly duties which in tribal life bound rich and poor together and mitigated its harshness, he set himself to revive the power of religion. He began quietly, amongst his own relatives, his intimates, his friends, seeking sympathy and support. Gradually his sphere widened, until he began to speak publicly. There is no doubt that he had been at one time a worshipper of the native gods, and probably he began by seeking to revive the native religion, the worship of the god of the Ka'ba. But for him, thinking over the problem of human life afresh, perhaps with the influence of Christianity and Judaism already upon him, or at least such indirect influence as had penetrated into Arabia, God, even if symbolised by the Lord of the Ka'ba, could not be simply one among many gods. He was the Creator, and there could be only one creator. So he became the messenger of Allah, the one God, summoning his people to the worship of the Creator, the Giver of all the good gifts of life, Author of all things which made life possible and of life itself. For this purpose he used the arguments which could be drawn from nature, making lists of the things essential to life for which man was dependent on a power beyond himself, and demanding that man should recognise this dependence, receive Allah's gifts gratefully, show reverence and worship, and act bountifully as he himself had been bountifully dealt with. There was no asceticism in this religion. What I regard as an early passage of the Qur'ān, one of those passages which, originally unrhymed, has been rather drastically annotated and made to rhyme, vi, 139 f., is directed against heathen taboos in the matter of food; and even at the beginning of the Medinan period his doctrine in this matter was, "Eat of what is in the earth as lawful and good" (ii, 163). His appeal was simply for grateful acceptance of Allah's gifts, worship of Allah, and humble obedience to Allah's laws.

Alas! he found that these appeals affected only the few. Allah's mercy falling on good soil produces a crop, but of bad soil the crop is scanty. Bad soil requires other treatment, and ignoble souls require some other incentive than appeals to their generosity. Refusal to respond, and finally bitter opposition, drove him to threats. Material for these

24

he found where his mind had turned from the first, in the religious ideas of those who were already worshippers of the one God, and mainly in the popular eschatology and apocalyptic ideas of Christianity. By these ideas he himself was certainly impressed. The resurrection, the judgment, the future life became revealed certainties for him. But he was never conquered by apocalyptic details. These he uses with perfect freedom as suits his purpose. His judgment scenes are not incoherent rhapsodies —though by the very freedom with which he revised and altered them they have often come to be in much confusion. They are deliberate, well-composed, and most effective lashings of the conscience. They are secondary, not primary in his thought. They are "sanctions" for a religion rooted in nature and experience. The fundamental thing in Muhammad's religion was, to begin with, and continued to be, worship of, and obedience to, the One God of supreme power and majesty.

(With the idea that he had political objects in his mission from the start, either in Grimme's form, that he aimed at a religious socialism, or in Winckler's, that he ambitiously aimed at uniting Arabia by the worship of one god and obedience to himself, I have not thought it necessary to deal. I have found no basis for it in the Qur'ān, and it seems to me to confuse the result with the beginning. The truth in it is that Muhammad had great political gifts and aimed always at well-defined objects, with intense earnestness, but with cool calculation. There can, however, be no doubt that his object from the first was a religious one, and religious it remained fundamentally to the end, in spite of the political manœuvring in which he became involved, and the political success which he ultimately gained. What he sought, and what he succeeded in enforcing in Arabia, was the triumph of Allah, and of the religion of Allah.)

HEBREW AND YIDDISH BOOKS OF THE BOURGEOIS COLLECTION IN GLASGOW UNIVERSITY LIBRARY.

By Mr. David Atlas, M.A.

The Semitic section of the Henri Bourgeois Collection in Glasgow University Library consists of about 410 volumes, mostly modern publications. These comprise 163 volumes of Hebrew books, 71 of Yiddish, 9 of Judæo-Spanish (Ladino), 8 of Judæo-Arabic, 2 of Judæo-Persian, 28 of Arabic, 1 of Maghribi, 13 of Maltese, 6 of Ethiopic, 6 of Coptic, 23 of Syriac, and 79 volumes in various European languages dealing with some aspect of Semitic study.

Though non-Semitic in origin, Yiddish is grouped with the Semitic owing to its having become during the centuries an accredited vehicle of Jewish thought and self-expression, developing in this capacity side by side with Hebrew. The case is similar with Judæo-Spanish and Judæo-Persian.

Of the minor Semitic languages, the Maltese and Neo-Syriac books are perhaps of special interest. Maltese offers instructive comparisons with Arabic. A poem by Dwardu Cachia is entitled "Malta mehlusa

16

ABŪ LAHAB AND SŪRA CXI

Uri Rubin

The studies of Sūra CXI [1] have not yet arrived at satisfactory results, hence the meaning of this sūra is still obscure. The present study tries to present a better basis for its understanding.[2]

1. *The date and background of the sūra*

Sūra CXI deals with Abū Lahab, whom all the Muslim sources identify as Muḥammad's paternal uncle, 'Abd al-'Uzzā b. 'Abd al-Muṭṭalib of the clan of Hāshim.

The clue to the date and background of this sūra is to be found in a tradition recorded by al-Wāqidī (d. 207/823).[3] This tradition is about al-'Uzzā, the greatest deity of Quraysh, whose sanctuary was at Nakhla, near Mecca. Quraysh also worshipped al-Lāt whose sanctuary was at al-Ṭā'if. A third deity, Manāt, whose sanctuary was at Qudayd, was worshipped mainly by the people of Yathrib (al-Madīna). All three were known as ' daughters of Allāh ' (*banāt Allāh*).[4]

The tradition of al-Wāqidī relates that the custodian (*sādin*) of the sanctuary of al-'Uzzā was Aflaḥ b. al-Naḍr al-Shaybānī of the tribe of Sulaym.[5] Before his death, Aflaḥ told Abū Lahab that he was afraid lest al-'Uzzā should be neglected once he was dead. Upon hearing this, Abū Lahab said : ' Do not grieve ; I shall attend to her after you go '. After that, Abū Lahab used to say : ' If al-'Uzzā triumphs, I have already earned a " hand " [6] which she has (to my credit) with her, for attending upon her,[7] and if Muḥammad triumphs over al-'Uzzā—which I do not believe will happen—then be it my nephew (who has a " hand " to my credit with him) '. Thereupon, Allāh revealed Sūra CXI.

This tradition had been noticed by Barth,[8] but he seems to have overlooked its great significance. Al-Wāqidī chose to record this tradition within

[1] J. Barth, ' Abū Lahab ', *EI*, first ed. ; A. Fischer, *Der Wert der vorhandenen Koranübersetzungen und Sura* CXI, Leipzig, 1937 ; D. Künstlinger, ' Eschatologisches in Sura 111 ', *OLZ*, XLI, 7, 1938, 407–10 ; T. Lohmann, ' Abū Lahab (Sura CXI) ', *Zeitschrift für Religions und Geistwelt Geschichte*, XVIII, 1966, 326–48 ; R. Paret, *Der Koran, Kommentar und Konkordanz*, Stuttgart, 1971, 529. J. Wansbrough in his *Quranic studies* (Oxford, 1977) does not refer to our sūra. This is quite disappointing, because a scholar who denies any historical connexion between the Qur'ān and the ' Arabian prophet ' ought to say something about the identity of Abū Lahab and his wife.

[2] References to the commentaries quoted in the following pages : al-Ṭabarī, *Jāmi' al-bayān fī tafsīr al-Qur'ān*, Būlāq, 1323/1905, XXX, 217–21 ; al-Ṭabarsī, *Majma' al-bayān fī tafsīr al-Qur'ān*, Beirut, n.d., XXX, 266–71 ; al-Zamakhsharī, *al-Kashshāf 'an ḥaqā'iq al-tanzīl*, Cairo, 1968, IV, 295–7 ; al-Bayḍāwī, *Anwār al-tanzīl wa-asrār al-ta'wīl*, Cairo, 1955, 317 ; al-Rāzī, *al-Tafsīr al-kabīr*, repr., Tehran, n.d., XXXII, 166–73 ; Abū Ḥayyān, *al-Baḥr al-muḥīṭ*, Cairo, 1328/1910, VIII, 524–7 ; Ibn Kathīr, *Tafsīr al-Qur'ān al-'aẓīm*, Beirut, 1966, VII, 399–402 ; al-Ālūsī, *Rūḥ al-ma'ānī*, repr., Beirut, n.d., XXX, 259–65.

[3] See al-Wāqidī, *Kitāb al-maghāzī*, ed. J. M. B. Jones, London, 1966, III, 874. See also al-Azraqī, *Akhbār Makka*, ed. Wüstenfeld, I, 81–2.

[4] Details about those deities are to be found in J. Wellhausen, *Reste arabischen Heidentums*, Berlin, repr. 1961, 24 ff.

[5] The Banū Shaybān of Sulaym were the confederates of the clan of Hāshim. See Ibn Hishām, *al-Sīra al-nabawiyya*, ed. al-Saqā, al-Abyārī, Shalabī, four vols., repr., Beirut, 1971, I, 86.

[6] The meaning of ' hand ' will be explained below.

[7] *in taẓhar al-'uzzā, kuntu qad ittakhadhtu yadan 'indahā bi-qiyāmī 'alayhā.*

[8] Barth, loc. cit. Fischer did not refer to it at all.

14

a chapter dealing with the destruction of the sanctuary of al-'Uzzā in the year 8/629, shortly after the conquest of Mecca. This led Barth to conclude that according to al-Wāqidī, Abū Lahab was still alive after the conquest of Mecca.[9] Thereby he rejected this tradition as a false one, because Abū Lahab had actually died long before, immediately after the battle of Badr. The truth is, however, that this tradition belongs to the time when both Abū Lahab and Aflaḥ b. al-Naḍr were still alive, that is, before the Hijra of Muḥammad to al-Madīna.[10] Al-Wāqidī placed this tradition within a later chapter dealing with the actual destruction of al-'Uzzā, after the conquest of Mecca, because the conversation between the *sādin* of al-'Uzzā and Abū Lahab referred to the same subject, i.e. the forthcoming end of al-'Uzzā.

A second version of the same story is recorded by Ibn al-Kalbī.[11] Ibn al-Kalbī located the story in its proper chronological place, that is, immediately after the abrogation of Muḥammad's temporal recognition of the ' daughters of Allāh '. This event was known as the affair of the ' Satanic verses '. In these verses, Muḥammad had recognized the divinity of al-Lāt, Manāt, and al-'Uzzā, and especially their authority to intercede with Allāh for their believers. Some time later, these verses were abrogated, being ascribed to Satan's influence upon the prophet. They were replaced by new verses denying the existence of these three deities (Qur'ān LIII, 19–23).[12]

Ibn al-Kalbī relates that Muḥammad's denial of al-'Uzzā was a great blow to Quraysh (*fa-shtadda dhālika 'alā Quraysh*); thereafter he recounts the story about Abū Lahab. According to Ibn al-Kalbī, however, the person to whom Abū Lahab talked was Abū Uḥayḥa Sa'īd b. al-'Āṣ, and not Aflaḥ b. al-Naḍr. At the time of the declaration of the ' Satanic verses ', this Abū Uḥayḥa was a very old man.[13] Ibn al-Kalbī's version contains some remarkable details. According to this version, Abū Lahab assured Abū Uḥayḥa that the veneration of al-'Uzzā would not cease after his death. Thereupon Abū Uḥayḥa said: ' Now I know that I have a successor (*khalīfa*) '. And he admired Abū Lahab's eagerness for her worship.

The conclusion to be drawn from Ibn al-Kalbī and al-Wāqidī is that Sūra CXI was revealed in Mecca after Muḥammad no longer recognized al-'Uzzā, when Abū Lahab, on his part, took it upon himself to defend and support this goddess against Muḥammad's new monotheistic course. In this connexion it may be noted that according to Ibn Isḥāq,[14] our sūra was revealed after Abū Lahab had abandoned Muḥammad and the rest of the Hāshimites in the ravine (*shi'b*) of Abū Ṭālib, where they had been put under a boycott by Quraysh. Abū Lahab had joined Quraysh in expressing his wish to support al-'Uzzā. These events took place in the seventh year of Muḥammad's prophecy, i.e. only a

[9] See also Lohmann, art. cit., 330.

[10] That Aflaḥ b. al-Naḍr was Abū Lahab's contemporary, and not the last *sādin* of al-'Uzzā who was killed by Khālid after the conquest of Mecca, was already pointed out by Wellhausen, op. cit., 38. The last *sādin* was named Dubayya b. Ḥaramī, see Ibn al-Kalbī, *Kitāb al-aṣnām*, ed. Aḥmad Zakī Bāshā, Cairo, 1914, 25 ff.

[11] *Aṣnām*, 23; cf. also Wellhausen, op. cit., 36.

[12] On the ' Satanic verses ', see al-Ṭabarī, *Tafsīr*, XVII, 131 ff. (on Qur'ān XXII, 52); *idem*, *Tārīkh*, Cairo, 1939, II, 75–7 (from Ibn Isḥāq and other sources); Ibn Kathīr, *al-Bidāya wa 'l-nihāya*, repr., Beirut, 1974, III, 90–1; al-Zurqānī, *Sharḥ al-mawāhib al-laduniyya*, repr., Beirut, 1973, I, 279 ff.; Ibn Shahrāshūb, *Manāqib Āl Abī Ṭālib*, Najaf, 1375/1956, I, 46; al-'Asqalānī, *Fatḥ al-bārī bi-sharḥ Ṣaḥīḥ al-Bukhārī*, Būlāq, 1300/1883, VIII, 332–4; al-Qāḍī 'Iyāḍ, *al-Shifā' bi-ta'rīf ḥuqūq al-Muṣṭafā*, Cairo, 1950, II, 106 ff.; Ibn Sa'd, *al-Ṭabaqāt al-kubrā*, Beirut, 1960, I, 205–6; Ibn Sayyid al-Nās, *'Uyūn al-athar*, repr., Beirut, n.d., I, 120–1; W. M. Watt, *Muḥammad at Mecca*, Oxford, 1953, 102 ff.; Paret, op. cit., 461.

[13] See Ibn Sa'd, op. cit., I, 205. On his last illness see ibid., IV, 95–6.

[14] Ibn Hishām, op. cit., I, 376.

short time after the abrogation of the 'Satanic verses'.[15] Abū Lahab was probably anxious to secure his economic position which was threatened by the boycott of his clan. By leaving the ravine of Abū Ṭālib, he could maintain his connexions with Quraysh and their sanctuaries.

That the revelation of Sūra CXI was caused directly by Abū Lahab's departure from Hāshim, may also be concluded from the Qur'ānic codex of Ubayy b. Ka'b.[16] This codex reportedly contained an additional verse, located between verses 1 and 2 of our sūra:

ḥālafa 'l-bayta 'l-waḍī'a 'alā 'l-bayti 'l-rafī'i
fa-shughila bi-nafsihi, thumma shughila
'He became allied to the inferior house against the exalted house, and he was occupied only with himself, and indeed he was'.

By the 'exalted house' the clan of Hāshim is probably meant, which Abū Lahab abandoned, allying himself with a certain unspecified clan, which is considered inferior to Hāshim. Some early verses ascribed to Ḥassān b. Thābit shed more light on the matter.[17] These verses condemn Abū Lahab for forsaking Muḥammad and stress at the same time that Abū Lahab was not a true son of Hāshim, being, in fact, the son of a person from the tribe of Liḥyān (to whom his mother had been married before marrying 'Abd al-Muṭṭalib). The clan of Hāshim is described as being high with noble traits, while Abū Lahab is described as being low with his shame.[18] Both these verses and Ubayy's verse allude to the fact that Muḥammad was deeply injured when Abū Lahab abandoned him.[19] This may lead to the conclusion that before leaving Muḥammad, Abū Lahab had bestowed his protection upon the prophet and extended to him much aid and support. Muḥammad's attack upon the 'daughters of Allāh' and the boycott of Hāshim forced upon Abū Lahab a completely different attitude towards the prophet. Muḥammad's dismay was fully expressed in Sūra CXI which was then revealed.

2. *Verse 1: tabbat yadā Abī Lahabin wa-tabba*

The most intriguing phrase in verse 1 is *yadā Abī Lahabin* 'the two hands of Abū Lahab'. According to the above-mentioned tradition of al-Wāqidī, Abū Lahab had supported al-'Uzzā and thus gained a 'hand' which was with her to his credit. The Arabic clause expressing it runs as follows: *kuntu qad ittakhadhtu yadan 'indahā. Yad* here means *ni'ma*, that is to say: 'favour' or 'benefaction'. The meaning of the whole clause is: 'I did her a favour (*yad*) and she is obliged to reward me for it'. The expression *ittakhadha 'indahum yadan* is explained by Lane [20] as follows: 'He did to them a benefit,

[15] According to al-Wāqidī, the proclamation of these verses occurred in the fifth year, i.e. two years before the boycott of Hāshim (Ibn Sa'd, op. cit., I, 206, 209). Therefore the abrogation must have happened shortly before the boycott. Al-Ṭabarī, on his part, mentions the affair of the 'Satanic verses' only after the beginning of the boycott. See *Tārīkh*, II, 74, 75 ff. See also al-Zurqānī, op. cit., I, 278 ff.

[16] A. Jeffery, *Materials for the history of the text of the Qur'ān*, Leiden, 1937, 180. Quoted from Jeffery by Fischer, p. 10, without any comment.

[17] See Ḥassān b. Thābit, *Dīwān*, ed. W. 'Arafāt, London, 1971, I, p. 390, no. 214.

[18] *wa-lākinna Liḥyānan abūka warithtahū/ wa-ma'wā 'l-khanā minhum fa-da' 'anka hāshimā/ samat hāshimun lil-makrumāti wa-lil-'ulā/ wa-ghūdirta fī ka'bin mina 'l-lu'mi jāthimā.*

[19] That Abū Lahab's conduct during the period of the boycott of Hāshim had a serious effect on Muḥammad is indicated also in some early verses ascribed to Abū Ṭālib (Ibn Hishām, op. cit., II, 11). In these verses Abū Ṭālib urges Abū Lahab not to abandon his nephew, stressing the importance of his protection. Abū Ṭālib swears by the 'house of Allāh' (the Ka'ba) that the Hāshimites will protect the prophet till the end. The background of these verses can easily be established, as the *shi'b* is mentioned in the last verse.

[20] *An Arabic–English lexicon*, s.v. *a.kh.dh.*

16

or favour, as though he earned one for himself in prospect, making it to be incumbent on them as a debt to him'. It follows that *yad* in this context denotes simultaneously the benefaction and its prospective reward. Al-Wāqidī's tradition leads to the conclusion that the Qur'ān has labelled Abū Lahab's attendance upon al-'Uzzā as *yad*, that is to say, an honourable act of help and support, for which he deserved a due recompense from this goddess.

The Qur'ān, however, mentions the 'two hands' of Abū Lahab. This is due to the fact that not only a single act of support is meant, but rather all Abū Lahab's good deeds, including those which were performed for Muḥammad's sake. For there is some evidence that at a certain stage, Abū Lahab bestowed protection upon Muḥammad.[21] Still, although the Qur'ān refers to all Abū Lahab's good deeds, it has nevertheless preferred the dual form, *yadā*, to the plural, *aydī*. *Yadā*, it seems, was much more natural, since the concrete meaning of *yad* (a hand) had not been wholly neglected. Hence, it was impossible to mention more than two 'hands' of a single person.

Abū Lahab had indeed several 'hands' to his credit in Mecca. As a generous wealthy man,[22] this was quite to be expected of him. Ibn Isḥāq has preserved for us some early verses in which Abū Lahab appears as a most generous and helpful person.[23] The verses are ascribed to Ḥudhayfa b. Ghānim, whom Abū Lahab redeemed after he had been seized for a debt of 4,000 dirhams. We shall adduce but one verse.[24] In this verse Abū Lahab is called Ibn Lubnā, after his mother Lubnā bint Hājar of Khuzā'a:[25]

wa-lā tansa mā asdā bnu Lubnā fa-innahū
qada sdā [26] *yadan maḥqūqatan minka bi 'l-shukrī*
'And do not forget what Ibn Lubnā has granted, for he has granted a "hand" that deserves your thankfulness'.

The original meaning of the phrase *yadā Abī Lahabin* was preserved not only in the above-mentioned tradition of al-Wāqidī, but also in some rare exegetical traditions included in the direct commentaries on our sūra. The commentary of al-Ālūsī (p. 261) contains the following passage:

wa-fī 'l-ta'wīlāt al-yadu bi-ma'nā 'l-ni'ma. wa-kāna yuḥsinu ilā 'l-nabī (ṣ) *wa-ilā quraysh wa-yaqūlu: in kāna 'l-amru li-Muḥammadin fa-lī 'indahu yadun, wa-in kāna li-qurayshin fa-ka-dhālika*
'There are some interpretations saying that *yad* denotes benefaction. (Abū

[21] Ibn Sa'd, op. cit., I, 211. It is related that Abū Lahab protected Muḥammad only after Abū Ṭālib had died, i.e. much later than the revelation of Sūra CXI. It is more likely, however, that Muḥammad had enjoyed the protection of Abū Lahab before the revelation of this sūra which marked the end of the friendly relations with his uncle. The present form of the account apparently reflects a Shī'ī tendency to promote the impression that as long as Abū Ṭālib ('Alī's father) was alive, he was Muḥammad's only protector. At any rate, both Abū Ṭālib and Abū Lahab are said to have earned something in return for their kind attitude towards Muḥammad. Abū Ṭālib, who died as an unbeliever, was said to be only in the shallow fire of hell (*ḍaḥḍāḥ*). Abū Lahab was said to have water to ease his torture in hell as a reward for setting free his slave Thuwayba, who was Muḥammad's wet-nurse. See al-Suhaylī, *al-Rawḍ al-unuf*, ed. 'Abd al-Ra'ūf Sa'd, Cairo, 1971, III, 67; al-'Asqalānī, *Fatḥ al-bārī*, IX, 124–5. On Abū Lahab and Thuwayba see also al-Bukhārī, *Ṣaḥīḥ*, Cairo, 1958, VII, 12; Ibn Sa'd, op. cit., I, 108; al-Bayhaqī, *Dalā'il al-nubuwwa*, ed. Muḥammad 'Uthmān, Cairo, 1969, I, 120; Ibn al-Jawzī, *al-Wafā bi-aḥwāl al-Muṣṭafā*, ed. 'Abd al-Wāḥid, Cairo, 1966, I, 107; al-'Asqalānī, *al-Iṣāba fī ma'rifat al-ṣaḥāba*, ed. al-Bijāwī, Cairo, 1970, VII, 549; al-Zurqānī, op. cit., I, 138.

[22] See e.g. Ibn Sa'd, op. cit., I, 93: *wa-kāna jawādan.*

[23] Ibn Hishām, op. cit., I, 184 ff.

[24] ibid., 187.

[25] ibid., 115; Ibn Sa'd, loc. cit.

[26] For: *qad asdā.*

Lahab) used to perform good deeds for the benefit of the prophet and Quraysh. He used to say: " if the victory is with Muḥammad, I have a 'hand' to my credit with him, and if the victory is with Quraysh, the same applies to them " '.[27]

Finally, it may be remarked that *yad* denoting benefaction, occurs in a further Qur'ānic passage as well. Qur'ān IX, 29 says: *qātilū 'lladhīna lā yu'minūna bi-llāhi ... mina 'lladhīna ūtū 'l-kitāba ḥattā yu'ṭū 'l-jizyata 'an yadin.* The true meaning of the phrase *al-jizyata 'an yadin* has been pointed out by M. M. Bravmann.[28] Bravmann, contrary to Kister's opinion,[29] renders this verse as follows: 'combat those non-believers who are possessors of a book (i.e. Christians and Jews) until they give the reward due for a benefaction (since their lives are spared)'. There is, however, some difference between the two verses. The phrase *yadā Abī Lahabin* refers mainly to the supporter himself, i.e. Abū Lahab, whereas the expression *'an yadin* refers to those who were granted the benefaction, who must make a reward for it. Besides, in Qur'ān IX, 29 *yad* means a benefaction consisting in sparing somebody's life, whereas in our sūra, *yad* means benefaction in the sense of material support. In both cases the benefaction must be duly rewarded or recompensed.

Our sūra is directly connected with Sūra LIII which abrogates Muḥammad's former recognition of al-'Uzzā's existence. Verse 1 conveys the idea that the 'hand' which Abū Lahab believed he had to his credit with al-'Uzzā, has become worthless; he can no longer count on al-'Uzzā's reward for serving and supporting her, as she became a false goddess due to the abrogation of the 'Satanic verses'. At the same time, the Qur'ān, as a retaliation against Abū Lahab who abandoned Muḥammad for his own interests, proclaims the end of his credit with Muḥammad, the latter being no longer obliged to reward Abū Lahab for his former protection. The word which signifies the new condition of Abū Lahab's 'hands' is *tabbat.* Qatāda (d. 118/736),[30] as quoted by al-Ṭabarī, interprets it as *khasirat,* i.e. 'failed to produce profits or reward; became worthless'. The explanation of *tabbat* as *khasirat* accords with the Qur'ān itself, in which the infinitive *tatbīb* is replaced by *takhsīr* (Qur'ān XI, 101: *wa-mā zādūhum ghayra tatbībin*; XI, 63: *fa-mā tazīdūnanī ghayra takhsīrin*). According to a further interpretation recorded on the authority of Yamān b. Ri'āb,[31] *tabbat* means: 'have become devoid of any benefit (*ṣafirat min kulli khayrin*)'.[32] Similarly, one of al-Ṭabarsī's interpretations says that verse 1 means: 'his hands have not gained any benefit at all, and he himself incurred loss as well, i.e. he has been lost in all respects (*wa-ma'nāhu annahu lam taktasib yadāhu khayran qaṭṭu, wa-khasira ma'a dhālika huwa nafsuhu, ay tabba 'alā kulli ḥālin*)'.

The final thing to be explained concerning verse 1 is the meaning of the name 'Abū Lahab', i.e. 'the father of flame'. According to Lohmann,[33] 'Abū Lahab' stands for the person who was first to kindle the fire, that is to say, the first person of Quraysh to break off friendly relations with Muḥammad.

[27] Abū Muslim (probably al-Kashshī, d. 292/904, see Sezgin, *GAS*, I, 162), as quoted by al-Rāzī, says that *yadā abī lahabin* means his fortune (*ya'nī mālahu*) which is also denoted by the expression *dhāt al-yad*. This interpretation is close to the interpretation of *yad* as *ni'ma*, in the sense of material support.
[28] See M. M. Bravmann, *The spiritual background of early Islam*, Leiden, 1972, 199 ff.
[29] See M. J. Kister, ' " *'An yadin* " (Qur'ān, IX, 29) ', *Arabica*, XI, 3, 1964, 272–8.
[30] Sezgin, *GAS*, I, 31 ff.
[31] On whom see al-Dhahabī, *Mīzān al-i'tidāl*, Cairo, n.d., IV, 460.
[32] See al-Ṭabarsī, al-Rāzī, and Abū Ḥayyān.
[33] Lohmann, art. cit., 334.

18

This explanation cannot be accepted for the simple reason that there is nothing to suggest that 'fire' symbolizes the conflict with the prophet, since this conflict, in its early stages, was by no means warlike. On the other hand, Lohmann is quite correct in assuming that 'Abū Lahab' has become the name (*kunya*) of Muḥammad's uncle only as a result of this sūra, not being known before. In general, a man's *kunya* is mentioned in his honour.[34] Abū Lahab's case, however, is different. Al-'Asqalānī[35] explains: 'the *kunya* in itself does not indicate glorification, since in some cases, the personal name may be more honourable than the *kunya* (. . . *inna 'l-takniya lā tadullu bi-mujarradihā 'alā 'l-ta'ẓīm bal qad yakūnu 'l-ismu ashrafa mina 'l-takniya*)'. This, indeed, seems to be true: the Qur'ān, in order to degrade Abū Lahab, has refrained from addressing him by his personal name, 'Abd al-'Uzzā, which signified his honour as servant of al-'Uzzā. The Qur'ān has chosen to name him 'the father of flame', thus suggesting that instead of being rewarded by al-'Uzzā at the Last Judgement for his service, he, being deprived of the intercession of that false goddess, will burn in the flames of hell. Thus the surname 'Abū Lahab' fits in with the general context of verse 1.

In conclusion, verse 1 may be rendered as follows: 'Abū Lahab's credit for his grand deeds has been lost, and he (himself) has been lost'.

3. *Other interpretations of verse 1*

The greater part of the Muslim commentaries on verse 1 contains new interpretations deviating from its true meaning. This deviation seems to be due to a deliberate modification of the meaning of this verse. The reason for this seems to be connected with verse 3 of our sūra: *sa-yaṣlā nāran dhāta lahabin* 'He shall be burned in a fire of flame'. Originally, this verse describes Abū Lahab's failure to gain his prospective reward for serving al-'Uzzā, on the one hand, and for protecting Muḥammad, on the other. Being deprived of his reward, the fire of hell has become his only prospect.[36] After Muḥammad's death, however, Muslim theologians gradually developed a new perception of verse 3, and consequently of the whole sūra. Their postulate was that Abū Lahab, being mentioned in a special Qur'ānic chapter, relating also his fate in hell, must have sinned greatly against Muḥammad and Islam, for which hell was to be his punishment.

This view had much bearing on verse 1. Firstly, the meaning of the 'hands' of Abū Lahab was changed from grand deeds of favour and support to hostile actions carried out by those hands against no other than Muḥammad himself. Thus the 'hands' regained their concrete meaning, while *tabbat* came to signify the failure of those hostile deeds. In this way Abū Lahab grew akin to the rest of the Qurashīs who had allegedly persecuted the prophet in Mecca.

The first step towards this new understanding of verse 1 seems to be reflected in a tradition traced back to Ibn 'Abbās. This tradition is recorded by al-Rāzī: 'Ibn 'Abbās said: he (i.e. Abū Lahab) used to send away people who had come to see (the prophet), saying that (Muḥammad) was a sorcerer (*sāḥir*). Those people used to turn back, not suspecting the truth of his words, since he was the head of the clan, and used to treat Muḥammad like a father. However,

[34] Goldhizer, *Muhammedanische Studien*, Halle a.S., I, 1889, 267 (English tr., *Muslim studies*, I, London, 1967, 242).

[35] *Fatḥ al-bārī*, VIII, 387.

[36] This verse seems to be the main reason for the Mu'tazila's rejection of our sūra, because it excludes from the outset any possibility of repentance on the part of Abū Lahab. See e.g. al-Rāzī on this verse. This point has not yet been explained by Western scholars who dealt with the Mu'tazilī attitude towards our sūra. See I. Goldziher, *Vorlesungen über den Islam*, 207; Fischer op. cit., 15 ff.; Barth, art. cit., 329.

when Sūra CXI was revealed, Abū Lahab became angry and showed his enmity, causing people to grow suspicious and to disbelieve in what he had said about the prophet. Thus his efforts (against the prophet) failed, and his aim was missed. And perhaps the " hand " has been mentioned because he used to strike with it on the shoulder of the person who had come to see the prophet, saying: " turn back, for Muḥammad is possessed (*majnūn*) ". Usually, when a man sends another man away, he puts his hand on the latter's shoulder, pushing him away '. Al-Rāzī records a further interpretation on the authority of 'Aṭā': '*tabbat* means: " has been defeated (*ghulibat*) "; (Abū Lahab) believed that his hand would (triumph) over (Muḥammad), and he would expel him from Mecca, humiliating and defeating him (but his own hand has been defeated) '.

Verse 3 of our sūra has a pure eschatological significance. This stimulated more new interpretations attaching a similar meaning to verse 1 as well. Thereby, verse 1 was treated as though dealing not only with the failure of Abū Lahab's worldly sins against the prophet, but also with his prospective punishment in hell. Al-Ṭabarsī interprets: ' his deeds have proved unsuccessful, and he himself has failed, being condemned to hell ' (*khasira 'amaluhu wa-khasira huwa bi 'l-wuqū'i fī 'l-nār*).[37]

Verse 1 was eventually interpreted as if referring solely to the world to come, *tabbat* being no longer interpreted as denoting a present worldly disadvantage, but rather as an invocation (*du'ā'*) for the same, due to come upon Abū Lahab in hell. This interpretation is reflected in the reading (*qirā'a*) of 'Abdullāh b. Mas'ūd: *tabbat yadā abī lahabin wa-qad tabba*; ' may the hands of Abū Lahab be lost, and indeed he has been lost '. This *qirā'a* is based on a structure of invocation common in old Arabic; it contains two verbs, the latter being preceded by *wa-qad*, denoting the inevitability of the invocation expressed by the first. Al-Ṭabarī adduces two examples of this structure: *ahlakaka 'llāhu wa-qad ahlakaka; ja'alaka ṣāliḥan wa-qad ja'alaka.*[38]

In acquiring the meaning of invocation, the phrase *tabbat yadāhu* was assimilated later on to genuine Arabic phrases of invocation connected with ' hands ', such as *shallat yadāhu* and *taribat yadāhu*. Unlike the Qur'ānic expression *tabbat yadāhu*, these phrases are to be found in many verses of old Arab poetry.[39] In the following *rajaz* verse, the Qur'ānic phrase *tabbat yadāhu* has already been adapted to its new usage of invocation. According to *Lisān al-'Arab* (s.v. *tbb*), this verse refers to somebody who has bought *fasw*, i.e. a commodity from which no great utility is derived.

akhsir bihā min ṣafqatin lam tustaqal
tabbat yadā ṣāfiqihā mādhā fa'al
' What a great loss (was caused by) this deal that was not abrogated,
May the hands of him who made this deal be lost, what has he done! '[40]

[37] See also al-Suhaylī, op. cit., II, 109.

[38] Regarding *tabbat* as an invocation, Fischer considered this *qirā'a* to be the original one. Paret (op. cit., 529), however, has shown that the *lectio difficilior* is not *wa-qad tabba* (Ibn Mas'ūd) but rather *wa-tabba*, thus affirming that Ibn Mas'ūd's reading is secondary. The *qirā'a* of Ibn Mas'ūd was indeed known as an ' easy ' one, containing many explanatory additions to the original text. See al-Suhaylī, loc. cit. See also I. Goldziher, *Richtungen*, 8 ff.

[39] See references in Fischer, op. cit., p. 20, n. 1.

[40] Fischer, loc. cit., adduces this verse as an illustration that *tabbat yadā abī lahabin* is an invocation. This verse, however, seems to be a later reflection of a somewhat similar *rajaz* verse included in the original story about the person who bought *fasw*. This man, so the story goes, was named Baydara; he bought the *fasw* of the tribe of Iyād. The original *rajaz* verse referring to him does not yet have *tabbat yadāhu* but still: *shallat yadāhu*. See e.g. Ibn Durayd, *Jamharat al-lugha*, Hyderabad, 1344/1925, I, 23.

20

The view that verse 1 invokes evil upon Abū Lahab is put forward by many traditions, some of which are widely current in the various commentaries on our sūra. This view represents, in fact, the consensus (*ijmā'*) of the Muslim scholars with regard to the meaning of verse 1. The main idea of the traditions presenting this view is that the phrase *tabbat yadā abī lahabin* forms an antiphony to the invocation *tabban lahu* uttered by Abū Lahab himself before the revelation of the sūra. One of the earliest of these traditions is that of Ibn Isḥāq.[41] According to Ibn Isḥāq, Abū Lahab used to say: 'Muḥammad promises me things that I do not see, which he says will come after my death. What has he actually put in my hands (except promises)?'. Then he would blow on his hands and say: 'May you be lost (*tabban lakumā*). I see in you nothing of what Muḥammad says'. Therefore Allāh revealed the sūra.

According to more developed traditions, Abū Lahab directed the imprecation not to his own self, but rather to the Islamic religion. A tradition to this effect is recorded by al-Ṭabarī on the authority of Ibn Zayd (d. 182/798).[42] Abū Lahab allegedly uttered the words *tabban li-hādhā min dīnin tabban*, when Muḥammad refused to grant him an exceptional position among the Muslims, as a reward for his embracing Islam.

The most current traditions, however, are those relating that Abū Lahab's curse was directed to Muḥammad himself. These traditions say that when Muḥammad was ordered to start warning his nearest relations of the Last Judgement (Qur'ān XXVI, 214: *wa-andhir 'ashīrataka 'l-aqrabīna . . .*), he summoned them all in order to convey his mission. Upon hearing his words, Abū Lahab said: 'Is this what you summoned us for? May you be lost (*tabban laka*)'. Thereupon Sūra CXI was revealed. This story implies that Sūra CXI was revealed at the very beginning of Muḥammad's prophetic activity. Al-Ṭabarī records no less than five versions of this story, four of which are from al-A'mash (d. 148/765),[43] with an *isnād* traced back to Ibn 'Abbās.

This story was admitted into the canonical *ḥadīth*,[44] as well as into books of *asbāb al-nuzūl*.[45] Its secondary nature is attested most clearly by the fact that in the earlier versions of the story about the beginning of Muḥammad's mission among his fellow tribesmen, there is not a single word concerning Sūra CXI.[46]

In later versions of the above traditions, Abū Lahab's hostile acts against the prophet assume a more aggressive nature. According to al-Zamakhsharī and al-Bayḍāwī, Abū Lahab not only abused the prophet, but also picked up a stone with the intention of throwing it at him, thus provoking the Qur'ānic damning of his hands.[47] Explaining why the Qur'ān has mentioned the hands of Abū Lahab, al-Ṭabarsī and al-Rāzī quote a tradition on the authority of the *ṣaḥābī* Ṭāriq al-Muḥāribī,[48] according to which Abū Lahab used to follow the

[41] Ibn Hishām, op. cit., I, 376.
[42] Sezgin, *GAS*, I, 38.
[43] ibid., 9.
[44] See al-Bukhārī, op. cit., VI, 140, 221–2; al-Tirmidhī, *Ṣaḥīḥ* (in *'Āriḍat al-aḥwadhī*, by Ibn al-'Arabī), XII, 259. See also Ibn Sa'd, op. cit., I, 74–5, 200.
[45] e.g. al-Wāḥidī, *Asbāb al-nuzūl*, Cairo, 1968, 261–2.
[46] See al-Ṭabarī, *Tārīkh*, II, 62–3 (from Ibn Isḥāq). Cf. also Ibn Sa'd, op. cit., I, 187.
[47] A similar story is told about the wife of Abū Lahab who, after the revelation of the sūra, intended to throw a big stone at Muḥammad. Allāh, however, concealed the prophet from her. See Ibn Hishām, op. cit., I, 381–2. Cf. al-'Asqalānī, *Fatḥ al-bārī*, VIII, 567; al-Ḥākim al-Naysābūrī, *al-Mustadrak 'alā 'l-ṣaḥīḥayn*, Riyāḍ, 1388/1968, II, 361; al-Bayhaqī, op. cit., I, 443–4; Ibn al-Jawzī, op. cit., I, 325; al-Suyūṭī, *al-Khaṣā'iṣ al-kubrā*, ed. Harās, Cairo, 1967, I, 318–19; Ibn Sayyid al-Nās, op. cit., I, 102–3; Ibn Shahrāshūb, op. cit., I, 61; al-Khargūshī, *Sharaf al-Nabī*, MS BM Or. 3014, fols. 40a, 127a.
[48] On whom see *Iṣāba*, III, 511.

prophet and throw stones at him, when the latter preached Islam to Arab tribesmen in the market of Dhū 'l-Majāz.[49] This tradition was already recorded by al-Tirmidhī.[50] An earlier version of the same story, however, does not mention any such act on the part of Abū Lahab, nor is there any allusion to the connexion of this event with our sūra.[51] A further tradition, recorded by al-Rāzī, relates that Abū Lahab had torn off the 'hands' (i.e. the front legs) of a kid (*jady*) that believed in Muḥammad, and this brought about the cursing of his own hands in the Qur'ān. This legendary tradition applies the most aggressive touch to Abū Lahab's negative image.[52]

The view that verse 1 invokes evil upon Abū Lahab eventually caused a considerable change in the meaning of *tabbat* and *wa-tabba*. Al-Zamakhsharī explains these verbs not in the meaning of *khasira*, but rather in the sense of *halaka*, i.e. 'to perish'. Al-Bayḍāwī explains that *tabāb* means *khusrān* (i.e. failure or loss) that brings about *halāk* (i.e. perdition).

The shift from *khasira* to *halaka* accords with the general tendency illustrated above, to conform verse 1 to the eschatological spirit of verse 3. This tendency is most evident in one of Bayḍāwī's interpretations, to the effect that the perdition of Abū Lahab's two hands stands for his own total perdition in this world as well as in the world to come (*dunyāhu wa-ukhrāhu*). This interpretation is closely connected with another interpretation offered by al-Zamakhsharī.

> *wa 'l-murād: halāk jumlatihi ka-qawlihi ta'ālā: bi-mā qaddamat yadāka*
> 'The meaning (of the perdition of Abū Lahab's hands) is the perdition of his whole person; this is like the verse (Qur'ān XXII, 10): "for what your two hands have done"'.

This interpretation takes the 'two hands' to be a synecdoche, i.e. denoting the whole person to whom they belong. It may be noted, however, that the

[49] A Shī'ī tradition relates that al-'Abbās participated with Abū Lahab in these deeds. Abū Ṭālib defended the prophet against them both. See Ibn Shahrāshūb, op. cit., I, 51.

[50] Quoted from al-Tirmidhī in *Iṣāba*, loc. cit.

[51] See Ibn Hishām, op. cit., II, 64–5; Ibn Sayyid al-Nās, op. cit., I, 101; Ibn Kathīr, op. cit., III, 41; Ibn Shahrāshūb, op. cit., I, 51. Cf. also Ibn Sa'd, op. cit., I, 216. In the course of time, Abū Lahab's name was included in the list of those Qurashīs who plotted to kill the prophet before the Hijra. See Ibn Sa'd, op. cit., I, 228. In Ibn Hishām, II, 125, his name is still absent from that list. Similarly, later sources (Ibn Shahrāshūb, I, 66–7, cf. Ibn Sayyid al-Nās, I, 113) include his name in the list of the *mustahzi'ūn*, from which his name is still absent in the earlier sources (e.g. Ibn Hishām, II, 50–1; al-Ṭabarī, *Tafsīr*, XIV, 48–9. See also al-Bayhaqī, op. cit., II, 85–6; al-Suyūṭī, op. cit., I, 365; Ibn al-Jawzī, op. cit., I, 329–30; al-Khargūshī, op. cit., MS Tübingen M.a. VI, 12, folios 44b–45a). It is also worthy of note that in later sources Abū Lahab is said to have performed deeds which were ascribed originally to Abū Jahl (of Makhzūm), probably due to the likeness of the names. In the earlier sources it is related that Abū Jahl plotted to kill Muḥammad with a stone, while the latter was absorbed in prayer (Ibn Hishām, op. cit., I, 319–20; see also al-Bayhaqī, op. cit., I, 438–40; al-Suyūṭī, op. cit., I, 315–16, 320–1; Ibn al-Jawzī, op. cit., I, 327; al-Khargūshī, op. cit. (BM), fol. 114b; Wensinck, *A handbook of early Muhammadan tradition*, 7, and also the commentaries on Sūra CXVI). In later sources the same story is transferred from Abū Jahl to Abū Lahab. See Ibn Shahrāshūb, op. cit., I, 68–9.

[52] Finally Abū Lahab has become the archetype of Muḥammad's enemies, whom all the Muslims are urged to curse. Ibn Kathīr (*Bidāya*, III, 41) informs us that Sūra CXI was recited on the *minbars* being included in the exhortations and the Friday sermons. And see further Fischer, op. cit., *passim*, Lohmann, art. cit., 339, 331–2. It is interesting to observe, however, that certain circles (probably of the Shī'a) produced several traditions to the effect that Muḥammad had forbidden the Muslims to curse the members of his own family. This had been done after Abū Lahab's daughter had complained to the prophet of being insulted by the Muslims for being the offspring of the 'fire-wood of hell' (*ibnat ḥaṭab al-nār*). According to some traditions the prophet announced on that occasion that his intercession (*shafā'a*) would save all his blood relations at the Last Judgement. See al-'Asqalānī, *Iṣāba*, VII, 634 ff.; al-Khargūshī, op. cit. (Tübingen), 18b, (BM) 50b–51a; al-Zurqānī, op. cit., I, 185–6; Ibn Ḥajar al-Haytamī, *al-Ṣawā'iq al-muḥriqa*, Cairo, 1965, 172.

22

comparison with Qur'ān XXII, 10, is unjustified, since *yadāka* there and elsewhere in the Qur'ān, has its own independent meaning, being used in a figurative sense, in connexion with the performance of deeds (*qaddamat*).[53]

4. *Verse 2: mā aghnā ʿanhu māluhu wa-mā kasaba*

The crucial phrase in verse 2 is *wa-mā kasaba*. Barth translated: '. . . und was er erworben hat'. Fischer (p. 25) and Lohmann (p. 326) followed suit. The truth is, however, that the verb *kasaba* in the Qur'ān does not usually denote 'to gain' or 'to earn', but rather 'to act' or 'to perform deeds of some importance'. Although this metaphorical usage of the verb *kasaba* has been pointed out by Western scholars,[54] it has not yet been noticed that *kasaba* has the same meaning in our sūra as well. The phrase *wa-mā kasaba* refers to Abū Lahab's grand deeds, namely his service to al-ʿUzzā and his protection of Muḥammad. These were the works that did credit to him and provided him with the 'hands' mentioned in the previous verse.

This true meaning of *wa-mā kasaba* was preserved for us in one tradition only. This tradition is recorded on the authority of Qatāda, the same Qatāda whose interpretation of verse 1 also preserved some of its original meaning (see above). The tradition of Qatāda is recorded by al-Zamakhsharī. It says: '(*mā kasaba* means) his deeds which he believed were of some benefit to him. It is like (Allāh) said (Qur'ān XXV, 23): "and we turned to the deeds they had performed . . ." (*ʿamaluhu 'llādhī ẓanna annahu minhu ʿalā shay'in ka-qawlihi: wa-qadimnā ilā mā ʿamilū min ʿamalin*)'. The *ʿamal* of Qur'ān XXV, 23, which, according to Qatāda, resembles the *ʿamal* of Abū Lahab, consists indeed in grand works which are proclaimed worthless by the Qur'ān because of the disbelief of those who carried them out.[55]

In close association with the grand works of Abū Lahab, the Qur'ān also mentions his wealth (*māluhu*). In this context *māluhu* must be taken as referring to the fortune Abū Lahab spent to perform his grand works of aid and support. *Māl* consisted mainly of camels and sheep, and Abū Lahab indeed used to bestow camels upon the needy, among them the above-mentioned Hudhayfa b. Ghānim.[56] Abū Lahab's *māl* was probably spent also for the sake of al-ʿUzzā. That *māl* was indeed used for such religious purposes, is indicated by a passage in al-Azraqī's *Akhbār Makka*.[57] Khālid b. al-Walīd, it is related, once told Muḥammad that his father used to offer up his best wealth (*bi-khayri mālihi*) to al-ʿUzzā.

The main idea of verse 2 is that neither the wealth Abū Lahab had spent, nor the grand works he had performed could prevent the ultimate loss of the 'hands' he hoped to preserve to his credit with both al-ʿUzzā and Muḥammad.

[53] Fischer also believes that *yadā* is a synecdoche, hence, *yadā Abī Lahabin* denotes: *Abū Lahab*. But this explanation is obviously wrong, as it does not explain why the Qur'ān speaks both of the hands of Abū Lahab (*tabbat*) and of Abū Lahab himself (*wa-tabba*). This repetition can be intelligible only if a clear distinction between the 'hands' of Abū Lahab and the person himself is assumed.

[54] Paret, op. cit., 22; Bravmann, op. cit., 107 ff.

[55] cf. al-Ṭabarī, *Tafsīr*, XIX, 3. Commenting on Qur'ān XXV, 23, al-Zamakhsharī says that the works of the unbelievers were such as doing good to the kindred, helping the suffering, entertaining guests, redeeming prisoners, and other such noble and good deeds (*wa-aʿmāluhum 'llatī ʿamilūhā fī kufrihim min ṣilati raḥimin wa-ighāthati malhūfin wa-qirā ḍayfin wa-mannin ʿalā asīrin wa-ghayri dhālika min makārimihim wa-maḥāsinihim*). And see further Qur'ān XIV, 18, where the *ʿamal* of the unbelievers is mentioned in connexion with their *kasb*: *mathalu 'lladhīna kafarū bi-rabbihim aʿmāluhum ka-ramādin ishtaddat bihi 'l-rīḥu fī yawmin ʿāṣifin lā yaqdirūna mimmā kasabū ʿalā shay'in*.

[56] Ibn Hishām, op. cit., I, 185, l. 12. As an owner of a large number of camels, Abū Lahab was able to practise *qimār*; see *Aghānī*, Būlāq, repr. Beirut, 1970, III, 100, IV, 19.

[57] I, 81.

This idea is conveyed by the phrase *mā aghnā ʿanhu*. Al-Bayḍāwī explains: *nafyun li-ighnā'i 'l-māli ʿanhu ḥīna nazala bihi 'l-tabābu* 'Negation of the benefit of his wealth when the loss (of his hands) was inflicted upon him'.

It is important to remark that with much the same words the Qur'ān denies elsewhere the benefit of the grand works of the ancient people of Thamūd who had erected monuments of stone for their protection, which, however, were soon destroyed. Qur'ān XV, 84 reads: *fa-mā aghnā ʿanhum mā kānū yaksibūna*. And see also XXXIX, 50; XL, 82.

Finally, verse 2 may be thus translated: 'the fortune (that he had spent) and the grand works that he had performed did not help him (to preserve his hands).'

5. *Other interpretations of verse 2*

The same reasons as caused the above-mentioned changes in the meaning of verse 1 have produced like changes in the meaning of verse 2. Like *yadā Abī Lahabin*, the phrase *wa-mā kasaba* was soon presented as denoting Abū Lahab's hostile actions against the prophet. Al-Ḍaḥḥāk (d. 105/723),[58] as quoted by al-Zamakhsharī, says that the phrase *wa-mā kasaba* means Abū Lahab's 'evil deeds i.e. his conspiracy against the messenger of Allāh (*wa-ʿamaluhu 'l-khabīthu yaʿnī kaydahu fī ʿadāwati rasūl allāh*)'. The interpretation of al-Ḍaḥḥāk perceives the phrase *wa-mā kasaba* in the meaning of *ʿamal al-khabīth*, which expression, like *kasb al-khabīth*, was quite common in pre-Islamic poetry.[59]

This interpretation soon adjusted itself to the eschatological meaning which became dominant in all the further interpretations of verse 2. *Wa-mā kasaba*, in the meaning of *kasb al-khabīth*, was associated with Abū Lahab's children, on grounds of some Qur'ānic passages containing the idea that at the Last Judgement neither wealth (*māl*) nor children (*awlād*) would save the unbelievers from hell (e.g. III, 10, 116; LVIII, 17). No less than five traditions putting forth this meaning of *wa-mā kasaba* are recorded by al-Ṭabarī. The most detailed one is recorded on the authority of Maʿmar b. Rāshid (d. 154/770).[60] This tradition relates that Abū Lahab's two sons once quarrelled with each other while at Ibn ʿAbbās's home. On trying to stop them, Ibn ʿAbbās was pushed by them on to his bed. Then he ordered that Abū Lahab's evil *kasb* be sent out of his house (*akhrijū ʿannī 'l-kasba 'l-khabītha*). In short, this tradition ascribes to Ibn ʿAbbās the interpretation that the phrase *wa-mā kasaba* stands for Abū Lahab's children.[61]

The same interpretation of *wa-mā kasaba* is widely current in later commentaries. Al-Ṭabarsī furnishes us with the following explanation: 'it means his sons because the sons of a man are part of his earnings (*kasb*). They were mentioned because Abū Lahab had said: "if what Muḥammad says about hell is true, I shall redeem myself (from hell) by means of my wealth and my sons"'. Al-Zamakhsharī adds a *ḥadīth* ascribing to the prophet the following statement: 'the best food that man eats is that which comes from his earnings (*kasb*); his children are part of his earnings'.[62]

[58] Sezgin, *GAS*, I, 29.

[59] Bravmann, op. cit., 110 ff.

[60] Sezgin, *GAS*, I, 290.

[61] See also al-Ṭabarī, *Tafsīr*, XXV, 86, where *mā kasabū* is explained as *māl wa-wuld*. In other cases, however, al-Ṭabarī did not refrain from explaining *kasaba* in the sense of *ʿamila*. See e.g. XIV, 34; XXIV, 9, 57.

[62] See also al-Nabhānī, *al-Fath al-kabīr*, Cairo, n.d., I, 292 (from al-Bukhārī's *Tārīkh*, al-Tirmidhī, al-Nasā'ī, and Ibn Māja). Cf. al-Sulamī, *ʿUyūb al-nafs*, ed. E. Kohlberg, Jerusalem, 1976, 101.

24

With the accommodation of verse 2 to the eschatological meaning, the expression *mā-aghnā ʿanhu* was no longer conceived as past tense but rather as referring to Abū Lahab's future punishment in hell. Al-Ṭabarsī interprets: 'neither his wealth nor his *kasb* helped him against Allāh's punishment (*ay mā nafaʿahu wa-lā dafaʿa ʿanhu ʿadhāba 'llāhi māluhu wa-mā kasabahu*'. Al-Ṭabarī regards *mā aghnā* as an interrogation denoting the question: 'what was the benefit of his wealth and to what extent did it protect him from Allāh's anger?'. It is interesting to observe, however, that elsewhere in the Qur'ān, al-Ṭabarī usually interprets *mā aghnā* as an ordinary past tense, denoting *lam yughni*.[63] In our sūra the eschatological point of view caused him to deviate from his usual manner of interpretation.[64]

6. *The miraculous aspects of the sūra*

The sons of Abū Lahab played a special role in Muḥammad's life. According to Ibn Qutayba,[65] Muḥammad's daughter Ruqayya had been married to Abū Lahab's son ʿUtba, but by order of his father he broke off the marriage. Muḥammad's daughter Umm Kulthūm had been married to Abū Lahab's son ʿUtayba, and he also was ordered by his father to do the same. According to Ibn Saʿd, this conduct on the part of Abū Lahab was caused by the revelation of our sūra.[66]

One of Abū Lahab's sons paid a heavy price for thus insulting the prophet. A legendary tradition relates that Muḥammad invoked Allāh to make Abū Lahab's son be killed by a predatory animal. Before long, this son was mauled by a lion.[67] Earlier versions of this story relate, however, that Abū Lahab's son suffered this fate because he had announced his rejection of Sūra LIII.[68] The connexion with Sūra LIII is not surprising, as this is the very sūra which abrogates the 'Satanic verses'. It is a further indication that Abū Lahab and his family took much interest in securing the worship of al-ʿUzzā.

The legendary story of the end of Abū Lahab's son finally found its way into the commentaries on Sūra CXI. Al-Bayḍāwī labels this sūra as *ikhbār ʿan al-ghayb*, thus associating it with a long series of miraculous stories about Muḥammad's outstanding powers to forecast the future, which are to be found in almost every book dealing with Muḥammad's prophet signs (*dalāʾil al-nubuwwa*).[69] Al-Bayḍāwī explains that the sūra foretells the end of Abū

[63] Al-Ṭabarī, *Tafsīr*, VIII, 142 (on Qur'ān VII, 48); XXIX, 40 (on LXIX, 28); XIV, 34 (on XV, 84); XXIV, 9 (on XXXIX, 50); XXVI, 18 (on XLVI, 26); XII, 68 (on XI, 101).

[64] In two more cases al-Ṭabarī has interpreted *mā kasaba* as an interrogation and not as past tense, due to interrogative pronouns found in the Qur'ānic text. See ibid., XXIV, 57 (on Qur'ān XL, 82), XIX, 71 (on XXVI, 207).

[65] *Kitāb al-maʿārif*, ed. al-Ṣāwī, Beirut, 1970, 62.

[66] Ibn Saʿd, op. cit., VIII, 36, 37. According to another source (*Aghānī*, XV, 2) it was the wife of Abū Lahab who ordered the breaking off of the marriage.

[67] Al-Suhaylī, op. cit., III, 68; al-Bayhaqī, op. cit., II, 96–7. See also al-Khargūshī, op. cit. (Tübingen), fol. 87b, (BM) fol. 124b. Another source says that Abū Lahab's son was killed by the lion because of his being one of the *mustahziʾūn* (p. 21, n. 51, above); see al-Ṭabarī, *al-Dīn wa 'l-dawla fī ithbāt nubuwwat al-Nabī Muḥammad*, ed. ʿĀdil Nuwayhiḍ, Beirut, 1973, 67. A distinction must be made between the son that was killed by a lion and the other two sons of Abū Lahab who survived their father and embraced Islam after the conquest of Mecca. The Muslim traditionists are a little puzzled as to what the exact name of each of the sons was, as their names were quite similar: ʿUtba, ʿUtayba, and Muʿattib. See al-Suhaylī, loc. cit. Sometimes the sources mention a son named Lahab, obviously a secondary derivation from the father's nickname. See *al-Dīn wa 'l-dawla*, loc. cit.; al-Naysābūrī, *Mustadrak*, II, 539; al-Bayhaqī, op. cit., II, 96.

[68] Al-Ṭabarī, *Tafsīr*, XXVII, 24; see also al-Suyūṭī, op. cit., I, 367–9; Ibn Shahrāshūb, op. cit., I, 71. Cf. *Aghānī*, XIII, 153.

[69] See e.g. *al-Dīn wa 'l-dawla*, 76 ff.; al-Suyūṭī, op. cit., II, 372 ff., III, 3 ff.; Ibn al-Jawzī, op. cit., 305 ff.; Ibn Kathīr, *Bidāya*, VI, 182 ff.

Lahab's son, to whom the expression *wa-mā kasaba* refers. In the same context, Bayḍāwī also relates the story of the end of Abū Lahab himself, who died shortly after Badr,[70] as though the sūra predicts his own death as well. Thus the sūra obtained its miraculous nature, and in some cases, as in the *Mustadrak* of al-Ḥākim,[71] a version of the story about the son of Abū Lahab [72] is given predominance over other traditions.

The miraculous features of our sūra as viewed by Muslim scholars are illustrated to the full in a passage in Ibn Kathīr's commentary: 'The learned men say that there is an evident miracle in our sūra and a clear proof of the prophecy, because since the revelation of the verses in which the misfortune and disbelief of Abū Lahab and his wife were foretold, they have not been led to embrace Islam, neither secretly nor openly. Thus it was the strongest of all the dazzling hidden proofs of the visible prophecy'.

7. *Verse 4: wa-'mra'atuhu ḥammālata 'l-ḥaṭabi*

Verse 4 runs as follows: 'And his wife (shall also burn); She is a fire-wood carrier'.[73]

This verse deals with the wife of Abū Lahab who, being the sister of Abū Sufyān, belonged to the highest rank of Meccan society. The original significance of the appelation *ḥammālat al-ḥaṭab* given to her in the Qur'ān was again preserved for us by Qatāda. His interpretation as quoted by al-Rāzī, reads: 'She (i.e. the wife of Abū Lahab) used to condemn the prophet for being poor, therefore she was condemned for being a wood gatherer (*qawlu qatādata: innahā kānat tu'ayyiru rasūla 'llāhi bi 'l-faqri fa-'uyyirat bi-annahā kānat taḥtaṭibu*)'. A more complete version of the same interpretation is recorded by al-Ṭabarī, without, however, mentioning its source: 'Some say: "she used to condemn the prophet for being poor, *herself being in the habit of gathering wood*, therefore she was condemned for being a wood gatherer" (*wa-qāla ba'ḍu-hum: wa-kānat tu'ayyiru rasūla 'llāhi bi-l-faqri wa-kānat taḥṭibu fa-'uyyirat bi-annahā kānat taḥṭibu*)'.[74]

Qatāda's interpretation implies that the wife of Abū Lahab used to perform such works as were connected with the gathering of fire-wood, which occupation gave the Qur'ān an opportunity for dishonouring her. It must be remembered that wood gathering was regarded as one of the most despicable works, carried out by women of the lowest rank.[75] The question arises, how did it come about that a woman of the rank of Abū Lahab's wife did such work. The explanation (al-Ālūsī, 263) that she was too miserly to employ servants to do the work for her, seems to be over-simplified.

The real solution is to be found in Wellhausen's *Reste arabischen Heidentums.* On pp. 40–1 Wellhausen quotes a passage from Isaak of Antioch (fifth century A.D.) about the ways in which the Arabs used to worship al-'Uzzā. Isaak identifies al-'Uzzā with *Kawkabta*, i.e. Venus who was also named 'the queen of heaven'. Isaak compares the Arab worship of al-'Uzzā with the Jewish

[70] Concerning his death, see al-Ṭabarī, *Tārīkh*, II, 159–60 (from Ibn Isḥāq); Ibn Sa'd, op. cit., IV, 73–4; al-Suhaylī, op. cit., III, 66 ff.; Ibn Sayyid al-Nās, op. cit., I, 267 ff.; *Aghānī*, IV, 32–3.

[71] *Mustadrak*, II, 539.

[72] See the same version also in al-Bayhaqī, op. cit., II, 96; Ibn al-Jawzī, op. cit., I, 348.

[73] This translation is based on the reading *ḥammālata 'l-ḥaṭabi*, which signifies *dhamm*, and not on *ḥammālatu 'l-ḥaṭabi*. For further details see the commentaries.

[74] Fischer, op. cit., 34, quoted Qatāda's interpretation from al-Rāzī, without noticing its complete version in al-Ṭabarī. Therefore he seems to have misunderstood its significance. See below, p. 27, n. 77.

[75] Fischer, op. cit., 35 ff.; Lohmann, art. cit., 344.

26

worship of the ' queen of heaven ' as described in Jeremiah vii, 18. The passage in Jeremiah seems to be most instructive: ' The children gather wood, and the fathers kindle the fire, and the women knead their dough to make cakes to the queen of heaven . . .'. Wellhausen finds evidence that the Arab customs of the worship of al-'Uzzā indeed resembled Jeremiah's description. This may well lead us to believe that the appelation *ḥammālat al-ḥaṭab* refers to the active part Abū Lahab's wife took in the worship of al-'Uzzā. Unlike Jeremiah, the Qur'ān assigns the task of gathering the fire-wood not to Abū Lahab's children, but rather to his wife, thus exposing the despicable nature of the works this aristocratic woman used to carry out in honour of al-'Uzzā, together with her whole family.

At this stage a more coherent understanding of the significance of the surname ' Abū Lahab ' is possible. Perhaps it does not so much refer to the fire of hell in which he is doomed to burn, as to the fire he used to kindle when worshipping al-'Uzzā. This observation produces a significant correlation between his surname ' Abū Lahab ' and his personal name, 'Abd al-'Uzzā.

8. *Other interpretations of verse 4*

The secondary interpretations of verse 4 are based on patterns similar to those of the secondary interpretations of the previous verses of our sūra. The appelation *ḥammālat al-ḥaṭab* gained a new meaning, more appropriate to the wife of a person who was believed to have been Muḥammad's enemy. The original meaning of this appelation, denoting religious action for the sake of al-'Uzzā, was totally neglected.

The following tradition seems to mark the first step towards the new understanding of *ḥammālat al-ḥaṭab*, presenting it as referring to hostile actions Abū Lahab's wife allegedly carried out against the prophet. This tradition, recorded by al-Ṭabarī, is also traced back to Qatāda: *kānat tanqulu 'l-aḥādītha min ba'ḍi 'l-nāsi ilā ba'ḍin* ' She used to pass on rumours from one person to another '. *Ḥammālat al-ḥaṭab* is understood here in its metaphorical sense, i.e. ' the rumours carrier ', or rather ' the slanderer '. The same interpretation, in much more explicit words (*kānat tamshī bi 'l-namīma*) is recorded by al-Ṭabarī on the authority of Mujāhid (d. 104/722) and 'Ikrima (d. 105/723).

Far more elaborate are the traditions which no longer conceive of *ḥaṭab* as fire-wood—neither concretely nor metaphorically—but rather as a bundle of thorns (*ḥuzmat shawk*), which the woman allegedly used to throw in Muḥammad's way, thus wounding his feet. This interpretation of *ḥammālat al-ḥaṭab* was preferred by al-Ṭabarī, who has recorded several traditions of this kind, tracing them back to Ibn 'Abbās, al-Ḍaḥḥāk, Ibn Zayd, and others.[76]

Al-Zamakhsharī explains that the action of throwing the bundle of thorns was described by the Qur'ān as the gathering of fire-wood in order to expose its inferior nature (. . . *wa-taṣwīran lahā bi-ṣūrati ba'ḍi 'l-ḥaṭṭābāti min al-mawāhini*). In other words, al-Zamakhsharī holds that *ḥaṭab* really denotes fire-wood but only in a figurative sense, symbolizing the bundle of thorns. Al-Bayḍāwī

[76] See also Ibn Hishām, op. cit., I, 380. A similar action, namely the throwing of offal in front of Muḥammad's door, is ascribed to Abū Lahab and 'Uqba b. Abī Mu'ayyiṭ. See Ibn Sa'd, op. cit., I, 201. It may be further remarked that in some later traditions Abū Lahab's wife is even presented as taking an active part in the plots of Quraysh to kill the prophet. The person who allegedly defended the prophet against this woman was no other than Abū Lahab himself. See al-Katikānī, *Tahsīr al-burhān*, on our sūra (reference from M. J. Kister). This tradition seems to express the anti-Umayyad feelings of the Shī'a.

explains likewise (*taṣwīran lahā bi-ṣūrati 'l-ḥaṭṭābati 'llatī taḥmilu 'l-ḥuzmata wa-tarbiṭuhā fī jīdihā taḥqīran li-sha'nihā*).[77]

Like the former verses of our sūra, verse 4 was finally interpreted in the eschatological sense. The wood gathering was presented as the woman's punishment in hell for her worldly sins against Muḥammad. Interpretations to this effect are given by al-Zamakhsharī and al-Bayḍāwī. They interpret *ḥaṭab* as signifying the trees and thorns of hell, i.e. the *Zaqqūm* and *Ḍarī'* (Qur'ān XLIV, 43; LXXXVIII, 6).

9. *Verse 5: fī jīdihā ḥablun min masadin*

Verse 5 may be thus translated: 'On her neck there is a cord made of fibres'.

The word *jīd* usually denotes a woman's neck from the aesthetic viewpoint, i.e. the place on which ornaments and the like are hanging.[78] Therefore, Qatāda's interpretation of this verse seems, once again, to be faithful to its original meaning. His interpretation is recorded by al-Ṭabarī. It says that *ḥablun min masadin* stands for *qilāda min wad'in*—'a necklace made of sea-shells'.[79] According to al-Ḥasan al-Baṣrī (d. 110/728) as quoted by Abū Ḥayyān, the necklace was made of *kharz*, which is the same as *wad'*.

Abū Ḥayyān also quotes the explanation of Ibn 'Aṭiyya [80] to the effect that the necklace was described by the Qur'ān as a cord of fibres in order to reproach the woman and to stress how detestable it was to use it (*wa-innamā 'abbara 'an qilādatihā bi-ḥablin min masadin 'alā jihati 'l-tafā'uli lahā wa-dhikri tabarrujihā fī hādhā 'l-sa'yi 'l-khabīthi*).

The reason for the Qur'ān's disapproval of the woman's necklace becomes clear in the light of Wellhausen's survey of old Arab practices of magic and witchcraft.[81] Wellhausen [82] mentions that magic powers were attributed to all kinds of ornaments and especially to sea-shells, viz. *kharz*, *wad'*, or *jaz'*. Hence it is clear that the Qur'ān disapproves of the woman's necklace because of its magical intentions. It was probably regarded by its owner as securing the protection of al-'Uzzā against evil powers. The usage of such a necklace was reproached by the Qur'ān as a part of its general rejection of witchcraft,[83] which was considered in Islam the core of Paganism.[84] The Qur'ān brings this magical necklace down to the rank of an ordinary simple cord (*ḥabl*) made of rough fibres (*min masadin*).

The correlation between verses 4 and 5 is now obvious: both verses reprove the Pagan practices carried out by the wife of Abū Lahab who participated with her husband in the veneration of al-'Uzzā. The Qur'ān views these practices as common, despicable actions suitable for women of the lowest rank.

[77] Fischer, op. cit., 35, holds that *ḥammālat 'l-ḥaṭab* is a mere curse directed to that aristocratic woman in order to humiliate her by alleging her to be a wood-carrier. He (p. 34) believes he finds this meaning in the interpretations of Qatāda and al-Bayḍāwī. But neither seems to support his view, as they both assume that *ḥammālat al-ḥaṭab* stands for a real action carried out by the woman, be it gathering of fire-wood (Qatāda) or of thorns (al-Bayḍāwī). Strangely enough, Fischer (p. 32) places al-Zamakhsharī's interpretation in a separate group, notwithstanding its resemblance to al-Bayḍāwī's interpretation, which is actually an abstract of the former.

[78] Al-Suhaylī, op. cit., II, 113.

[79] Fischer has totally ignored this outstanding interpretation.

[80] D. 542/1147. See Brockelmann, *GAL*, Supp. I, 732.

[81] *Reste*, 159 ff.

[82] ibid., 165.

[83] See Qur'ān CXIII, 4.

[84] Wensinck, op. cit., s.v. 'magic'.

10. *Other interpretations of verse 5*

The tendency to confine the meaning of our sūra to the hostility of Abū Lahab and his wife towards the prophet gave rise to new interpretations of *ḥablun min masadin* as well. A tradition traced back to Sa'īd b. al-Musayyab (d. 94/713) says: 'She (i.e. Abū Lahab's wife) had a luxurious necklace of pearls, and she said: "I shall disburse it for the assault on Muḥammad" (*kānat lahā qilāda fākhira min jawhar fa-qālat: la-unfiqannahā fī adāwat Muḥammad*)'. This tradition is recorded by al-Ṭabarsī, Abū Ḥayyān, and Ibn Kathīr.

Another interpretation seems to be based simply on an erroneous understanding of the context of our verse. The cord was quite naturally associated with the fire-wood of the former verse, as though being used for tying and carrying it. Its original figurative sense was eventually neglected. Thus, al-Ḍaḥḥāk, as quoted by al-Ṭabarī, interprets: '... this was the cord which she used for gathering the fire-wood'.[85] This interpretation is, however, impossible; as was already mentioned, the word *jīdihā* indicates clearly that *ḥablun* does not stand for a load with which the woman's neck is burdened, but rather for a certain kind of ornament hanging on her neck, having no relation to the fire-wood of the former verse. Whenever the Qur'ān speaks of carrying loads the word used is not *jīd* but rather *'unuq*.[86]

The most current interpretation of *ḥablun min masadin* is again the eschatological one. Although not assuming any connexion between the cord and the wood, it nevertheless considers our verse as speaking of a heavy load which the woman shall carry in hell as a punishment for her worldly sins. The *jīd* is understood in the meaning of *raqaba*, namely a neck carrying a burden, while the cord is conceived of as the load itself. The whole scene is inspired by Qur'ān LXIX, 32 which speaks of a 'chain whose length is seventy cubits (*silsila dhar'uhā sab'ūna dhirā'an*)', which is used in hell for torturing sinners. Thereby *masad* is understood as denoting 'iron'. This word, originally denoting the rope of the well, gained the meaning of 'iron' because it occurs in old poetry in close association with the iron axis of the pulley of the well, around which the rope is coiled.[87]

Most of the eschatological traditions of this kind, as recorded by al-Ṭabarī, are traced back to 'Urwa b. al-Zubayr (d. 94/713). These traditions relate that *ḥablun min masadin* stands for 'an iron chain whose length is seventy cubits'. A tradition on the authority of Sufyān says that it stands for 'a rope on her neck, in hell, like a collar, seventy cubits long'. The original significance of *masad* being the rope of the bucket, is preserved in a further eschatological tradition recorded by al-Suhaylī.[88] It says: 'she will be handled in hell like a bucket. She will be lifted to the top of hell by the rope on her neck, then downwards to its bottom again, and so on for ever and ever'. As an integral part of hell, the *ḥabl* is sometimes depicted as though made of fire (al-Ṭabarī). Summing up, al-Ṭabarsī interprets *masad* as a cord of rough fibres, burning like fire, heavy like iron, with which her neck is burdened to increase her torture.

Thus, the eschatological spirit finally overwhelmed all the parts of our sūra.

[85] See also Fischer, op. cit., 35, 42; Lohmann, art. cit., 346; Künstlinger, art. cit., 408.
[86] e.g. XVII, 29; XXXIV, 33; etc.
[87] e.g. al-Suhaylī, op. cit., II, 111 ff.
[88] II, 111.

17

SIMPLE NEGATIVE REMARKS ON THE VOCABULARY OF THE QUR'ĀN

Robert Brunschvig

From the Middle Ages to our day the vocabulary of the Qur'ān has been the object of two main kinds of studies: determining the exact meaning of the words on the one hand and detecting loans from languages other than Arabic on the other.[1] This twofold research does not exhaust the subject matter; not at all. Portions of Qur'ānic vocabulary have been methodically examined in various ways, with varying luck, by contemporary scholars.[2] However, there remains much, on more than one aspect, which needs to be looked at once again, and without doubt also to be initiated. I would like to suggest briefly a way of approaching the problem which might seem paradoxical but which, it is hoped, will be fruitful: the *negative* way, i.e. stating not what is but rather that which *is not* in the Qur'ān. Every negative method has its dangers, but this is not a sufficient reason to renounce it forever. Once the difficulties and traps have been located and determined as clearly as possible, areas sufficiently large to justify continuing the investigation remain.

As we are dealing with the Qur'ān, it is the 'Uthmānic vulgate [20] which will be used as the fundamental text. However, we must ask ourselves whether recorded variants outside that vulgate might not modify useful facts as well as the conclusions to be drawn from them. After a summary search, which would have to be taken up again in more detail for a more thorough research, it appears that such a study would be in vain for this stage of first considerations: non-'Uthmānic variants which have come down to us are, from the point of view of vocabulary, of only minor importance. A chronological approach, taking into account the successive dates (whether certain or probable) of the verses of the Book, would be more successful. In the present study, however, a chronological approach is redundant since the text of the Qur'ān as a whole is the

---

[1] In our time especially Jeffery, *The Foreign Vocabulary of the Qur'ân*, Baroda, 1938

[2] Notably Torrey, *The Commercial-theological Terms in the Koran*, Leyden, 1892; Talaat, *Die Seelenlehre des Korans (mit besonderer Berücksichtigung der Terminologie)*, Halle, 1929; Sister, *Metaphern und Vergleiche im Koran*, Berlin, 1931; Sabbagh, *La Métaphore dans le Coran*, Paris, 1943.

2

subject of a negative examination, rather than as segments according to the time of their revelation.

A negative examination in relation to what, seeing as there are no prose writings from the same period?[3] And what would be the value of negative observations on a document whose scope and variety, however remarkable, can only tread limited dimensions? A point of reference might be ancient Arabic poetry with all the uncertainties related to it as well as the added disadvantage inherent in its being poetry. In these pages we will almost always refer to classical Arabic prose, what there is of it, which is reliably recorded from the second and third centuries AH onwards: a gap in time and also in space. Of course, such a comparison also involves other problems and is situated in a different area. Furthermore, the evidence is such that the vocabulary of one single book, however rich, could not be compared with that of a whole language which is used in a wide variety of fields. Stating a deficiency usually is or becomes significant only if used with complementary pieces of evidence. The first of these is that general or specific subjects dealt with in the Book surprise us by not using this or that term which is habitually used in the language dealing with that subject. [21] One could raise an objection to this method, which will apply to all arguments *e silentio*, and which, in the present case, will make the comparatively high number of unique occurrences all the more sensitive. Such unique occurrences exist within the Qur'ān as well as in relation to it: the difference is slight, between one and zero, and one can appreciate the subtlety of the criterion which, situated on the margin of a unit, causes the passage from being to nothingness. The best way to parry this menacing attack is to lay the emphasis on prudence, to make observations only on those words of the literary language which are used most widely and, in addition, not to assign any value to their absence from the Qur'ān unless very serious presumptions, in the absence of certainty, lead us to dismiss the hypothesis of coincidence.

To begin with we will approach phenomenon which, while properly a matter for morphology, is also part of the lexicon to a certain extent. The diminutive is alive in the Arabic language at all times and in every place, lovingly as well as disparagingly. Its basic classical form is *fu'ayl*, and ancient grammarians delight in long discourses on all the aspects which this scheme covers when applied to all possible nominal forms. Medieval and modern dialects have multiplied the number of morphological types

[3] On a strictly scientific level one could not consider the 'prophetic ḥadīths' as valid evidence regarding Arabic prose at the time of Muhammad.

used as diminutives, more exactly as hypocoristics,[4] by using suffixes from other languages than Arabic, if necessary.[5] The Qur'ān knows diminutives of the form *fu'ayl*, insofar as several proper nouns have to be considered as such: *Shu'ayb* (passim), *'Uzayr* (9:30), *Quraysh* (106:1), *Ḥunayn* (9:25), and without doubt one would be justified to count *Sulayman* (passim) with these. But where common nouns are concerned, the only example of the diminutive to be found is – and it appears that this remark has not been made until the present day – in the set phrase *ya bunayya*, which is the most common way of saying "O my son" in classical Arabic. In each of the six verses where it appears (11:42; 12:5; [22] 31:13, 16, 17; 37:102) it is put into the mouth of a patriarch or a prophet. Three chapters of the Proverbs of Solomon in the Bible already began with this "O my son" which has an almost ritual ring at the beginning of texts of wisdom.[6] How can it be explained that, with the exception of this one instance, the Qur'ān in all its forceful and fiery passages does not make use of diminutives, these terms *par excellence* of the language of emotion? Might it not be possible to risk the hypothesis that they were felt, whether indistinctly or clearly, to possess a certain vulgarity unworthy of the revealed word, or at least unacceptable in earnest prose? This would also emphasise the fact that a particularly elevated style was claimed by the Qur'ān from the very beginning.

But let us proceed to the vocabulary proper. In the first place, there are many words – besides particular loans from foreign languages – whose absence is to be explained by the social and cultural developments which took place between Qur'ānic and later times. Some examples among these should be emphasised because of their particular importance and because their absence is rather unexpected. *Amīr* and *qā'id*, military leaders of organised armies, are cases in point (the root *q w d* is completely missing), as is *adab*[7] (the root *' d b* is completely missing). Later *adab* will be used to express a complex and frequently occurring notion, which will develop from "knowledge of the world" to "Humanities". The Qur'ān does not express the notion of "time" by means of the most current classical term *zamān* (variant: *zaman*), even though for "place" the banal *makān* is used frequently. Later, *makān* and *zamān* will form

[4] Littmann, *Arabische Hypokoristika, in Studia Orientalia I. Pedersen ... dicata,* Copenhagen, 1953, pp. 193–9

[5] See especially Nöldeke, in his *Persische Studien, I (Sitzungsberichte d. k. Akademie der Wissenschaften*, Vienna, vol. CXIV, 1888); García Gómez, *Hipocoristicos árabes y patronimicos hispánicos,* in *Arabica*, 1954, pp. 131–5.

[6] Horovitz, *Koranische Untersuchungen*, Berlin-Leipzig, 1926, p.135

[7] It has been suggested that *adab* and denominatives derived from it could be explained as originating with the plural of *da'b* (cf. EI[2], I, p. 180) a term which is used in the language of the Qur'ān.

4

a common locution together. To express a "moment" of time the common terms *ḥīn*, *ān*, *waqt* are used; for "hour" there is *sāʿa*; for "duration" in time, *amad* or *mudda* and for the "passage of time fate", *dahr*.[8] [23] Do we have to assume that *zamān*, which is an old word in other Semitic languages, was not at home in the Arabic of old[9] and only acquired citizenship there when a more rational notion of "time" developed?

It would be helpful, as an annex or supplement to this sort of absence, to point out words which are found in the Qur'ān, but whose basic classical meaning definitely or probably did not exist at the time the Qur'ān was revealed. This is certainly the case for *qāḍī* in the sense of "*cadi*" [i.e., judge]. Must we not, in the domain of the law, add the verb *wajaba* = "to be obliged to; to be obligatory", whose absence would be well-nigh unthinkable in the classics, but which is still unknown to the Qur'ān? This is a remarkable fact, and there is only one instance (22:36) where there might be some doubt, although the verb is used in the etymological sense of "to fall, crumble".[10] Also, what idea could turn out to be more indispensable to the Book than that of obligation and duty, which, indeed, is expressed in various ways? It might also be that the words denoting "kind" and especially "species", which will be dealt with later, should be added to the present category from the point of view of semantic development.

However, the essential point of the negative evidence which will be set up here is supported by vocabulary whose early use and meaning is not called into question by any historical or philological evidence. Let us explore this. We will take, randomly, one consonant of the alphabet: *n*. Among the roots which occur most frequently in the classical language – and we do not need any statistics to prove this – there are easily thirty, all beginning with *n*, which are not used in the Qur'ān, even though one would be perfectly justified in expecting to find them there:
[24]

n b gh – to burst forth, to excel
n b l – flash; merit
n b h – alertness, attention
n t j – to give birth, to produce
n t n – bad smell
n j b – nobility

[8] Neither *ʿasr* or *ʿahd*, which are found in the Qur'ān, are used in the sense of 'age, epoch'.

[9] My colleague and friend R. Blachère kindly assures me that the word is not, or barely, found in the ancient poetry.

[10] Compare semantically the French 'incomber; échoir' (to be incumbent on; to fail, run aground')

5

n j z – completion
n ḥ f – thinness, meagreness
n ḥ w – direction
n d b – invitation; lament for the dead
n d r – scarcity
n z h – abstention; charm, pleasantness
n s j – to weave
n s q – to tidy, to arrange·
n s m – breath
n sh d – entreaty, prophetic recitation
n ẓ m – to arrange
n ʻ sh – to relieve, to comfort
n q d – criticism; money
n q ṭ – point
n q l – to transfer
n q y – purity
n k y – to hurt, to injure
n m w (or *n m y*) – to grow, to increase
n h b – to pillage
n h d – to attack
n h z – to be close, to seize
n h ḍ – to stand (up)
n h l – to quench one's thirst
n w ṭ – to hang (up)
n w ʻ – species, kind
n w y – to tend to, to intend[11]

By deliberately saying "roots" rather than "words", we have multiplied the number of absences considerably. And we could easily extend the list, without any effort. It would be no problem to proceed in the same way for every initial consonant, i.e. for the whole lexicon. Is this not the proof that the Qur'ān only comprises a limited section of the most widely used classical vocabulary?

Now we have to ask ourselves whether there is a way of classifying and interpreting the facts. We cannot deny that with our present knowledge about the state of the language, and in particular of the obscure question of dialects, there are still many explanations which we either have not yet found or which would appear too daring. In many instances it would seem that we do not yet have the right to venture any further than a

[11] For these three last radicals there is, however, one single instance: *nawa'* – kernels, cores.

6

simple summary. However, our curiosity becomes even further piqued after observing the repeated use of certain terms whose common synonyms are [25] consistently lacking. The following examples should be noted: the Qur'ān uses *ḥūt* = "fish" several times, but never *samak(a)*;[12] we find, for "merchandise", *biḍāʿa* or *tijāra* (which also means "commerce"), but never *silʿa*; the notion of "usefulness" is expressed frequently by the root *nfʿ*, never by words of the root *fyd*; the idea of "justice, equity" is expressed several times by the roots *ʿdl* or *qsṭ*, but never by words of the root *nṣf*; for the notion of "changing, replacing" we find the root *bdl* very frequently, but never the root *ʿwḍ*. Are we dealing here with common phenomena which reflect the state of a language at a given time and in a given environment, or may we venture to believe that at least some among them are due to the Prophet, without having even the vaguest idea the reason why?

On the other hand, one might feel more at ease with the latter hypothesis if one were in a position to suspect that some of the words which, according to all probability, were widely used in ancient Arabia, are missing for reasons of style and of thought, the distinction between which is often subtle. In the concrete domain, it is perhaps at first the Prophet's mental vision which is our concern, but even from there, omissions in the language can be observed which are probably intended. Concerning certain notions with an ethical resonance, doubt dwindles and it is easy to admit that elimination from the lexicon corresponds to a conscious attitude which closely agrees with the new religion.

The evocation of nature is so frequent in a number of suras, so gripping and so colourful that an inventory of the arsenal of words describing the various aspects of nature appears at first to be very well stocked. There are indeed fields, such as the description of landscapes on earth, whose vocabulary is rich and varied, and where the absence of certain common terms is all the more surprising. These are obviously not absences like *thalj* = "snow", or [26] *ghāba* = "forest",[13] words which would surprise in Arabia. But is it not strange that the Qur'ān does not contain the name of the "sand", *raml* (once there is "a lot of sand", *kathīb* (53:14)?[14] And that, with just one exception: *badw* (12:100; in the Biblical story of Joseph), it does not give any of the common nouns for the "desert" which exist: *ṣaḥrāʾ*, *qafr*, *barriyya*, *mahmah*, *falāl*, *majhal*, *fayfāʾ* (*mafāza* is

[12] Landberg, *Glossaire Datînois*, p. 1100, has noted that 'ancient poetry in classical Arabic' commonly uses *ḥūt* and not *samak*.

[13] *ayka*, which appears four times in the text, always describes the 'shrubs' in the land of Madyan.

[14] Concerning the southern Arabic name *Aḥqāf* (46:21), which is traditionally translated as 'dunes' but really only means 'mountains', cf. EI^2, vol. I, p. 265.

7

used, but only in the sense of "refuge")? Maybe the hapax *qīʿa* (24:39), associated with *sarāb* = "mirage" can be interpreted in this sense. Is the search for a particular style responsible for this avoidance? It is difficult to find an explanation for it on the level of ideas.

On the contrary, it might be possible that a definite attitude of thought was responsible for some omissions which would be difficult to disregard. The Qur'ān has a vivid sense of the great phenomena of nature and emphasises repeatedly the succession of day and night, but does not attach itself to the change of the seasons: the words *sayf* "summer" and *shitā'* "winter" occur only once and then in connection with one another in one of the oldest suras (104:2), in the context of the Meccan caravan. No mention is made of either "autumn", *kharīf*, or, and this is much more amazing, the famous "spring", *rabīʿ*, of the desert and the steppes, which revives the pastures and fills man and beast with life. The exclusive importance which was given to the lunar cycles and the reform of the calendar in favour of a strictly lunar year (9:36) tally with this tendency to relegate phrases relating to the seasons to the shade. It would not be long until the famous markets of pre-Islamic Arabia suffered a similar fate. It may also be that a tendency to reject the favourite topics of secular poetry comes to light in this remarkable dismissal of the word *rabīʿ*. Such a tendency could easily motivate other omissions as well, for example, that of *badr* = "full moon" and of *anwā'* = "stars announcing rain". However, it is also not impossible to see in these two last [27] instances an implicit reprobation of rites and beliefs which should be eradicated.[15]

Let us now look at the human body, and then at the vegetable and animal kingdoms. Several very common nouns for body parts are missing. We hesitate to mention those whose absence might comfortably be ascribed to coincidence, such as *ḥajīb* – "eyebrow", *ṣudgh* = "temple", *warik* = "hip", *fakhdh* = "thigh". The "shoulder", *katf* or *ʿātiq* or *mankib*, is also missing; only the plural *manākib* appears in one verse (67:15) where it describes the vast expanse of the surface of the earth. It is more disturbing that the "liver", *kabid*, is never mentioned. In only one instance we find *kabad* (91:4), from the same root, with the figurative meaning "misery". The liver plays such a major role in ancient Semitic thought as well as in the traditional Arabic expression of ideas[16] that to find it missing causes substantial surprise. Here again the question of

---

[15] For *anwā'* see Pellat in *Arabica*, 1955, p. 30. Some hadiths and the *Lisān al-ʿArab*, I, 170, bottom, list Islam's condemnation of the belief in stars which bring rain.

[16] Mainly Merx, *Le rôle du foie dans la littérature des peuples sémitiques*, in *Florilegium...Melchior de Vogüé*, Paris, 1909, pp. 429–44 (this reference was kindly provided to me by Mr William Marçais).

8

style on the one hand and idea on the other poses itself, but again we cannot solve it. The reply would be easier concerning another basic term which does not appear in the Qur'ān either, namely the "date", *tamr*. Palm trees are evoked frequently, as is only to be expected in Arabia, with their trunks, their leaves, their wrapped flowers and their tops laden with fruit. The Book has words for "bunches of dates", *qinwān*; for "kernels", *nawā'*; also, for "the outer membrane of date kernels", *qiṭmīr*; or "hollow split" (in the palm tree trunk) *naqīr*; and "fibre of palm bark", *fatīl*, the three last ones with the figurative meaning of a minimal quantity. Dates as such, however, are only ever found as *ruṭāb*, "fresh (dates)" (19:25), or in the phrase *thamarāt al-nakhīl* "fruit of palm trees" (16:67). It is probable that the most ordinary name of the date in its edible state would have lowered the style of this prose which aims at creating an effect. In the third field, moving on to the animal kingdom, we have to stress the absence of the word *faras* = "horse". It is not that [28] the Qur'ān does not know these animals, but in the various instances they are mentioned it is always in the collective *khayl*. While the "ass" is in the Book, in the singular as well as in the plural, the "camel" is found in the singular only once, *jamal* (7:40), in a Biblical expression. The "horse" is even more resolutely taken not as an individual animal, but as species or forming a group, or as "cavalry" even, more frequently than "horses".[17] This is undoubtedly a trait of Muhammad's mental vision.

Muhammad's subconscious thought was mainly determined by his intellectual and social environment. The following observations about three discrete series of basic notions are certainly linked to this subconscious thought.

1. Firstly, that of "order, arrangement, classification". None of the roots which usually express this notion, *n ẓ m*, *n s q*, *r t b*, are to be found in the Qur'ān. As far as the universe and physical and biological phenomena are concerned, the Qur'ān most definitely puts the emphasis on the marvel of its structure and the chain of being: there is no flaw or crack in the skies and on this earth there is an organic development which is as complex as it is harmonious. However, perfection of the structures and dynamic balance, which testify to God's actions, are not perceived from the point of view of a logical or hierarchical division or a strict regularity. The idea of "keeping in order", *ḍ b ṭ*, is missing, as well as the most common classical Arabic terms for "species, kind": *naw'*, *ṣinf*, *fann*, (and *ḍarb* in this sense), to

[17] It is uncertain whether the *'ādiyāt* = 'gallopping ones' (100:1) are 'female camels' or 'mares'.

say nothing of the loan *jins* = genus. Only the plural *alwān*, actually meaning "colours", is found in a few instances, and in various cases the term *zawj*, pl. *azwāj*, which means "couple" or "half of a couple" is used.[18] There can be no doubt that the idea of "species, kind" had not yet reached the stage of abstraction.

2. Second, it is a piquant observation that while the notions of "hunger", *jūʿ*, *makhmaṣa*, *masghaba*, and of "thirst", *ẓamā'*, are widely represented in the Qur'ān, the roots [29] most commonly used meaning "to sate one's hunger", *ṣ b ʿ*, "to quench one's thirst", *r w y*, *n h l*, are not found at all. The one controversial example, from the root *r t ʿ* = "to eat and drink to repletion" (12:12, again in the story of Joseph), cannot stand up against this. At this point the temptation is great to cite the scarcity of food resources in Arabia as part of the background
3. This Book comes from a merchant community, and trade and counting have given it many words and metaphors. It is significant that allusions to the world of artisans, on the other hand, are very rare. The majority of words describing workers in their various professions are lacking; *fakhkhār* = "potter", which is quoted once (55:14), most likely under the influence of the Bible in the context of God the creator, is a rare exception. Whole roots are missing in this field. One would search in vain for words derived from *n s j* or *ḥ w k* = "to weave", and the usual terms for "warp" or "weft" of a cloth are not found either. The shepherd's work, apart from a few commonplaces, is hardly more common: *j z z* = "to shear" and *ḥ l b* = "to milk" are not found at all. There is slightly more precision concerning agriculture, with the notions of "labouring, sowing, harvesting" present, but *gh r s* = "to plant" is missing and, in particular, whenever "cereal" or "grains" in general are mentioned, the most commonly used terms for "wheat", *qamḥ* or *burr* or *ḥinṭa*, "barley", *shaʿīr*, and "flour", *daqīq*, are missing. The situation is the same for milling and the most usual roots associated with it, *ṭ ḥ n* and *r ḥ y*. There is, on the one hand, a certain underlying disdain for and spontaneous aversion to manual work, a trait which is entirely in keeping with the Arab mentality at the time and, indeed, for a long time to come. On the other hand, there is a apparent uneasiness which leads to an exclusion of technology as well as the profession of the shepherd and the farmer.

In the context of *badr* and *anwā'* we have alluded above to a possible explanation through a conscious change in beliefs. It is almost certain

---

[18] *Aṭwār^an* (71:14) means without doubt 'by stages', rather than 'of various kinds'.

10

that the dawning Islam and the behaviour it recommended justify other omissions in the lexicon in several directions. The Qur'ān never names the famous Arab "vendetta", *tha'r*, but tries to replace it with [30] legal retaliation (hence the sentence "there is life for you in retaliation" (2:179)) or with pecuniary compensation. In addition, retaliation does not have its ancient name of *qawad* but is expressed by a euphemism which primarily means "compensation": *qiṣāṣ*. An echo of the reforms in favour of women can be seen in the naming of the "marriage settlement" which is presented several times as "reward due" to the wife, *farīḍa*, *'ujūr*, or even, in one instance (4:4), as a "legal gift" which is lawfully hers, *ṣaduqāt* (classical *ṣadāq* is derived from this term). The ancient term *mahr* is never used, although it has survived in Muslim law (as a synonym of *ṣadāq*). In this case the intention is certainly to anchor firmly in people's minds the idea that the marriage settlement belongs to the woman herself and not – as did the original *mahr* – to her father or guardian.

Islam confirmed slavery, but endeavoured to reduce and alleviate it, and it is in this spirit that one has to understand Qur'ānic terminology dealing with this subject. It was hardly possible not to use *'abd* = "male slave" and *ama* = "female slave"; furthermore, are not all humans God's "slaves"? However, the Book refrains from using terms derived from the root *r q q* meaning "slave" and "slavery" in a purely legal sense. Not even the notion of "freeing" – which is recommended as a pious action – is expressed by technical terms derived from the root *' t q*, but obstinately by the paraphrase "freeing a neck", *taḥrīr raqaba* (4:92; 5:89; 58:3). Thus the deliverance and accession of the freed person to the full – normal – state of the "free man", *ḥurr*, are marked more forcefully.

Besides isolated words there are whole groups of words or roots whose absence can be legitimately explained by the changes in moral values which Qur'ānic preaching intended to induce in the audience. Roots which express the "praise" of living, *m d ḥ*, or dead humans, *r th y* and *n d b*, as well as those meaning "satire", *h j w*, or "adjuration or reciting of verses", *n sh d*, are kept out, because they were too closely related to Arab notions or practices [31] which the Book condemned either openly or implicitly. The absence of *m d h* is compensated by the abundant use of *s b ḥ*, *ḥ m d* and *sh k r*, specifically for "to glorify" and "to praise gratefully" the Lord above all others. The concepts of "nobility" and "honour" also have to pay tribute to this negative inventory: neither the roots *sh r f* or *n j b* for the former, nor the term *'ird* for the latter are found, as they might have brought to mind dominating pre-Islamic attitudes which, in the end, survived tenaciously in spite of Islam.

The idea of "male courage, bravery" must be added to these astonishing omissions, because none of the classical Arabic words expressing this idea are found in the Qur'ān: *basāla, jarā'a, jasāra, ḥamāsa, shajā'a, ṣarāma, murū'a, najāda.* The words meaning "force" and "strength", on the other hand, are present, and also – characteristically for Islam – the "steadfastness or firmness of the soul", *ṣ b r.*[19] This proves that in the Qur'ān martial virtues are valued less for prowess and physical feats, aspects which made them glorious in the times of the forebears, but that submission to God's will and faith in God, during the attack as well as on the defence, are the true military merits. Along the same lines, it is surprising that the Qur'ān, where wars take up so many pages, should be so very reticent in describing battles and only uses a fairly limited military vocabulary. The typical root, *gh z w* (which is the origin of the French word "razzia", meaning "raid"), only appears once (3:156), where it is perpetrated by the Infidels; the idea of "taking captive" is expressed by *'s r* and never by *s b y*. It is particularly striking that roots as common as *h j m, w th b* and *n h d* for "attack" or *n h d* for "pillage" are missing, that *rimāḥ* = "lances" is a hapax (in 5:94 in connection with hunting and not with war) and that *sayf* = "sword" does not appear at all. While the idea of "fighting" is frequent, the Qur'ān prefers to use the verb *qātala*, which does not have any specific colouring, or *jāhada* to stress the Islamic nature of the fighting.

It is a matter for historians of Arabic to undertake a study which would be the complementary opposite of the present attempt: [32] which are the elements of the Qur'ānic vocabulary which the classical language has not adopted? Such an undertaking might be thought absurd, at first sight even sacrilegious: once the Qur'ān had been accepted as a model its lexicon would naturally have been integrated into the classical heritage. There is indeed an abundance of Qur'ānic quotations and allusions, but does that mean that the vocabulary of the Qur'ān is blended in and naturalised? We believe we are justified in expressing strong reservations in that respect. A number of Qur'ānic words would, if confronted with current usage of classical *'arabiyya*, appear to be "unusual", *gharīb*, in the eyes of Arab lexicographers as well as our own.

But let us leave this problem for the time being and be content with the hope that our negative observations have convinced our readers that the vocabulary of the Qur'ān is still open for investigation driven by curiousity.

---

[19] It will be noted that the Qur'ān does not use the root *wr'* which would be so widely exploited later in the sense of 'pious abstention'.

18

INTRODUCTION: AN ASSESSMENT OF AND PERSPECTIVES ON THE STUDY OF THE QUR'ĀN

Mohammed Arkoun

[A man will not understand all of the law until he perceives many dimensions to the Qur'ān] (ḥadīth).

[v] THE QUR'ĀN IS INVOKED, more often than not, by millions of faithful believers in order to legitimate their actions, support their struggles, establish their aspirations, nourish their hopes, perpetuate their beliefs, and affirm their collective identities in the face of the homogenizing forces of industrial civilization. We know how the Muslim countries from Indonesia to Morocco were forced to develop an ideology of struggle in order to liberate themselves after the Second World War. This phenomenon did not cease with the restoration of political independence; in addition to the recurring strategies of political and economic domination in the real world, the difficulties of nation building imposed on each country have led to the increasingly pressing recourse to religion as an ideological tool for the leaders, a political base for opposition elements, and an instrument for the promotion of new groups in society.[1]

Several extremely broad phenomena—the proliferation of mosques (in Western societies too), the abundance of the faithful in the places of ritual, the return to the norms of Islamic law, the frequency of international gatherings, and the major success of apologetic works for publishers, etc.—have forced observers to speak of a "renaissance" of Islam and to take note of its expansion, "revolutionary" efficacy, the return to the divine, and the revival of the sacred. One will note clearly the Western origin of these expressions, which are incomprehensible outside of the socio-cultural context that has been promoted by the forces of secularization. Muslims can take pride, therefore, and brim with confidence in their religion, which has put in check the hegemonic theories of Western reason. The ideological demand of the West in crisis is encountering an equivalent demand in Muslim societies in conflict with underdevelopment and new forms of domination. This unacknowledged

---

[1] Cf. M. Arkoun, "Religion et société d'après l'exemple de l'Islam", *Studia Islamica* 55 (1982), 5–59.

complicity in the manipulation of intellectual, spiritual, and moral values with political and economic ends has particularly serious consequences for the Islamic side: the damage caused there is seen at the level of precariousness of intellectual life and cultural capital.

[vi] One would expect that the Qur'ān, given that it is solicited in all areas and read and interpreted by all of the social actors regardless of their cultural level or doctrinal competence, would be made the object of scientific investigation on the basis of new linguistic, historical, anthropological, theological, and philosophical research. One would also expect an intellectual renaissance, if not a revolution, to accompany the multiple militant discourses, in order to explain their genesis, functions, and significances, and as well as to exercise control of them. Rather, we will see that there is a overlapping imbalance between the day-to-day ideological consumption of the Qur'ān and the incorporation, by *liberal* (independent) and *critical* thought, of all of the contemporary problems that face not just Muslims, but rather all individuals who are concerned about reviving our knowledge of the religious phenomenon.

What I mean by "liberal and critical thought" will be understood when I discuss the approaches to Qur'ānic studies in what follows below. I will begin by undertaking an entirely intellectual survey of these studies; in order to illustrate the imbalance about which I have just spoken I will rely upon two texts that are quite representative of the two major currents of research: the *Itqān fī 'ulūm al-Qur'ān* ["Quest for Certainty in the Qur'ānic Sciences"] of the erudite polygraph al-Suyūṭī (d. 911/1505) and the article "Ḳur'ān" by A.T. Welch in the second edition of the *Encyclopaedia of Islam*.

The Qur'ānic Sciences According to al-Suyūṭī

Why choose an author of the ninth/fifteenth century in order to present a survey of the curiosities, problems, and knowledge of the Qur'ān in the Islamic tradition? Is it not unfair to compare an old text bound by classical Muslim erudition and a very recent text by a Western scholar?

This approach is warranted precisely because it is not a question of a comparative evaluation of two intellectual and scientific practices, but rather a critical analysis of each of them in order to locate better the topics that remain *unthinkable* and extend to the *unthought* in one or the other case. Several reasons have led me to remain with the *Itqān* rather than investigate a more recent work by a Muslim scholar. In 1954 Ṣubḥī al-Ṣāliḥ published a manual the title of which resembles that of al-Suyūṭī's book: *Mabāḥith fī'ulūm al-Qur'ān*, ["Studies in the Qur'ānic

Sciences"]; but by his own admission this book is limited to a simplified presentation of that which was taught by "the virtuous forefathers and the pious and good scholars" (p. 5). The documentation gathered and used by al-Suyūṭī is infinitely richer, more reliable, and more receptive to all of the sciences that had been developed over nine centuries by generations of specialists. One can also, thanks to the *Itqān*, have a precise idea of the problems that were encountered, the solutions found, and the limits fixed by the tradition of Islamic thought. The manual of Ṣubḥī al-Ṣāliḥ, like many other works of the same genre, has the merit, above all else, of showing that the collective synthesis furnished by al-Suyūṭī has not been surpassed; intellectually, one discerns among our contemporaries a hardening of dogmatic opinion, a contraction of information, and an excessive simplification of the issues at stake. **[vii]** In a manner like that of al-Ṭabarī in his great *Tafsīr*, the author of the *Itqān* has largely drawn upon an immense literature, which includes information that would have been lost or remained unknown for a long time had it not been for him.

We shall not engage in a detailed analysis of this work of over 1500 pages, but shall instead limit ourselves to the table of contents, which consists of 80 "categories" (*naw'*) enumerated by the author himself in the following order:[2]

1. Knowledge of the Meccan and Medinan [parts of the Qur'ān]
2. Knowledge of [the parts of the Qur'ān] revealed while at home and while on a voyage
3. That of the Qur'ān revealed during the daytime and at night
4. That of the Qur'ān revealed in the summer and in the winter
5. That of the Qur'ān revealed in bed while the Prophet was asleep
6. That of the Qur'ān revealed on earth and in the sky
7. The first revelation
8. The last revelation
9. The causes/occasions of revelation
10. That of the Qur'ān revealed via the words of a Companion
11. Fragments revealed multiple times
12. That of which the legal qualification was posterior to the revelation and that of which the revelation was posterior to the qualification

[2] I am using the edition of Muḥammad Abū l-Faḍl Ibrāhīm, 4 vols. (Cairo: Maktabat dār al-turāth, 1974–75). I have declined to transcribe the Arabic terms because it would require reproducing the entire table of contents. I have retained, though, some useful indications.

4

13. Knowledge of that revealed in fragments and that revealed in its entirety
14. That of the Qur'ān revealed with or without angelic accompaniment
15. That which had been revealed to certain prophets and that which had not been revealed to anyone prior to the Prophet (Muḥammad)
16. Modalities of revelation
17. The names of the Qur'ān and the titles of the Sūras
18. Collection and organization of the Qur'ān
19. Number of Sūras, verses, words, and letters
20. Those who knew the Qur'ān by heart and their transmitters
21. High *isnād* and low *isnād*

22–27. Readings transmitted through multiple channels (*mutawātir*), by more than two people (*mashhūr*), by very few people (*āḥād*), by a single authority (*shādhdh*), with fictitious traditions (*mawḍū'*), and traditions bearing insertions (*mudraj*)

28. Knowledge of when to pause and resume (pertaining to rhythmic unity)
29. What is contiguous in wording but unrelated in meaning
30. Inflection (*imāla*), the vowel "a", and what is midway between the two
31. Assimilation (*idghām*), manifestation (*iẓhār*), obscuring (*ikhfā'*), and transformation (*al-iqlāb*)
32. Elongation and shortening (of a short or long ending)
33. Weakening of the *hamza*
34. How should one use the Qur'ān
35. Rules for modulating recitation and the reciter
36. Knowledge of rare and obscure words
37. Employment of words from outside the Ḥijāz
38. Use [in the Qur'ān] of non-Arabic words
39. Terms that have multiple meanings (*wujūh*) and terms with a consistent meaning (*naẓā'ir*)
40. Useful words that an exegete must know
41. The Inflection (*i'rāb*) of the Qur'ān
42. Important rules that the exegete must know
43. The exact and the ambiguous (*al-muḥkam wa-l-mutashābih*)
44. What is brought forward and what has been delayed (in syntax)
45. General enunciations and specific enunciations
46. Imprecise enunciations and clear enunciations
47. Abrogating and abrogated verses

48. [viii] That which makes things difficult and which involves divergences and contradiction
49. The indeterminate and the determinate
50. The explicit and implicit
51. The modes of interpolation
52. Real meaning and figurative meaning
53. Similes and metaphors
54. Metonyms and allusions
55. Limitation and particularization
56. Conciseness and emphasis
57. Declarative sentences and all other forms of sentences (*al-khabar wa-l-inshā'*)
58. Stylistics of the Qur'ān
59. The division of verses
60. The opening of Sūras
61. The end of Sūras
62. The adaptation of verses to Sūras
63. The ambiguous verses
64. The inimitability of the Qur'ān
65. The sciences elaborated on the basis of the Qur'ān
66. The parables of the Qur'ān
67. The sermons of the Qur'ān
68. The polemics of the Qur'ān
69. The names, *kunyas*, and family names mentioned in the Qur'ān
70. The indeterminate verses
71. The names that are an object of revelation
72. The virtues of the Qur'ān
73. The most eminent passage of the Qur'ān
74. The unique enunciations of the Qur'ān
75. The properties that are unique to the Qur'ān
76. Orthography and rules for the copying of the Qur'ān
77. Knowledge of its exegesis, interpretation, the evidence of its nobility and one's need for it
78. Conditions and rules for the exegete
79. Oddities of exegesis
80. The classes of exegetes

This long enumeration of titles permits us to make several decisive observations, which we will group in three themes of research and reflection: 1) an organization of the knowable; 2) technical skills and religious reason; 3) the thinkable, the unthinkable, and the unthought in the sciences of the Qur'ān.

6

An Organization of the Knowable

The *Itqān*, like all of the works of al-Suyūṭī, exhibits all of the characteristics of the mode of scholastic composition that was self-imposed by the encyclopediasts who collected the inherited knowledge of the classical period. The encyclopediasts themselves only reproduced the ways of exposition long used by the specialists of the sciences for the examination of specific cases (*masa'il*): jurists, theologians, exegetes, and grammarians. The structure of the works of al-Ghazālī, al-Māwardī, al-Juwaynī, Abū Ya'lā, Fakhr al-Dīn, al-Rāzī, etc., is very significant in this regard.[3] Each case necessitates the exhaustive enumeration of facts that are **[ix]** limited to a tradition of transmission; the totality of the related cases is assembled under a *naw'*, a category of knowledge that constitutes both a speciality (a vocabulary, a writing, some means of acquisition, procedures of research and teaching) and a field more or less neatly carved out from the order of knowledge.

The 80 *naw'* of the *Itqān* comprise, as do other like-sized monographs, options for separate collection or transmission each in its own right. Each *naw'* consists of a variety of chapters, remarks, and notes. The appearance of being exhaustive, the care for detail, the casuistry, and the taxonomy give the feeling of a confident erudition that is complete, convenient of access, and couched in contemporary usage. In consideration of the diversity and order of the titles and the contents that they cover, it is clear that we stand before a brilliant array of knowledge, inconveniently dispersed under rubrics that can be reduced to the divisions better associated with the specialties established by the great classical works. It is nonetheless possible to reorganize the material of the *Itqān*, not only in a modern classification of the sciences, but rather in conformity with the Arabic-Islamic disciplines as al-Suyūṭī knew them (or could have known them). It is not a question of redoing the work in a manner to our liking, but rather it is a better approach to the organization of the knowable upon which all discussions of the Qur'ān to this day depend, including those of Western scholars:

Issues of chronology: *naw'* 2–8, 12–13, 15, 47
Modes of revelation: 9–10, 13, 14, 16
Collection and transmission: 17–27
Formal presentation of the definitive recension (*muṣḥaf*): 17, 60–62, 76
Prosody and textual units: 13, 15, 28–35, 59–61

[3] In the exegetical literature methodology is shaped by the necessity of relying upon textual units ranging from one verse to several verses.

Lexical topics: 36–39
Syntax: 41–42
Logical–semantic analysis: 42–46, 48–50, 63
Rhetoric and style: 52–58, 64, 66–68, 70, 74
Exegesis: 42, 77–80
Sciences derived from the Qur'ān: 65
Historical notations: 69, 71
Propitiatory values: 72, 73, 75

One notes a clear disproportion between the space accorded to syntax and lexicology, the emphasis of which benefits rhetoric, on the one side, and the logical–semantic analysis (requisite for the deducation of the legal qualifications, i.e. the *aḥkām* in *fiqh*), on the other. Prosody fills the practical needs for the memorization and recitation of the text, while chronology and modes of revelation have direct implications for the development of Islamic religious law, the *sharīʿa*. In other words, nine centuries of the development of the sciences of the Qur'ān have resulted in a body of practical knowledge designed to nourish the belief in a divine foundation of the Law, the super-natural character of the Speech of God, and the irreproachable conditions of its transmission and reproduction. The *Itqān* completes a slow filtering process of selection and condensation of facts, points of view, definitions, [x] explanations, and the types of knowledge that progressively came to constitute the *orthodoxy* and *orthopraxy* in connection with the Qur'ān. The knowable, thus organized and delimited, refers to:

1. That which is *possible* to know thanks to the works and teachings of the scholars cited by al-Suyūṭī at the heading of each *nawʿ* (scholars who themselves were true to the teachings of the Prophet and the pious ancestors)
2. That which is indispensable to acquire in order to think, speak, and live in conformity with the Qur'ān; in other words as a *mukallaf*, one who is responsible before God
3. That which cannot be transgressed without reaction by the Community, which bases its identity on the sum of knowledge recapitulated in the *Itqān* and assimilated by each believer in the form of psychological, ritual, and corporal practices (*habitus*).[4]

[4] One cannot insist too much (with the force of ritual repetition) upon the importance of the incorporation of the rhythmic structure, the affective and esthetic power, and the semantic contents (for those who understand the Arabic) of the Qur'ān. It is this that makes it so difficult for the practicing Muslim to put himself at the necessary intellectual distance in order to approach these facts as objects of analysis.

8

Technical Skills and Religious Reason

Among the technical skills used by the scholastic tradition, which includes al-Suyūṭī, one notices many levels of linguistic analysis: lexicology, morphology, syntax, semantics, rhetoric, and prosody. Even though topics concerning the chronology and transmission of the Qur'ān were raised, it is difficult to speak of a "historicity" in the *Itqān*. One is struck, on the contrary, by the triumph of an ahistorical point of view on all of the problems that are approached. In other words, the instructive discussions on the circumstances of the revelation, transmission, and elaboration of the *muṣḥaf*, or even the evolution of its lexicology, are abandoned, or reduced to a few scattered notations. These notations are always offered as "solutions" that since the fourth/tenth century have defined the Muslim creed. It is not sufficient to state here that later scholars, such as al-Suyūṭī, are satisfied with the faithful reproduction and conservation of the principle teachings of the classical masters in a didactic form; beyond the well-known dependence of the imitators (*muqallidūn*) upon the initiators (*mujtahidūn*), these scholars conform to a religious reason (which emerged at the beginning of the Qur'ānic discourse) that strives to control the significations of the discourse by means of a diverse array of technical skills that have been established by numerous authors at other times. Can one say that the reason at work in the Qur'ānic discourse is the same as that employed by a Ḥasan al-Baṣrī, a Qāḍī 'Abd al-Jabbār, a Ghazālī, and Ibn Khaldūn, and, here, a Suyūṭī? Which relations hold together the religious reason with the technical reasons requisite in each of the sciences, such as grammar, logic, history, mathematics, etc? Is there a unilateral borrowing by the former from the latter, or, eventually, a retroaction of these ones on those?

One of the constant characteristics of religious reason is that it seeks to construct a practical coherence within a closed theological domain without questioning the presuppositions, postulates, and convictions that make possible the discursive activity *inside* this domain. This is why religious reason [**xi**] lives in perpetual tension with scientific reason; the latter, applied to positive, discernable, and observable objects, can and must account for all of its operations. Here it is necessary to draw attention to an ambiguity which is so threatening to the spirit and which has been exploited on a vast scale for many years by the dominant Islamic discourse.

The relations between religious reasons and scientific reason do not need to be defined in terms of the superiority of one over the other (it is this that has for centuries made theological reason dogmatic and so given rise to the militant reaction of scientific reason), nor with the illusion of objectivity that assigns to each of them their domains of competence, roles, and specific procedures. It is also unnecessary to define them in terms of the relentless polemic that in the secular West characterizes the debate between the Church and State, spiritual and temporal, the religious and the secular. We may begin, philosophically, with the idea of "an affective knowledge" acquired and realized by "the affective conscience".[5] Each individual defines himself by means of a certain equilibrium (or disequilibrium), which manifests itself between the affective conscience and the intellectual conscience. The philosopher explores the occasion of these two consciences and their cognitive status: must one think, with the Heideggerian current, that man "rises to being beginning with 'there is' and that being is always for thinking and not for anything in itself"? Or can we say (with F. Alquié) that "the fundamental conviction in man is the certitude of being in a substantive sense of this word: that is, the belief that there exists an independent anterior reality to our soul cannot without due rigor be qualified, but rather may find itself, without absurdity, hypothetically specified as matter or as God"?[6]

I will leave this philosophical problem open, contrary to F. Alquié, in order to return to the concrete objects of this study, namely the revealed texts of monotheistic religions and the history of the consciences that they have engendered. We know with what force the Qur'ān instills and feeds the fundamental conviction that there exists a being "anterior to our soul, independent of it" and a heavily qualified (correctly so) point that the soul, which is invested in all parts by the attributes of God (i.e., the names and regulations, *al-asmā' wa-l-aḥkām*, explicitly articulated by Him in a clear Arabic language), must only assimilate and reproduce that which henceforth would be transcendent Knowledge. The 73rd *naw*' of the *Itqān* treats, as we have seen, the most eminent passages in the Qur'ān: it is interesting to remark that religious reason retained, in the first place, the verses and Sūras whose ontological content is the most dense and decisive (for example, the Verse of the Throne and Sūra 112 speak of the pure faith or unicity). These verses convey the immediate sense of authority and compulsion that God is One, living, speaking present, life-giving, thus relying, in other words, on an irrefutable affective knowledge, but which continues to cause a philosophical problem that religious reason engages in a multiplicity of paths or challenges to the social imagination, such as individual fantasies, false facts, and beliefs accredited with the consensus of good spirit, the "values" of the dominant class, etc. All of this prevails over and influences the initial

[5] Cf. F. Alquié, *La conscience affective* (Paris: J. Vrin, 1979).
[6] F. Alquié, "Le savoir affectif", *Le Monde-Dimanche*, 27 June 1982, xi.

10

ontological intuition. Furthermore, religious reason continues to invoke itself formally [**xii**] in order to justify its errors, dogmatics and renunciations.

The *Itqān* furnishes many illustrations of the ease by which religious reason agrees, when it is applied unwittingly, to orthodox reason. Following venerable ancient precedent, al-Suyūṭī cites apocryphal traditions to support his argument; on the other hand, in order to bolster his own authority he himself feels compelled to criticize the same practice when it is used by his predecessors. One technical skill—*ḥadīth* criticism—changes its role: in place of serving as a strict regulator of the authenticity of Prophetic *ḥadīth*, the condition of which is itself the key to this foundational ontological Presence, *ḥadīth* criticism becomes an instrument of mimetic outbidding between the doctors and the rival schools. Each author reproduces the arguments, texts, and sacred names within each of the major Sunnī, Shī'ī, and Khārijī orthodoxies, and then for the Ḥanafī, Mālikī, Shāfi'ī, Mu'tazilī, Ja'farī, and Zaydī (etc.) sub-orthodoxies. Al-Suyūṭī does not escape this necessity, and thus does not perceive the ruptures caused by the introduction of his orthodox reason in connection with religious reason, as in the case of what is postulated in the ontological verses of the Qur'ān: historical rupture (which does not necessarily entail spiritual rupture) with the life and real/actual work of the Prophet; linguistic rupture with the system of language manifest in the Qur'ān; cultural rupture with the advent of great commentaries such as those of al-Ṭabarī or Fakhr al-Dīn al-Rāzī (both cited in the *Itqān*, the former more than the latter, but always for minor issues); intellectual rupture with the opinions (attitudes) of a Jāḥiẓ, a Tawḥīdī, an 'Abd al-Jabbār, an Ibn Sīnā, an Ibn Rushd, etc.; scientific rupture with the theorizing effort of a Jurjānī on the rhetoric of Qur'ānic discourse.

We arrive, finally, at the question as to whether the *Itqān* and all of the similar literature composed prior to and after it, permits a knowledge *of* the Qur'ān or rather simply assembles the indispensable scholarly learning *about* the Qur'ān. It remains for us today, in either case, that the methods, approaches, problems, skills and intellectual attitudes used in this literature are obsolete, inadequate, and insufficient. If we are to undertake new investigations aimed at achieving new readings of the Qur'ān for the purpose of securing a place for the Qur'ān within broader contemporary movements of scientific research and philosophical reflection, than we must return to the three concepts I mentioned earlier: the thinkable, the unthinkable, and the unthought in the sciences of the Qur'ān.

The Thinkable, the Unthinkable, and the Unthought

In working with these three concepts, which are as alien to Islamic thought as they are to Orientalist research, my aim consists of two inseparable objectives: to enrich the history of thought by setting forth cognitive, intellectual, and ideological markers of the tensions between the schools of thought; and to invigorate contemporary Islamic thought by focusing on the problems it has ignored, the taboos it has erected, the frontiers it has drawn, and the horizons where it has stopped and beyond which it refuses to gaze. All of this has been done in the name of that which has been imposed progressively as the unique truth.

[xiii] If we begin with the chronological and epistemological observation that the *Itqān* gives us, we can distinguish three turning points where the borders between the thinkable, the unthinkable, and the unthought were shifted, with regards to the Qur'ān:

1. The time of the revelation (AD 610–32)
2. Collection and fixation of the *muṣḥaf* (AH 12–324/AD 632–936)
3. The time of orthodoxy (324–/936–)

Before we explore each of these three moments, we must explain what the notions of thinkable, unthinkable, and unthought cover. For the past few years the history and thought of Arabic literature have oscillated between linear descriptive expositions of men and works, and the leap (perilous for many) towards structural and semiotic analysis. These latter studies remain limited to a few influential theses or essays by the new criticism, especially in France.[7] In both of these cases recourse to social criticism and historical psychology continues to be neglected. Social criticism and historical psychology not only link, in a lively manner, the descriptive method and the structural, but also give rise to unexplored regions of historical reality in a sociological and anthropological perspective.[8] The conscience (mythical, historical, social, economic, political, philosophical, moral, aesthetic, religious, etc.), reason and irrationality, imagination and imaginary, meaning, natural and supernatural, profane and sacred, etc., all have a history that has not yet been studied in its own right. It is because we ignore everything up to the distinction be-

[7] As for works relevant to the Qur'ān, I will note L. Gasmi, *Narrativité et production du sens dans le texte coranique: le récit de Joseph*, These 3e cycle, Paris III, 1978.

[8] A. Miquel has the distinction of going far in this direction with regards to Arabic geographical literature and the *Thousand and One Nights*; he has begun a very promising inquiry on the *majnūn: Une histoire d'amour fou.* M. de Certeau recently published a fine work that takes advantage of the orientations that I have mentioned here: *La fable mystique* (Paris: Gallimard, 1982).

12

tween mythical and historical conscience, rational and imaginary, that the current dominant trend of Islamic thought *can* study the Qur'ān as though the tools of modern reason were in every way identical with the reason of the work in Qur'ānic discourse and the epistemological environment of the Prophet. This is the meaning of my inquiry into the wonders in the Qur'ān.[9]

We can follow the shifts of the borders between consciousness and unconsciousness, rational and imaginary, and thus thinkable, unthinkable, and unthought, in order to reorient research in this new direction. The thinkable of a linguistic community at a given time is that of which it is possible to think and express with the help of the available mental equipment. This definition immediately indicates that it is not possible to think and express [all of the same thoughts] in the same time period and in the same social-cultural space because of the limits of a cognitive nature and modes of intelligibility true to living social-cultural systems. It can also be traced to the fact that the subject of the enunciation (the author) has integrated, in the form of self-censure (**xiv**], the constraints conveyed by the dominant ideology. (In this second case, "deviant" and "subversive" authors can give value to an unthinkable idea, at their own risk, by transgressing against the social-cultural system that is jealously guarded by the community.) Finally, this definition of the thinkable is due to the tension of thought attached to the region of the inexpressible and unfathomable opacity of being (cf. the poetic and prophetic discourse that drives towards this region).

We could give many examples to illustrate this analysis, but we shall limit ourselves here to that of the Qur'ān. Everything that pertains to monotheism was *unthinkable* in the Arabic social discourse prior to the revelation. This explains, on the one hand, the subversive character of Qur'ānic discourse, and on the other, the climate of polemics and radical contestation for the divine authenticity of the message delivered by Muḥammad, which was perceived by the protagonists of the conflict as the destruction of ancestral beliefs. The conflict of active force over some twenty years did not have, as a final goal, the simple substitution of one social-political force for another one in a group of institutions and an intangible cognitive order,[10] but rather the subversion was fundamentally related to the thinkable of a society and to a time in which all symbolic resources were being disenfranchised to the advantage of a

---

[9] [This study is Chapter V of Arkoun's *Lectures du Coran* (Paris: G.-P. Maisonneuve et Larose, 1982)].

[10] The actions of the Prophet, despite his subversive aspirations, did not entirely eliminate the tribal system and values with which he was connected; on the contrary, he used the elements of the Arab society to his advantage in order to assign them to a new destiny.

model of historical action unknown in the Arabic language.[11] This is why both the structure and discourse of the Qur'ān reflect the configuration of social-political forces in its midst: it is an "epic narrative" where the subject–object relationship (the quest for salvation) is entirely dependent upon the giver–recipient (God–men, by means of Muḥammad and the prophets), with the Giver being "the actor who utilizes *justice* with enough power to impose upon his opposite the obligations vis-a-vis the obligations that he has decided to watch his execute".[12] The terms that disqualify the opponents of the quest (the infidels) in th eununciations of state or descriptions only achieve their full negative value because they depend upon enunciations of action, by which I mean "predetermined modalities such as *power*, *obligation*, *knowledge*, and *will*".[13] In other words, the narrative and discursive construction of the Qur'ānic enunciations is located simultaneously in the daily life of the "faithful" (i.e. acting as recipients-subjects-actors), at their victorious historical action against the "unbelievers" (opponents), and at the organization of the imaginary already in place by the "people of the Book" (*ahl al-kitāb*). Here the narrative is not limited to mere manipulation of miraculous people, dramatic situations, mythic productions with dramatic finales, nor aesthetics and recapitulations, but rather it is generated by a concrete history at the same time as it is generating a new axis for *another* concrete history: it signals the unthinkable of the preceding history, by defining the groups, means, and the boundaries of an infinite thinkable.

[**xv**] We cannot limit ourselves, either historically or anthropologically, to this semiotic presentation; if we are not careful, it can corroborate opposition to the theological essense, which has definitively won the acceptance of the infinite thinkable of the Qur'ān over the false, subjective thinkable that is accompanied by an immense unthought towards the infidels (cf. the famous bipolar opposition that developed in all Islamic discourse on the basis of Qur'ānic concepts such as *islām/jāhilīya, nūr/ẓulumāt, ahl al-kitāb/ummīyūn*, which enter into some of the opposing structures). We are aware of how the spirit of orthodoxy surreptitiously annexes the results of a science by preemptively declaring that it does not alter any of the teachings previously acquired by the traditional disciplines.[14] It is necessary, then, to repeat forcefully, always

[11] It is necessary to specify the Arabic language, since Aramaic, Syriac, Hebrew, and Greek had already long expressed analogous subversions to the universal ancient Near East.

[12] J.C. Coquet, *Sémiotique. L'Ecole de Paris* (Paris: Hachette Université, 1982), 54.

[13] *Ibid.* See also Chapters III and V.

[14] I have often heard this observation from all those who ignore the entire field of semiotics and have decided to have no interest in it. The intellectual discipline that it requires has a great liberating virtue with regards to the power that all languages exert without the user being aware of it.

14

with the intention for the Muslim reader who is overwhelmed by theological schemas and correct refutations in the dogmatic spirit, that semiotic analysis is limited to the deconstruction of the linguistic, narrative, and discursive mechanisms that generate meaning and affect the listener or reader. What we uncover, even in Qur'ānic discourse, is a thorough mastery of the mechanisms whose effects of the produced meaning have acted and continue to act upon the consciences at the most varied linguistic and cultural roots. This science does not prejudge any of the values of the thinkable, the heard, the unthinkable, nor even the nature of the unthought in cultural systems that are marginalized or eliminated by the organization of the thinkable and the imaginary introduced by the Qur'ān. In considering this polemical and theological disqualification, the historian must reconsider each situation of confrontation, just as in Arabic, between the "savage" cultural configuration and the *Islamic* strategy of "domestication". We are beginning a long and difficult investigation into the unthinkable and unthought aroused in different societies at the times of various meetings, by the manipulation of the thinkable and the Qur'ānic imaginary. We find again the valuable distinction between Qur'ānic fact and Islamic fact, Qur'ānic discourse and Islamic discourse, and the semiotics of religious discourse and semiotics of theological discourse;[15] and we are brought back to the above-mentioned examination of the three turning point moments in the life of the Qur'ān.

The attitudes concerning the Qur'ānic fact, and the languages that clearly express them, changed at each of these three moments. The essential challenge for us today, proceeding from the knowledge assembled in the *Itqān*, is the necessity to cut through the sedimentary layers of the Islamic imaginary that were constructed in the first four centuries of the *hijra* in order to gain access to the time of the revelation. The conscience that is submissive to the tradition is unfamiliar with this problem, and we have seen that al-Suyūṭī does not feel ill at ease to base all of his information on chains of transmission whose authenticity is recognized by the Sunnī community. In other words, he uses, with complete confidence, what Franz Rosenthal has called "knowledge triumphant".[16] The time **[xvi]** of the revelation is the inaugurating time of a new, universal, historic era that is itself oriented towards an eschatological future. The time of mythical essence is nevertheless described as a series of dated terrestrial events, manipulated and used as

---

[15] Cf. *Ecole de Paris*, 39; *Sémiotique et Bible* 12 (1978), on theological discourse. For the Qur'ānic fact, see Chapter I of my *Lectures du Coran* and my *Pensée arabe*, 2nd ed. (Paris: Presses universitaires de France, 1979), 5–18.

[16] F. Rosenthal, *Knowledge Triumphant: the Concept of Knowledge in Medieval Islam* (Leiden: E.J. Brill, 1970).

normative references for the judgments and conduct of each believer. The acts of the collection and fixation of the *muṣḥaf* are reported likewise as external operations, enacted with care and integrity, which protected the contents of the Message from decay and all disputation. The *Itqān* provides an abundance of material for anyone who wishes to show how classical Islamic thought, as systematized by the guardians of orthodoxy, used materials, procedures, and an historiographical corpus in order to *dehistoricize* both the time of the revelation and the collection of the *muṣḥaf*. This project consists of a vast collective operation that mobilized the *'ulamā'* (*fuqahā'*, *ḥadīth* transmitters, theologians, exegetes, historians, philologists, and rhetoreticians) after the Companions and Successors, the Caliphal state, and the social *imaginaire* that further supported traditional religious sensibilities.

We thus find ourselves confronted with an extremely powerful organization of a mythical-religious thinkable hemmed in by a chronology at once closed (2–324/622–936) and open to a "before" and an "after" of eternity. This thinkable is rigid, limited, and therefore suitable for a more extended and essential unthought in proportion to what one finds at the time of orthodoxy. Al-Suyūṭī only mentions the name of Abū Bakr ibn Mujāhid in order to point out that he did not discuss "phonetic reduction" (*takhfīf*) in his treatise of the seven readings of the Qur'ān (*musabba 'a*). This is a clear example of the dehistorization of the *muṣḥaf*, because Ibn Mujāhid was responsible for the reform in 324/936 that ended the rivalries of the scholars of Qur'ān recitation.[17] If we knew better the vicissitudes that led to this reform and the consequences of the definitive fixation of the text, we would be able to attack one of the great problems that has been trapped in the unthought by Islamic thought: the historicity of a discourse that became a canonical corpus and a generator of transcendence. The transformation of the Qur'ānic discourse into multiple discursive forms of Arabic culture in relation to a state and society in the course of expansion, took place at the cost of epistemic and epistemological ruptures that the modern historian continues to understand and describe poorly.[18] This attitude, like that of al-Suyūṭī, has long been content to recapitulate *positive* knowledge acquired by the tradition of erudition without questioning the intellectual conditions (i.e. the type of reason in the text) at work, and thus the validity of this knowledge. There is much epistemological continuity, as we shall see with the *Encyclopaedia of Islam* article, between Islamic reason and the philological and historicist reason of the nineteenth century. I know that the former

[17] Al-Suyūṭī, *Itqān*, I, 323.

[18] Cf. *La Pensée arabe*, and "The Concept of Islamic Reason", in *Critique*.

16

is more intransigent than the latter with respect to textual criticism and the clear distinction between authentic and **[xvii]** apocryphal information, but this rigor comes at the same exorbitent cost as that of religious reason, namely the impossibility of the criticism of knowledge and the opening of new dimensions of the mythical conscience and social imaginary, in one case, and the philosophical weights and goals of historicity, in the other.[19]

The most significant event worthy of our attention, after that of the codification of the seven Qur'ānic readings by Ibn Mujāhid, is the publication in 1924 in Cairo of the standard edition of the Qur'ān. The diffusion on such a vast scale of the received text will increase even more the unthinkable in the domains of the great theological problems and the new directions of research into the distinction between Qur'ānic fact and Islamic fact. We might even reach the point of losing interest in the rhetorical and historical knowledge that were still of interest at the time of al-Suyūṭī. From now on, the text is applied to all of the problems of daily life and has received an immediate meaning from diverse actors in the discourse of social mobilization, such as the accountable politician, the militant of the party, the teacher at school, the professor at the university, the writer, the essayist, the amateur, the recent convert, the student (especially of the social sciences!), and the journalist. The former religious personnel (*muftī*, *imām*, preacher, *qāḍī*, doctor of the law) have not maintained the same significance as they did in earlier times, and only in post-revolutionary Iran has their control been so encroaching on society. But the Word of God, even in the case of Iran, has been reduced to a mere instrument of secular power, social control, and ideological orientation. The liturgical recitation of the Qur'ān, without doubt, has increased as a consequence of religious practice, but the degree of corruption of religious expression for political and social ends, even at the level of the individual mosques, remains to be documented.

We will have a more precise idea of the current modes of consumption of the standard text by consulting the vast corpus that constitutes the *Actes du Séminaire de la pensée islamique*, organized each year (since 1969) by the Algerian Ministry of Religious Affairs. I have indicated previously, in two works, the socio-cultural and ideological baggage of these gatherings where "authorized" representatives (by their religous or university roles, their traditional knowledge, and their orthodoxy) are brought together from all of the Muslim communities throughout the

[19] One must not confuse the historicity practiced by the humanities and social sciences with that which cultivates positive rationalism. Cf. M. Arkoun: "Islam et l'historicité", in *Critique*. See also F. Furet, *Penser la Révolution française* (Paris: Gallimard, 1979).

world.[20] All of the panels reveal a unanimity of opinion on well-worn themes, strategies of practical studies, defended positions, and developed ideas, so that one can speak of a general Islamic discourse of the contemporary Muslim community (*umma*). Even though this unity only exists politically in a precarious manner, its semiotic existence is largely attested by structural and functional convergences of an immense discourse located across the planet in the most varied milieus. The traditional boundaries between Shī'īs and **[xviii]** Khārijīs are toned down or explicitly minimized by the representatives of these two rival currents to Sunnī Islam.

The fifteenth Seminar held in Algeria in September 1981 was devoted entirely to the 'Qur'ān. The program of works and principle panels published in the journal *al-Risāla* (1401/1981, no. 5) and various issues of *al-Aṣāla*, allows one to define the techniques and directions of the thinkable that are imposed upon the general Islamic discourse. The program included the following points:

1) The Qur'ān
   Its revelation
   Its commitment to writing
   Its expression as a book (corpus)
   Its collection
   Its memorization
   Its recitation
   Its teachings (i.e. pedagogical transmission)
2) Understanding the Qur'ān
   Exegesis: foundations and methods
   Translation of the meaning of the Qur'ān; and evaluation of translators, authorized topics and goals
3) The Noble Qur'ān (*karīm*) in our world today
   Its teaching at different school levels
   Its transmission (as a message)
   How to renew our bond with the Qur'ān in ritual, social relations, education, knowledge, culture, and civilization
   The future of human society with the Qur'ān as the guide

The first section discusses yet again, at best, the body of knowledge fixed by the *Itqān* and faithfully repeated in various contemporary manuals and textbooks. It refutes, at times, the "attacks" of the Orientalists on

20 "Le IXe Séminaire de la Pensée islamique: Tlemcen, 1974", *Maghreb-Machrek* 70 (1976); "Le XIVe Séminaire de la Pensé islamique: Alger, 1980", *Maghreb-Machrek*, 74 (1980).

18

the topic of the order of Sūras and verses, but it does not approach further anything that touches upon the history of the corpus. We raise the point again that the philological method practiced with remarkable fecundity in the West since the sixteenth century has been relegated to the realm of the unthinkable and unthought whenever it approaches the fundamental sources (*uṣūl*) of the Islamic discourse, and, in particular the Qur'ān and *ḥadīth*. The refutations never use philogical or historical arguments in the modern sense, but rather invariably make use of the authority of the texts that are precisely the subjects under discussion, namely the Qur'ān and *ḥadīth*, as well as an historical scheme that has stabilized since the fourth/tenth century under the pressure of an orthodox theology. This is how, as we have seen, all religious reason works.[21]

The attitude towards the old and contemporary exegietical literature, as with the problem of translations, reveals **[xix]** the continuity of a group of convictions about the uniqueness of the Arabic language, which all modern linguistics vehemently deny. One supposes, simultaneously, that the "authorized" exegete—here as elsewhere, the filter of the traditional orthodoxy intervenes—can *deliver* the canonical unique meaning, which can be exploited either ethically or legally, and is attached to each word, expression, and verse in the Qur'ān (cf. the paraphrasing method of al-Ṭabarī, but that one cannot possibly transmit adequately into another language anything other than the general meanings (*ma'ānī*), because of the transcendental quality of the Arabic of the Qur'ān.[22] Semiotic analysis unveils the mechanics of this *reading*, which disconnects the foundational text or tutor (= the Qur'ān, as it is for the Bible or Gospels) from the social-historical processes of its textualization in order to produce other texts (the open series of commentaries, ranging from those of al-Ṭabarī or Ja'far al-Ṣādiq, to fantastic manipulations, such as those that "prove" that all scientific discoveries were already mentioned in the Qur'ān) with the help "of a paradigmatic and syntagmatic memory" capable of reproducing "a group of codified, axiological structures and recurrent ideological schemes".[23] The paradigms and syntagmes applied

[21] Cf. the reassessment of this controversy in the light of the works of J. Schacht and I. Goldziher.

[22] We shall return to the problem of translation shortly below; it is necessary to distinguish between the theological objection raised against all translations and the linguistic difficulties inherent in any translation of a religious text of mythical structure, or of poetry. As for the Qur'ān, the legislative and narrative discourses are more translatable than the prophetic discourse. The most insurmountable problems are tied to the inevitable recontextualization of a text translated in the culture of the acquired language, although this holds true for all modern readers (non-linguist and non-historian) who read a text in its original language whose socio-cultural location is at a far removed historical time. In the case of the Qur'ān, this is compounded by the fact that it is a singular expression in its level of language.

[23] E. Landowski, "Le discours politique", in *Ecole de Paris*, 170.

here are indissociable linguistics and meta-linguistics for the reason of powerful intervention of the imaginary organization of the world, such that it results from the semiotic role of the foundation text and secondary texts. This is what illustrates clearly the current technique of verse citation, of the *ḥadīth,* and more generally, the texts whose theological authority is recognized. The citation presuppposes and prolongs a *homogenous space–time* that truly belongs to the imaginary and religous reason: this is why it does not matter if the cited fragment is detached from its linguistic context and the initial situation of its enunciation. We will also go as far as to split the semantic content of the cited fragment in order to retain only the articulable value of the principle theme (spiritual, ethical, legal, historical) of the new text.[24] Regarding each case, or each text, designed to support and guide the history of the group and manipulate the virtual meanings of the foundational text, we can say that the traditional method of study functions by means of social-historical efficiency, and that it loses the theoretical knowledge of the means of its manipulation in the course of this endeavor. Finally, there arises a priority thinkable, in modern thought, **[xx]** that is often retracted in the polemical confrontations. How do we interpret and, eventually, get beyond the recurring competition between the pragmatism and the empiricism of religious reason, which asserts a transcendent, intangible knowledge, through recourse to the methodology and theory of modern scientific reason, and in such a way as to pursue the project of a positive knowledge based upon a perpetual application of self-criticism?

Religious reason pursues, nonetheless, its own imperial, regulatory, proud path in its discourses, while being submissive, impotent, and opportunistic with the facts. This appears clearly in the general Islamic discourse in the form of the protest against "the professionals of intellectual aggression", the increased destruction wrought by technology, modern economic imperialism, and the rupture with the educational system, seen from the angle of the religious practices whose absence would reduce Islam to mere nomenclature. Likewise, it is manifest when it reaffirms, with vehemence, its profession of the exclusive and universal truth, and calls for the radical reform of the thoughts and manners of political regimes and economic systems. It is aware of the collective hopes and pleas that have the mobilizing virtue of the former mahdisms and messianisms, while it relies entirely upon modern means—imported,

[24] One will find a good example of this study, which fissures the initial coherence of the text and presupposes a homogenous space-time for the new manufactured coherence, in A. Saḥnoun, "'Ibād al-Raḥmān", in *Al-Risāla*, 5–6; and Muḥammad al-Ṣadīq, "Inṣn al-Qur'ān wa-insān al-Shayṭān", *Al-Aṣāla* 91 (1981), 107–11. One will also find many examples in the Tunisian journal *Al-Hidāya*.

20

tacitly appreciated, rigorously exploited, and yet paradoxically condemned whenever a coherent thought ventures into the religous domain—of social control and historical production.[25]

The general Islamic discourse applies several other principles, postulates, and logical-semantic presuppositions that are not intermingled with the articles of the profession of faith, and that continue to inform every reader of the Qur'ān today.[26] I have shown their directive action in several contexts.[27] Finally, I must stress the need to link the permanence of the cognitive system formed in the classical period, not with an exceptional epistemological validation or an incomparable ontological anchor (as religious reason so desires), but with the permanence of the social-economic and political conditions exercised by Arabic-Islamic thought.[28]

Assets and Limits of Orientalism

Has not Orientalism proven to be so iconoclastic that it merely confirms the complaints of the guardians of Sunnī orthodoxy? Has it forced open several doors that had been bolted shut, or is it satisfied with the application to the Qur'ān of principles, methods, and questions [**xxi**] that were typically used by research universities in the West between 1850 and 1960?[29]

I shall begin, as I did previously, with the outline offered by A.T. Welch at the beginning of his article:

1) Etymology and Synonyms
   a) Derivation and Qur'ānic usage
   b) Synonyms in the Qur'ān
2) Muḥammad and the Qur'ān

[25] I have mentioned, in broad strokes, the postulates and principles of study generating the general Islamic discourse and seeking to readjust the Qur'ānic enunciations to uncharted waters in societies in the process of development. The degree of appropriateness of such a reapplication to the selected texts remains to be seen.

[26] Cf. the 21 articles of faith reported by Ḥasan Khalīfa, "Hādhihi 'aqīdatuka ayyuhā l-muslim", *Al-Risāla*, 12–13. See my analysis in *L'Islam, hier–demain*, 2nd ed. (Paris: Buchet/Chastel, 1982), 155–75.

[27] See *Lectures du Coran*, Chapter III; and *passim* in *Pour une critique de la raison islamique*.

[28] Cf. *La Pensée arabe*, 19–78.

[29] Rudi Paret has assembled 48 texts published between 1923 and 1971 by a variety of Orientalists: cf. *Der Koran* (Darmstadt: Wissenschaftliche Buchgesellschaft, 1975). We have also, with the article of the *Encyclopaedia of Islam* (2nd ed.), two representative documents of the methods, goals, viewpoints, and results that one can call "Orientalist Qur'ānology". It is unfortunate that a rich compilation such as *Der Koran* has not been translated into Arabic, as the issues it contains help to make known the necessary recourse to philological methods.

3) History of the Qur'ān after 632
   a) The "collection" of the Qur'ān
   b) Variant readings and Companion codices
   c) Establishment of the canonical text and readings
4) Structure
   a) The Sūras and their names
   b) The verses
   c) The *basmala*
   d) The mysterious letters
5) Chronology of the text
   a) Historical references in the Qur'ān
   b) Traditional Muslim dating
   c) Modern Western dating
6) Language and style
   a) Language of the Qur'ān
   b) Foreign vocabulary
   c) Rhymes and refrains
   d) Schematic forms and multiple accounts
7) Literary forms and major themes
   a) Oaths and related forms
   b) Sign-pasages
   c) Say-passages
   d) Narratives
   e) Regulations
   f) Liturgical forms
   g) Other forms
8) The Qur'ān in Muslim life and thought
9) Translation of the Qur'ān
   a) The orthodox doctrine
   b) Translations into specific languages

The author has read and exploited thoroughly all of the Orientalist literature on this subject. One is struck by the constant references to early documentation and the negligible attention paid to Muslim scholarship that is chronologically contemporary, but epistemologically scholastic. The results, which have been collected in the course of over a century of research, are expressed with clarity and conciseness, so that the article offers a critical survey and a starting point for either new research, or questions that have been ignored until now.

[xxii] It is to be noted that aspects of this outline are similar to those of the *Itqān*, which is cited throughout the article, as it is in most Orientalist works. We find the same care as that displayed by al-Suyūṭī

22

towards the description and inventory of the knowledge and problems relating to the final form of the revelation in the *muṣḥaf*, or definitive corpus. We remain on the exterior and at a superficial level of the text when we inquiry into the vocabulary, morphology, syntax, and style. The formal approach is more evident when the author studies the mysterious letters, division of verses, and the order, length, and titles of the Sūras. It is also evident in the observations concerning whether a Sūra begins with the *basmala* or not. The literary forms and primary themes come in the same paragraph, as it is a requirement of an encyclopedia article on a given subject that one writes in a manner that is more precise and modern than the style of the contents of the works under examination. We remain, on the contrary, in the scheme of traditional literary criticism, which separates language and style, and literary forms and themes. These comments will assume their full meaning when we mention the directions of contemporary research, and they need not impede the recognition of the positive contributions made by the philological methodology.

Orientalist erudition, in contrast with the de-historicized Muslim exegesis, erudition, and avoidance of the problems related to the constitution of the *muṣḥaf* when they transcend the contents of the received text, is limited *exclusively* to positive facts of the history of the Qur'ān after 632 and the linguistic and historical context of the verses. The intransigence between these two points of view is radical:[30] no bridge can be forged between them so as to allow the approach extolled in our discussion to integrate the theological demands of Believers, the philological imperative of the positive (but not positivist) historian, the explanatory perspective of anthropology, and the critical control of philosophy. Under these conditions it is hardly astonishing that Muslims have always rejected (albeit without serious examination, in most cases) the most instructive contributions of the Orientalists.

Theodor Nöldeke had the great distinction of introducing, for the first time since the fourth/tenth century, the inevitable question of historical criticism of the Qur'ānic text. [*Über den Ursprung des Qorāns*, 1909].

[30] The concessions of vocabulary, such as "Holy Book" or "Book of God", "Muslim position", or "revelation", only introduce a false sense of neutrality with regard to the Believers in which one "respects" the claims (vis-à-vis non-Muslim studies) that maintain the illusion of "objectivity" and a critical distance that is perfectly amenable to philological sensibilities. The entire vocabulary of the Believer must be deconstructed and put in epistemological perspective so that it can be stripped of the epistemological casing that serves as a watertight compartment between the orthodox thinkable and the heterodox unthinkables. The Orientalist habitually responds to this objection as though it were the responsibility of the Muslims, and not himself! The generation of Nöldeke and Goldziher, at the time of colonial power, was not bothered by the need for such caution, which today is more often an *alibi* for all those who refuse to take into consideration the new inquiries of the humanities and social sciences.

The fact that this work has not yet found an Arabic translator is just one more indication of the "unthinkable" imposed by orthodox reason. The works of Arthur Jeffery, Rudi Paret, Régis Blachère are located in the philological and historicist line drawn by the German school. John Burton[31] **[xxiii]** and John Wansbrough[32] have enriched the discussion recently, even though they came to diametrically opposite conclusions.[33] The works of the latter author and those of Harris Birkeland,[34] despite the lack of consensus upon this topic among the Orientalists, have enriched philological analysis with a curiosity that is appropriate for social criticism. The problems of authenticity become socio-cultural facts that carry the meaning for the knowledge of each of the groups of the "sectarian milieu",[35] each of which was confronted by simultaneous milieus and for whom political victory changed *their own* polemical truth, in relationship with the transcendental orthodox Truth. The *ḥadīth* were summoned and produced on the basis of the needs of the time and place with various *isnāds* that were not stabilized until the end of the fourth/tenth century. Each time this work was accomplished by the elite clerics, and it resulted in the fixation of the region of the thinkable for all of the movements and groups who referred their identity back to the Qur'ān.[36]

The two most important problems that have been approached by means of philology are the chronology of the Sūras and the verses, and then the organization, after the death of the Prophet, of the revealed enunciations.[37]

---

[31] *The Collection of the Qur'ān* (Cambridge: Cambridge University Press, 1977).

[32] *Quranic Studies: Sources and Methods of Scriptural Interpretation* (Oxford: Oxford University Press, 1977).

[33] One may also benefit from the discussion on the works of J. Van Ess in Michael Cook, *Early Muslim Dogma: a Source-Critical Study* (Cambridge: Cambridge University Press, 1981). One should also consult the reviews by J. Van Ess of the works of Burton and Wansbrough, respectively, in the *Times Literary Supplement* 8 September 1978, 997, and *Bibliotheca Orientalis* 35 (1978), 349–53, where many of the essential problems concerning the earliest commentaries (prior to al-Ṭabarī) are mentioned. When, for example, did exegetes begin to cite poetry in order to clarify the meaning of the Qur'ān?

[34] [Harris Birkeland, *Old Muslim Opposition against Interpretation of the Koran* (Oslo: H. Aschehoug, 1955); *idem, The Lord Guideth: Studies on Primitive Islam* (Oslo: H. Aschehoug, 1956).]

[35] John Wansbrough, *The Sectarian Milieu: Contents and Composition of Islamic Salvation History* (Oxford: Oxford University Press, 1978).

[36] If the Qur'ān achieved the consensus of the Muslims, then the *ḥadīth* witnessed two fixations that were clearly different: that of the Sunnīs (the works of al-Bukhārī and Muslim, recognized in the fourth/tenth century) and those of the Shī'a (the works of al-Kūlīnī and Ibn Bābūwayhi, recognized at the same time). See M. Arkoun, "Pour un remembrement de la conscience islamique", in *Ctitique*. As for the works of the stabilization and accomplishment of al-Ṭabarī, see Claude Gillot, *La sourate al-Baqara d'après le commentaire de Ṭabarī*, Thèse 3e cycle, Paris III, 1982.

[37] One may profit from the comments of A.T. Welch on the meaning of *Qur'ān* and *kitāb*, the structure of verses, the languages of the Qur'ān, the passages which included "signs" and the passages that have "say" (although the remarks are insufficient from the semiotic viewpoint).

24

The jurist-theologians were extremely interested in the former, as it was necessary to make the verses that treated the same subject (such as wine) in an exact sequence in order to elaborate legal rules (*aḥkām*). This was not, strictly speaking, a question of history, for John Burton has tried to show how the jurists could play with historical reality while in the process of manipulating traditions in the course of their research.[38] This demonstrates just how necessary it is for us to reevaluate the literature concerning the occasions for Revelation (*asbāb al-nuzūl*), those of abrogation (*al-nāsikh wa-l-mansūkh*), and all traditions that have been applied by exegetes, so that we can reconstitute the true history of the Qur'ānic text. We continue to adhere to the notion that each Sūra corresponds to an original textual unity, which can be qualified as either Meccan or Medinan. The reality is far more complex, and the examination of this question must use formal (prosody, syntax, vocabulary), thematic, and historical criteria in order to designate [**xxiv**] the textual units that exist inside complete Sūras. The studies of Blachère, which employed the works of his predecessors, remain very insufficient. It is possible to proceed to the chronology and exegesis of the transmitted enunciations in the canonical closed corpus.[39] The loss of decisive manuscripts and works will always impede the achievement of inscrutable solutions, but Islamic thought, which is so attached to studying the Qur'ān "in the virginal freshness of the Revelation" (*ghaḍḍan kamā unzila*), can no longer continue to ignore the extreme fecundity of historical inquiry.

It is important to articulate what is really at stake of this quest in order to put an end to, if possible, the sterile out-of-date polemics against the Orientalist philologists.[40] It is neither a question of disqualifying the positions and knowledge consecrated by a secular tradition, nor of satisfying curiosity—in reality negligible—for uncovering merely the chronological order of the verses and Sūas. What is at stake, which is unrecognized by researchers who are only preoccupied with "establishing the facts", is linguistic, historical, legal, theological, and philosophical.

---

[38] See the difficult discussion on *naskh al-ḥukm wa-l-tilāwa* and *naskh al-tilāwa dūna l-ḥukm*, in Burton, *Collection of the Qur'ān*, 131.

[39] For the meaning of this expression, see 42–45.

[40] From the point of view of the desired renewal of Islamic thought, there is good reason to be suspicious of the literature that appears to be favorable towards the Islamic tradition, such as K. Cragg's *The Event of the Qur'ān: Islam and Its Scripture* (London: Allen and Unwin, 1971), and his *The Mind of the Qur'ān: Chapters in Reflection* (London: Allen and Unwin, 1973), as well as W.C. Smith's *On Understanding Islam: Selected Studies* (The Hague: Mouton, 1981). One should be wary, in general, of the literature of Islamic-Christian dialogue that supresses all of the problems related to sociological, anthropological, linguistic, and philosophical cricitism. See P. Kemp, "Désapprendre l'Orientalisme", *Arabica*, 30 (1983), 1–35.

This can be shown with the help of verses IV:12 and IV:176, which have just been the object of an interesting study.[41] I do not agree with the author's over-confident and in my opinion premature conclusions, but I must stress the heuristic value of all investigation that challenges the transmitted reports by al-Ṭabarī, especially those found in his *Tafsīr*.

The two verses in question deal with inheritance (*al-farā'iḍ*). The portion of verse IV:12 that reads *wa-in kāna rajulun...* has divided the commentators to such a degree that al-Ṭabarī devotes to it seven pages and includes 27 witnesses (*shawāhid*) to try and clarify the meaning of the word *kalāla*, which only appears in the Qur'ān twice.[42] It is concerned first with a linguistic exercise in the form of a semantic inquiry into the meaning of *kalāla*, as well as a syntactic one on the syntagme *wa-in kāna rajulun yūrathu kalālatan aw imra'atun* (final received reading) or *yūrithu kalālatan aw imra'atan...waṣīyatin yūṣī bishā* (in the place of the final recension *yūṣā*). The *yūrathu/imra'atun/yūṣā* group is in opposition to the *yūrithu/imra'atan/yūṣī* one. D.S. Powers has illustrated well how al-Ṭabarī consolidates the "orthodox" reading by omitting the link between the commentary of IV:12 and the important reports that are mentioned only in relationship with IV:176, which in turn send the reader back to the solutions given previously in IV:12. This is the linguistic method; as for the historic one, it is no less important: How, and in what setting(s), were the variant readings supporting *yūrithu* and *yūṣī* found? This debate is so important becuse [**xxv**] it concerns here the control of the priority of the distribution of the property to the male descendents. The rejected reading permits the property to go to other lineages, on the female side, especially if one extends the meaning of daughter-in-law or fiancée to *kalāla*. It is therefore indispensable to reconstruct the system of inheritance in practice in Arabia at the time of the Prophet in order to compare it with those of the Iraqi and Syrian milieus in the first century AH. We will see if the first jurists did not read the verse in the meaning that is required for a rigid agnatic system.[43] It is not necessary to give a definitive answer to this question in order to have a glimpse of the theological and philosophical stakes of philological inquiry. One finds, *theologically* speaking, a serious debate over the createdness of the Qur'ān that has been buried by scholastic orthodoxy.

[41] D.S. Powers, "The Islamic Law of Inheritance Reconsidered: a New Reading of Q. IV.12b", *Studia Islamica* 55 (1982), 61–94.

[42] The second occurrence is IV:176.

[43] This appears to have been done by Powers in a dissertation that I could not consult: *The Formation of the Isamic Law of Inheritance*, Ph.D., Princeton, 1979 [published as *Studies in Qur'ān and Ḥadīth: the Formation of the Islamic Law of Inheritance* (Berkeley and Los Angeles: University of California Press, 1986].

26

This debate arose because the Word of God was delivered in an Arabic language used by men in society; deviant readings that were ideologically contrary to the initial intention of the revelation were thus always possible. We cannot escape several great difficulties of a *philosophical* nature: the vision of transcendence fed by the Revelation and incessantly repeated in the profession of faith, is, at the same time, compromised by the immanent needs within social-historical existence. These necessities assign the roles of regulation, legitimation, and sanctification in terms of religion, and they must not be confused with the ideal definitions, aspirations of the Absolute [One], the striving toward perfection, and the spiritual ethos of all religions. We should not loose sight of the fact that the representations and operations disguising reality and conditioning the social *imaginaire*, at the level of playing a role in the production, manipulation, and consumption of meaning, do so in a manner far more decisive than the pseudo-certitudes elaborated by reason in their discursive activities of syntactical, semantic, and stylistic analyses. We must also recall their activity in the construction of transmissions for *re*-presenting the truth communicated *in illo tempore*, logical deductions (*qiyās*) of the *aḥkām*, and so forth.[44]

We have come quite far from the cold, formal, academic (not to say scholastic) discussions of A.T. Welch in his article that neglect to present the philological method as a primary, indispensable technique and springboard for the purpose of richer and richer elaborations. It remains for us to show now, taking into account all that has been said up to this point, what should and can be the approaches for Qur'ānic studies today.

Approaches

I will present the following outline in order to allow the reader to proceed to a methodological confrontation between the two paths of Muslim science and Orientalist erudition: **[xxvi]**

1. Synchronous Explorations
   (a) The linguistic status of the Qur'ānic discourse
      i. Speech, statement, enunciation, discourse, text
      ii. Qur'ānic discourse, canonical closed corpus, interpreted corpus
      iii. Prosodic structures or forms of expression

[44] I shall return to this point at length in a study curently under preparation on *Sīra et Histoire*.

iv. Syntactic structures, grammatical tools
v. Vocabulary: lexical networks; systems of connotations; denotations, structural semantics
vi. Rhetoric: metaphorical organization of Qur'ānic discourse
vii. Survey of the typology of Qur'ānic discourse: Prophetic, narrative, legislative, polemic, hymnic or liturgical discourse; sermons, threats, promises

(b) Semiotic analyses: Forms and contents
i. Place of communication; study of enunciation, models of agency; primary agent – recipient – subject; agent – recipient – subject I; agent – recipient – subject II; transcendental enunciation; state of the recipient
ii. Inventory and hierarchy of the cultural codes; citation of the codes; new directions of codes; axiological or directing isotopes; central or satellite isotopes[45]
iii. Forms and structures of the report, or the mechanisms of the production and reproduction of meaning; logical–semantic organization of values; power of the report
iv. Symbol, sign, concept, word: the levels of the manifestation of signification

(c) Social-critical analyses
i. Social process of the enunciation and textualization[46]
ii. Social antagonisms and the bipolarity of discourse (*mu'min* as opposed to *kāfir*)
iii. Prominent groups, marginal groups, and the discourse of power (cf. Sūra IX); strategy of inclusion/exclusion by which the new group of *mu'minūm* impose an infringing social-historical dynamic, generating meaning, a consensus on the meaning, which henceforth ranges from orthopraxy (= the correct action) to orthology (= the correct speech, = appropriate expression)
iv. The living Qur'ān: changing social implications of the mentioned contents; social groups; levels of culture and expansion of the Qur'ānic imaginary;
v. Transformation of the dialectic (social, historical, languages, thought) into a hierarchy: (divine logos, orthology, orthopraxy)
vi. Sociology and metamorphosis of the sacred; strategies of socialization and sanctification

[45] See A. Kilito, *Récits et codes culturels dans les Maqāmāt de Hamadhānī et Ḥarīrī*, Thèse d'État, Paris III, 1982.
[46] See Chapters II, IV, and VII of *Lectures du Coran.*

28

vii. Transcendence, structure, and history

(d) Psycho-critical analyses

i. The rational, irrational, and the imaginary

ii. Mythical conscience, religious conscience, collective unconscious; the guiding power of the Qur'ānic discourse and the Qur'ānic discourse as a place of mental projection (cf. mythical discourse)

iii. The spatial–temporal frameworks of the representation and perception; multiplicity of times and imaginary topography of the world

iv. The ways and levels of knowing

v. The natural, supernatural, mystery, divine, sacred, and profane

vi. Fiction and non-fiction, legend and history, earth and heaven, this life and future life, the cosmic order

vii. Angel, man, *jinn*; masculine and feminine; free man and slave; Faithful/Believer, infidel, and lawless rebel

viii. The modality of being: power, knowledge, action/behavior, possession, desire to be, desire not to be [**xxvii**]

2. Diachronic Explorations

(a) The work of each of the societies of the Book in themselves

i. Powers of the Divine logos and languages of human powers, or of the Word of God to the interpreted corpus on the following diagram

$$\frac{WG \rightarrow QD \rightarrow OCC \rightarrow IC \rightarrow th \rightarrow el \quad \text{Icy} = \textit{Mukallafūn}{=}\textit{mu'minūn}}{}$$

whereby WG = Word of God; QD=Qur'ānic discourse; OCC=Official Closed Corpus; IC=Interpreted Corpuses; th=Terrestial History; el=Eternal Life; ICy=Interpreters of the Community[47]

ii. The tension of relation to meaning/relation to forces; authority as a case of all legitimation and powers of domination and expansion

iii. Islamic reason and concurrent reasons or mimetic rivalries of groups vieing for the monopoly of authority and the powers

iv. The historicity and understanding of the Book or the production of the revealed text

---

[47] See Arkoun, *Religion et société*, 33–37.

Qur'ānic Studies: a Survey of Past and Future Approaches 29

(b) The Scriptural tradition and ethno-cultural traditions
   i. Notion of the living tradition: when the believer cites the tradition (= transmitted Islamic *sunna* and *ḥadīth*) it refers to a *reality* as if it was lived and articulated by the founding ancestors; this reality is transhistorical and transcultural from the view of the believers; it is the recurrence of the Divine logos in history. At this level it tends to be substituted for local traditions and to eliminate them
   ii. The resistance of local traditions, or the dialectics of Islām/Jāhilīya and legitimate state/lawless rebels
   iii. Principles of studying "Islamic" history: the problem of the dominant cause: political, economic, spiritual, and ideological
   iv. Structural discontinuities, epistemological ruptures, recurrences of the religious
   v. Strategies of theological authorities to annul historicity and the revival of concrete history

3. Anthropological Approaches
   (a) Societies, cultures, and religions in the Ancient Near East; in the Mediterranean; contacts with the Far East
   (b) The notion of revelation in the Semitic tradition
   (c) Categories of thought and themes of Knowledge in the monethistic Revelation (Bible, Gospels, Qur'ān)
   (d) The concept of the society of the Book
   (e) Myths, rites, languages, and thoughts in the societies of the Book
   (f) Techniques of thought, techniques of the body; ways of personal or collective realization among the societies of the Book
   (g) The imaginary and its influences on the societies of the Book
   (h) Graphic reason, audio-oral reason in the societies of the Book
   (i) Economies, societies, and ideologies
   (j) Violence, the sacred, and signification in the societies of the Book
   (k) The pure and impure, sacred and profane; justice and injustice
   (l) Conditions and processes of transition of the society of the Book to the secular society; the problem of the reversibility of this evolution
   (m) Note: This group of anthropological approaches is only indicative of that which must be included in research integrating the example of [**xxviii**] Islam in place of being trapped in an Oriental foreignness, as has already been done with Western thought,

30

primarily in the cases of Jewish and Christian theological thought

4. Philosophy and the Religious Fact
   (a) The Qur'ānic fact and the Islamic fact: critical review of all of the research conducted under the preceding rubrics
   (b) First, the categories bequeathed by the history of ideas: Eastern and Western philosophy; classical metaphysics; dogmatic theology, serving as systems of control, limitation, exclusion, normalization, and reproduction of thoughts, beliefs, and values
   (c) Integration of the Islamic example into the general movement of contemporary research and reflection

A careful perusal of this program outline will lead easily to the following observations:

1) The *epistemology* of Orientalist erudition applied to the Qur'ān is no longer grounded in the past—like that of the Muslim learning—but to the new organization of knowledge that has come into currency since the 1950s and 60s. Its epistemology, by being limited to the historicity of facts, pulverized a living tradition, nurtured skepticism, and aroused polemic against its method of exploiting earlier sources (even though Muslims using the same method have made good progress in recovering the written testimony of their culture, which had been mutilated and suppressed by the zealousness of the Believers or rulers)

2) This program outline allows for a degree of expansion of the *unthought*, not just in Islamic thought, but also in the more advanced thought of the West. Virtually none of the mentioned chapters has been treated in the approaches that we employ, neither in Islamic studies nor in the social sciences of religons.[48] Religious thought is still a prisoner of traditional theology, which continues to age with respect to the frontiers of the unthinkable. The integration of the Qur'ānic, Gospel, and Biblical facts as facts of revelation remains unthinkable for each tradition in relation to the others.

3) The inauguration of such a vast unreasonable program requires, *strategically*, as we have have already mentioned, a freedom of thought, of writing, and publishing, which cannot yet be undertaken in contemporary Muslim societies. This is the reason why this program integrates the totality of the attitudes, cultural practices, horizons of thought, symbolic resources, writings, and oral traditions to which these societies

[48] Compare *Archives des sciences socials des religions*, CNRS.

make reference. It redirects this totality into a recapitulatory, liberal, critical, and creative knowledge all at once, because it is concerned with a knowledge open to positive acquisitions of past, attentive to the current conquests and future promises, hostile to mystifications, myth-making, ideologies, and sanctifications, but always struggling for an appropriateness that is clearer between the real, the acted, and the spoken. This knowledge is [**xxix**] no less than a project for the emancipation of the human condition, conceived and developed by the prophets, perpetuated, and recast (who will dare say increased and enriched?) by modern revolutionary movements. Crises, regressions, progressions, negligence, destruction, setbacks, mutilations, alienations, oppressions, liberations, hopes, despairs, victories over ignorance, hunger, servitude, death: all of this must be analyzed, thought about, and organized by a reason that truncates neither the living Absolute testified to be the [religious traditions], nor the positive fact of history, societies, biology, and the world.

4) The four major elements of research are, *methodologically*, inseparable and aim for a coherent view based on a complex differential reality that is lived globally by each individual and society. Specialization is inevitable, in practice, but the generalist thinkers must re-establish the severed links, the continuities, the articulations that are imperceptible for the specialists, and the overarching visions that guide the future. Our summary program only seeks to translate the extreme flexibility, the overall strategies, and the semantic and semiotic complexity of the Qur'ānic discourse. One would break this simultaneously unifying and dividing dynamic, if one limits oneself to the examination of isolated objects and decontextualized units (verses, fragments, Sūras separated from the inaugural social process of their enunciation for the purposes of arguments and illustrations applied to variant textualizations). One of the merits of the *Itqān* is that it has assembled material relating to the majority of the disciplines that have developed in relation to the Qur'ān; our program merely seeks to complement this work and bring it up to date.

5) When we elicit and articulate several traditional and modern disciplines and methodologies, we do so to get past the theoretical rigidities and reductionism that is reproached by the humanities and social sciences. We wish to avoid the base thematic curiosity of the historian of ideas, the etymologism and literalism of classical exegesis, the disincarnate and logistical formalism of structuralism, and the limits of the semiotic practice that removes the logical-semantic forms of signification within the psycho-social condition from their production and function. We also seek to avoid the dissolvent relativism, the ethnographic view of anthropology (which is limited to "other" cultures), and the regionalism and

arbitrary divisions of philosophy and classical theology. This position explains why none of the seven essays in this book exhausts any or all of the possible paths. This tentative, interrogative, attentive allure behind this course of research is a methodological and epistemological decision, dictated by the complexity of the subject, the backwardness of the field, the inadequacy of documentation, and the theoretical barriers inside each discipline.

6) We would suppress a fundamental quality of the Qur'ānic text were we not to engage in interdisciplinary research: its ability to signify, in order to provide it with a permanent meaning, an 'objectivity', to in other words, a number of readings that are already in practice and always advocated. The great commentary of al-Rāzī, for example, makes reference to several readings, but juxtaposes them without engaging in a critical review of each of them. We find in his commentary **[xxx]** lexical and grammatical readings, existential readings based upon traditionally transmitted stories, and legal, philosophical, "scientific" (or what was called scientific knowledge at his time), and literary (= *i'jāz*, rhetoric) readings. A commentary such as this one is far more interesting to us today for the purpose of studying the ability of the Qur'ān to signify in a historical, social, and cultural context far different than that of Arabia in the seventh century, than for the purpose of researching the interpretations or exegeses based on the Word of God. This is why all of the commentaries accumulated up until now by Muslims—regardless of their school of thought or sectarian affiliation—must be used for a history of the *imaginaire* and Islamic reason, more than as a source *of the* meaning that would have been most accessible to past generations. In other words, these texts should be freed from the constraints of historicity inherent in the act of understanding.

7) It is clear that the cognitive strategy thus put in place and practised with prudence will strip away all of the epistemological armor of classical thought in all cultures, including, of course, that of the West. The competent sovereign subject relying upon the transcendent Word of God believes that he has taken all reality and expressed it in an appropriate, stable language, properly articulated in the syntax and semantics of the language made transcendental by the Revelation.[49] An eternal sovereign Reason consisting of all of the orders of truth correponds to this stable substantialist ontology. This is why the sovereign subject is attached to the linguistic, semiotic, sociological, and historical constraints manifest

[49] See the theory of the Arabic language developed by al-Shāfi'ī in his *Risāla* [trans. Majid Khadduri, *Al-Shāfi'ī's Risāla: Treatise on the Foundations of Islamic Jurisprudence* (Baltimore: Johns Hopkins University Press, 1961), 88–95].

in each perception and each enunciation. This is what manipulates and is manipulated across networks of actors, syntactic positions, and thematic roles, which define the moments of communication. The study of the texts, and, even more, of all of the societies of the Book—each one under the same rubric as all of the others (even though the resistance is stronger in the case of the normative privilege attached to the Book)—will find itself changed.

Muslims reject this epistemological rupture because it is, with respect to the West, an Islam with a capital "I" that neither invents nor follows its own historical trajectory. This objection and pretension warrants a serious examination. If this rejection reflects the great historical time lag between the evolutions of the respective Islamic and Western societies, than it is not only understandable, but is actually an unavoidable necessity. We shall remark, though, that it is expressed by the dominant ideological discourse in order to lead us to think that Islamic societies can adopt a system of exchange, production and consumption along Western lines without suffering the inevitable destructive and homogenizing effects, because Islam is anchored in an ontology that is truer than those of Judaism and Christianity. This ontology is historically unbroachable, and suitable to guarantee the perennial survival of the sovereign subject and the constituent reason.[50] **[xxxi]** The evolution of the Arabic language, dislocation of traditional solidarities/allegiances, militant nationalism, the burden of demographic considerations that has lead to the explosion of cities to the detriment of the countryside and nomads, the demands of industrialization, the valuing of all transactions in monetary terms, and the emergence of the bureaucracy and proletariat, all attest to the profound changes that have been implemented without a corresponding change in scientific thought (i.e. the thought of which we refuse categories and procedure). We are thus in a contradictory situation that exacerbates itself and leads towards no solution. We also forget that the monotheistic ontology and the cognitive system that it implies have prevailed throughout the centuries in the West, and that it continues to influence large sectors of these communities while allowing various great scientific currents to thrive. The task of Islamic thought is to relinquish apologetic discourse aimed at the anesthesia of the human

[50] Sa'īd Ramaḍān al-Būṭī, one of the great activists of the general Islamic discourse, and professor of the Faculty of Theology of Damascus, defines this perennial nature in "Mas'alat al-tasayyub wa-l-tamadhdhub wa-l-i'tizām", in *al-Risāla*, 9–10. He says vigorously that Muslims must remain attached to the teachings of a founder of a school (*imām*) for issues that concern religious observances (*'ibādāt*), and that one may approach the four sanctified schools—without adding a single one to the four—on issues that concern *mu'āmalāt*, or general rules and laws that are applicable to society.

34

spirit in order to take its proper role in the current struggle for the reconstruction of meaning, for a better grasp of the destiny of mankind in each society and in the universal movement of history. I do not hold that the displacements wrought by contemporary thought in the intellectual arena are all philosophically legitimate, nor do I consider that they render all traditional culture obsolete. Rather, they only require a radical rethinking of the conditions of emergence, circulation, and efficiency of the meanings in societies.

8) There remains a problem to be discussed briefly, which appears different from the preceding ones, but in fact lies close enough to them so that we may include it here: the issues of the translation of the Qur'ān. The recent tendency of the expansion of Isam includes a need for translations of the Qur'ān into all languages. Publishers encourage this movement for the obvious reason of profitability. Old translations are re-edited, or eclectic versions, which are presented as new products, are collected.[51] All of the transpositions in circulation to this day are conceived and executed, *at best*, in the spirit of the principles of classical philology, and we are well aware of the criticisms and exigencies of linguistics in this domain.[52] If we were to proceed in a systematic manner with all of the indicated approaches in our outline, we would still need to provide and find a system of cultural connotations, and metaphor for each language that would be equivalent to those of the Arabic language of the Qur'ān. The limits of linguistics have supported the long-lived hostility of Muslims toward the translation of their inimitable Book. It is necessary to realize that what we are calling the "semantic destiny" of the Qur'ānic message is very different from that of the teachings of Christ: the latter spoke in Aramaic, and very quickly his enunciations were transformed into Greek, then Latin, and in the sixteenth century into German by Luther. Each change of the linguistic code has brought about a change in the cultural code, from the point of view that it has given birth to new religious sensibilities. **[xxxii]** It is there that we must research the origins of the historical concept in the West. Once again, it can be foreseen that Arab and non-Arab national traits will be imprinted more and more strongly in the religious field that was established by the Qur'ān. It is another area of transformation, tension, and therefore, reflection and investigation.

Where are the teams of scholars from the various disciplines who have converted to the new scientific spirit that we have just discussed? Where

[51] See J.D. Bensheikh, "Sourate al-kahf: neuf traductions du Coran", *Analyses Théories*, 1980/no. 3, 2–50.

[52] See H. Meschonnic, *Cinq rouleaux* (Paris: Gallimard, 1970); *Jona et le significant errant* (Paris: Gallimard, 1981); *Sémiotique et Bible*, 182 no. 26.

can we find the cultural environment, university support, and the informed public that will encourage the systematic achievement of the program outlined here? How can we unite the efforts of specialists who are already numerous, although dispersed in many institutions in each county? It is not easy to coordinate teaching and research projects in France (or anywhere else where the Arabists are not numerous) into a hierarchy based on pressing needs and overly neglected domains.

It appears to me that the most difficult obstacle to overcome is the intellectual conservatism manifest in Arabic and Islamic studies. Many scholars feel reluctant to lead the studies of old Arabic sources by means of the exploitation of the scientific production most often located in the Western domains. A prevalent idea in Arab societies is that the efforts at Arabization must be imposed, above all else, on the domain of exact sciences and technology, tools that are indispensable for economic development. However, it is in the humanities and social sciences that the Arabs must draw upon their rich heritage. For ideological reasons it has not been determined yet at what point the act of knowing is *one*.

We will have to wait for a long time, no doubt, before the outlined chapters of social criticism, psycho-criticism, and social and cultural anthropology become a reality. My goal, above all, is to introduce the possibilities and stimulate young researchers. This is why I thought that it was a good idea to assemble seven essays in this volume that have been published in works of limited access. These articles are inseparable from many others that I brought together in a volume entitled *Pour une critique de la raison islamique*, to which I have made reference several times in this essay. This project in its entirety is a critical study—in the philosophical sense—of the conditions that have been products of Islamic thought throughout its long history. I ask the reader not to come to conclusions on each portion independent of the others, including those I have already published. I have long endeavored to live a historical solidarity while thinking liberally and fully—in the best tradition of *ijtihād*—about the conditions of existence of the societies of the Book. Historians, philosophers, sociologists, psychologists, and theologians have thoroughly explored Christianity, and this has benefited the revolutions, social-economic upheavals, and intellectual audacity that have shaped the history of the West since the sixteenth century. It is also true, no doubt, that it has overwhelmed for good certain aspects of the message delivered by Jesus in Palestine, where some of the most unanticipated turnarounds were accomplished. Islam, and thus the Qur'ān, have remained sheltered from all that was put into question by modernity until the nineteenth century, and it is still necessary to specify that colonial domination has stifled intellectual life, ossified tradition, [**xxxiii**], and

36

favored the nature of certain local identities, such that it did not give way to currents of innovative thought. The struggle for liberation, and then for national construction, have created the current situation: movements that describe themselves as Islamic base their claims throughout on the slogan binding the secular inseparability of Islam—state—world = *dīn—dawla—dunyā.*[53] The majority of the militants in these movements are over 35 years old and grew up in a climate of militant ideology that emphasized the value of the recovery (or the conquest) of power, at the expense of the study of *meaning*, and justification of the rights of certain men with respect to the rights of God (*ḥuqūq Allāh*). The role of transcendence, which is the substance of the greatness of the Qur'ān, was diminished in relative importance to the legal codes established by the *fuqahā'*. One may well understand why a renewal of Qur'ānic studies is imperative: in the terrifying semantic disorder in place in all contemporary societies, we are in dire need to better understand, in order to better control, the relationships between "*meaning and power*", and "*violence and sacred*". These two themes have been introduced, but certainly not exhausted, by G. Balandier and R. Girard. To repeat: the great religions are always located on the side of meaning and the sacred, in that they preach peace, love, and the quest for the Absolute, such as in a sermon or political discourse. It remains to be understood why these teachings themselves serve so often to legitimate the worst acts of violence and the confiscation of meaning.

[53] See Chapter VI of *Lectures du Coran*.

19

SOUND, SPIRIT, AND GENDER IN *SŪRAT AL-QADR*

Michael Sells

By the night when it shrouds
And the day when it reveals
And what made the male and the female
(*sūrat al-layl*, 92:1–3)[1]

FEW WHO HAVE INTRODUCED THE QURʾAN to those not conversant with Arabic can have escaped the feeling that, whatever the strengths of the translations used (if they are in fact translations at all), what is heard is only an echo, often distorted, of what is there.[2] Contemporary focus upon the oral and aural nature of the Qurʾan has brought this translation gap into higher profile. Several intertwined issues have been raised: Qurʾanic self-description as an "Arabic" Qurʾan (*Qurʾānan ʿArabiyyan*); the role of oral tradition in its transmission; the insistence within Islam upon reading and reciting it in the original Arabic; the pervasiveness within Islamic life of its recitation; and the importance within Qurʾanic recitation of the art of *tajwīd* ("making right") which puts forward the conventions of proper articulation.[3]

In memory of Professor Fazlur Rahman. Special thanks are due Mahmoud Ayoub, Rick Colby, John Eisele, Ken Fromm, Th. Emil Homerin, Mustansīr Mir, Azim Nanji, John Seybold, Ruth Tonner, and Michael Zwettler for their comments on earlier drafts. This study was enabled in part through research grants from Haverford College.

[1] Qurʾanic citations follow numbering of the Egyptian standard edition. Unless otherwise noted, translations are those of the author.

[2] See Fazlur Rahman, "Translating the Qurʾan," *Religion and Literature* 20 (1988): 23–30; and Samuel Zwemer, "Translations of the Koran," *Studies in Popular Islam: A Collection of Papers Dealing with the Superstitions and Beliefs of the Common People* (New York: Macmillan, 1939). Zwemer contrasts Muslim hesitancy to translate the Qurʾan or use translation to the plethora of translations of the Christian Bible (into 1008 languages by Zwemer's count). Cf. *EI*$_2$ 5:428a–32b, s.v. "Kurʾan" (sect. 9, "Translations of the Kurʾan").

[3] Cf. William Graham, *Beyond the Written Word: Oral Aspects of Scripture in the History of Religion* (Cambridge: Cambridge University Press, 1987), 79–115; Kristina Nelson, *The Art of Reciting the Qurʾan* (Austin: University of Texas Press, 1985); Frederick Denny, "The Adab of Qurʾan Recitation: Text and Context," in *International Congress for the Study of the Qurʾan*, ed. Anthony Johns, Australian National University, Canberra, 8–13 May 1980, ser. 1, 2nd ed. (Canberra: Australian National University [1981]); idem, "Exegesis and Recitation: Their Development as Classical Forms of Qurʾanic Piety," in *Transitions and Transformations in the History of Religions: Essays in Honor of Joseph M. Kitagawa*, ed. Frank E. Reynolds and T. M. Ludwig (Leiden: E. J. Brill, 1980), 91–123; idem and R. L. Taylor, eds., *The Holy Book in Comparative Perspective* (Columbia: University of South Carolina Press, 1985); Lamyāʾ al-Farūqī, "Tartīl al-Qurʾān al-Karīm," in *Islamic Perspectives: Studies in Honor of Maw-*

Even so, applied literary studies of the Qurʾan, especially of the Qurʾan in its aurality, are rare. Contemporary "literary" approaches have been concerned with source criticism, with how the Qurʾan was composed,[4] rather than with how the Qurʾanic text generates meaning. The literatures devoted to *iʿjāz al-qurʾān* (the inimitability of the Qurʾan) and *faḍāʾil al-qurʾān* (the excellences of the Qurʾan) offer strong anecdotal affirmation concerning the sound quality of the Qurʾan, but traditional analysis focuses upon rhetorical features usually unrelated to the interaction of sound and meaning.[5] Simply put, what is the relation of sound to sense in the Qurʾan? To pose this question is to pose again the specific question of *tawāzun*, what we might call "textual harmonics," and the more general question of *naẓm*, a word commonly rendered as "composition," but which might allude as well to that dynamic principle that gives the Qurʾan its distinctive quality, to what will here be called the Qurʾanic voice.[6]

This discussion examines meaning in the Qurʾan as it is generated across four principal axes or modes of discourse: semantic, acoustic, emotive, and gendered. Though the four modes are separated for the purpose of exposition, no one of them exists independently of

lānā Sayyid Abul Aʿlā Mawdūdī, ed. Khurshid Ahmad and Zafar Ansari (London: Islamic Foundation, U.K.; and Jedda, 1979), 105–21; Labīb al-Saʿīd, *Al-Jamʿ al-Ṣawtiyy li l-Qurʾān al-Karīm* (Cairo: Dār al-Kātib al-ʿArabī), 324–30; Khalil Semaan, "*Tajwīd* as a Source in Phonetic Research," *Wiener Zeitschrift für die Kunde des Morganlandes* 58 (1962): 112–20.

[4] Cf. John Wansbrough, *Qurʾanic Studies: Sources and Methods of Scriptural Interpretation* (Oxford University Press, 1977); idem, *The Sectarian Milieu* (Oxford University Press, 1978). Even those interpretations not explicitly concerned with source analysis tend to focus primarily upon historical issues, the modern equivalent of the issues explored in *asbāb an-nuzūl* commentaries. For an interesting exchange on the Wansbrough approach, see Andrew Rippin, "Literary Analysis of Qurʾan, Tafsir, and Sira: The Methodologies of John Wansbrough," and Fazlur Rahman, "Approaches to Islam in Religious Studies: Review Essay," in *Approaches to Islam in Religious Studies*, ed. Richard Martin (Tucson: University of Arizona Press, 1985), 151–63, 189–202.

[5] Bāqillānī ignores suras such as *al-zalzala* and *al-qāriʿa*, which most resemble *sūrat al-qadr* in their acoustical and semantic resonances. He also ignores *sūrat al-qadr* itself. Cf. Abū Bakr Muḥammad ibn al-Ṭayyib al-Bāqillānī, *Iʿjāz al-Qurʾān*, ed. As-Sayyid Aḥmad Saqr (Cairo: Dār al-Maʿārif, 1981). Zamakhsharī discusses some of these passages, but from a largely rhetorical perspective: Maḥmūd ibn ʿUmar al-Zamakhsharī, *Al-Kashshāf ʿan Ḥaqāʾīq Ghawāmiḍ al-Tanzīl wa ʿUyūn al-Aqāwīl fī Wujūh al-Taʾwīl* (Beirut: Dār al-Kitāb al-ʿArabī, 1947). In his *Faḍāʾil al-Qurʾān*, Ibn Kathīr relates traditions concerning the importance of proper recitation and the power of sound quality, but does not integrate such issues into his *tafsīr* proper: Ismaʿīl ibn ʿUmar ibn Kathīr, *Tafsīr al-Qurʾān al-ʿAẓīm*, vol. 7 (Beirut: Dār al-Fikr, 1966). Cf. Muḥammad ibn Ismāʿīl al-Bukhārī, *Al-Ṣaḥīḥ*, vol. 3 (Cairo: Muṣṭafā al-Bābī, 1953), 162–69. For a translation of Abū Ḥāmid al-Ghazālī's discussion of the *faḍāʾil*, see Muhammad Abul Quasem, *The Recitation and Interpretation of the Qurʾan: Al-Ghazālī's Theory* (London: Kegan Paul, 1982), pp. 18–33. In "The Qurʾan as Literature," *Religion and Literature* 20 (1988): 49–64, Mustansir Mir makes the following point (p. 49): "But, one might ask, does there not exist, at least in Arabic, a large number of works dealing with the literary qualities of the Qurʾan? Such works certainly exist. But most of them are, in respect of their orientation, premises, and structure, works of theology rather than of literary criticism, a typical example being *The Inimitability of the Qurʾan* by the medieval scholar Abū Bakr al-Bāqillānī (950–1013)."

Perhaps the specific issues examined below were too close to the heart of the experience of Qurʾanic discourse to gain the objectivity, the otherness, that would lead to academic inquiry. In this regard, see F. Denny, "Adab" (cited above, n. 3), p. 143, where the author describes the queries concerning his interest in Qurʾanic recitation that came from those who were learning and practicing it: "There was the sense in these queries that a Western student of Islam should be devoting his energies to understanding and appreciating the great themes of the Qurʾan and the history of their interpretation and application to the community."

The interpretation offered here is the first of several based upon years of teaching the Qurʾan to students not conversant with Arabic. The teaching makes use of a series of transliterated passages and interlinear word-for-word translations used in conjunction with cassettes of Qurʾanic reciters. After the students have heard the recitation and are able to relate sound to text, a word-for-word analysis of the text is presented, with particular attention to what is lost in translation.

[6] The atomistic view of Arabic poetry that is reflected in classical Arabic theory has been discussed in a number of recent studies. Cf. G. van Gelder, *Beyond the Line: Classical Arabic Literary Critics on the Coherence and Unity of the Poem* (Leiden: Brill, 1982); W. Heinrichs, "Literary Theory: The Problem of Its Efficiency," in *Arabic Poetry: Theory and Development*, ed. G. E. von Grunebaum (Wiesbaden: Otto Harrassowitz, 1973), 19–69; R. Scheindlin, *Form and Structure in the Poetry of al-Muʿtamid Ibn ʿAbbād* (Leiden: Brill, 1978); and J. Stetkevych, "Arabic Poetry and Assorted Poetics," in *Islamic Studies: A Tradition and Its Problems*, ed. Malcom Kerr (Malibu, Calif.: Undena Publications, 1980).

the others. Though other forms of literature might also be generated across the same modes, the goal here is a better understanding of the distinctive role they play in Qurᵓanic discourse.

(1) The semantic mode will include the lexical, syntactical, and thematic aspects of the text. For the sake of analysis, the term is used narrowly to indicate the discursive level of meaning, that level most accessible to translation.

(2) The acoustic mode evokes the problematic relationship of the Qurᵓan to poetry. Several Qurᵓanic passages (21:5, 37:36, 52:30, 69:41) reflect and refute the contention of some of Muhammad's contemporaries that the Qurᵓanic revelation was poetry. There are clear differences between the Qurᵓan and early Arabic poetry, most notably the Qurᵓan's lack of regular meter. Yet by some commonly held modern criteria—compactness and intensity—at least some Qurᵓanic passages can be classified as poetic. Roman Jakobson's suggestion that the poetic function of language should by no means be limited to poetry seems particularly relevant at this point.[7]

Early Arabic poetry is in part built around a tension between syntactical rhythm and metrical rhythm. The analysis below suggests that the Qurᵓan substitutes for that dynamic a heightened reliance upon the tension between syntactical rhythm and phonological cohesion,[8] the tying together of a unit of language through acoustical echoes, and, when cohesion extends over parallel lines, through phonological parallelism.[9] Of interest here will be the art of recitation, *tajwīd*, an essential aspect of the oral and aural text of the Qurᵓan. While many acoustical effects might still be present with a reading that ignores *tajwīd*, they would

[7] Roman Jakobson, "Linguistics and Poetics," in *Style in Language*, ed. Thomas A. Sebeok (Cambridge, Mass.: M.I.T. Press, 1960), 358–59.

[8] Of course, early Arabic poetry also contains various forms of phonological cohesion, but the Qurᵓan, with its lack of meter, seems to rely on them more strongly. The more easily identified effects would include interior echo, alliteration, assonance, consonance, euphony. In the article, "Sound in Poetry," from the *Princeton Encyclopedia of Poetry and Poetics* (Princeton: Princeton Univ. Press, 1965), 785–86, sound effects are divided into 17 categories—underpinning, counterpoising, rubricating emphasis, tagging, correlation, implication, diagramming, sound-representation, illustrative mime, illustrative painting, passionate emphasis, mood-evocation, expressive mime, expressive painting, ebullience, embellishment, and incantation—most of which can be applied to the Qurᵓan. However, the division of sound timbre into discreet figures tends toward the atomizing result noted in reference to classical Arabic criticism (above, n. 6). The effect of Qurᵓanic sound play often lies in its operation between and across such discrete categories.

[9] Analysis of parallelism has tended to focus upon grammatical parallelism at the expense of phonological parallelism. For some recent work on parallelism in Biblical criticism and related areas, see S. A. Geller, "Were the Prophets Poets?" *Prooftexts* 3 (1983): 211–21; idem, "A Poetic Analysis of Isaiah 40:1–2," *Harvard Theological Review* 77 (1984): 413–20; James Kugel, *The Idea of Biblical Parallelism: Parallelism and Its History* (New Haven: Yale Univ. Press, 1981); Adele Berlin, *The Dynamics of Biblical Parallelism* (Bloomington: Indiana Univ. Press, 1985); Robert Alter, *The Art of Biblical Poetry* (New York: Basic Books, 1985), esp. ch. 6, "Prophecy and Poetry," where parallelism is usually viewed through its grammatical expression; Dennis Pardee, *Ugaritic and Hebrew Poetic Parallelism: A Trial Cut* (Leiden: Brill, 1988); and Clarissa Burt, "Parallelism in Post-Jahiliyya Arabic Poetry," a paper presented to the American Oriental Society, Atlanta, 3/27/90, which focuses more strongly on phonological parallelism. See also the short discussion by Luis Alonso-Schokel to be found in the article "Sound," in *The Hebrew Bible in Literary Criticism*, ed. A. Preminger and E. Greenstein (New York: Ungar, 1986), 225–26, excerpted from *Vetus Testamentum Supplement* 7 (1959): 155–56. After a discussion of such sound figures as alliterative hendiadys, alliterative word pairs, alliterative parallel sentences, sound concatenation, sound-chiasm, and vowel reiteration, the author remarks: "These examples are selected from richer material. Unfortunately we are apt not to find such patterns very impressive. As moderns we are used to reading softly poetry that is intended to reverberate and resound. Moreover, this sort of observation is scarcely cultivated in biblical scholarship." See also L. Finkelstein, "The Hebrew Text of the Bible: A Study of its Cadence Symbols," in *Symbols and Society*, ed. L. Bryson et al. (New York: 1955), 409–26. Of special interest will be an effect similar to paronomasia, an effect built less upon verbal play at the level of lexeme and morpheme, as in the case of punning, than upon the play of sound figures at the submorphemic and transmorphemic levels. For a treatment of paronomasia at the more traditional morphemic and lexical level, see H. Reckendorf, *Über Paronomasie in den Semitischen Sprachen* (Verlag Alfred Ropelmann: Giessen, 1909); and the *New Oxford Annotated Bible with the Apocrypha* (Oxford: Oxford University Press, 1973), 1527, where the example given is the play on the name "Gilgal" and the verb *galah* (to go into exile) in *ki haggilgal galoh yighleh*. For a broader conception of paronomasia, see Jakobson, "Linguistics and Poetics" (n. 7 above).

be muted. *Tajwīd* underscores them and will serve as a useful index in the analysis.[10]

(3) The Qurʾan is imbued with a range of acoustically modulated emotive distinctions that are lost in translation.[11] In the abstract, only very general patterns of sound symbolism can be discerned. In the passages discussed below, for example, dense patterns of long *a*'s tend to be semantically open and emotively high-pitched, at times moving toward a sense of pure emotion, the phonetic equivalent of certain English interjections. The emotive charge is more supple than the interjection, however, not being confined to a particular lexical unit. This preliminary characterization is vague and hypothetical. The analysis will give it more specificity by tracing the sound figure through three vectors of amplification: (i) through intratextual phonological parallelism as the sound is repeated, echoed, and inverted throughout an extended passage; (ii) through the sound's intertwining with the semantic aspects of the text and its consequent adoption of certain semantic overtones; (iii) through the intertextual resonance of the sound figure with other key texts in the Qurʾan on the acoustical, lexical, and thematic planes.

(4) Of special interest to this study is the tension between natural gender and grammatical gender, as well as the tension between animate and inanimate. The grammatical gender of Arabic offers a double possibility for each pronoun and inflection when translated into the natural gender system of English: masculine and neuter or feminine and neuter, depending upon the individual case. In normal cases no problem arises: an inanimate object is translated by the neuter "it." However, in some passages of Qurʾanic Arabic, a subtle personification seems to inhere in many of the pronouns that on first glance have an inanimate referent. While there is at least anecdotal discussion within the classical *tafsīr* concerning the value of the Qurʾanic sound, to my knowledge the kind of gender dynamic discussed here is not a subject of classical *tafsīr*.

What follows is a close reading of *sūrat al-qadr*, one of the best known and most beloved passages in the Qurʾan. The expectation is that *sūrat al-qadr* has something to tell us about the importance of the role of the four modes in the generation of the Qurʾanic voice, and that the model of interplay offered here might engage dimensions of meaning in *sūrat al-qadr*, and, by extension, in other Qurʾanic passages, that elude traditional forms of literary analysis. No claim is made concerning quantitative difference in the occurrence of particular language units in the Qurʾan vs. other seventh-century Arabic texts, or in *sūrat al-qadr* vs. other passages in the Qurʾan.[12] Nor is any position taken on the debates over the acoustic arbitrariness of the linguistic sign and the evolutionary development of grammatical gender in Arabic.[13] The focus of this

[10] For an overview of *tajwīd*, see Ahmed Gouda, "Qurʾanic Recitation: Phonological Analysis" (Ph.D. diss., Georgetown Univ., 1988). Qurʾanic recitation will be treated here on the ideal level; actual differences in recitation style and dialectical influences on pronunciation will not be an issue. The acoustical distinctions are robust, i.e., made of several strands of acoustical effect. Though one or another strand might be influenced by a local difference, it is doubtful that the entire complex would be altered. The analysis is based upon contemporary recitation and the rules of *tajwīd* as they have been codified and applied in the basic style preserved in the *murattal* form. No position is taken on the question of whether or not contemporary recitation represents an unbroken and stable tradition from the time of Muhammad to the present. Like the questions of the sources and manner of composition of the Qurʾan, the question of possible historical developments in recitation is of secondary interest to the question posed here, i.e., how the Qurʾan as we know it—however it came to be—generates meaning.

[11] As opposed to the Vedas—to which the Qurʾan has been compared in its resistance to translation and the insistence of those who hold it sacred on the oral and aural character of the text (Graham, 80, 88)—the Qurʾanic involvement in emotion is striking. The role of emotion is a fundamental substantial difference between the two recitation traditions. Another difference is in scope; though the Vedic and Qurʾanic traditions are similar in their insistence upon the text in its oral performance in its original language, the Vedic tradition differs in limiting access to that form to an elite of brahmins, while the Qurʾanic text (see Graham, 96–109), pervades every aspect of Islamic life and society.

[12] For two recent systematic approaches, see Angelika Neuwirth, *Studien zur Komposition der mekkanischen Suren* (Berlin and New York: Walter de Gruyter, 1981), and Pierre Crapon de Caprona, *Le Coran aux sources de la parole oraculaire: Structures rhythmique des sourates mecquoises* (Paris: Publications Orientalistes de France, 1981). See also Issa J. Boullata, "The Rhetorical Interpretation of the Qurʾan: *iʿjāz* and Related Topics" in *Approaches to the History of the Interpretation of the Qurʾan*, ed. A. Rippin (Oxford: Clarendon Press, 1988), 139–57.

[13] For a critique of the more radical Saussurian position on the arbitrariness of the verbal sign, see R. Jakobson, *Six Lectures on Sound and Meaning* (Cambridge, Mass.: M.I.T. Press, 1979). For a review of research suggesting some cross-cultural evidence for sound symbolism, see R. Jakobson and Linda Waugh, *The Sound Shape of Language* (Bloomington:

study is the manner in which certain sound-units and patterns, that may be unexceptional in themselves, are transformed into meaningful sound figures through their implication in other constructs and their deployment through particular passages.

Though stress is placed in the beginning upon the three non-semantic elements, the second half of the essay focuses more on the semantic area. The distinction among the four modes, and the distinction between sound and meaning is provisional. No single mode exists by and in itself. Each takes on shape in combination with the others. In this sense we might speak of two kinds of semantics: semantics more narrowly defined (surface semantics) and a broader definition of semantics that will include the acoustic, emotive, and gender modes. The emphasis upon aspects of the Qur'anic text that have been underplayed in traditional analysis is not meant to sacrifice meaning to sound, but to contribute to a more multidimensional conception of meaning within the Qur'an.

سُورَةُ الفَدْرِ مَكِّيَّةٌ

بِسْمِ اللَّهِ الرَّحْمَنِ الرَّحِيمِ

إِنَّا أَنزَلْنَاهُ فِي لَيْلَةِ الْقَدْرِ ﴿١﴾

وَمَا أَدْرَاكَ مَا لَيْلَةُ الْقَدْرِ ﴿٢﴾

لَيْلَةُ الْقَدْرِ خَيْرٌ مِنْ أَلْفِ شَهْرٍ ﴿٣﴾

تَنَزَّلُ الْمَلَائِكَةُ وَالرُّوحُ فِيهَا بِإِذْنِ رَبِّهِم مِّن كُلِّ أَمْرٍ ﴿٤﴾

سَلَامٌ هِيَ حَتَّىٰ مَطْلَعِ الْفَجْرِ ﴿٥﴾

Sūrat al-Qadr

1 *Innā anzalnāhu fī laylati l-qadr*
2 *wa mā adrāka mā laylatu l-qadr*
3 *laylatu l-qadri khayrun min alfi shahr*
4 *tanazzalu l-malā'ikatu wa r-rūḥu fīhā bi idhni rabbihim min kulli amr*
5 *salāmun hiya ḥattā maṭlaʿi l-fajr*

The Sura of *Qadr*

1 We sent it down on the night of *qadr*
2 And what could let you know what the night of *qadr* is
3 The night of *qadr* is better than a thousand months
4 The angels and the spirit come down on it by leave of their lord from every *amr*
5 Peace it is until the rise of dawn

A plain-sense reading might have the following outline. The divine voice proclaims that it has sent something down upon the night of *qadr*, a night that is better than a thousand months. On that night, angels and the spirit descend by leave of their lord according, through, from, or with the *amr*. The night is said to be peace, a peace that lasts until the break of dawn. Yet even such a bare-boned reading is not without interpretive difficulties. The terms *qadr* and *amr* present problems for translation. The syntax at the end of verse 4 is ambiguous. The antecedents of the pronouns pose intricate problems of interpretation. On the grammatical and rhetorical level, these issues have been covered in the *tafsīr* works and in Theodor Lohmann's overview of *sūrat al-qadr*.[14] I will not repeat the earlier

---

Indiana Univ. Press, 1979), 177–237. Though this study presupposes no position on the sound value of any Arabic phoneme in itself, it is interesting to note that the suggestions here, particularly in the association of *a*-sounds with emotive intensity, echo one of the strongest cross-cultural equivalences. See for example, Jakobson's and Waugh's discussion of synaesthesia, pp. 188–93. For the question of gender, see Muhammad Hasan Ibrahim, *Grammatical Gender* (The Hague: Mouton, 1973); A. J. Wensinck, "Some Aspects of Gender in the Semitic Languages," *Verhandelingen der Koninklijke Nederlandsche Akademie van Wetenschappen te Amsterdam, Afdeeling Letterkunde*, 26 (1927): 1–60; L. Drozdik, "Grammatical Gender in Arabic Nouns," *Graeco-latina et Orientalia* 5 (1973): 217–46; M. Féghali and A. Cuny, *Du genre grammatical en sémitique* (Paris, 1924).

[14] For the overview of *sūrat al-qadr*, see Theodor Lohmann, "Die Nacht al-Qadr: Übersetzung und Erklärung von Sure 97," *Mitteilungen des Instituts für Orientforschung* 15 (1969): 275–85. For historical questions surrounding the night of *qadr* and its possible role as a new year's festival in pre-Islam, see K. Wagtendonk, *Fasting in the Koran* (Leiden: Brill, 1968); Lohmann, 281–83, and A. J. Wensinck, *Arabic New-Year and the Feast of Tabernacles* (Amsterdam, 1925). Whether *sūrat al-qadr* is Meccan or Medinan is in dispute, but acoustically *sūrat al-qadr* parallels Qur'anic passages usually associated with the early Meccan period (with the exception of *sūrat al-zalzala*). Such similarity does not imply that there is any temporal connection among these passages. The order of Qur'anic revelation is not relevant to the issues raised here. Of the *tafsīr* works, I have found two to be particularly useful: Fakhr al-Dīn al-Rāzī, *Al-Tafsīr al-Kabīr*, vol. 32 (Cairo: Iltizām ʿAbd al-Raḥmān Muḥammad, n.d.), 27–37

discussion, but will draw upon it when relevant to the issues of sound and meaning being discussed here.

In the rendition above, I have followed common practice in rendering as "it" the *hu* of verse 1, the *hā* of verse 4, and the *hiya* of verse 5. In this way not only *sūrat al-qadr*, but the Qurʾan as a whole, is most often rendered into English, with only those pronouns whose antecedents are unambiguously animate translated into masculine and feminine English pronouns. Yet there are possibilities here of an alternate reading, one that operates as an undertone beneath the surface semantics of the texts. Some later commentaries suggest that the antecedent of the *hu* in verse 1 might be Gabriel.[15] This suggestion is at odds with the preponderance of Qurʾanic language of *tanzīl* where the object in other cases is clearly the Qurʾan, and it is at odds with the preponderance of early *tafsīr*. Even so, in many *tafsīr* discussions, Gabriel and the sending down of the Qurʾan are so closely related that a reference to one may imply a reference to the other. Nor is the standard reading of the antecedent as the Qurʾan without problems. One school of interpretation suggests that the Qurʾan was sent down from the preserved tablet (*al-lawḥ al-maḥfūẓ*) to the lowest heaven (*al-samāʾ al-dunyā*) on the night of *qadr*, and then revealed to Muhammad over a period of twenty or twenty-three years, or, in an alternate version, that each year the part of the Qurʾan to be revealed that year was sent down to the lower heaven. Another school suggests that only the first revelation of Muhammad's prophecy was sent down on the night of *qadr*. It has been pointed out that the Qurʾanic term *anzala* usually denotes the sending down of something to earth and that the purely cosmic event of sending down the Qurʾan to the lowest heaven would have been a purely transcendent event. It would not likely have generated the combination of the cosmic and the intimate that underlies this and other of the shorter suras. On the other hand, there is no justification in the text itself for any *first* revelation being sent down.[16] Also of interest is a third perspective

---

and Muḥammad ibn Aḥmad al-Qurṭubī: *Al-Jāmiʿ li Aḥkām al-Qurʾān*, vol. 28 (Cairo, 1962), 130–38. Also consulted were the following: Muḥammad ibn Jarīr al-Ṭabarī, *Jāmiʿ al-Bayān ʿan Taʾwīl al-Qurʾān*, vol. 30 (Cairo, 1953), 258–62; Zamakhsharī, *Al-Kashshāf*, vol. 3 (cited above, n. 5), 282–83; Ibn Kathīr, *Tafsīr*, vol. 7 (cited above, n. 5), 330–41; ʿAbd Allāh ibn ʿUmar al-Bayḍāwī, *Anwār al-Tanzīl wa Asrār al-Taʾwīl*, vol. 2 (Osnabruck: Biblio Verlag, 1968), 411–12; Al-Faḍl ibn al-Ḥasan al-Ṭabarsī, *Majmaʿ al-Bayān fī Tafsīr al-Qurʾān*, vol. 9 (Beirut, 1379 A.H.), 516–21; Aḥmad ibn Muḥammad al-Khafājī, *Ḥāshiyat al-Shihāb: ʿInāyat al-Qāḍī wa Kifāyat al-Rāḍī ʿalā Tafsīr al-Bayḍāwī*, vol. 8 (Beirut: Dār Ṣādir, n.d.), 382–84; ʿAbd al-Karīm ibn Hawāzin al-Qushayrī, *Laṭāʾif al-Ishārat* (Cairo: Al-Hayʾa al-Miṣriyya al-ʿĀmma li al-Kitāb, 1983), 750–51; Muḥammad al-Ṭabāṭabāʾī, *Al-Mizān fī Tafsīr al-Qurʾān*, vol. 20 (n.p., 1974), 330–34; Ismāʾīl Ḥaqqī Bursevi, *Tafsīr Rūḥ al-Bayān*, vol. 10 (Beirut: Dār al-Fikr, n.d.), 479–86; Niẓām al-Dīn al-Ḥasan ibn Muḥammad Nīsābūrī, *Gharāʾib al-Qurʾān wa Raghāʾib al-Furqān*, vol. 30 (Cairo: Muṣṭafā al-Bābī, 1962–), 141–49; Maḥmūd ibn ʿAbd Allāh al-Alūsī, *Rūḥ al-Maʿānī fī Tafsīr al-Qurʾān al-ʿĀẓīm*, vol. 10 (Beirut: Dār al-Fikr, 1978), 241–56; ʿAlī ibn Ibrāhīm al-Qummī, *Tafsīr Qummī*, vol. 2 (Najaf: Maṭbaʿat Najaf, 1387 A.H.), 431–32.

[15] Khafājī, 382; the antecedent of the *hu* is said to be, by common consent, the Qurʾan, but it is noted that some have suggested Gabriel. In *The Meaning of the Glorious Qurʾan* (Beirut: Dār al-Kitāb al-Lubnānī, 1970), 814, Marmaduke Pickthall, who situates himself in the interpretive tradition of the Azhari Shaykh Muṣṭafā Marāghī, flatly assimilates the *rūḥ* to Gabriel or other angels by glossing *rūḥ* as "Gabriel, or, as some commentators think, a general term for angels of the highest rank." Ahmed Ali translates *rūḥ* in this instance as "grace": *Al-Qurʾān: A Commentary Translation* (Princeton: Princeton Univ. Press, 1988), 544. For a discussion of *rūḥ* in the Qurʾan see Thomas O'Shaughnessy, *The Development of the Meaning of Spirit in the Koran* (Rome: Pont. Institutum Orientalium Studiorum, 1953). O'Shaughnessy provides a commentary on each Qurʾanic proof text, a commentary concerned primarily with the possible extra-Qurʾanic sources for the differing Qurʾanic treatments of *rūḥ*. Earlier treatments include D. B. MacDonald, "The Development of the Idea of Spirit in Islam," *Acta Orientalia* 9 (1931): 307–51; and E. E. Calverley, "Doctrines of the Soul (*Nafs* and *Ruḥ*) in Islam," *Moslem World* 33 (1943): 254–65, a revision of Wensinck's article *Nafs* in EI_1, 3:827–30. For Calverley and Wensinck, *rūḥ* is a "special angel messenger and a special divine gift" (Calverley, 254). MacDonald makes a four-set division: passages in which the *rūḥ* is identified with Jibrīl; with a "personality apart from the angels" (70:4, 78:38, 97:4); with the "Angel of Revelation" (2:87, 253; 5:110; 16:102)—and here he cites various opinions on 2:87 (Jibrīl, the spirit of ʿĪsā, the *injīl*, the "Most Great Name of Allah by which ʿĪsā raised the dead," the "*kalām* by which the *dīn* or the *nafs* are vivified to eternal life and purified from sins"; and four passages (16:2; 17:85; 40:15; 42:52) where *rūḥ* is combined with *amr*, where it can mean *waḥī*, the Qurʾan, a spiritual influence rather than a person (pp. 308–14, with verse numbers adjusted to the Egyptian standard). For *tafsīr* treatments of the word *rūḥ* in 2:87 see Mahmoud Ayoub, *The Qurʾan and Its Interpreters*, vol. 1 (Albany: State Univ. of New York Press, 1984), 124–25.

[16] See Lohmann, 277–78. The case for the antecedent of *hu* in verse 1 being the Qurʾan is centered on the parallels with 44:1–3: *ḥm / wa l-kitābi l-mubīn / innā anzalnāhu fī laylatin*

whereby the Qur'an would have been revealed to Muhammad, not verbally, but in a trans-verbal, even trans-conscious experience in which the words were inchoate.[17]

More common than the identification of the *hu* with Gabriel is the identification of the *rūḥ* (spirit) in verse 4 with Gabriel or other high angels.[18] Again, the hypostasizing interpretation suggests a movement toward a more animate and personified gender construction within the text, a construction that remains in tension with the non-animate reading. These intimations of personification form one side of a latent gender dynamic, the other side of which is provided by the feminine gender constructions dependent upon the construct *laylat al-qadr*.

Before beginning the close reading, it might help to have an overview of the sura's syntactical, phonological, and rhythmic grids. I have divided the sura into two basic grids. As is often the case with the shorter suras, a strong metric sense is to be found toward the end of the verses, while the beginning of the verses tend to be more variable and less metric.[19] The first grid

---

mubārakatin innā kunnā mundhirīn and 2:184: *shahru ramaḍāna l-ladhī unzila fīhi l-qur'ān*. The major tension is between the tradition related through Ibn ᶜAbbās that the night of *qadr* was the occasion for the sending down of the Qur'an from the preserved tablet to the earthly heaven and then revealed by Gabriel to Muhammad over a period of 23 years, and that related through al-Shaᶜbī (who is also placed by Ṭabarī as relating the opposing tradition) that the night of *qadr* was the occasion of the first revelation. Cf. Ṭabarī, 258 (who gives 20 years for the full revelation in Ibn ᶜAbbās's version); Ṭabarsī, 518 (who gives 23 years to the Ibn ᶜAbbās tradition); and Rāzī, 27–28. The difference between the 20 and 23 year prophecy results from the disagreement over how long a period of interruption in prophecy was experienced by Muhammad shortly after his prophetic call. Cf. A. Guillaume, *The Life of Muhammad: A Translation of Ibn Isḥāq's Sīrat Rasūl Allāh* (Oxford: Oxford Univ. Press, 1955), 111–12. Rāzī's discussion gives a good example of the tortured logic employed to make Ibn ᶜAbbās's postulate of a descent to the lowest heaven plausible, in view of the absence of textual backing. Wensinck tends toward accepting the Ibn ᶜAbbās tradition, pointing out the equal lack of textual backing for any reference to a first revelation: Wensinck, 1–3.

[17] See the traditions of ᶜĀ'isha (in Bukhārī, *Ṣaḥīḥ, bad' al-waḥī*) and Abdallah ibn ᶜUmar (in Ibn Ḥanbal, *Musnad*). Titus Burckhardt gives a discussion of this perspective that serves as an interpretive translation for the elliptical commentary attributed to Ibn ᶜArabī, but probably by his commentator, ᶜAbd al-Razzāq al-Kāshānī (d. 730/1329). According to Burckhardt, the Qur'an descends in an undifferentiated form upon the body of the prophet rather than the mind, since the "relatively undifferentiated nature" of the body is related to pure cosmic potentiality: "In the same way the state of perfect receptivity—the state of the Prophet when the Qur'an 'descended'—is a 'night' into which no distinctive knowledge penetrates: manifestation is here compared to day. This state is also 'peace' because of Divine Presence which comprehends in their immutable plenitude all the first realities of things—all the Divine 'Commands'." This reading, sensitive to both the Sufi interpretation and the undertones of the sura to be discussed below, is partially clouded by the expressions taken from R. Guenon, whereby the night is equivalent to "*caro* and not *mens*." Cf. T. Burckhardt, *An Introduction to Sufi Doctrine*, tr. D. M. Matheson (Lahore: Sh. Muhammad Ashraf, 1959), 43–44; see also Burckhardt's discussion of *rūḥ*, pp. 19–21. For the passage on which Burckhardt bases his reading, see Muḥyī ad-Dīn ibn al-ᶜArabī [?], *Tafsīr al-Qur'ān al-Karīm*, ed. Muṣṭafā Ghālib (Tehran, 1979), 831: *laylatu l-qadri hiya l-binyatu l-muḥammadiyyatu ḥāla iḥtijābihi ᶜalayhi as-salām, fī maqāmi l-qalb baᶜda sh-shuhūdi dh-dhātī*, "The night of *qadr* is the Muhammadiyyan constitution in the condition of his being veiled, peace upon him, in the station of the heart after the pre-essential manifestation." The "Muhammadiyyan" is a category used throughout Ibn al-ᶜArabī's works to refer to that Sufi station of "no station," beyond all differentiated categories and knowledge, and to Sufis who attain that station. I discuss this concept in detail in "Ibn ᶜArabī's Garden among the Flames: A Reevaluation," *History of Religions* 23 (1984): 287–315. The term may be used in a somewhat different manner in this commentary, but to equate the *binya l-muḥammadiyya fī maqāmi l-qalb* with the Christian notion of "flesh" seems to me problematic.

[18] Rāzī, 32, follows popular interpretation in reading the *rūḥ* as *jibrīl*, but he lists the following alternative interpretations: 1) a great angel; 2) a group of angels invisible (to other angels), except on *laylat al-qadr*; 3) another group of creatures, neither angel nor human; 4) ᶜĪsā; 5) the Qur'an; 6) *al-raḥma* (compassion); 7) the most exalted of the angels; 8) the recorder-angels (*ḥafaẓa, kirāmūn kātibūn*).

[19] For a good overview of the complex question of Qur'anic rhythm, see Caprona, 178–212. Caprona attempts to find a metrical system that will function for the early Meccan suras. The analysis here bases itself upon the more traditional contrast between metrical sections of verses and those which seem resistant to metrical analysis. The attempt to quantify the Qur'anic verse is laden with complexities. Thus for example, the end-syllables (*qadr, shahr, amr, fajr*) are subject to the recitation phenomena of *naql* or *itbāᶜ*, the pronunciation of an intercalated vowel—reflecting either the dropped final vowel or the previous vowel—between the final two consonants: (*qadir* or *qadar*, etc.). Cf. W. Wright, *A Grammar of the Arabic Language*, vol. 2 (Cambridge: Cambridge Univ.

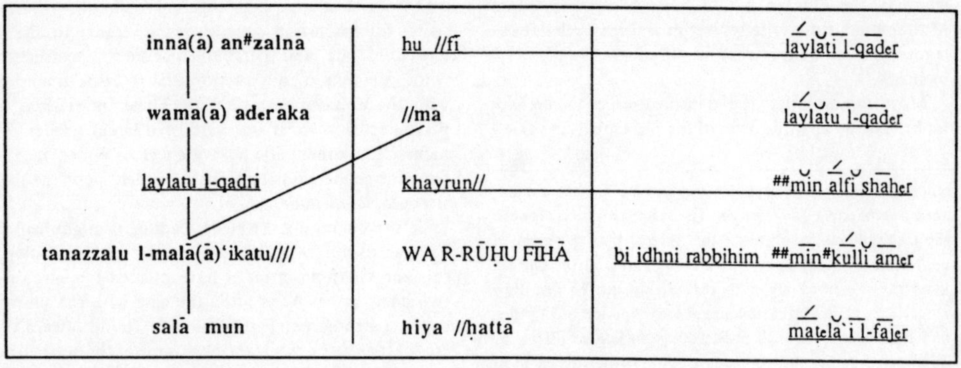

Key: e Anaptyctic Vowel (naql, itbā', qalqala). //// Rhythmic Break (ā) madd

Nasalization (ikhfā') **bold**: first grid based on /ā/ dominate phonic cohesions

Strong Nasalization (ghunna, idghām) underline: second grid based on closed syllables, rhythmic cohesion

// Syntactical Caesura central section: central axis, aspirate dominated phonic cohesion

Fig. 1a.

consists of the first parts of verses 1, 2, 4, and 5, which are held together by a tight phonological parallelism built around the /ā/, open syllables, and nasals. The second grid consists of the last parts of each verse and all of verse 3. Each verse ends with a strongly metric and accentual rhythm, and a phonology based on wide consonantal variety and on closed as opposed to open syllables.

Verse 4 is complex. Its ending (*min kulli amr*) fits in strongly with the second grid, and part of its early section fits in phonologically with the first grid. But its central section, *wa r-rūḥu fīhā*, is left in an anomalous position, stranded as it were in the center of the verse. Alternatively, verse 4 can be divided into two sections, with the *wa r-rūḥu fīhā* at the end of the first section, where it would almost fit rhythmically, but contrast phonologically (its long open syllables in marked contrast to the closed syllables of *min alfi shahr* and *min kulli amr*). The long open syllable (*hā*) at the end would hang over the margin set by the rhyme (*tasjīʿ*) syllables, giving it a special marking.[20] However verse 4 is treated, the phrase *wa r-rūḥu fīhā* is at the center of a series of converging semantic and acoustic pressures. It becomes the dominant term within a third category that includes terms that fall between the two dominant grids for one reason or another: the *hu* in verse 1 and second *mā* in verse 2, *khayrun* in verse 3, *wa r-rūḥu fīhā* in verse 4, and *ḥattā* in verse 5. (See figs. 1a and 1b.)

The reading is divided into three sections. The first focuses upon phonological cohesion and parallelism as it is constructed through *sūrat al-qadr*. The second ties those features to thematic aspects of the sura and thematically parallel passages elsewhere in the Qur'an. The third section traces key sound figures from *sūrat al-qadr* through other, phonologically parallel passages with similar implied personifications.

Press, 1859–62 [1967]), 372; Caprona, *Le Coran*, 230; and Henri Fleisch, *Traité de philologie arabe*, vol. 1 (Beirut: Imprimerie Catholique, 1961), 175–78. Adding to the difficulty are the effects of *tajwīd*, not only the *madd*, but also the *ghunna* and *ikhfā'* and *qalqalqa*, which also affect duration. With major methodological difficulties left unsolved, any rhythmic points made here must necessarily be *ad hoc* and tentative.

20 Caprona, 228–34, divides the verse into two rhythmic units, the first of which ends with *wa r-rūḥu fīhā*. Arberry, 345, translates the sura by dividing verse 4 in the same way.

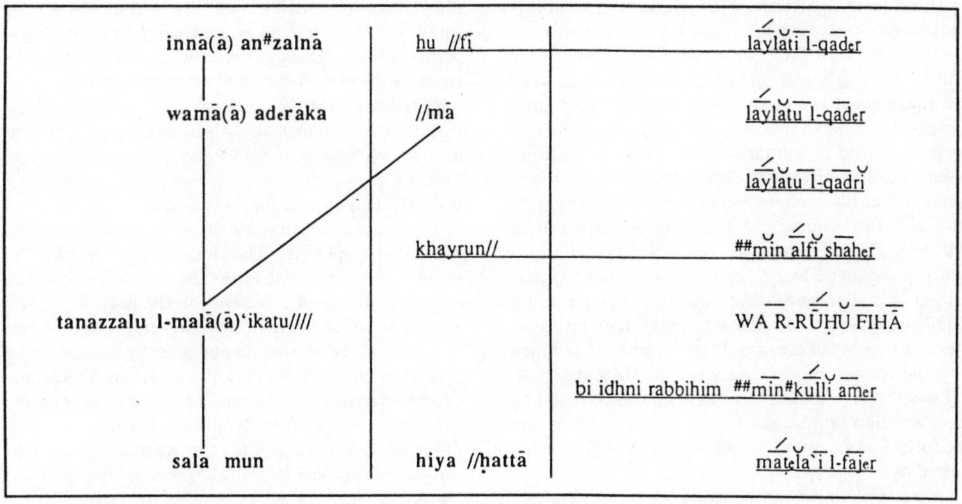

Key: e Anaptyctic Vowel (naql, itbā', qalqala).
Nasalization (ikhfā')
Strong Nasalization (ghunna, idghām)
// Syntactical Caesura
//// Rhythmic Break
(ā) madd
bold: first grid based on /a/ dominate phonic cohesions
underline: second grid based on closed syllables, rhythmic cohesion
central section: central axis, aspirate dominated phonic cohesion

Fig. 1b.

I

Verse 1: *innā anzalnāhu fī laylati l-qadr*

The first half of verse 1 contains various permutations of *a*-sound and *n*-sound combinations: *in/nā/an/zal/nā/*. The particle-pronoun combination *innā* is untranslatable, yet is critical. The doubled *n* in *innā*, lengthened and nasalized by the *tajwīd* convention of *ghunna* is followed by an /ā/ which is in turn extended by the *tajwīd* lengthening (*madd*) that occurs when an /ā/ precedes a *hamza*. The closed and nasalized *nn* provides a tension and withheld energy that is released in the following /ā/ in a moment of semantic-acoustical intensity.

The initial *innā* would not generate such a commentary were its effects not amplified by the following syllables. The acoustical effects of the *ghunna* and *a*-vowel combination are recast in a new permutation: *an/zal/nā*. The result is an intricately intertwined series of echoes, partial echoes, inverse echoes, tensions and releases, constructed of *a*- and *n*- sounds and hinging on the liquid /l/.[21] These effects are amplified by the anti-metrical and lapidary rhythm of the five consecutive long syllables—the continued sequence of long syllables forcing the reciter and hearer to dwell upon the aural aspects of the sound-unit.

---

[21] Perversely, the descriptive language tends to become more laborious the more supple and subtle are the original sound effects being described. The following description is offered as a supplement. The *an* and the final *nā* are partial inverse echoes of one another. The initial /ā/ is followed by a closed syllable, *anz* enhanced by *ikhfā'* (nasalized combination of the /n/ with the following /z/). This initial *an* combines qualities of the *nn* and of the *nā* from the previous word *innā*. The *an* is partially echoed by the final *nā* in *anzalnā* with its /n/ followed by an open /ā/. This acoustical mirroring or inverse imaging is embedded within an oblique repetition (the closed *in* syllable of *innā* partially repeated by the closed *an* of *anzalnā*) and by a pronounced exact repetition (the *nā* of *anzalnā* echoing the *nā* of *innā*), the latter repetition intensified further by the *madd* lengthening of the original *nā*. The

The acoustical intensity of the phrase *innā anzalnā* is balanced by a semantic openness. The sura begins without an antecedent for the pronoun "we." The listener will have no difficulty identifying the Qur'anic "we," but the introduction of a pronoun without stated antecedent in the first verse of a chapter gives to the discourse a sense of authority and solemnity. Identity needs no announcement. The *pluralis majestatis* is generated at the combination of two morphemes (*inna* and *nā*). The echoing and extension of the nasalised /ā/ throughout the first two verses generates a transmorphemic sound figure that extends beyond any particular lexical or morphemic boundary. The result is a combination of sound and sense, emphasis and naturalness, arising out of the sound texture and not confined to a particularized interjection like the standard translations "lo" or "indeed"—a sense of subjectivity and proclamation beyond anything captured by the purely rhetorical description of the Qur'anic first person plural as a "royal we."[22]

After the sequence of *a-* and *n*-sounds in *innā anzalnā*, the *hu* marks a phonological shift which, though unremarkable in itself, will take on significance within the sura. Syntactically the word clearly belongs with the first half of the verse: *innā anzalnāhu*. However, its phonological cohesion—its shift from the previous phonemes along with its ease in fitting in with the aural texture of the second half of the verse—pulls it toward the second half of the verse. Rhythm seems to reinforce the pull toward the second half. A quantitative scansion of verse 1 yields: – – – – –/(hu) – – ⏑ – –, which would put the *hu* in the second half, yielding a 10/10 balance. This placement would fit the metrical sense of the end of the sura: after the thick series of long syllables, the *hu* fits in with the final part of the verse to form a more metrically natural unit.[23] With the lengthening effects of *madd* and *ghunna*, considerations of quantitative balance would pull the *hu* even more strongly toward the second half.

The tension surrounding the *hu* is compounded by its semantic openness. The lack of antecedent for the *nā* in *anzalnāhu* foreshadows the even more charged case of an unstated antecedent in the case of *hu*. The second occurrence within a single verse of a pronoun without a stated antecedent puts a heavy burden on the second pronoun. In the case of the *nā*, the divine voice can be inferred as the antecedent. Though the consensus of commentary and the plain-sense interpretation of the text would suggest the Qur'an as the antecedent for *hu*, the difficulties in interpretation pointed out above keep *hu* from achieving semantic closure.[24]

The /ī/ of *fī* and the flow of liquids (*lay/la/til/qadr*) in four successive syllables offer a sonic contrast to the first half of the verse, reinforcing the position of the *hu* between the two halves. The *hu*, pulled in one direction by syntactical rhythm and in the other by phonological cohesion, metrical rhythm, and quantitative balance, lacking in specified antecedent, becomes the matrix of semantic, acoustic, emotive, and gender energy within verse 1. This tension and centrality are further heightened by the resonance of *hu* with other aspirates along the central axis of the sura. The multi-sourced resonance around the word *hu* calls attention to the latent ambivalence between its animate and inanimate possibilities. By contrast, the feminine gender of *laylat al-qadr*, and consequently the possibility of a personification, is not yet highlighted by any gender marked pronoun or inflection.

Verse 2: *wa mā adrāka mā laylatu l-qadr*

The expression *mā adrāka mā* is used here, as elsewhere in the Qur'an, to mark a term that is not expected to be immediately understood. With its long *a*'s and nasals the *mā adrāka mā* is phonologically parallel to

liquid /l/ occurs within *anzalnā* as a hinge on which the echoing, mirroring, and reduplication swing. Finally, just as the tension of the *nn* in *innā* is released in the *alif-hamza* combination that follows it, so in somewhat less intense a way the tension of the *nz* is released in the following *alif*, the intermediary *zāl* serving as a mediation of the acoustical and semantic play of tension and release. Of course, such effects become semantically and acoustically significant only insofar as they are picked up and amplified throughout the sura. It would be easy to imagine contexts in which such a phrase would be completely unexceptional, or in which its phonological character would inhibit rather than enhance the discursive resonance. It is interesting to compare this verse to 44:3 (above, n. 17) which is itself made up of an extraordinary thick use of nasals and long *a*'s.

[22] In line with his dominant interest in determining how the Qur'an was composed, Nöldeke suggests that in this case, as in others involving suras beginning with *innā*, we might be dealing with the fragment of a sentence, whose first part is lost. Cf. Theodor Nöldeke, *Geschichte des Qorāns*, vol. 1 (Hildesheim: Georg Olms Verlag, 1970), 92–93.

[23] See Nelson, 9–13, and Gouda, 288–93, for discussions of rhythmic and metrical shifts in the Qur'an.

[24] Again, Rāzī's commentary is among the more complete, with a full discussion of the rhetorical elements that bring about a sense of *ta'dhīm*: the lack of specified antecedent, the use of the plural, etc. See Rāzī, 27.

the *innā anzalnā* of verse 1. In each case we have a repetition of a nasal and long vowel (*nā . . . nā, mā . . . mā*) and in each case the first long vowel is lengthened by a *madd* due to a following *hamza*. The interior undertones, inverse echoes, and partial echoes of the nasalized *ạ*-sounds of *innā anzalnā* also find correspondences with the interior acoustics of *mā adrāka mā*, with the /r/, enhanced by the *tajwīd* effect of *qalqalqa* (*a-d-ə-rā-ka*), playing the role of liquid hinge corresponding to the /l/ in *anzalnā*.

As with verse 1, there is a tension between syntactical rhythm and phonological cohesion. Syntactically, the verse falls into two parts, with a caesura after *adrāka*: (*wa mā adrāka* // *mā laylatu l-qadr*), putting the second *mā* in the second half of the verse. However, the cohesion of long-*a* sounds and nasalized consonants ties the *mā* to the first half of the verse, rather than to the second. This attachment is reinforced by the phonological parallelism between the units *innā anzalnā* and *mā adrāka mā*. Quantitative balance leaves the *mā* in the hovering between the first and second halves of the verse.[25] Like the *hu* in verse 1, the second *mā* is in tension between a syntactical pull forward toward the second half of the verse, and phonological cohesion that pulls it back, and a complex quantitative harmonics that seems to pull in both directions.

Verse 3: *laylatu l-qadri khayrun min alfi shahr*

The meaning of *laylat al-qadr* is questioned, but direct answer is deferred. The *mā adrāka mā* ends in a deeper sense of questioning, rather than in any quick resolution. Instead of explaining what the night of *qadr* might be, the text repeats the phrase *laylat al-qadr* for the third time—this time at the beginning of the verse, and then offers the comparison to a thousand months. The verse is framed by two phrases *laylatu l-qadri* and *min alfi shahr* which belong rhythmically and phonologically with the verse ends of the sura. The two phrases surround the rhythmical and semantic pivot, *khayrun*, with its spondaic weightiness. The verse is made up entirely of short and closed syllables, in contrast to the previous verses, which were dominated by open, long *a*'s. This phonic texture interrupts the emotive pitch set by the beginnings of the first two verses, while the repetitions of the construct *laylat al-qadr* reinforces the sense of anticipation.

The acoustic effects mirror a thematic sense of anticipation. The night of *qadr* is said to be better than a thousand months. In two cases the Qurʾan makes a similar remark concerning the transformation of temporal categories in connection with the spirit. The opening verses of *sūrat al-maʿārij* (70:4) combine a reference to the *yawm ad-dīn* with the suggestion that the angels and the *rūḥ* rise upon a day whose length is fifty thousand years. In the second (32:5) a day is said to equal two thousand years by normal calculation. The reference occurs in a passage describing the divine *amr* and the creation of the primordial human (*al-insān*) through the breathing of *rūḥ* into its shape. *Rūḥ* is thus connected with three moments—the creation of the first human, the *yawm ad-dīn*, and the prophetic experience of the night of *qadr*—and in each of the three moments temporal categories are transformed.[26] The significance of this transformation is as yet partially veiled by the acoustic matter-of-factness of the phonemic pattern, by the lack of specific reference at this point to the spirit, and by the lack of any enactment of this implied temporal transformation. All three of these elements occur in the following verse.

Verse 4: tanazzalu l-malāʾikatu wa r-rūḥu fīhā bi idhni rabbihim min kulli amr

tanazzalu l-malāʾikatu. Verse 4 is the longest, most complex within the sura. It begins with a change in tense and voice, from the perfect, transitive *anzalnā* in verse 1 to the imperfect, intransitive *tanazzalu* (*tatanazzalu*), a shift that occurs within the repetition of the same verbal root. The comparison of a day to a thousand months that was made in verse 3 suggested the transformation of temporal linearity into a point of absolute present. The sudden shift from perfect to imperfect enacts that change.[27] The identical action is presented once as completed, once as in process, once transitive, once as intransitive. The shift in tense and

[25] Again, the results depend upon how one counts the *madd*: ⏑ – (–) – – ⏑ *mā* – ⏑ – –.

[26] While many commentators interpret the comparison of the night to a thousand months as simply being an indication of the greatness of the night, Qurṭubī, 131, cites a tradition that seems to get more to the heart of the way such comparisons are used in these passages. In this tradition, the comparison indicates that the night of *qadr* is a night equal to all time, *jamīʿ ad-dahr*.

[27] The Christian mystics, John the Scot Erigena and Meister Eckhart, both emphasized the combination of perfect and imperfect tenses as essential to an intimation of the "eternal moment," the moment that for Eckhart always has occurred and always is occurring, and which in his Christian interpretation corresponds to the eternal birth of the son of God in the soul: *semper nascitur, semper natus est* (Cf. Meister Eckhart, *Die deutschen und lateinischen Werke* (Stuttgart and Berlin: W. Kohlhammer, 1936), LW, *Comm. Jn.* 3:9–10.

voice, not unusual in itself, becomes pronounced when heard through its resonances with the aural, emotive, and gender aspects of the passage.

The words *tanazzalu l-malāʾikatu* mark a shift in phonological timbre from that of the preceding verse. The three *a*-sounds in *malāʾikatu*, with a long *a* lengthened by a *madd*, bring back the phonetic pattern of verse 1, with echoes of the /a/'s in "*innā anzalnāhu.*" The /z/ (strengthened through *ikhfāʾ*) and the /l/ in *anzalnāhu* are amplified into a droning, doubled /z/ and a sequence of three /l/s in *tanazzalu l-malāʾika.* This acoustic reverberation and its modulation through the acoustics of the sura as a whole intensify the connection between the shift in tense and mood and the enactment of the temporal transformation anticipated in the previous verse.

wa r-rūḥu fīhā. Lohmann has suggested that verse 4 is an "alien body" in the sura, pointing out that it "explodes" the hymnic rhythm of the sura through its lengthy and prosaic *Erklärung*.[28] Of interest here is not the cause of the rhythmic "explosion," but its literary effect. After the tightly structured rhythms of verses 1–3, the rhythm does break down in verse 4, particularly with the sequence of three short syllables in *malāʾikatu*, resulting in a rhythmic hiatus between *malāʾikatu* and the following conjunctive phrase, *wa r-rūḥu fīhā*. The sense of being cut off from the previous phrase is further enhanced by the position of *wa r-rūḥu fīhā* within the verse, and sura as a whole, and by its distinctive phonology, the sequence of long vowels: the /ū/ that seems amplified rather than interrupted by the *ḍamma*, the /ī/ and the /ā/:

– – ⌣ – – ⌣ – (–) ⌣ ⌣ ⌣   – – ⌣ – –   ⌣ – ⌣ – ⌣ – – – ⌣ –

tanazzalu l-malāʾikatu / wa r-rūḥu fīhā / bi idhni rabbihim min kulli amr

Wa r-rūḥu fīhā is balanced on either side by phrases that are quantitatively similar, especially when one takes into consideration the *madd* in *malāʾika*. The most evident reading of this verse would not separate *tanazzalu l-malāʾika* from *wa r-rūḥu fīhā*, but would read them together as a unit: "The angels and the spirit come down upon her by leave of their lord through every *amr*." An alternative, acknowledged in some later *tafsīr* literature, places *wa rūḥu fīhā* in a circumstantial relation: "The angels come down—the spirit with them—upon her by leave of their lord from every *amr*."[29] This interpretation is admittedly weak, from the point of view of surface semantics, but when looked at in view of the rhythmic and phonological break after the word *malāʾikatu* and the position of the *wa r-rūḥu fīhā* within the phrase and within the verse as a whole, it may well have a rationale that is not purely syntactical and which may operate more as a semantic undertone than as an interpretive option. In the circumstantial undertone, the unit *wa r-rūḥu fīhā* would be balanced syntactically between the two phrases that together form a complete expression: *tanazzalu l-malāʾikatu bi idhni rabbihim min kulli amr*.

If we divide the verse into two sections (as in fig. 1b), the phrase *wa r-rūḥu fīhā* finds itself isolated and marked in yet another manner. It fits rhythmically between the preceding and following verse-ends, which are themselves in phonological, syntactical, and rhythmic parallelism with one another, but its open syllables contrast dramatically with their closed syllables. As mentioned above, the *hā* in *fīhā* hangs over the margin established by the rhythmic boundary, giving it a particularly strong marking.

Whether verse 4 is counted as one unit or two, the phrase *wa r-rūḥu fīhā* is at the center of a variety of phonological and rhythmic stresses. At this point, I would suggest that a third possibility might be heard: "*the spirit upon or within her*," i.e., the night of *qadr*. Keeping the night as *hā*'s antecedent and combining such a reading with the circumstantial syntax would make the central action that of spirit coming upon the night of *qadr* or upon the personification of the night. The action would be related in a grammatically oblique manner, surrounded by the main sentence which relates the secondary action—the angelic accompaniment as it were. Such a possibility has little justification on the level of surface syntax. Rather, the rhythmic "explosion" exerts a strong enough pressure against the syntactical flow of the verse to allow a semantic undertone

[28] Lohmann, 283: "In diesem Zusammenhang erscheint V. 4 als ein Fremdkörper, der dieses rhythmische Preislied durch eine längere prosaische Erklärung sprengt. Sowohl in seiner äußeren Form als auch in seinem Inhalt erweist sich V. 4 als ein späterer Zusatz." Even Caprona, whose metric system is very flexible, is led to concede a rhythmic breakdown (*une arythmie*) at this point: Caprona, 230. He then goes on to suggest a cause: "On serait donc tenté de se demander par exemple si *tanazzalu l-malāʾikatu* n'aurait pas été substitué, par erreur de lecture peut-être d'un *ductus* très primitif, à une autre formule qui rétablirait les isochronies. . . ."

[29] See Khafājī, 384, who considers this the weaker possibility. Qurṭubī, 133, suggests that the intent of the verse in question is indicated by the parallel in 16:2: *yunazzalu l-malāʾikatu bi r-rūḥi min amrihi.*

that would be otherwise untenable. This suggestion will be given additional weight when we turn later in the essay to resonances with other Qur'anic passages.

The central location of *wa r-rūḥu fīhā* in the verse and of *ḥu* in this clause, and the resulting pivotal position of the *ḥu* on the syntactical, semantic, and acoustical levels, set up a reverberation with the other aspirates that occur along the phonological and rhythmic central axis of the sura: the /*ḥ*/ of the *ḥatta* in the following verse, and the *hu* of *anzalnāhu* in verse 1. While the *ḥu* in *rūḥu* is not pronominal, and while the *ḥu* of *rūḥu* is a different phoneme from the *hu* of verse 1, a partial correspondence is generated by the repetition of the *fī* + feminine construction: *hu fī laylati l-qadr* in verse 1 and the *ḥu fīhā* in verse 4, by the centrality of each sound unit within its respective verse, and by the aural dynamic of the sura as a whole. The effect of the complex echoing between *hu fī* and *ḥu fīhā* may be the generation, as an undertone of a transmorphemic sound symbol, the aspirate *ḍamma*. Such a figure might echo the association of spirit and breath that is evoked by the resonance of this passage with parallel passages elsewhere in the Qur'an.[30]

Above, I rendered the *fīhā* as "on it." The phrase is normally interpreted as indicating the *time* of the coming down of the angels (they come down during the night of *qadr*, or, according to the subtext, when the spirit was upon the night of *qadr*). But it can also be read as indicating the locus or receptor of the revelation, as in the symbolic interpretation attributed to Ibn al-ʿArabī (above, n. 17). Translated as feminine, the *hā* would have as its antecedent the *laylatu l-qadr* in a quasi-personified sense. The spirit would be upon her or entering into her, the latter interpretation giving clear implications of insemination and conception, as associated with the story of Maryam and the spirit. Within such an undertone the *fī* would become not only an indicator of temporal or spatial relation but a pivot for the gender interplay.

bi idhni rabbihim min kulli amr. The final section of verse 4 presents a very different texture: syntactically loose, lexically ambiguous, acoustically rapid. The final phrase, *min kulli amr*, is in a strong acoustic relation to the previous phrase, forming a run of closed syllables, doubled consonants, and *kasras*: *bi idhni rabbihim min kulli amr*. The *idghām* (the assimilation of the *mīm* of *rabbihim* into the *mīm* of *min*) and the *ikhfā'* (between the *nūn* and the *kāf*) both add to the sense of doubling and elongation. After the sequence of open syllables in the first and central sections of the verse, this final sequence of /i/'s, closed syllables and geminate consonants comes as a strong contrast: *bi-idh-ni rab-bi-him-min-kul-li-amr*. It also parallels syntactically, phonologically, rhythmically, and accentually, the last part of the previous verse (with ## indicating *ghunna*, and # indicating *ikhfā'*).

un##min alfi shahr

– ⏑ – ⏑ –

bi idhni rabbihim##min #kulli amr

– – – ⏑ –

The *min* clause is syntactically ambiguous. It could imply that the angels (and the spirit) come down in possession of *amr*, as a result of *amr*, or as a manifestation, part, vestige of, or wholly made up of, *amr*. The syntax here is so loose that some traditions place the phrase *min kulli amr* with the following verse (i.e., "in every affair it is peace").[31] Syntactical ambiguity is heightened by lexical indeterminacy in the word *amr* (command, order, dispensation, matter, affair, business at hand), one of the most fluid terms in the Qur'an. This ambiguity is reinforced by the phonic parallel with the last part of the previous verse (*min alfi shahr*), with its intimations of a transformation of temporal categories. Following the rhythmic break earlier in the

---

[30] See below, pp. 254–55. The power of acoustic correspondences can be heard in the way syntax is overriden in Sufi use of the *tahlīl* as a *dhikr*. *Lā ilāha illā llāh* is composed of the kind of intense aural texture being discussed here, in this case a run of *l*'s and long *a*'s very similar to the run of *n*'s and long *a*'s that occurs in several places in *sūrat al-qadr*. A certain Sufi use of the *tahlīl* as a *dhikr* begins with the chanting of the entire refrain, and then proceeds to drop off phonemes from the beginning until reaching a culmination in the chant "*hu, hu*." While strictly speaking the *hu* is merely the last consonant of the word *allah* and the grammatical inflection for the nominative, when it is isolated within the *dhikr* it becomes indistinguishable from the pronominal *hu*/*huwa* (he), the divine beloved, and is chanted in each outbreath within the meditatively and rhymically controlled breathing cycle of the *dhikr*. This usage does not invent the association, it merely allows what was a semantic undercurrent within the aural texture of the words to come to the surface.

[31] Qurṭubī, 134. An alternative reading gives *imr'*, "person," i.e., the spirit is sent down to every person. Cf. Qurṭubī, 134, Khafājī, 384–85, and Ṭabāṭabā'ī, 330–35. In this case, some interpret the *min* as meaning *ʿalā*.

252

verse, we now have a syntactical and lexical looseness that seems close to semantic breakdown.[32]

Verse 5: salāmun hiya ḥattā maṭlaᶜi l-fajr

In the previous four verses, each of the four major movements—semantic, acoustical, emotive, and gendered—has been treated as intertwined with the others and as having its own semi-autonomous dynamic. With the first two words of verse 5, it is as if all four movements come together upon the key tonic chord. Or one might compare the first four verses to a network of streams, dams, and rivers, of tensions and releases of tensions. The final confluence takes place at the beginning of verse 5.

The semantic indeterminacy at the end of verse 4 results in a build-up of tension that is released climactically with the first two words of the final verse: *salāmun hiya*. The statement seems to follow directly from verse 3: *wā mā adrāka mā laylatu l-qadr . . . salāmun hiya*, in a manner directly parallel to 101:10–11: *wa mā adrāka mā hiya* [*al-hāwiya*] / *nārun ḥāmiya*. The expression is syntactically charged. Commentators have glossed it as *salāmatun hiya* or *khayrun hiya* (peaceful or good is the night). It is hard to hear the phrase without hearing—at least on the subliminal level—the echoes of the *salāmun ᶜalā*.[33] This echo is compounded by the emphatic position of *salāmun* at the beginning of the verse. Some traditions evoke the angels greeting every pious human, or one another, on the night of peace. Such an interpretation could be read as a dramatization of the semantic tension within the expression and the expectation of *salāmun ᶜalā* that it sets up.[34]

Compounding the effect further is the rhythmic and phonemic quality of *salāmun*. The central long *a* echoes the long-*a* sounds of the preceding verses and gathers the emotive charge associated with them. More specifically, the combination short *a*, consonant, long *a*, sets up a chain of assonance reaching back through the sura: *salā* (in *salāmun*), *malā* (in *malāᵓika*, verse 4), *kamā* (from *adrāka mā*, verse 2) and *wamā* (from *wa mā adrāka*, verse 2). The *mā*'s of verse 2 are in turn linked to the *nā*'s of verse 1 by phonological parallelism. Of particular interest is the assonance of *salā* with *malā*, with its repetition of the entire *a*/*l*/*ā* combination. Throughout these various echoes, the long-*a* sound is being filtered and intensified to the emotive pitch of some Arabic interjections (*yā*, *alā*, *ayyuhā*) that are themselves built upon /ā/, yet here it escapes confinement to any single lexical unit.[35]

Any expectation of *salāmun ᶜalā* engendered by the *salāmun* at the beginning of the verse is broken with the word *hiya*. The immediate syntactical expectation is neglected in favor of an expectation more deeply embedded within the dynamics of the sura as a whole, bringing out a more latent possibility and giving a sense of surprise, of newness, to the *hiya*.[36] In such an enhanced position, the ambivalence between animate and inanimate readings achieves articulation. If we translate the *hiya* as "it," the evident antecedent is the night: "the night is peace." With the alternate translation, "she," we can sense not only the *hiya* but all the pronouns struggling toward a more personified and mythic sense.[37]

[32] Cf. J. Baljon, "The *'Amr* of God' in the Koran," *Acta Orientalia* 23 (1959): 7–18, and Lohmann, 284. In another context, Rahman suggests that *min amrihi* should be translated only as "from the command of the lord" when it is used in connection with the spirit: Rahman, 29.

[33] There are at least sixteen Qurᵓanic occurrences of *salāmun ᶜalā* and one of *salāmun laka*, which make up the majority of occurrences of the form *salāmun* acting as a *mubtadiᵓ* or in a syntactically analogous position; the one interesting exception, along the lines of *salāmun hiya*, being *salāmun qawlan* (36:58). Rāzī, 36–37, offers one of the clearer and more extensive outlines of possible interpretations.

[34] Qurṭubī, 134: "According to al-Shaᶜbī, the angels . . . pass by each believer and say: *as-salāmu ᶜalayka ᶜayyuhā l-muᵓminu*. And it is also said that the angels greet one another in it (i.e., in the night of destiny)." Again, these early traditions tend to ignore any possibility of personification, and thus we find no reference to the night as the possible recipient of the greeting or good news.

[35] For Islamic interjections—interestingly called *aṣwāt* (tones or sounds)—see Wright, 1:194. See also the *nūniyya* of Ibn Zaydūn, verses 2 and 8. This poem achieves its emotively intense character by combining themes from both the classical poetic and the Qurᵓanic traditions (such as the Qurᵓanic theme of the *qiyāma* and the poetic theme of the departure of the beloved), and especially by combining the aural effects of classical and *badīᶜ* prosody with those of the Qurᵓan. Note particularly the intensive use of the long *a* in verse two: *allā wa qad ḥāna ṣ-ṣubḥu l-bayni ṣabbaḥanā* / *ḥaynun fa qāma binā li l-ḥayni nāᶜinā*. Cf. Ibn Zaydūn, *Diwān* (Beirut: Dār Ṣādir, 1975), 9.

[36] See Khafājī, 384, for another alternative, that the antecedent of *hiya* is the *rūḥ*, a possibility that is thematically remote but which may have plausibility at the level of semantic and phonic undertone, especially in view of the extremely charged nature of *rūḥ* (see below, section II).

[37] The inclination toward personification of "*layla*" may well be heightened by the almost complete homonymy between *layla* and the personal name *laylā*, which is also the name of the most famous beloved of the classical poetic tradition. The

The two sides of verse 5, *salāmun hiya*, and *maṭlaᶜi l-fajr* hinge on the pronoun *ḥattā*. This word is tied grammatically to what follows, and the rhythm of natural syntax places the pronoun with the second part of the verse, as does the alliteration between *ḥattā* and *maṭlaᶜ*. Yet there is also a phonic cohesion of the /a/ with the first half of the verse. Though the pull in both directions is not as strong as it was with the *hu* in verse 1, the *mā* of verse 2, or the *khayrun* in verse 3, it is strong enough to echo its more effective predecessors, and it is amplified by the placement of *ḥattā* at the quantitative center of the verse.

The harmonic balance heard in the sphere of gender is echoed in two more areas as the sura ends. In balance with the sending down and coming down (*tanzīl* and *tanazzul*) is the "rise" (*maṭlaᶜ*) of daybreak. And in balance with the night is the breaking of dawn (*fajr*). The Qur᾿an (17:12) refers to the alternation of day and night as a sign (*āya*), the interpretation of which is of vital importance and which is bound up with destiny. The word *fajr* has a range of meanings, many of which involve the notion of a violent transformation.[38] This sense of a shock is intensified by the position of *fajr* as the final rhyming end-word of the sura, a rhyme which is itself quite accented and non-euphonic.[39] The last three words of the sura are balanced precisely between the calm of night and the lyricism of the general image of night yielding to day, on the one hand, and a sense of foreboding concerning the break, or breaking, of the day. The rhyming of *fajr* with the thrice-repeated *qadr*, with *shahr*, and with *amr* accents the relationship among the oscillation of day and night, the relativity and collapsing of time, and the Qur᾿anic understanding of *qadr*.

The phonological reading has yielded a variety of tentative sound and sense relations. In the following sections I relate them more directly to the semantic and thematic aspects of the sura, and to other phonologically and semantically parallel passages within the Qur᾿an.

point here is not that the hearer or reciter thinks of the personal name *laylā* during the recitation of *sūrat al-qadr*, but that the homonymy between the two words can contribute to the tendency toward personification, especially in combination with other linguistic motivations. The widespread existence of punning within Arabic suggests the latent semantic force of complete and partial homonymy.

[38] Cf. Ibn Manẓūr, *Lisān al-ᶜArab* (Beirut: Dār Ṣādir, n.d.), 5:45–48.

[39] For the rarity of this particular *tasjīᶜ*, see Lohmann, 226. For some comments on the use of the term *tasjīᶜ* rather than *qāfiya* in discussions of Qur᾿anic rhyme, see Farūqī, 105–6.

II

The word *rūḥ* appears less than two dozen times in the Qur᾿an,[40] almost always in one of three contexts: creation, prophecy, and the *yawm ad-dīn*. Though the three moments are presented as separate, they are intertwined—thematically, lexically, and acoustically.[41]

(1) The creation motif includes both the creation of the primordial human and the conception of Jesus. In the first case (15:29, 32:9), the primordial human (*insān* or *bashar*), made from mud or clay (*ṭīn*), is the receiver of the *rūḥ* breathed into it by the creator: *nafakhtu fīhi min rūḥī*. The language of the Maryam episode is almost identical, only this time it is Maryam into whom the spirit is breathed (21:91, 66:12): *nafakhnā fīhā* [or *fīhi*] *min rūḥinā*. Another tie between the conception of Jesus and the creation of Adam can be heard in (19:17): *fa arsalnā ilayhā rūḥanā fa tamaththala lahā basharan sawiyyan*, "We sent down to her our spirit and it took the appearance of a formed human." The phrase *basharan sawiyyan* is the exact phrase used in the creation story to indicate the human form brought to life by the inbreathing of the spirit. Here the *bashar* becomes the form taken by the spirit, which in 21:91 and 66:12 was breathed into Maryam.[42] We note here an interesting gender dynamic. In one case it is *insān* or

[40] O'Shaughnessy, 13–15, lists 20 instances, with the Arabic citations and translations. ᶜAbd al-Bāqī's *Al-Muᶜjam al-Mufahris* (Cairo: Kitāb al-Shaᶜb, n.d.), 326, gives the same citations, but numbers them as 21 separate references, giving a separate citation to the two occurrences of the word in 17:85 (17:87 by O'Shaughnessy's numbering, based upon Fluegel).

[41] Sura 32, for example, begins with a mention of Muhammad's prophecy (1–3). It moves suddenly to creation and the breathing of the spirit into the primordial human (4–9), and then, in a final sudden shift, to the *yawm ad-dīn* (10–11).

[42] For the creation of the primordial human, see 32:8, 15:28–29, and the very similar 38:71–72, the latter of which reads: *idh qāla rabbuka li l-malā᾿ikati innī khāliqun basharan min ṭīn fa idhā sawwaytuhu wa nafakhtu fīhi min rūḥī fa qaᶜū lahu sājidīn*, "When your lord said to the angels: 'I am going to create humankind from mud. When I have formed it/him and breathed into it/him, then fall before it/him in prostration.'" For the Maryam episodes, see 66:12 and the almost identical 21:91, the latter of which reads: *wa l-latī aḥsanat farjahā fa nafakhnā fīhā min rūḥinā wa jaᶜalnāhā wa bnahā āyatan li l-ᶜālimīn*. 66:12 is almost identical but brings out more strongly the implications of spiritual insemination by replacing the *fīhā* with *fīhi*. The antecedent for the masculine pronoun would most naturally and logically be *farjahā*. Muḥyī al-Dīn ibn al-ᶜArabī recognized the power of the gender dynamic in the Qur᾿an and refers to it often in his *Fuṣūṣ*,

bashar who receives the spirit—a gender-non-specific term that is usually rendered gender-specific in the personification of the *insān* as Adam.[43] In the other case it is Maryam who receives the spirit, a spirit that in another passage personifies itself (*tamaththala*) as *bashar*. Finally, in another passage, Jesus himself, who is the result of that inbreathing, is called the spirit (4:171).

(2) In the second moment, the *rūḥ* is associated with the sending down (*tanzīl*) of prophetic revelation, as in 16:2: "He sends down the angels with the spirit from his *amr* to whichever of his servants he wills." The spirit of transcendence, *rūḥu l-quds* (16:102) is linked to the prophecy of Muhammad. The *rūḥ* is also seen as a support (*ta*ʾ*yīd*) for the prophecy of Jesus, son of Maryam (2:87, 2:253, 5:110). These verses are in tension with those mentioned above in which Jesus himself is called the spirit (4:171). The spirit-as-support passages and the Jesus-as-spirit passage echo, acoustically and lexically, the description of the creation of Jesus through the spirit's insemination of Maryam.[44] The *rūḥ*-prophecy passage is the subject *par excellence* of our essay, *sūrat al-qadr*.

(3) Qurʾanic passages related to the *yawm al-dīn* allude to the spirit-creation and spirit-prophecy passages, for example, 70:4: "The angels ascend—and the spirit—to him on a day whose extent is fifty thousand years." The equation of this day to fifty thousand years recalls the statement in *sūrat al-qadr* that the night of *qadr* is better than a thousand months.[45] In both the prophetic moment and the moment of final return, a particular delimited span of time is compared to a much larger span. In each case the relationship between the *rūḥ* and the angels is unspecified. The imagery, syntax, vocabulary, and acoustics of one mirrors the other.

70:4 *taʿruju l-malāʾikatu wa r-rūḥu ilayhi*
97:4 *tanazzalu l-malāʾikatu wa r-rūḥu fīhā*

Here the "coming down" that occurs on the night of *qadr* is balanced by the "rising" that occurs on the day of *dīn*, the feminine indirect object counterbalanced by the masculine indirect object (*fīhā, ilayhi*). These intertextual correspondences and inversions reinforce the intratextual polarity noted above in *sūrat al-qadr* between the coming down of the angels and the rising (*maṭlaʿ*) of dawn. The intertwining of the two passages leads to the sense of something hidden within the intensely lyrical imagery of daybreak coming after a night better than a thousand months. It may allude to the break of the day equal to fifty thousand years or, in another version, to a thousand years—the rising of the spirit back to its source at the *yawm ad-dīn*.

Through such aural, syntactic, and thematic intertwining among the *rūḥ* passages involving creation, revelation, and *yawm ad-dīn*, of which the above example is only one of many that could be cited, the spirit takes on a temporal multivalence. The occurrence of the term *rūḥ* within these three distinct moments engenders an intertextual acoustical-semantic dynamic that plays against the separation of the three moments and transforms normal understandings of time.[46] The

especially in the sections on Jesus and Muhammad. See Ibn al-ʿArabī, *Fuṣūṣ al-Ḥikam*, ed. A. A. Affifi (Cairo: Dar Iḥyāʾ al-Kutub al-ʿArabiyya, 1946).

[43] Phyllis Trible's argument concerning the gender nonspecificity of the Biblical Adam in the first creation account might have some bearing on issues in Qurʾanic interpretation, as well. See Phyllis Trible, *God and the Rhetoric of Sexuality* (Philadelphia: Fortress Press, 1978); idem, *Texts of Terror: Literary-Feminist Readings of Biblical Narratives* (Philadelphia: Fortress Press, 1984).

[44] For an interesting interpretation of this issue, see Ibn al-ʿArabī, *Fuṣūṣ*, 138–50. Ibn al-ʿArabī notes that Jesus is called spirit and that he brings together the spirit as life force (as seen in his conception) and the spirit as prophetic support. This nexus of associations provides him with an interpretation of the life-producing miracles associated with the prophecy of Jesus. The text is translated in Ibn al-ʿArabī, *The Bezels of Wisdom*, tr. R. W. J. Austin (New York: Paulist Press, 1980), 172–86.

[45] It also recalls the statement (32:5) equating the day to a thousand years: *yudabbiru l-amra mina s-samāʾi ilā l-arḍi thumma yaʿruju ilayhi fī yawmin kāna miqdāruhu alfa sanatin min mā taʿuddūn*, "He directs the *amr* from the heaven to the earth/then it goes up to him on a day whose extent is a thousand years by your calculations." It is not clear whether the thousand years modifies the going up only, or can refer back to the directing of the *amr* as well, though most translations choose the former. See also 78:38 (*yawma yaqūmu r-rūḥu wa l-malāʾikatu ṣaffan*, "a day the spirit rises—the angels in ranks"). In these two cases the aural factors that heighten the circumstantial possibility are not as pronounced, however. In 78:38, the syntactical places of *al-rūḥu* and *al-malāʾikatu* are inverted.

[46] This intertwining of semantic and acoustic fields between the *yawm ad-dīn* and *laylat al-qadr* is then compounded by a similar aural and semantic intertwining between creation and the *yawm ad-dīn*. In *sūrat al-infiṭār*, the apocalyptic imagery associated with the *yawm ad-dīn* is immediately followed by a reference to the creation (*khalq*) and formation (*taswiya*) of humankind, themes and terms closely aligned in *sūrat al-sajada* with the inbreathing of the spirit into humankind.

We can give only a brief example here of the constant reflection of semantic fields and key terms (*āya, amr, sawwā,*

yawm ad-dīn is both a second creation and a second revelation, the moment when what is hidden within the earth, behind the spheres, within the tombs, and within the breasts of humankind is revealed. While this revelation can be seen in temporal terms as happening in the future, from the divine perspective this secret is already known—as is emphasized in the continual references to the divine as the *ʿalīm* (knower), *samīʿ* (hearer), *baṣīr* (seer), and the *khabīr* (the one skilled in knowing human intentions). The mediator between this atemporal perspective and the temporal is the *rūḥ*. From the temporal perspective these are three distinct moments, but from the eternal perspective they seem, as it were, embedded one within the other, a phenomenon foretold and enacted by the embedding of the acoustical-semantic fields of each within the other.

This embedding of the three archetypal moments one within the other is mediated through the polarity of day and night, a primary image within *sūrat al-qadr*, as well as a sign or archetype, an *āya*. Day and night are also frequently evoked in the oaths that begin many of the shorter suras.[47] In one case, the rhyme is identical with that used in *sūrat al-qadr*, the emphatic and difficult closed syllable ending in "r":

1 By the dawn
2 and ten nights
3 and the even and the odd
4 and the night when it is dispelled
5 is there not in that an oath for one of insight (*ḥijr*)?[48]

(*sūrat al-fajr*, 89:1–5)

Implicit in the alternation of day and night is a transformation from temporal triplicity (creation, revelation, *yawm ad-dīn*) to the duality of day and night—or into a complex triplicity of day, night, and day, with the triple and dual, the odd and the even, combined into one movement. The transformation from triplicity to polarity to primordial unity beyond temporal distinction is centered upon the *rūḥ*.

The connection between *rūḥ* and *qadr* in *sūrat al-qadr* suggests that this transformation of time into a primordial unity is an aspect of *qadr*. Through the *mā adrāka mā*, the Qurʾanic voice acknowledges that the meaning of *qadr* is obscure. In the pre-Islamic vocabulary, *qadara* meant "to decree or allot." The term naturally becomes associated with fate and with wealth (a good "lot"). The commentators offer two major possibilities, *qadr* as power or empowerment on the one hand, or divine determination on the other. Another double possibility also presents itself: the night as the night that is determined or decreed in advance, or the night in which the determination of future events is contained. *Qadr* seems to be situated between empowerment (*qudra*) and fate (*qadar*).[49] Translators of the Qurʾan have tended to choose terms like "power" for *qadr*, terms that express only one side of the semantic field. It is my view that "destiny" might come closer to expressing the mutivalence of the term, though no single English term would seem sufficient.[50]

---

istawā, nafakha, bashar, waḥī, malāʾika). Thus, *waḥī*, which often denotes *revelation*, is used in *sūrat al-zalzala* in connection with the *yawm ad-dīn*, and in a manner that cannot help bring to mind other spirit passages linking spirit to *conception* (*biʾanna rabbaka awḥā lahā*).

47 For a summary and discussion of oaths in the Qurʾan, see A. Yusuf Ali, *The Holy Quran: Text, Translation, and Commentary* (New York: Hafner Publishing, 1946), 2:1784–88.

48 *wa l-fajr*
wa layālin ashr
wa sh-shafʿi wa l-watr
wa l-layli idhā yasr
hal fī dhālika qasamun li dhī ḥijr

Here we note a buildup of verse length that reaches its apogee in the following verse:

a lam tara kayfa faʿala rabbuka bi ʿād.

"Don't you see what your lord did with ʿĀd?"

At this climactic point the end-rhyme shifts to the emotively intense *ʿād*, with its long *a* in emphatic position at the end of the verse.

49 The intertwinings and intersections of connotations among *qadr, qudra,* and *qadar* are explored by Ibn Manẓūr, *Lisān al-ʿArab*, 5:74–80.

50 *Qādir* can be used in the more univocal sense of "having capability" or "being able" (17:99, 36:81). The notions capability and measurement are stressed by Zamakhsharī, unsurprisingly in view of the Muʿtazilī denial of *qadar*: *Asās al-Balāgha*, ed. ʿAbd al-Raḥmān Maḥmūd (Qum, n.d.), 357. Arberry, 345, translates *qadr* as "power." Syed Abdul Latif chooses "glory": *Al-Quran Rendered into English* (Hyderabad: The Academy of Islamic Studies, 1969), 528. T. B. Irving (Taʿlim ʿAlī) translates it as "power" but titles the sura "Power (or Fate)": *The Qurʾan: The First American Version* (Brattleboro, Vt.: Amana Books, 1988), 383. Ahmad Ali chooses "determination": *Al-Qurʾān: A Contemporary Translation*, 544. Richard Bell translates *qadr* as power, but then remarks: "The common translation of the phrase has been retained; 'Night of Decree' would perhaps correspond better to the sense." R. Bell, *The Qurʾān: Translated, with a Critical Re-arrangement of the Surahs*, vol. 2 (Edinburgh: T. & T. Clark, 1937 [1960]), 669. Guillaume, 111, chooses "destiny." For a good discussion of the ambivalences within the use of the term *qadr* here, see Lohmann, 280: "Die Nacht Al-Qadr ist nicht nur eine ganz bestimmte, im Heilsplan Gottes

The uncertainty over the meaning of *qadr* is reflected in the uncertainty over which night in Ramadan constitutes the night of *qadr*, a question that is at the center of most classical exegeses of the sura. The classical interpreters emphasize the storing up of future events in the *laylat al-qadr*, a phenomenon that represents the containment of a span of time (whether one year or all time) within a single moment. The confusion over which *odd*-numbered night is the night of *qadr*—and in most interpretations the night could fall on several odd-numbered nights in the last part of Ramadan[51]—relates this temporal transformation to the alternations of day and night, odd and even. The maintaining of the vigil on what is held to be the night of *qadr* imbues the occasion with a sense of the dissolution of normal temporal boundaries, as if it were a ritual performance, a living out of the temporal transformation that is textually performed within *sūrat al-qadr* and across its intertextual reverberations with other *rūḥ* passages in the Qurʾan.[52]

III

In order to discuss the significance of *rūḥ* and *qadr* in *sūrat al-qadr*, I departed from the close reading of the sura to trace some intertextual resonances through other passages. Though reference was made to acoustic, emotive, and gender intertwinings in the *rūḥ* passages involving creation, prophecy, and the *yawm ad-dīn*, it is beyond the scope of this article to trace such intertwinings in the manner followed in the close reading of *sūrat al-qadr*. Yet an instance of close reading is necessary to demonstrate more clearly the nexus between the acoustic, emotive, and gender modes on the one hand, and the thematic on the other.

Along with the alternation of day and night, the alternation of male and female is central to *sūrat al-qadr*. Just as the spirit is associated with the transformation of temporal categories, so in the close reading of *surat al-qadr* and in the discussion of the three primordial moments, the *rūḥ* (which can be grammatically either masculine or feminine) has emerged at the center of a complex gender dynamic. The *rūḥ* serves as a mediation between the limitations of individual entity and something more universal. While it may be interpreted as an individual personality or agent, such as Gabriel, it resists being limited to any single entity. The effort to find a single entity corresponding to *rūḥ* has meant a dividing up of the term among several possibilities, with consequent concern over their incompatibility, a shattering of the meaning into a set of isolated reifications.[53]

Here we might reconsider the concept of sign (*āya*) in the Qurʾan. It may be that the concept refers not only to signs within the world, but self-referentially to the Qurʾan's own generation of meaning. Those features called signs and those items that the Qurʾanic voice swears by (day and night, odd and even, male and female) indicate central modes of Qurʾanic signification. The dynamic of gender would be not only a sign within the world, but a central aspect of Qurʾanic semantics. Not only would the Qurʾan point to the sign, it would speak through it.

The archetypal nature of the alternation of day and night, and odd and even, was reflected in a Qurʾanic oath quoted above. In another Qurʾanic oath, that alternation is tied to the polarity of male and female, and it is this oath that should lead back to the harmonics of gender:

1 *wa l-layli idhā yaghshā*
2 *wa n-nahāri idhā tajallā*
3 *wa mā khalaqa dh-dhakara wa l-unthā*
sūrat al-layl (92:1–3)

1 By the night when it shrouds
2 And the day when it reveals
3 And what made the male and female

Some translations follow the classical *tafsīr* in interpreting the *mā* in verse 3 as a substitute for *man*, and thereby translate it as "He" or "Him."[54] Aural, emotive,

---

von Anfang an genau festgesetzte Nacht, in der mit der Herabsendung des Korans an Muhammed begonnen worden ist, sondern auch die Nacht, in der das weitere Schicksal von Welt und Mensch in allen Einzelheiten festgelegt wird."

[51] See Ṭabāṭabāʾī, 333–34.

[52] Qushayrī, 750, relates, without explanation, the following evocative verses in the same rhyme as the sura:

ya laylatan min layālī d-dahrī / qābaltu fīhā badrahā bi badrī
wa lam yakun ʿan shafaqin wa fajrin / ḥattā tawallat bikra d-dahrī

[53] This effect is particularly strong in O'Shaughnessy, cited above, n. 15.

[54] Rāzī, 198, is most matter of fact in making the substitution: *mā bi maʿnā man*. Qushayrī, 3:735, is equally quick to substitute: *ay man*. Pickthall, 808, 812, renders the last verse, "And by Him who made the male and the female," and translates the *mā* similarly in 95:7 and 91:5. Arberry, 341, renders it, "And That which created the male and the female."

and gender connotations and interplays are not considered important enough to give pause to such a substitution. A justification for the substitution that would validate the literary and artistic quality of the text is not offered. However, in this case, and it might be argued, in other cases as well,[55] the substitution is problematic. Throughout the Qurʾan, third person reference to Allah is made through the masculine/neuter. In the absence of any sustained theological justification for viewing the deity as male, the choice can be considered conventional. However, in this passage the subject matter is not just creation in general, but *the creation of gender*. The "*man*" substitution theory leads to the translation of the *mā* as "Him." Though we might recognize the "Him" as conventional, the contradiction involved with a grammatically *male* referent creating gender is rhetorically and stylistically awkward. A sounding through the four modes of analysis of the other possibility—taking *mā* seriously as *mā*—will suggest the plausibility of rendering to the *mā* its own textual integrity.

The neuter and inanimate character of *mā* and the syntactical ambivalence between the relative pronoun and the interrogative pronoun are vital for the correspondences and allusions that give the verse its vitality. These correspondences are compounded by the important assonance between the *mā* and long *a* of *unthā*, and by the strong end-assonance of *yaghshā* and *tajallā* in the previous verses.

Wa mā khalaqa reverberates in turn against passages elsewhere in the Qurʾan. In *sūrat al-zalzala*, the earth is portrayed as being caught up in a cosmic shaking. After two verses based upon /ā/ and the *lahā* rhyme, the third verse shows a powerful phonetic parallelism both with the surrounding verses of the sura, and with the "*wa mā khalaqa*": *wa qāla l-insānu mā lahā*. The most cosmic moment is combined with the most intimate speech, as if a person were asking about the state of a woman's birth pangs: "and a person will ask 'what is with her.'" The verses that follow bring the semantic and acoustical charge of the /ā/ and the *Cālahā* assonance (*zālahā, qālahā, mā lahā, bārahā, ḥā lahā*) to the breaking point, allowing the *mā* of *mā lahā* an unlimited resonance as an undertone. Within this resonance is a unification among the moments of creation, revelation, and *yawm ad-dīn*, especially in verse 5: *biʾanna rabbaka awḥā lahā*: "how your lord inspired her." Taken from context, one would almost think Maryam was meant, and the connection of Jesus with the *yawm ad-dīn* takes on a compelling logic. Creation, revelation, and the *yawm ad-dīn* are three moments seen in terms that often imply an insemination, a conception, and a birth, often in terms of the gender dynamic heard in *sūrat al-qadr* in the above analysis. The radical *w/ḥ/y* used in reference here to the *yawm ad-dīn* ties the passage to the moment of revelation. The aural, emotive, and gender resonances of the sound-units, such as *mā lahā* and *awḥā lahā*, link this *yawm ad-dīn* passage even more strongly to creation (*wa mā khalaqa*) and revelation, as well as to *sūrat al-qadr*. The forming of an aspirate *ḍamma* from the *hu* in *hu fī* and the *ḥu* in *rūḥu fīhā* in *sūrat al-qadr* would find its analogue on the feminine side by the formation of an aspirate /ā/ from the *ḥā* and the *hā* in *awḥā lahā*, an effect reinforced by the incantational repetition of *lahā* throughout *sūrat al-zalzala*.[56]

The *mā* assumes a similarly central role in *sūrat al-qāriʿa*, a sura with two key feminine-gendered parties

---

One solution is to read the *mā* as *maṣdariyya*. Cf. Maulvi Muhammad Ali, *The Holy Qurʾan: Containing the Arabic Text with English Translation and Commentary* (Surrey, England: 1917), 1196: "And the creating of the male and female." For a similar translation, see *The Quran: An English Translation of the Meaning of the Quran*, checked and revised by Mahmud Y. Zayid (Dar al-Choura: 1980). While this translation does not fall into gender contradiction and does not collapse the *mā* into *man*, it nevertheless loses—as translations seem fated to lose—the aural resonances between the *mā* in this passage and other important passages with acoustically charged usages of *mā*. Ahmad Ali translates the verse, "And what He created of the male and female." While grammatically possible, this interpretation must create an antecedent for the subject of *khalaqa* that is not only not in the text, but seems to go against the oath style. See also Ahmad Ali, 539. Irving's version, p. 378, reads: "and whatever has created the male and the female." For an illustration of the extraordinary ambivalence within the tradition concerning this *mā*, see the traditions relating to Abū Dardāʾ: Bukhārī, 3:154.

[55] Other cases are to be found in 95:7 and 91:5, 6, 7, the latter of which is especially resonant with the passage in *sūrat al-layl*.

[56] *idhā zulzilati l-arḍu zilzālahā*
wa akhrajati l-arḍu athqālahā
wa qāla l-insānu mā lahā
yawmaʾidhin tuḥaddithu akhbārahā
biʾanna rabbaka awḥā lahā

It is interesting to note that while the play of aspirates is located in *sūrat al-qadr* along the central axis, it occurs in *sūrat al-zalzala* (and *sūrat al-qāriʿa*, see below) within the *tasjīʿ* endings. The interchangeability of central position and end position can also be seen by comparing the interior *tasjīʿ* of *sūrat al-zalzala* (*zulzilat, akhrajat, qālat*) with the end-verse *tasjīʿ* of *sūrat al-infiṭār* (*nfaṭarat, ntatharat, sujjirat, buʿthirat*).

(*qāriᶜa* and *hāwiya*). The first three verses of the sura show a progressive build-up of acoustic and emotive associations with the *mā* and the /ā/: *al-qāriᶜa / mā l-qāriᶜa / wa mā adrāka mā l-qāriᶜa*, "the *qāriᶜa*, what is the *qāriᶜa*, what can let you know what the *qāriᶜa* is?" The phonic patterns of these verses are then intensified throughout the sura, combined with the imagery of the *yawm ad-dīn*, culminating in the final verses: *fa ummuhu hāwiya / wa mā adrāka mā hiyah / nārun ḥāmiya*. Again we hear an aspirate /ā/ combination at the point when the undertone of gender dynamic is most strong, with *hāwiya*, *mā hiya* and *ḥāmiya* in a robust phonological, rhythmic, and accentual parallelism. The undertone of partial personification is further strengthened by the unusual word *hāwiya*, with its complex semantic field (a woman bereft of her children, an abyss, with etymological associations of emptiness, air, and desire), and equally complex syntactical range (from "his mother is a *hāwiya*" to the possibility of a curse "may his mother be *hāwiya*").[57]

Thematic and lexical resonances that were heard among the three moments of spirit, creation, revelation, and the *yawm ad-dīn*, are now also heard through phonological parallelism. Returning to *sūrat al-qadr*, we find in the *wamā* of *wa mā khalaqa* the *aCā* sequence that was the phonological tonic of *sūrat al-qadr* (*salā*, *malā*, and, precisely, *wamā*). In each of the three moments, the semantic, emotive, and acoustic energies fall upon units of sound and meaning that are complex and gender-charged. When it is not dismissed through the substitution of *man* for *mā*, the *mā* in *sūrat al-layl* can be heard in its interplay between animate and inanimate, and relative and interrogative. Its phonological correspondences with other passages give it the highest emotive charge. An aural analysis has followed a trail that ties *sūrat al-layl* together with the *rūḥ* passages of each of the three moments: creation, prophecy, and *yawm ad-dīn*. In each case it is implicated in the gender dynamic associated with the *rūḥ*.

Keeping in mind these acoustical resonances, and the thematic resonances involving women conceiving, giving birth, or bereft of their children, we might return to the *salāmun hiya*. Richard Bell made the following elliptical comment on *sūrat al-qadr*: "In some ways what is here said of it [the night of *qadr*] suggests that some account of the Eve of the Nativity may have given rise to it."[58] Bell does not give his reasons for making such a speculation. The above analysis suggests a connection, but a connection that would run against the frequent treatment of Qurᵓanic themes as borrowings from Biblical traditions. Through an intricate webbing of echoes, allusions, resonances across the four modes of discourse and across a variety of passages the Qurᵓan seems to have evoked an experience of *bushrā* similar to that found in the χαῖρε, κεχαριτωμένη (Hail, Blessed one) of Luke 1:28. When we compare the various texts tied together through these resonances and hear their undertone of gender dynamic, we arrive at a sustained gender figure in which a series of partially personified female referents (the earth, the *hāwiya*, the night of *qadr*) and a related female character (Maryam) are to be found at the center of the experiences of prophecy, creation, and the *yawm ad-dīn*. This figure is not announced on the level of surface semantics. It is a moving figure, evoked by, but not confined to, particular lexical, morphemic, and syntactical units. It can be heard through the resonances, echoes, undertones, and interstices of the Arabic text in recitation.[59] It is lost when translated into an English discourse dominated by masculine and neuter gender.[60]

---

[57] Cf. Ibn Manẓūr, 15:373, and Qurṭubī, 167.
al-qāriᶜa
mā l-qāriᶜa
wa mā adrāka mā l-qāriᶜa
yawma yakūnu n-nāsu ka l-farāshi l-mabthūth
wa takūnu l-jibālu ka l-ᶜihni l-manfūsh
fa ammā man thaqulat mawāzīnuh
fa huwa fī ᶜishatin rāḍiya
wa ammā man khaffat mawāzīnuh
fa ummuhu hāwiya
wa mā adrāka mā hiyah
nārun ḥāmiya.

A fuller treatment of *sūrat al-qāriᶜa* is given by M. Sells, "Sound and Meaning in *Sūrat al-Qāriᶜa*," a paper presented to the Middle East Studies Association, Toronto, Nov. 1989, which is now being revised for publication. One important difference between *sūrat al-qāriᶜa* and *sūrat al-qadr* is the highly prominent role played by the distinction between pharyngealized and non-pharyngealized /ā/ within *sūrat al-qāriᶜa*. The pharyngealized /ā/ occurs only once in *sūrat al-qadr* (in *adrāka*), and though the effect of the pharyngealization in *sūrat al-qadr* is not insignificant, it is not strong enough to warrant specific discussion in the present essay.

[58] Bell, 669.

[59] It might be of interest to compare the hypothesis of an implicit personification that can only be heard within the undertones and interstices of certain Qurᵓanic passages concerning prophecy, creation, and the *yawm ad-dīn*, with the following words concerning Maryam (19:17): *fa ᵓttakhadhat min dūnihim ḥijāban*.

[60] A similar loss of gender interplay occurs in the English translations of a wide variety of post-Qurᵓanic Islamic texts. The conventional use of the masculine for the deity, the

This essay has explored dimensions of Qurʾanic meaning neglected in critical literature, though often acknowledged on the informal and personal level. It has recently been said that "studying the Qurʾan as literature—and purely as literature—is not unlike setting foot on new territory."[61] It might be argued that such an exploration should be put off until larger methodological and hermeneutical difficulties are resolved. Delay can serve, however, only to reinforce the current isolation of the Qurʾan from literary discussion. The effect of this isolation on perceptions and representations of Islamic culture can hardly be underestimated. It may be that others will hear these figures differently, or will hear different figures. Complete homogeneity of response to the more subtle undertones of a text is not to be expected and may not be desired. What does seem needed is an ongoing discussion of the wider regions of semantic multidimensionality within the Qurʾan. *Wa llāhu samīʿun ʿalīm.*[62]

insistence on translating *insān* as "man" with its resulting masculine grammatical field of pronouns and inflections, rather than as "human" or "person," and the loss of the feminine pronominal and inflectional field created by terms like *nafs* and *dhāt*, all serve to transform the play of gender within Arabic Islamic texts into a monotonically masculine-gendered English discourse.

[61] Mir, 49.

[62] Abd al-Bāqī, 360, lists some 32 examples of the combination of *samīʿ* and *ʿalīm* within the Qurʾan. When the proper noun Allāh is used, the names are put in the indefinite. When the pronoun is used, the names are put in the definite: *allāhu samīʿun ʿalīm* and *huwa s-samīʿu l-ʿalīm*. At this point it might be of interest to point out the consistent resistance encountered by this author in attempting to use a critical vocabulary based on sound rather than sight. On each rereading I found myself to have used expressions (we see, can be seen, point of view, perspective, focus) based on visual metaphors when describing aural effects. The habits ingrained through engagement with traditional Western critical vocabulary seem particularly resistant to discussion of aural aspects of meaning.

20

THE APOCALYPSE OF ISLAM

Norman O. Brown

We can read the Bhagavad Gita in translation, and Confucius; we cannot read the Koran. Carlyle has perfectly articulated the response of every honest Englishman: "I must say, it is as toilsome reading as I ever undertook. A wearisome confused jumble, crude, incondite; endless iterations, long-windedness, entanglement; most crude, incondite;—insupportable stupidity, in short! Nothing but a sense of duty could carry any European through the Koran. . . . With every allowance, one feels it difficult to see how any mortal ever could consider this Koran as a Book written in Heaven, too good for the Earth; as a well-written book, or indeed as a *book* at all."

In the twentieth century the work of syncretism is beginning to change the picture: the work above all of Louis Massignon, the mystically minded Roman Catholic, and Henri Corbin, the mystically minded Protestant. Louis Massignon called sura 18 the apocalypse of Islam. The solemn recitation of sura 18 every Friday is all that Islam has in the way of weekly liturgy corresponding to the Christian Eucharist. In Islam the Body is the Book, and the part that represents the whole is sura 18.[1]

SURA 18—THE CAVE
REVEALED AT MECCA

In the name of Allah, the Beneficent, the Merciful.

Lecture for the Facing Apocalypse Conference, Salve Regina College, Newport, R.I., June 1983. Published in *Social Text*, no. 8 (Winter 1983–1984), 155–170. Also in V. Andrews, R. Bosnak, and K. W. Goodwin, eds., *Facing Apocalypse* (Dallas, 1987), 137–162. Reprinted by permission of Spring Publications.

70 / The Apocalypse of Islam

1. Praise be to Allah Who hath revealed the Scripture unto His slave, and hath not placed therein any crookedness.

2. (But hath made it) straight, to give warning of stern punishment from Him, and to bring unto the believers who do good works the news that theirs will be a fair reward.

3. Wherein they will abide for ever;

4. And to warn those who say: Allah hath chosen a son,

5. (A thing) whereof they have no knowledge, nor (had) their fathers. Dreadful is the word that cometh out of their mouths. They speak naught but a lie.

6. Yet it may be, if they believe not in this statement, that thou (Muhammad) wilt torment thy soul with grief over their footsteps.

7. Lo! We have placed all that is in the earth as an ornament thereof that we may try them: which of them is best in conduct.

8. And lo! We shall make all that is therein a barren mound.

9. Or deemest thou that the People of the Cave and the Inscription are a wonder among Our portents?

10. When the young men fled for refuge to the Cave and said: Our Lord! Give us mercy from Thy presence, and shape for us right conduct in our plight.

11. Then We sealed up their hearing in the Cave for a number of years.

12. And afterward We raised them up that We might know which of the two parties would best calculate the time that they had tarried.

13. We narrate unto thee their story with truth. Lo! they were young men who believed in their Lord, and We increased them in guidance.

14. And We made firm their hearts when they stood forth and said: Our Lord is the Lord of the heavens and the earth. We cry unto no god beside Him, for then should we utter an enormity.

15. These, our people, have chosen (other) gods beside Him though they bring no clear warrant (vouchsafed) to them. And who doth greater wrong than he who inventeth a lie concerning Allah?

16. And when ye withdraw from them and that which they worship except Allah, then seek refuge in the Cave; your Lord will spread for you of His mercy and will prepare for you a pillow in your plight.

17. And thou mightest have seen the sun when it rose move away from their cave to the right, and when it set go past them on the left, and they were in the cleft thereof. That was (one) of the portents of Allah. He whom Allah guideth, he indeed is led aright,

and he whom He sendeth astray, for him thou wilt not find a guiding friend.

18. And thou wouldst have deemed them waking though they were asleep, and we caused them to turn over to the right and the left, and their dog stretching out his paws on the threshold.

19. If thou hadst observed them closely thou hadst assuredly turned away from them in flight, and hadst been filled with awe of them.

20. And in like manner We awakened them that they might question one another. A speaker from among them said: How long have ye tarried? They said: We have tarried a day or some part of a day, (Others) said: Your Lord best knoweth what ye have tarried. Now send one of you with this your silver coin unto the city, and let him see what food is purest there and bring you a supply thereof. Let him be courteous and let no man know of you.

21. For they, if they should come to know of you, will stone you or turn you back to their religion; then ye will never prosper.

22. And in like manner We disclosed them (to the people of the city) that they might know that the promise of Allah is true, and that, as for the Hour, there is no doubt concerning it. When (the people of the city) disputed of their case among themselves, they said: Build over them a building; their Lord knoweth best concerning them. Those who won their point said: We verily shall build a place of worship over them.

23. (Some) will say: They were three, their dog the fourth, and (some) say: Five, their dog the sixth, guessing at random; and (some) say: Seven, and their dog eighth. Say (O Muhammad): My Lord is best aware of their number. None knoweth them save a few. So contend not concerning them except with an outward contending, and ask not any of them to pronounce concerning them.

24. And say not of anything: Lo! I shall do that tomorrow.

25. Except if Allah will. And remember thy Lord when thou forgettest, and say: It may be that my Lord guideth me unto a nearer way of truth than this.

26. And (it is said) they tarried in their Cave three hundred years and add nine.

27. Say: Allah is best aware how long they tarried. His is the invisible of the heavens and the earth. How clear of sight is He and keen of hearing! They have no protecting friend beside Him, and He maketh none to share in His government.

28. And recite that which hath been revealed unto thee of the Scripture of thy Lord. There is none who can change His words, and thou wilt find no refuge beside Him.

72 / The Apocalypse of Islam

29. Restrain thyself along with those who cry unto their Lord at morn and evening, seeking His countenance; and let not thine eyes overlook them, desiring the pomp of the life of the world; and obey not him whose heart We have made heedless of Our remembrance, who followeth his own lust and whose case hath been abandoned.

30. Say: (It is) the truth from the Lord of you (all). Then whosoever will, let him believe, and whosoever will, let him disbelieve. Lo! We have prepared for disbelievers Fire. Its tent encloseth them. If they ask for showers, they will be showered with water like to molten lead which burneth the faces. Calamitous the drink and ill the resting-place!

31. Lo! as for those who believe and do good works—Lo! We suffer not the reward of one whose work is goodly to be lost.

32. As for such, theirs will be Gardens of Eden, wherein rivers flow beneath them; therein they will be given armlets of gold and will wear green robes of finest silk and gold embroidery, reclining upon thrones therein. Blest the reward, and fair the resting-place!

33. Coin for them a similitude: Two men, unto one of whom We had assigned two gardens of grapes, and We had surrounded both with date-palms and had put between them tillage.

34. Each of the gardens gave its fruit and withheld naught thereof. And We caused a river to gush forth therein.

35. And he had fruit. And he said unto his comrade, when he spake with him: I am more than thee in wealth, and stronger in respect of men.

36. And he went into his garden, while he (thus) wronged himself. He said: I think not that all this will ever perish.

37. I think not that the Hour will ever come, and if indeed I am brought back unto my Lord I surely shall find better than this as a resort.

38. And his comrade, while he disputed with him, exclaimed: Disbelievest thou in Him Who created thee of dust, then of a drop (of seed), and then fashioned thee a man?

39. But He is Allah, my Lord, and I ascribe unto my Lord no partner.

40. If only, when thou enteredst thy garden, thou hadst said: That which Allah willeth (will come to pass)! There is no strength save in Allah! Though thou seest me as less than thee in wealth and children.

41. Yet it may be that my Lord will give me better than thy garden, and will send on it a bolt from heaven, and some morning it will be a smooth hillside,

42. Or some morning the water thereof will be lost in the earth so that thou canst not make search for it.

43. And his fruit was beset (with destruction). Then began he to wring his hands for all that he had spent upon it, when (now) it was all ruined on its trellises, and to say: Would that I had ascribed no partner to my Lord!

44. And he had no troop of men to help him as against Allah, nor could he save himself.

45. In this case is protection only from Allah, the True. He is best for reward, and best for consequence.

46. And coin for them the similitude of the life of the world as water which We send down from the sky, and the vegetation of the earth mingleth with it and then becometh dry twigs that the winds scatter. Allah is Able to do all things.

47. Wealth and children are an ornament of life of the world. But the good deeds which endure are better in thy Lord's sight for reward, and better in respect of hope.

48. And (bethink you of) the Day when We remove the hills and ye see the earth emerging, and We gather them together so as to leave not one of them behind.

49. And they are set before thy Lord in ranks (and it is said unto them): Now verily have ye come unto Us as We created you at the first. But ye thought that We had set no tryst for you.

50. And the Book is placed, and thou seest the guilty fearful of that which is therein, and they say: What kind of a book is this that leaveth not a small thing nor a great thing but hath counted it! And they find all that they did confronting them, and thy Lord wrongeth no one.

51. And (remember) when We said unto the angels: Fall prostrate before Adam, and they fell prostrate, all save Iblis. He was of the Jinn, so he rebelled against his Lord's command. Will ye choose him and his seed for your protecting friends instead of Me, when they are an enemy unto you? Calamitous is the exchange for evil-doers!

52. I made them not to witness the creation of the heavens and the earth, nor their own creation; nor choose I misleaders for (My) helpers.

53. And (be mindful of) the Day when He will say: Call those partners of Mine whom ye pretended. Then they will cry unto them, but they will not hear their prayer, and We shall set a gulf of doom between them.

54. And the guilty behold the Fire and know that they are about to fall therein, and they find no way of escape thence.

74 / The Apocalypse of Islam

55. And verily We have displayed for mankind in this Qur'an all manner of similitudes, but man is more than anything contentious.

56. And naught hindereth mankind from believing when the guidance cometh unto them, and from asking forgiveness of their Lord, unless (it be that they wish) that the judgement of the men of old should come upon them or (that) they should be confronted with the Doom.

57. We send not the messengers save as bearers of good news and warners. Those who disbelieve contend with falsehood in order to refute the Truth thereby. And they take Our revelations and that wherewith they are threatened as a jest.

58. And who doth greater wrong than he who hath been reminded of the revelations of his Lord, yet turneth away from them and forgetteth what his hands send forward (to the Judgement)? Lo! on their hearts We have placed coverings so that they understand not, and in their ears a deafness. And though thou call them to the guidance, in that case they can never be led aright.

59. Thy Lord is the Forgiver, Full of Mercy. If He took them to task (now) for what they earn, He would hasten on the doom for them; but theirs is an appointed term from which they will find no escape.

60. And (all) those townships! We destroyed them when they did wrong, and We appointed a fixed time for their destruction.

61. And when Moses said unto his servant: I will not give up until I reach the point where the two rivers meet, though I march on for ages.

62. And when they reached the point where the two met, they forgot their fish, and it took its way into the waters, being free.

63. And when they had gone further, he said unto his servant: Bring us our breakfast. Verily we have found fatigue in this our journey.

64. He said: Didst thou see, when we took refuge on the rock, and I forgot the fish—and none but Satan caused me to forget to mention it—it took its way into the waters by a marvel.

65. He said: This is that which we have been seeking. So they retraced their steps again.

66. Then found they one of Our slaves, unto whom We had given mercy from Us, and had taught him knowledge from Our presence.

67. Moses said unto him: May I follow thee, to the end that thou mayst teach me right conduct of that which thou hast been taught?

68. He said: Lo! thou canst not bear with me.

The Apocalypse of Islam / 75

69. How canst thou bear with that whereof thou canst not compass any knowledge?

70. He said: Allah willing, thou shalt find me patient and I shall not in aught gainsay thee.

71. He said: Well, if thou go with me, ask me not concerning aught till I myself mention of it unto thee.

72. So the twain set out till, when they were in the ship, he made a hole therein. (Moses) said: Hast thou made a hole therein to drown the folk thereof? Thou verily hast done a dreadful thing.

73. He said: Did I not tell thee thou couldst not bear with me?

74. (Moses) said: Be not wroth with me that I forgot, and be not hard upon me for my fault.

75. So the twain journeyed on till, when they met a lad, he slew him. (Moses) said: What! Hast thou slain an innocent soul who hath slain no man? Verily thou hast done a horrid thing.

76. He said: Did I not tell thee that thou couldst not bear with me?

77. (Moses) said: If I ask thee after this concerning aught, keep not company with me. Thou hast received an excuse from me.

78. So they twain journeyed on till, when they came unto the folk of a certain township, they asked its folk for food, but they refused to make them guests. And they found therein a wall upon the point of falling into ruin, and he repaired it. (Moses) said: If thou hadst wished, thou couldst have taken payment for it.

79. He said: This is the parting between thee and me! I will announce unto thee the interpretation of that thou couldst not bear with patience.

80. As for the ship, it belonged to poor people working on the river, and I wished to mar it, for there was a king behind them who is taking every ship by force.

81. And as for the lad, his parents were believers and We feared lest he should oppress them by rebellion and disbelief.

82. And We intended that their Lord should change him for them for one better in purity and nearer to mercy.

83. And as for the wall, it belonged to two orphan boys in the city, and there was beneath it a treasure belonging to them, and their father had been righteous, and thy Lord intended that they should come to their full strength and should bring forth their treasure as a mercy from their Lord; and I did it not upon my own command. Such is the interpretation of that wherewith thou couldst not bear.

84. They will ask thee of Dhu'l-Qarneyn. Say: I shall recite unto you a remembrance of him.

76 / The Apocalypse of Islam

85. Lo! We made him strong in the land and gave him unto every thing a road.

86. And he followed a road

87. Till, when he reached the setting-place of the sun, he found it setting in a muddy spring, and found a people thereabout: We said: O Dhu'l-Qarneyn! Either punish or show them kindness.

88. He said: As for him who doeth wrong, we shall punish him, and then he will be brought back unto his Lord, who will punish him with awful punishment!

89. But as for him who believeth and doeth right, good will be his reward, and We shall speak unto him a mild command.

90. Then he followed a road

91. Till, when he reached the rising-place of the sun, he found it rising on a people for whom We had appointed no shelter therefrom.

92. So (it was). And We knew all concerning him.

93. Then he followed a road

94. Till, when he came between the two mountains, he found upon their hither side a folk that scarce could understand a saying.

95. They said: O Dhu'l-Qarneyn! Lo! Gog and Magog are spoiling the land. So may we pay thee tribute on condition that thou set a barrier between us and them?

96. He said: That wherein my Lord hath established me is better (than your tribute). Do but help me with strength (of men), I will set between you and them a bank.

97. Give me pieces of iron—till, when he had levelled up (the gap) between the cliffs, he said: Blow!—till, when he had made it a fire, he said: Bring me molten copper to pour thereon.

98. And (Gog and Magog) were not able to surmount, nor could they pierce (it).

99. He said: This is a mercy from my Lord; but when the promise of my Lord cometh to pass, He will lay it low, for the promise of my Lord is true.

100. And on that day We shall let some of them surge against others, and the Trumpet will be blown. Then We shall gather them together in one gathering.

101. On that day We shall present hell to the disbelievers, plain to view,

102. Those whose eyes were hoodwinked from My reminder, and who could not bear to hear.

103. Do the disbelievers reckon that they can choose My bondmen as protecting friends beside Me? Lo! We have prepared hell as a welcome for the disbelievers.

The Apocalypse of Islam / 77

104. Say: Shall We inform you who will be the greatest losers by their works?

105. Those whose effort goeth astray in the life of the world, and yet they reckon that they do good work.

106. Those are they who disbelieve in the revelations of their Lord and in the meeting with Him. Therefore their works are vain, and on the Day of Resurrection We assign no weight to them.

107. That is their reward: hell, because they disbelieved, and made a jest of Our revelations and Our messengers.

108. Lo! those who believe and do good works, theirs are the Gardens of Paradise for welcome,

109. Wherein they will abide, with no desire to be removed from thence.

110. Say: Though the sea became ink for the Words of my Lord, verily the sea would be used up before the Words of my Lord were exhausted, even though We brought the like thereof to help.

111. Say: I am only a mortal like you. My Lord inspireth in me that your God is only One God. And whoever hopeth for the meeting with his Lord, let him do righteous work, and make none sharer of the worship due unto his Lord.

❧

In the farrago of sura 18 the bewildered Western mind discerns and fastens onto three mysterious episodes—one cannot call them narratives—(1) The Sleepers in the Cave (vs. 9–26), (2) Moses' journey (vs. 61–83), and (3) Dhu'l-Qarneyn's wall against Gog and Magog (vs. 84–99).

The Sleepers in the Cave:

ASHAB al-KAHF, "those of the cave." This is the name given in the Kur'an, and in later Arabic literature, to the youths who in the Christian Occident are usually called the "Seven Sleepers of Ephesus." According to the legend, in the time of the Christian persecution under the Emperor Decius (249–51), seven Christian youths fled into a cave near Ephesus and there sank into a miraculous sleep for centuries, awoke under the Christian Emperor Theodosius (c. 437 A.D.), were discovered and then went to sleep for ever. Their resting place and grave was considered, at any rate since the beginnings of the 6th century A.D., as a place of worship.[2]

Dhu'l-Qarneyn, literally the "two-horned," is Alexander the Great, as in Syriac legend of the sixth century A.D., in which

Alexander says to God: "I know that thou hast caused horns to grow upon my head, so that I may crush the kingdoms of the world with them." In late classical antiquity—in between Christ and Muhammad—apocalyptic syncretism, Judeo-Christian-Hellenistic, expanding on lines laid down in the biblical books of Daniel and Revelation, absorbed the figure of Alexander into its sequence of world conquerors. Gog and Magog are biblical figures of eschatological terror. In Ezekiel 38 and 39, Gog and Magog represent peoples of the north who are let loose against the peaceful land of Israel, unwalled and undefended, with a great army of countless troops. In Revelation 20:7, "When the thousand years are over, Satan will be let loose from his prison and will come out to seduce the nations in the four quarters of the earth and to muster them for battle, yes, the hosts of Gog and Magog." Koranic commentary, in the spirit of the modern historian W. W. Tarn, sees in Alexander a prophet of the unity of mankind as well as a world conqueror, and thus a prefiguration of Muhammad himself. Early Christian tradition, and Jewish tradition as early as Josephus, identified Gog and Magog with barbarian peoples to the north, locked away behind iron gates at the Caspian Sea by Alexander the Great, but destined to break loose at the end of time.[3]

The episodes of the Sleepers in the Cave and Dhu'l-Qarneyn's Wall palpably allude to preexistent legends. The episode of Moses' journey is more complex. The most bafflingly elliptical of the three episodes, and the centerpiece of the sura, introduces a new Moses, a Moses who like Gilgamesh and Alexander is committed to the quest for the Fountain of Life: "I will not give up until I reach the point where the two rivers meet" (v. 61). The new Moses, having become a seeker, submits to spiritual direction by a mysterious master who bewilders Moses through a series of Zen-like absurd actions, finally justified by his privy knowledge of the secrets of predestination.

Again we have to do with preexistent materials, but here the action is positive confusion. To begin with, confusion between Moses and Alexander; not the historical but the mythical Alexander of the Alexander Romance, a complex literary production, completed about 300 C.E., giving voice to eschatological dreams close to the heart of late classical antiquity. Alexander goes in quest of the Fountain of Life. By the merest chance his cook discovers the fountain: he was preparing a dried fish by cleaning it in a fountain; the fish came to life again and swam away. The cook jumps in and gains immortality. He tells Alexander the story, but they cannot find the fountain again.

The Koran, with its creative confusion of Moses and Alexander, in a characteristically abrupt and monumental gesture, breaks with Judaic ethnocentrism and reprojects the prophetic tradition on a new transcultural, universal, world-historical plane. At the same time, by making Moses a seeker on the same plane as the pagan Alexander, the Koran defines a limitation in Moses and in the Halakhic Judaism of which he is the author: he lacks eternal life. In so doing the passage mobilizes, without naming, the powerful contrast, latent in Jewish tradition, between Moses and Elijah—Elijah the most popular figure in the legendary world of postbiblical Judaism: Elijah who did not, like Moses, die in sight of the Promised Land but who never died, being caught up to heaven in a chariot of fire; Elijah the omnipresent Comforter-Spirit present at every Jewish circumcision ceremony and every Jewish Passover; Elijah the herald and helper of the Messiah at the time of the return; Elijah, who knows the secrets of heaven and is claimed as the direct source of revelation by Jewish mystics including Kabbalists. The Koran sends Moses to Elijah's school—"it was taught in Elijah's school," Jewish mystics say.[4]

To represent what Moses learned in Elijah's school, the Koran has recourse to a folktale, type no. 759 in Aarne and Thompson's *Types of the Folktale*: "God's Justice vindicated." Thompson's paradigm is the Christian story of the angel and the hermit, very popular among Oriental Christians about the middle of the fifth century: "An angel takes a hermit with him and does many seemingly unjust things (repays hospitality by stealing a cup; inhospitality by giving a cup; hospitality by throwing his host's servant from a bridge and by killing the host's son). The angel shows the hermit why each of these was just." Just as the Koran transplants the Christian legend of the Seven Sleepers and the Hellenistic legend of Alexander into a new Koranic context, so it is drawing here on the vast ocean of traditional Talmudic Midrashic Haggadic wisdom.

> First of all the story of Rabbi Akiba, who was often made to feel the truth of his favorite maxim: "Whatever God does He does for the best." Once he was compelled to pass the night outside the town walls because he was refused any hospitality in the town. Without a murmur he resigned himself to this hardship, and even when a lion devoured his ass, a cat killed his cock, and the wind extinguished his candle he only said: "Gam Zu Letovah" (This, too, must be for a good purpose). When morning dawned R. Akiba learned how true his words were. A band of robbers had attacked the town and carried its inhabitants into captivity, but he had escaped. Thus the fact of getting no accommodation in the town, as well as the killing of his ass and cock, turned out to be a blessing from God, otherwise the ass or the cock could easily have betrayed his whereabouts.[5]

Conventional Western commentators, who are quite sure there is nothing new in the Koran, assume without hesitation that the folktale is to be taken literally and that all that is going on in the passage is the transmission of conventional Haggadic piety. A detailed study of the Jewish and Muslim theodicy legends by Haim Schwarzbaum shows that sura 18, taken literally, offers nothing new to justify the ways of God to men. What is new is the sura's promotion of Haggadic folklore material to the status of revelation, its transgression or confusion of the boundary separating Haggadah and Torah. The Koran, with characteristic monumentality, reduces the folktale to its archetypal essence and makes evident its folktale form, thereby alerting the intelligence to the problem of interpretation. Folktales, like dreams, are not to be interpreted literally. And the content of the folktale—the episodes of the ship, the youth, and the wall—tells us in the most literal, even crude way, three times reiterated, that there is a distinction between "what actually happened," events as seen by the eye of historical materialism, and "what is really going on," events sub specie aeternitatis, as seen by the inward, clairvoyant eye, the second sight. The form and the content of the folktale oblige us, as they have obliged all subsequent Islamic culture, to make the distinction between literal meaning and something beyond—in Islamic terminology between *zahir* and *batin*, between outer (exoteric) and inner (esoteric); between external-visible-patent and internal-invisible-latent; between materialist and spiritual meanings.[6]

Sura 18 is the apocalypse of Islam: the heart of its message, not displayed on the surface, is the distinction between surface and substance, between *zahir* and *batin*. The context in which the folktale is embedded contains further paradoxical revelations for those who have eyes to see and are alert to read between the lines as well as in them. The context obliges us to identify prophecy (the prophet Moses) with the literal or external view of events (the ship, the youth, the wall) and to attribute the deeper view into the hidden reality to a mysterious other servant of God; not a prophet, or a prophet of the Elijah type as opposed to the Moses type. The context also obliges us to associate the mysterious other with the water of life—or where the two waters meet, the water of life and the water of death.

Sura 18 opens up, silently, majestically, in the heart of the Koran the question, What lies beyond or after the Koran? For Muhammad, like Moses, is a prophet. Muhammad is the seal of prophecy; what comes after prophecy? Prophecy is delivered in the form of a book, a scripture. But everything including the Book has an exterior (*zahir*) and an interior (*batin*). Especially the Book, according to the Prophet himself. Of Ibn Abbas, one of the most respected sources of Hadith (traditions about the Prophet), it is said: "One day while standing on Mt. Arafat he made an allusion to the verse 'Allah it is who hath created seven heavens, and of the earth the like thereof' (65:12) and turned to the people saying 'O men! if I were to comment before you on this verse as I heard it commented upon by the Prophet himself you would stone me.' " There is therefore a basic distinction between *ta'wil*, the symbolic and hermeneutic interpretation of the inner meaning, and *tafsir*, the literal explanation of the external aspect of the Book.[7] In the subsequent history of Islam, sura 18 became the basis for the elaboration of a distinction between prophecy and another transcendent or esoteric kind of wisdom; a kind of wisdom which in the fullness of time came to be most notoriously represented by, on the one hand, the Sufi master (*pir*) and, on the other, the Shiite imam. Whereas the cycle of prophecy is over (Muhammad is the seal of prophecy), the cycle of *wilayat* continues, which Seyyed Hossein Nasr tells us, for want of a better term, may be translated as the "cycle of initiation" and also "sanctity."[8] For want of a better term: the translation has to be in terms of Western Judeo-Christian religious experience. "Initiation" is closer to Shiite notions: Sufi masters are often more like Christian saints. The Shiite imam represents a principle of authoritative guidance in interpretation of the revelation; the Sufi *pir* represents a principle of mystic illumination which supplements the legislative or imperative mood of prophecy.

The text of sura 18 leaves us with a riddle: who is the mysterious other to whom Moses turns for guidance, "one of Our slaves, unto whom We had given mercy from Us, and had taught him knowledge from Our presence" (v. 66). Although he is like Elijah, he is not exactly Elijah; the Koran with a characteristically majestic gesture leaves him unnamed. The Koran leaves us with a riddle, or an assignment, to find him. The ellipses in the Koran are pregnant with the future. Very soon, within the first century, Muslim traditions and commentary on the Koran had given a name to the "Servant of God" who initiates Moses—al-Khadir, or Khidr, the Green (the sacred color of Islam), or Evergreen; taking their cue not from the reminiscence of Elijah but from the bold Koranic association of the servant with the Fountain of Life in the Alexander Romance. The name, the Evergreen, while naming, preserves his unnamable, unhistorical or suprahistorical, archetypal or folkloristic essence. In traditional Muslim piety, Khidr, like Elijah, enjoys eternal life and invisible omnipresence. Like Elijah he participates in the small rituals of domestic life and in the great public liturgies. Every Friday he prays in five different places—Mecca, Medina, Jerusalem, Quba (southeast of Medina), and Tur Sina (Sinai). For the annual fast of Ramadan he is in Jerusalem; for the hajj (pilgrimage) he is always in Mecca. The eternal protector of the community will appear at the Return at the head of the armies of the Mahdi, who will fill the earth with justice even as it is now full of injustice.[9] In Islam the umbilical cord which connects "popular superstition" with avant-garde esoteric, theosophic speculation has not been cut; and Khidr is that cord. The Sufis attribute their illuminations to the inspiration of Khidr: Corbin's book on Ibn Arabi, the mastermind of Sufistic theosophy, *Creative Imagination in the Sufism of Ibn Arabi*, is organized around the two questions—Who is Khidr? What does it mean to be a disciple of Khidr? The rendezvous of Moses and Khidr becomes the prototype of all those later mystic voyages in the company of a spiritual guide; including, when Western Civilization becomes strong enough to absorb into its own system some of the strong medicine of Islam, Dante under the guidance of Virgil and Beatrice. The visionary journey of the *Divine Comedy* is an appropriation of the Islamic *miraj*, the Ascension of the Prophet; the poet inherits the prophetic task of rescuing the Eternal Gospel from ecclesiastical deformations.[10]

The postbiblical Haggadah shows the efforts of Jewish orthodoxy to reduce Elijah's stature and to counter the excessive veneration accorded to him in apocalyptic Jewish sectarianism and Christian circles. It was denied that Elijah had ever gone up to heaven, biblical evidence to the contrary notwithstanding. Elijah's habit of revealing divine secrets to pious mortals once earned him a severe punishment of sixty lashes of fire. The Koran goes the other way. Without impairing its veneration for Moses as a prophetic figure, it endorses the eschatological longings and mystic revelations associated with the figure of Elijah, without naming him. But the orthodox Sunni *ulama* regress to the posture of Halakhic Judaism. The official theologians of Islam, we are told, are and always have been averse to these excesses of the popular Khidr belief; even as the Talmudic rabbis tried to put down the popularity of Elijah. "There are two things I hate about the orthodox canonists," says the mystic master Shadhili. "They say that Khidr is dead and that Hallaj was an infidel"—Hallaj the martyred prototype of Sufi mysticism, the subject of Massignon's masterpiece. Who is Khidr? How much does he know? These are questions neoorthodox Sunni Islam can do without. The great

Egyptian modernist, or neofundamentalist, Islamic reformer Rashid Rida attacked the Friday liturgy of sura 18 as a degenerate innovation (*bida*), a departure from the original Sunna, the hallowed practice of primitive Islam. Rashid Rida also condemns as subjective interpretation all *ta'wil* which claims to find a hidden sense beyond the literal, and he restricts Koranic exegesis to simple literalist commentary, *tafsir*.[11]

The controversy between literalism and mysticism in the interpretation of the Koran is aboriginal in Islam, and reaches into the split in the core of the Prophet's followers over the succession to his leadership. The rejected leader Ali is to be identified not simply with the principle of hereditary legitimacy, but also with the assertion of charismatic authority after the Prophet, and with inspired interpretation after the Koran. Sura 18 is pregnant with the Sunni-Shiite split and the whole subsequent history of Islam.

The Koran is pregnant with the future. It is only in the light of later developments that we can find the riddle, the question—Who is Khidr?—in sura 18. Later Islamic traditions linked the occult spirit of Khidr with the Seven Sleepers and with Dhu'l-Qarneyn's wall. Khidr is the Director of the Seven Sleepers, their watchdog; together they form a community of apotropaic or intercessory saints whose virtue saves the city, like those ten just men for whose sake the Lord would have, at Abraham's intercession, spared Sodom. They repair breaches in the wall against Gog and Magog that Dhu'l-Qarneyn built. The weekly liturgical recitation of sura 18 is to invoke the spirit of Khidr and join the communion of saints in their action of repairing that wall. The fight (*jihad*) against Gog and Magog is an eschatological reality, but not in the future. In the Islamic sense of time we are always in the last days.

The interpenetration works both ways: Khidr is assimilated to the Seven Sleepers: he is an anchorite who has to flee from persecution and lives, exempt from death, having found the Fountain of Life, concealed in a remote island; like Kevin, of increate God the servant, in *Finnegans Wake*. The melting or merging—"confusion"—of Khidr and the Seven Sleepers generates mystical—i.e., nonliteral—interpretations of that sleep. The literalists,

Christian or Islamic, cite the story as "proof" of the resurrection, literally understood as life after death. Seen with the inward eye, to be immured alive in a cave is an image of saintly or eremite withdrawal from the world, taking refuge with Allah; and sleep the image of that extinction of self, that condition of being lost in God which characterizes the saint (*wali*) as distinct from the prophet (*nabi*); in the Night of Unction, the Night of the Heavenly Ascension, the blessed Night, the Night of Enshrouding which is also the Night of Power; the Dark Night of the Soul which is also the Night of *Finnegans Wake.*[12]

The spirit of Khidr is eschatological as well as mystical. The Sleepers Awake at the end of time, to figure together with Khidr in the Return of the Mahdi. History becomes a night, or seven nights. And everything is their sleep: The Seven Sleepers can represent the seven prophets who periodize world history—Adam, Idris, Noah, Abraham, Moses, Jesus, and Muhammad. The text explicitly provokes millenarian calculations: "which of the two parties would best calculate the time that they had tarried"; "it is said they tarried in their Cave three hundred years and add nine"; "say: Allah is best aware how long they tarried" (vs. 12, 26–27).

It is Shiite exegesis that has made the most elaborate eschatological interpretations of sura 18. The Sleepers hidden in the cave are the Koranic authority for the Shiite notion of the *ghayba*, or occultation, of the Hidden Imam. In the Ithna'ashari, or Twelver Shiites, the occultation becomes the principle on which they base their periodization of the whole of post-Koranic history. We are living in the occultation, which began with the disappearance, or sleep, of the Twelfth Imam in 874 C.E. and will last till his reappearance, or reawakening, with the Mahdi at the end of time. Modern times are divided into the lesser occultation, which lasted from 874–941 C.E., in which the imam, although invisible, was still in regular touch with visible representatives of his authority; and the greater occultation, which began in 941 C.E. and is still our present condition, in which communication with the imam is irregular, rare, unpredictable, miraculous. In this vision of history modernity means the disappearance of authority (authoritative guidance in the interpretation of scripture). The Shiite notion of the Hidden Imam is to be understood in analogy with folktale no. D1960.2. in Stith Thompson's index: Barbarossa, king asleep in a mountain, will awake one day to succor his people. Thus interpreted, the legend of the Seven Sleepers contains the perpetual threat of an eschatological outbreak. For example, the Seven Sleepers are seven imams of the Ismaili Shiites hidden in the cave, the womb of Fatima, and guarded over by their watchdog, Ali. The great Shiite insurrection (resurrection) on behalf of social justice in the ninth and tenth centuries C.E., which succeeded in establishing the Fatimid anticaliphate in Egypt, was commenced in the 309th year of the Hegira, as prophesied in sura 18:26.[13]

Massignon calls Sura 18 the apocalypse of Islam. But sura 18 is a résumé, epitome of the whole Koran. The Koran is not like the Bible, historical, running from Genesis to Apocalypse. The Koran is altogether apocalyptic. The Koran backs off from that linear organization of time, revelation, and history which became the backbone of orthodox Christianity and remains the backbone of the Western culture after the death of God. Islam is wholly apocalyptic or eschatological, and its eschatology is not teleology. The moment of decision, the Hour of Judgment, is not reached at the end of a line, nor by a predestined cycle of cosmic recurrence; eschatology can break out at any moment. Koran 16:77: "To Allah belong the secrets of the heavens and the earth, and the matter of the Hour is as the twinkling of an eye, or it is nearer still." In fully developed Islamic theology only the moment is real. There is no necessary connection between cause and effect. The world is made up of atomic space-time points, among which the only continuity is the utterly inscrutable will of God, who creates every atomic point anew at every moment.[14] And the Islamic mosque discards the orientation toward time essential to a Christian church: "The space," says Titus Burckhardt, "is as if reabsorbed into the ubiquity of the present moment; it does not beckon the eye in a specific direction; it suggests no tension or antinomy between the here below and the beyond, or between earth and heaven; it possesses all its fullness in every place."[15]

The rejection of linearity involves a rejection of narrative. There is only one decent narrative in the Koran: sura 12, "Joseph," acclaimed by condescending Western Orientalists: for once Muhammad overcame his temperamental incoherence and managed to do it right. The strict sect of the Kharidjis, on this point and on others the voice of rigorous Islamic consistency, condemned sura 12 on the ground that narrative has no place in revelation.[16] The Koran breaks decisively with that alliance between the prophetic tradition and materialistic historicism—"what actually happened"—which set in with the materialistically historical triumph of Christianity. Hence the strangely abortive and incoherent character of the pseudonarratives in sura 18. Something happened, but this strange revelation manages not to reveal what or why. In fact the impossibility of history as "what actually happened" becomes the theme of an abrupt interruption in the narrative at vs. 23–25: the Sleepers; how many were there? The Lord only knows.

"Recalls of former times" are an integral component of Koranic revelation, but as Massignon's Muslim disciple Nwyia says in his indispensable study of the mystic tradition of Koranic exegesis, "recalls of former times" does not mean history:

> Schooled in the Koran, Muslim consciousness is spontaneously ahistorical, that is to say mythic. It takes up events of the past in approximately the same way as the apocryphal gospels adapt the gospel narratives. When Muslim consciousness takes up for its own ends an event borrowed from the Bible or Judeo-Christian hagiography, it in most cases cannot resist effecting a transvaluation by introducing fabulous details or otherwise transforming the meaning. Passing from one hand to another in a chain of Muslim transmission the historical event evaporates and all that is left is a vague memory submerged in a story which has become mythic.[17]

The use of the term *mythic*, with its Hellenic origins and overtones, may be questionable. At any rate apocryphal: not obsessed with the question, what really happened; willing to surrender to the fiction that is more real. Gibbon delighted in the irony that the Immaculate Conception of the Virgin, the Dogma of 1854, is first offered as a salvific image in the Koran (3:35–36). The Koran, with its angels and jinns, is pregnant also with the *Arabian Nights*; and with Rumi's *Masnavi*, that synthesis of Koranic inspiration and *Arabian Nights* imagination.[18]

In sura 18, in the Koran, there is a mysterious regression to a more primitive stratum, archetypal, folkloristic, fabulous, apocryphal. Historical material is fragmented into its archetypal constituents and then subjected to displacement and condensation, as in dreams. It is a rebirth of images, as in Revelation, or *Finnegans Wake*. In becoming unhistorical, it becomes elliptical: "And they forgot their fish; and it took its way into the waters, being free." The fish appears suddenly from nowhere, as in dreams; no causal explanation, no narrative coherence. The fish becomes a symbolic, or the archetypal, fish, the same one you see on California bumper-stickers; or in the mediaeval jingle *piscis assus Christus passus*. Moses and Elijah meet; Moses and Alexander merge, or "reamalgamerge" (*Finnegans Wake*, 49), not on the plane of materialistic historicism—what actually happened—but in the world of archetypal images, that world in which Moses and Alexander meet because they are both two-horned. In sura 19:25–26, Mary giving birth under a palm tree on the desert is also Agar the wife of Abraham; and in sura 3 Mary is also Miriam the sister of Moses. In this condensation Western scholarship sees only confusion—who is who when everybody is somebody else; as in *Finnegans Wake*. Massignon speaks of transhistorical, or metahistorical, telescoping; systematic anachronism. Islam is committed by the Koran to project a metahistorical plane on which the eternal meaning of historical events is disclosed. It is that plane on which Moses and Elijah are seen conversing with Jesus in Matthew 17; that plane on which Dante's *Divine Comedy* unfolds; and Blake's prophetic books; and *Finnegans Wake*. History sub specie aeternitatis.[19]

There is an apocalyptic or eschatological style: every sura is an epiphany and a portent; a warning, "plain tokens that haply we may take heed" (24:1). The apocalyptic style is *totum simul*, simultaneous totality: the whole in every part. Marshall Hodgson, in *The Venture of Islam*—still the outstanding and only ecumenical Western history—says of the Koran, "Almost every element which goes to make up its message is somehow present in any given passage." Simultaneous totality, as in *Finnegans Wake*. Or, more generally, what Umberto Eco calls "The Poetics of the Open Work": "We can see it as an infinite contained within finiteness. The work therefore has infinite aspects, because each of them, and any moment of it, contains the totality of the work." Eco is trying to characterize a revolution in the aesthetic sensibility of the West: we are the first generation in the West able to read the Koran, if we are able to read *Finnegans Wake*. In fact Carlyle's reaction to the Koran—"a wearisome confused jumble, crude, incondite; endless iterations, long-windedness, entanglement"—is exactly our first reaction to *Finnegans Wake*. The affinity between this most recalcitrant of sacred texts and this most avant-garde of literary experiments is a sign of our times. Joyce was fully aware of the connection, as Atherton shows in the most exciting chapter of *The Books at the Wake*; I particularly like his discovery in the *Wake* of the titles of 111 of the 114 suras.[20]

In both the Koran and *Finnegans Wake* this effect of simultaneous totality involves systematic violation of the classic rules of unity, propriety and harmony; bewildering changes of subject; abrupt juxtaposition of incongruities. Sura 18 is a good example. In addition to the melange of pseudonarratives, there are two intrusive parables ("similitudes," vs. 33 and 46) to remind us of the Day of Judgment; intrusive allusions to the current circumstances of the Prophet (his grief, v. 6; his lack of children, v. 40); and one intrusive pointer on pious decorum or etiquette in speech (vs. 24–25). Like *Finnegans Wake* the Koran rudely insists on indecent conjunctions. The Sura on Light (24), in the words of Hodgson, contains the most ethereal passage of visionary mysticism juxtaposed with what might seem the most sordid, dealing with matters of etiquette, with sexual decency, and in particular with an accusation of infidelity levied against a wife of the Prophet. The whole texture is one of interruption (Joyce's "enterruption"); collision (Joyce's "collideorscape"); abrupt collage, or bricolage, of disconnected ejaculations, *disjecta membra*, miscellaneous fragments. The widely accepted tradition is that the

Koran was collected, after the death of the Prophet, not only from the "hearts of men" but also from pieces of parchment or papyrus, flat stones, palm leaves, shoulderblades and ribs of animals, pieces of leather and wooden boards. In the words of *Finnegans Wake*, "A bone, a pebble, a ramskin; chip them, chap them, cut them up allways; leave them to terracook in the muttering pot" (*FW*, 20).[21]

Hence, it does not matter in what order you read the Koran: it is all there all the time; and it is supposed to be all there all the time in your mind or at the back of your mind, memorized and available for appropriate quotation and collage into your conversation or your writing, or your action. Hence the beautiful inconsequentiality of the arrangement of the suras: from the longest to the shortest. In this respect the Koran is more avant-garde than *Finnegans Wake*, in which the overall organization is entangled in both the linear and the cyclical patterns the novel is trying to transcend.

Every sura is an epiphany and a portent; and therefore not beautiful but sublime. Again He speaks in thunder and in fire! What the thunder said. Dumbfounding. Wonderstruck us at a thunder, yunder. Well, all be dumbed! (*FW*, 47, 262). In the Koran as in *Finnegans Wake* there is a destruction of human language. To quote Seyyed Hossein Nasr:

> Many people, especially non-Muslims, who read the Quran for the first time are struck by what appears as a kind of incoherence from the human point of view. It is neither like a highly mystical text nor a manual of Aristotelian logic, though it contains both mysticism and logic. It is not just poetry although it contains the most powerful poetry. The text of the Quran reveals human language crushed by the power of the Divine Word. It is as if human language were scattered into a thousand fragments like a wave scattered into drops against the rocks at sea. One feels through the shattering effect left upon the language of the Quran, the power of the Divine whence it originated. The Quran displays human language with all the weakness inherent in it becoming suddenly the recipient of the Divine Word and displaying its frailty before a power which is infinitely greater than man can imagine.[22]

In Islamic apologetics the miracle is not the incarnation of God, but a book. The miraculous character of the Koran is self-evident in the immediate effect of its style, its *idjaz*, literally "the rendering incapable, powerless"; the overwhelming experience of manifest transcendence, compelling surrender to a new world vision.[23] The bewilderment is part of the message: "Through the windr of a wondr in a wildr is a weltr as a wirbl of a warbl is a world" (*FW*, 597).

How do you start a new civilization—in the seventh or the twentieth century C.E., with all that history weighing like an Alp on the brains of the living? Out of the rubble of the old; there is no other way. "He dumptied the wholeborrow of rubbages on to soil here" (*FW*, 17). Massignon speaks of the farrago of folklore (*fatras folkloriste*) in the Koran. First you trash or junk the old, as in *Finnegans Wake*, or the Koran; reducing preexistent traditions to rubble. Muslim piety, for whom the Koran is the suprahistorical word of God, is troubled by the question of the relation of the Koran to preexistent traditions. Western historicism, with its well-honed methods of source criticism—*Quellenforschung*—is only too delighted to lose itself in tracing the Koran to its sources, with the usual nihilistic result: the Koran is reduced to a meaningless confusion. Meaning is attributed to the original sources, but in sura 18 it has been "mutilated almost beyond recognition" and mechanically combined "in a most artificial and clumsy manner." Schwarzbaum refers to Muhammad as making a brave show with "borrowed trappings."[24] The notion that Muhammad was a charlatan, who stole from the treasury of Western Civilization and passed off his plagiarisms on his unsophisticated bedouin audience as the voice of God, is still very much alive at the back of Western minds.

Muslim piety need not be so troubled, nor Western scholarship so complacent and condescending. Sura 18 with its imperious restructuring of Christian Hellenistic and Judaic tradition is not troubled. It is a prototypical model of Islamic syncretism. The Koran is not an operation of high cultural continuity, the *translatio* of the legacy of Greece and Rome (or Jerusalem), or the appropriation of the jewels of Egypt as we make our Exodus, as in Augustine's *De Civitate Dei.* To start a new civilization is not to introduce some new refinement in higher culture but to change the imagination of the masses, the folk who shape and are shaped by folklore and folktales. Prophecy is an operation in what Vico called vulgar metaphysics. The Islamic imagination, Massignon has written, should be seen as the product of a desperate regression back to the primitive, the eternal pagan substrate of all religions—that proteiform cubehouse the Ka'ba—as well as to a primitive pre-Mosaic monotheism of Abraham. The Dome is built on the Rock. Islam stays with the dream-life of the masses, the eschatological imagination of the lowly and oppressed. The dream-life of the masses, discarded by the elite of the Enlightenment as superstition—the stone which the builders rejected—becomes in the twentieth century the Golden Bough for the return to the archetypal unconscious, *quod semper*, *quod ubique*, *quod ab omnibus*. Here Comes Everybody.[25]

Sura 18, and the Koran as a whole, like *Finnegans Wake*, shows us preexistent traditions, Jewish, Christian, Hellenistic, pulverized into condensed atoms or etyms of meaning: the abnihilisation of the etym (*FW*, 353). Out of this dust the world is to be made new. We are once amore as babes awondering in a wold made fresh where with the hen in the storyaboot we start from scratch (*FW*, 336). In the words of Muhammad Iqbal in his *Javid-nama*—that syncretistic (*West-östlich*) resumption of the Koranic, Dantesque, Faustian journey through all worlds and all history—

> the Koran—
> a hundred new worlds lie within its verses,
> whole centuries are involved in its moments. . . .
> A believing servant himself is a sign of God,
> every world to his breast is as a garment;
> and when one world grows old upon his bosom,
> the Koran gives him another world!

The Koran is not responsible for the way Islam developed into a closed system and for the drily rational spirit of the Sunni *ulama* who turned all the luxuriant cosmic imagery of the Koran into legalistic prose. In the tragic view of history taken by the Shiites, things went wrong from the moment the Prophet died. The problem is, What comes after the prophet? The question is, Who is Khidr? And, What does it mean to be a disciple of Khidr?—the question at the heart of Sura 18. Pursuing that question, Ibn Arabi said that he had plunged into an ocean on whose shore the prophets remained behind standing.[26]

NOTES

1. L. Massignon, *Opera Minora*, 3 vols. (Paris, 1969): "L'Homme Parfait en Islam et Son Originalité Eschatologique," 1:107–125; "Elie et Son Rôle Transhistorique, Khadiriya, en Islam," 1:142–161; "Le Temps dans la Pensée Islamique," 2:606–612; "Les 'Sept Dormants' Apocalypse de l'Islam," 3:104–118; "Le Culte Liturgique et Populaire des Sept Dormants Martyres d'Ephèse (Ahl al-Kahf): Trait d'Union Orient-Occident Entre l'Islam et la Chrétienté," 3:119–180. The translation is that of M. M. Pickthall, *The Meaning of the Glorious Koran* (London: George Allen and Unwin).

2. *Encyclopedia of Islam*, s.v. "Ashab al Kahf." A juicier account of this "insipid legend of ecclesiastical history," which is often retaled early in bed and later in life down through all Christian and also Muslim minstrelsy, is Gibbon, *Decline and Fall*, chapter 33, *sub fin.*

3. *Encyclopedia of Islam*, s.v. "al-Khadir." *Encyclopedia Judaica*, s.v. "Gog and Magog." G. Cary, *The Medieval Alexander* (Cambridge, 1956), 130. Cf. F. Pfister, *Kleine Schriften zum Alexanderroman* (Meisenheim, 1976), 143–150.

4. *Encyclopedia Judaica*, s.v. "Elijah."

5. H. Schwarzbaum, "The Jewish and Moslem Versions of Some Theodicy Legends," *Fabula* 3 (1959–1960): 127.

6. S. H. Nasr, *Ideals and Realities of Islam* (Boston, 1972), 58. I. Goldziher, *Die Richtungen der islamischen Koranauslegung* (Leiden, 1920), 182.

7. Nasr, *Ideals and Realities*, 58–59.

8. Ibid., 87.

9. Massingnon, *Opera Minora* 1:151–152.

10. W. Anderson, *Dante the Maker* (New York, 1982), 277.

11. *Encyclopedia Judaica*, s.v. "Elijah." *Hastings Encyclopedia of Religion and Ethics*, s.v. "Khidr," 695. Massignon, *Opera Minora*

1:148. Goldziher, *Richtungen*, 335. *Encyclopedia of Islam*, s.v. "Islah," 147.

12. Koran 44:3; 92:1; 97:1. Massignon, *Opera Minora* 2:354; 3:104–118. H. Ritter, *Das Meer der Seele* (Leiden, 1955), 588–589.

13. Massignon, *Opera Minora* 3:104–118. *Encyclopedia of Islam*, s.v. "Ghayba," "Ithna'ashari."

14. M. G. S. Hodgson, *The Venture of Islam* (Chicago, 1974), 1:443. Massignon, *Opera Minora* 1:108; 2:606.

15. T. Burckhardt, *Art of Islam: Language and Meaning* (London, 1976), 19.

16. W. M. Watt, *Bell's Introduction to the Qur'an* (Edinburgh, 1977), 46.

17. P. Nwyia, *Exégèse Coranique et Langage Mystique* (Beirut, 1970), 74.

18. Cf. Massignon, "Le Folklore chez les Mystiques Musulmanes," *Opera Minora* 2:345–352.

19. Massignon, *Opera Minora* 1:109; cf. 1:143 and 3:143.

20. M. G. S. Hodgson, "A Comparison of Islam and Christianity as Framework for Religious Life," *Diogenes* 32 (1960): 61. U. Eco, *The Role of the Reader* (Bloomington, Ind., 1979), 63. J. S. Atherton, *The Books at the Wake* (Carbondale, Ill., 1974), chapter 12.

21. Hodgson, "A Comparison," 62. Watt, *Bell's Introduction*, 32.

22. Nasr, *Ideals and Realities*, 47–48.

23. *Encyclopedia of Islam*, s.v. "Idjaz."

24. *Hastings Encyclopedia of Religion and Ethics*, s.v. "Khidr," 694. Schwarzbaum, "Theodicy Legends," 135.

25. Massignon, *Opera Minora* 1:158–159, 162–163; 3:128, 143.

26. M. Iqbal, *Javid-nama*, trans. A. J. Arberry (London, 1966), ll. 1132–1140. Hodgson, *Venture of Islam* 1:392. Goldziher, *Richtungen*, 217.

21

METHOD AGAINST TRUTH ORIENTALISM AND QUR'ĀNIC STUDIES

S. Parvez Manzoor

The Orientalist enterprise of Qur'ānic studies, whatever its other merits and services, was a project born of spite, bred in frustration and nourished by vengeance: the spite of the powerful for the powerless, the frustration of the 'rational' towards the 'superstitious' and the vengeance of the 'orthodox' against the 'non-conformist'. At the greatest hour of his worldly-triumph, the Western man, co-ordinating the powers of the State, Church and Academia, launched his most determined assault on the citadel of Muslim faith. All the aberrant streaks of his arrogant personality – its reckless rationalism, its world-domineering phantasy and its sectarian fanaticism – joined in an unholy conspiracy to dislodge the Muslim Scripture from its firmly entrenched position as the epitome of historic authenticity and moral unassailability. The ultimate trophy that the Western man sought by his dare-devil venture was the Muslim mind itself. In order to rid the West forever of the 'problem' of Islam, he reasoned, Muslim consciousness must be made to despair of the cognitive certainty of the Divine message revealed to the Prophet. Only a Muslim confounded of the historical authenticity or doctrinal autonomy of the Qur'ānic revelation would abdicate his universal mission and hence pose no challenge to the global domination of the West. Such, at least, seems to have been the tacit, if not the explicit, rationale of the Orientalist assault on the Qur'ān.

That Orientalism was a naked discourse of power and that its epistemology was a crude charade of legitimizing ethnocentric arrogance, is no longer a point of contention with any knowledgeable student of Islam or of modern history. Thus, it is neither inapt nor squeamish to construe the Orientalist enterprise as a frontal, at times even subversive, 'behind the lines', assault on the Qur'ān; for, the only distinguishing mark of the Orientalist approach is its vengefulness and hatred. Seldom, if ever, has any sacred scripture of a universal faith been treated with such pathological animosity as the Orientalists handled the Qur'ān. Far from showing even the perfunctory reverence that in cases like these is otherwise *de rigueur*, the Orientalist launched his 'iconoclastic' attack with such fanaticism that compared to it even the crusaders' fury pales to nothing. Indeed, brave would be the person who today would defend the Orientalist method for studying the Muslim Scripture as being the natural mode of apprehension of the rationalist man. If it was 'rationalist', it was of a supremely arrogant European kind. Indeed, in all its emotional moorings, the Orientalist method was visibly vindictive, partisan and squint-eyed (cf. our review-essay: 'Islam and Orientalism: The Duplicity of a Scholarly Tradition', in *MWBR*, Vol. 6, No. 1, pp. 3–12). Of all the sacred texts of the world, it singled out the Qur'ānic revelation for carrying out its senseless act of vandalism that shocked

34

even its own champions. For instance, a scholar like Ignaz Goldziher, hardly to be accused of pro-Islamic partiality, had to cry out in protest, exclaiming: 'What would be left of the Gospels if the Qur'ānic methods were applied to them?'

To condemn the entire legacy of Orientalism, at least its enterprise of Qur'ānic studies, as an outburst of psychopathic vandalism may seem harsh in our more 'ecumenical' times. It might even be dangerous. Such a wholesale dismissal of a solidly scholarly tradition, for instance, may become for us a facile substitute for critical and nuanced analysis. Indeed, there are signs that some of us are doing just that: dismissing Orientalism entirely and cavalierly rather than studying it and analysing it. Whatever the rewards of such emotional escapism, the stance adopted here (see the Introduction to the Bibliography) is diametrically opposed to any sentiment of self-indulgence. In our opinion, there is no substitute for the defeat of Orientalism but on the epistemological battlefield. Only by checkmating the Sovereign of the Orientalist cognitive pieces will the Muslim be able to pursue the games of his own choosing. Having said that, it also remains incontestable that any earnest-minded reader, Muslim or otherwise, who has the patience to sit through the irreverent inanities or petty squabblings of its mediocre discourse, will come to the realization that indeed there is something sick and sickening about the Orientalist hatred of Islam and the Muslims. If nothing else, the Muslim finds it impossible to forgive the Orientalist for the tone he employed in his discourse. It remains painful to this day.

With the balance-sheet in hand, we now know that Orientalism has failed in all its major objectives. If by its frontal attack on the Qur'ān it sought to make a breach in the fortification of the Muslim faith, it has failed miserably. If by its 'rationalist' epistemology, it had hoped to make a dent in the Islamic personality, the evidence today spells the death of such nefarious designs. Muslims today are rallying around the banner of their faith and revelation with firmer commitment than prior to the Orientalist assault. If some odd Orientalist benignly strove to make Muslim conscience more in alignment with the canons of modernity, his disenchantment must be great because Muslims today are challenging the moral and epistemological foundations of modernity itself. Even if by his disinterested observation, from a doctrinally safe distance of course, the Orientalist had aspired to unravel the mystery of the numinous, he stands totally humiliated today. Neither his method nor his rationality, it appears irrefutable now, will ever solve the riddle of the revelation. More pitiable than all that, the edifice of colonial power-structure, which sustained and protected the Orientalist hoax, has been pulverized by the emancipatory forces of history. There exists, thus, neither the intellectual nor the political space for carrying out the Orientalist discourse today. Little wonder, then, that even the old Orientalist establishments are having a face-lift now and the Muslim is being admitted to their closed sessions. In short, whatever the Orientalist had hoped to gain by his academic endeavours has not come to fruition at all. Thanks to the historical development, thus, the Muslim may now analyse the cognitive and emotional disorders of the Orientalist personality within a less infected emotional atmosphere than would have been

35

possible in the hey-days of the Orientalist hegemony.

Ignoring the historical roots of modern Orientalism which reach as far back as the polemical marshes of medieval Christianity, we should turn our attention to the nineteenth century, which saw the appearance of a number of biographies of the Prophet, notably by Gustav Weil (1843), Muir (1861) and Sprenger (1861–65). Obviously these biographical works also contained some introductory material relevant to the study of the Qur'ān **[83, 131]** (the bold numerals within square brackets refer to listings in the Bibliography) which later crystallized into a separate discipline of its own. Sprenger and Weil also laid the foundation of the chronology of the Qur'ānic text – something which was elaborated by every subsequent scholar till it reached the cul-de-sac of its own making. Earlier, in 1834, Gustav Flügel's recension of the Qur'ānic text had already provided Orientalist scholarship with one of its indispensable tools. With regard to Qur'ānic studies, however, the most notable event of nineteenth-century Orientalism was the publication of Nöldeke's seminal work, *Geschichte des Qorans*, in 1860 [**88**]. It was under the auspices of the Parisian Académie des Inscriptions et Belle-Letteres that a competition on the best monograph on the Qur'ān was announced in 1857. Of the three scholars who were attracted by the subject, Aloys Sprenger, Michele Amri and Theodore Nöldeke, the latter won the prize and out of this effort was born the most seminal work of the Orientalist scholarship on the Qur'ān.

From its inception, Orientalist scholarship conceived of its principal task as the establishment of the chronology of the Qur'ānic text. With Nöldeke this, perhaps the only 'scientific' so to speak, motif of Western Qur'ānic studies gets fully crystallized. Following Weil [**131**], Nöldeke proposed a chronological scheme, dividing the revelation into three Makkan and one Madinan periods, that has gained widespread acceptance since then. Apart from the four-period standard chronology, there were other systems as well, most notably the ones proposed by Muir (five Makkan, including one pre-Prophetic (!), and one Madinan phases) [**83**], Grimme and Hirschfeld [**51**]. Notwithstanding all their differences from the Muslim datings, however, the early European chronologies are nothing but variations of the traditional schemes. A more radical – and preposterous – re-arrangement of the Qur'ānic text was later suggested by the eccentric Scotsman, Richard Bell [**16–20**]. Taking his cue from Hirschfeld that in dating the Qur'ān one must take notice of the individual pericopes rather than entire *sūras*, Bell undertook a verse-by-verse examination and even tried to recast the entire text of the Qur'ān in his own mould! The peculiar theory which the Scottish crackpot laboured all his life to substantiate concerned the revision of the text by the Prophet himself in Madina. One of Bell's more quixotic suggestions was that whilst some passages were being revised, the Prophet instructed his scribes to note them down on the back of the sheets that already had the verses that were being replaced on them. Later editors, not willing to discard any shred of the revelation, therefore, inserted the old verses back in the text as it were. Consequently, Bell tried to explain every possible break in the text on the basis of some discarded 'scrap' that had got into the Qur'ān by mistake!

36

Whatever his ingenuity at the rehabilitation of the original arrangement, Richard Bell, paradoxically, brought the Western attempt to establish a textual chronology of the Qur'ān to a complete halt. Like the proverbial snake, Orientalism bit its own tail. All that one can say today is, in the authoritarian opinion of the *Encyclopaedia of Islam* [72] ('Al-Ḳur'ān', s.v.) that 'it is not possible to put the *sūras* as wholes in chronological order, or to determine the exact order of the passages on any major teaching . . .!

The reasons for the Orientalist obsession with dating and chronology are not far to seek. At its most obvious, the theme of chronology which itself is a category of history, provides a chain of temporal, and hence causal, 'explanations' for the 'phenomenon' of the Qur'ān. Not only does such a 'natural' order of events obviate the need for any supernatural and transcendental agency, which is the claim of the Muslim perception, but with the introduction of the category of 'sequential time' in the workings of the Sacred, the notions of historical relativity or relative truth are also reinstated at the heart of our cognition. If the Qur'ān itself may be understood as a chronological sequence of events, then whatever truth that it proclaims cannot be but temporal, and hence fallible. To introduce the category of 'secular' time in the 'sacred' event of the revelation is, thus, to 'con-fuse' temporality with eternity. It is not accidental that Muslims, who are fully committed to the 'historicity' of the Sacred Descent (*Nuzūl*), the Event of the Qur'ān, have never confounded the Sacred times of the Revelation with the 'secular' times of profane history. True enough, the Revelation took place in historical times, but inasmuch as the Sacred entered into history, it radically metamorphosed history and temporality. Thus, for the Muslim, the nature of time and history is fundamentally different during the Event of the Revelation, during the Sacred Mission of the Prophet, because then God guided the affairs of the Community in a uniquely direct way. Insofar as the Orientalist epistemology is unable to concede the possibility of the Sacred intervening in human history during the time of the Prophecy, its system of chronology does not cross-sect the Muslim perception of the sacred times but merely runs parallel to it. All that the Orientalist can accomplish by his method is to posit a category of 'history' which encircles but never enters the sacred times of the Prophecy. Clearly, therefore, the Orientalist method is unable to arbitrate the issue of 'historical truth': all it is able to achieve is the confusion of the two order of realities – profane times and sacred history. Given its ideological commitment, it may not be unfair to assume that the ultimate objective of the Orientalist chronological exercise is not to pronounce any judgement on the 'truth' of the Qur'ān but to spread confusion concerning its temporality and hence confound the unperceptive believer.

Along with chronology, the other major theme of Orientalist scholarship with 'scientific' pretensions is, what may be broadly termed as, 'textual and linguistic studies'. Since linguistic analysis and explanation has been the mainstay of Muslim exegetical tradition, one expects that not only would Muslims find the modern Orientalist approach congenial to their traditional temper but that the Western effort would also be able to enrich Muslim self-understanding itself. And indeed, to some extent, it is so. Modern scholarship, possessing a much broader knowledge of comparative Semitic philology and even of other classical languages, not to speak of the more sophisticated methods of linguistic analysis that are at its disposal, is in an infinitely better position to shed light on 'obscure' words and terms that have baffled traditional commentators. In many cases, modern knowledge is indeed a boon. It has provided more plausible explanations, given more solid etymologies and traced more foreign words than was possible for the traditional Muslim scholars. And yet, there is always a polemical and derogatory side to the Orientalist effort. Not only does it assume a total cultural void in pre-Islamic Arabia but in terms of discretion it also labours under the assumption that the traditional Muslim view, influenced as it is by theological and dogmatic considerations, must of necessity be discarded. Invariably, out of the two or more plausible explanations, Western scholars compulsively pick up the one which is farthest from the accepted Muslim opinion [**60**]. Alas, there can be no other reason for this but the pathological, Islamophobic trait of the Orientalist personality.

Undoubtedly, within the matrix of linguistic, textual and chronological studies, the most ambitious project of Orientalist scholarship was to produce a 'critical' text of the Qur'ān. To a Muslim, uncompromisingly conditioned by the authority of the *mutawātir* tradition, such scholarly hybris strikes as suicidal, if not downright blasphemous. Such, however, is the lure of the 'critical' approach for the Orientalist that everything that is normative and axiomatic for the Muslim tradition has to be rejected with impunity, even if it tolls the death of impartiality or of 'scholarship'. In any case, the moving force behind this project was Arthur Jeffery, who had earlier pursued this line of research vigorously [**59**]. Together with a team of German scholars and on the basis of the surviving manuscripts from the earliest times, Jeffery was busy preparing 'the critical text of the Qur'ān', when his project was brought to a halt by the Allied bombing of Munich during World War II. All the manuscripts and other material that had been assembled with such painstaking fanaticism were utterly destroyed. Charles Adams mourns the loss in these words: 'The degree of loss was so great that it may never again be possible to mount a similar effort. The problem is further compounded by the deaths of most of the persons involved. To my knowledge, no extensive critical work on the text of the Qur'ān is now being undertaken in either the Muslim or the Western worlds.' Whatever the validity of the mock-sentiment of bereavement above, our readers ought to know that the highly praised critical dimension of Jeffery's project consisted of nothing more than documenting all the textual variations – usually no more than dialectical or vocal divergences that in no way affect the sense and meaning of the extant 'Vulgate' – that had, wittingly or unwittingly, crept into the Muslim works on the Qur'ān. Obviously, the most paramount tenet of Orientalist 'reason' is scepticism. To distrust vengefully everything that is consensual and conformist in the Muslim tradition and to espouse passionately everything that is deviant and freakish is the epitome of sacred canons of Orientalist 'criticism'!

38

Purely philological and lexical research, of course, is impossible without situating linguistic terms and expression in a historical and cultural milieu. It is here that the ingenuity [**4, 8, 48, 121, 128, 132, 133**], polemics [**3, 13–20, 35–6, 37, 39, 41–2, 50, 52, 54–6, 59–62, 64, 68, 75–6, 80–2, 87, 90–4, 100, 109, 112, 113, 120, 122, 124–6, 132**], derision [**90–4**], irony [**101**] and the proverbial Islamophobia (almost everyone) of Orientalism find their full rein. Within this paradigm, thus, by far the greatest part of the Orientalist effort is devoted to tracing 'the origins of the Qur'ān and the sources of its teaching'. The rationale behind committing all the resources of Orientalism to this project is, no doubt, polemical through and through. Epistemologically, it is grounded in a materialistic metaphysics that does not recognize the possibility of the Transcendent acting in human history, just as, dogmatically, it is unable to concede that God speaks to anyone but to His 'own people'. Given this fortuitous union of the sceptical and the Biblical, it is not surprising that, in studying the Qur'ānic revelation, even the most committed theist from among the People of the Book wears the agnostic mask. Scholars, otherwise fanatically opposed to weighing the mystery of revelation on the scale of reason, approach the Qur'ān with ideological premises and methodological practices that are strict taboos in their own homes. It is this duplicity of the Biblical, read Christian, personality that Goldziher finds objectionable. For the Muslim, however, the hybris of the Chosen is little different from the pre-judice of the Saved.

Unfortunately, the 'ecumenical' promise, which the theme of 'Judaeo-Christian antecedants of the Qur'ān' undoubtedly holds, was callously flouted in the annals of Orientalism. Sectarian passions were sanctified in the name of 'method' and all search for 'truth' was expelled from its academic precincts. Uppermost in these concerns was the eagerness to 'prove' that the Qur'ān was a poor replica of the Bible and that the Prophet was no more than a confused 'forger' of the Judaeo-Christian revelation! If Jewish doctors strove to prove 'the Jewish Foundations of Islam' [**122**, cf. even, **13, 44, 52, 55–6, 68, 113, 120**], Christian clerics felt obliged to outbid them in demonstrating its 'Christian Origins' [**3, 14, 20, 60, 62, 87, 90–4, 129, 132**]. Central to this type of perception is a radical sensitivity that has been sanctified in the name of religious exclusivism. God speaks only to the children of Israel and inasmuch as the Arabian Prophet is an *outsider*, God could not have addressed him directly, is the gist of this stance. (Even the few odd 'conciliatory' schemes of revelation, that have come to us from Jomier [**65**] Massignon or Moubarac [**81–2**], unblushingly tout for the 'racial' rationale!)

Only from such a sentiment of racial-religious exclusiveness may the Orientalist reproach to the Prophet and the Qur'ān be justified: the Arabian outsider 'appropriates' the truth of the Bible and 'forges' it into a revelation of his own! Everything Qur'ānic that corroborates earlier scriptures, thus, is viewed as 'borrowing' and everything that the Qur'ān modifies of their contents is dismissed as 'deviant' and 'distortive'. Should one, on the other hand, accept – even phenomenologically and not doctrinally – that the 'founder' of Islam stands at the end of a long chain of religious personalities, best described as 'prophetic' according to the typology of the Near East, then the whole edifice of Biblical

Orientalism crumbles to the ground. In the latter case, it would be absurd to speak about 'derivations', 'borrowings', 'distortions', even 'misunderstandings', as the Qur'ānic revelation too would be recognized as expounding the common truth of 'monotheism' (according to the Muslim opinion, even arbitrating it) rather than 'transgressing' the preserve of Judaeo-Christianity. Clearly, at the heart of the Orientalist vision lies the conviction of the *non-conformity* of the Qur'ānic revelation and the racial 'heresy' of the Prophet of Islam. By all standards, it is a dogmatic conviction and has nothing to do with the claims of method.

Forgotten also in the source-historical discourse of Orientalism is the inconvenient fact that the Qur'ān categorically proclaims its affinity with earlier revelations, including the Biblical, and that for the Muslim, convinced as he is of the unity of the *content* as well as the *source* of all revelations, the evidence of Judaeo-Christian antecedents of the Qur'ānic themes causes little doctrinal discomfort. Inasmuch as the Qur'ān and other scriptures exhibit overlapping of themes and motifs, even of linguistic expressions, it is due to the identity of the Transcendent Source of this knowledge and not attributable to any vagaries of its human recipients. For, not to claim externality for the Source of one's own – as well as for that of the others' – truth is to negate the 'revelation principle' itself. Indeed, it is tantamount to denying the existence of a transcendent order of knowledge and reducing the revelation to the imminent workings of the human mind. (Is the truth of Judaism (or Christianity) from God or is it a product of the Jewish (or Christian) genus?) In claiming that the truth of the Qur'ān is a borrowed, human, truth, whereas that of Judaism (or Christianity) is the revealed, divine, truth, the Orientalist reveals himself to be a dogmatic partisan of the Biblical tradition. Or, in his zeal to deprive the Muslim scripture of its transcendent moorings, he ends up by denying the possibility of revealed, extra-sensory, knowledge *über haupt*. Thus, despite his fondness of running with the hare and hunting with the hound, as it were, the Orientalist may claim methodological validity either for all the historical revelations or for none at all. Denying the revelation-principle in the case of the Qur'ān and upholding it in that of the Bible hardly makes the Orientalist method more 'scientific'. At heart, and behind all the masks of academic respectability, the Orientalist always remains, either a dogmatist or an atheist! In both cases, his methodological perception does violence to the Islamic faith and is unable to arbitrate the question of the Islamic truth.

The dogmatic principle of the uniqueness of the Biblical tradition, the darling of the Orientalist method, as mentioned earlier, cannot be maintained in the nascent discipline of phenomenology of religions. If anything, the phenomenological perception has a tendency to posit a typological and taxonomic kinship between all 'Semitic', 'Prophetic' or 'Western' religions [**78**]. (In perceiving this unity, the modern discipline, thus, comes very close to the Qur'ānic notions of the Abrahamic faiths.) In a sense, then, one of the most cogent refutations of the Orientalist method has, unwittingly, arisen within the Western worldview. It is not accidental, thus, that in studying Islam, Biblical Orientalism is loathe to employ the phenomenological methodology. Even here, however,

40

there is no mistaking about the Islamophobic emotionality of Orientalism. Thus, whatever phenomenological studies of Islam that have been carried out within the Orientalist tradition have not been free of the Biblical bias [**64, 79, 104**]. At times, they have even been unable to rise above the Biblical calling to polemicize against Islam [**37, 90**]. Committed as it is to the recovery of religious *meaning*, the new discipline of phenomenology of religions does show scholarly promise and, if handled properly, it may elicit insights that, *mutatis mutandis*, may enrich Muslim self-perception itself [**48**]. As yet, however, this potential remains largely untapped.

Notwithstanding the appearance of certain dogmatically, if not ideologically, neutral, even conciliatory tracts [**45, 65,** also **35–6**], the 'academic' temper of Orientalist scholarship has grown more sceptical with time [**75–6, 107–8, 125–6, 132**]. Today, the most radical demand for the revision of Orientalist legacy comes in the field of chronology and concerns the authenticity of the Qur'ānic text itself! We have seen that with Richard Bell tolls, no pun intended, the death-knell of the chronological movement of Orientalism. Henceforth, only an Exodus could save the chosen ones of its pure faith from the accursed captivity of chronology in the Arabia of history and lead them to the Promised Land, the no-man's Jerusalem, of literary analysis. Orientalism's new deliverer was to be John Wansbrough [**124–6**]. The new methodology and its wholesale rejection of the traditional chronological framework is as candid an admission of defeat on the part of the Orientalist establishment as it is a unilateral breach of the scholarly contract between Muslim sources and modern methods. The gist of Wansbrough's astounding thesis is that the Qur'ān is a 'composite' document containing within its covers a number of strands of sectarian Jewish polemics, that its present form and structure were crystallized during the ninth century of the Christian era and that it may or may not incorporate anything of the Prophet's own inspiration or revelation! Clearly, such a cataclysmic conjecture can only be sustained by making chaos out of the order of Islamic history. Not surprisingly, therefore, Wansbrough has to disown the entire corpus of Muslim historiography in order to strike a bargain with the merchants of 'literary analysis'. Only such a quantum jump ensures the Orientalist of reaching the orbit of a higher polemical charge!

With Wansbrough, the triumph of *method* over *truth* is complete. Along with the bathwater of Orientalist chronology, one now throws out the baby of Islamic history as well. The Qur'ān, thus unanchored from its historic moorings, now becomes amenable to any kind of methodological torture and the Orientalist scholar is absolved of any chronological responsibility. He may now dismiss the entire formative history of Islam as a hoax, and yet be free from the burden of advancing a single plausible reason for this colossal self-deception. He may play any kind of scholarly charade, and as long as he keeps on producing the rabbit of method from his academic hat, there is no end to his jugglery, nor any reprimand for his jestery. The divorce of history and method that is the seed of Wansbrough's literary analysis, however, is bringing a mixed harvest to the, now largely abandoned, manor-house of Orientalism. If, on the one hand, there is a vanguard assault to pulverize the mansion of Islamic history into the rubble of 'salvation history', most notably in the works of Patricia Croone and Michael Cooke, there is also, on the other hand, growing evidence of the reliability of the Muslim tradition [**85–6**]. Oddly enough, Wansbrough's own pupil, John Burton is also proclaiming, most paradoxically and more than any traditional Muslim claim, that the entirety of the Qur'ān in its present textual arrangement is the work of the Prophet himself! Understandably, the Orientalist establishment has reacted with caution, circumspection and scepticism to Wansbrough's highly provocative, nay tendentious, hypothesis. The *Encyclopaedia of Islam*, for instance, sums up the majority-view of the Orientalists as: 'Neither [Wansbrough nor Burton] has given convincing reasons for his own hypothesis, or for the shared assertion that the Muslim accounts should be rejected altogether' [**72**]. More outspoken dismissals of Wansbrough's brazen assertions have not been lacking either. R. B. Serjeant, for instance, expresses the gist of the counter-argument against Wansbrough as such: 'An historical circumstance so public [as the appearance of the Qur'ānic revelation] cannot have been invented'! (For a very firm, pithy and scholarly rebuttal of Wansbrough's 'methodology', see: Fazlur Rahman: 'Approaches to Islam in Religious Studies: Review Essay', in R. C. Martin (ed.): *Approaches to Islam in Religious Studies*, Arizona, 1985, pp. 189–202; also the same author's: 'Some Recent Books on the Qur'ān by Western Authors', in *The Journal of Religion*, Vol. 61, No. 1 (January 1984), pp. 73–95, as well as his more general work, *Major Themes of the Qur'ān*, (Chicago, 1980).)

Out of the vast corpus of Orientalist works, only a few deal with the *contents* of the Qur'ān, and even these are peripheral to the Orientalist effort and worldview. Apart from some recent Christian works that go a long way towards the revision of earlier Islamophobic sentiments [**35–6, 45, 65**], there is one scholar whose work recommends itself highly to the Muslims. Against all the canons of Western academism, the Japanese scholar Izutsu, as an outsider to Orientalism and sharing none of its historical prejudices or emotional phobias, has allowed the Qur'ān to speak for itself [**57–8**]. The result also speaks for itself! The moral élan of the Qur'ānic worldview, ritually masked by the Orientalist method, here shines through with dazzling luminosity. Professor Izutsu's work provides the most cogent argument against the claim that the truth of a scripture is accessible only to those who are inside its sacred tradition.

In the end, the uncomfortable question that has to be faced by any earnest-minded Muslim critic of Orientalism: Has the Orientalist enterprise brought nothing of value to Islam? Is there anything in its vast scholarly output that helps us elicit some insights about our own situation today or of our collective enterprise in history? Critical, even irreverential and pathologically Islamophobic, though the Orientalist may have been in dealing with our heritage, has he nothing to contribute to our self-criticism? So far, we have ignored the Orientalist reproach. Because of its foreign origin, its missionary trappings and its colonial designs, we have, rightly, dismissed Orientalism as the pathological fallacy of the Western religious, political and cultural megalomania. Nonetheless, we cannot remain immune forever against the claims of its method that are being proffered in the name of 'universal' reason itself. Sooner or later, authentic Muslim effort will have to approach the Qur'ān from methodological assumptions and parameters that are radically at odds with the ones consecrated by our tradition. If we are not to follow in the footsteps of the Western man to the wasteland of scepticism, disbelief and despair, we had better learn from the nemesis of Orientalism that the only proper method for the study of the Qur'ān is the one that allows its truth to speak for itself.

A Note on the Bibliography

No bibliography that aims at being *critical* can ever be *comprehensive*. In bibliographic science, just as in other branches of knowledge, all-inclusiveness and selection are founded on contradictory principles. Only by renouncing one's right to be critical and selective may one attain comprehensiveness, just as in order to achieve critical acumen one has to say good-bye to comprehensiveness. In the preparation of this short bibliography, thus, certain principles of selection and omission have been strictly adhered to. First of all, it has been accepted that in listing the modern works on the Qur'ān, language serves as no meaningful criterion of classification. No doubt, limiting Qur'ānic studies to works written in the (ill-defined) Western languages may act as some primitive principle of selection, (cf.: *Islamic Studies – Publish and Perish*, by Munawar A. Anees, *MWBR*, Vol. 2, No. 5 (Winter 1985), pp. 55–68); nevertheless, the illicit union that such an ideologically neutral linguistic criterion sanctions between Muslim works that are firmly committed to the 'Divine' nature of the Qur'ānic revelation and those by non-Muslims for whom the Qur'ān is no more than a document of human 'literature', cannot be condoned at all. Indeed, by no stretch of the imagination can the criterion of linguistic classification be considered a critical principle of Muslim bibliography.

Given the guiding function of bibliographies, therefore, the most logical system of classification for the Muslim would be the one that strictly separates Muslim works on the Qur'ān from those by non-Muslims. For, one need hardly insist that there is no methodology available today which can bridge the epistemological chasm between the two worldviews. Accordingly, the present bibliography lists only those works that are products of the non-Muslim effort – a few odd ones that innocuously display Muslim sounding names not excepting! More than that, it further restricts the non-Muslim effort to those studies that, following some perverted logic of their own, purport to be *critical* of the Qur'ān, or at least of the Muslim 'dogma' concerning its 'Divine' authorship. Such an attitude is pre-eminently associated with the academic worldview of Orientalism, that is, with its historical, linguistic, textual and source-critical methodologies and its vengeful emotional parameters. Orientalism, however, is not some kind of a protean body of 'knowledge' that includes the entirety of Christian and Jewish polemics against Islam: it is a historically specific epistemological enterprise and must be treated as such. Consequently – and in contradis-

43

tinction to the earlier views expressed in the *MWBR* that would regard even John of Damascus as the arch-protagonist of Orientalism (cf.: M. M. Ahsan's critique of Orientalism, Vol. 6, No. 2 (Winter 1986), p. 7), the present bibliography uncompromisingly limits itself to the Western academic effort of, say, the last hundred years. It even makes no mention of the current embryonic, post-Orientalist, phase of Qur'ānic studies in the West, which deserves a separate critique of its own.

Though firmly circumscribed within the Orientalist parameters of Qur'ānic studies, the present bibliography posits a further distinction between the Orientalist's own perception of the Qur'ān and his critical account of the Muslim's response to his Scripture. The focus of interest here as well as in the accompanying essay is the former studies; the latter, for instance, the Orientalist view of the classical works of *tafsīr*, as a rule, have been omitted. Needless to say, despite the application of these, stringent, criteria of selection and exclusion, anomalies remain. The most eye-catching of these is that the present listing excludes from its 'Qur'ānic studies' framework nearly all the biographies of the Prophet written in the West. Now, obviously, not only is there a lot of overlapping of the two themes – the Prophet's biography and the study of the Qur'ān – in the actual Western studies, it is impossible even from a strictly traditional Muslim vantage point to keep the two neatly separated. Clearly, to give a biographical account of the Prophet's mission without alluding to its Qur'ānic moorings or to discuss the contents of the Qur'ān without taking cognizance of its anchorage in the Prophet's *sīra* and in the historical vicissitudes of the nascent Muslim community would be, epistemologically speaking, an impossible feat. Nevertheless, inasmuch as Western accounts of the Prophet pre-eminently concern themselves with the Prophet's personality and insofar as they adduce the Qur'ānic evidence merely for the sake of elucidating or comprehending that personality, they belong, strictly speaking, to the genre of '*sīra* studies', and hence have been excluded from the present list. Consequently, only those studies whose proper focus is the Qur'ān, and whose reference to the Prophet's life is merely for the sake of understanding the phenomenon and contents of the Revelation, have been included here. Not only is the traditional Muslim distinction between the Prophetic *Sunna* (one of whose exegetical disciplines is the historiographically conceived *sīra* literature) and the Qur'ānic Revelation essential to safeguard the Muslim dogma about the 'divine' nature of the Qur'ān, upholding this division makes sense in the classification scheme of Orientalist scholarship as well. It also explains the present arrangement. Of course, it goes without saying that for a profound understanding of the Orientalist psychology, its enterprise of Qur'ānic studies cannot be insulated from its perception of the Prophecy. The latter, however, demands a more comprehensive and independent treatment than can be accorded here.

Other inconsistencies are of less fundamental import. For instance, it was found advisable not to exclude from the present list a seminal work like number 46 that deals with the main currents of Muslim exegesis, merely because it does not fit the above criterion. After all, the work is very crucial to the understanding of the scholarly tenor of the Orientalist thought and should therefore be compulsory reading for

44

the Muslim student of Orientalism; hence its inclusion. There are also a few other instances of such ambiguities. In addition to the objective and explicit criteria of selection mentioned above, certain judgements of a personal nature have also been exercised in the making of this list. Orientalist studies that are either unoriginal, repetitious or extremely difficult to access have not been given a place in this compilation – no matter how dutifully and repetitiously they may be listed in conventional literature. In short, the guiding principle behind this effort – and its sole vindication – has been its utility to the ordinary Muslim reader. It is earnestly hoped that this critical introduction and bibliographical guideline to the Orientalist enterprise of Qur'ānic studies will provide the Muslim reader with a list that he is actually able to *use* and not burden him with yet another compilation which is for the sake of compilation alone. Bibliographies can be a self-gratifying end of spurious scholarship and unless the compiler can actually appraise the works he lists there is no sense to his listings. Composing bibliographies to the n–th degree of citations is the most unredeeming and meaningless charade of empirical and normless modern scholarship. The less the Muslim emulates this fad the better. In short, every Muslim effort at bibliographical compilation must also constitute a critical attempt to assess the contents of the presented literature. Otherwise, the Muslim risks drowning in, what Ibn al-ʿArabī very aptly calls, 'the sea of names'.

Finally, a few words about the linguistic diversity of the source-material presented here. For any critical study of the 'classical' phase of Orientalism, familiarity with the German language is indispensable. No serious student of Orientalism, the Muslim included, thus, may remain ignorant of the German language. Notwithstanding the growing number of English translations – thanks especially to the assiduity of the ex-patriate Judaeo-Germanic community now settled in the United States – the main achievements of German Orientalism remain out of reach for the English-speaking student. For him, there is also the problem of the sizeable literature existing in French which cannot be ignored either (good, functional summaries, however, are available in the two editions of the *Encyclopaedia of Islam*). Given the predominantly anglophone, and to a much lesser extent, francophone, nature of the Muslim scholar, it is indeed a sad fact. Whatever the limitations of the ordinary Muslim scholar, however, linguistic diversity is a fact of the Orientalist 'way of life' that simply cannot be wished away. Great care, however, has been taken to include in the present bibliography only those works that are absolutely essential to the comprehension of the Orientalist mentality and scholarship and that their linguistic diversity be limited to English, French and German – the traditional trinity of tongues whose functional knowledge has been made obligatory for every student of humanities at European universities. Spanish, Italian, Dutch and Scandinavian studies of the Qur'ān in native tongues, accordingly, have been left out. No matter how daunting the prospects of mastering foreign European tongues may appear to the Muslim student, for a critical appraisal of Orientalist enterprise such an effort is indispensable. The present bibliographical introduction merely provides a faint indication of the toilsome task ahead.

45

Abbreviations:
BOAS – Bulletin of the School of Oriental and African Studies
JAL – Journal of Arabic Literature
JAOS – Journal of the American Oriental Society
JRAS – Journal of the Royal Asiatic Society
JSS – Journal of Semitic Studies
MW – Muslim World
OLZ – Orientalistische Literaturzeitung
WZKM – Wiener Zietschrift für die Kunde des Morgenlandes
ZDMG – Zietschrift der Deutschen Morgenländischen Gesellschaft

Some Notable Translations of the Qur'ān by Orientalists

English

1. ARBERRY, Arthur John, *The Koran Interpreted,* 2 vols., London, 1955.

2. BELL, Richard, *The Qur'ān*, 2 vols., Edinburgh, 1937–39.

3. PALMER, Edward Henry, *The Qur'ān*, 2 vols., Oxford, 1880. (Appeared in the 'The Sacred Books of the East' series; edited by Max Müller.)

4. RODWELL, John Meadows, *The Koran*, Hertford (London), 1861.

5. SALE, George, *A Comprehensive Commentary on the Qur'ān*, London, 1882–96. (Includes a full translation of the text.)

Besides the complete tranlations mentioned above, many other Orientalist scholars, notably Jeffery, Lane, Muir, Nicholson and Schroeder, have attempted partial and selective translations of the sacred text.

French

1. BLACHÈRE, Régis, *Le Coran*, 3 vols., Paris, 1947–50.

2. MASSON, Denise, *Le Coran*, Paris, 1967.

German

1. HENNING, Max, *Der Koran*, Leipzig, 1901. (Later revised by Annemarie Schimmel, Stuttgart, 1962.)

2. PARET, Rudi, *Der Koran*, Stuttgart, 1962.

3. RÜCKERT, Friedrich, *Der Koran*, Frankfurt, 1888.

Italian

1. BAUSANI, Alessandro, *Il Corano*, Florence, 1955.

Dutch

1. KRAEMERS, Johannes Hendrik, *De Koran*, Amsterdam, 1956.

Swedish

1. ZETTERSTÉEN, Karl Vilhelm, *Koranen*, Stockholm, 1917.

(For details concerning all subsequent editions and reprints as well as reviews, *vide* O.I.C. Research Centre For Islamic History, Art and Culture: *World Bibliography of Translations of the Meanings of the Holy Qur'ān*, Istanbul, 1406/1986.)

Some Standard Tools of Qur'ānic Scholarship in the West

The Text

Corani Textus Arabicus, Leipzig, 1834.

Prepared by Gustav Flügel, the standard text of Western scholarship differs from the commonly employed Muslim version (Al-Fu'ād edition, Cairo, 1342/1923) only in the numeration of the verses.

Secondary Aids

1. FLÜGEL, Gustav, *Concordantiae Corani Arabicae*, Leipzig, 1842.

2. KASSIS, Hanna, E., *A Concordance of the Qur'ān*, Berkeley, University of California Press, 1983. Supercedes and replaces the earlier standard.

3. PENRICE, John, *A Dictionary and Glossary of the Koran*, London, 1873. (Reprinted by Praeger Publishers New York and Washington in 1971.)

4. LANE, Edward W., *An Arabic-English Lexicon*, London and Edinburgh, 1863–93. New Edition: London, 1955–57 and 1968. Another new edition: Cambridge, Islamic Text Society, 1984.

5. WRIGHT William, *A Grammar of the Arabic Language*, Cambridge, 1896.

6. *Index Islamicus*, London, 1906, still continuing.

46

Books and Articles

1. ABBOT, N., *Studies in Arabic Literary Papyri*. Vol I: Historical Texts. Chicago, 1957.

2. ———, *Studies in Arabic Literary Papyri*. Vol II: Qur'ānic Commentary and Tradition. Chicago, 1967.

3. AHRENS, K., 'Christliches im Qoran', *ZDMG*, 84 (1930), pp. 15–68, 149–90.

4. ALLARD, M., 'Une méthode nouvelle pour l'étude du Coran', in *Studia Islamica*, 15 (1961), pp. 5–21.

5. ———, *Analyse conceptuelle du Coran sur cartes perforées*, Paris, 1963.

6. AUGAPFEL, J., 'Das *Kitab* im Qoran', *WZKM*, 29 (1915), pp. 384–93.

7. BAKKAR, D., *Man in the Qur'ān*, Amsterdam, 1965.

8. BALJON, J., 'The "Amr of God" in the Koran', in *Acta Orientalia*, 23 (1959), pp. 7–18.

9. ———, *Modern Muslim Koran Interpretations*, Leiden, 1961.

10. BARTH, J., 'Studien zur Kritik und Exegese des Qorans', in *Der Islam*, 6 (1915–16), pp. 113–48.

11. BARTHOLD, W. W., 'Der Koran und das Meer', in *ZDMG*, 83 (1929), pp. 37–43.

12. BAUER, H., 'Über die Anordnung der Suren und über die geheimnisvollen Buchstaben im Qoran', in *ZDMG*, 75 (1921), pp. 1–20.

13. BAUMSTARK, A., 'Jüdischer und christlicher Gebetstypus im Koran', in *Der Islam*, 16 (1927), pp. 229–48.

14. BECK, E., *Das christliche Mönchtum im Qoran*, Helsinki, 1946.

15. ———, 'Die Gestalt des Abraham am Wendepunkt der Entwicklung Muhammeds', in *Muséon*, 65 (1952), pp. 73–94.

16. BELL, R., 'The Style of the Qur'ān', in *Transactions of the Glasgow University Oriental Society*, 9 (1942–44), pp. 9–15.

17. ———, 'A duplicate in the Koran: the composition of sūrah xxiii', in *MW*, 18 (1928), pp. 227–33.

18. ———, 'Muhammad and Divorce in the Qur'ān', in *MW*, 29 (1939), pp. 55–62.

19. ———, 'Sūrat-al-Ḥashr: a study of its composition', in *MW*, 38 (1948), pp. 29–42.

20. ———, *Bell's Introduction to the Qur'ān*, (ed. M. W. Watt), Edinburgh, 1970. (Recasting of the 1953 edition.)

21. BEESTON, A. F. L., 'The "Men of Tanglewood" in the Qur'ān', in *JSS*, 13 (1968), pp. 253–5.

22. ———, 'Ships in a Qur'ānic Simile', in *JAL*, 4 (1973), pp. 94–6.

23. BELLAMY, J. A., 'The Mysterious Letters of the Koran', in *JAOS*, 93 (1973), pp. 267–85.

24. BIJLEFELD, W. A., 'A prophet and more than a prophet? Some observations on the Qur'ānic use of the terms "prophet" and "apostle"', in *MW*, 59 (1969), pp. 1–28.

25. BIRKELAND, H., *The Lord Guideth: studies on primitive Islam*, Oslo, 1956.

26. ———, 'The Interpretation of Sūrah 107', in *Studia Islamica*, 9 (1958), pp. 13–29.

27. BISHOP, E., 'The Quran Scrolls and the Qur'ān', in *MW*, 48 (1958), pp. 223–36.

28. BLACHERE, R., *Introduction au Coran*, Paris, 1959. (1947)

29. BOUMAN, J., *Gott und Mensch im Koran*, Darmstadt, 1977.

30. BRUNSHVIG, R., 'Simples remarkes négatives sur le vocabulaire du Coran', in *Studia Islamica*, 5 (1956), pp. 19–32.

31. BUHL, F., Art. 'Qoran', in *Enc. Isl.* (First Edition).

32. ———, 'Zur Koranexegese', in *Acta Orientalia*, 3 (1925), pp. 97–108.

33. BURTON, J., *The Collection of the Qur'ān*, Cambridge, 1977.

34. CALVERLEY, E., 'The Grammar of *Sūra 'l-Ikhlāṣ*, in *Studia Islamica*, 8 (1957), pp. 5–14.

35. CRAGG, K., *The Event of the Qur'ān*, London, 1971.

36. ———, *The Mind of the Qur'ān*, London, 1973.

37. CROLLIUS, A. A. R., *The Word in the experience of Revelation in Qur'ān and Hindu Scriptures*, Rome, 1974.

38. DENNY, F., 'The Meaning of the *Umma* in the Qur'ān', in *History of Religions*, 15 (1975), pp. 34–70.

39. EICHLER, P. A., *Die Dschinn, Tuefel und Engel im Koran*, Leipzig, 1928.

40. FARIS, N. A. and GLIDDEN, H. W., 'The Development of the Meaning of the Koranic *Hanif*', in *The Journal of the Palestinian Oriental Society*, 19 (1939–40), pp. 1–13.

41. GAUDEFROY-DEMOMBYNES, M., 'Sur quelques noms d'Allah dans le Coran', in *Bulletin de l'Ecole Pratique des Hautes Études*, (1929), pp. 1–21.

42. ———, 'Le sens de substantif *ghayb* dans le Coran', in *Méllanges Louis Massignon*, Damascus, 1957, II, pp. 245–50.

43. GÄTJE, H., *Koran und Koran exegese*, Zurich, 1971. (Eng. tr. by A. T. WELCH, *The Qur'ān and Its Exegesis*, Berkeley and London, 1977.)

47

44. GEIGER, A., *Was hat Mohammed aus dem Judentuhum aufgenommen?*, Bonn, 1833 (new edition, Leipzig, 1902.) (Eng. tr. by F. M. Young, *Muhammad and Judaism*, New York, 1970.)

45. GIULIO, B-S., *The Koran in the Light of Christ*, Chicago, 1977.

46. GOLDZIHER, I., *Die Richtungen der islamischen Koranauslegung*, Leiden, 1920.

47. GOOSENS, E., 'Ursprung und Bedeutung der koranischen Siglen', in *Der Islam*, 13 (1923), pp. 191–226.

48. GRAHAM, William, A., '*Qur'ān* as Spoken Word: An Islamic Contribution to the Understanding of Scripture', in *Approaches to Islam in Religious Studies*, ed. Richard C. Martin, The University of Arizona Press, Tucson, 1985, pp. 23–40.

49. HADDAD, Y. Y., 'An Exegesis of *Sūra* Ninety-Eight', in *JAOS*, 97 (1977), pp. 519–30.

50. HENNINGER, J., *Spuren christlicher Glaubenswahrheit im Koran*, Schönbeck, 1951.

51. HIRSCHFELD, H., *New Researches in the Composition and Exegesis of the Qoran*, London, 1902.

52. ———, *Jüdische Elemente im Koran*, Berlin, 1878.

53. ———, *Beiträge zur Erklärung des Qorans*, Leipzig, 1886.

54. HOROVITZ, J., 'Das Koranische Paradies', in *Scripta Universitatis atque Bibliothecae Hierosolymitanarum*, Jerusalem, 1923, pp. 1–13.

55. ———, 'Jewish proper names and derivatives in the Koran', in *Hebrew Union College Annual*, 2 (1925), pp. 145–227. (Reprint, Hildesheim, 1964.)

56. ———, *Koranische Untersuchungen*, Leipzig, 1926.

57. IZUTSU, T., *God and Man in the Koran: semantics of the Koranic weltanschauung*, Tokyo, 1964.

58. ———, *Ethico-Religious Concepts in the Qur'ān*, Montreal, 1966.

59. JEFFERY, A., *Materials for the History of the Text of the Qur'ān*, Leiden, 1937.

60. ———, *the Foreign Vocabulary of the Qur'ān*, Baroda, 1938.

61. ———, 'The Mystic Letters of the Koran', in *MW*, 14 (1924), pp. 247–60.

62. ———, 'The Qur'ān as a Scripture', in *MW*, 40 (1950), pp. 41–55, 106–34, 185–206, 257–75.

63. JOMIER, J., 'Le nom divin "al-Raḥmān" dans le Coran', in *Mélanges Louis Massignon*, Damascus, 1957, II, pp. 361–81.

64. ———, *Bible et Coran*, Paris, 1959. (Eng. version, tr. by ARBEZ: *The Bible and the Koran*, New York, 1964.)

65. ———, *Les grandes themes du Coran*, Paris, 1978.

66. JOHNS, A. H. (ed.), *International Congress for the Study of the Qur'ān*, Canberra, 1982.

67. JONES, A. 'The Mystical Letters of the Qur'ān', in *Studia Islamica*, 16 (1962), pp. 5–11.

68. KATSH, A. I., *Judaism in Islam: Biblical and Talmudic Backgrounds of the Qur'ān and its Commentaries*, New York, 1954.

69. KÜNSTLINGER, D., '"Kitāb" und "ahlu l-kitabi" im Qoran', *Rocznik Orientalistyczny*, 4 (1926), pp. 238–47.

70. ———, 'Die Namen der Gottes-Schriften im Qoran', *Rocznik Orientlistyczny*, 13 (1937), pp. 72–84.

71. ———, 'Sura 95', in *OLZ*, (1936), pp. 1–3.

72. ḲUR'ĀN. Articles in the *Enc. Isl.* (New Edition) by Welch A. T., Paret, Rudi and Pearson, J. D.

73. LEHMANN and PEDERSEN, 'Der Beweis für die Ausstehung im Koran', in *Der Islam*, 5 (1914).

74. LICHTENSTADTER, I., 'Origin and Interpretation of some Koranic Symbols', in *Arabic and Islamic Studies in honour of Hamilton A. R. Gibb*, (ed. G. Makdisi), Leiden, 1965, pp. 426–36.

75. LÜLIG, G., *Kritisch-Exegetische Untersuchung des Qurantextes*, Erlangen, 1970.

76. ———, *Über den Ur-Qur'ān*, Erlangen, 1974.

77. MARTIN, Richard C., 'Understanding the Qur'ān in Text and Context', in *History of Religions*, 21 (1981–82), pp. 361–84.

78. MASSON, D., *Le Coran et la revelation judeo-chretienne*, 2 vols., Paris, 1958.

79. ———, *Monotheisme coranique et monotheisme biblique*, Paris, 1976.

80. MICHAUD, H., *Jésus selon le Coran*, Lausanne, 1960.

81. MOUBARAC, Youakim, *Abraham dans le Coran*, Paris, 1958.

82. ———, *Le Coran et la critique occidentale*, Beirut, 1972–3.

83. MUIR, W., *The Coran, its Composition and Teaching; and the Testimony it bears to the Holy Scriptures*, London, 1878.

84. NAGEL, Tilman, 'Vom "Qoran" zur "Schrift" – Bells Hypothese aus religionsgeschitlicher Sicht', in *Der Islam*, 60 (1983), pp. 143–65.

48

85. NEUWIRTH, A., *Studien zur Komposition der mekkanischen Suren*, Berlin and New York, 1981.

86. ———, 'Das Islamische Dogma der Unnachahmlichkeit des Korans in Literaturwissenschaflicher Sicht', in *Der Islam*, 60 (1983), pp. 166–83.

87. NWIYA, P., *Exegese coranique et langage mystique*, Beirut, 1970.

88. NÖLDEKE, T., SCHWALLY, F., BERGSTRÄSSER, G., PRETZL, O., *Geschichte des Qorans*, 3 vols., Leipzig, 1909–38. (Reprint: Hildesheim, 1961.)
(This seminal Orientalist work of Qur'ānic studies appeared for the first time in 1860. A second edition, revised and enlarged first by Nöldeke's pupil, F. Schwally, and later by Bergsträsser and Pretzl, was published intermittantly in 1909, 1918 and 1938. A photocopied reprint of all the three volumes was issued at Hildesheim in 1961.)

89. OPITZ, K., *Die Medizin im Koran*, Stuttgart, 1906.

90. O'SHAUGHNESSY, T., *The Koranic Concept of the Word of God*, Rome, 1948 (*Biblica et Orientalia* xi).

91. ———, *The Development of the Meaning of Spirit in the Koran*, Rome, 1953.

92. ———, 'The seven names for hell in the Qur'ān', in *BOAS*, 24 (1961), pp. 444–69.

93. ———, 'Creation from nothing and the teaching of the Qur'ān', in *ZDMG*, 120 (1970), pp. 274–80.

94. ———, 'God's throne and the biblical symbolism of the Qur'ān', in *Numen*, 20 (1973), pp. 202–21.

95. PARET, R., *Muhammed und der Koran*, Stuttgart, 1957.

96. ———, *Der Koran: Kommentar und Konkordanz*, Stuttgart, 1971.

97. ———, (ed.), *Der Koran*, Darmstadt, 1975.

98. ———, 'Der Koran als Gesichtsquelle', in *Der Islam*, 37 (1961), pp. 26–42.

99. ———, 'Sura 109', in *Der Islam*, 39 (1964), pp. 197–200.

100. PARRINDER, G., *Jesus in the Qur'ān*, London, 1965.

101. PEDERSEN, J., Review of *E. Meyer*: Ursprung und Geschichte der Mormonen. Mit Exkursen über die Anfange des Islams und des Christentums (Halle, 1912) in *Der Islam*, 10 (1914), pp. 110–15.

102. RAHBAR, D., *God of Justice: a study of the ethical doctrines of the Qur'ān*, Leiden, 1960.

103. RÄISÄNEN, H., *Das koranische Jesubild*, Helsinki, 1971.

104. ———, *The idea of Divine hardening* (in the Bible and the Kur'an), Helsinki, 1972.

105. RINGGREN, H., 'The Conception of Faith in the Qur'ān', in *Oriens*, 4 (1951), pp. 1–20.

106. ———, 'Die Gottesfurcht im Koran', in *Orientalia Suecana*, 3 (1954), pp. 118–34.

107. RIPPIN, A., 'The Qur'ān as Literature: Perils, Pitfalls and Prospects', in *MESA Bull*, 10 (1983), pp. 38–47.

108. ———, 'Literary Analysis of *Qur'ān*, *Tafsīr*, and *Sīra*: The Methodologies of John Wansbrough', in *Approaches to Islam in Religious Studies*, ed. Richard C. Martin, Arizona, 1985.

109. RIVLIN, J., *Gesetz im Koran, Kultus und Ritus*, Jerusalem, 1934.

110. ROBERTS, R., *The Social Laws of the Qur'ān*, London, 1925.

111. ROSENTHAL, F., 'Nineteen', in *Analecta Biblica*, 12 (1959), pp. 304–18.

112. RUDOLPH, W., *Die Abhängigkeit des Qorans von Judentum und Christentum*, Stuttgart, 1922.

113. SCHAPIRO, I., *Die haggadischen Elemente im erzählenden Teil des Korans*, Frankfurt, 1907.

114. SCHEDL, C., 'Probleme der Koranexegese', in *Der Islam*, 58 (1981), pp. 1–14.

115. SEALE, M., 'The Mysterious Letters in the Qur'ān', in *Akten des XXIV. Internationalen Orientalisten-Kongresses, München 1957*, Wiesbaden, 1959, pp. 276–79.

116. ———, Qur'ān and Bible: Studies in Interpretation and Dialogue, London, 1978.

117. SEZGIN, F., *Geschichte des arabischen Schriftums*, vol. I., Leiden, 1967.

118. SIDERSKY, D., *Les origines des légendes musulmanes dans le Coran*, Paris, 1933.

119. SISTER, H., *Metaphoren und Vergleiche im Koran*, Berlin, 1931.

120. SPEYER, H., *Die biblischen Erzählungen im Qoran*, Gräfenhainichen, s.d. (reprint, Hildesheim, 1961.)

121. TORREY, C., *The Commercial-theological terms in the Koran*, Leiden, 1892.

122. ———, *The Jewish Foundation of Islam*, New York, 1933 (reprint 1967).

123. WAGTENDONIK, K., *Fasting in the Koran*, Leiden, 1968.

124. WANSBROUGH, J., 'Arabic rhetoric and Qur'ānic exegesis', in *BOAS*, 31 (1968), pp. 469–85.

125. ———, *Qur'ānic Studies*, Oxford, 1977.

126. ———, *The Sectarian Milieu*, Oxford, 1979.

127. WATT, W. M., 'The dating of the Qur'ān: a review of Richard Bell's theories', in *JRAS*, (1957), pp. 46–56.

128. ———, 'The Christianity criticized in the Qur'ān', in *MW*, 57 (1967), pp. 197–201.

129. ———, *Companion to the Qur'ān*, London, 1967.

130. ———, 'On Interpreting the Qur'ān', in *Oriens*, 25–6 (1976), pp. 41–7.

131. WEIL, G., *Historisch-kritische Einleitung in den Koran*, Leipzig, 1844. (Second revised edition appeared in 1872.)

132. WELCH, A. T., 'Muhammad's understanding of himself: The Koranic data', in *Islam's Understanding of Itself*, (ed. Hovannisian, R. and Vyronis, S.), Malibu, California, 1983, pp. 15–52.

133. WIDENGREN, G., *The Ascension of the Apostle and the heavenly Book*, (Uppsala Universitets Årsskrift, 1950:7), Uppsala, 1950.

134. ———, 'Holy Book and Holy Tradition in Islam', in *Holy Book and Holy Tradition*, ed. Bruce, F. F. and Rupp, E. G., Manchester, 1968, pp. 210–36.

135. YAHUDA, A. S., 'A Contribution to Qur'ān and Ḥadīth Interpretation', in *I Goldziher Memorial Volume*, Budapest, 1948, I, pp. 280–308.

INDEX

Compiled by Meg Davies (Registered Indexer, Society of Indexers)

study of 297–332
'Uthmānic vulgate 285, 385
vocabulary 285–95
and youth and old age 177–95
see also chronology; recitation; revelation; Scripture; style; sūras; translations
qur'ān , earliest meaning xvii, 148 n.80, 159–75
Qur'ānic studies *see* scholarship, Qur'ānic
Al-Qurṭubī, Muḥammad b, Aḥmad, *Tafsīr* xxv, 337–8 n.14, 343 n.26, 344 n.29, 345 n.31, 346 n.34, 353 n.57
Al-Qushayrī, Abū al-Qāsim 'Abd al-Karīm b. Hawāzin 173 n.61, 337–8 n.14, 350 nn.52,54

Rabbinic Jews
and eschatology 7–8
and Jews as chosen people 46
and prediction 5
and Qumran sect 11, 17
and river *Sambatyon* 68
Rabin, Chaim xiii, 1–20, 88
Al-Raḥīm, and *al-Raḥmān* 197–8, 204
Al-Raḥmān
as Creator 207
and eschatology 205–7, 209
and Meccan period 199, 200–3
pre-Islamic use 207, 208 n.40, 209, 210–11
in the Qur'ān xvii, 197–212
and *al-Raḥīm* 197–8, 204
and religious ideas 204–10
and revelation 208
as unique 208
used in proper names 202–3
Rahman, Fazlur xxvi n.57, 333 n.2, 334 n.4, 346 n.32, 389
rajaz 214, 219, 221, 223, 233, 275
rasūl (apostle)
as community's representative 151
Jesus as 25
Muḥammad as 57–8, 146–7, 153–6
in Qur'ān xvii, 31, 139, 141–57
Ratramnus of Corbie 76
Rauf, Muḥammad Abdul 112 nn.23,24
Al-Rāzi, Fakhr al-Dīn 31, 302, 306, 328
and old age 192, 195
and *sūra* 97 337 n.14, 338–9 n.16, 339 n.18, 342 n.24, 346 n.33, 350 n.54
and *sūra* 111 269 n.2, 273 n.27, 273 n.32, 274–7, 281
Al-Rāzī, Zayn al-Din Muḥammad b. Abī Bakr 219 n.32, 241 n.105, 242 n.113, 243 n.118, 244 n.120
reason, religious 304–6, 311–15, 319, 328
recitation (*tajwīd*)
of *ḥadīth qudsī* 161
of Qur'ān 159, 161–75, 253, 311, 312, 333, 341
see also sound
Reckendorf, H. 335 n.9
redaction criticism 254–5
Reese, W. 76
Reicke, B. 3 n.1
religion
natural 157, 262–7
see also dīn
religions
unity of 100, 101, 102
see also history of religions
resurrection, and 'signs' 260–4, 267
revelation
Divine Saying as 161
and first Meccan period 11, 40–5, 96–7
to Jesus 25, 56, 96
and Medinan period 52–60
and Muḥammad 22–3, 25, 26, 29–31, 33 n.9, 37, 96–9, 307–8, 338–9
and narrative 373
and Orientalism 386–7
and prophets 59, 148–9, 154–5, 157, 208
and *qur'ān* 160–1
and *rūḥ* 348–9, 351–3
and second Meccan period 16, 45–51
theory of 2, 159–60
unity of 100
and use of *al-Raḥmān* 208
rhyme 261–4, 266
mono-rhyme 221, 233, 240, 245
in Qur'ānic *saj'* 25, 220–3, 243, 244, 247–9
syntactical and metrical 335
Richter, Wolfgang 254
Rida, Rashid 370
Ringgren, Helmer xv n.19, 112 nn.23,24, 113 n.26
and meaning of *islām* 85–7, 89
Rippin, A. xi–xxvi, 334 n.4
Al-Riqāshī, 'Abd al-Ṣamad Ibn al-Faḍl 243
Ritter, H. 380 n.12
ritual, Jewish 99–100
Robert of Ketton xi

INDEX OF QUR'ĀNIC REFERENCES

Note: Quranic references are to the Cairo edition, except for the chapters by Bell and Rabin which use the Flügel numbering.